CW00601211

First edition published 1992
First colour edition published 1998 by

Ordnance Survey® and George Philip Ltd
Romsey Road   a division of Octopus Publishing Group Ltd
Maybush   Michelin House, 81 Fulham Road,
Southampton   London SW3 6RB
SO16 4GU

ISBN 0-540-07560 4 (hardback)
ISBN 0-540-07561 2 (spiral)

To the best of the Publishers' knowledge, the information in this
atlas was correct at the time of going to press. No responsibility
can be accepted for any errors or their consequences.

The representation in this atlas of a road, track or path is no
evidence of the existence of a right of way.

**The mapping between pages 1 and 152 (inclusive) in this atlas
is derived from Ordnance Survey® Large Scale and Landranger®
mapping, and revised using OSCAR® and Land-Line® data.**

Ordnance Survey, OSCAR, Land-line and Landranger are registered
trade marks of Ordnance Survey, the national mapping agency of
Great Britain.

Printed and bound in Spain by Cayfosa

Digital Data

The exceptionally high-quality mapping
found in this book is available as digital
data in TIFF format, which is easily
convertible to other bit-mapped (raster)
image formats.

The index is also available in digital form
as a standard database table. It contains
all the details found in the printed index
together with the National Grid reference
for the map square in which each entry
is named and feature codes for places
of interest in eight categories such as
education and health.

For further information and to discuss
your requirements, please contact the
Ordnance Survey Solutions Centre on
01703 792929.

Key to map symbols

III

(22a)	**Motorway** (with junction number)
	Primary route (dual carriageway and single)
	A road (dual carriageway and single)
	B road (dual carriageway and single)
	Minor road (dual carriageway and single)
	Other minor road
	Road under construction
	Pedestrianised area
DY7	**Post code boundaries**
	County and Unitary Authority boundaries
	Railway
	Tramway, miniature railway
	Rural track, private road or narrow road in urban area
	Gate or obstruction to traffic (restrictions may not apply at all times or to all vehicles)
	Path, bridleway, byway open to all traffic, road used as a public path

The representation in this atlas of a road, track or path is no evidence of the existence of a right of way

105 **Adjoining page indicators**
(The colour of the arrow indicates the scale of the adjoining page – see scales below)

85

143

152

The map areas within the pink/blue bands are shown at a larger scale on the page, indicated by the red/blue blocks and arrows

Walsall	**British Rail station**
	Midland Metro
(M)	**Metrolink station**
	Underground station
D	**Docklands Light Railway station**
M	**Tyne and Wear Metro**
	Private railway station
	Bus, coach station
◆	**Ambulance station**
◆	**Coastguard station**
◆	**Fire station**
◆	**Police station**
✚	**Accident and Emergency entrance to hospital**
H	**Hospital**
+	**Church, place of worship**
i	**Information centre** (open all year)
P P&R	**Parking, Park and Ride**
PO PO	**Post Office**
Prim Sch	**Important buildings, schools, colleges, universities and hospitals**
River Medway	**Water name**
	Stream
	River or canal (minor and major)
	Water
	Tidal water
	Woods
	Houses
House	**Non-Roman antiquity**
VILLA	**Roman antiquity**

Acad	**Academy**	Ct	**Law Court**	PH	**Public House**
Crem	**Crematorium**	L Ctr	**Leisure Centre**	Recn Gd	**Recreation Ground**
Cemy	**Cemetery**	LC	**Level Crossing**	Resr	**Reservoir**
C Ctr	**Civic Centre**	Liby	**Library**	Ret Pk	**Retail Park**
CH	**Club House**	Mkt	**Market**	Sch	**School**
Coll	**College**	Meml	**Memorial**	Sh Ctr	**Shopping Centre**
Ent	**Enterprise**	Mon	**Monument**	TH	**Town Hall/House**
Ex H	**Exhibition Hall**	Mus	**Museum**	Trad Est	**Trading Estate**
Ind Est	**Industrial Estate**	Obsy	**Observatory**	Univ	**University**
Inst	**Institute**	Pal	**Royal Palace**	YH	**Youth Hostel**

■ The dark grey border on the inside edge of some pages indicates that the mapping does not continue onto the adjacent page
■ The small numbers around the edges of the maps identify the 1 kilometre National Grid lines

The scale of the maps is 5.52 cm to 1 km (3½ inches to 1 mile)

0		¼		½		¾		1 mile
0		250 m		500 m		750 m		1 kilometre

The scale of the maps on pages numbered in red is 11.04 cm to 1 km (7 inches to 1 mile)

0		220 yards		440 yards		660 yards		½ mile
0		125 m		250 m		375 m		½ kilometre

The scale of the maps on pages numbered in green is 2.76 cm to 1 km (1¾ inches to 1 mile)

0	¼	½	¾	1 mile
0	250 m	500 m	750 m	1 kilometre

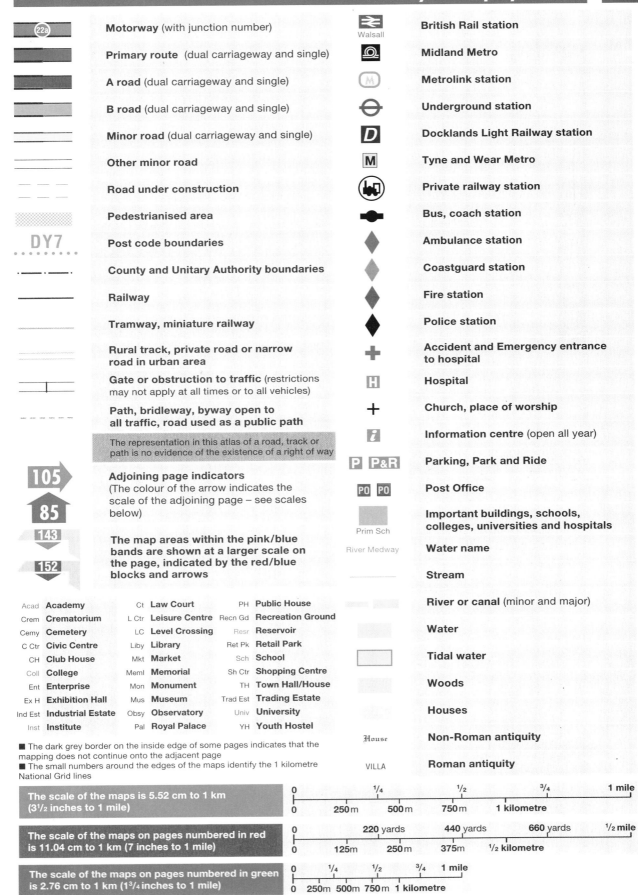

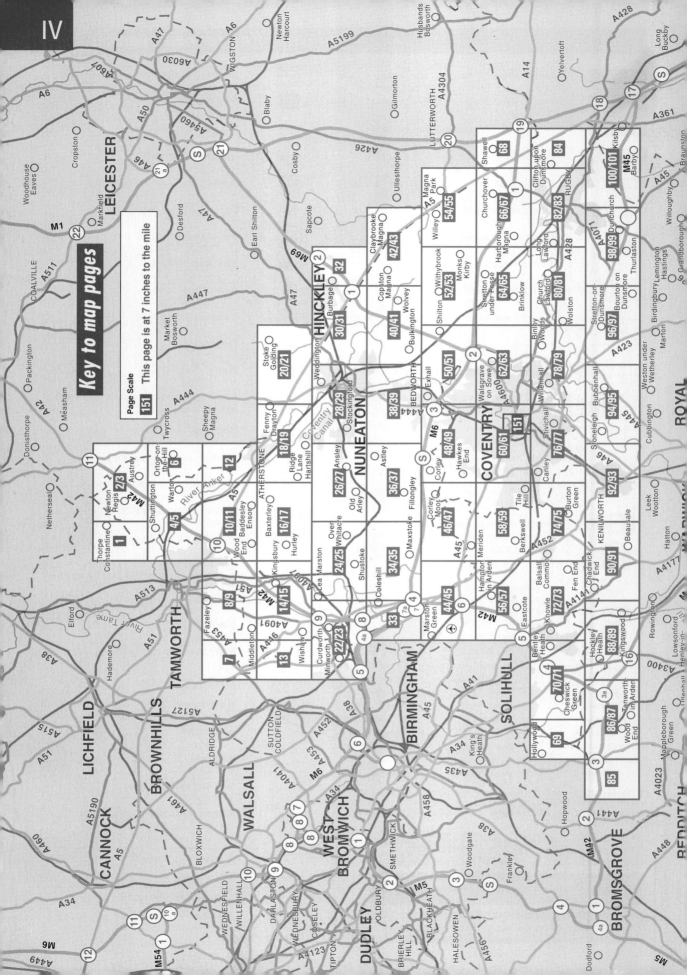

Key to map pages

Page Scale
151 This page is at 7 inches to the mile

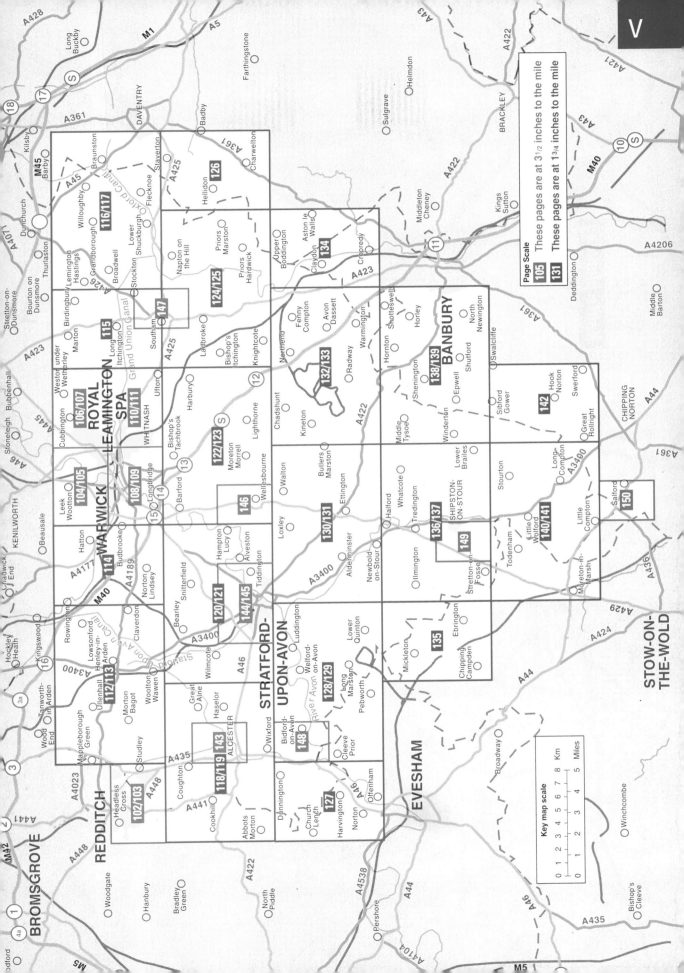

V

BROMSGROVE

REDDITCH

STRATFORD-UPON-AVON

ROYAL LEAMINGTON SPA

WARWICK

BANBURY

SHIPSTON-ON-STOUR

STOW-ON-THE-WOLD

EVESHAM

KENILWORTH

CHIPPING NORTON

Page Scale
105 These pages are at 3½ inches to the mile
131 These pages are at 1¾ inches to the mile

Key map scale
Km 8 7 6 5 4 3 2 1 0
Miles 5 4 3 2 1 0

116/117
126
124/125
134
147
115
105/107
110/111
132/133
138/139
142
104/105
108/109
122/123
130/131
136/137
149
140/141
150
114
120/121
144/145
146
112/113
118/119 143
148
128/129
127
102/103
135

Long Buckby
Kilsby
Barby
Dunchurch
Willoughby
Braunston
Flecknoe
Staverton
Badby
Farthingstone
Helmdon
Sulgrave
Middleton Cheney
Kings Sutton
Deddington
Middle Barton
Thurlaston
Leamington Hastings
Grandborough
Broadwell
Lower Shuckburgh
Stockton
Napton on the Hill
Priors Marston
Priors Hardwick
Hellidon
Charwelton
Upper Boddington
Aston le Walls
Claydon
Cropredy
North Newington
Swalcliffe
Bourton on Dunsmore
Birdingbury
Marton
Ladbroke
Bishop's Itchington
Knightcote
Fenny Compton
Avon Dassett
Warmington
Shotteswell
Horley
Horton
Shutford
Hook Norton
Swerford
Stretton-on-Dunsmore
Weston under Wetherley
Long Itchington
Southam
Harbury
Ufton
Lighthorne
Chadshunt
Kineton
Radway
Middle Tysoe
Shenington
Epwell
Sibford Gower
Great Rollright
Cubbington
Whitnash
Bishop's Tachbrook
Moreton Morrell
Wellesbourne
Walton
Butlers Marston
Ettington
Halford
Whatcote
Tredington
Lower Brailes
Stourton
Long Compton
Leek Wootton
Barford
Loxley
Alderminster
Ilmington
Todenham
Little Wolford
Little Compton
Salford
Beausale
Hatton
Budbrooke
Norton Lindsey
Snitterfield
Hampton Lucy
Alveston
Tiddington
Newbold-on-Stour
Stretton-on-Fosse
Moreton-in-Marsh
Chadwick End
Hockley Heath
Kingswood
Rowington
Claverdon
Bearley
Wilmcote
Lower Quinton
Mickleton
Ebrington
Broadway
Tanworth in Arden
Ullenhall
Henley-in-Arden
Morton Bagot
Wootton Wawen
Great Alne
Haselor
Chipping Campden
Wood End
Mappleborough Green
Studley
Wixford
Bidford-on-Avon
Welford on Avon
Long Marston
Pebworth
Cleeve Prior
Headless Cross
Cookhill
Coughton
ALCESTER
Dorsington
Cleeve Prior
Abbots Morton
Church Lench
Norton
Offenham
Harvington
Woodgate
Hanbury
Bradley Green
North Piddle
Pershore
Winchcombe
Bishop's Cleeve

M1
M45
M40
M5
M42
M6

A428
A5
A422
A43
A421
A361
A45
A425
A426
A423
A423
A4206
A361
A44
A4177
A4189
A3400
A46
A441
A4023
A448
A435
A4538
A4104
A424
A429
A436
A4540

Oxford Canal
Grand Union Canal
Stratford upon Avon Canal
River Avon

17
18
S
10
S
11
12
13
14
15
16
3a
3
1
4a
S

Route planning

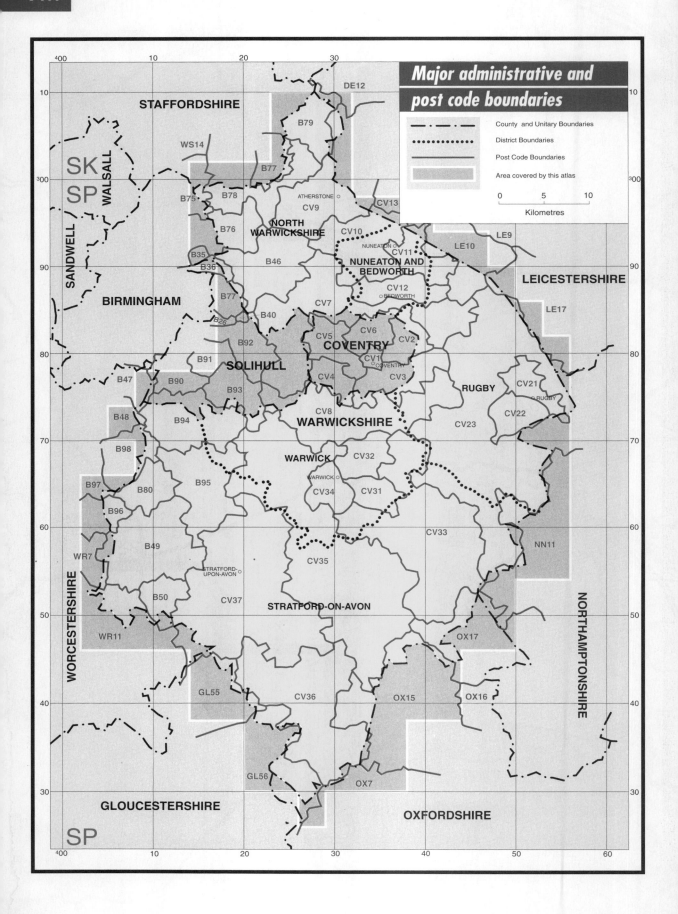

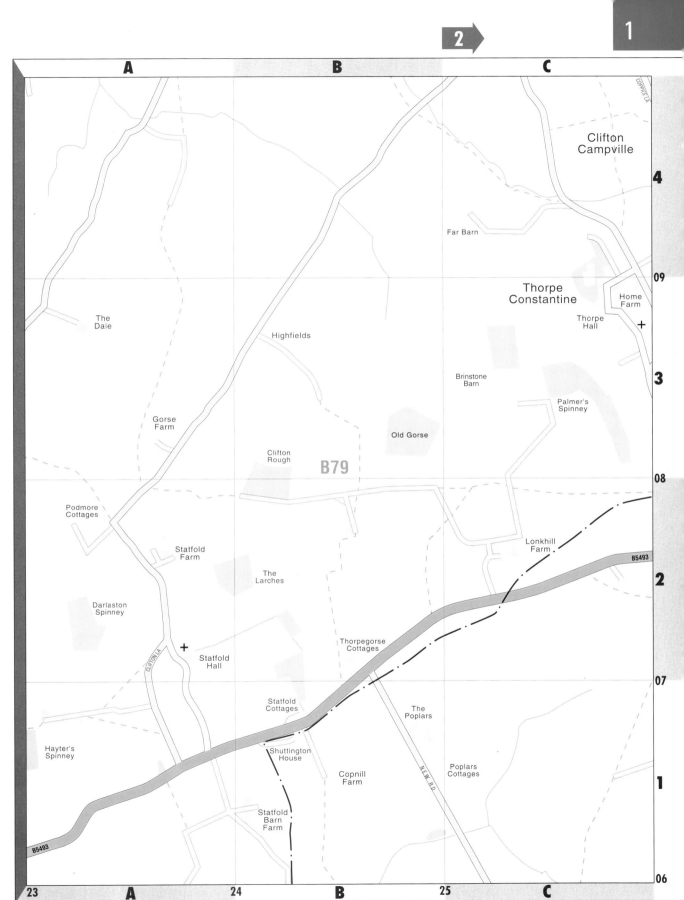

A   B   C

Clifton
Campville

Far Barn

Thorpe
Constantine

Home
Farm

Thorpe
Hall

Brinstone
Barn

Palmer's
Spinney

The
Dale

Highfields

Old Gorse

Gorse
Farm

Clifton
Rough

B79

Podmore
Cottages

Statfold
Farm

The
Larches

Lonkhill
Farm

B5493

Darlaston
Spinney

Thorpegorse
Cottages

Statfold
Hall

CLIFTON LA

Statfold
Cottages

The
Poplars

Hayter's
Spinney

Shuttington
House

Copnill
Farm

NEW RD

Poplars
Cottages

Statfold
Barn
Farm

B5493

23   A   24   B   25   C   06

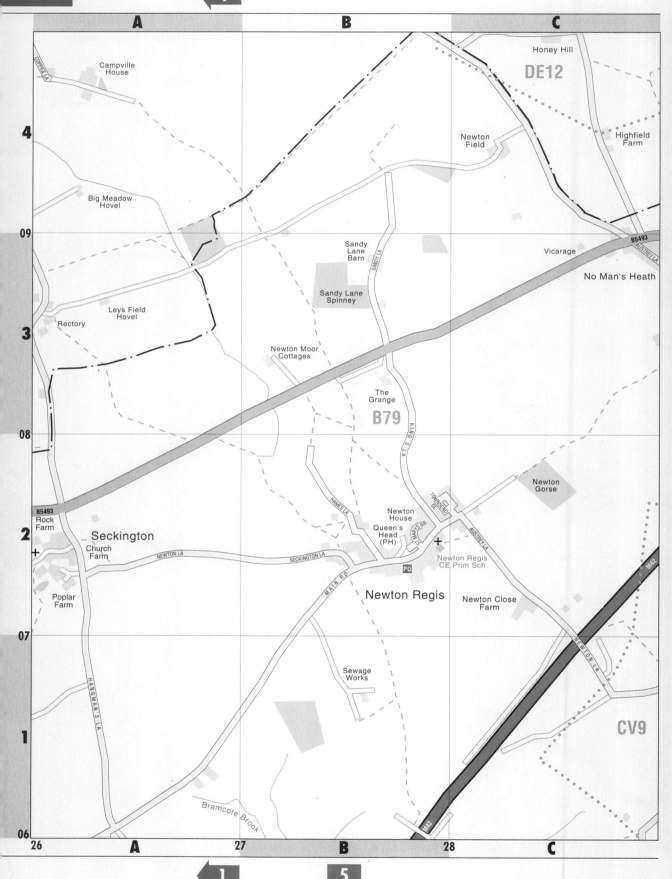

Honey Hill

DE12

Campville
House

Newton
Field

Highfield
Farm

Big Meadow
Hovel

Sandy
Lane
Barn

Vicarage

No Man's Heath

Sandy Lane
Spinney

Leys Field
Hovel

Rectory

Newton Moor
Cottages

The
Grange

B79

Newton
Gorse

Newton
House

Queen's
Head
(PH)

B5493

Rock
Farm

Seckington

Church
Farm

NEWTON LA

SECKINGTON LA

Newton Regis
CE Prim Sch

PO

Newton Regis

Newton Close
Farm

M42

Poplar
Farm

MAIN RD

Sewage
Works

CV9

Bramcote Brook

M42

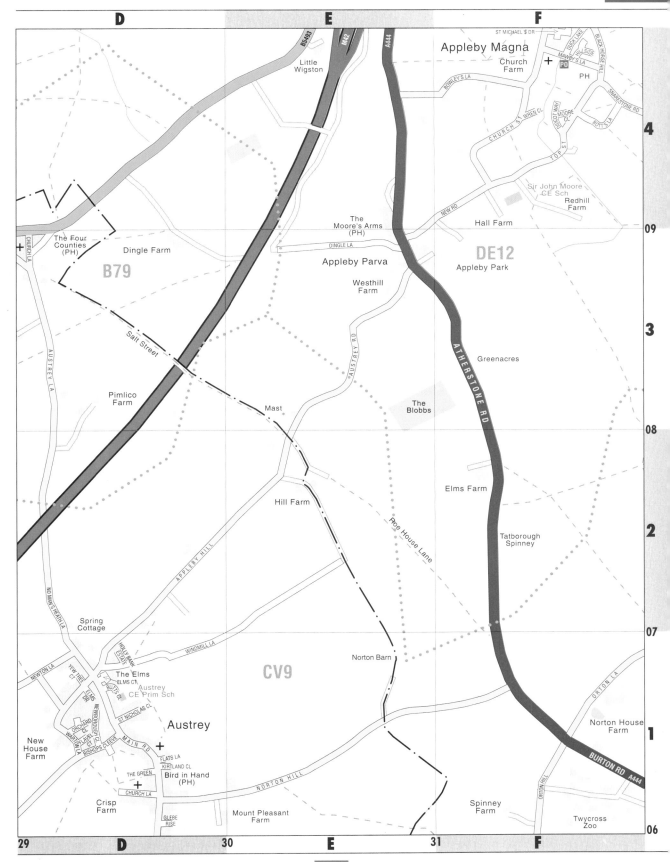

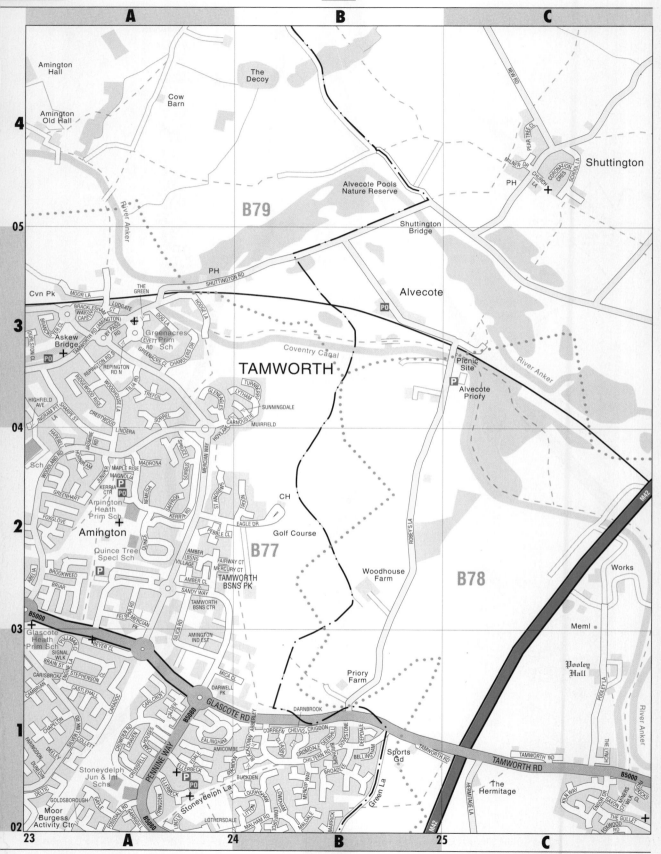

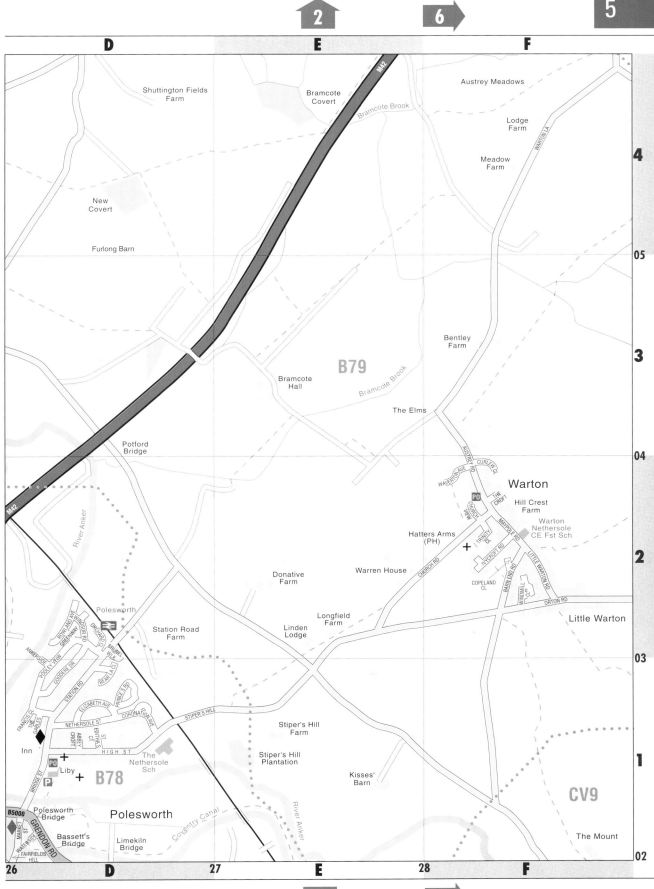

D E F

4
05
3
04
2
03
1
02

Shuttington Fields Farm

Bramcote Covert

Austrey Meadows

Bramcote Brook

Lodge Farm

Meadow Farm

WARTON LA

New Covert

Furlong Barn

Bentley Farm

B79

Bramcote Brook

Bramcote Hall

The Elms

M42

Potford Bridge

AUSTREY RD

CURLEW CL

Warton

WAVERTON AVE

PO

THE CROFT

CHURCH VIEW

Hill Crest Farm

Warton Nethersole CE Fst Sch

River Anker

Hatters Arms (PH)

TRINITY CL

MAYPOLE RD

Polesworth

Station Road Farm

Donative Farm

Warren House

CHURCH RD

IVYCROFT RD

BARN END RD

LITTLE WARTON RD

Little Warton

COPELAND CL

WINDMILL CL

ORTON RD

Longfield Farm

Linden Lodge

ROWLAND AVE

WINDSOR RD

GREENWAY

ORCHARD CL

BRUNEL WAY

ANKERSIDE CL

PYDLEY VIEW

GOODERE DR

STATION RD

BEAR LA

PRINCE'S RD

ELIZABETH AVE

CORONATION AVE

Stiper's Hill

Stiper's Hill Farm

FRANCIS CT

GABLES

NETHERSOLE ST

EDITHA S CT

ST EDITHA S

HIGH ST

ABBEY CROFT

The Nethersole Sch

Stiper's Hill Plantation

Inn

PO

Liby

P

B78

Kisses' Barn

River Anker

CV9

B5000

MARKET

GRENDON RD

WATERSIDE

Polesworth Bridge

Polesworth

Coventry Canal

FAIRFIELDS HILL

Bassett's Bridge

Limekiln Bridge

The Mount

26 D 27 E 28 F

A

B

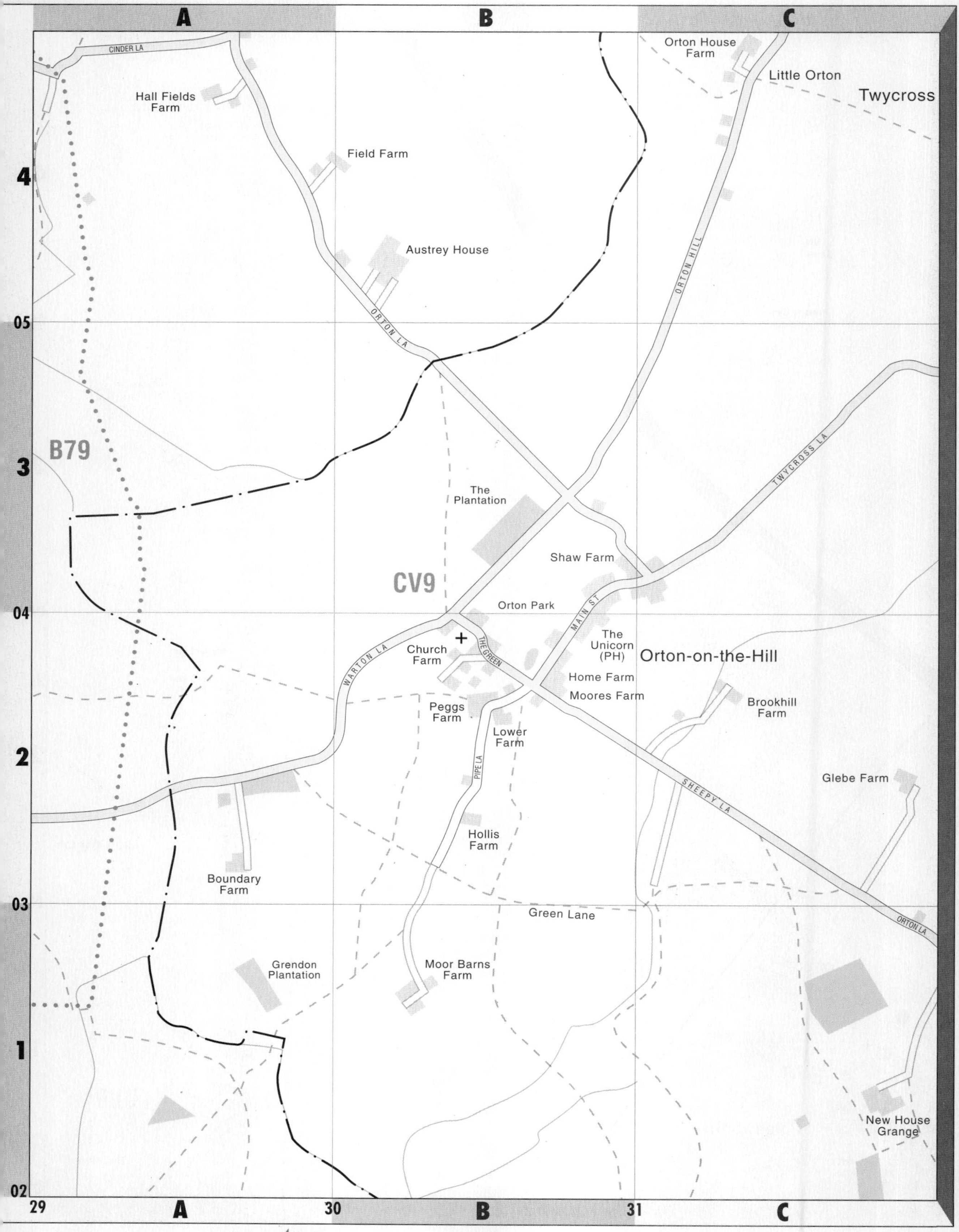

C

CINDER LA

Hall Fields
Farm

Orton House
Farm

Little Orton

Twycross

Field Farm

4

Austrey House

ORTON LA

ORTON HILL

05

TWYCROSS LA

B79

3

The Plantation

Shaw Farm

CV9

Orton Park

MAIN ST

04

+

The
Unicorn
(PH)

Orton-on-the-Hill

WARTON LA

Church
Farm

THE GREEN

Home Farm

Brookhill
Farm

Moores Farm

Peggs
Farm

PIPE LA

Lower
Farm

2

SHEEPY LA

Glebe Farm

Hollis
Farm

03

Boundary
Farm

Green Lane

ORTON LA

Grendon
Plantation

Moor Barns
Farm

1

New House
Grange

02

29

A

30

B

31

C

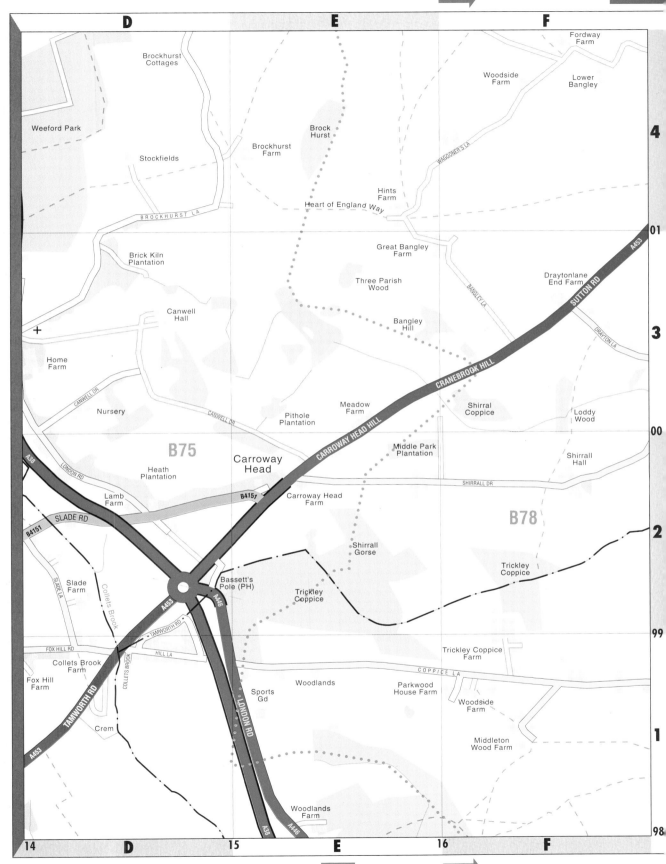

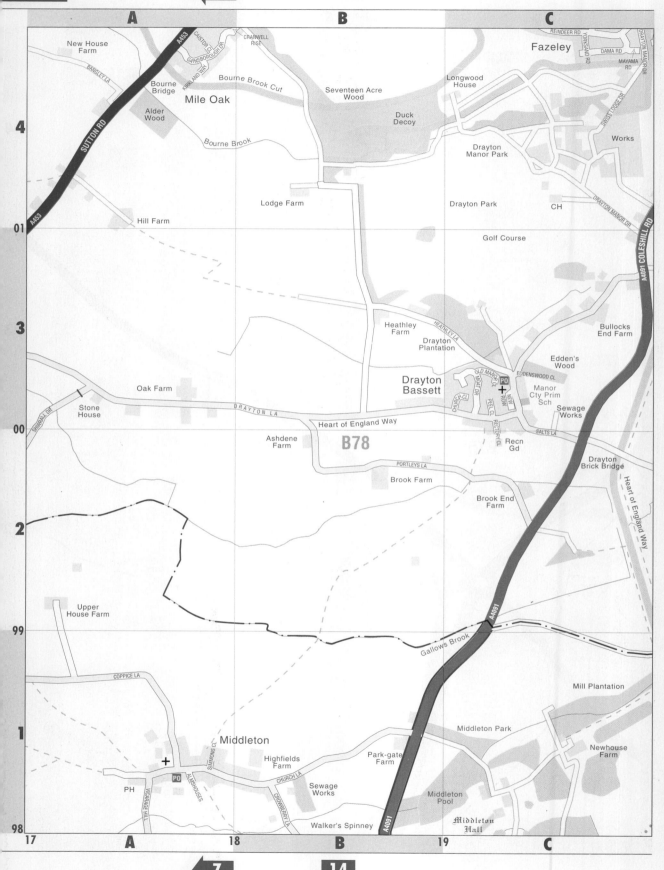

Fazeley

Mile Oak

New House Farm

Bourne Bridge

Alder Wood

Bourne Brook Cut

Seventeen Acre Wood

Longwood House

Duck Decoy

Drayton Manor Park

Works

Hill Farm

Lodge Farm

Drayton Park

CH

Golf Course

Heathley Farm

Drayton Plantation

Bullocks End Farm

Edden's Wood

Oak Farm

Stone House

Drayton Bassett

Manor Cty Prim Sch

Sewage Works

Drayton La

Heart of England Way

B78

Recn Gd

Drayton Brick Bridge

Ashdene Farm

Portleys La

Brook Farm

Brook End Farm

Upper House Farm

Gallows Brook

Mill Plantation

Coppice La

Middleton

Highfields Farm

Park-gate Farm

Middleton Park

Newhouse Farm

PH

PO

Church La

Sewage Works

Middleton Pool

Middleton Hall

Walker's Spinney

A4091

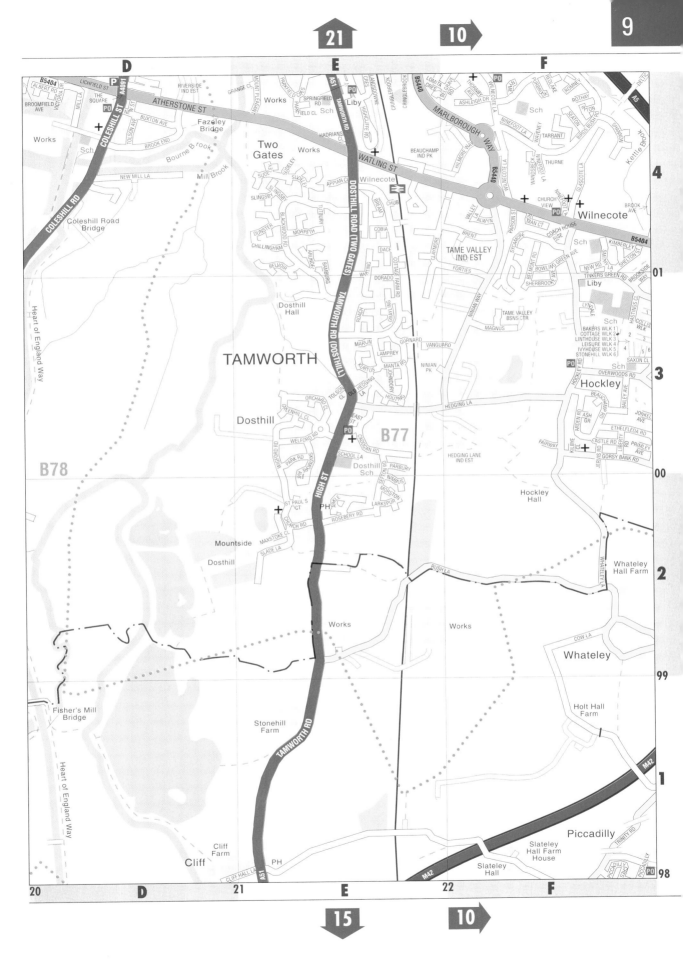

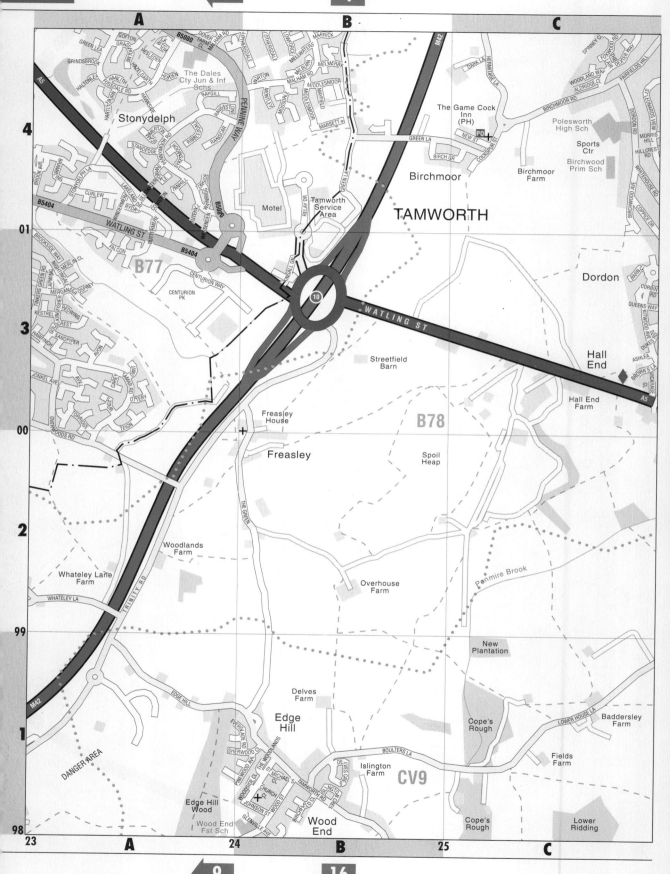

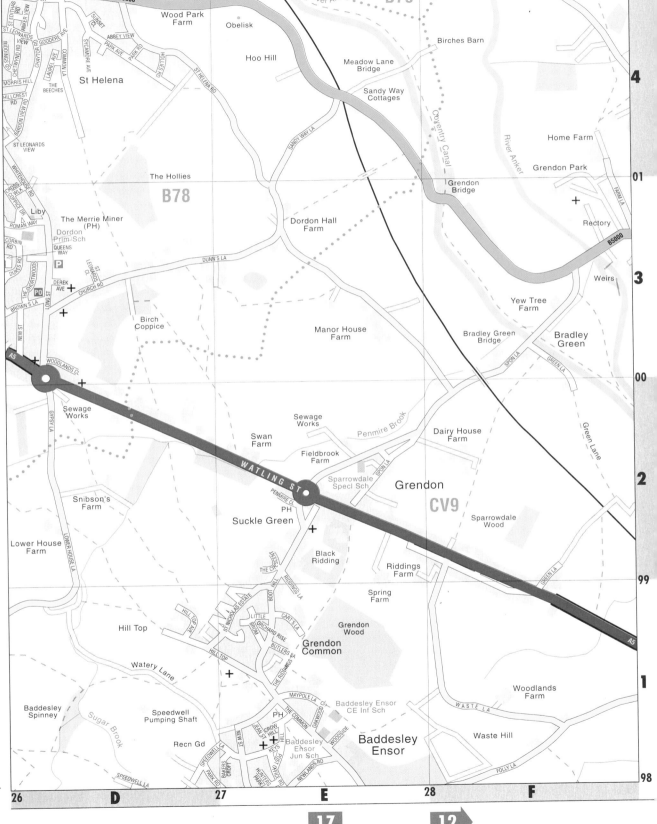

5 | 12

D | E | F

GRENDON RD **B5000**
FAIRFIELDS HILL
POTTERS LA
LIME KILN
Wood Park Farm
Obelisk
River Anker
B79
Birches Barn

ST EDITHS RD
ANKER VIEW
ST LEONARDS VIEW
RIDDINGS
MORRIS HILL
CHETWYND RD
HILLCREST RD
CHAYTOR
GOODERE AVE
LAUREL AVE
SYCAMORE AVE
PARK AVE
PARK RD
ABBEY VIEW
SUNSET DR
HOLLIES RD
St Helena
Hoo Hill
Meadow Lane Bridge
Sandy Way Cottages

4

THE BEECHES
ST LEONARDS VIEW
BARDON VIEW RD
WHITEHOUSE RD
Liby
COMMON LA
ST HELENA RD
SANDY WAY LA
Coventry Canal
River Anker
Home Farm
Grendon Park

The Hollies
B78
Grendon Bridge
Rectory
FARM LA
B5000

01

CROSS WLK
COPPICE DR
ROMAN WAY
CORBIN RD
DUKES RD
The Merrie Miner (PH)
Dordon Prim Sch
QUEENS WAY
The Shortwoods
P
P0
DEREK AVE
CHURCH RD
ST LEONARDS CL
DUNN'S LA
Dordon Hall Farm
Yew Tree Farm
Weirs

3

NEW ST
BROWN'S LA
LONG ST
Birch Coppice
Manor House Farm
Bradley Green Bridge
SPOON LA
Bradley Green
GREEN LA

A5
WOODLANDS CL
Sewage Works
Swan Farm
Sewage Works
Penmire Brook
Dairy House Farm
Green Lane

00

GYPSY LA
Snibson's Farm
LOWER HOUSE LA
Fieldbrook Farm
Sparrowdale Specl Sch
SPOON LA
Grendon
CV9
Sparrowdale Wood

2

Lower House Farm
WATLING ST
PENMIRE CL
PH
Suckle Green
THE CROSS
Black Ridding
Riddings Farm
GREEN LA

99

Hill Top
THE CROSS
RIDDINGS LA
BOOT
ST NICHOLAS ESTATE
LITTLE BRUM
CART'S LA
ORCHARD RISE
BUTLERS LA
THE RIDDINGS
HILL TOP AVE
HILL TOP
Grendon Common
Spring Farm
Grendon Wood
Woodlands Farm
WASTE LA

1

Watery Lane
Baddesley Spinney
Sugar Brook
Speedwell Pumping Shaft
Recn Gd
MAYPOLE LA
THE COMMON
NEW ST
CROW HILL
PH
JEAN'S LA
POST OFFICE RD
Baddesley Ensor Jun Sch
OAKWOOD
WOODSIDE
Baddesley Ensor CE Inf Sch
Baddesley Ensor
Waste Hill
FOLLY LA

SPEEDWELL LA
BAKERS CROFT
PARK RD
HUNTERS PARK
NEWLANDS RD
A5

98

26 | D | 27 | E | 28 | F

17 | 12

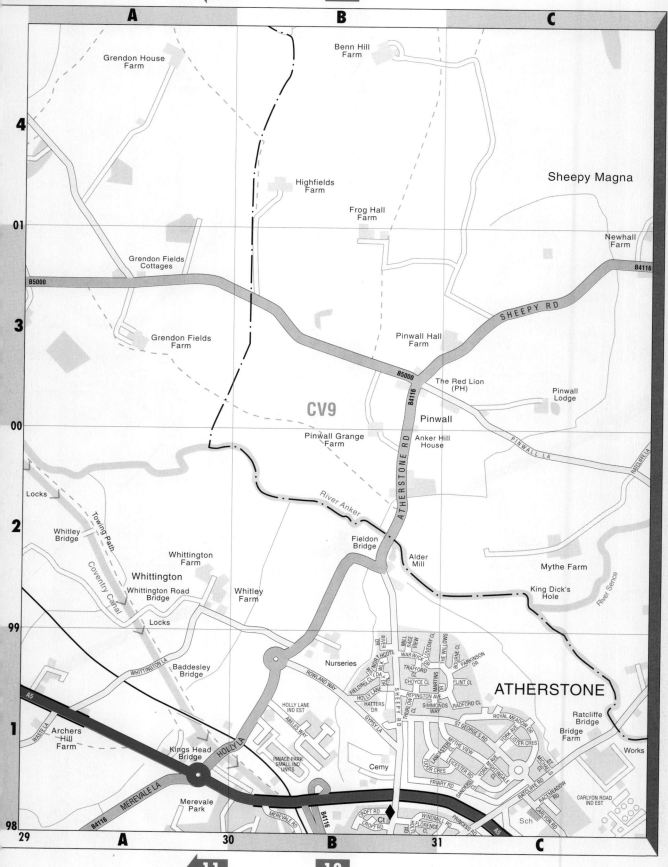

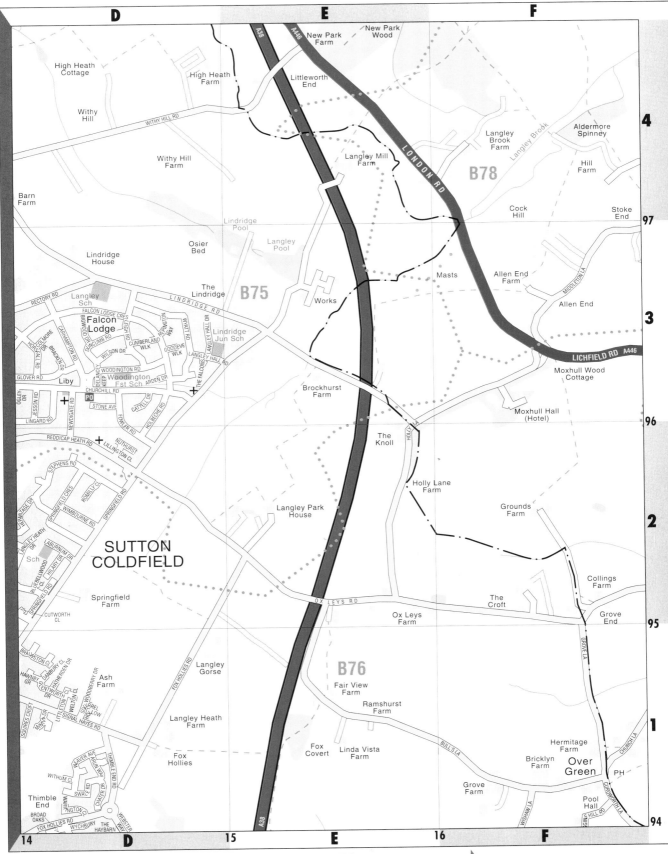

7
14
22
14

D E F

4
97
3
96
2
95
1
94

New Park Farm
New Park Wood
High Heath Cottage
High Heath Farm
Littleworth End
Withy Hill
WITHY HILL RD
Langley Mill Farm
Langley Brook Farm
Langley Brook
Aldermore Spinney
Hill Farm
Withy Hill Farm
B78
LONDON RD
A446
A38
Cock Hill
Stoke End
Barn Farm
Lindridge Pool
Osier Bed
Langley Pool
Masts
Allen End Farm
Allen End
MIDDLETON LA
Lindridge House
The Lindridge
LINDRIDGE RD
B75
Works
LICHFIELD RD A446
Moxhull Wood Cottage
RECTORY RD
Langley Sch
FALCON LODGE CRES
Falcon Lodge
BIGWOOD DR
DUNCOMB RD
CUMBERLAND WLK
WYATT RD
GOODEVE WLK
REPINGTON WAY
WILSON DR
LANGLEY HALL RD
THE FALCONS
Lindridge Jun Sch
HORSECROFT DR
BRACKNELL
CARHAMPTON RD
WOODINGTON RD
DELANCY KEEP
Woodington Fst Sch
ARDEN DR
Brockhurst Farm
GLOVER RD
Liby
CHURCHILL RD
CATTELL RD
HOLBECHE RD
Moxhull Hall (Hotel)
OGLEY DR
JESSON RD
NEWDIGATE RD
PO
STONE AVE
FOWLER RD
LINGARD RD
The Knoll
HOLLY LA
REDDICAP HEATH RD
LILLINGTON CL
NUTHURST
Holly Lane Farm
STEPHENS RD
Grounds Farm
ROMILLY CL
SPRINGFIELD CRES
WIMBOURNE RD
SPRINGFIELD RD
HERMITAGE DR
Langley Park House
SUTTON COLDFIELD
LANGLEY HEATH DR
LABURNUM DR
Sch
HILARY DR
BLUEBELLWOOD CL
Collings Farm
Springfield Farm
The Croft
Grove End
CUTWORTH CL
OX LEYS RD
Ox Leys Farm
GROVE LA
BRAMSTON CL
DANBURY CL
HETHERTON DR
Langley Gorse
FOX HOLLIES RD
B76
Fair View Farm
HAWNBY GR
WELTON CL
KENTWORTH DR
SQUIRREL HOLLOW
WOODBERRY DR
Ash Farm
Ramshurst Farm
SQUIRES CROFT
LITTLETON CL
SIGNAL HAYES RD
BULL S LA
Hermitage Farm
CHURCHILL LA
Langley Heath Farm
Bricklyn Farm
Over Green
DUNWORTH LA
WEAVER AVE
WITHUM CL
THIMBLE END RD
CHARTER RD
Fox Hollies
Fox Covert
Linda Vista Farm
PH
Thimble End
WARRINGTON CL
WEBSTER WAY
Grove Farm
WISHAW LA
Pool Hall
VESEY HILL RD
BROAD OAKS
FOX HOLLIES RD
WYCHBURY
THE HAYBARN

14 D 15 E 16 F

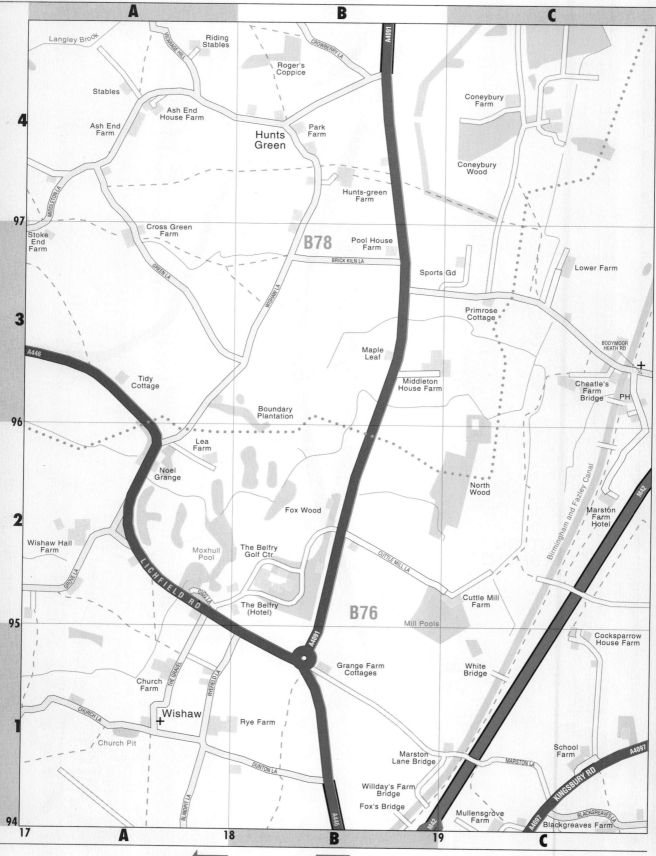

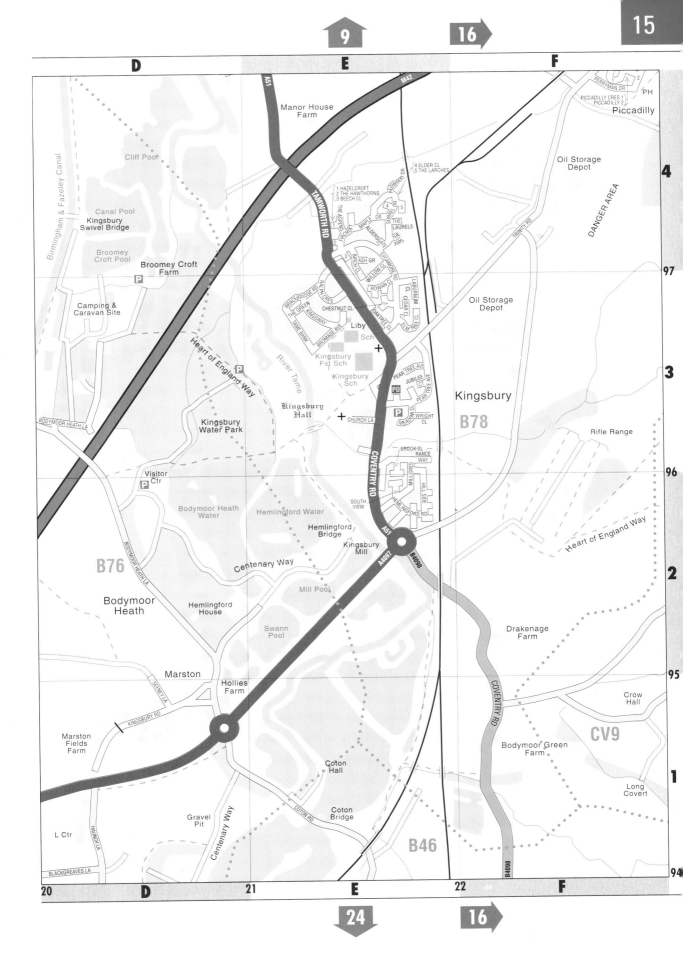

A   B   C

WOOD ST

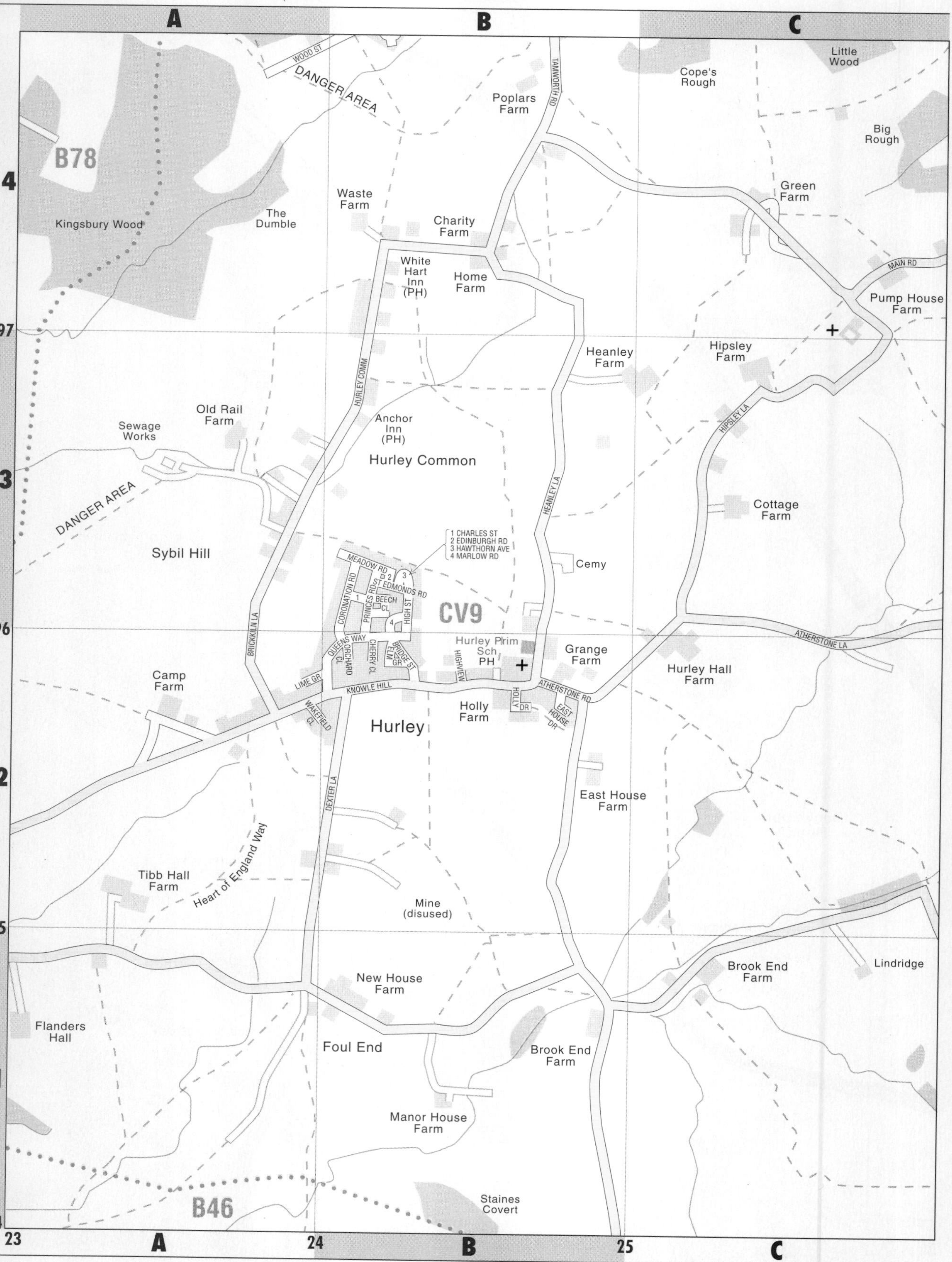

DANGER AREA

Poplars Farm

TAMWORTH RD

Cope's Rough

Little Wood

Big Rough

B78

4

Kingsbury Wood

The Dumble

Waste Farm

Charity Farm

Green Farm

White Hart Inn (PH)

Home Farm

MAIN RD

Pump House Farm

97

HURLEY COMM

Heanley Farm

Hipsley Farm

Sewage Works

Old Rail Farm

Anchor Inn (PH)

HIPSLEY LA

3

DANGER AREA

Hurley Common

HEANLEY LA

Cottage Farm

Sybil Hill

1 CHARLES ST
2 EDINBURGH RD
3 HAWTHORN AVE
4 MARLOW RD

MEADOW RD

ST EDMONDS RD

Cemy

Cemy

CV9

CORONATION RD

PRINCE RD

BEECH CL

HIGH ST

96

BRICKKILN LA

QUEENS WAY

ORCHARD CL

CHERRY CL

ELM GR

BRIDGE ST

Hurley Prim Sch

Grange Farm

ATHERSTONE LA

Camp Farm

LIME GR

KNOWLE HILL

HIGHVIEW

PH

Hurley Hall Farm

WAKEFIELD CL

Hurley

HOLLY DR

EAST HOUSE DR

ATHERSTONE RD

2

DEXTER LA

Holly Farm

East House Farm

Heart of England Way

Tibb Hall Farm

Mine (disused)

95

New House Farm

Brook End Farm

Lindridge

Flanders Hall

Foul End

Brook End Farm

1

Manor House Farm

Staines Covert

B46

94

23   A   24   B   25   C

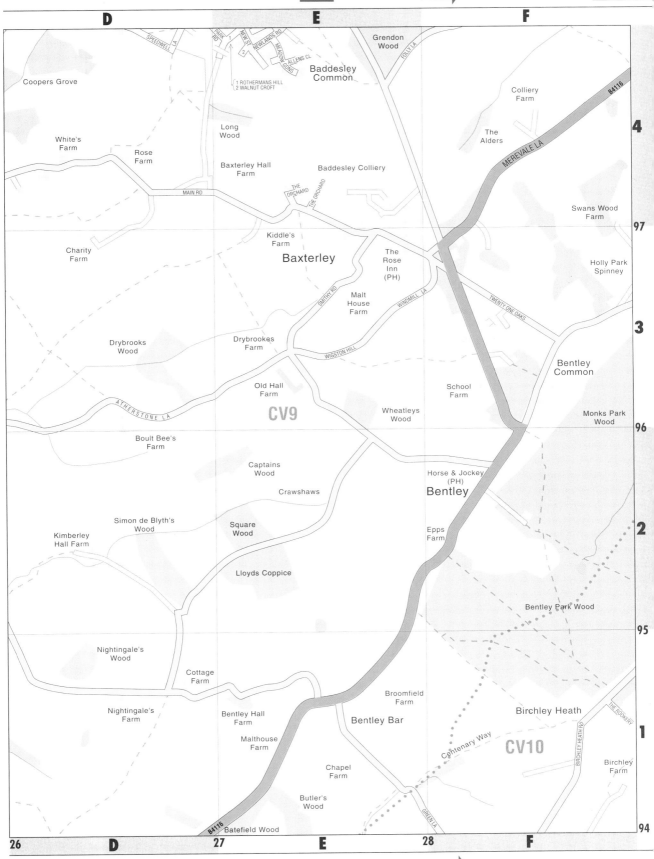

D E F

Coopers Grove

Grendon Wood

Baddesley Common

1 ROTHERMANS HILL
2 WALNUT CROFT

Colliery Farm

White's Farm

Long Wood

Rose Farm

The Alders

MEREVALE LA

B4116

4

Baxterley Hall Farm

Baddesley Colliery

Swans Wood Farm

97

MAIN RD

THE ORCHARD

THE ORCHARD

Kiddle's Farm

Baxterley

The Rose Inn (PH)

Holly Park Spinney

Charity Farm

SMITHY RD

Malt House Farm

WINDMILL LA

WIGSTON HILL

TWENTY ONE OAKS

3

Drybrooks Wood

Drybrookes Farm

Bentley Common

ATHERSTONE LA

Old Hall Farm

CV9

Wheatleys Wood

School Farm

Monks Park Wood

96

Boult Bee's Farm

Captains Wood

Horse & Jockey (PH)

Bentley

Crawshaws

Simon de Blyth's Wood

Square Wood

Epps Farm

2

Kimberley Hall Farm

Lloyds Coppice

Bentley Park Wood

95

Nightingale's Wood

Cottage Farm

Broomfield Farm

Birchley Heath

THE ROOKERY

Nightingale's Farm

Bentley Hall Farm

Bentley Bar

Centenary Way

CV10

BIRCHLEY HEATH RD

1

Malthouse Farm

Chapel Farm

GREEN LA

Birchley Farm

B4116

Butler's Wood

Batefield Wood

94

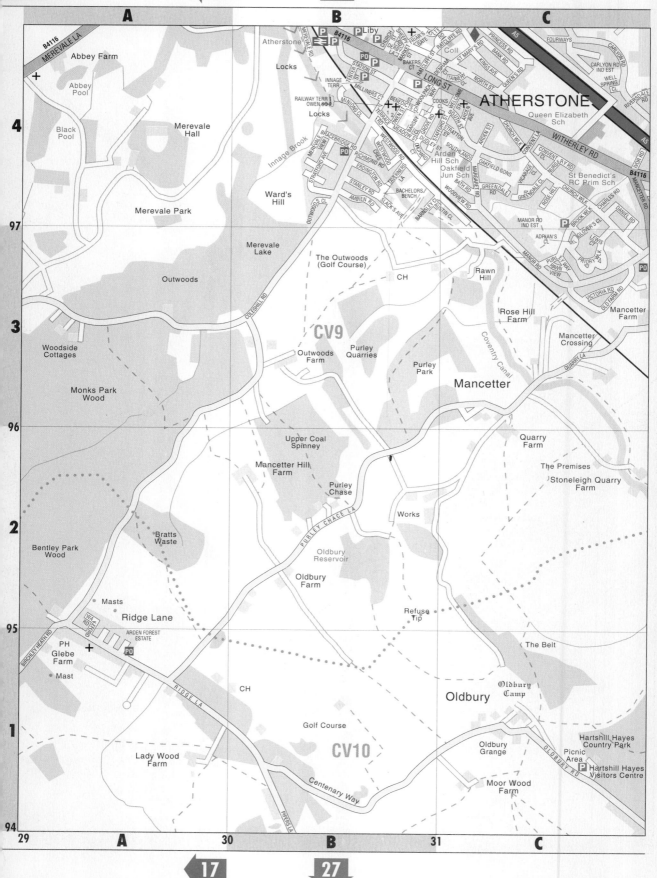

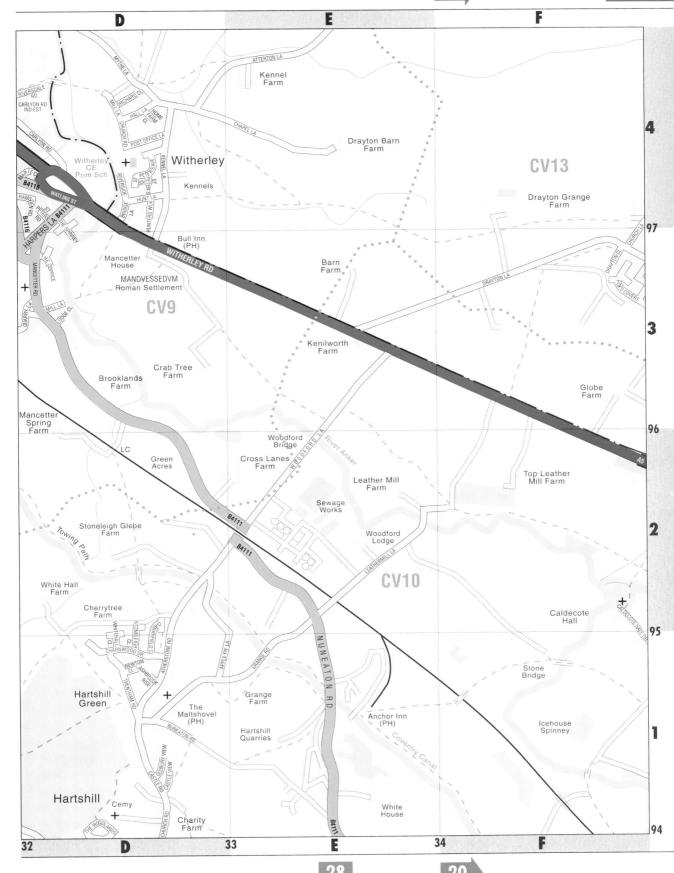

D E F

RIVERSDALE RD
CARLYON RD IND EST
CARLYON RD
ATTERTON LA
Kennel Farm
CHAPEL LA
Drayton Barn Farm
CV13
MYTHE LA
ORCHARD CL
HALL LA HOME FARM CL
MILL LA
CHURCH RD
POST OFFICE LA
Witherley CE Prim Sch
Witherley
ST PETERS CL
ST PETERS RD
KENNEL LA
Drayton Grange Farm

4

MAR LE CL
B4116
WATLING ST
RAMSDEN RD
B4116
HARPERS LA
B4111
RIVERSIDE
ST PETERS WLK
HUNT LA
HUNTERS WLK
THE SPINNEY
Kennels
97
CHURCH CL
DRAYTON CL
FOX'S COVERT

Bull Inn (PH)
WITHERLEY RD
Barn Farm
DRAYTON LA

MANCETTER RD
Mancetter House
THE COPPICE
MANDVESSEDVM Roman Settlement
CV9
MILL LA
LODGE CL
QUARRY
Kenilworth Farm
Globe Farm

3

Crab Tree Farm
Brooklands Farm

96
A5

Mancetter Spring Farm
LC
Green Acres
Woodford Bridge
WOODFORD LA
River Anker
Cross Lanes Farm
Leather Mill Farm
Top Leather Mill Farm

Towing Path
Stoneleigh Glebe Farm
B4111
Sewage Works
Woodford Lodge
LEATHERMILL LA

2

B4111
CV10

White Hall Farm
Cherrytree Farm
WHITEHALL CL
STONELEIGH CL
ASHFIELD CL
ATHERSTONE RD
CHARNWOOD DR
ASHBROOK RISE
NEWTON CL
TRENTHAM RD
APPLE PIE LA
GRANGE RD
NUNEATON RD
Caldecote Hall
CALDECOTE HALL LA

95

Hartshill Green
The Maltshovel (PH)
NUNEATON RD
Grange Farm
Hartshill Quarries
Stone Bridge
Anchor Inn (PH)
Coventry Canal
Icehouse Spinney

1

Hartshill
Cemy
CASTLE RD
OLDBURY VIEW
CASTLE VIEW
CHURCH RD
THE WOODLANDS
Charity Farm
B4111
White House

94

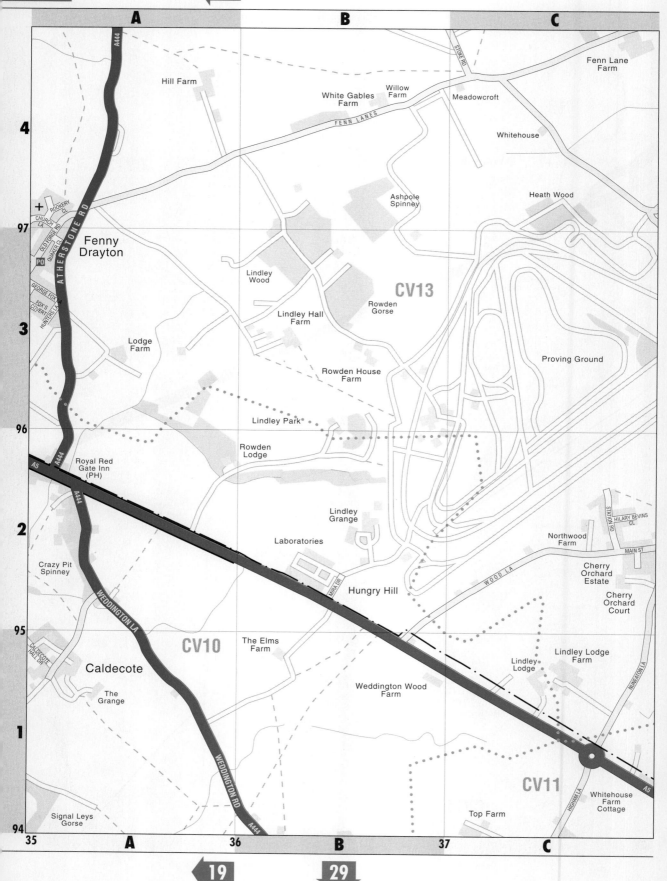

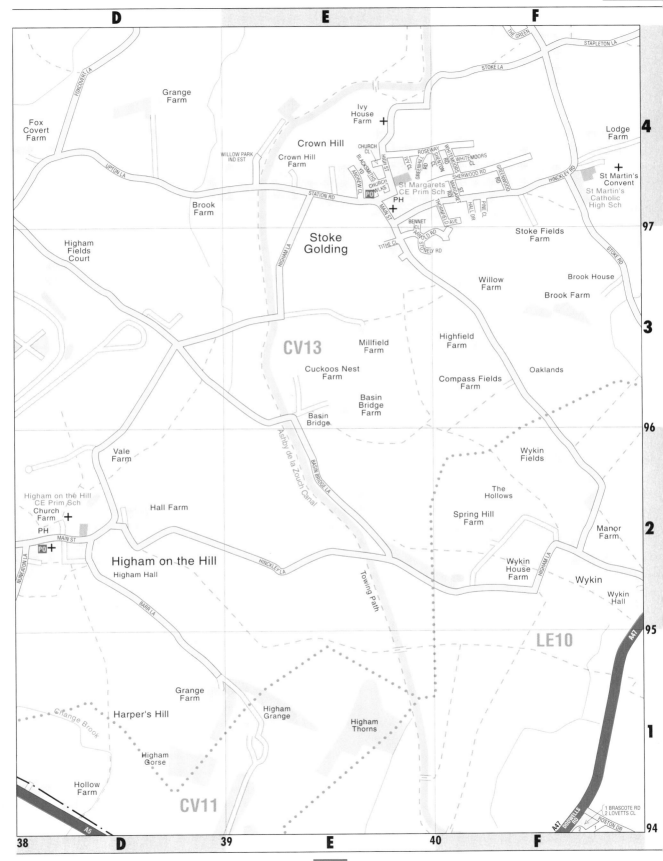

D E F

4

97

3

96

2

95

1

94

38 D 39 E 40 F

Fox Covert Farm

Grange Farm

FOXCOVERT LA

UPTON LA

Brook Farm

WILLOW PARK IND EST

Crown Hill Farm

Crown Hill

Ivy House Farm

CHURCH CL

ROSEWAY

WHITMOORS CL

Whitmoors CL

SHERETON RD

GREENHILL RD

HIGH ST

IVY CL

BLACKSMITHS CL

ANDREW CL

PO

CHURCH WLKS

St Margarets CE Prim Sch

SHERWOOD RD

ST MARGARET RD

THORNFIELD AVE

HALL DR

PINE CL

GREENWOOD RD

HINCKLEY RD

STOKE LA

THE GREEN

STAPLETON LA

Lodge Farm

St Martin's Convent

St Martin's Catholic High Sch

STOKE RD

STATION RD

MAIN ST

PH

BENNET CL

ASHFORD RD

STONELY RD

TITHE CL

Stoke Golding

Stoke Fields Farm

Higham Fields Court

HIGHAM LA

Willow Farm

Brook House

Brook Farm

CV13

Millfield Farm

Highfield Farm

Oaklands

Cuckoos Nest Farm

Compass Fields Farm

Basin Bridge Farm

Ashby de la Zouch Canal

BASIN BRIDGE LA

Basin Bridge

Wykin Fields

Vale Farm

The Hollows

Spring Hill Farm

Wykin House Farm

HIGHAM LA

Manor Farm

Wykin

Higham on the Hill CE Prim Sch

Church Farm

PH

PO

NUNEATON LA

MAIN ST

Hall Farm

HINCKLEY LA

Higham on the Hill

Higham Hall

BARR LA

Towing Path

Wykin Hall

LE10

A47

DOUGLES RD

A47

Grange Brook

Harper's Hill

Grange Farm

Higham Grange

Higham Thorns

Higham Gorse

Hollow Farm

CV11

A5

1 BRASCOTE RD
2 LOVETTS CL

ROSTON DR

30

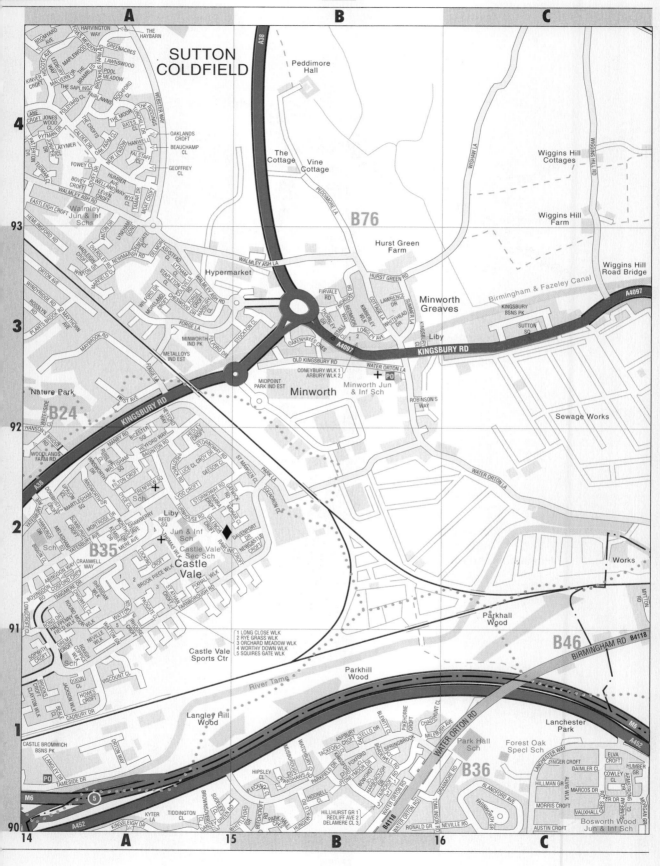

SUTTON COLDFIELD

B76

Peddimore Hall

Wiggins Hill Cottages

Wiggins Hill Farm

Wiggins Hill Road Bridge

The Cottage

Vine Cottage

Hurst Green Farm

Birmingham & Fazeley Canal

A4097

Minworth Greaves

Hypermarket

KINGSBURY RD

Kingsbury Bsns Pk

Sutton Sq

Liby

Minworth Ind Pk

Metalloys Ind Est

Midpoint Park Ind Est

Minworth

Old Kingsbury Rd

Coneybury Wlk 1
Arbury Wlk 2

Minworth Jun & Inf Sch

Robinson's Way

Water Orton La

Nature Park

B24

Sewage Works

KINGSBURY RD

B35

Liby Reed Sq Jun & Inf Sch

Castle Vale Sec Sch

Castle Vale

Davenport Dr

Newcastle Croft

Water Orton La

Works

Parkhall Wood

B46

BIRMINGHAM RD B4118

1 LONG CLOSE WLK
2 RYE GRASS WLK
3 ORCHARD MEADOW WLK
4 WORTHY DOWN WLK
5 SQUIRES GATE WLK

Castle Vale Sports Ctr

River Tame

Parkhill Wood

M6

Lanchester Park

A452

Langley Hill Wood

Castle Bromwich Bsns Pk

PO

Water Orton Rd

Park Hall Sch

Forest Oak Specl Sch

B36

Bosworth Wood Jun & Inf Sch

M6

A452

1 HILLHURST GR 1
2 REDLIFF AVE 2
3 DELAMERE CL 3

B4118

Water Orton Rd

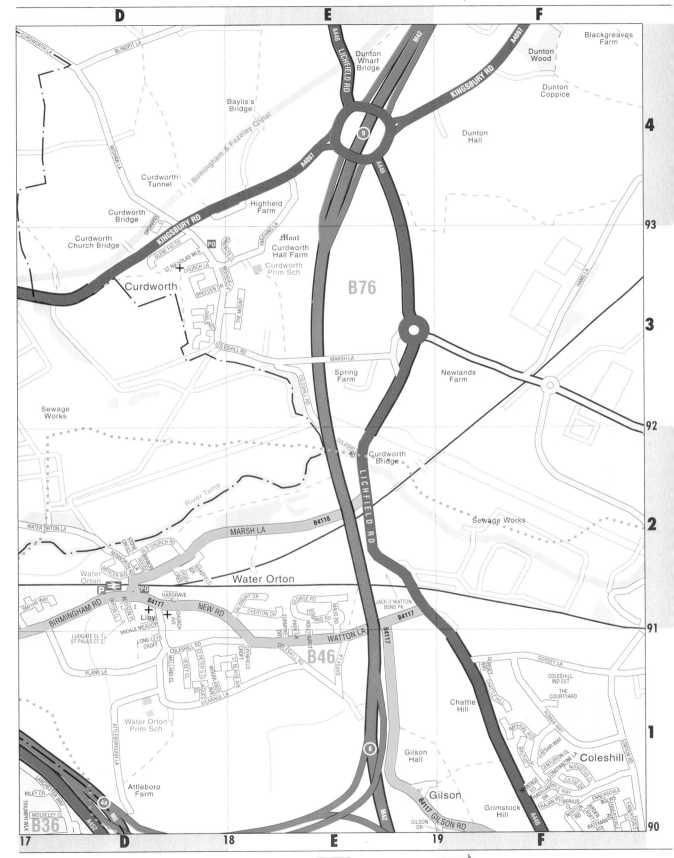

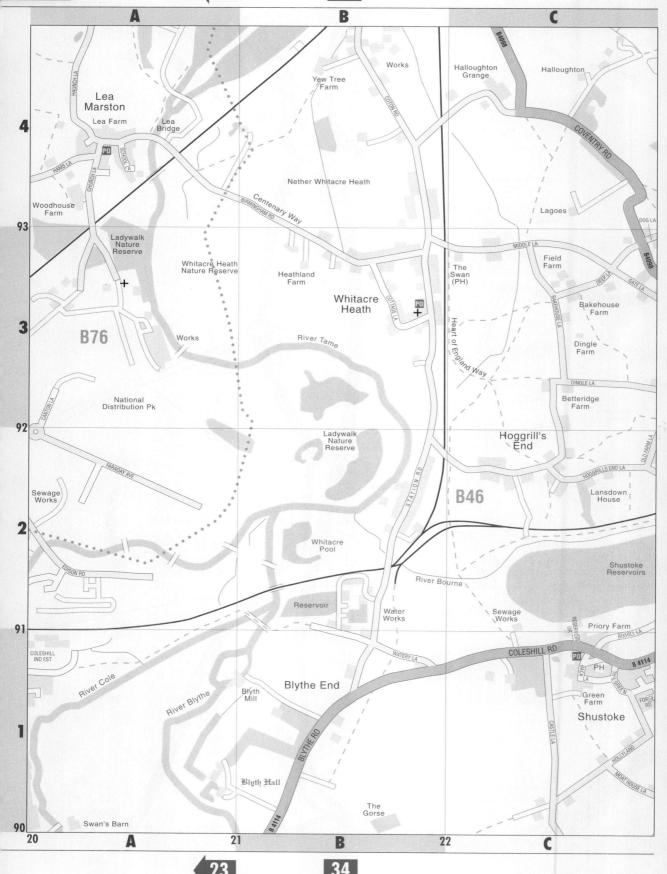

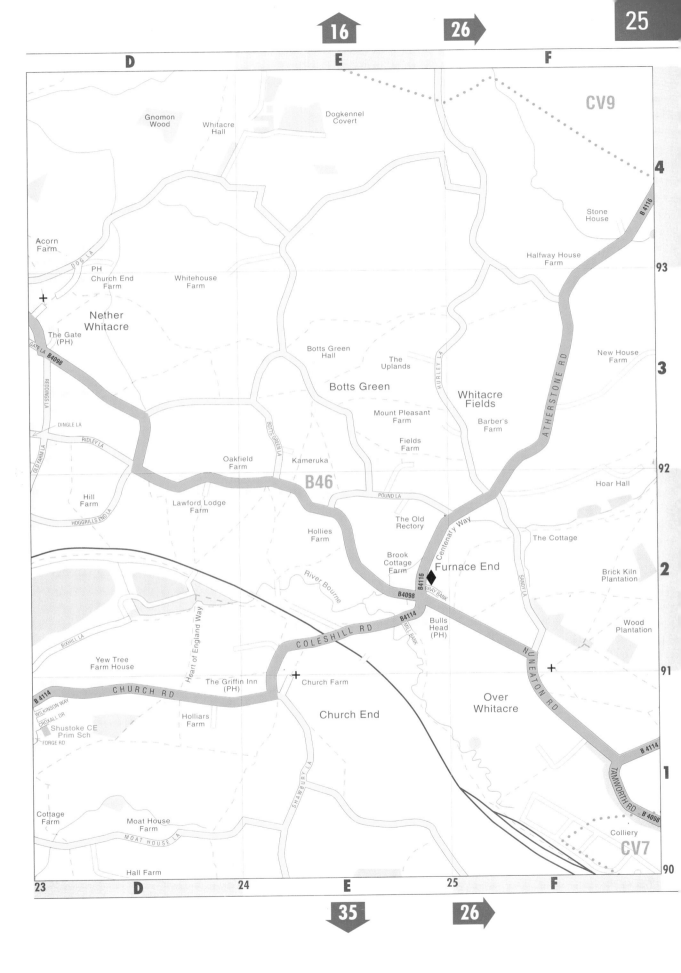

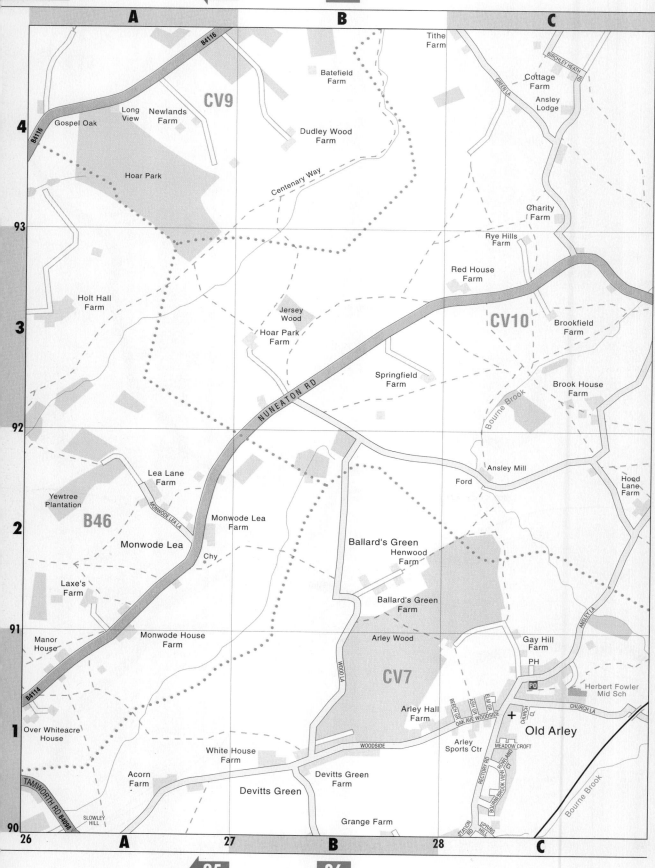

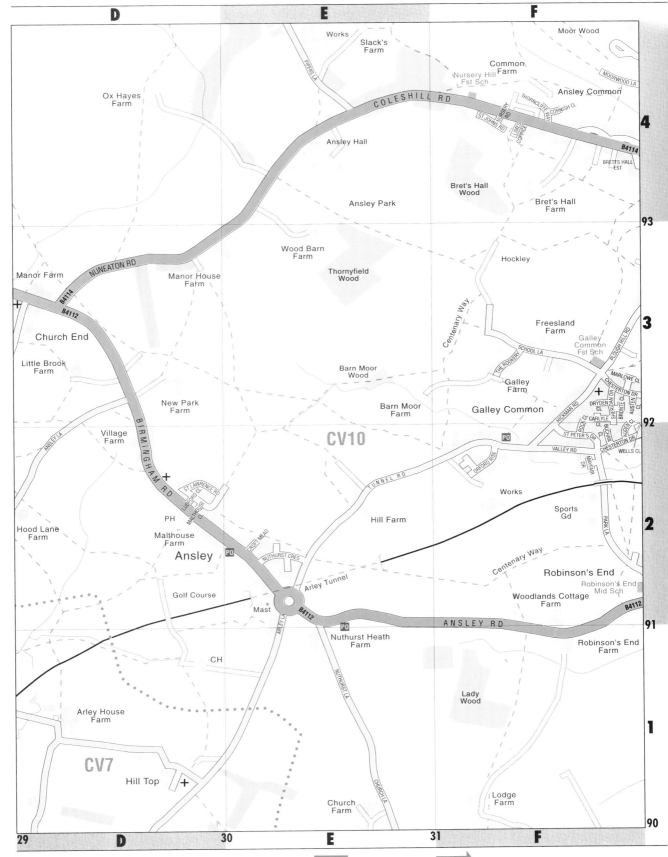

D   E   F

Works

Moor Wood

Slack's
Farm

Common
Farm

MOORWOOD LA

Nursery Hill Fst Sch

Ansley Common

THORNCLIFFE RD

PIPERS LA

CORNISH CL

COLESHILL RD

ST JOHNS RD

NURSERY RD

LIMES COPPICE

B4114

4

BRETTS HALL
EST

Ox Hayes
Farm

Ansley Hall

Bret's Hall
Wood

Bret's Hall
Farm

93

Wood Barn
Farm

Ansley Park

Hockley

Thornyfield
Wood

Centenary Way

Freesland
Farm

NUNEATON RD

Manor Farm

Manor House
Farm

Galley
Common
Fst Sch

3

PLOUGH HILL RD

B4114

SCHOOL LA

THE ROOKERY

MARLOWE CL

B4112

Church End

Barn Moor
Wood

Galley
Farm

MARLOWE CL

CHESTERTON DR

Little Brook
Farm

Barn Moor
Farm

Galley Common

DRYDEN CL

BRONTE CL

AUSTEN CL

ANSLEY LA

New Park
Farm

HICKMAN RD

ROCK CL

CARLYLE

BUCHAN

SPENCER CL

92

BIRMINGHAM RD

Village
Farm

St PETER'S DR

CHESTERTON DR

CV10

PO

WELLS CL

ORFORD RISE

VALLEY RD

MAYFAIR DR

St LAWRENCE RD

LUPTON CL

Hood Lane
Farm

TUNNEL RD

Works

Sports
Gd

PARK LA

2

MALTHOUSE CL

PH

Hill Farm

Malthouse
Farm

Centenary Way

Robinson's End

CROFT MEAD

Ansley

PO

Robinson's End
Mid Sch

NUTHURST CRES

Arley Tunnel

Woodlands Cottage
Farm

B4112

Golf Course

ARLEY LA

Mast

B4112

ANSLEY RD

91

PO

Nuthurst Heath
Farm

Robinson's End
Farm

CH

NUTHURST LA

Arley House
Farm

Lady
Wood

1

CV7

CHURCH LA

Hill Top

Lodge
Farm

Church
Farm

90

29   D   30   E   31   F

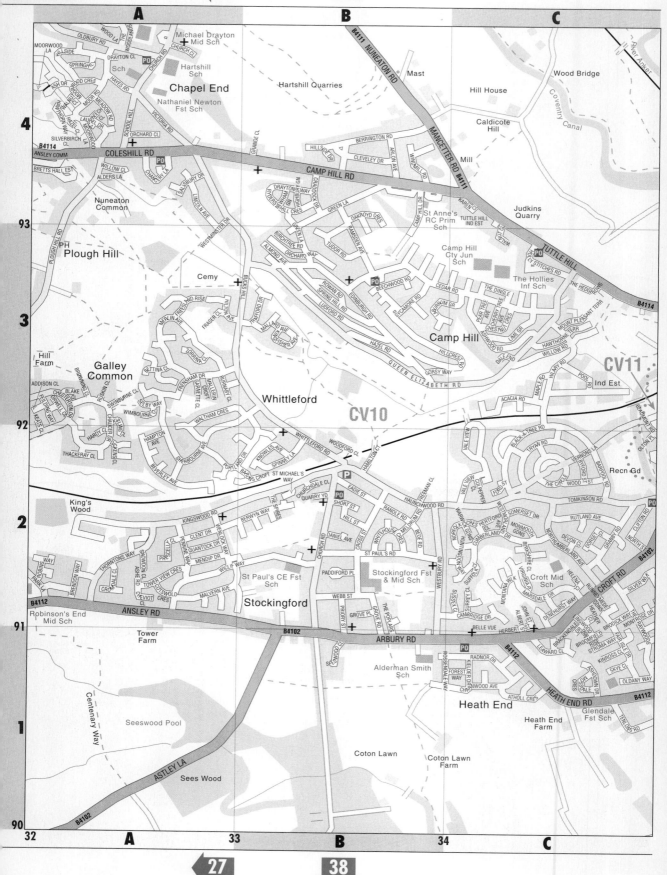

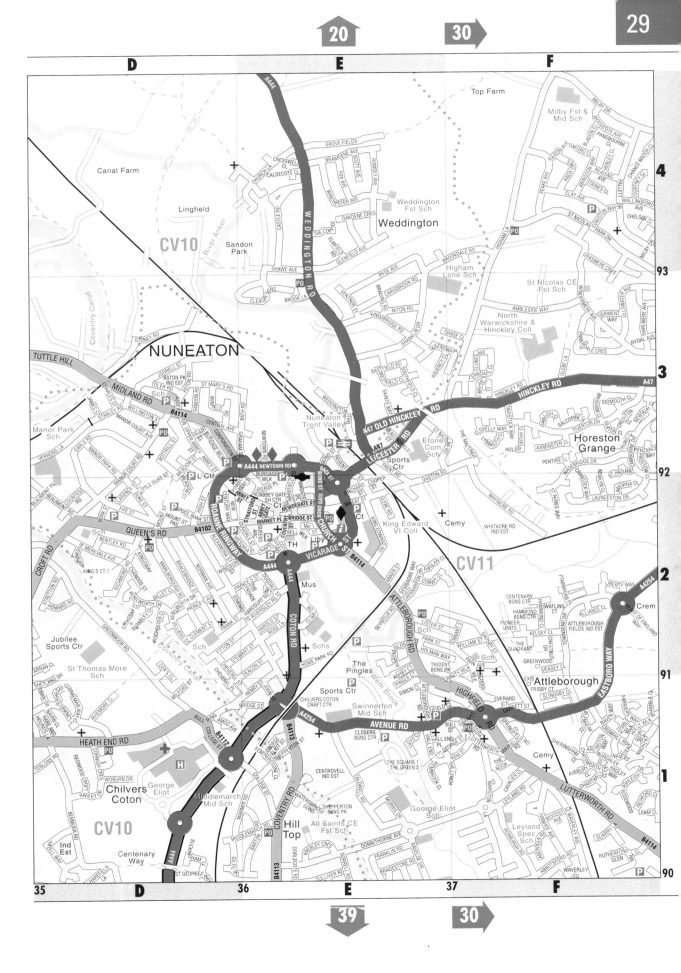

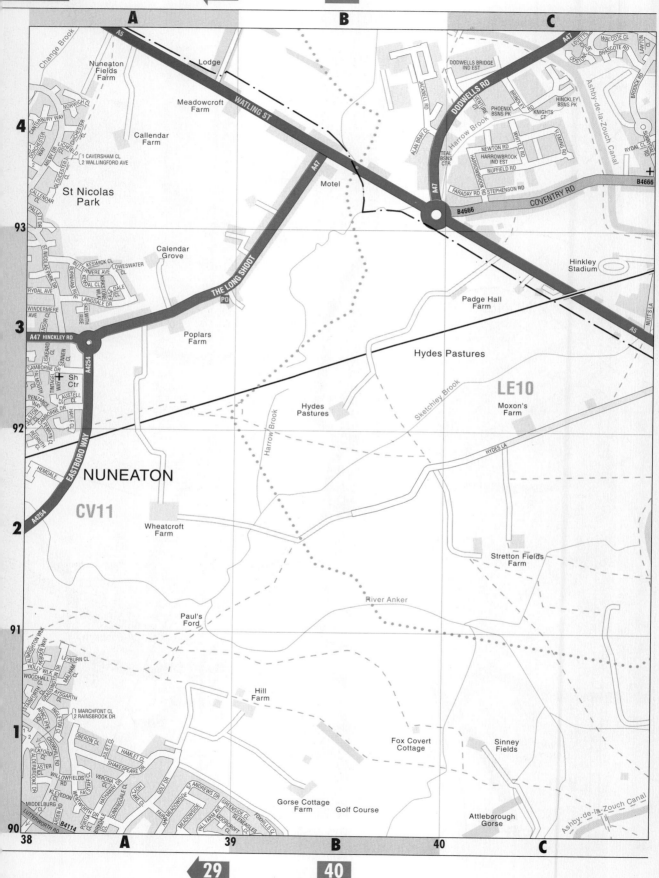

A   **B**   **C**

A5

Change Brook

Nuneaton
Fields
Farm

Lodge

WATLING ST

4

Meadowcroft
Farm

NORWICH CL

CANTERBURY WAY

DORCHESTER WAY

LICHFIELD

CHICHESTER

MILBY DR

GLOUCESTER CL

Callendar
Farm

CALLENDAR CL

PALLETT DR

1 CAVERSHAM CL
2 WALLINGFORD AVE

DODWELLS BRIDGE
IND EST

A47

JACKNELL RD

ALAN BRAY CL

DODWELLS RD

LOVETTS
CL

GROVE DR

WALCOTE CL

BRASCOTE RD

Ashby-de-la-Zouch Canal

Harrow Brook

VENTURE
CTR

BRINDLEY RD

PHOENIX
BSNS PK

HINCKLEY
BSNS PK

KNIGHTS
CT

WHITTLE RD

FLEMING RD

RYDAL CL

SHINFILL RD

St Nicolas
Park

Motel

TEAL
BSNS
CTR

HARROWBROOK

NEWTON RD

HARROWBROOK
IND EST

NUFFIELD RD

FARADAY RD

STEPHENSON RD

COVENTRY RD

B4666

93

A47

Calendar
Grove

THE LONG SHOOT

PO

ST NICOLAS PARK DR

KESWICK CL

LOWESWATER
CL

BUTTERMERE AVE

BURNHAM RISE

RYDAL AVE

KIRKSTONE

EASEDALE CL

LANGDALE DR

SKELWITH RISE

B4666

Padge
Hall
Farm

Hinkley
Stadium

A5

NUTT'S LA

3

A47 Hinckley Rd

A254

WINDERMERE
AVE

Poplars
Farm

Hydes Pastures

Sketchley Brook

LE10

FALMOUTH CL

CAMBORNE DR

TINTAGEL
WAY

Sh
Ctr

ST AUSTELL
CL

SENNEN CL

LISKEARD

Hydes
Pastures

Moxon's
Farm

92

PENZANCE
WAY

HELSTON

PENRYN CL

REDRUTH CL

CAMBORNE DR

EASTBORO WAY

HYDES LA

NUNEATON

HEMDALE

2

A4254

CV11

Wheatcroft
Farm

Harrow Brook

Stretton Fields
Farm

River Anker

91

ALBRIGHTON WLK

HERBERT WAY

LEYBURN CL

MALLOW CL

WOOLLY WLK

WOODHALL CL

GRASSINGTON
AVE

AYSGARTH
CL

Paul's
Ford

STAINCROFT

INGLEWAY

HAMLET CL

1 MARCHFONT CL
2 RAINSBROOK DR

Hill
Farm

OBERON CL

JULIET CL

SHAKESPEARE DR

Fox Covert
Cottage

Sinney
Fields

1

1

2

PICKFORD
CL

ASTER
CL

CROMWELL RD

WILLOWFIELDS
RD

VERONA
CL

HATHAWAY DR

ST ANDREWS DR

MEADOWSIDE

GREENSIDE CL

FOXHILLS CL

GLENEAGLES

LITHERBROOKE
CL

WENTWORTH DR

GOLF DR

KLEVEDON
CL

MIDDELBURG
CL

LUTTERWORTH RD

PORTIA CL

BRIDALE
CL

SUMMINGDALE CL

FAIRWAY

FALSTAFF CL

MOORCROFT

HLL FARM AVE

MEADOWBANK

Gorse Cottage
Farm

Golf Course

Attleborough
Gorse

Ashby-de-la-Zouch Canal

B4114

90

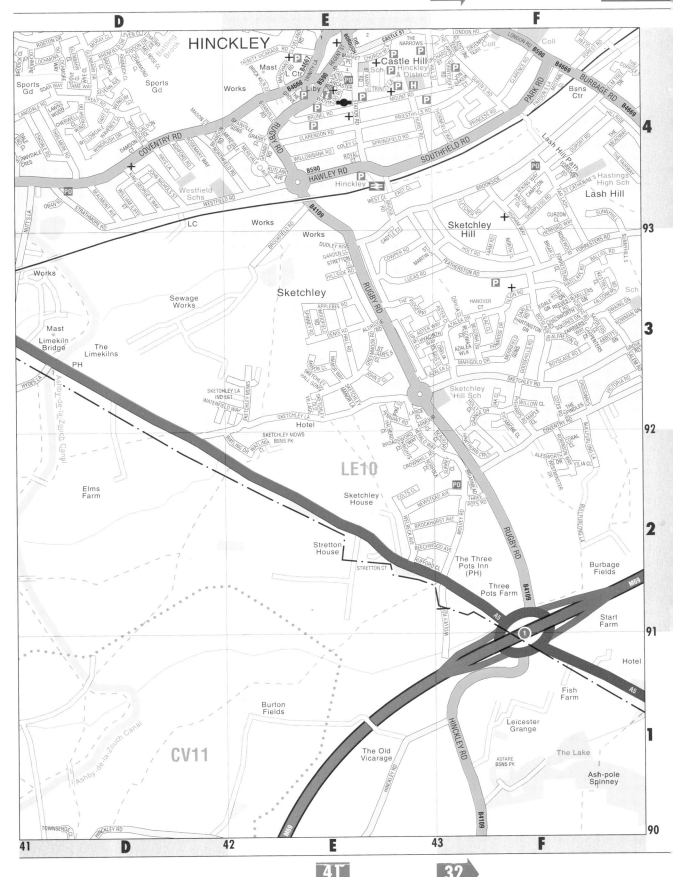

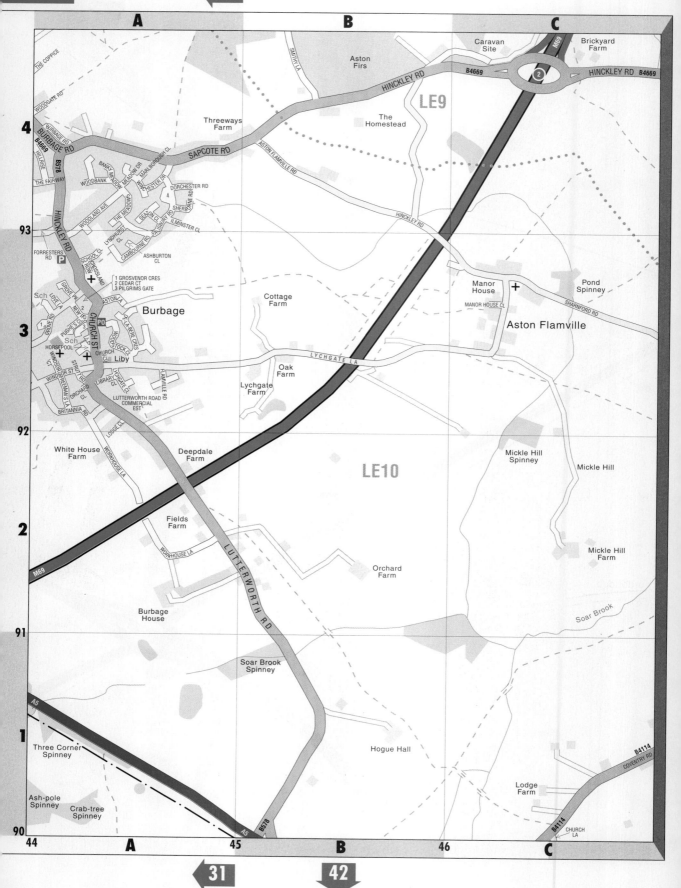

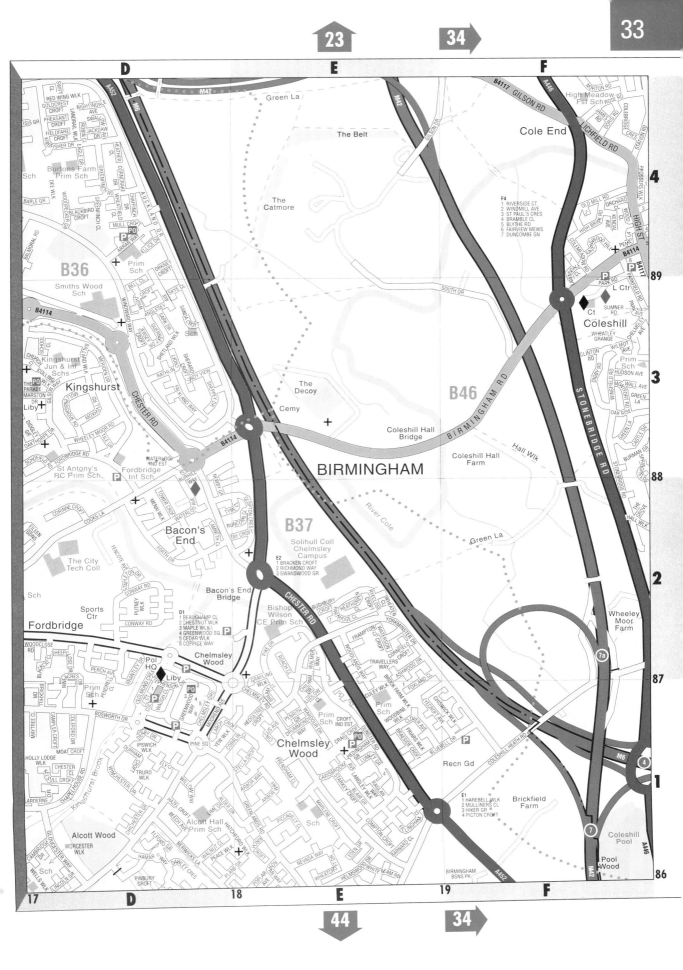

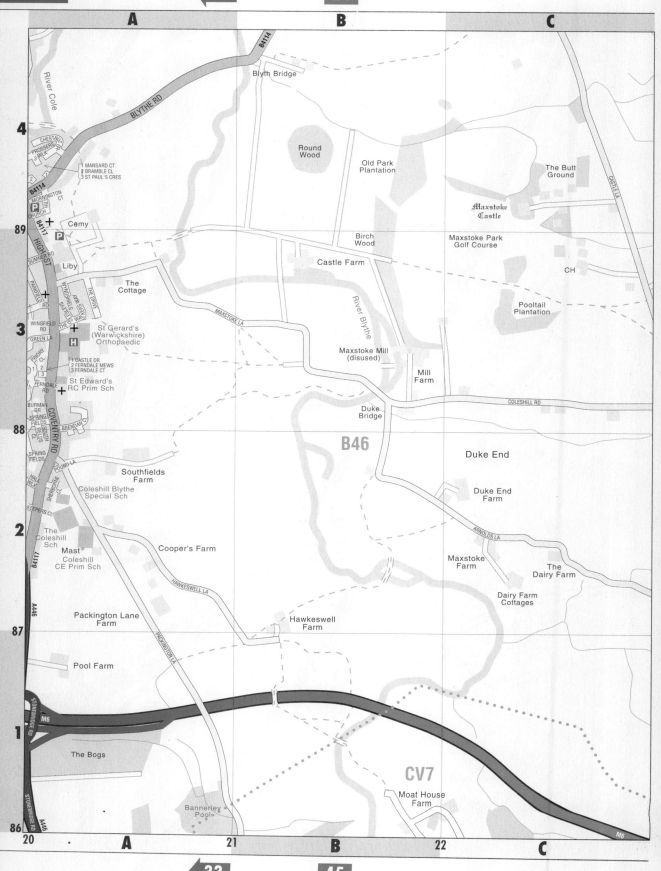

A   B   C

River Cole

BLYTHE RD

B4114

Blyth Bridge

Round Wood

Old Park Plantation

The Butt Ground

4

CHESTNUT GR
PROSSERS WLK

1 MANSARD CT
2 BRAMBLE CL
3 ST PAUL'S CRES

MORNINGTON CT

B4114

P
CHURCH

Maxstoke Castle

Cemy

89

Maxstoke Park Golf Course

B4117

HIGH ST

P

SUMNER RD

Liby

Birch Wood

Castle Farm

CH

River Blythe

Pooltail Plantation

WYNDSHIELS

THE DRIVE

The Cottage

MAXSTOKE LA

3

PARKFIELD RD

AVON WAY

THE CLOSE

WINGFIELD RD

GREEN LA

St Gerard's (Warwickshire) Orthopaedic

Maxstoke Mill (disused)

Mill Farm

H

PRIORY CL

1 CASTLE DR
2 FERNDALE MEWS
3 FERNDALE CT

St Edward's RC Prim Sch

Duke Bridge

COLESHILL RD

FERNDALE RD

BURMAN DR

SPRING FIELDS

BRENDON

B46

Duke End

88

SPRING FIELDS

SPRING FIELDS

POUND LA

Southfields Farm

Duke End Farm

COVENTRY RD

HALL WLK

SHERBOURNE CL

Coleshill Blythe Special Sch

ARNOLDS LA

KEEPERS CL

2

B4117

The Coleshill Sch

Mast
Coleshill CE Prim Sch

Cooper's Farm

Maxstoke Farm

The Dairy Farm

HAWKESWELL LA

Dairy Farm Cottages

A446

Packington Lane Farm

PACKINGTON LA

87

Hawkeswell Farm

Pool Farm

STONEBRIDGE RD

M6

1

The Bogs

CV7

Moat House Farm

A446

STONEBRIDGE RD

86

Bannerley Pool

M6

20   A   21   B   22   C

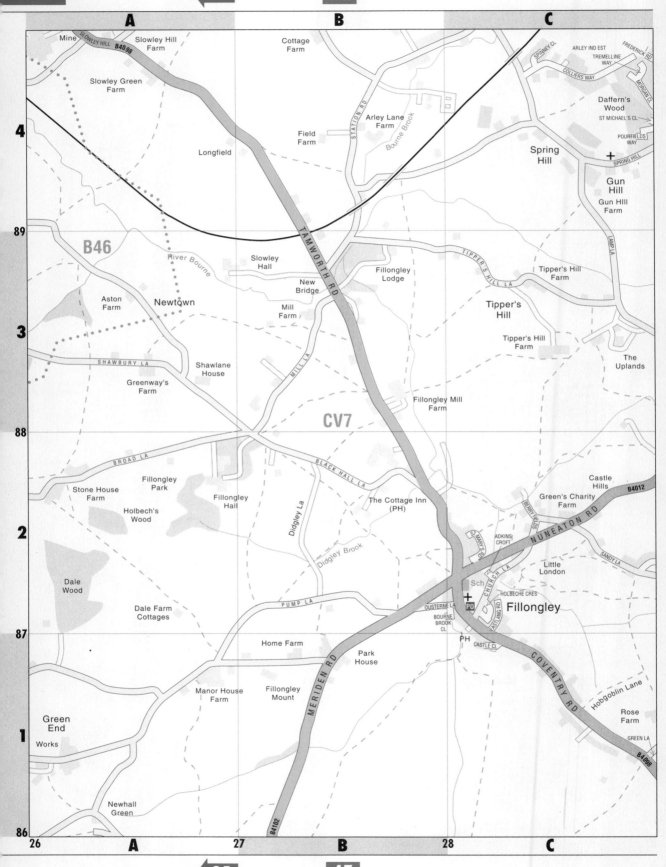

A   B   C

Mine
SLOWLEY HILL   B4098
Slowley Hill Farm
Cottage Farm
SPINNEY CL
ARLEY IND EST
TREMELLINE WAY
FREDERICK RD
COLLIERS WAY
MORGAN CL

Slowley Green Farm
Daffern's Wood
ST MICHAEL'S CL

STATION RD
Arley Lane Farm
POURFIELDS WAY

Field Farm
Longfield
Bourne Brook
Spring Hill
+ Spring Hill

4

Gun Hill
Gun Hill Farm

89   B46
River Bourne
Slowley Hall
Fillongley Lodge
TIPPER'S HILL LA
LAMP LA
Tipper's Hill Farm

New Bridge
TAMWORTH RD
Tipper's Hill

Aston Farm
Newtown
Mill Farm

Tipper's Hill Farm
3

SHAWBURY LA
Shawlane House
MILL LA
The Uplands

Greenway's Farm

CV7
Fillongley Mill Farm

88

BROAD LA
BLACK HALL LA
Castle Hills
B4012

Stone House Farm
Fillongley Park
Fillongley Hall
Didgley La
The Cottage Inn (PH)
Green's Charity Farm
BERRY FIELDS
NUNEATON RD

Holbech's Wood
Didgley Brook
ST MARY'S CL
ADKINS CROFT
SANDY LA

2
Little London

Dale Wood
Dale Farm Cottages
PUMP LA
CHURCH LA
Sch
HOLBECHE CRES
+ PO
Fillongley

87
OUSTERNE LA
BOURNE BROOK CL
EASTLING RD

Home Farm
MERIDEN RD
Park House
PH
CASTLE CL
COVENTRY RD

Manor House Farm
Fillongley Mount
Hobgoblin Lane
Rose Farm

1
Green End
Works
GREEN LA
B4098

B4102
Newhall Green

86

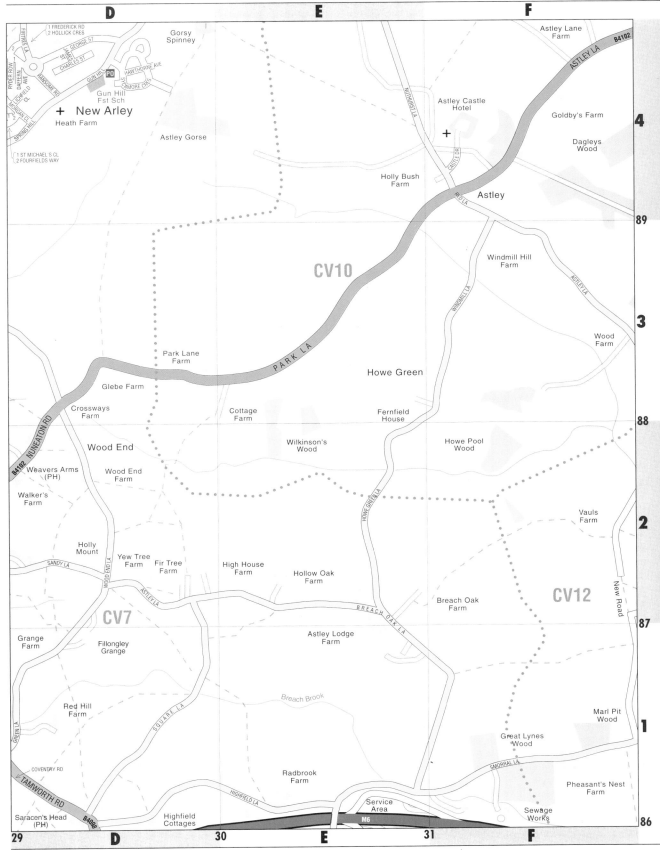

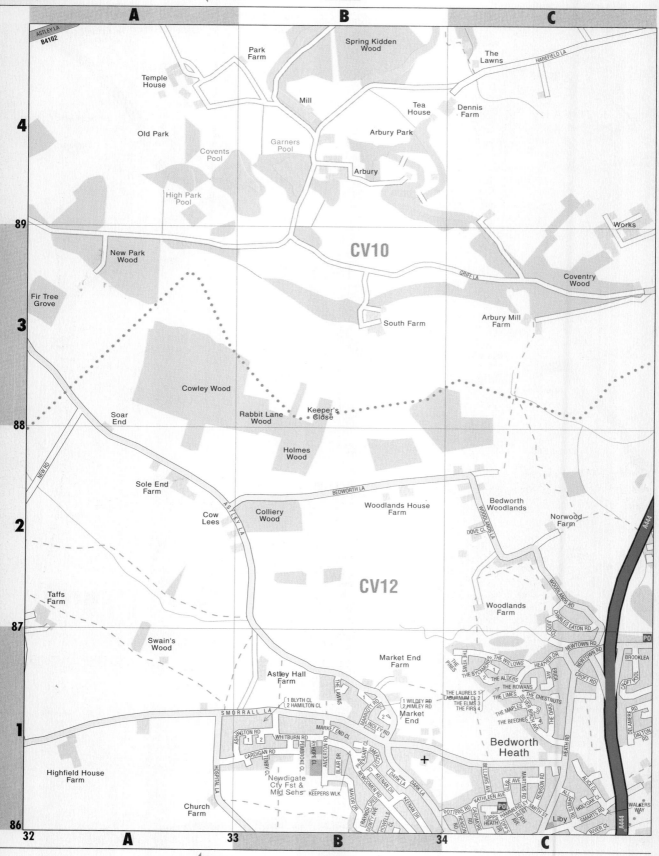

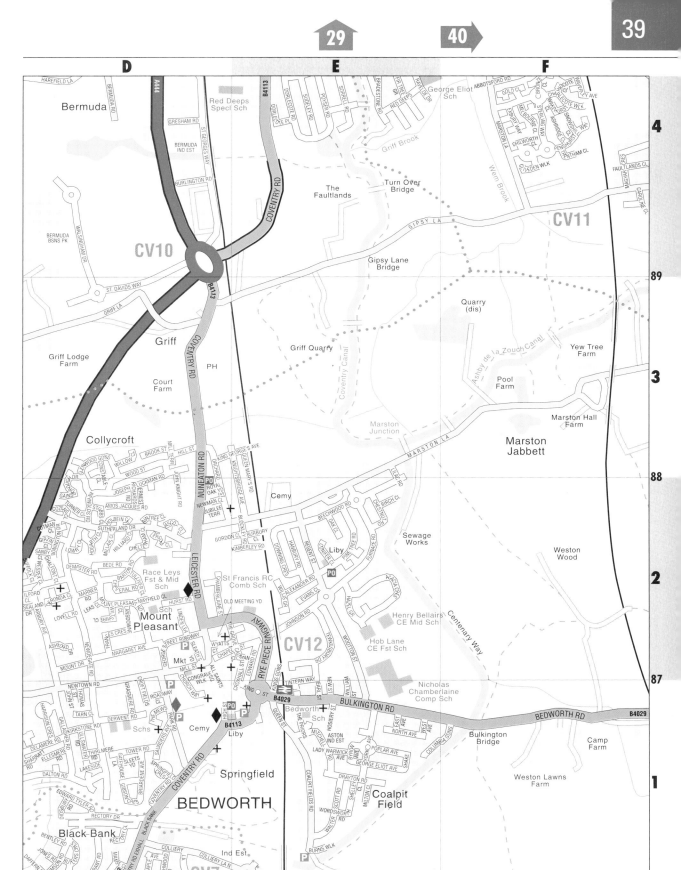

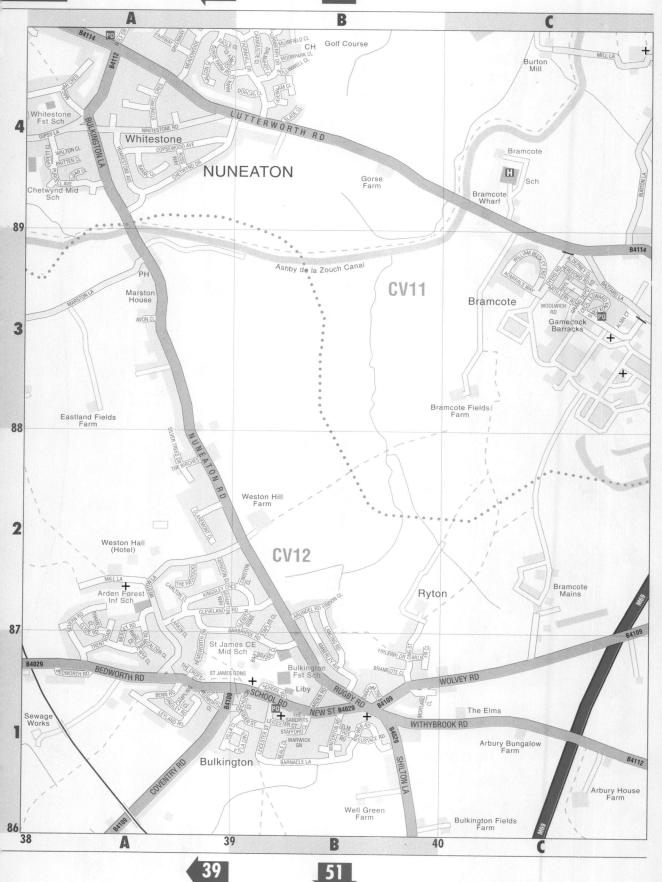

A | B | C

4

89

3

88

2

87

1

86

38 39 40

NUNEATON

Whitestone

CV11

CV12

Bramcote

Ryton

Bulkington

B4114
LUTTERWORTH RD
BULKINGTON LA
NUNEATON RD
Gorse Farm
Golf Course
Burton Mill
Bramcote Wharf
Bramcote Sch
Gamecock Barracks
Bramcote Fields Farm
Bramcote Mains
Ashby de la Zouch Canal
Marston House
Marston La
Eastland Fields Farm
Weston Hill Farm
Weston Hall (Hotel)
Arden Forest Inf Sch
St James CE Mid Sch
Bulkington Fst Sch
Liby
BEDWORTH RD
B4029
Sewage Works
COVENTRY RD
SCHOOL RD
NEW ST
RUGBY RD
WOLVEY RD
WITHYBROOK RD
SHILTON LA
The Elms
Arbury Bungalow Farm
Arbury House Farm
Well Green Farm
Bulkington Fields Farm
Whitestone Fst Sch
Chetwynd Mid Sch
B4109
B4112
M69

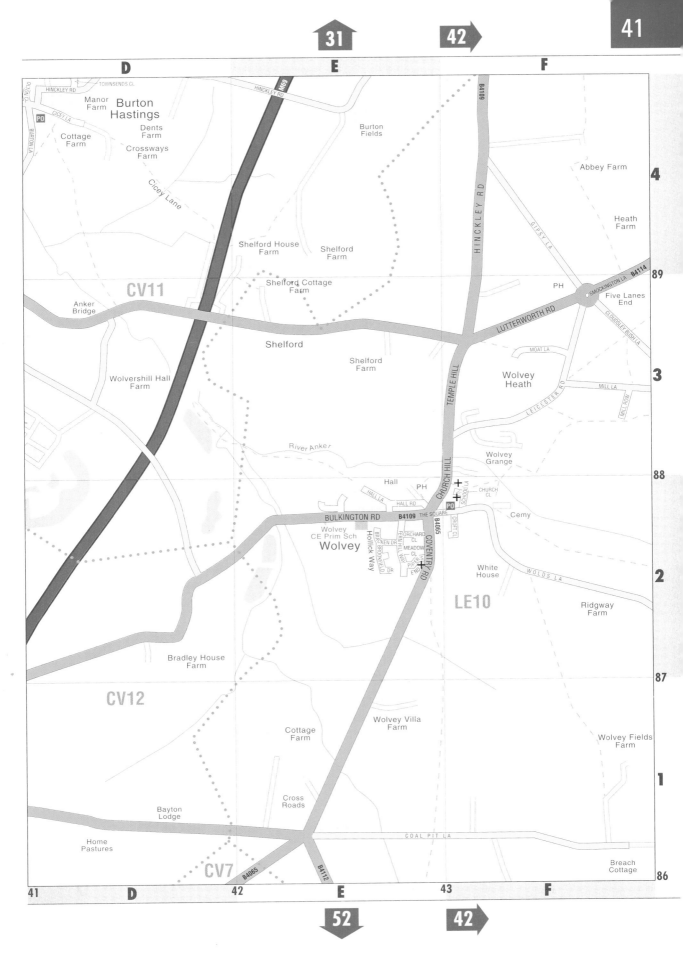

TOWNSENDS CL

Manor Farm

Burton Hastings

Dents Farm

Crossways Farm

Cottage Farm

HINCKLEY RD

CICEY LA

BURTON LA

PO

Cicey Lane

Burton Fields

B4109

HINCKLEY RD

Abbey Farm

4

Heath Farm

GIPSY LA

Shelford House Farm

Shelford Farm

Shelford Cottage Farm

CV11

Anker Bridge

Shelford

PH

LUTTERWORTH RD

Five Lanes End

SMOCKINGTON LA

B4114

89

CLOUDSLEY BUSH LA

MOAT LA

Wolvershill Hall Farm

Shelford Farm

TEMPLE HILL

Wolvey Heath

MILL LA

MILL ROW

3

LEICESTER RD

River Anker

CHURCH HILL

Wolvey Grange

88

Hall

PH

HALL LA

HALL RD

Wolvey CE Prim Sch

BULKINGTON RD

B4109

THE SQUARE

SCHOOL LA

CHURCH CL

PO

Cemy

BRACKEN DR

ORCHARD CL

DROIT CL

Wolvey

Hollick Way

BROOKFIELD

MEADOW CL

FERN HILL WAY

PIPERS END S

COVENTRY RD

B4065

White House

WOLDS LA

LE10

2

Ridgway Farm

Bradley House Farm

87

CV12

Cottage Farm

Wolvey Villa Farm

Wolvey Fields Farm

1

Cross Roads

Bayton Lodge

Home Pastures

COAL PIT LA

CV7

B4065

B4112

Breach Cottage

86

	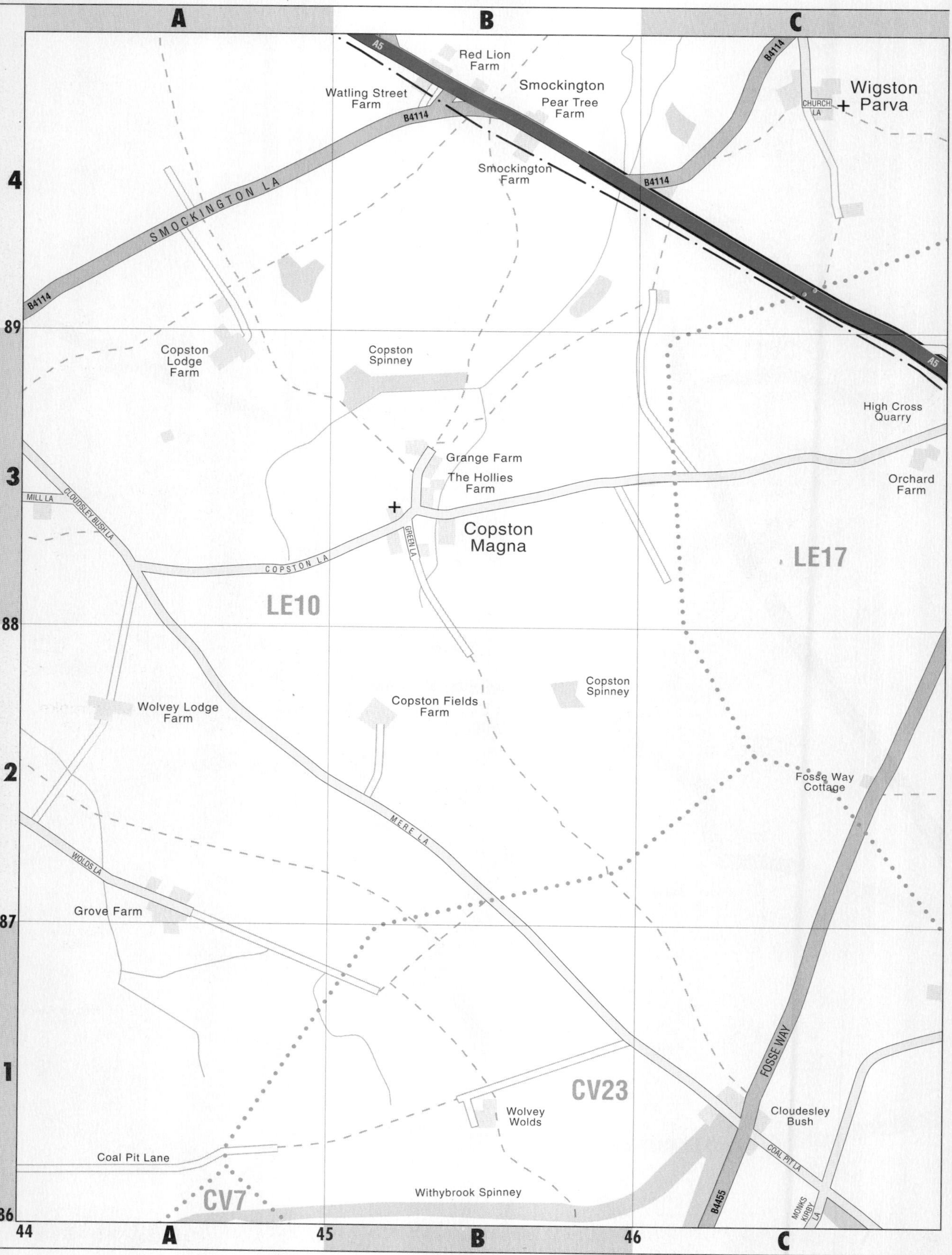 A	B	C

4

A5

Red Lion Farm

Watling Street Farm

Smockington

Pear Tree Farm

B4114

B4114

SMOCKINGTON LA

Smockington Farm

B4114

Wigston Parva

CHURCH LA

+

B4114

89

B4114

Copston Lodge Farm

Copston Spinney

A5

High Cross Quarry

3

MILL LA

CLOUDSLEY BUSH LA

Grange Farm

The Hollies Farm

+

Orchard Farm

COPSTON LA

GREEN LA

Copston Magna

LE17

LE10

88

Wolvey Lodge Farm

Copston Fields Farm

Copston Spinney

2

WOLDS LA

MERE LA

Fosse Way Cottage

87

Grove Farm

1

FOSSE WAY

CV23

Wolvey Wolds

Cloudesley Bush

COAL PIT LA

Coal Pit Lane

B4455

MONKS KIRBY LA

CV7

Withybrook Spinney

86

44	A	45	B	46	C

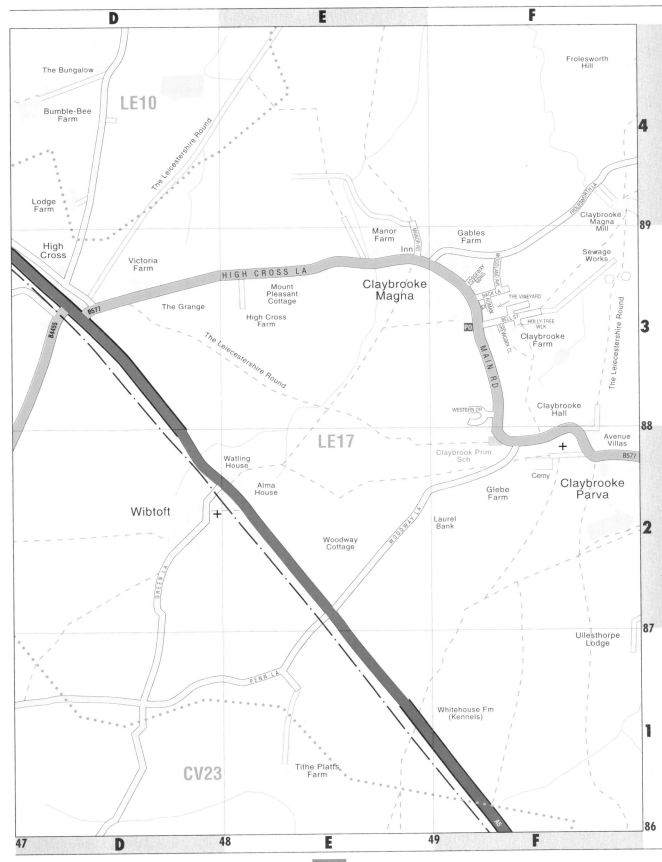

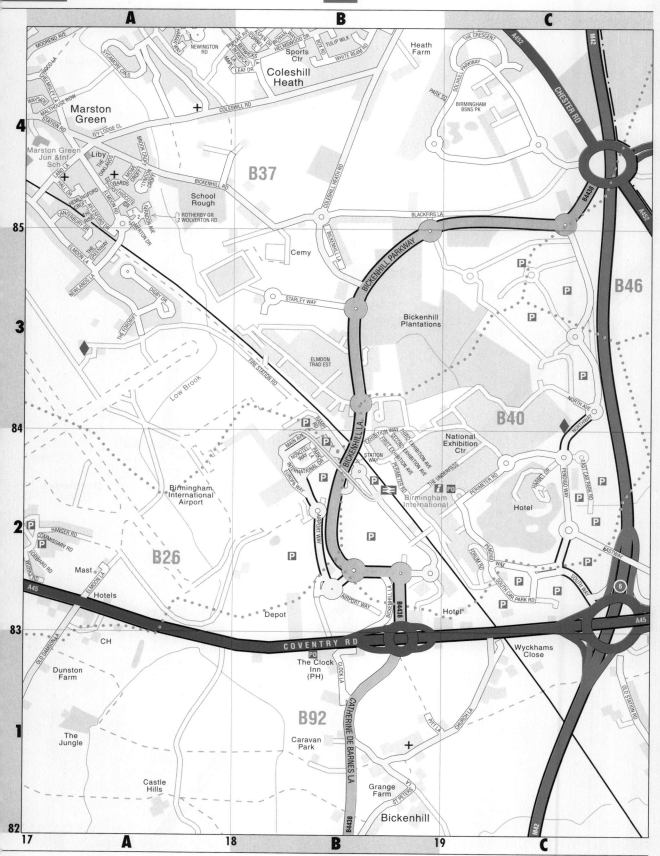

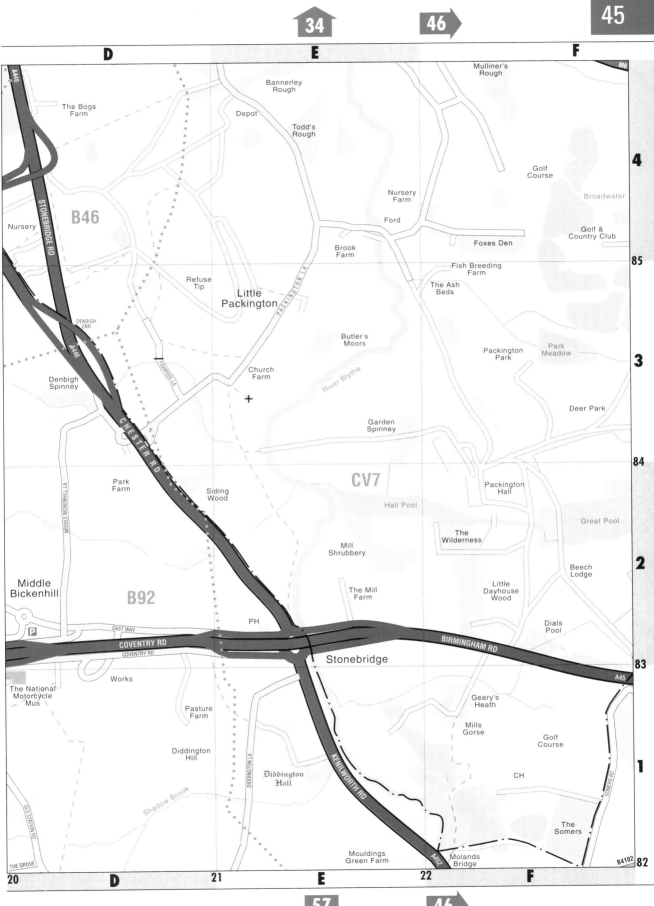

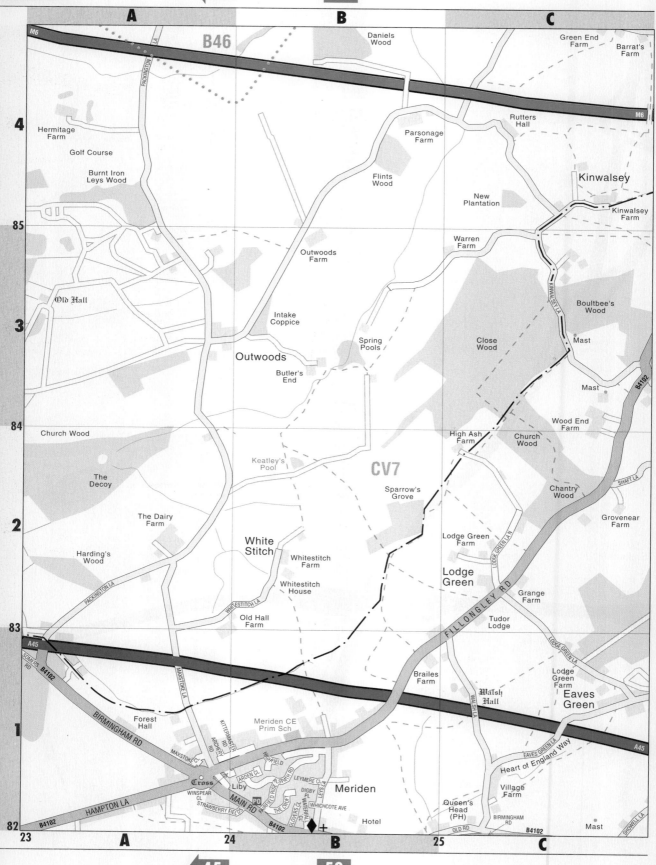

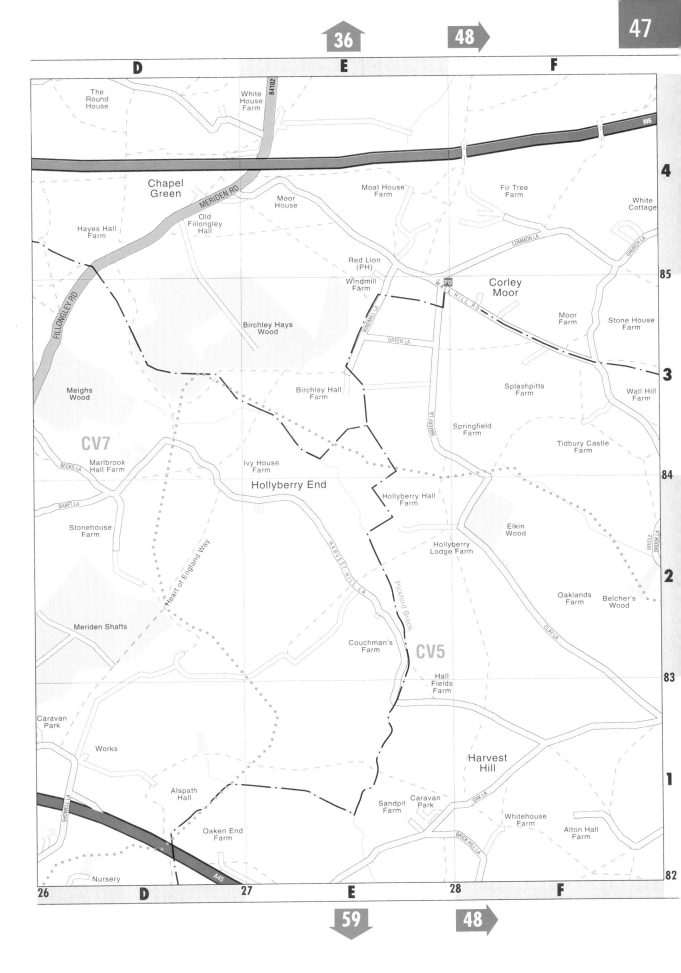

36
48

D   E   F

The Round House

White House Farm

B4102

M6

4

Chapel Green

MERIDEN RD

Moor House

Moat House Farm

Fir Tree Farm

White Cottage

Hayes Hall Farm

Old Fillongley Hall

COMMON LA

CHURCH LA

85

FILLONGLEY RD

Red Lion (PH)

Windmill Farm

PO

Corley Moor

Moor Farm

Stone House Farm

Birchley Hays Wood

WINDMILL LA

WALL HILL RD

GREEN LA

Wall Hill Farm

3

Meighs Wood

Birchley Hall Farm

Splashpitts Farm

CV7

WATERY LA

Springfield Farm

Tidbury Castle Farm

BECKS LA

Marlbrook Hall Farm

Ivy House Farm

84

SHAFT LA

Hollyberry End

Hollyberry Hall Farm

BRIDLE BROOK LA

Stonehouse Farm

Heart of England Way

Elkin Wood

2

Hollyberry Lodge Farm

HARVEST HILL LA

Pickford Brook

Oaklands Farm

Belcher's Wood

Meriden Shafts

Couchman's Farm

CV5

CLAY LA

83

Caravan Park

Hall Fields Farm

Works

Harvest Hill

1

SHOWELL LA

Alspath Hall

Sandpit Farm

Caravan Park

OAK LA

Whitehouse Farm

Alton Hall Farm

Oaken End Farm

BRICK HILL LA

A45

Nursery

82

26   D   27   E   28   F

59
48

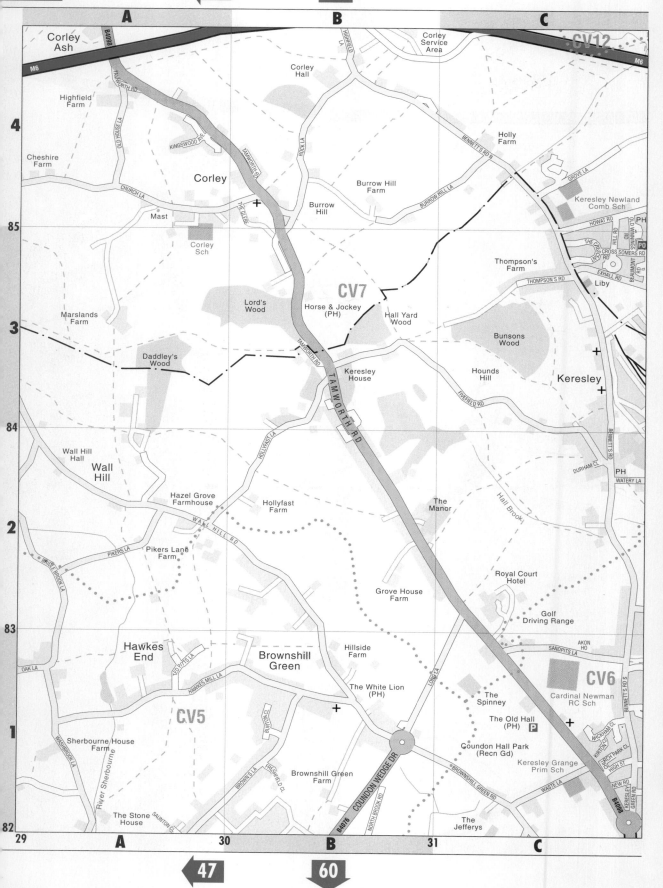

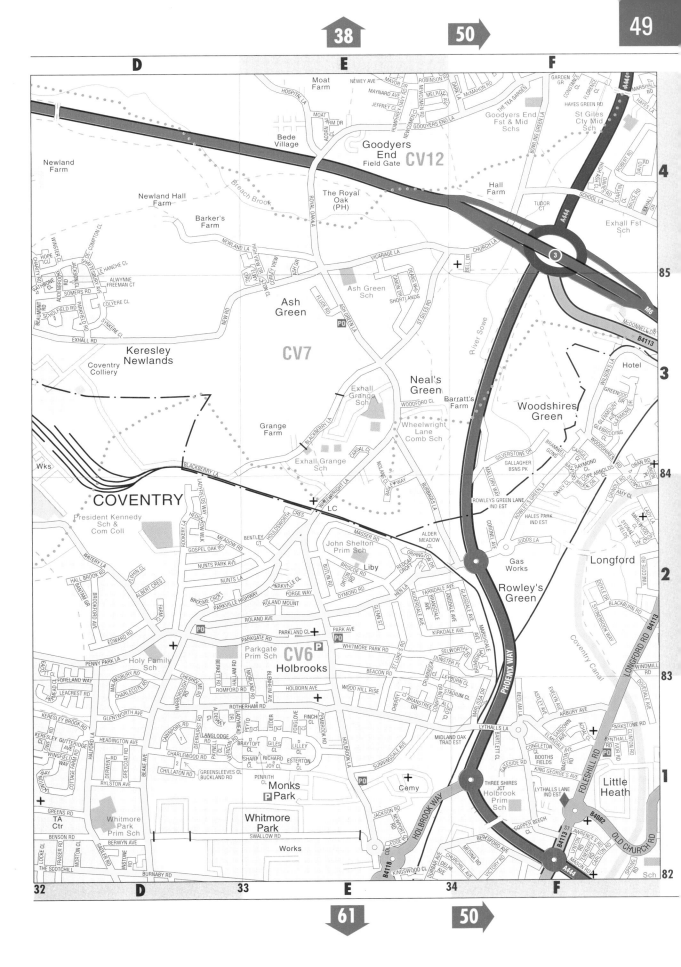

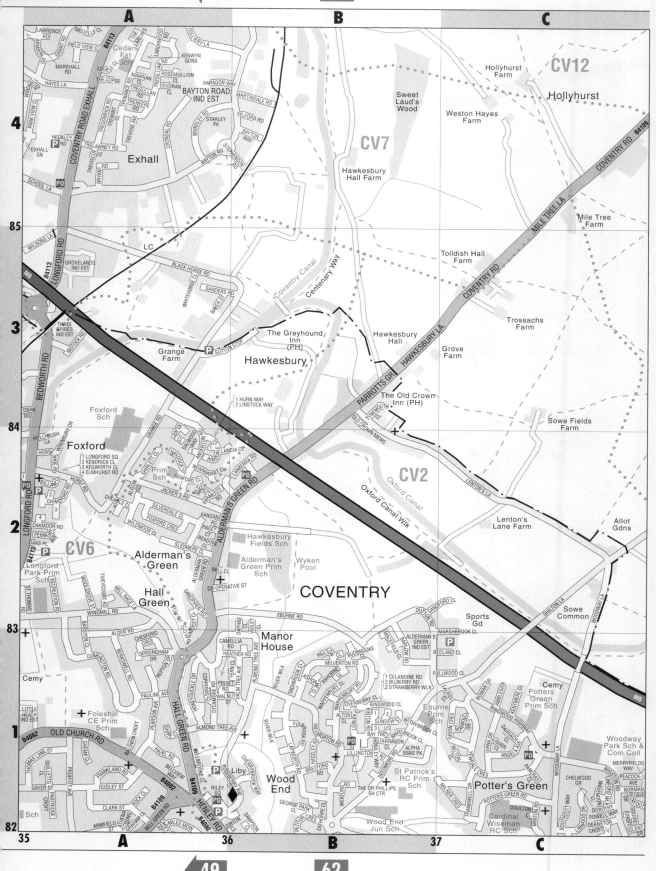

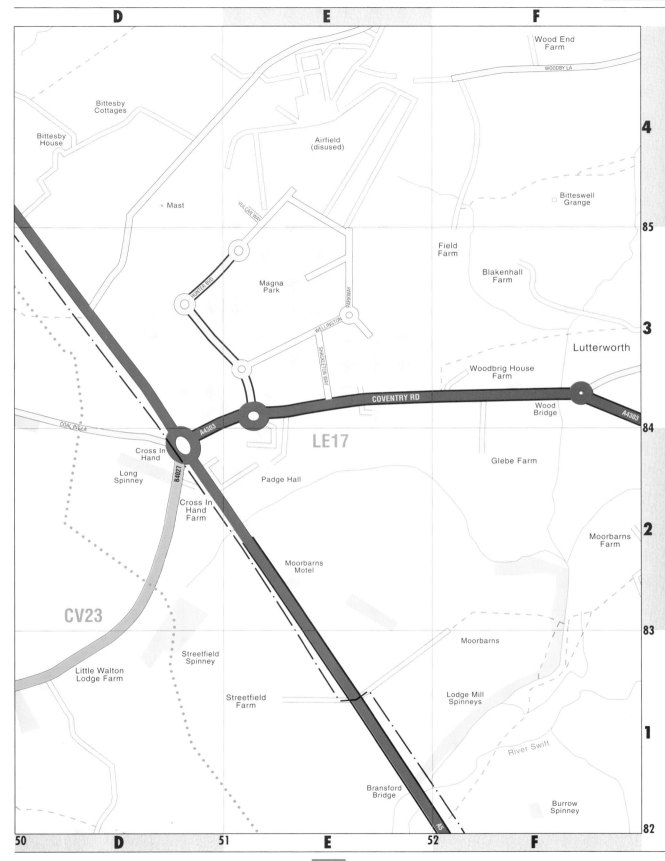

44

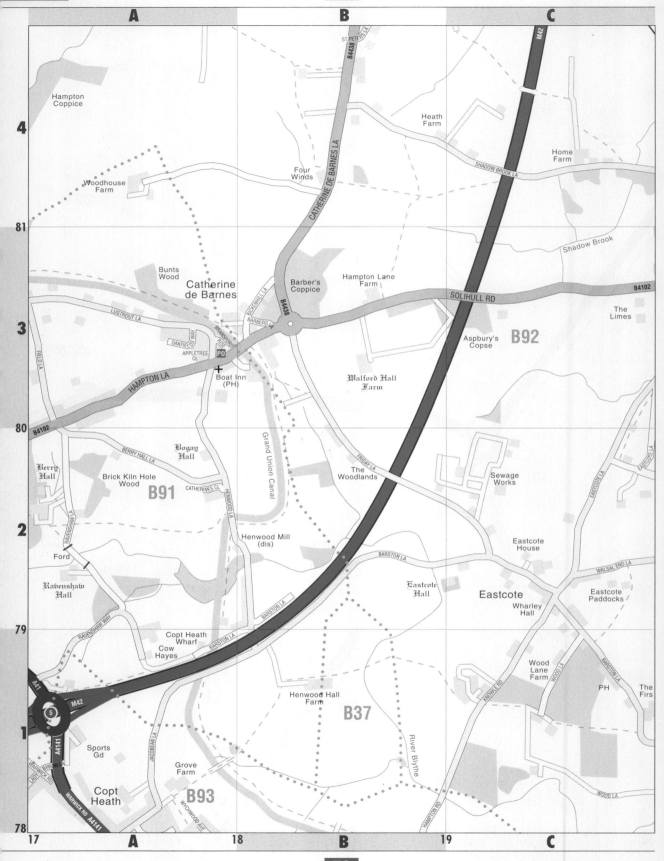

A   B   C

4

81

3

80

2

79

1

78

17   A   18   B   19   C

Hampton Coppice

Woodhouse Farm

Four Winds

St Peters La

B4438

CATHERINE DE BARNES LA

Heath Farm

SHADOW BROOK LA

Home Farm

Shadow Brook

M42

B4102

Bunts Wood

Catherine de Barnes

Barber's Coppice

Hampton Lane Farm

SOLIHULL RD

The Limes

LUGTROUT LA

BICKENHILL LA

BARBERS LA

B4438

Aspbury's Copse

B92

FIELD LA

BRANSONS RISE

OAKFIELDS WAY

APPLETREE CL

PO

Boat Inn (PH)

HAMPTON LA

Walford Hall Farm

BERRY HALL LA

Bogay Hall

Grand Union Canal

FRIDAY LA

Sewage Works

EASTCOTE LA

EASTCOTE LA

Berry Hall

Brick Kiln Hole Wood

B91

CATHERINES CL

HENWOOD LA

The Woodlands

RAVENSHAW LA

Henwood Mill (dis)

BARSTON LA

Eastcote House

WALSAL END LA

Ford

Eastcote Hall

Eastcote

Eastcote Paddocks

Ravenshaw Hall

RAVENSHAW WAY

BARSTON LA

Wharley Hall

BARSTON LA

Copt Heath Wharf

Cow Hayes

Wood Lane Farm

WOOD LA

KNOWLE RD

PH

The Firs

M41

M42

5

A4141

Sports Gd

JACOBEAN LA

Henwood Hall Farm

B37

River Blythe

HAMPTON RD

WOOD LA

WARWICK RD

LADY BYRON LA

Copt Heath

Grove Farm

WYCHWOOD AVE

WARWICK RD

A4141

B93

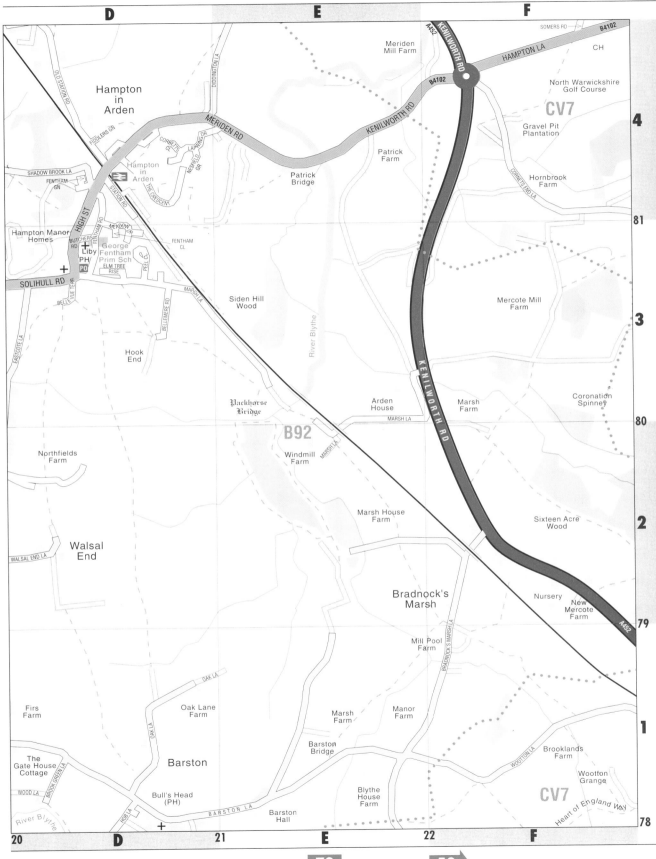

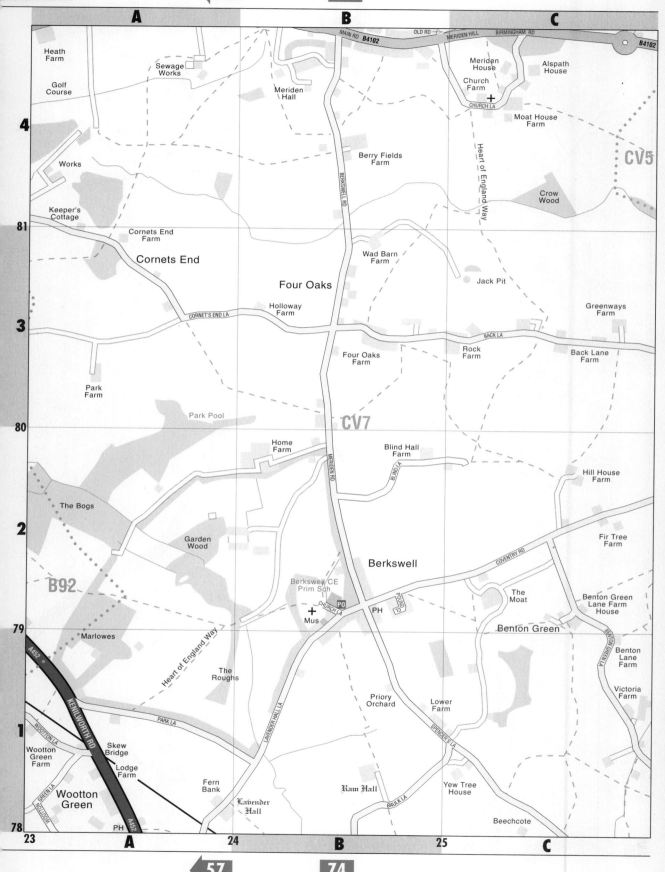

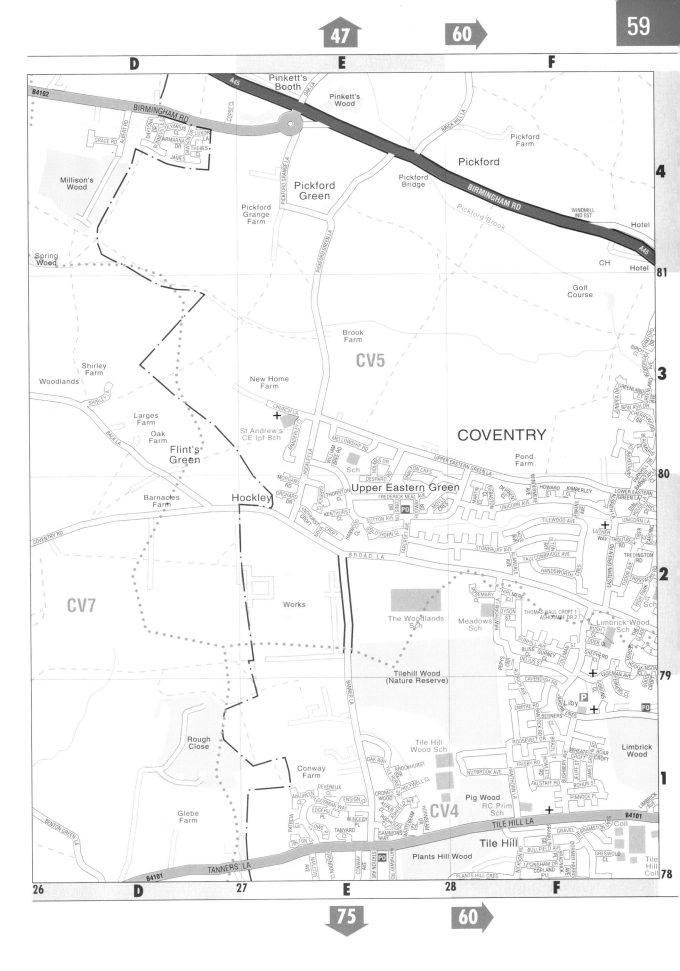

59 48

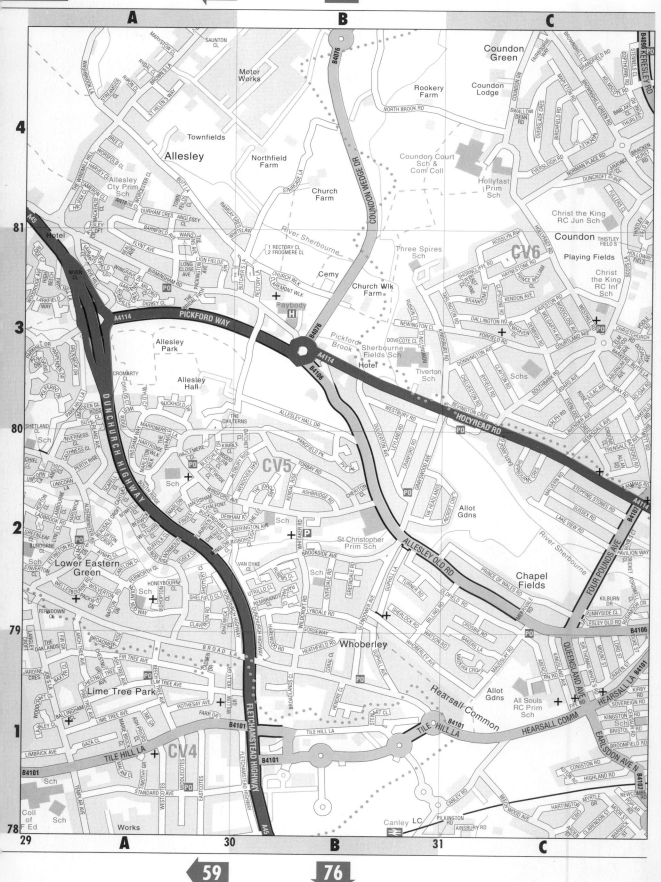

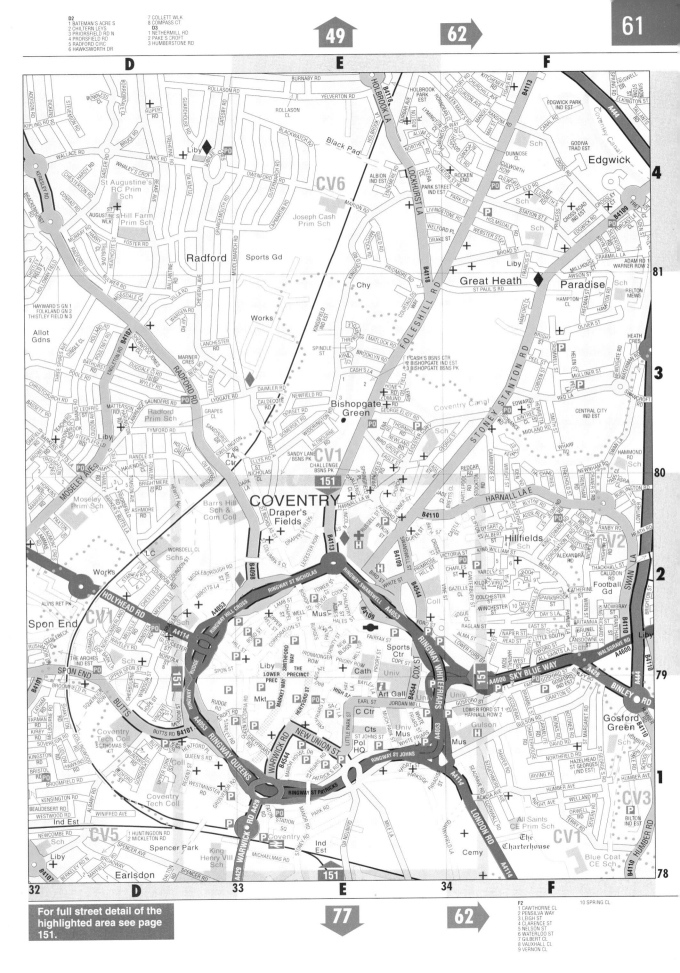

D2
1 BATEMAN'S ACRE S
2 CHILTERN LEYS
3 PRIORSFIELD RD N
4 PRORSFIELD RD
5 RADFORD CIRC
6 HAWKSWORTH DR

7 COLLETT WLK
8 COMPASS CT
D3
1 NETHERMILL RD
2 PAKE'S CROFT
3 HUMBERSTONE RD

F2
1 CAWTHORNE CL
2 PENSILVA WAY
3 LEIGH ST
4 CLARENCE ST
5 NELSON ST
6 WATERLOO ST
7 GILBERT CL
8 VAUXHALL CL
9 VERNON CL

10 SPRING CL

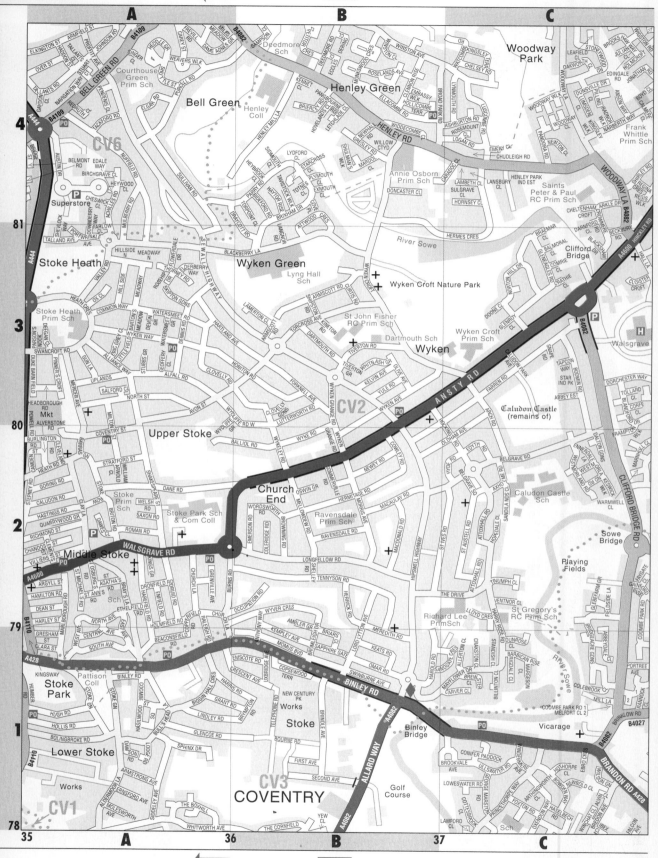

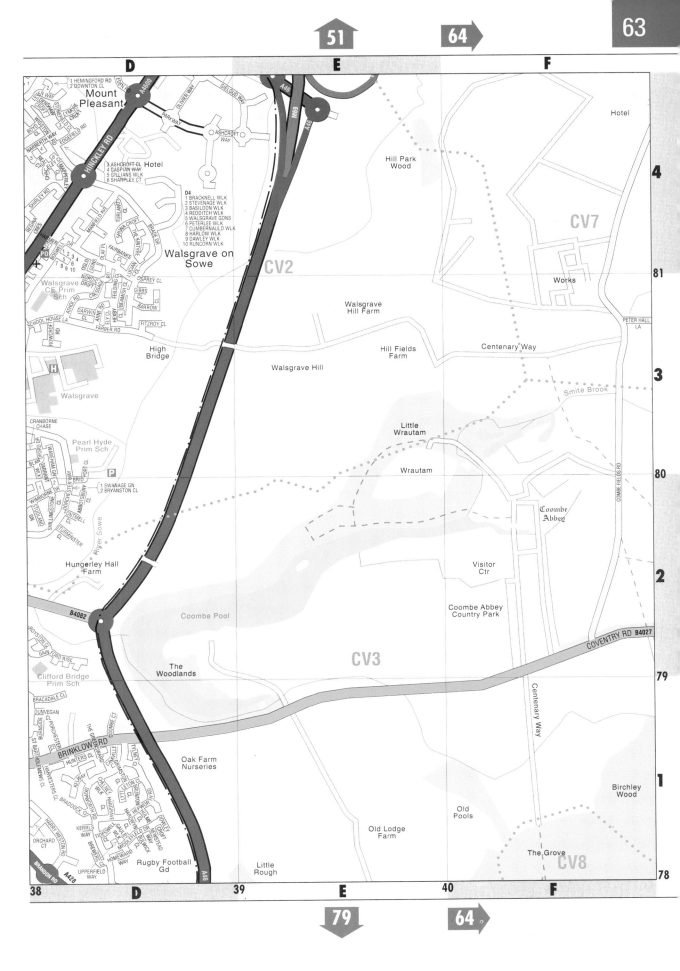

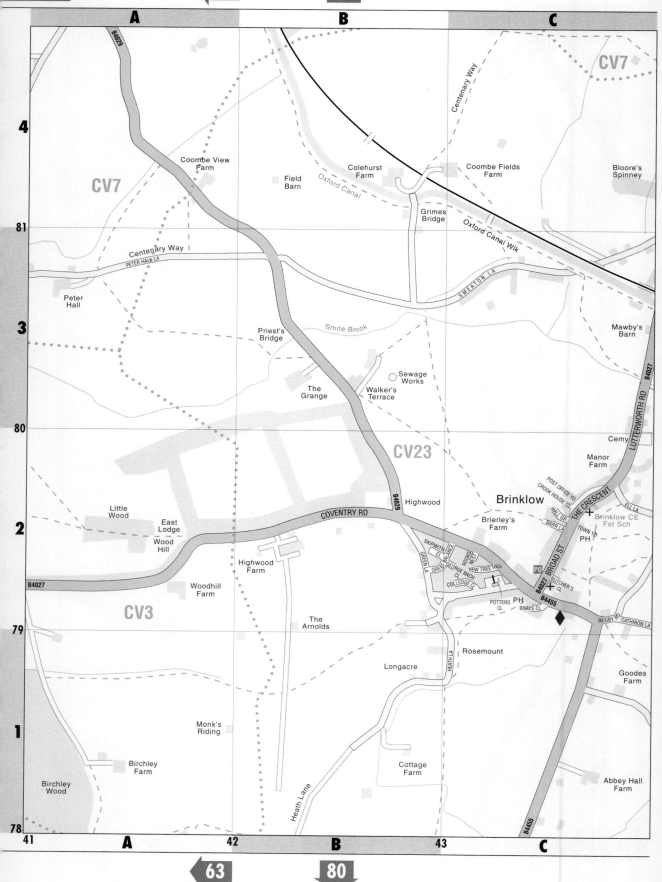

A   B   C

B4029

CV7

CV7

Coombe View Farm

Field Barn

Colehurst Farm

Oxford Canal

Coombe Fields Farm

Bloore's Spinney

4

Centenary Way

Grimes Bridge

Oxford Canal Wlk

81

Centenary Way

PETER HALL LA

SMEATON LA

Peter Hall

Mawby's Barn

3

Priest's Bridge

Smite Brook

The Grange

Walker's Terrace

Sewage Works

B4027

CV23

80

LUTTERWORTH RD

Cemy

Manor Farm

Little Wood

East Lodge

Wood Hill

B4029

COVENTRY RD

Highwood

Brinklow

Brierley's Farm

POST OFFICE YD

CROOK HOUSE YD

HALL GR

THE CRESCENT

Brinklow CE Fst Sch

ELL LA

BARR LA

TOWN YD

PH

2

Highwood Farm

SKIPWITH CL

ROOKS NEST

GREEN LA

GREAT BALANCE

GEORGE BACH

YEW TREE HILL

BROAD ST

B4027

PO

BUTCHER S

CL

Woodhill Farm

B4027

CV3

COLLEDGE CL

POTTERS CL

PH

BRAYS CL

B4455

RUGBY RD

CATHIRON LA

The Arnolds

79

Rosemount

Goodes Farm

Longacre

HEATH LA

Monk's Riding

1

Birchley Farm

Cottage Farm

Abbey Hall Farm

Birchley Wood

Heath Lane

B4455

78

41   A   42   B   43   C

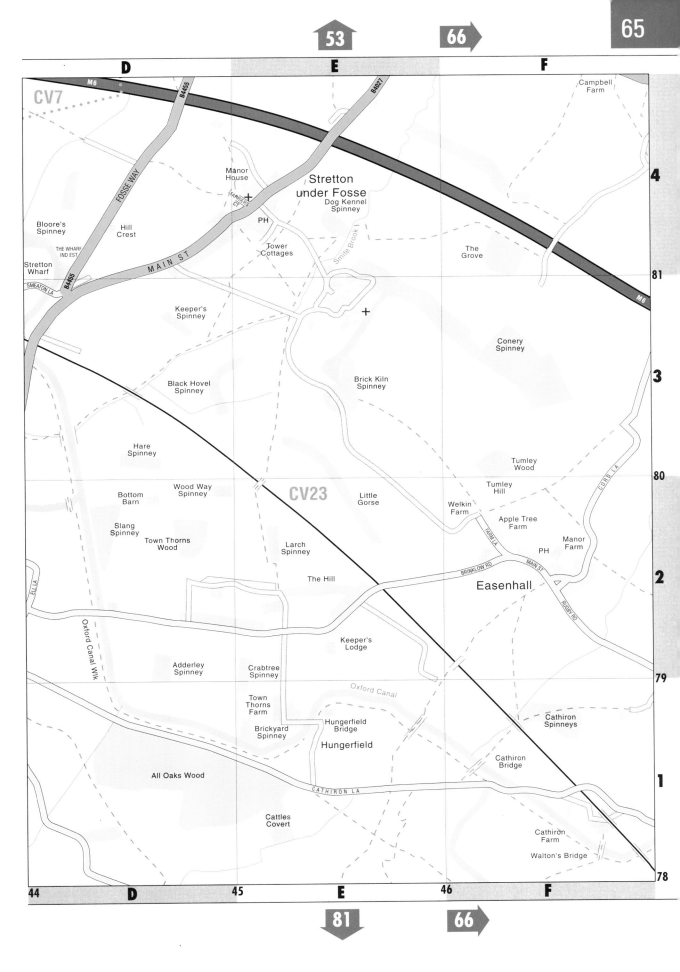

D   E   F

CV7

M6

B4455

Campbell Farm

FOSSE WAY

Manor House

FARRIERS CT

Stretton under Fosse

B4027

4

Dog Kennel Spinney

Bloore's Spinney

Hill Crest

PH

Smite Brook

The Grove

THE WHARF IND EST

Tower Cottages

Stretton Wharf

MAIN ST

B4455

SMEATON LA

81

M6

Keeper's Spinney

Conery Spinney

Black Hovel Spinney

Brick Kiln Spinney

3

Hare Spinney

Tumley Wood

Bottom Barn

Wood Way Spinney

CV23

Little Gorse

Tumley Hill

Welkin Farm

Apple Tree Farm

80

Slang Spinney

Town Thorns Wood

Larch Spinney

FARM LA

PH

Manor Farm

BRINKLOW RD

MAIN ST

ELLA

The Hill

Easenhall

2

RUGBY RD

Oxford Canal Wlk

Keeper's Lodge

Adderley Spinney

Crabtree Spinney

Oxford Canal

Cathiron Spinneys

Town Thorns Farm

Hungerfield Bridge

CORB LA

79

Brickyard Spinney

Hungerfield

Cathiron Bridge

All Oaks Wood

CATHIRON LA

1

Cattles Covert

Cathiron Farm

Walton's Bridge

78

44   D   45   E   46   F

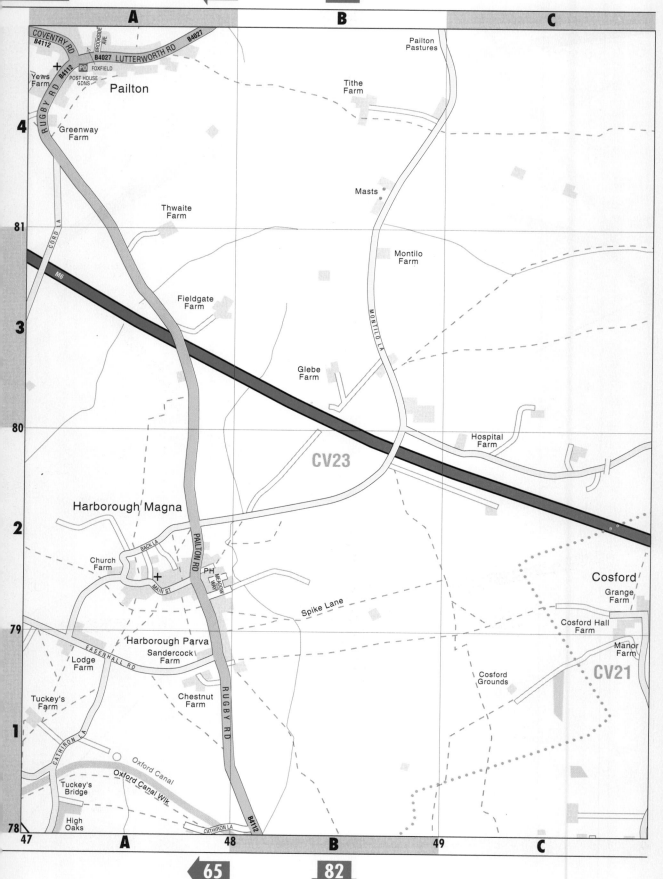

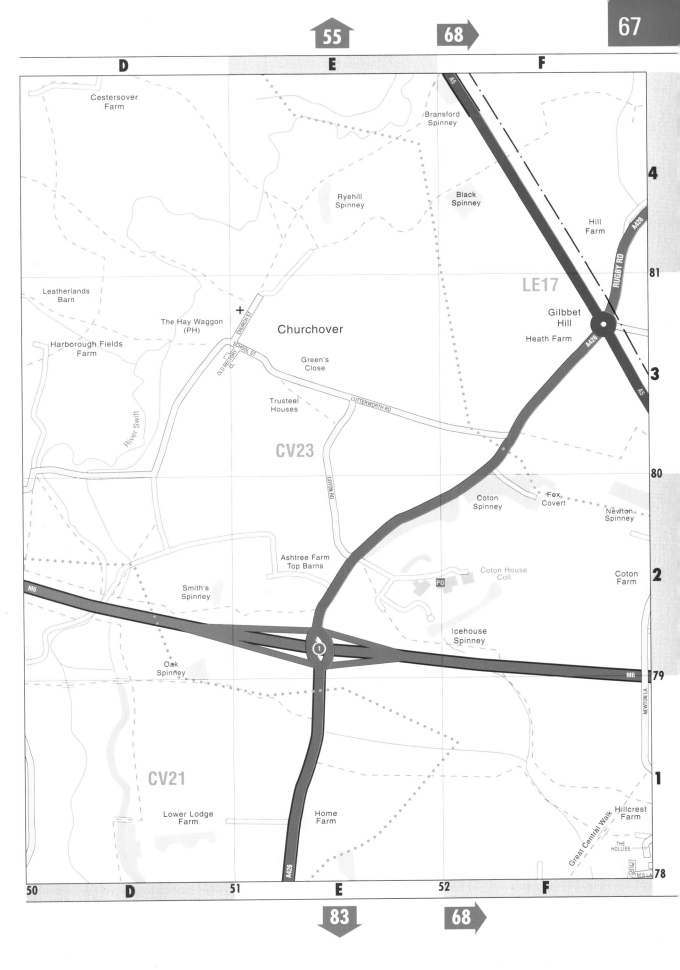

D
E
F

4

Cestersover
Farm

Bransford
Spinney

A5

Black
Spinney

Hill
Farm

A426

Ryehill
Spinney

81

LE17

Leatherlands
Barn

Gilbbet
Hill

The Hay Waggon
(PH)

Churchover

Heath Farm

A426

3

A5

Harborough Fields
Farm

CHURCH ST

SCHOOL ST

OLD RECTORY RD

Green's
Close

LUTTERWORTH RD

Trusteel
Houses

River Swift

CV23

COTON RD

80

Coton
Spinney

Fox
Covert

Newton
Spinney

Ashtree Farm
Top Barns

Coton House
Coll

Coton
Farm

2

Smith's
Spinney

PO

M6

Icehouse
Spinney

Oak
Spinney

1

79

M6

NEWTON LA

CV21

1

Lower Lodge
Farm

Home
Farm

Hillcrest
Farm

Great Central Walk

THE
HOLLIES

A426

PH
M.S.LA

78

50
D
51
E
52
F
78

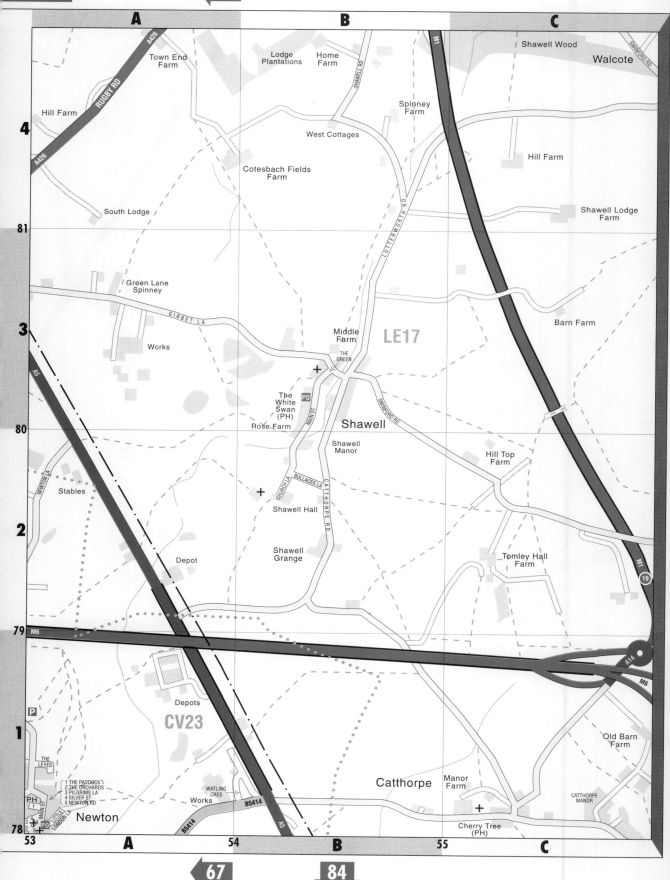

A426

Town End
Farm

RUGBY RD

Lodge
Plantations

Home
Farm

SWINNEL RD

M1

Shawell Wood

Walcote

SWINFORD RD

Hill Farm

Spinney
Farm

West Cottages

A426

Hill Farm

Cotesbach Fields
Farm

South Lodge

LUTTERWORTH RD

Shawell Lodge
Farm

81

Green Lane
Spinney

GIBBET LA

Barn Farm

3

A5

Works

Middle
Farm

LE17

THE
GREEN

The
White
Swan
(PH)

PO

MAIN ST

Rose Farm

Shawell

SWINFORD RD

80

Shawell
Manor

Hill Top
Farm

Stables

NEWTON LA

CHURCH LA

BULLACES LA

Shawell Hall

CATTHORPE RD

2

Depot

Shawell
Grange

Tomley Hall
Farm

M1

19

79 M6

A14

M6

Depots

CV23

1

P

THE
LEYES

Old Barn
Farm

WATLING
CRES

Catthorpe

Manor
Farm

CATTHORPE
MANOR

1 THE PADDOCK
2 THE ORCHARDS
3 PILGRIMS LA
4 SILVER ST
5 NEWTON RD

Works

B5414

PH

MAIN ST

LITTLE
LONDON LA

Newton

PO

A5

Cherry Tree
(PH)

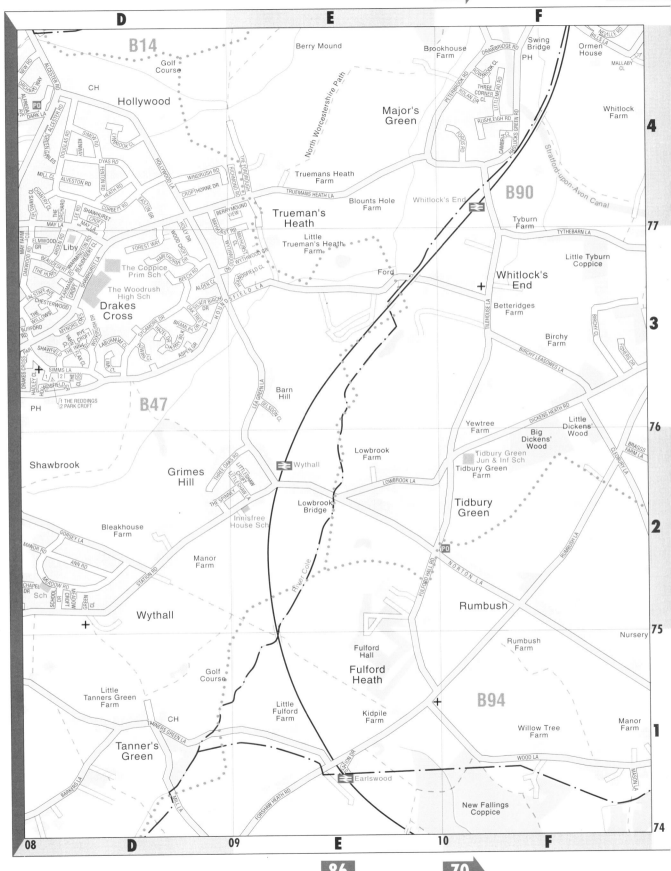

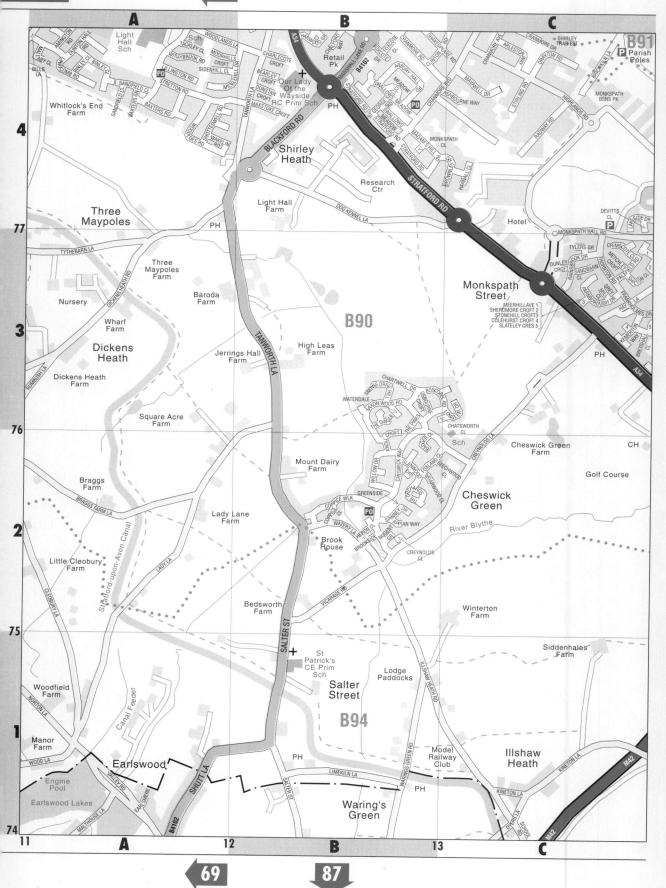

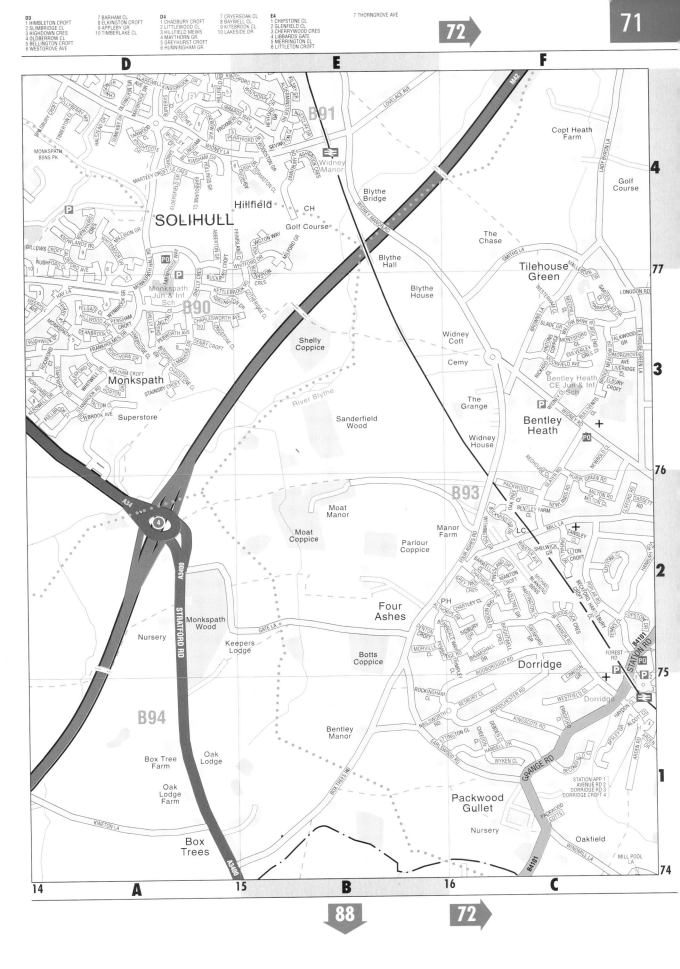

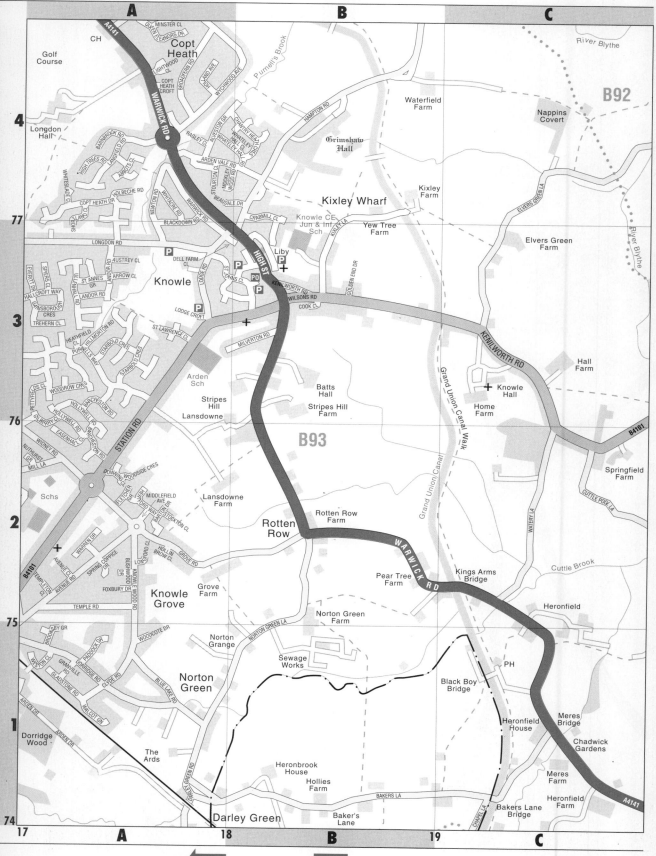

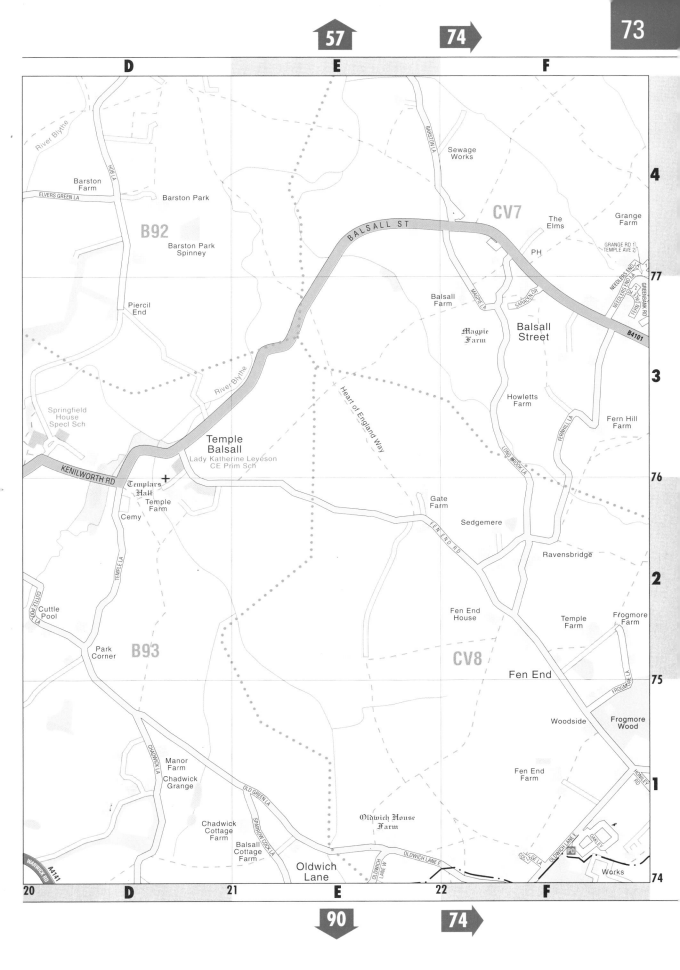

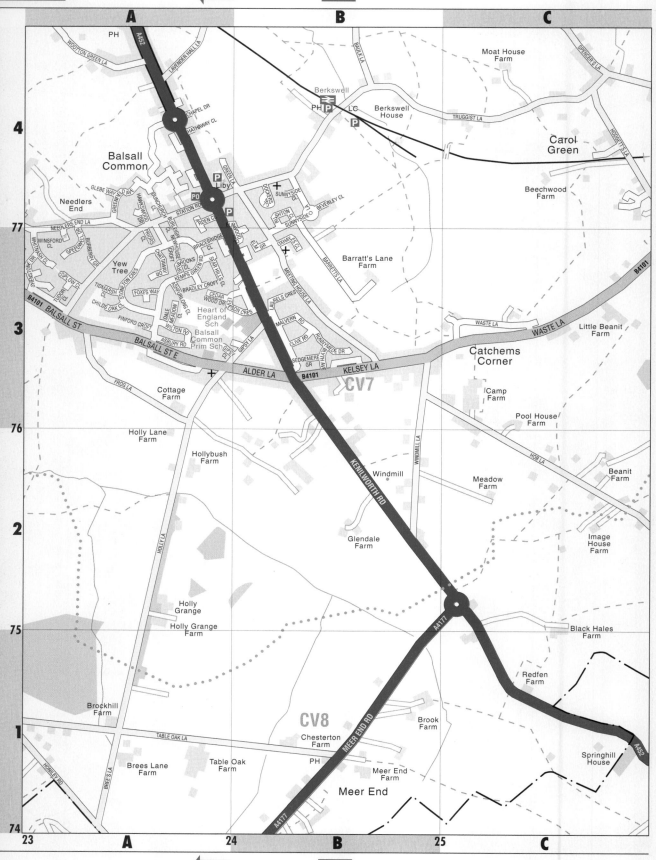

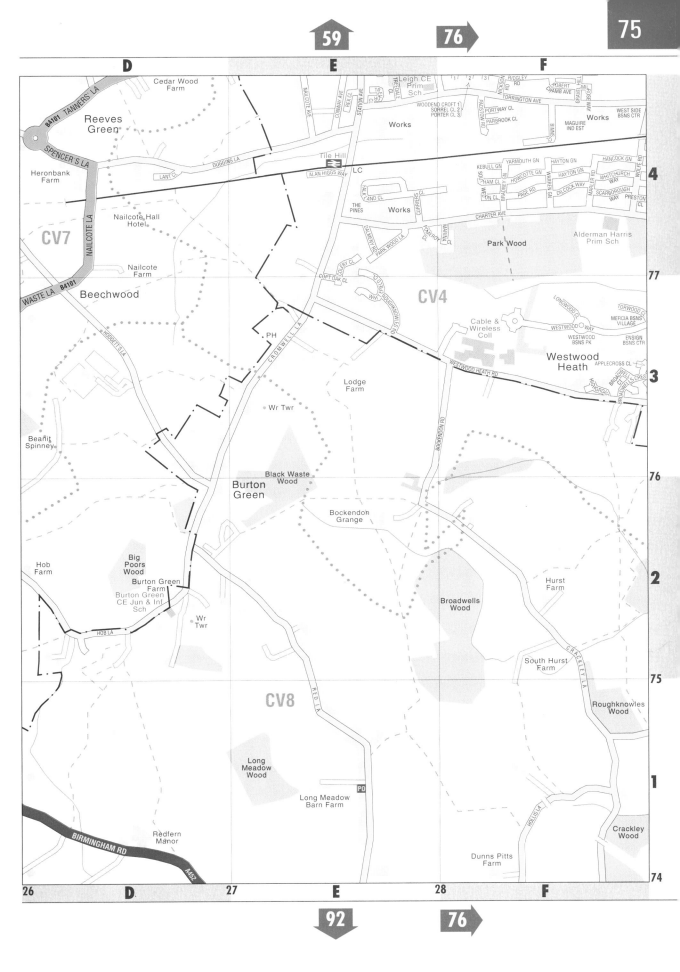

D
E
F

Cedar Wood Farm

Leigh CE Prim Sch

RIDGLEY

NICKSON RD

ROBERT CRAMB AVE

GOSEY WAY

WEST SIDE BSNS CTR

TORRINGTON AVE

Reeves Green

B4101 TANNERS LA

CONWAY AVE

REX CL

STATION AVE

TREEDALE CL

WOODEND CROFT 1
SORREL CL 2
PORTER CL 3

PARBROOK CL

PORTWAY CL

PAXTON RD

MAGUIRE IND EST

Works

BINNS CL

Works

SPENCER'S LA

NAILCOTE AVE

Tile Hill

DUGGINS LA

LANT CL

ALAN HIGGS WAY

LC

KEBULL GN

YARMOUTH GN

HAYTON GN

HANCOCK GN

WHITCHURCH WAY

WOLFE RD

4

Heronbank Farm

NAILCOTE LA

SOU...HAM CL

WE...ON CL

HONGCOTTE GN

BRADNEY

WARREN GN

HAYTON GN

PAGE RD

MARLER RD

DILCOCK WAY

SCARBOROUGH WAY

PRESTON CL

CV7

Nailcote Hall Hotel

THE PINES

Works

FALKLAND CL

CURRIERS CL

CHARTER AVE

77

Nailcote Farm

WASTE LA

B4101

Beechwood

DALMENY RD

PARK WOOD LA

POMEROY CL

MARINA CL

Park Wood

Alderman Harris Prim Sch

COPT OAK CL

COLLEY CL

WH...

ROUGHKNOWLES RD

CV4

LONGWOOD CL

WAY

TORWOOD CL

MERCIA BSNS VILLAGE

WESTWOOD WAY

HODGETTS LA

PH

CROMWELL LA

Cable & Wireless Coll

WESTWOOD BSNS PK

ENSIGN BSNS CTR

APPLECROSS CL

Westwood Heath

Lodge Farm

WESTWOOD HEATH RD

BOCKENDON RD

BROADWELLS CT

HIGGROVE

BROADWELLS CRES

3

Wr Twr

Beanit Spinney

Black Waste Wood

76

Burton Green

Bockendon Grange

Hob Farm

Big Poors Wood

Broadwells Wood

Hurst Farm

2

Burton Green Farm
Burton Green CE Jun & Inf Sch

Wr Twr

HOB LA

CRACKLEY LA

South Hurst Farm

75

CV8

RED LA

Roughknowles Wood

Long Meadow Wood

PO

1

Long Meadow Barn Farm

Crackley Wood

BIRMINGHAM RD

A452

Redfern Manor

HOLLIS LA

Dunns Pitts Farm

74

26
D
27
E
28
F

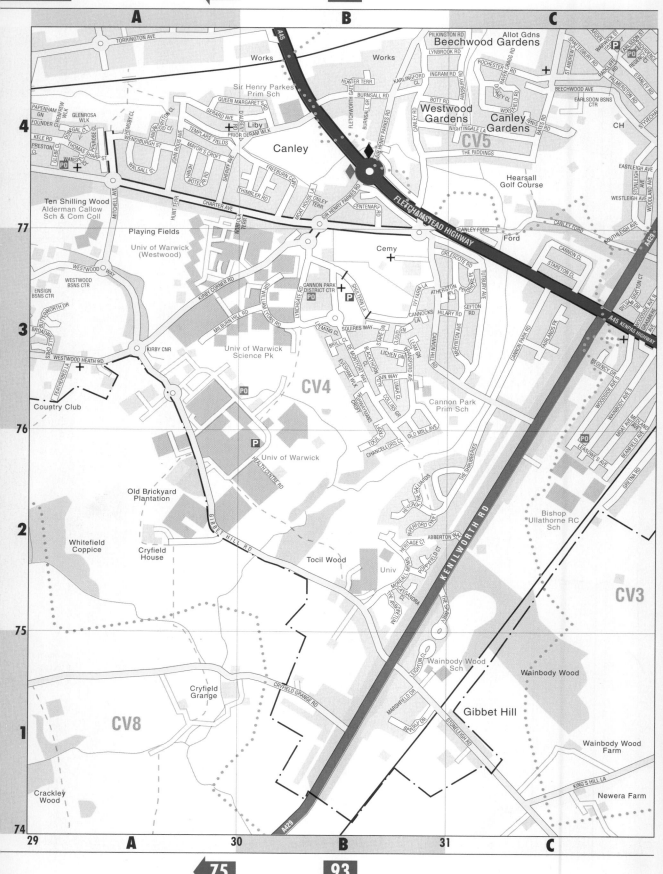

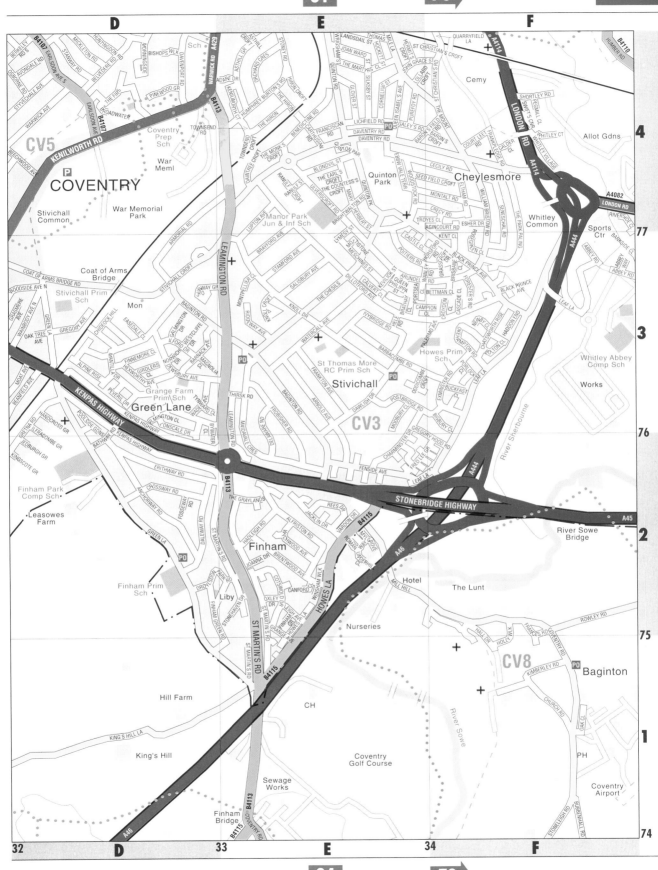

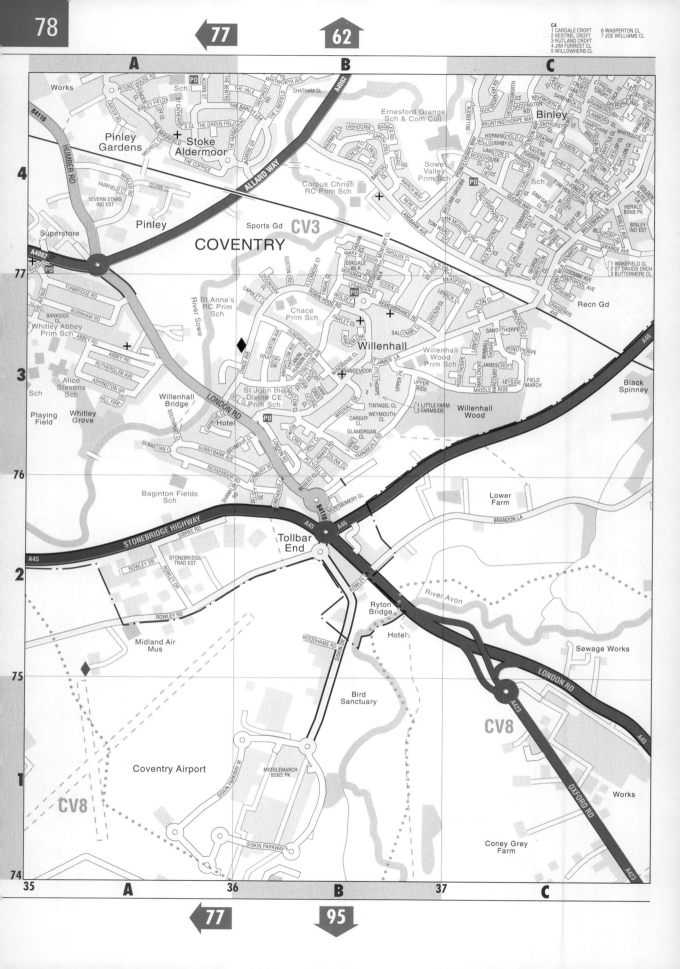

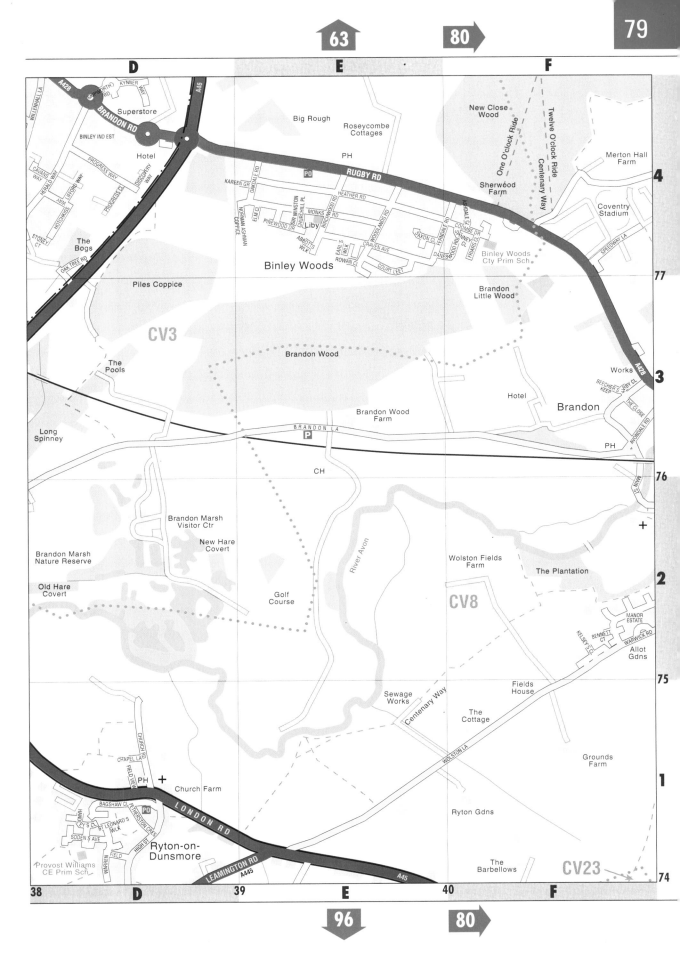

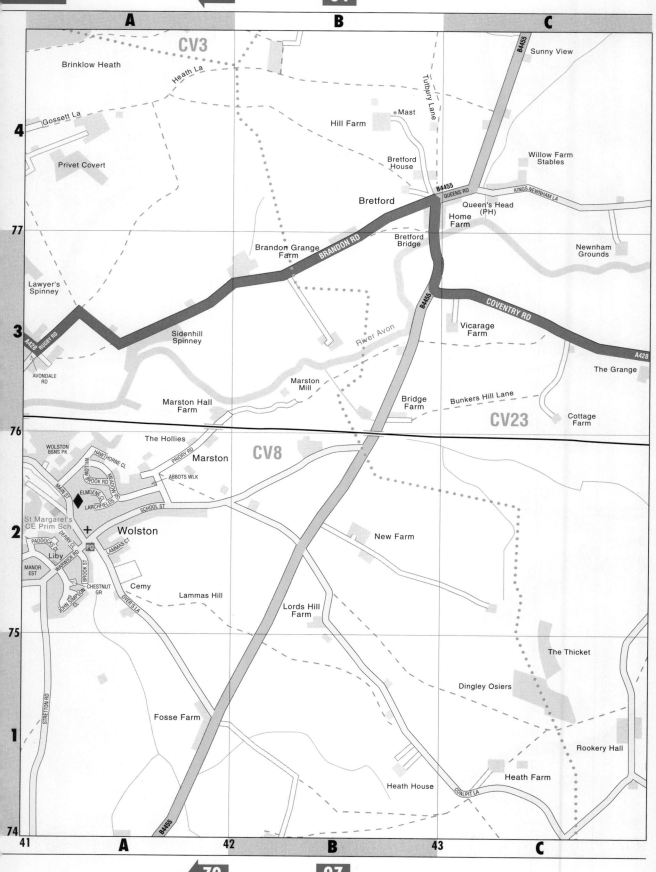

A   B   C

CV3

Brinklow Heath

Heath La

Gossett La

4

Privet Covert

Hill Farm

Mast

Tutbury Lane

B4455

Sunny View

Willow Farm Stables

Bretford House

Bretford

B4455

QUEENS RD

KINGS NEWNHAM LA

Queen's Head (PH)

Home Farm

Newnham Grounds

77

Brandon Grange Farm

BRANDON RD

Bretford Bridge

Lawyer's Spinney

COVENTRY RD

3

A428 RUGBY RD

Sidenhill Spinney

River Avon

B4455

Vicarage Farm

The Grange

A428

AVONDALE RD

Marston Mill

Bridge Farm

Bunkers Hill Lane

CV23

Cottage Farm

Marston Hall Farm

76

The Hollies

CV8

WOLSTON BSNS PK

HAWTHORNE CL

WILLOW

BROOK RD

MEADOW RD

PRIORY RD

Marston

ABBOTS WLK

ELMDENE CL

LARCHFIELDS

SCHOOL ST

MAIN ST

St Margaret's CE Prim Sch

2

DERBY CL

Wolston

LAMMAS CT

New Farm

PADDOCKS CT

Liby

WARWICK RD

BROOK ST

PO

MANOR EST

JOHN SIMPSON CL

CHESTNUT GR

Cemy

DYER'S LA

Lammas Hill

Lords Hill Farm

75

The Thicket

STRETTON RD

Dingley Osiers

1

Fosse Farm

Rookery Hall

Heath Farm

Heath House

COALPIT LA

B4455

74

41   A   42   B   43   C

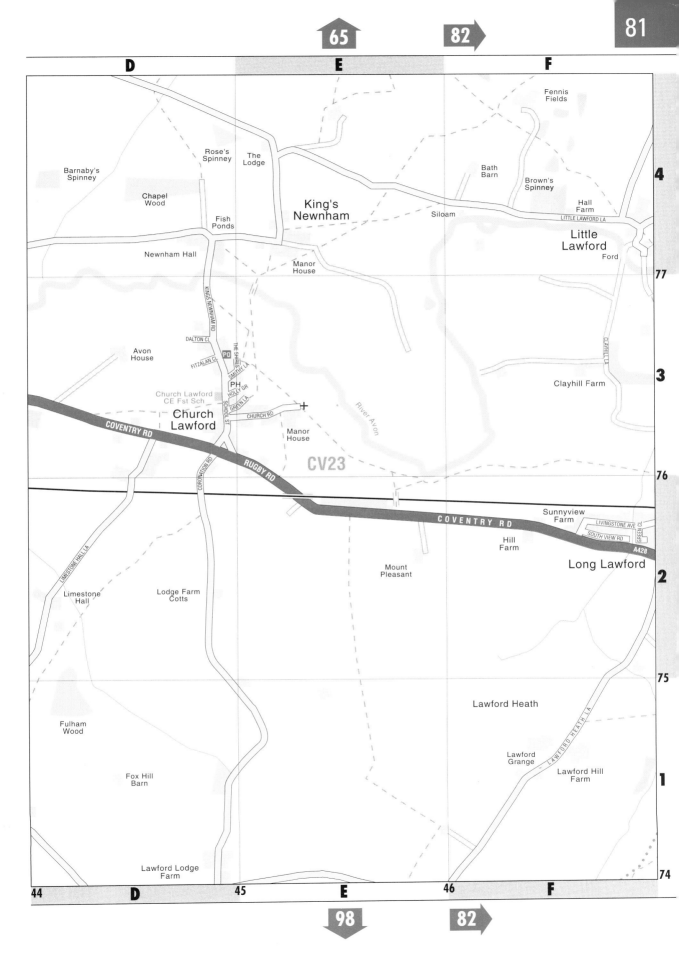

D
E
F

4

Fennis
Fields

Barnaby's
Spinney

Rose's
Spinney

The
Lodge

Bath
Barn

Brown's
Spinney

Chapel
Wood

King's
Newnham

Hall
Farm

Siloam

LITTLE LAWFORD LA

Fish
Ponds

Little
Lawford

77

Newnham Hall

Manor
House

Ford

KINGS NEWNHAM RD

DALTON CL

Avon
House

PO

THE SHIRES

FITZALAN CL

SMITHY LA

PH

HOLLY GR

GREEN LA

Clayhill Farm

CLAYHILL LA

3

Church Lawford
CE Fst Sch

SCHOOL ST

Church
Lawford

CHURCH RD

Manor
House

River Avon

COVENTRY RD

CORONATION RD

RUGBY RD

CV23

76

COVENTRY RD

Sunnyview
Farm

LIVINGSTONE AVE CL

GREEN CL

SOUTH VIEW RD

A428

Hill
Farm

Long Lawford

2

Limestone
Hall

LIMESTONE HALL LA

Lodge Farm
Cotts

Mount
Pleasant

75

Lawford Heath

Fulham
Wood

LAWFORD HEATH LA

Lawford
Grange

Fox Hill
Barn

Lawford Hill
Farm

1

Lawford Lodge
Farm

74

44
D
45
E
46
F

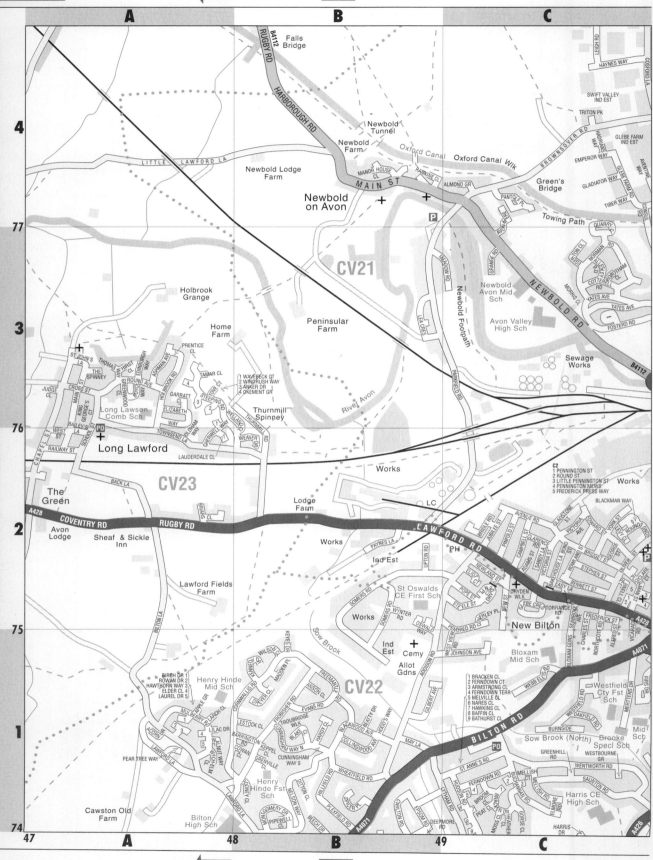

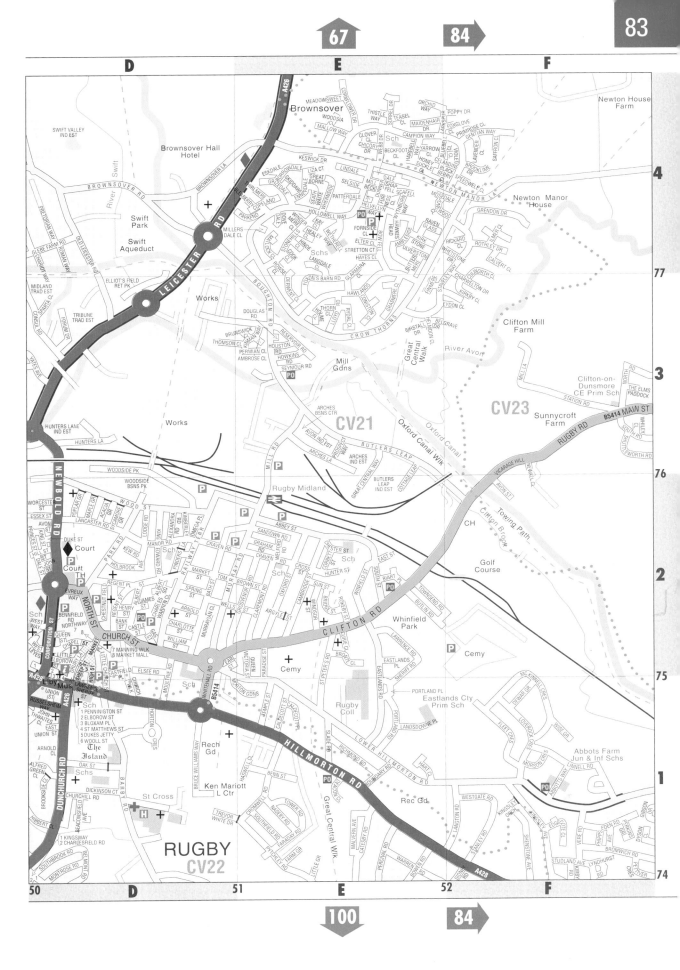

83
68

A
B
C
4
77
3
76
2
75
1
74
53
54
55
Mill Farm
B5414
Dow Bridge
A5
River Avon
LE17
STATION RD
Lilbourne Gorse
Lilbourne Furze
NEWTON RD
Dunsmore Farm
Lilbourne
RUGBY RD
BUCKWELL LA
Cemy
Almond Bank
NORTH RD
MANOR LA
CHURCH ST
Manor Farm
Dunsmore
Magpie Lodge Farm
ROBERTSON CL
HADFIELD CL
MAIN ST
LILBOURNE RD
Dunsmore House
PO
ORWELL CL
EVERARD CL
GOODACRE
ALLANS CL
ALLANS LA
SOUTH RD
Clifton Hall Farm
Dunsmore Hall Farm
CV23
HILLMORTON LA
Clifton upon Dunsmore
Dunsmore Home Farm
SHUTTLEWORTH RD
Clifton Court Farm
The Clifton Court Hotel
Masts
Oakridge Farm
Clifton Hall
Masts
The Meadows
HILLMORTON LA
Grange Farm House
Masts
Home Farm
Clifton Brook
Masts
Double Bridge
Oxford Canal
Towing Path
Oxford Canal Wlk
CV21
Rugby Radio Station
THE KENT
WAVERLEY RD
THE LOCKS
Hillmorton Locks
GWS
DR
ROBERT HILL CL
FEATHERBED LA
JENKINS RD
PINE GR
BRINDLEY RD
Normandy Farm
Masts
DYSON CL
JACKSON RD
COTON RD
THE MEWS
GAINSBOROUGH CR
BONNINGTON CL
1 LANDSEER CL
2 REYNOLDS CL
BROMWICH RD
PETTIVER CRES
WIGSTON RD
LEVER RD
SCHOOL ST
SCHOOL GDNS
CONSTABLE RD
FOX CL
LOWER ST

83
101

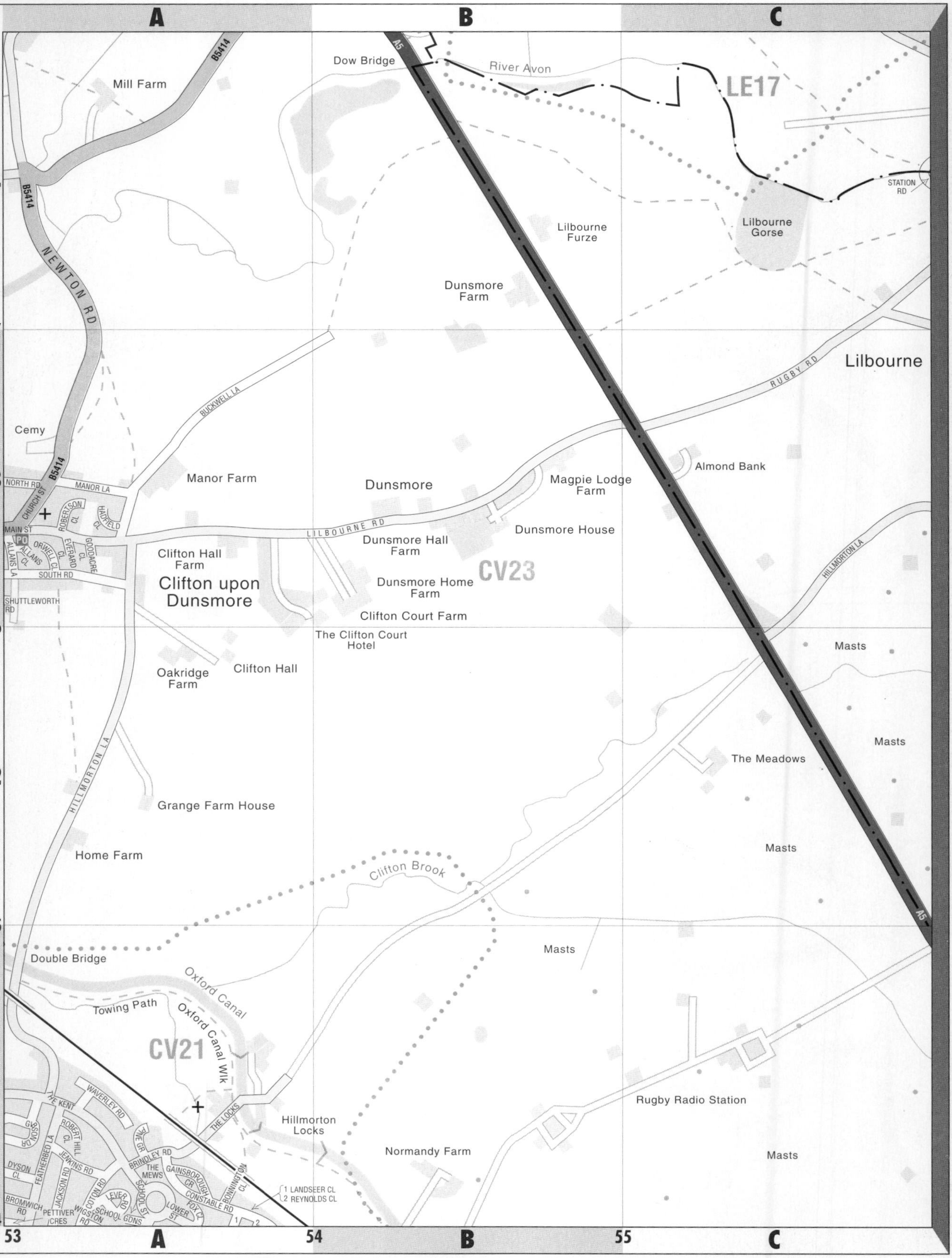

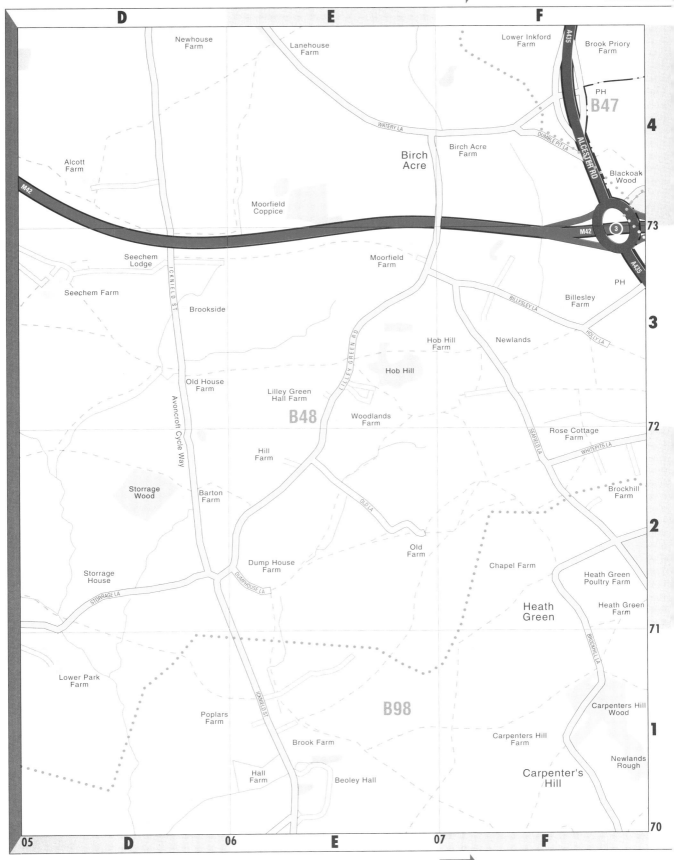

85

69

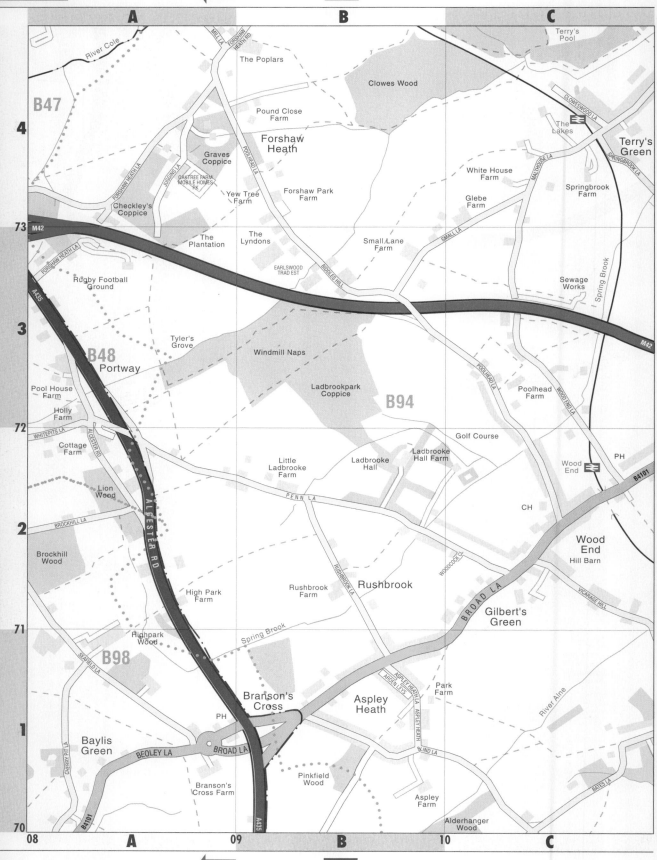

85

112

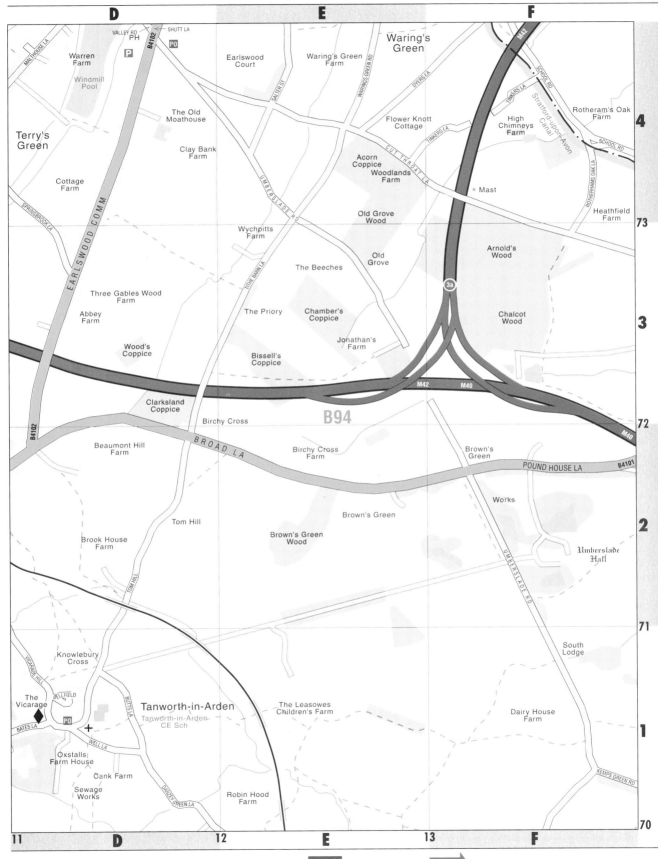

D **E** **F**

Waring's Green

M42

SHUTT LA
VALLEY RD
PH
P
B4102
PO

Warren Farm

Windmill Pool

Earlswood Court

Waring's Green Farm

WARINGS GREEN RD

DYERS LA

SCHOOL RD

TINKERS LA

Stratford-upon-Avon Canal

Rotheram's Oak Farm

Terry's Green

The Old Moathouse

Flower Knott Cottage

High Chimneys Farm

SCHOOL RD

4

Clay Bank Farm

SALTER ST

Acorn Coppice

Woodlands Farm

CUT THROAT LA

TINKERS LA

ROTHERHAMS OAK LA

Heathfield Farm

Cottage Farm

SPRINGBROOK LA

UMBERSLADE RD

Mast

73

EARLSWOOD COMM

Wychpitts Farm

Old Grove Wood

Arnold's Wood

Three Gables Wood Farm

THE BARN LA

The Beeches

Old Grove

3

Abbey Farm

The Priory

Chamber's Coppice

Chalcot Wood

Wood's Coppice

Bissell's Coppice

Jonathan's Farm

3a

B4102

Clarksland Coppice

Birchy Cross

M42 M40

M40

72

B94

BROAD LA

Birchy Cross Farm

Brown's Green

POUND HOUSE LA B4101

Beaumont Hill Farm

Works

2

Tom Hill

Brown's Green

Umberslade Hall

Brook House Farm

TOM HILL

Brown's Green Wood

UMBERSLADE RD

71

Knowlebury Cross

South Lodge

VICARAGE HILL

The Vicarage

BALLFIELD

BUTTS LA

Tanworth-in-Arden

Tanworth-in-Arden CE Sch

The Leasowes Children's Farm

Dairy House Farm

1

BATES LA

PO

WELL LA

Oxstalls Farm House

Cank Farm

DANZEY GREEN LA

Sewage Works

Robin Hood Farm

KEMPS GREEN RD

11 **D** **12** **E** **13** **F** **70**

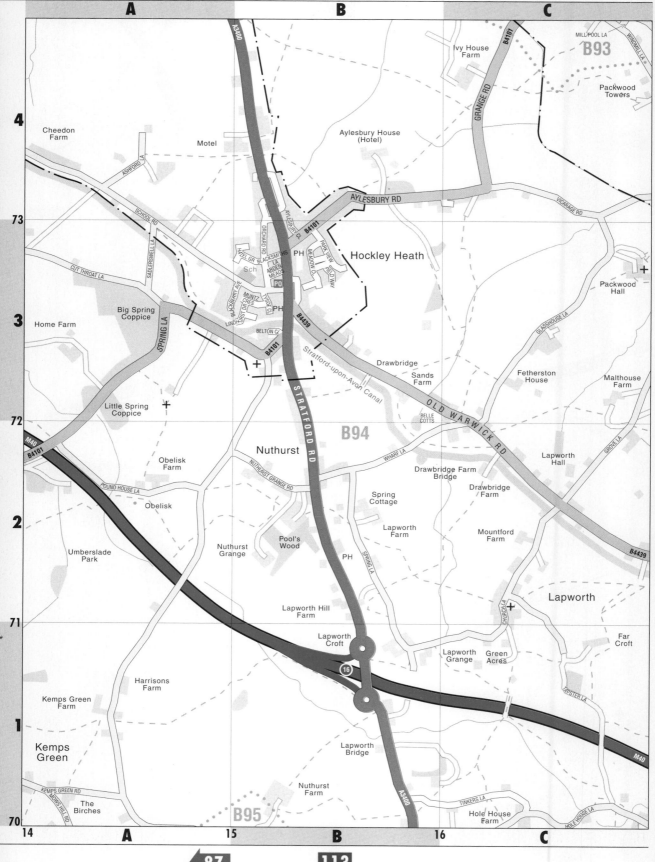

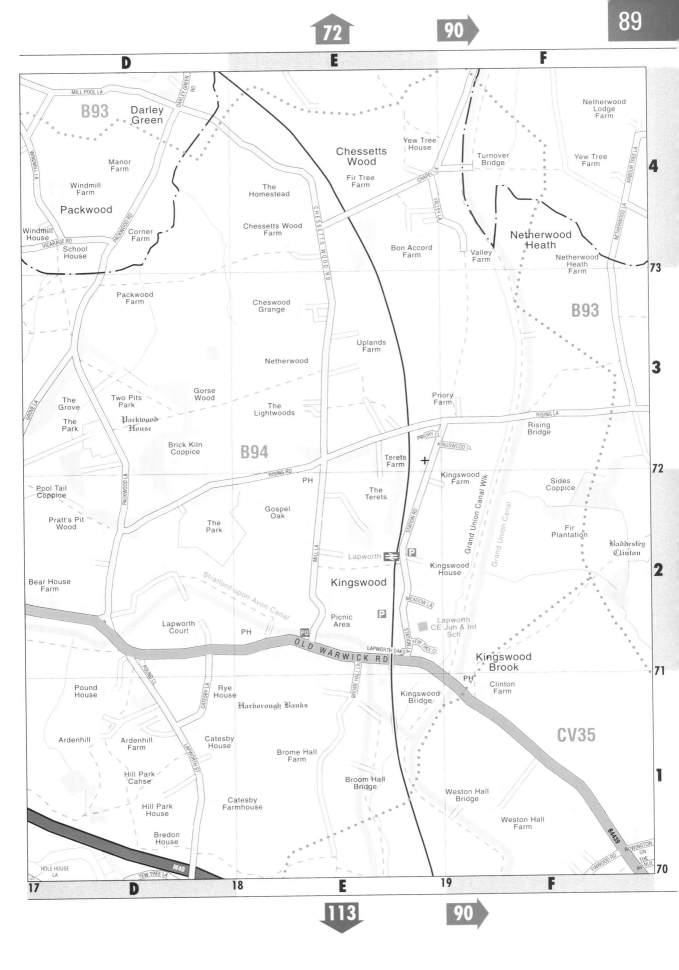

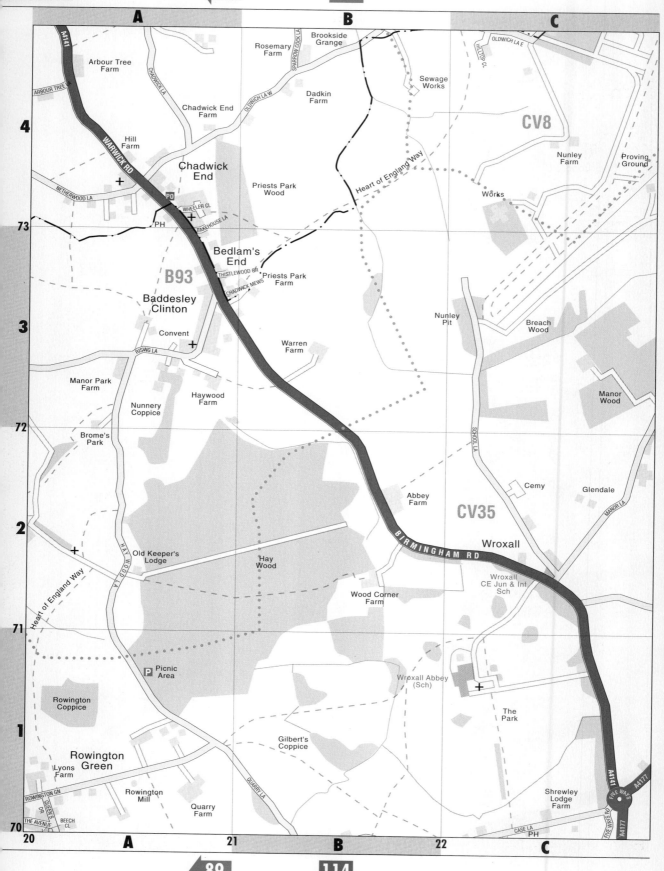

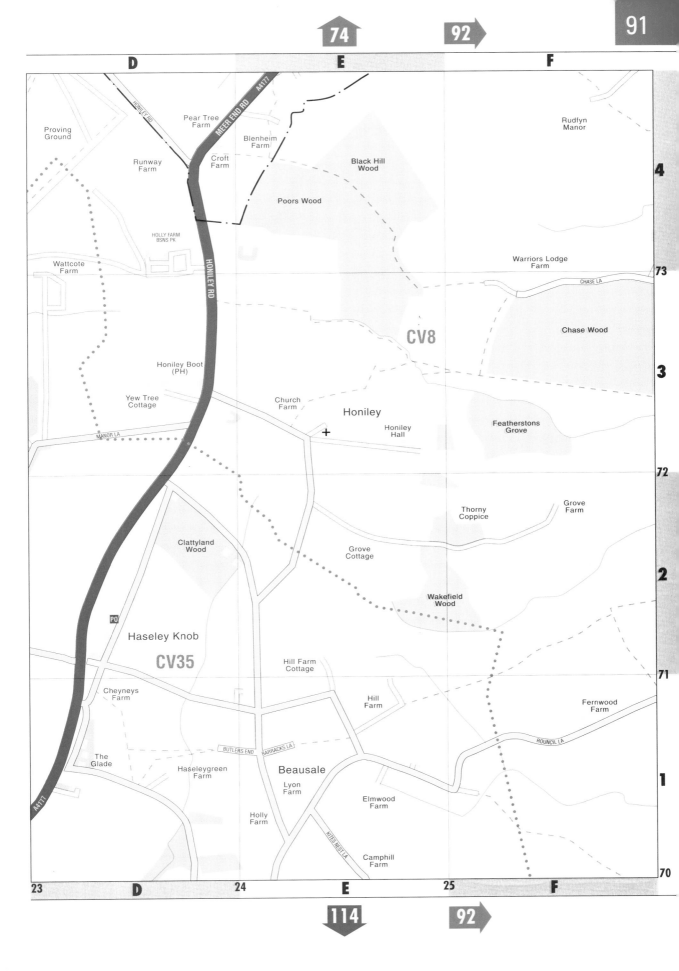

74
92

D   E   F

Proving Ground

Pear Tree Farm

MEER END RD

A4177

HONILEY RD

Blenheim Farm

Rudfyn Manor

Runway Farm

Croft Farm

Black Hill Wood

Poors Wood

4

HOLLY FARM BSNS PK

Wattcote Farm

Warriors Lodge Farm

CHASE LA

73

HONILEY RD

CV8

Chase Wood

Honiley Boot (PH)

3

Yew Tree Cottage

Church Farm

Honiley

MANOR LA

+

Honiley Hall

Featherstons Grove

72

Thorny Coppice

Grove Farm

Clattyland Wood

Grove Cottage

Wakefield Wood

2

PO

Haseley Knob

CV35

Hill Farm Cottage

71

Cheyneys Farm

Hill Farm

Fernwood Farm

ROUNCIL LA

The Glade

BUTLERS END

BARRACKS LA

Beausale

Haseleygreen Farm

Lyon Farm

Elmwood Farm

1

A4177

Holly Farm

KITES NEST LA

Camphill Farm

70

23   D   24   E   25   F

114
92

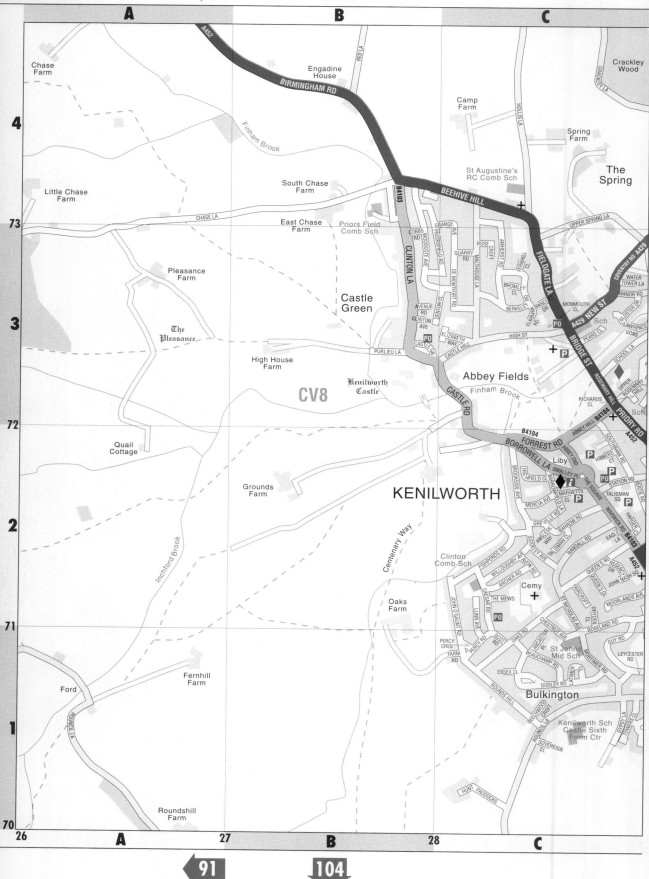

A B C

4

73

3

72

2

71

1

70

26 27 28

A B C

Chase Farm

Little Chase Farm

Crackley Wood

Engadine House

Camp Farm

Spring Farm

The Spring

St Augustine's RC Comb Sch

South Chase Farm

East Chase Farm

Priors Field Comb Sch

Castle Green

Pleasance Farm

The Pleasance

High House Farm

Kenilworth Castle

CV8

Abbey Fields

Finham Brook

Quail Cottage

Grounds Farm

KENILWORTH

Clinton Comb Sch

Oaks Farm

Fernhill Farm

Ford

Percy Cres

St Johns Mid Sch

Bulkington

Roundshill Farm

Kenilworth Sch Castle Sixth Form Ctr

Hunt Paddocks

BIRMINGHAM RD

BEEHIVE HILL

CLINTON LA

CASTLE RD

FORREST RD

BORROWELL LA

NEW ST

BRIDGE ST

FIELDGATE LA

PRIORY RD

COVENTRY RD

Finham Brook

Inchford Brook

Centenary Way

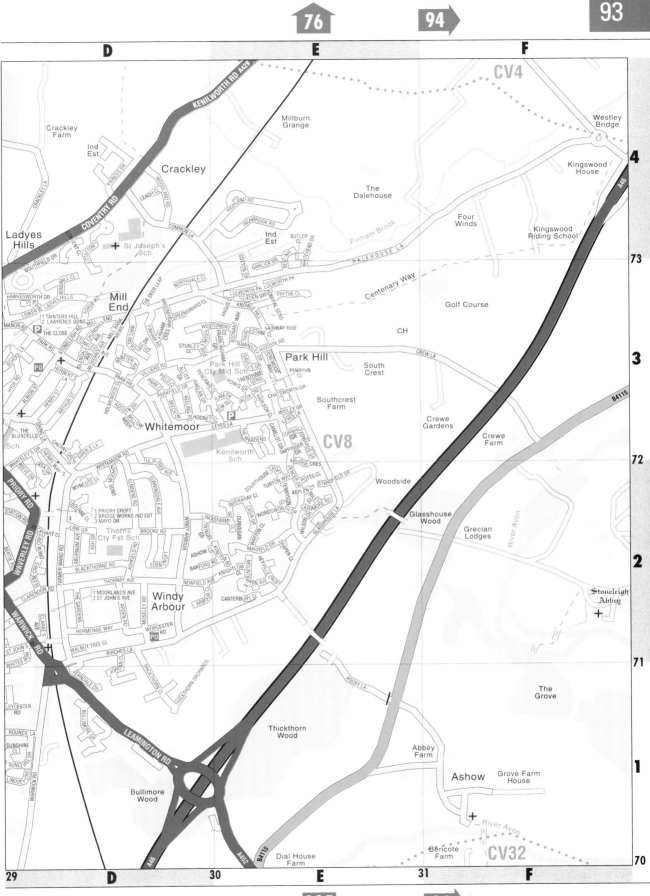

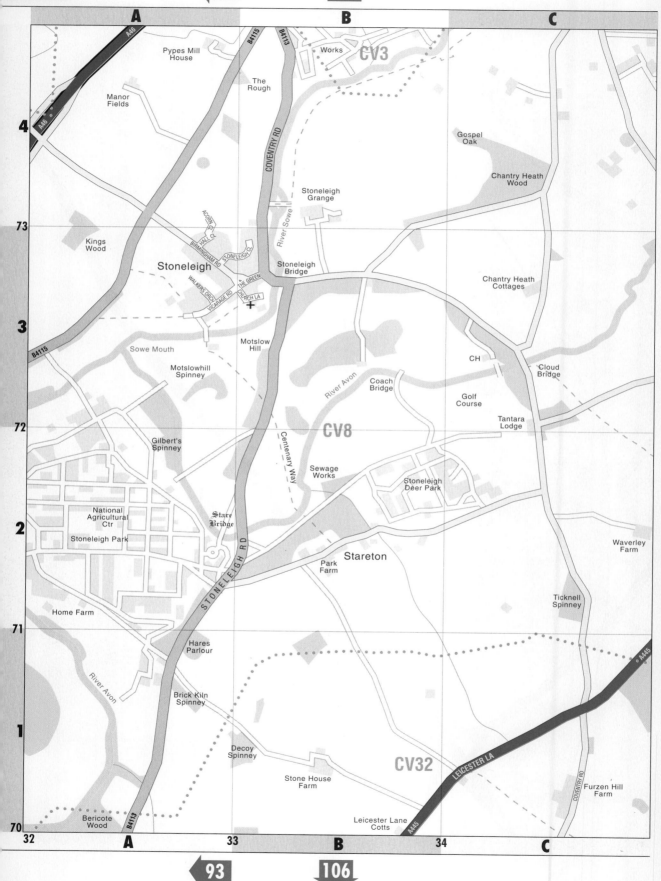

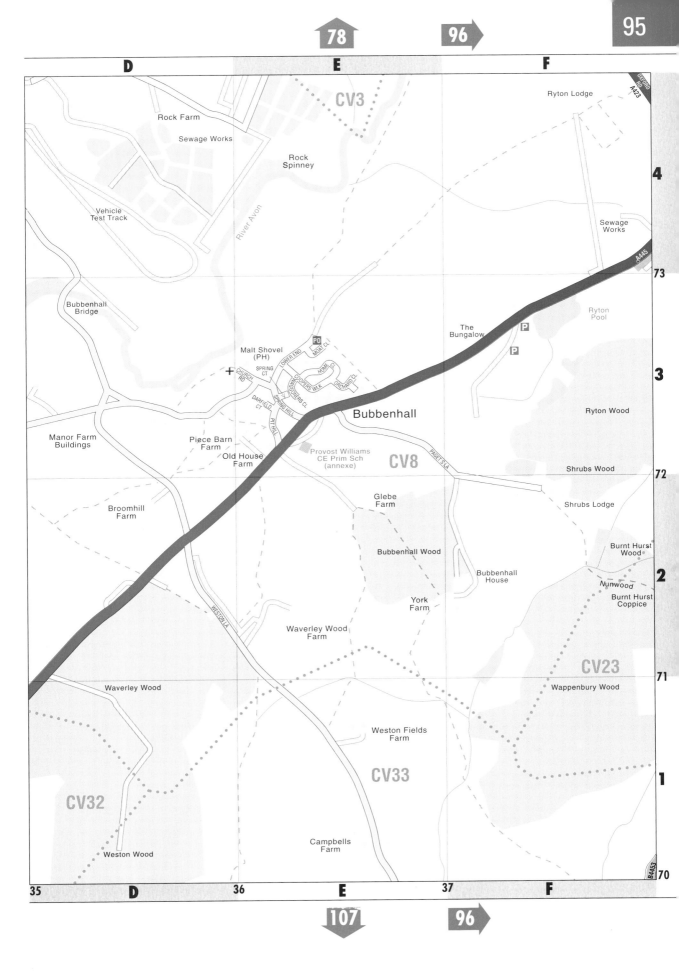

78
96
107
96

D   E   F

CV3

Rock Farm

Sewage Works

Ryton Lodge

Rock
Spinney

4

Vehicle
Test Track

River Avon

Sewage
Works

A423

OXFORD RD

A445

73

Bubbenhall
Bridge

Ryton
Pool

The
Bungalow

P

P

3

Malt Shovel
(PH)

PO

MOAT CL

Ryton Wood

CHURCH
RD

SPRING
CT

LOWER END

HOME CL

COOPERS WLK

WAGSTHERS CL

ORCHARD CL

DARFIELD
CT

SPRING HILL

PIT HILL

Bubbenhall

Manor Farm
Buildings

Piece Barn
Farm

Old House
Farm

Provost Williams
CE Prim Sch
(annexe)

CV8

PAGET'S LA

Shrubs Wood

72

Broomhill
Farm

Glebe
Farm

Shrubs Lodge

Bubbenhall Wood

Burnt Hurst
Wood

Bubbenhall
House

Nunwood

2

WESTON LA

York
Farm

Burnt Hurst
Coppice

Waverley Wood
Farm

CV23

71

Waverley Wood

Wappenbury Wood

Weston Fields
Farm

CV33

1

CV32

Campbells
Farm

Weston Wood

B4453

70

35   D   36   E   37   F

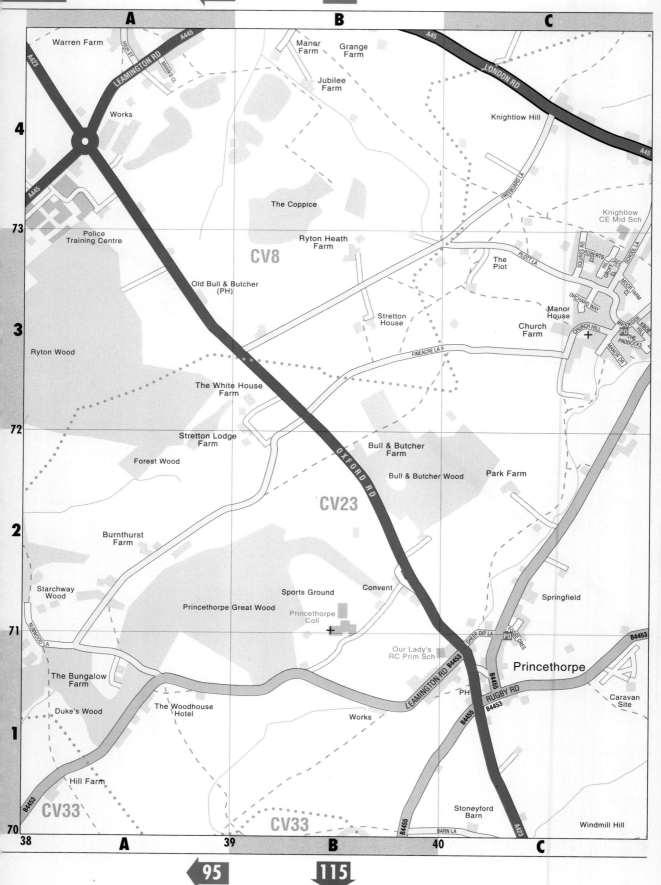

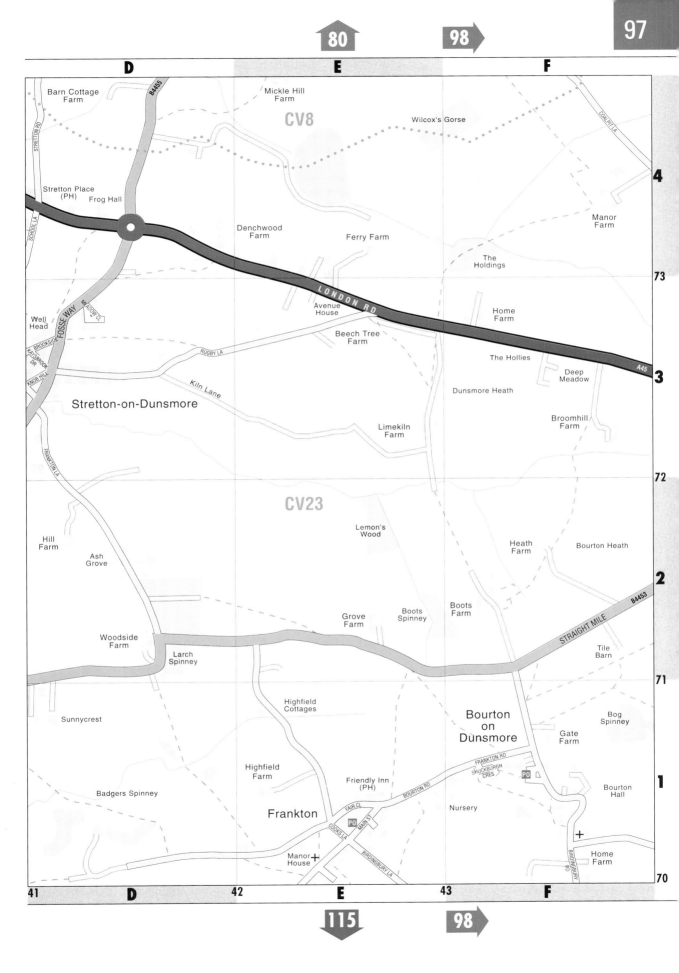

97
81

A   **B**   **C**

4

North Lodge Farm

Nursery

COALPIT LA

Lawford Heath

LAWFORD HEATH IND EST

Lawford Heath Farm

Rose Grove Farm

Works

Reservoir

CV22

73

Wolston Grange

THE CRESCENT

LAWFORD HEATH LA

THE RYELANDS

A4071

Cawston Farm

Potford's Dam Farm

Cawston Spinney

3

A45

Park Farm

South Lodge Farm

Blue Boar Farm

72

Nursery

LONDON RD

A4071

DUNCHURCH TRAD EST

Station Farm

B4453

A4071

Motel

CV23

The Mill House

Northampton Lane

2

B4453

STRAIGHT MILE

CH

Hotel

COVENTRY RD

A45

M45

B4429

Barnwells Barn Farm

Thurlaston

STOCKS LA

THE GARDENS

BEECH DR

MAIN ST

CHURCH WLK

Far Popehill Spinney

Golf Course

Poultry Farm

BIGGIN HALL LA

71

Popehill Spinneys

Biggin Hall

Little Mead

MOAT CL

PUDDING BAG LA

GRAYS ORCHARD

Hill Farm

Thurlaston Grange

Grange Farm

Biggin House

1

Draycote Fields Farm

Draycote Water (Reservoir)

CV22

70

44   **A**   45   **B**   46   **C**

Chapel Farm

97
116

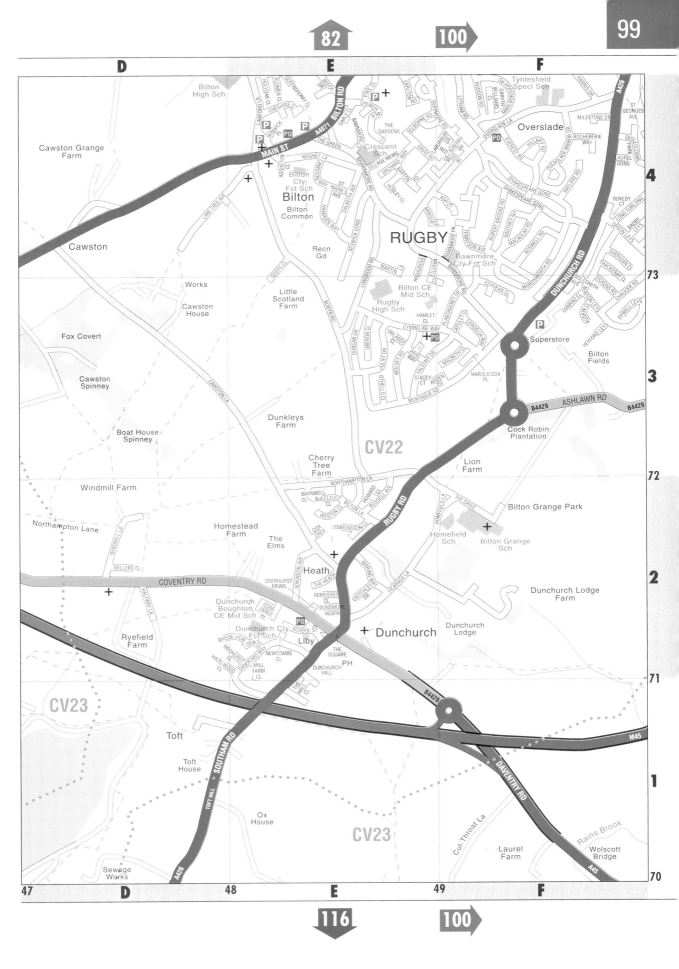

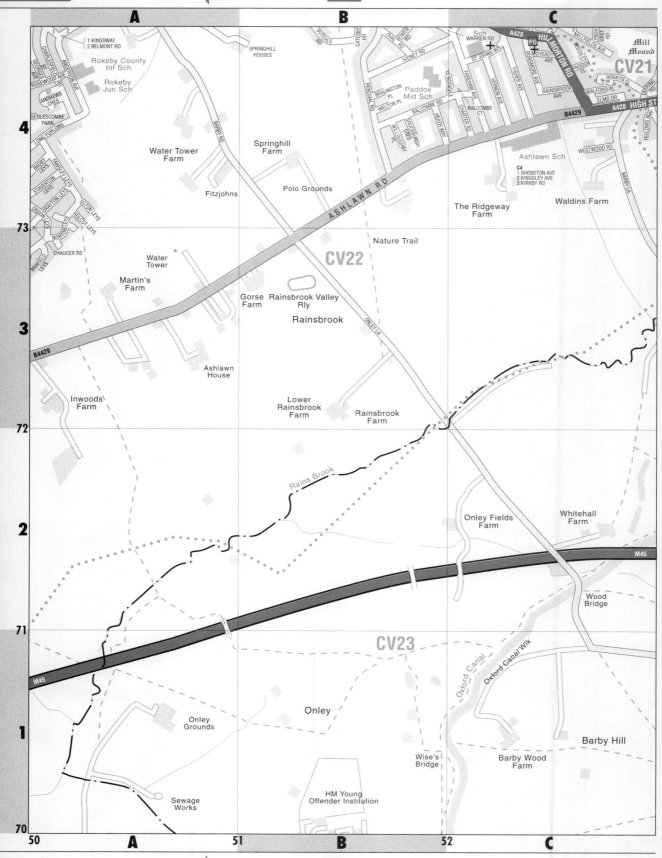

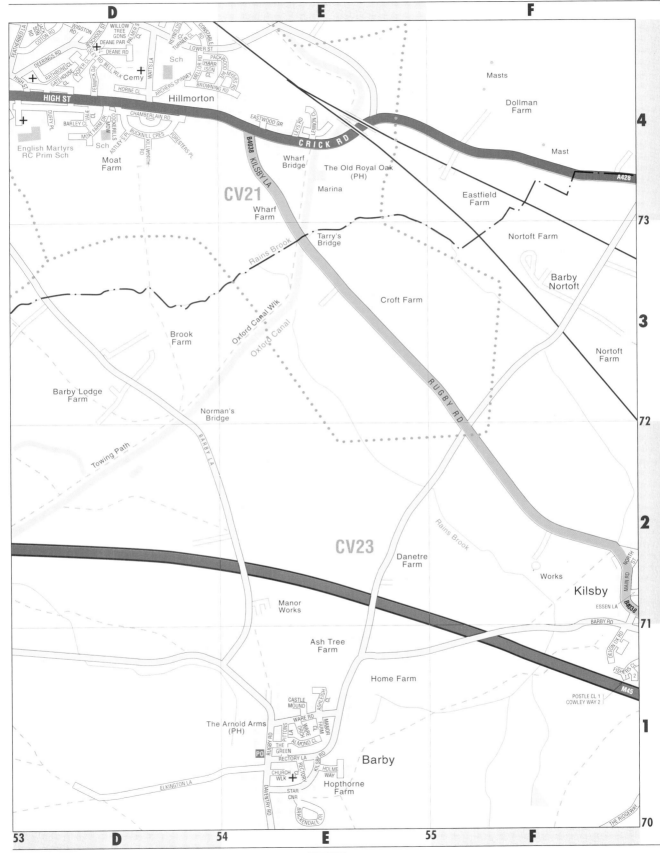

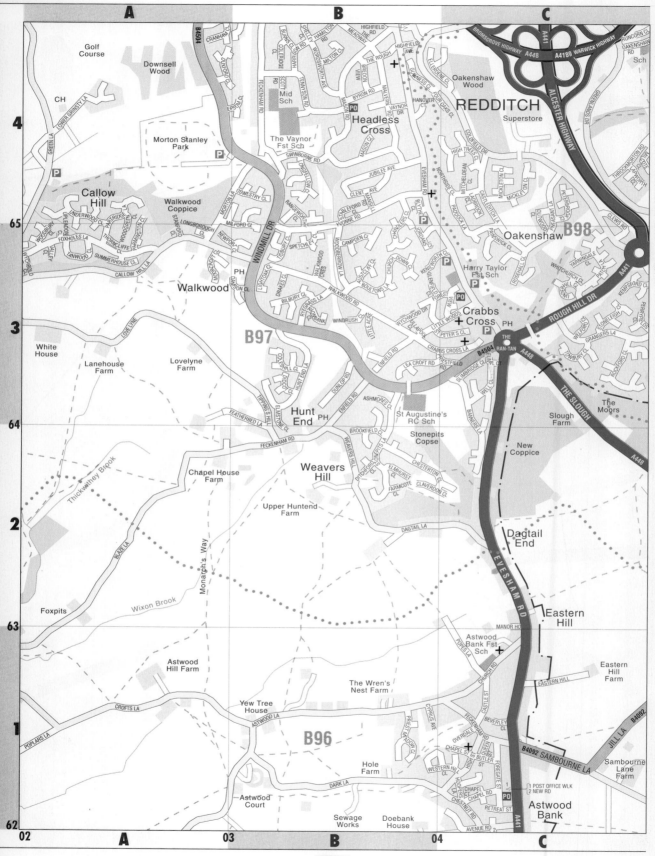

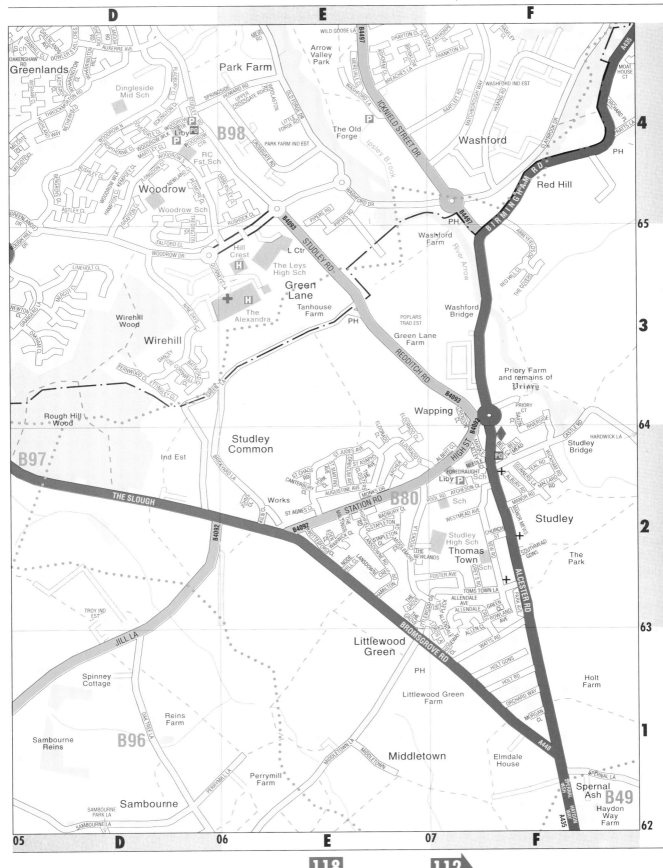

D   E   F

Greenlands

Dingleside
Mid Sch

Park Farm

Arrow
Valley
Park

WILD GOOSE LA

B98

The Old
Forge

Ipsley Brook

Washford

Park Farm Ind Est

Washford Ind Est

4

MOAT
HOUSE
CT

Woodrow

Liby
P
PO
P

RC
Fst Sch

Woodrow Sch

Red Hill

PH

65

Hill Crest
H

L Ctr

The Leys
High Sch

**Green
Lane**

Washford
Farm

River Arrow

ICKNIELD STREET DR

BIRMINGHAM RD

B4497

The
Alexandra
H

Tanhouse
Farm

PH

Washford
Bridge

Washford Dr

STUDLEY RD

B4083

PIPERS RD

Pipers Rd

Wirehill

Wirehill
Wood

POPLARS
TRAD EST

Green Lane
Farm

3

REDDITCH RD

B4093

Rough Hill
Wood

Priory Farm
and remains of
Priory

B97

Wapping

HIGH ST

CRENDON

B4092

PRIORY
CT

SAXON

RIVERSIDE

64

**Studley
Common**

Ind Est

BRICKYARD LA

GREEN LA

PO
BELL LA

MEAD

CASTLE RD

HARDWICK LA

Studley
Bridge

WICKHAM RD

ALBERT ST

NEEDLE

Liby
P

Foredraught
Sch

ALBURY RD

THE SLOUGH

B4092

ST JUDES AVE

ST CHADS
RD

CANTERBURY
CL

ST MARTINS

CORBIZUM AVE

ST ASAPHS
AVE

THE CLOISTERS

AUGUSTINE AVE

YORK

ARCHER CL

ELDORADO

ELDORADO CL

POOL RD

ATCHESON CL

Sch

MANOR RD

Studley

2

Works

ST AGNES CL

STATION RD

B80

WESTMEAD AVE

CHURCH
ST

SOUTHMEAD
GDNS

The
Park

KILN CL

MOTTLESFORD CL

ADMIN

B4092

BADBURY CL

STAPLETON
CL

BROOKS LA

Studley
High Sch

**Thomas
Town**

Sch

ALCESTER RD

THE MALTHOUSE

HIGHFIELD

STAPLETON
CL

EDEN CL

WARWICK CL

LANSDOWNE RD

NODE
HILL CL

LANSDOWNE
CRES

ELMORE

The
Newlands

FOSTER AVE

GREY'S RD

NEW RD

MANOR MEWS

HAMILTON

THE GROVE

TOMS TOWN LA

63

**Littlewood
Green**

BROMSGROVE RD

LITTLEWOOD CL

ALLEN CL

ALLENDALE
AVE

ALLENDALE CRES

GREEN
CL

ROWLAND
AVE

PARK AVE

WATTS RD

Holt
Farm

TROY IND
EST

JILL LA

Spinney
Cottage

Reins
Farm

B96

OAK TREE LA

HOLT GDNS

HOLT RD

ORCHARD WAY

MORGAN
CL

A448

1

PH

Littlewood Green
Farm

Sambourne
Reins

Perrymill
Farm

Middletown

MIDDLETOWN LA

MIDDLETOWN

Elmdale
House

SPERNAL LA

Spernal
Ash

B49

PERRYMILL LA

Sambourne

SAMBOURNE
PARK LA

SAMBOURNE LA

SPERNAL ASH

HAYDON WAY

A435

Haydon
Way
Farm

62

05   D   06   E   07   F

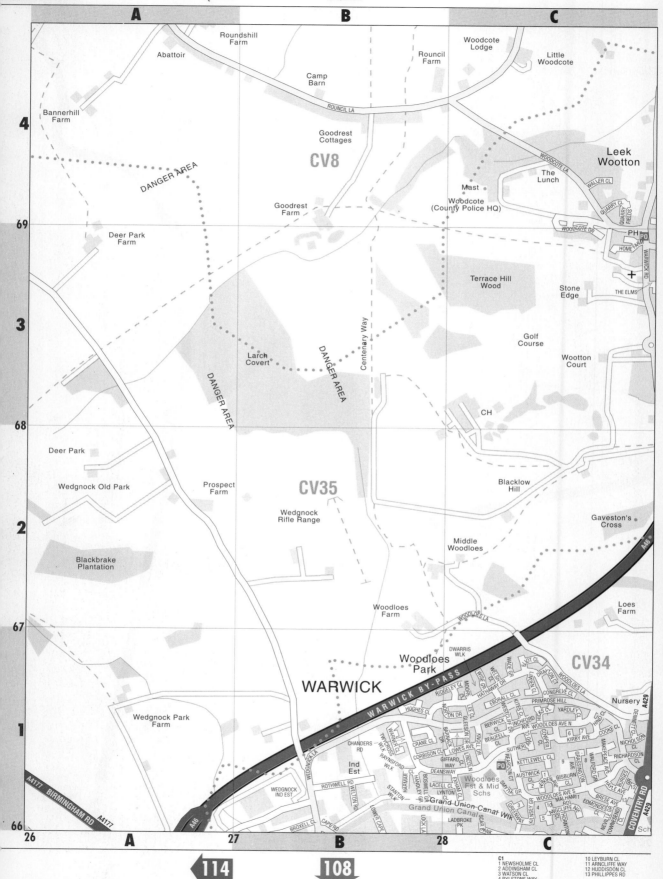
A   B   C

Roundshill
Farm

Abattoir

Camp
Barn

Rouncil
Farm

Woodcote
Lodge

Little
Woodcote

4

Bannerhill
Farm

ROUNCIL LA

Goodrest
Cottages

CV8

Leek
Wootton

WOODCOTE LA

The
Lunch

WALLER CL

DANGER AREA

Mast

QUARRY CL

QUARRY FIELDS

69

Deer Park
Farm

Goodrest
Farm

Woodcote
(County Police HQ)

WOODCOTE DR

HOME

PO

PH

WARWICK RD

Terrace Hill
Wood

Stone
Edge

THE ELMS

+

3

Larch
Covert

DANGER AREA

Centenary Way

Golf
Course

Wootton
Court

DANGER AREA

CH

68

Deer Park

Wedgnock Old Park

Prospect
Farm

CV35

Blacklow
Hill

Gaveston's
Cross

2

Blackbrake
Plantation

Wedgnock
Rifle Range

Middle
Woodloes

A46

Woodloes
Farm

WOODLOES LA

Loes
Farm

67

Woodloes
Park

DWARRIS WLK

CV34

Nursery

A429

WARWICK

WARWICK BY-PASS

WEST CL
WADE GR
OT CL
WOODLOES LA
CONGREVE CL
DRAY...ON CT
KITES CL

Primrose Hill

HATHAWAY DR
RIDGELEY CL
MOORS...
WISE GR
EBORALL CL

Yardley

1

Wedgnock Park
Farm

WEDGNOCK LA

HUGHES CL

CHANDERS
RD

TWYCROSS HD
WARNER CL

CRANE CL

CORBISON CL

NORTON DR
BARNACK

GIFFARD
WAY

LOWES AVE
LINCOLN CL
LYNTON CL

KNOLL DR

BERWICK
AVE
INCHFORD
BEAUFELL
SUTHERL...

WOODLOES AVE N
COOPER
KIRBY AVE

GRASSINGTON
AVE
WALFORD...

RICHARDSON
CL

Ind
Est

RAYNSFORD
WLK
JERMYN

DEANSWAY
LACELL CL
BOSWELL
HANDLEY...
SMYTHE GR

REARDON CT
KETTLEWELL CL
PO

6
7

MAKEPEACE AVE
NICHOLSON
CL

GISBURN
...

WEDGNOCK
IND EST

ROTHWELL RD
WELTON RD

STANTON
WLK

GREENWAY
WOODLOES AVE S

AUSTWICK

MALHAM 1
NGCLIFFE AV...
EDMONDES...

BRESE AVE
TOWNSEND...
BURGES...

HYLE AVE

66

A4177 BIRMINGHAM RD

A4177

A46

BROXELL CL

CAPE RD

LOWER CAPE

LOCK LA

LADBROKE
PK

SPAR...BANK

Grand Union Canal WIK
Grand Union Canal

Woodloes
Fst & Mid
Schs

MALHAM 1
RDL

EDMONDES...

A429

COVENTRY RD

Sch

26   27   28

A   B   C

C1
1 NEWSHOLME CL
2 ADDINGHAM CL
3 WATSON CL
4 RYLSTONE WAY
5 KILDWICK WAY
6 SHELDON GR
7 WEALE GR
8 HETTON CL
9 BUCKDEN CL
10 LEYBURN CL
11 ARNCLIFFE WAY
12 HUDDISDON CL
13 PHILLIPPES RD

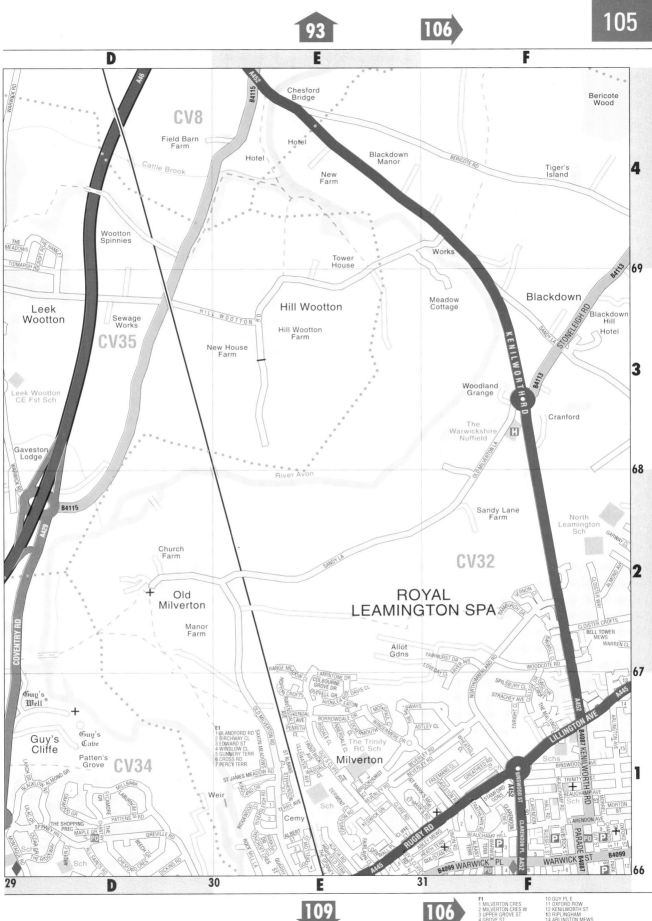

D
E
F

CV8

Field Barn
Farm

Cattle Brook

Chesford
Bridge

Hotel

Bericote
Wood

Hotel

Blackdown
Manor

BERICOTE RD

Tiger's
Island

4

New
Farm

Wootton
Spinnies

THE
MEADOWS

THE HAMLET

CROFT LA

WARWICK RD

TIDMARSH RD

Leek
Wootton

CV35

Sewage
Works

HILL WOOTTON RD

Tower
House

Hill Wootton

Hill Wootton
Farm

Works

Meadow
Cottage

Blackdown

B4113

69

Blackdown
Hill

STONELEIGH RD

SANDY LA

Hotel

3

Leek Wootton
CE Fst Sch

New House
Farm

Woodland
Grange

KENILWORTH RD

B4113

Cranford

Gaveston
Lodge

River Avon

OLD MILVERTON LA

The
Warwickshire
Nuffield

H

68

WARWICK RD

A46

A429

B4115

Church
Farm

SANDY LA

Sandy Lane
Farm

CV32

North
Leamington
Sch

GARWAY CL

ALMOND AVE

CLOISTER WAY

2

COVENTRY RD

Old
Milverton

Manor
Farm

RANGE MEADOW CL

LAMINTONE DR

COLBOURNE
GROVE DR

OVERELL GR

DAVIS CL

ROYAL
LEAMINGTON SPA

VERNON

BRAMBURGH GR

CLOISTER CROFTS

BELL TOWER
MEWS

WARREN CL

Allot
Gdns

FAIRHURST DR

RYLEY AVE

LOVEDAY CL

SPILSBURY CL

COLLEGE CL

COLLEGE CR

ORLOW

STRACHEY AVE

THE MALTINGS

WOODCOTE RD

67

Guy's
Well

Guy's
Cliffe

Guy's
Cave

Patten's
Grove

CV34

E1
1 BLANDFORD RD
2 BIRCHWAY CL
3 EDWARD ST
4 WINSLOW CL
5 GUNNERY TERR
6 CROSS RD
7 PERCY TERR

HOPTON CROFTS

RAVENSDALE CL

KENDAL
AVE

PENRITH

AVONLEA
CL

EATON
CL

BORROWDALE DR

ENNERDALE CL

DOCKEMOUTH CL

ASTLEY CL

NORTHUMBERLAND RD

The Trinity
RC Sch

OAKWAYS

SPRUL CT

EIGHBERRY

SAUL CT

Milverton

Schs

A452

A445

LILLINGTON AVE

B4087 KENILWORTH RD

ARLINGTON AVE

Trinity
Sch

BEAUCHAMP AVE

MORRELL ST

MORTON
ST

1

LARCH GR

ALMOND GR

SYCAMORE
GR

SPINNEY HILL

LABURNUM GR

MILLBRIK

PATTENS
RD

CHANTRY
HTS

LILAC GR

CEDAR GR

THE ROYSTON

MONTAGUE RD

ARDEN CL

ALL SAINTS RD

Sch

MAPLE GR

GREVILLE RD

BEECH GR

DICKINS RD

St James Meadow

Weir

Cemy

ULSWATER AVE

TERRY AVE

RIDGWAY CL

RUGERLY DR

FOXCROFT DR

OAKDENE CRES

QUARRY LA

ALBERT

NUTFIELD

ACACIA RD

HIGHFIELD

KESWICK GN

DERWENT CL

CLIFFE
CT

BROOKHURST

BEVERLEY RD

ST MARKS RD

STAMFORD GDNS

TREEMANS CL

GREATHEED RD

BINSWOOD ST

CLARENDON PL

BEAUCHAMP HILL

P

WARWICK
PL

P

CLARENDON SQ

RUSSELL ST

PARADE

TAVISTOCK ST

CHANDOS ST

PARK

B4087

WARWICK

ST

B4099

P

PO

P

B4099 WARWICK PL

A445

A452

66

29
D
30
E
31
F

F1
1 MILVERTON CRES
2 MILVERTON CRES W
3 UPPER GROVE ST
4 GROVE ST
5 WATERLOO PL
6 CLARENCE TERR
7 WINDSOR PL
8 BEDFORD ST
9 GUY PL W
10 GUY PL E
11 OXFORD ROW
12 KENILWORTH ST
13 RIPLINGHAM
14 ARLINGTON MEWS
15 BINSWOOD MANS

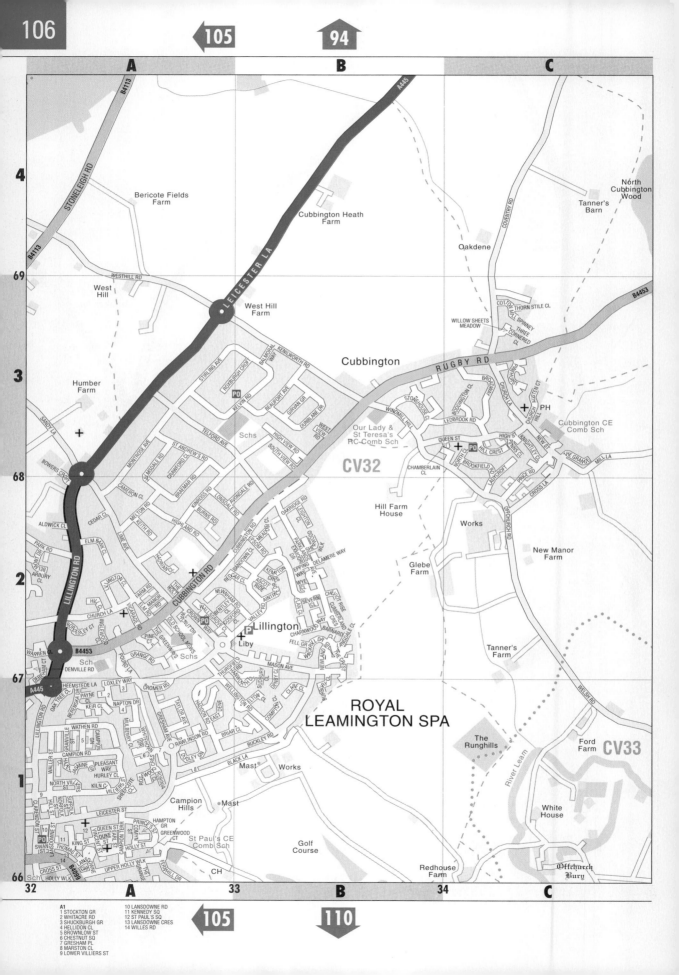

A1
1 STOCKTON GR
2 WHITACRE RD
3 SHUCKBURGH GR
4 HELLIDON CL
5 BROWNLOW ST
6 CHESTNUT SQ
7 GRESHAM PL
8 MARSTON CL
9 LOWER VILLIERS ST
10 LANSDOWNE RD
11 KENNEDY SQ
12 ST PAUL'S SQ
13 LANSDOWNE CRES
14 WILLES RD

95
115

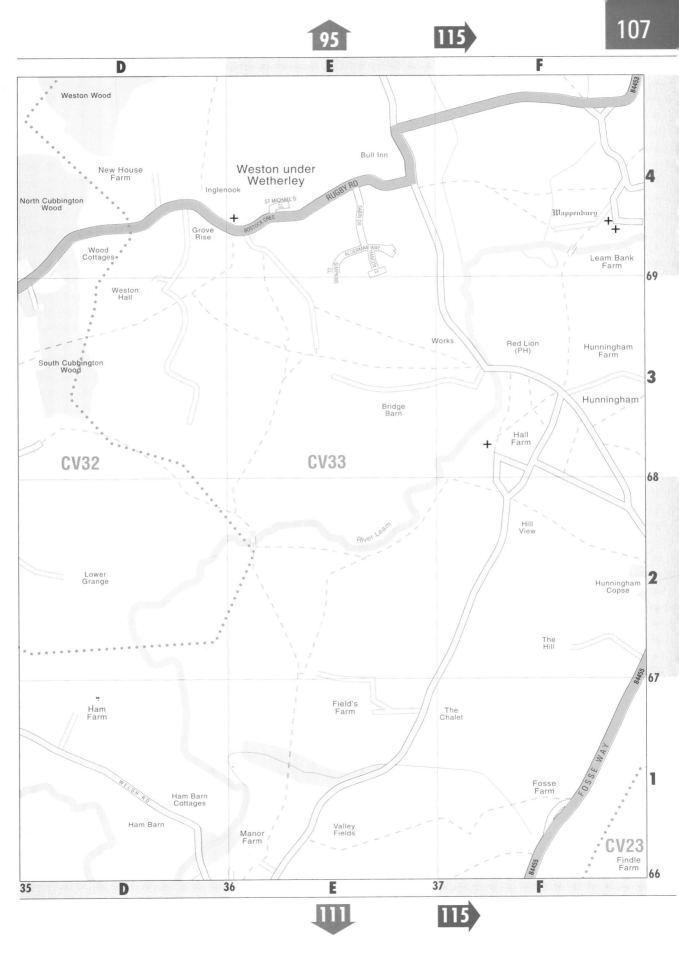

D   E   F

Weston Wood

New House Farm

North Cubbington Wood

Inglenook

Weston under Wetherley

Bull Inn

ST MICHAEL'S CL

RUGBY RD

BOSTOCK CRES

SABIN DR

Wappenbury

4

Grove Rise

ALDERMAN WAY

HANCOX CL

SIMPKINS CL

Leam Bank Farm

Wood Cottages

69

Weston Hall

Works

Red Lion (PH)

Hunningham Farm

South Cubbington Wood

3

Hunningham

Bridge Barn

CV32

CV33

Hall Farm

68

River Leam

Hill View

Lower Grange

Hunningham Copse

2

The Hill

67

Ham Farm

Field's Farm

The Chalet

1

WELSH RD

Ham Barn Cottages

Manor Farm

Valley Fields

Fosse Farm

B4455

FOSSE WAY

Ham Barn

CV23

Findle Farm

66

35   D   36   E   37   F

111
115

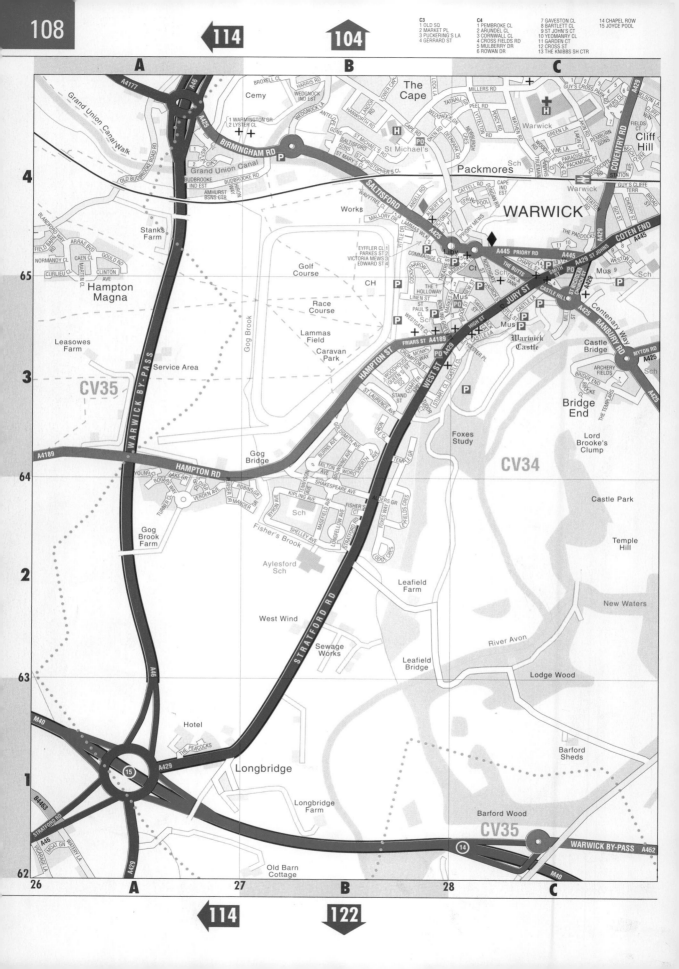

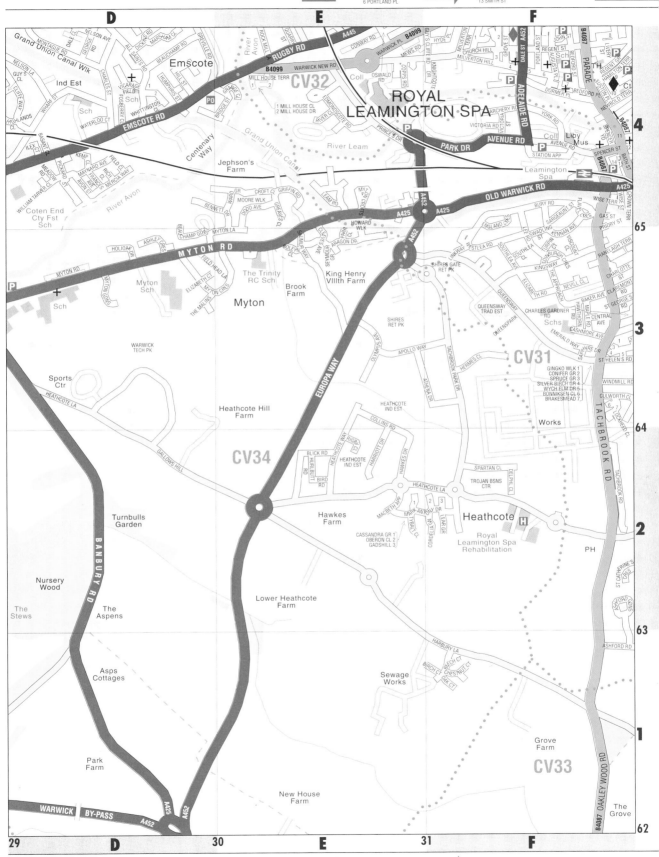

105
110
122
110

D4
1 ST EDITH S GN
2 AUSTIN EDWARDS DR

F4
1 WOODBINE ST
2 NEW BROOK ST
3 SOMERS PL
4 PORTLAND PLACE W
5 PORTLAND PLACE E
6 PORTLAND PL

7 ST PETER S RD
8 SATCHWELL WLK
9 ROSEFIELD WLK
10 ROSEFIELD PL
11 VICTORIA TERR
12 CHURCH WLK
13 SMITH ST

14 BATH PL
15 ABBOTTS ST

ROYAL LEAMINGTON SPA

Emscote

CV32

CV31

CV34

CV33

Heathcote

Myton

Grand Union Canal Wlk
Ind Est
EMSCOTE RD
Centenary Way
Jephson's Farm
River Avon
Coten End Cty Fst Sch
MYTON RD
Myton Sch
The Trinity RC Sch
Brook Farm
King Henry VIIIth Farm
WARWICK TECH PK
Sports Ctr
HEATHCOTE LA
Heathcote Hill Farm
EUROPA WAY
Turnbulls Garden
Nursery Wood
The Stews
The Aspens
Asps Cottages
Park Farm
BANBURY RD
WARWICK BY-PASS
A425
A452
New House Farm
Lower Heathcote Farm
Hawkes Farm
HEATHCOTE LA
Heathcote Ind Est
Sewage Works
Grove Farm
The Grove
OAKLEY WOOD RD
TACHBROOK RD
Royal Leamington Spa Rehabilitation
Works
Queensway Trad Est
SHIRES RET PK
SHIRES GATE RET PK
OLD WARWICK RD
Leamington Spa
PARK DR
AVENUE RD
ADELAIDE RD
PARADE
River Leam
Grand Union Canal
RUGBY RD
WARWICK NEW RD
B4099
A445
Liby Mus
Coll
River Avon

D   E   F

29   30   31

65   64   3   2   63   1   62   4

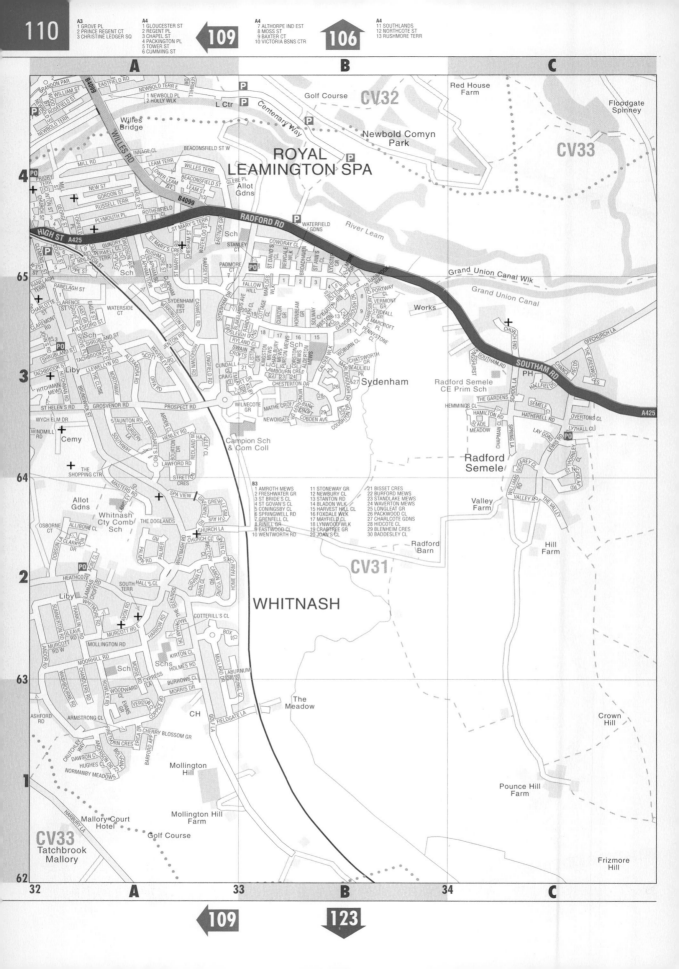

110

A3
1 GROVE PL
2 PRINCE REGENT CT
3 CHRISTINE LEDGER SQ

A4
1 GLOUCESTER ST
2 REGENT PL
3 CHAPEL ST
4 PACKINGTON PL
5 TOWER ST
6 CUMMING ST

109

A4
7 ALTHORPE IND EST
8 MOSS ST
9 BAXTER CT
10 VICTORIA BSNS CTR

106

A4
11 SOUTHLANDS
12 NORTHCOTE ST
13 RUSHMORE TERR

CV32

Golf Course

Red House Farm

Floodgate Spinney

CV33

Newbold Comyn Park

ROYAL LEAMINGTON SPA

RADFORD RD

River Leam

Grand Union Canal Wlk

Grand Union Canal

Works

SOUTHAM RD

A425

Sydenham

Radford Semele CE Prim Sch

Radford Semele

Campion Sch & Com Coll

Valley Farm

Hill Farm

B3
1 AMROTH MEWS
2 FRESHWATER GR
3 ST BRIDE'S CL
4 ST GOVAN'S CL
5 CONINGSBY CL
6 SPRINGWELL RD
7 GRENFELL CL
8 RINILL GR
9 EASTWOOD CL
10 WENTWORTH RD

11 STONEWAY GR
12 NEWBURY CL
13 STANTON RD
14 BLADON WLK
15 HARVEST HILL CL
16 FOXDALE WLK
17 MAYFIELD CL
18 LYNWOOD WLK
19 CRABTREE GR
20 JOAN'S CL

21 BISSET CRES
22 BURFORD MEWS
23 STANDLAKE MEWS
24 WAVERTON MEWS
25 LONGLEAT GR
26 PACKWOOD CL
27 CHARLCOTE GDNS
28 HIDCOTE CL
29 BLENHEIM CRES
30 BADDESLEY CL

CV31

Radford Barn

WHITNASH

Whitnash City Comb Sch

The Meadow

Crown Hill

Mollington Hill

Mollington Hill Farm

Pounce Hill Farm

CV33
Tatchbrook Mallory

Mallory Court Hotel

Golf Course

Frizmore Hill

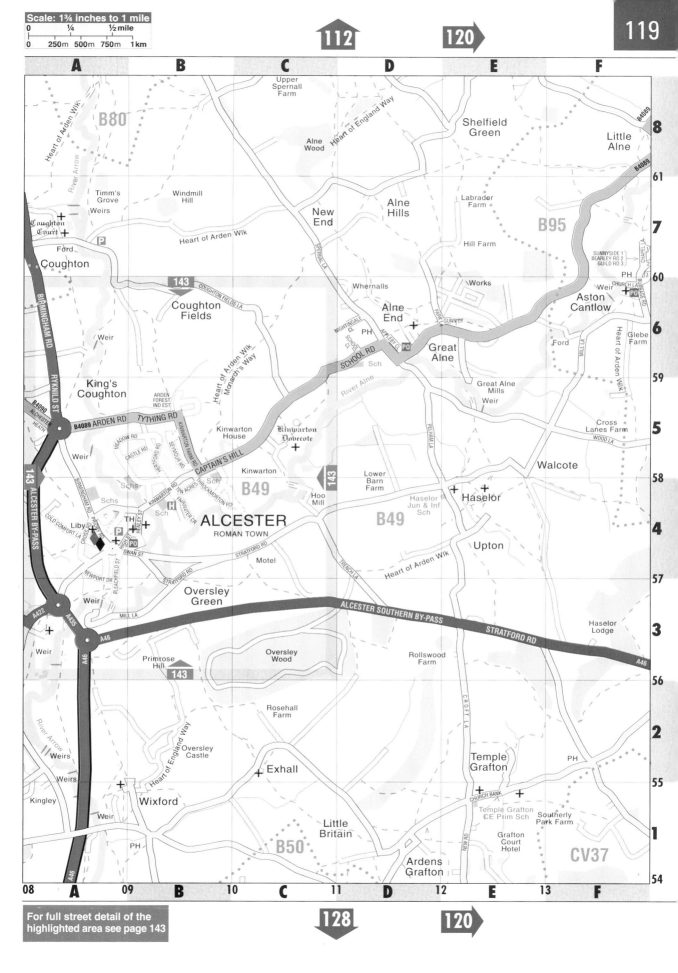

Scale: 1¾ inches to 1 mile

0   ¼   ½ mile
0   250m 500m 750m 1km

112
120
128
120

B80

Heart of Arden Wlk

Upper Spernall Farm

River Arrow

Alne Wood

Heart of England Way

Shelfield Green

Little Alne

B4089

B4089

Timm's Grove

Windmill Hill

New End

Alne Hills

Labrador Farm

B95

Weirs

Coughton Court

Heart of Arden Wlk

Ford

Coughton

P

143

Coughton Fields La

Whernalls

Hill Farm

Works

SUNNYSIDE 1
BEARLEY RD 2
GUILD RD 3

CHAPEL LA 1/2/3/4

Coughton Fields

Alne End

PH

Weir

Aston Cantlow

PH

BIRMINGHAM RD

RYKNILD ST

King's Coughton

Heart of Arden Wlk
Monarch's Way

SPERNAL LA

NIGHTINGALE CL
SCHOOL CL

School RD

Sch

APPLEBY C.

PO

Great Alne

PARK LA

GUNN CT

Ford

MILL LA

Glebe Farm

Heart of Arden Wlk

B4090

ALCESTER HEATH

B4089 ARDEN RD TYTHING RD

KINWARTON FARM RD

CAPTAIN'S HILL

ARDEN FOREST IND EST

Kinwarton House

Kinwarton Dovecote

River Alne

Great Alne Mills

Weir

Cross Lanes Farm

WOOD LA

143

Weir

MEADOW RD
CASTLE RD
HERTFORD RD
SEYMOUR RD

KINWARTON RD

Schs

Kinwarton

Sch

B49

Lower Barn Farm

PELHAM LA

Walcote

143

ALCESTER BY-PASS

COLD COMFORT LA

Schs

H

TEN ACRES
FAIRWATER CR
THROCKMORTON RD

Hoo Mill

Haselor Jun & Inf Sch

Haselor

COLD COMFORT LA
CROSS...

BIRMINGHAM RD
HENLEY ST
HIGH ST
PRIORY RD

Liby

TH

P

PO

Sch

ALCESTER
ROMAN TOWN

B49

Upton

SWAN ST
NEWPORT DR
BLEACHFIELD ST

STRATFORD RD

Motel

TRENCH LA

Heart of Arden Wlk

A422

A435

Weir

Oversley Green

STRATFORD RD
MILL LA

ALCESTER SOUTHERN BY-PASS

STRATFORD RD

Haselor Lodge

A46

A46

A46

Weir

Primrose Hill

143

Oversley Wood

Rollswood Farm

CROFT LA

River Arrow

Weirs

Heart of England Way

Rosehall Farm

Temple Grafton

PH

Weirs

Oversley Castle

Exhall

Temple Grafton CE Prim Sch

Church Bank

Southerly Park Farm

Kingley

Wixford

CHURCH BANK

MARSH RD

Grafton Court Hotel

CV37

Weir

PH

B50

Little Britain

Ardens Grafton

For full street detail of the highlighted area see page 143

A B C D E F

08 09 10 11 12 13

54 55 56 57 58 59 60 61

1 2 3 4 5 6 7 8

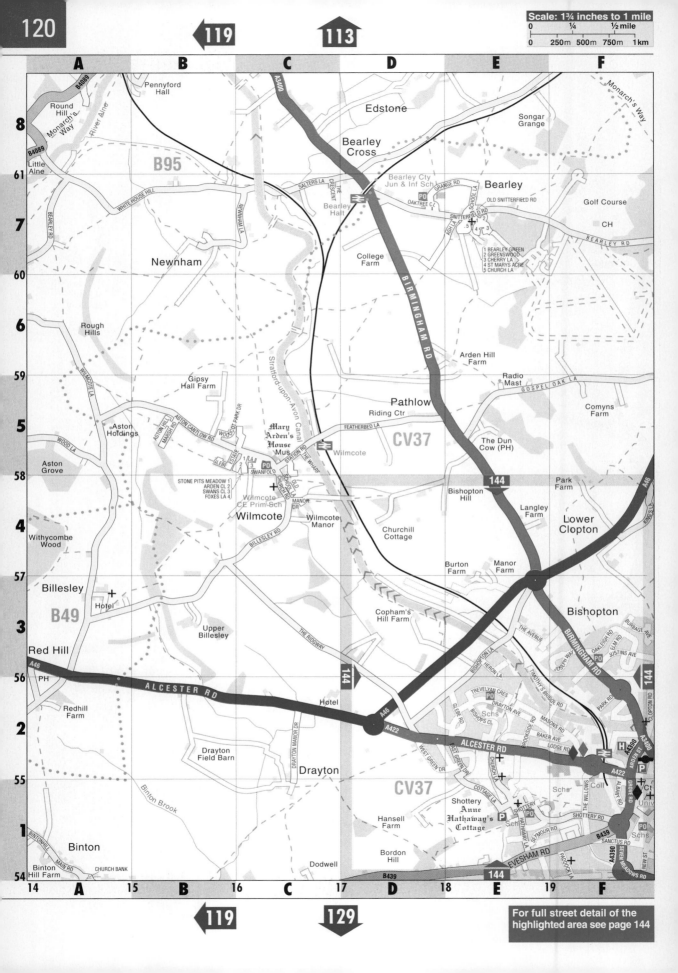

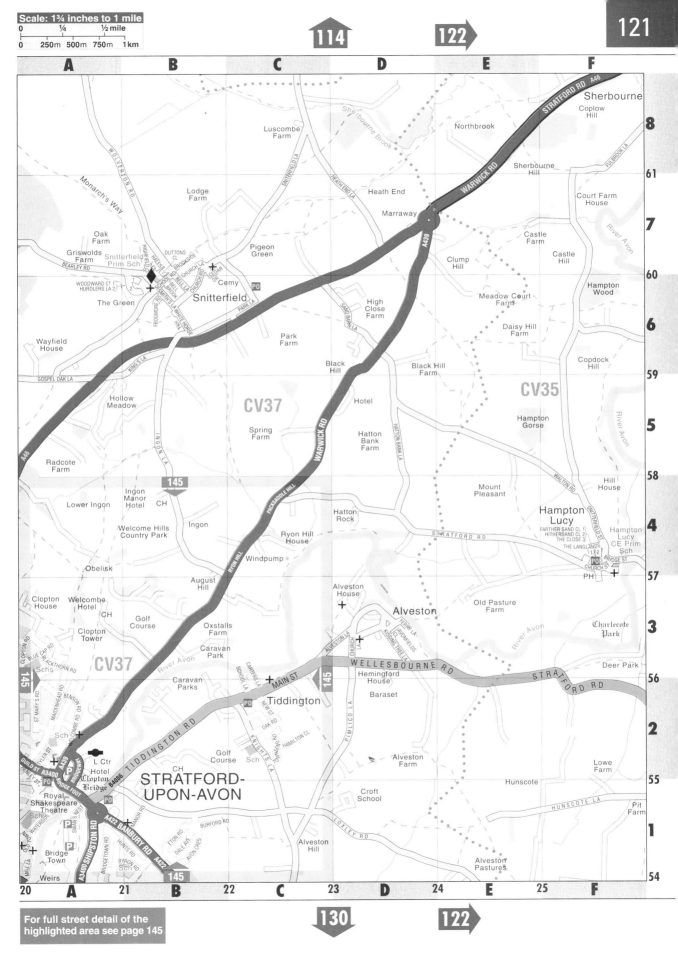

Scale: 1¾ inches to 1 mile

0   ¼   ½ mile
0   250m 500m 750m 1km

114   122

Sherbourne

Coplow Hill

Northbrook

Luscombe Farm

Sherbourne Brook

Heath End La

Sherbourne Hill

Court Farm House

Fulbrook La

Monarch's Way

Wolverton Rd

Lodge Farm

Snitterfield La

Heath End

Marraway

Castle Farm

Castle Hill

River Avon

Oak Farm

Pigeon Green

Clump Hill

Griswolds Farm

Snitterfield Prim Sch

Duttons Cl

Cedar Dr

Meadow Court Farm

Hampton Wood

Bearley Rd

High St

School La

Church Rd

Cemy

WOODWARD CT 1
HURDLERS LA 2

The Green

Froghmore Rd

Bell La

White Horse Hill

Park La

Snitterfield

PO

High Close Farm

Daisy Hill Farm

Copdock Hill

Wayfield House

King's La

Park Farm

Sand Barn La

Black Hill Farm

CV35

Gospel Oak La

Hollow Meadow

Black Hill

Hotel

Hampton Gorse

River Avon

Warwick Rd

A439

Warwick Rd

Stratford Rd

A46

Radcote Farm

Spring Farm

Hatton Bank Farm

Hatton Bank La

Mount Pleasant

Hill House

145

Ingon La

Ingon Manor Hotel

CH

Ingon

Hatton Rock

Walton Rd

Hampton Lucy

FARTHER SAND CL 1
HITHERSAND CL 2
THE CLOSE 3

Hampton Lucy CE Prim Sch

Lower Ingon

Welcome Hills Country Park

Ryon Hill House

Stratford Rd

Snitterfield St

THE LANGLANDS
1 2

Ryon Hill

Windpump

Obelisk

August Hill

PO

CHURCH ST

BRIDGE ST

PH

Clopton House

Welcombe Hotel

CH

Golf Course

Oxstalls Farm

Alveston House

Old Pasture Farm

Charlecote Park

Clopton Tower

CV37

Caravan Park

River Avon

Caravan Parks

Carters La

School La

Main St

FEBEK LA
GWONFIELDS
KISSING TREE LA

Alveston

Deer Park

145

Wellesbourne Rd

Stratford Rd

Blue Cap Rd

Blackthorn Rd

Schs

Maidenhead Rd

Benson Rd

Welcombe Rd

Tiddington

PO

Hemingford House

Baraset

St Mary's Rd

Tyler St

Sch

L Ctr Hotel

Tiddington Rd

New St

Oak La

Hamilton Cl

Church La

Alveston La

Pimlico La

Alveston Farm

Lowe Farm

GUILD ST

A3400

BRIDGEWAY

A439

BRIDGE FOOT

Clopton Bridge

B4086

Golf Course

Knight's La

Sch

Hunscote

STRATFORD-UPON-AVON

CH

Croft School

PO

Royal Shakespeare Theatre

SWAN'S NEST

A422 BANBURY RD

Manor Rd

Burford Rd

Loxley Rd

Hunscote La

Pit Farm

WATERSIDE

P

A3400 SHIPSTON RD

Bridgetown Rd

Hunt's Rd

Byron Rd Sch

Eton Ave

Dale Ave

Avon Cres

Alveston Hill

A422

Bridge Town

MILL LA

Weirs

145

Alveston Pastures

CV37

130   122

For full street detail of the highlighted area see page 145

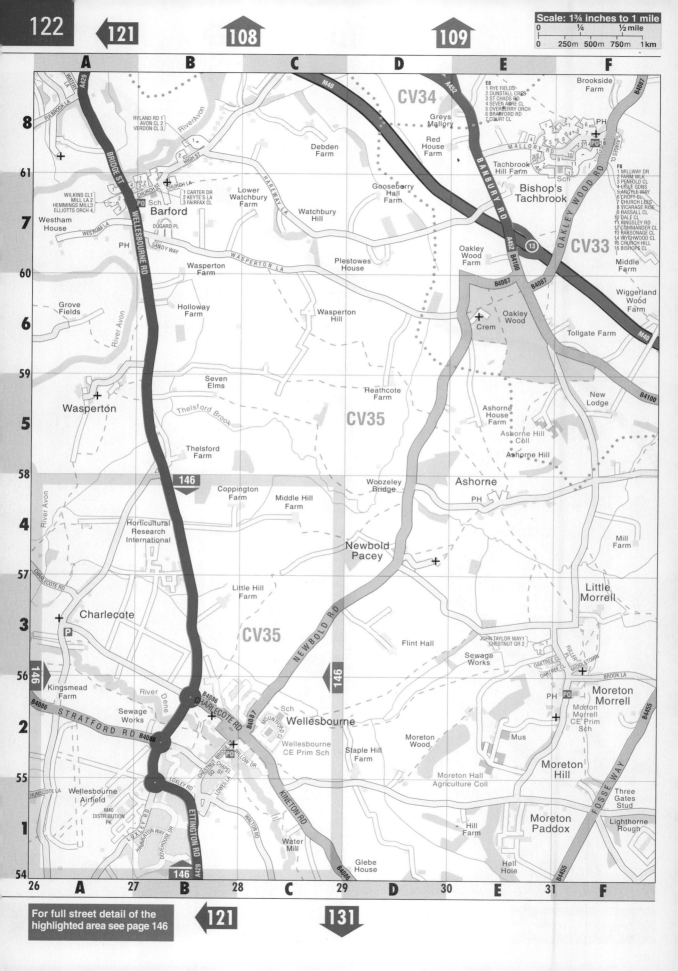

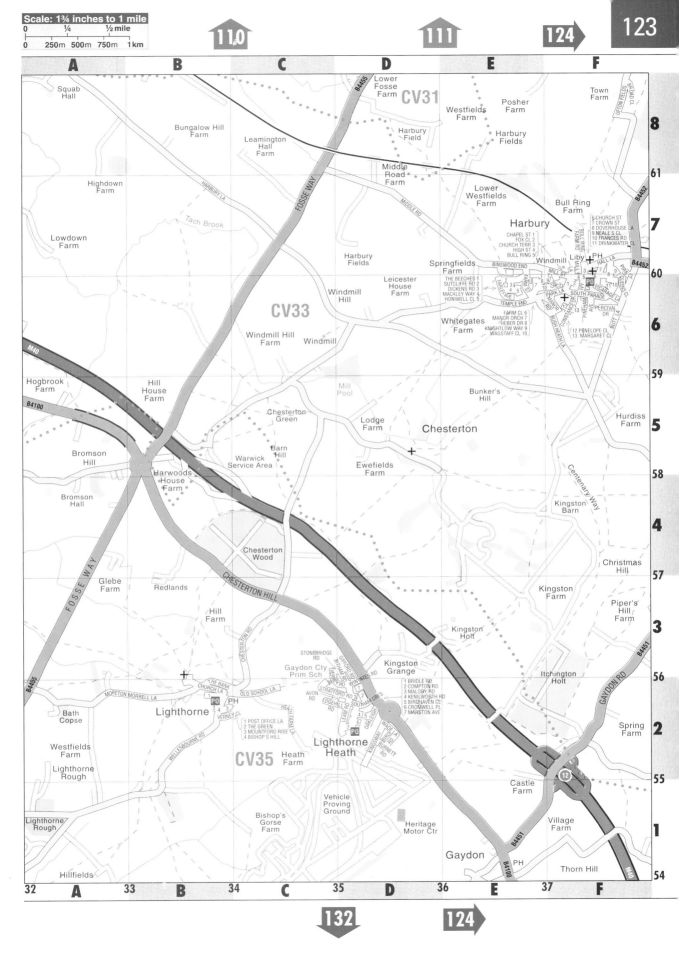

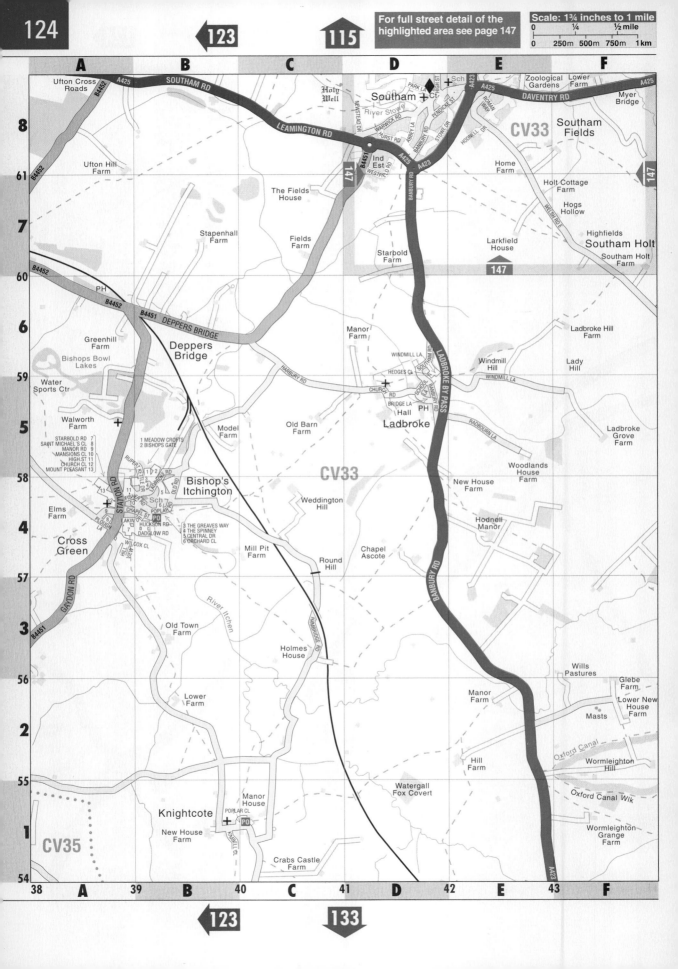

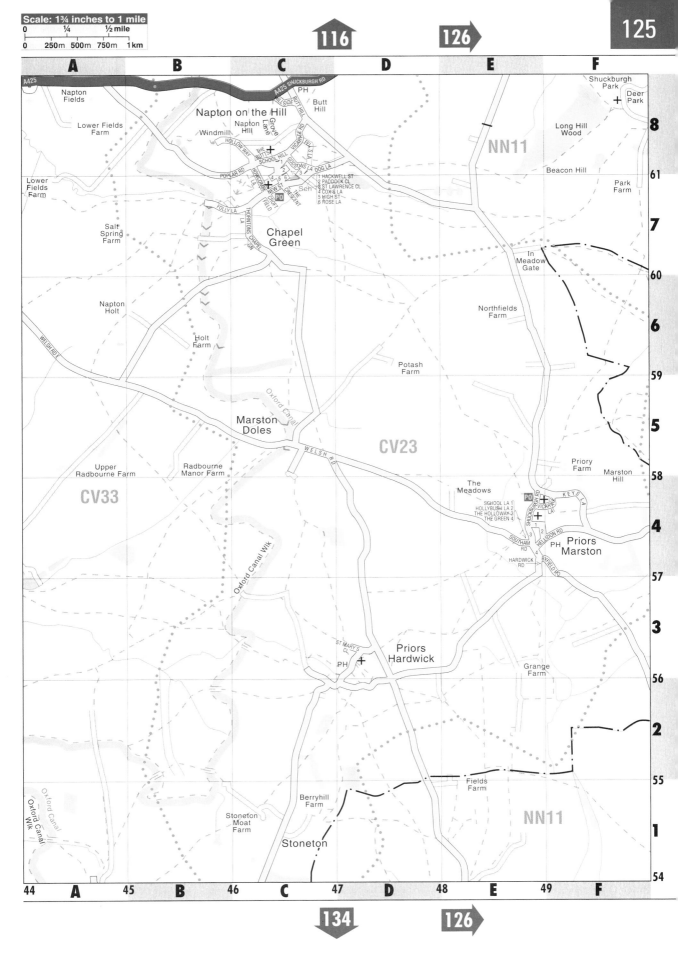

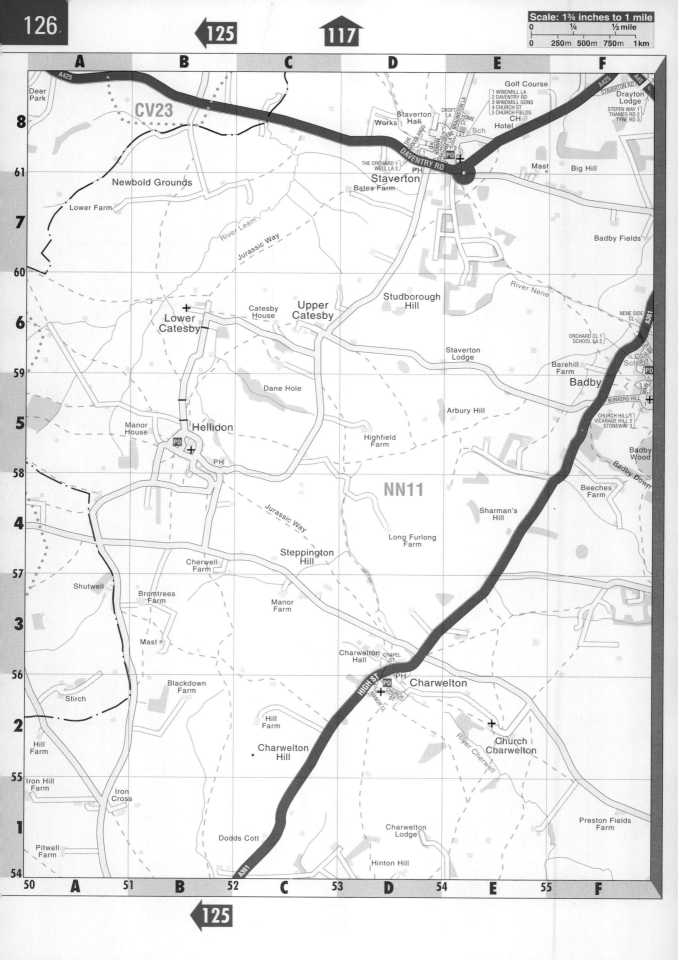

125
117

Scale: 1¾ inches to 1 mile

0   ¼   ½ mile
0   250m   500m   750m   1km

A   B   C   D   E   F

Deer Park

A425

CV23

8

Golf Course
1 WINDMILL LA
2 DAVENTRY RD
3 WINDMILL GDNS
4 CHURCH ST
5 CHURCH FIELDS

Staverton Hall
Works
CROFT LA
BRAUNSTON LA
HOME CL
Sch
CH Hotel

Drayton Lodge
STAVERTON RD
STEFEN WAY 1
THAMES RD 2
TYNE RD 3

Newbold Grounds

61

THE ORCHARD 1
WELL LA 2
PH
DAVENTRY RD
PO

Staverton

Mast   Big Hill

Lower Farm

Bates Farm

7

River Leam

Jurassic Way

Badby Fields

60

River Nene

NENE SIDE CL

A361

6

Lower Catesby

Catesby House

Upper Catesby

Studborough Hill

Staverton Lodge

ORCHARD CL 1
SCHOOL LA 2

59

Dane Hole

Barehill Farm

Sch
PO

Badby

5

Manor House

Hellidon

Highfield Farm

Arbury Hill

BUNKERS HILL

CHURCH HILL 1
VICARAGE HILL 2
STONEWAY 3

58

PO
PH

NN11

Badby Wood

Badby Down

Jurassic Way

Sharman's Hill

Beeches Farm

4

Long Furlong Farm

57

Cherwell Farm

Steppington Hill

Shutwell

Bromtrees Farm

Manor Farm

3

Mast

Charwelton Hall

CHAPEL ST

56

Blackdown Farm

PH
HIGH ST
PO
CHURCH ST

Charwelton

Stirch

MANOR CL

2

Hill Farm

Charwelton Hill

Church Charwelton

River Cherwell

Hill Farm

55

Iron Hill Farm

Iron Cross

1

Preston Fields Farm

Pitwell Farm

Dodds Cott

Charwelton Lodge

54

A361

Hinton Hill

50   A   51   B   52   C   53   D   54   E   55   F

125

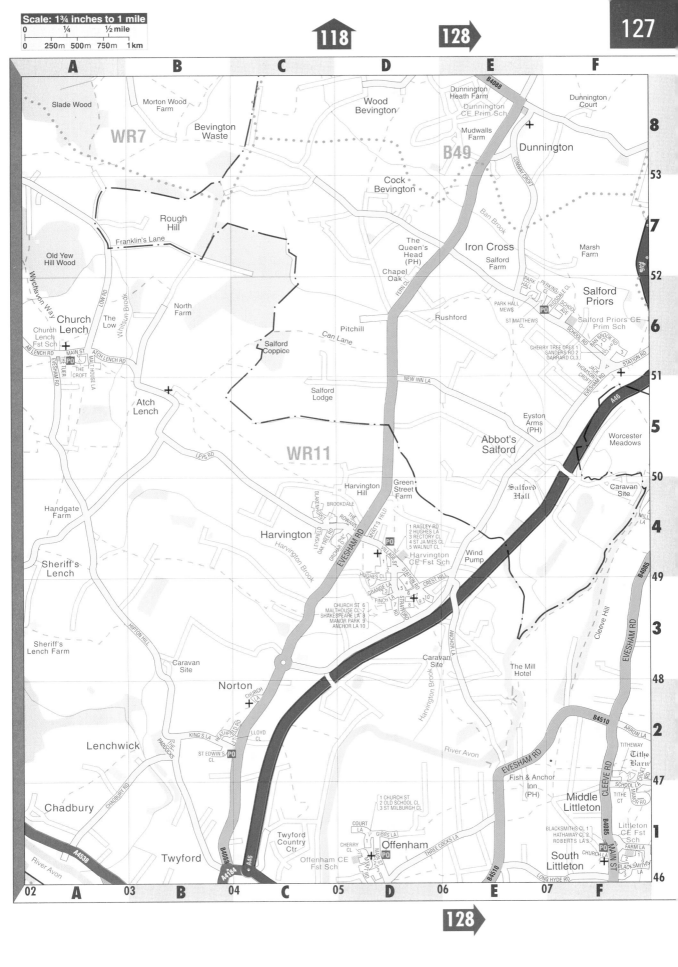

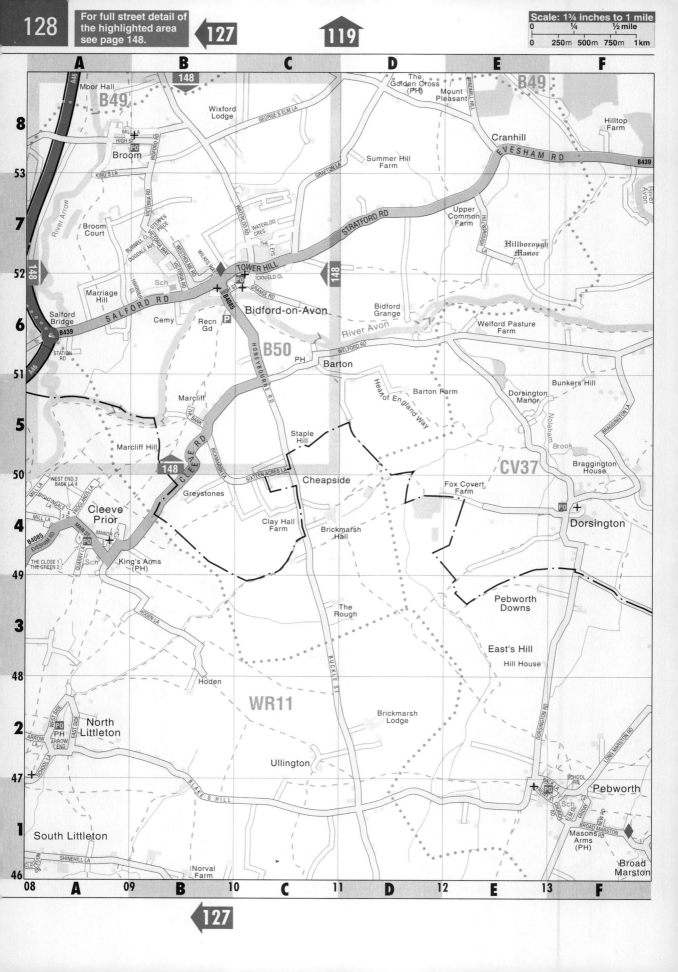

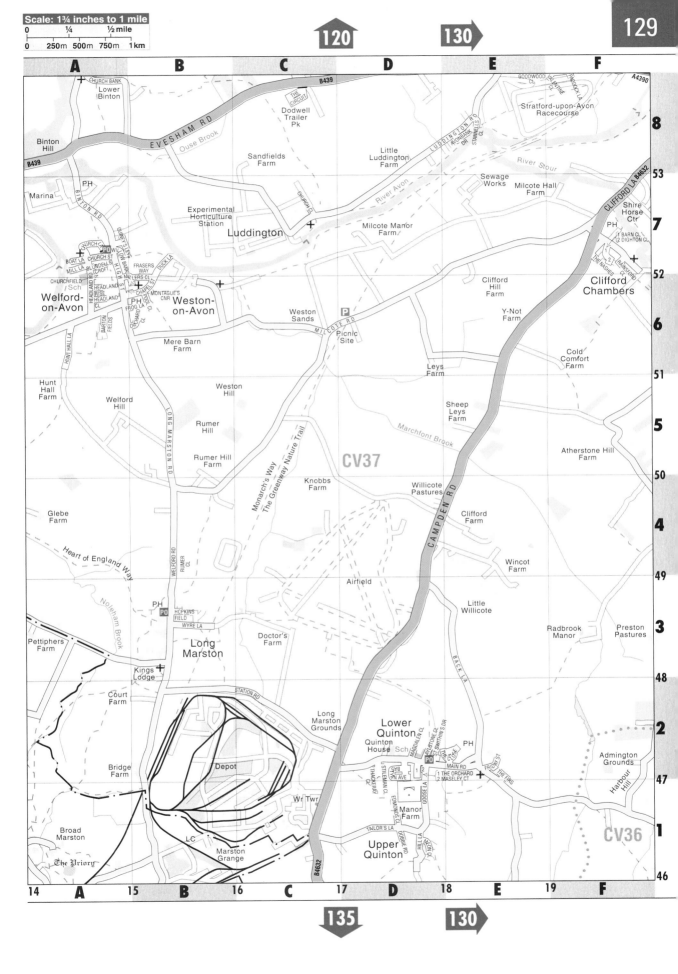

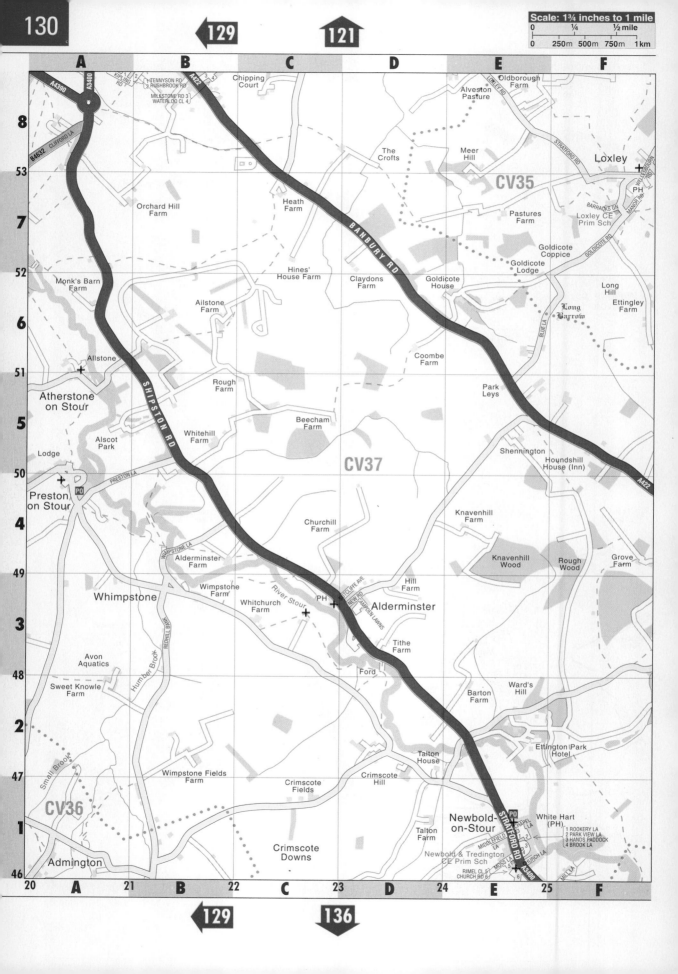

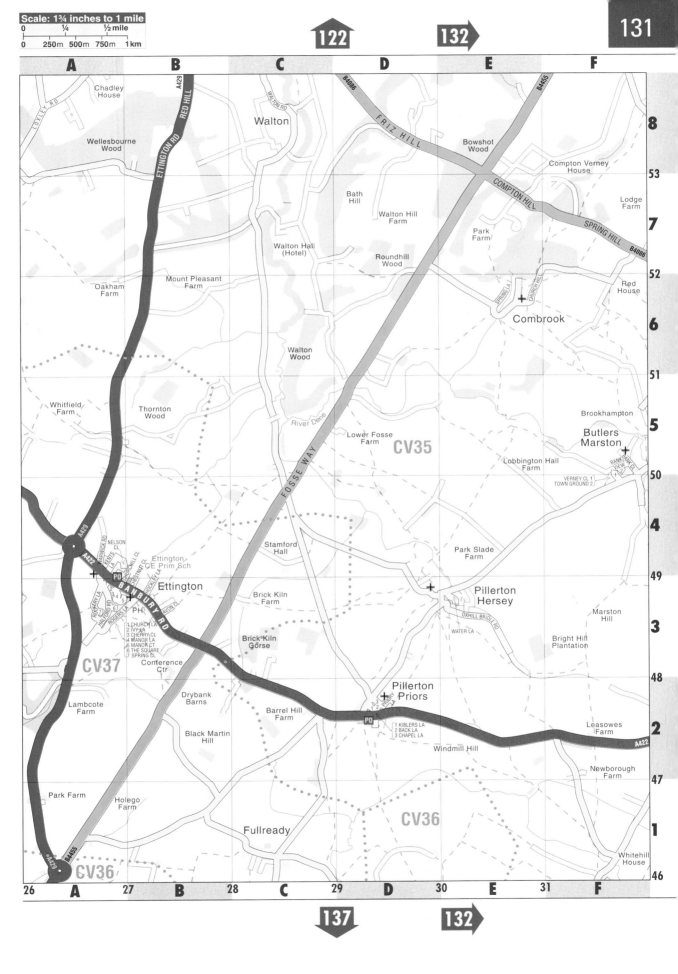

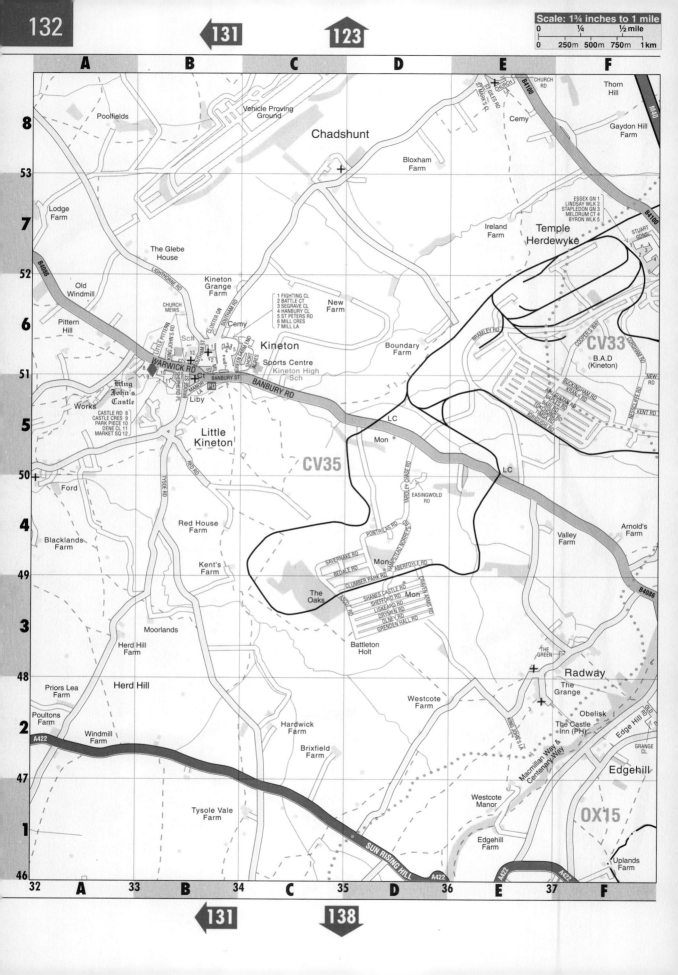

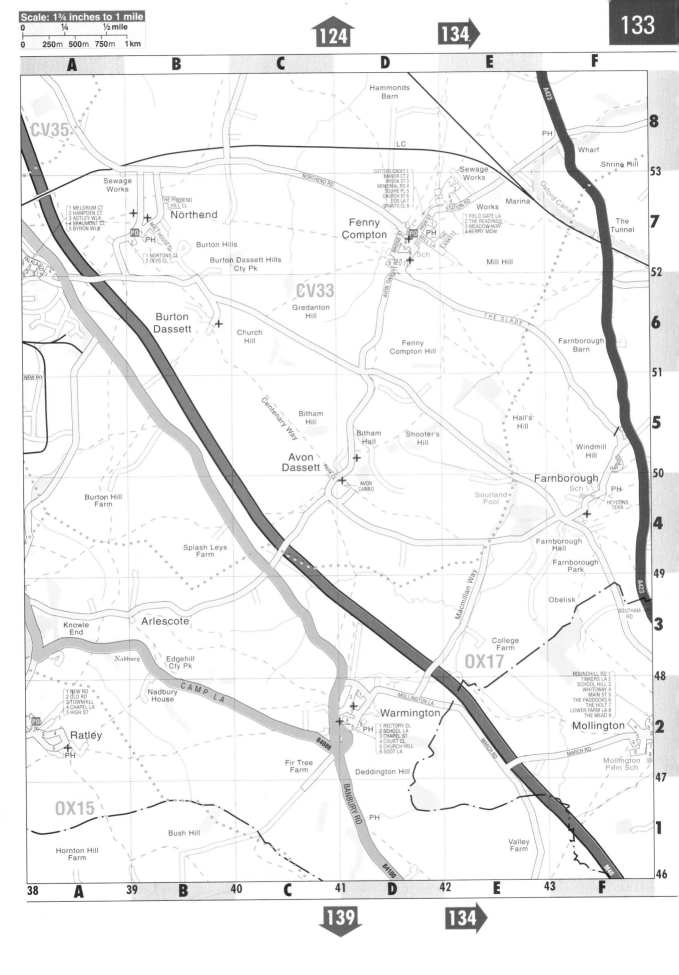

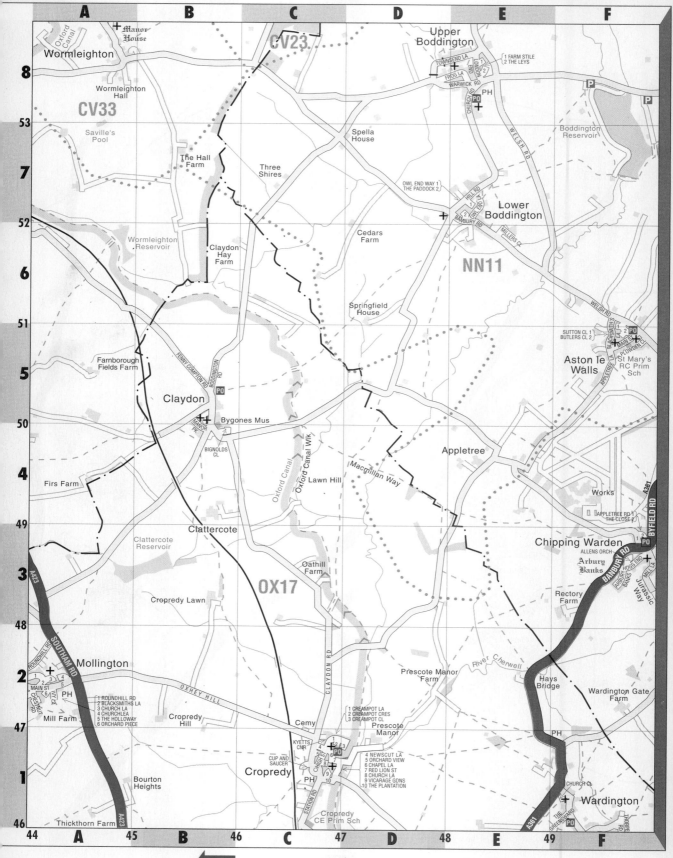

133
125

Scale: 1¾ inches to 1 mile
0   ¼   ½ mile
0   250m 500m 750m 1km

A   B   C   D   E   F

Wormleighton
Oxford Canal
Manor House
CV33
Wormleighton Hall
Saville's Pool
The Hall Farm
Three Shires
CV23
Upper Boddington
TOWNSEND LA
FROG LA
WARWICK RD
1 FARM STILE
2 THE LEYS
PH
PO
P
P
Boddington Reservoir

8
53
7
52
6
51
5
50
4
49
3
48
2
47
1
46

Spella House
Claydon Hay Farm
Wormleighton Reservoir
Cedars Farm
Springfield House
OWL END WAY 1
THE PADDOCK 2
HILL RD
BANBURY RD
Lower Boddington
NN11
MILLERS CL
SUTTON CL 1
BUTLERS CL 2
BLACKSMITHS
PLOWDEN CL
MAIN ST
PO
Aston le Walls
St Mary's RC Prim Sch
APPLETREE

Farnborough Fields Farm
FENNY COMPTON RD
BODDINGTON RD
Claydon
PO
MANOR
BYGONES MUS
BIGNOLDS CL
Oxford Canal
Oxford Canal Wlk
Lawn Hill
Macmillan Way
Appletree
Works
APPLETREE RD 1
THE CLOSE 2
A361
BYFIELD RD

Firs Farm
Clattercote Reservoir
Clattercote
Oathill Farm
OX17
Cropredy Lawn
A423
SOUTHAM RD
ROUNDHILL RD
Mollington
1 ROUNDHILL RD
2 BLACKSMITHS LA
3 CHURCH LA
4 CHURCH LEA
5 THE HOLLOWAY
6 ORCHARD PIECE
MAIN ST
CHESTNUT RD
PH
Mill Farm
OXHEY HILL
Cropredy Hill
CLAYDON RD
Cemy
KYETTS CNR
CUP AND SAUCER
Cropredy
PH
STATION RD
HIGH ST
1 CREAMPOT LA
2 CREAMPOT CRES
3 CREAMPOT CL
Prescote Manor Farm
Prescote Manor
4 NEWSCUT LA
5 ORCHARD VIEW
6 CHAPEL LA
7 RED LION ST
8 CHURCH LA
9 VICARAGE GDNS
10 THE PLANTATION
PO
River Cherwell
Hays Bridge
Wardington Gate Farm
Chipping Warden
ALLENS ORCH
Arbury Banks
ARBURY
JURASSIC WAY
MILL LA
PO
Rectory Farm
BANBURY RD
PH
Bourton Heights
Thickthorn Farm
A423
Cropredy CE Prim Sch
THE GREENSWARD
THORPE RD
CHURCH CL
Wardington
A361
PO

44   45   46   47   48   49

133

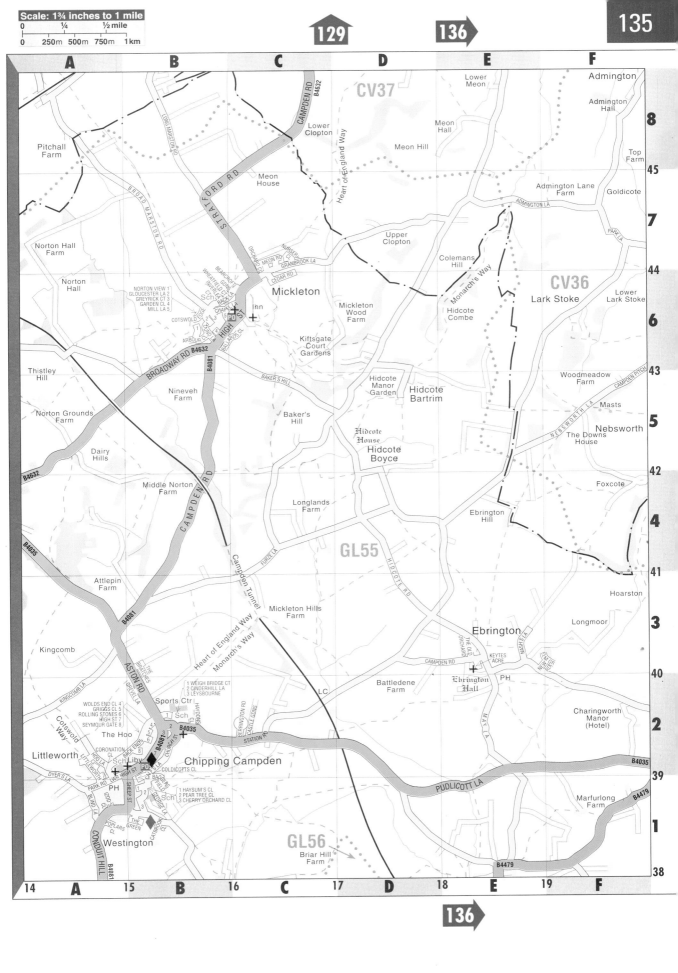

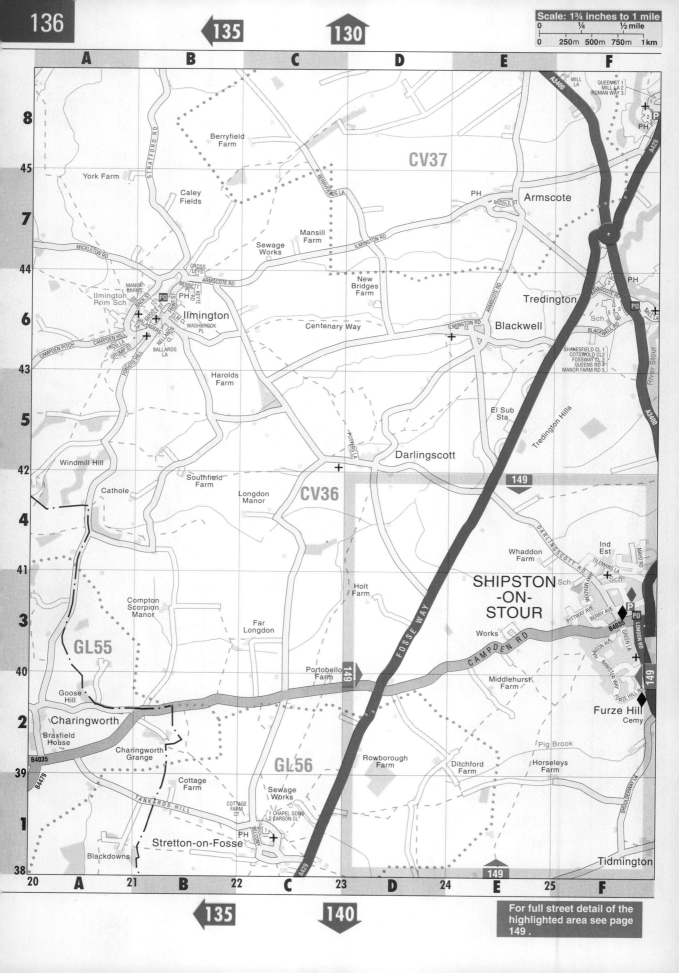

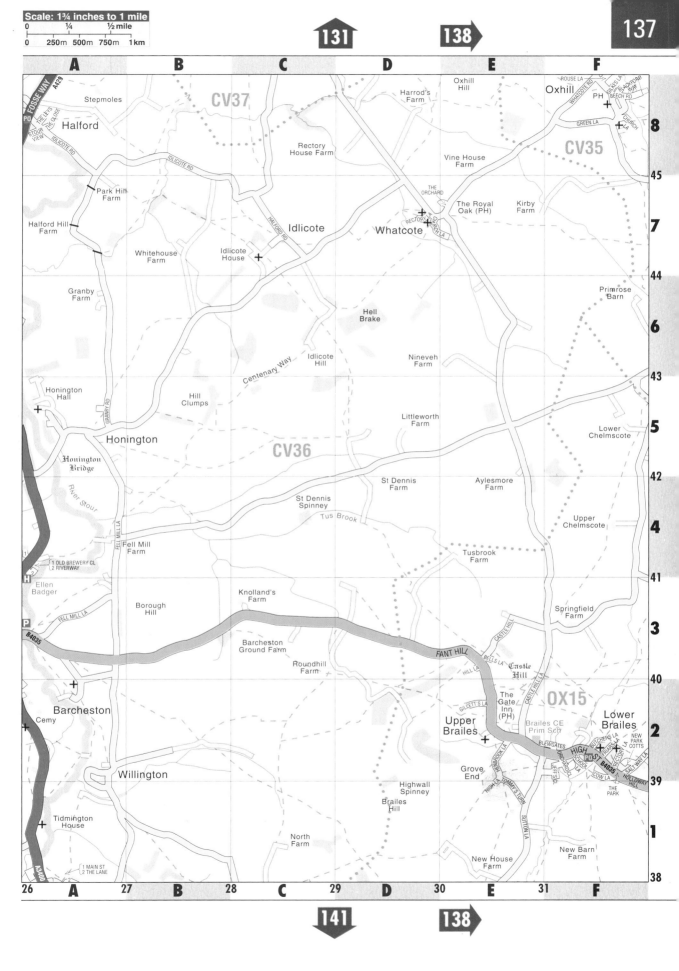

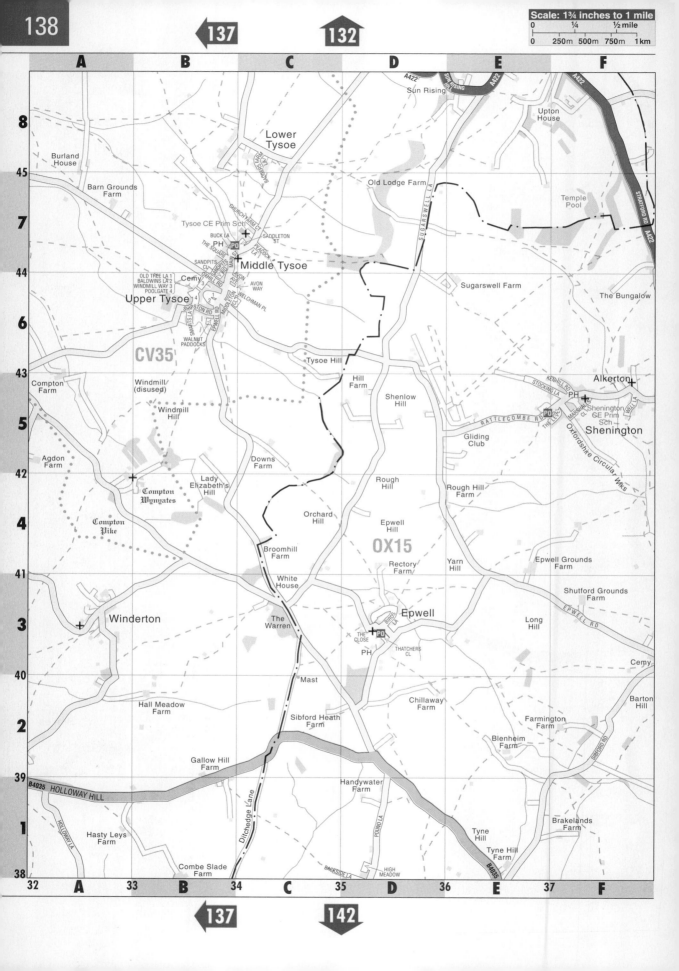

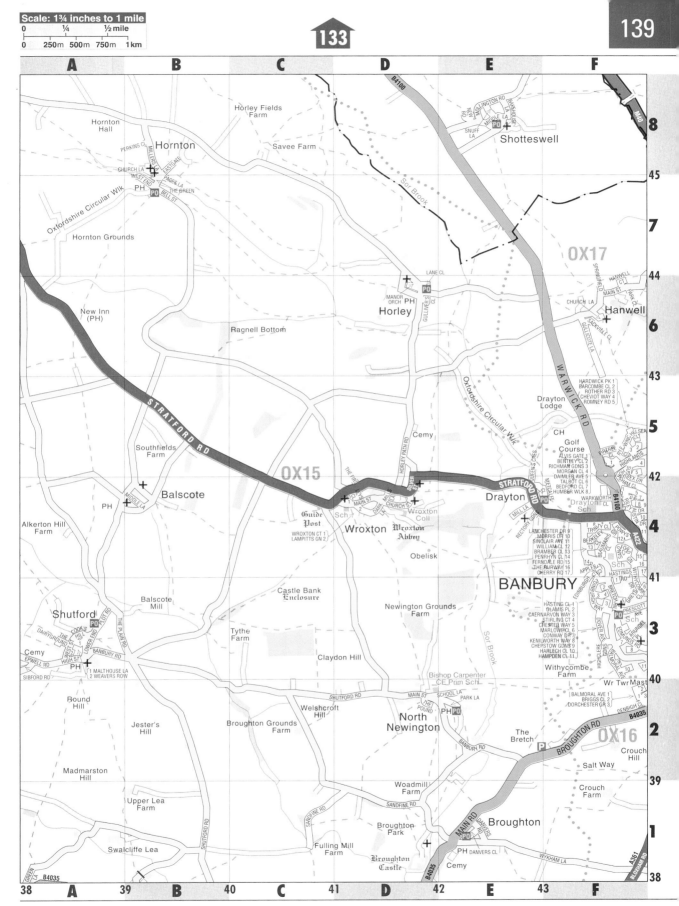

Scale: 1¾ inches to 1 mile

0   ¼   ½ mile
0 250m 500m 750m 1km

Hornton Hall

Horley Fields Farm

Savee Farm

Hornton

PERKINS CL
MILLERS LA
EASTGATE
CHURCH LA
WEST END
PAGES LA
THE GREEN
PH
PO
BELL ST

Oxfordshire Circular Wlk

Hornton Grounds

New Inn (PH)

Ragnell Bottom

STRATFORD RD

OX15

Southfields Farm

Balscote

PH
MIDDLE LA

Alkerton Hill Farm

B4100

Shotteswell

MOLLINGTON RD
BARTON RD
NEW RD
MIDDLE LA
PO
SNUFF LA

OX17

Sor Brook

Horley

MANOR ORCH
PH
LANE CL
PO
GULLIVERS CL

SPRINGFIELD
HANWELL
CT
MAIN ST
PARK RD
CHURCH LA
Hanwell

SACKVILLE CL
GULLICOTE LA

Oxfordshire Circular Wlk

Drayton Lodge

HARDWICK PK 1
BARCOMBE CL 2
ROTHER RD 3
CHEVIOT WAY 4
ROMNEY RD 5

CH
Golf Course

Cemy

Horley Path Rd

THE FIRS
MAIN ST
CHURCH ST
DARK LA
MILL LA

Guide Post

WROXTON CT 1
LAMPITTS GN 2

Wroxton

Wroxton Abbey
Wroxton Coll

Obelisk

PYTHE
WELL RD
HIGHLANDS
ALVIS GATE 1
BENTLEY CL 2
RICHMAN GDNS 3
MORGAN CL 4
DAIMLER AVE 5
TALBOT CL 6
BEDFORD CL 7
HUMBER WLK 8

STRATFORD RD

Drayton

QUEENS CRES
MEDCALFE
RECTORY DRIVE
MILL LA

WARWORTH
Drayton Sch

B4100

LANCHESTER DR 9
MORRIS DR 10
SINCLAIR AVE 11
WILLIAM CL 12
BRAMBER CL 13
PENRHYN CL 14
FERNDALE RD 15
THE FAIRWAY 16
CHERRY RD 17

BANBURY

Sch
HASTINGS RD

A422

Shutford

PO
COOKS HILL
DAIRYGROUND
WEST END
PLOT RD
LOWER END
THE PLAIN RD
HIGH ST
Cemy
EPWELL RD
PH
SIBFORD RD

1 MALTHOUSE LA
2 WEAVERS ROW

Banbury Rd

Balscote Mill

Tythe Farm

Castle Bank Enclosure

Claydon Hill

Newington Grounds Farm

Sor Brook

Bishop Carpenter CE Prim Sch

HASTING CL 1
GLAMIS PL 2
CAERNARVON WAY 3
STIRLING CT 4
CRESTER WAY 5
MARLOW CL 6
CONWAY DR 7
KENILWORTH WAY 8
CHEPSTOW GDNS 9
HARLECH CL 10
HAMPDEN CL 11

Withycombe Farm

Wr Twr Mast

Round Hill

Jester's Hill

Madmarston Hill

Upper Lea Farm

Swalcliffe Lea

B4035

SHUTFORD RD

SHUTFORD RD
MAIN ST
SCHOOL LA
PARK LA
THE POUND
PH PO

North Newington

Welshcroft Hill

Broughton Grounds Farm

SANDFINE RD

Fulling Mill Farm

Broughton Park

Woadmill Farm

SANDFINE RD

BANBURY RD

Broughton Castle

Cemy

MAIN RD
PO
DANVERS CL
PH
DANVERS CL
WYKHAM LA

BALMORAL AVE 1
BRIGGS CL 2
DORCHESTER GR 3
DENBIGH CL

The Bretch
P
BROUGHTON RD
B4035
OX16

Crouch Hill

Salt Way

Crouch Farm

Broughton

A361
BLOXHAM RD

GREEN
B4035

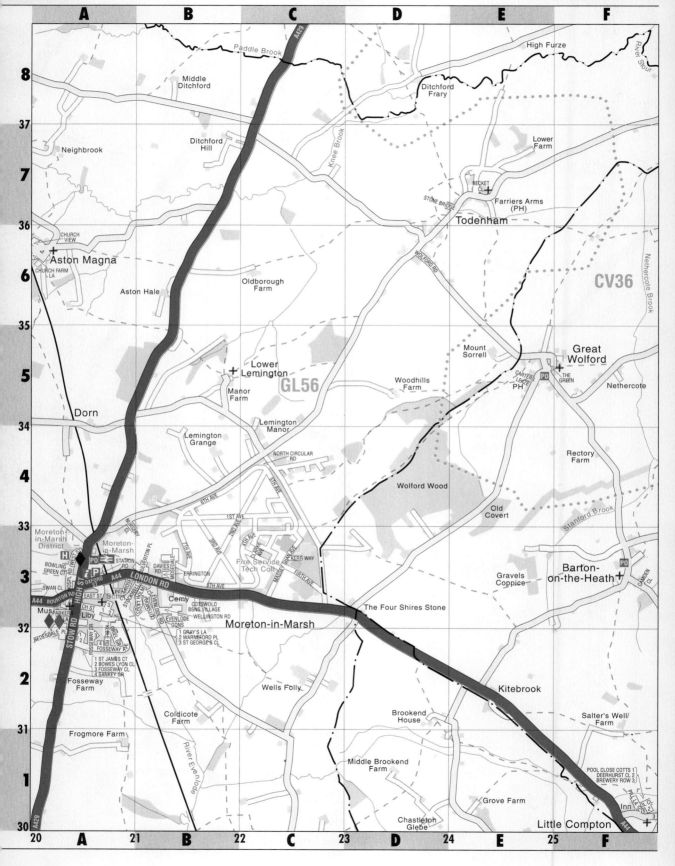

Scale: 1¾ inches to 1 mile

0   ¼   ½ mile
0   250m   500m   750m   1km

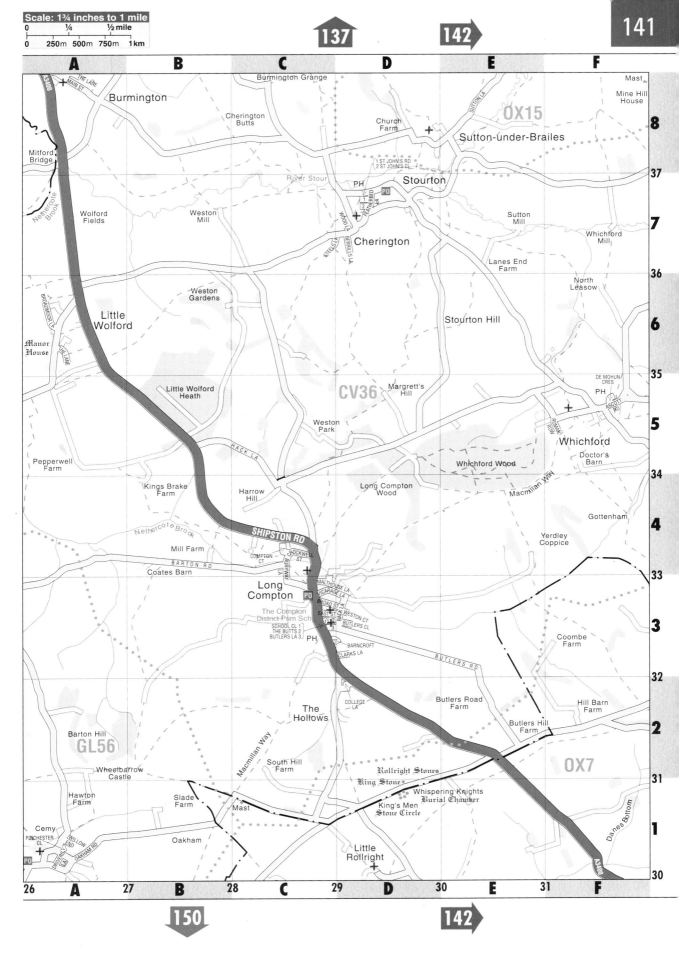

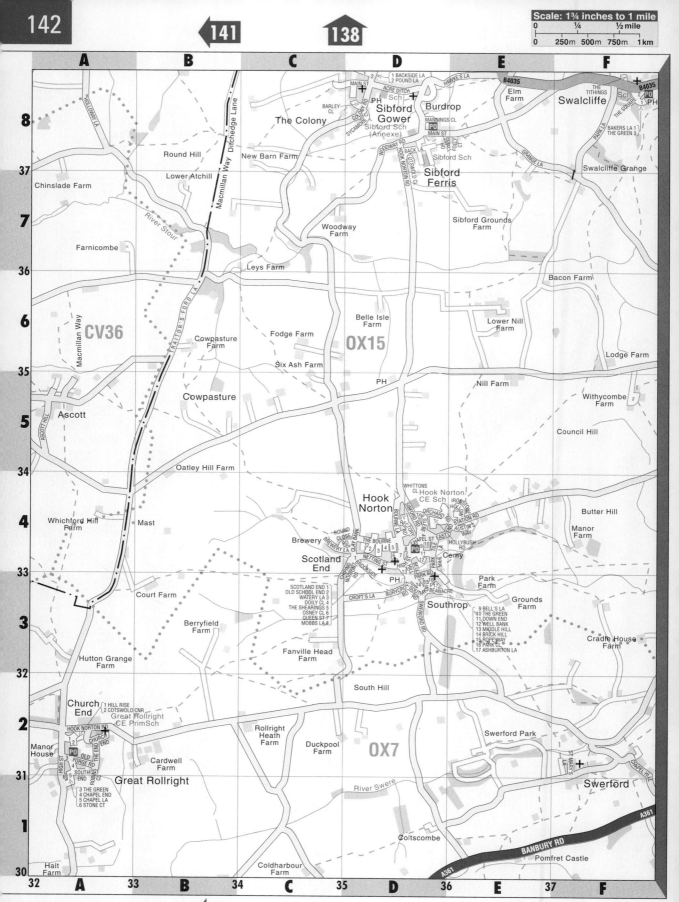

141
138

Scale: 1¾ inches to 1 mile
0 ¼ ½ mile
0 250m 500m 750m 1km

A B C D E F

8

37

7

36

6

35

5

34

4

33

3

32

2

1

30

Holloway La

Chinslade Farm

Round Hill

Lower Atchill

Macmillan Way Ditchedge Lane

River Stour

Farnicombe

Leys Farm

Macmillan Way

CV36

TRAITOR'S FORD LA

Cowpasture Farm

Fodge Farm

Six Ash Farm

Cowpasture

Ascott

ASCOTT LA

Oatley Hill Farm

Whichford Hill Farm

Mast

Court Farm

Berryfield Farm

Fanville Head Farm

Hutton Grange Farm

1 HILL RISE
2 COTSWOLD CNR

Church End

Great Rollright CE PrimSch

Manor House

PO

HIGH ST

THE END

CHURCH END

OLD FORGE RD

ROBBS

SOUTH END

3 THE GREEN
4 CHAPEL END
5 CHAPEL LA
6 STONE CT

Great Rollright

Cardwell Farm

Rollright Heath Farm

Duckpool Farm

South Hill

OX7

Halt Farm

Coldharbour Farm

1 BACKSIDE LA
2 POUND LA

MAIN ST

ACRE DITCH

HINXIE'S LA

The Colony

BARLEY CL

COLLINS'S RD

SYCAMORE CL

PH

Sibford Gower

Sibford Sch (Annexe)

Burdrop

MANNINGS CL

PO

MAIN ST

B4035

Elm Farm

Swalcliffe

THE TITHINGS

Sch

B4035

PO

PH

THE SQUARE

WOODWAY RD

COTSWOLD CL

BACK LA

HOOK NORTON RD

Sibford Sch

Sibford Ferris

GRANGE LA

PARK LA

BAKERS LA 1
THE GREEN 2

Swalcliffe Grange

New Barn Farm

Woodway Farm

Belle Isle Farm

OX15

Lower Nill Farm

Bacon Farm

Lodge Farm

PH

Nill Farm

Withycombe Farm

Council Hill

WHITTONS CL

Hook Norton CE Sch

IRON

HOLLY

Hook Norton

STATION RD

ORCHARD RD

AUSTIN'S WAY

Butter Hill

Manor Farm

BOURNE LA

CURT END

SIBFORD RD

BELL END

GORE

CHAPEL ST EAST

Brewery

Brewery RD

ROUND CLOSE

CLAY BANK

THE BOURNE

CHAPEL ST

TILE

HOLLYBUSH RD

PO

Cerny

Scotland End

2 3 4 5

1

NETTING ST

CHIPPING NORTON RD

BROOKSIDE

HIGH ST

BEANACRE

PARK RD

PARK LA

Park Farm

SCOTLAND END 1
OLD SCHOOL END 2
WATERY LA 3
DOILY CL 4
THE SHEARINGS 5
OSNEY CL 6
QUEEN ST 7
MOBBS LA 8

PH

CROFT'S LA

BURYCROFT RD

SOUTH RD

SWERFORD RD

Southrop

9 BELL'S LA
10 THE GREEN
11 DOWN END
12 WELL BANK
13 MIDDLE HILL
14 BRICK HILL
15 ROPEWAY
16 PARK CL
17 ASHBURTON LA

Grounds Farm

Cradle House Farm

Swerford Park

ST MARY'S LA

Swerford

CHAPEL HILL

Coltscombe

River Swere

Pomfret Castle

BANBURY RD

A361

A361

141

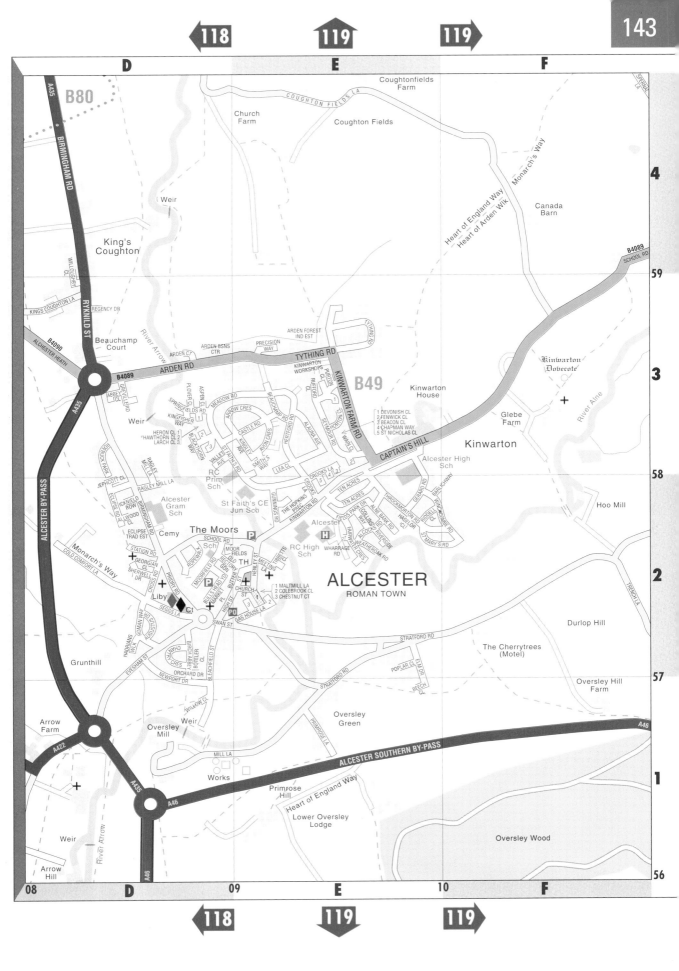

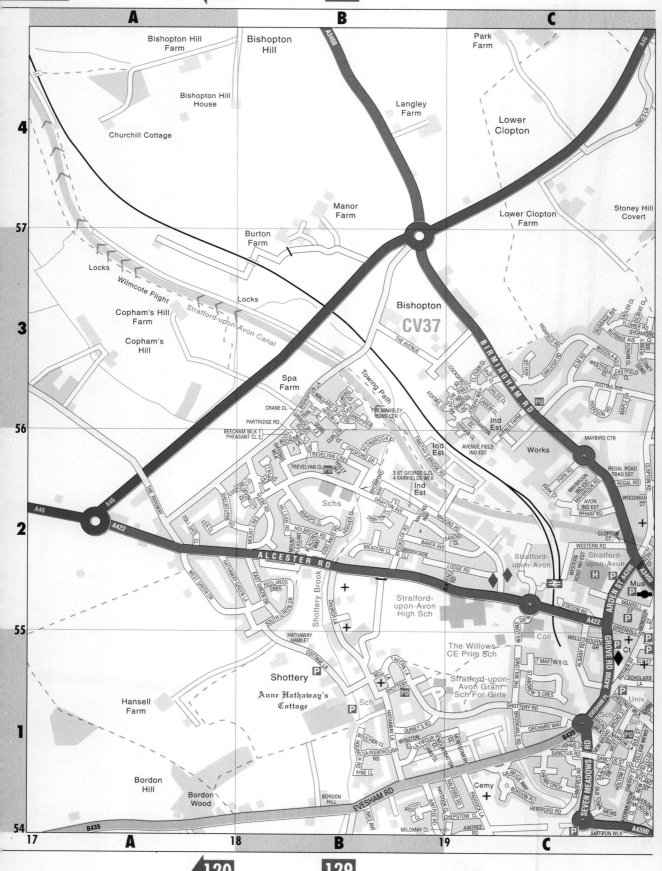

120 120

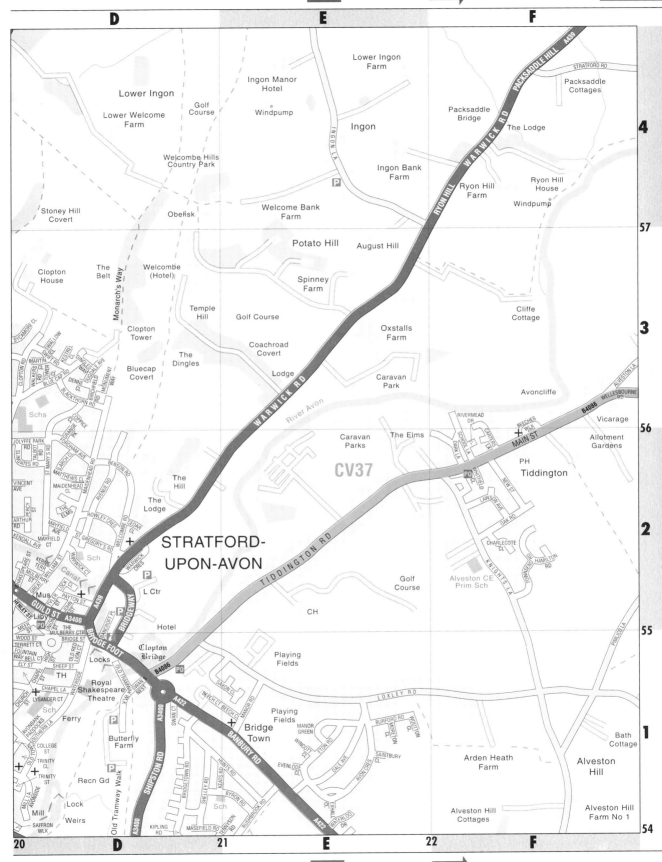

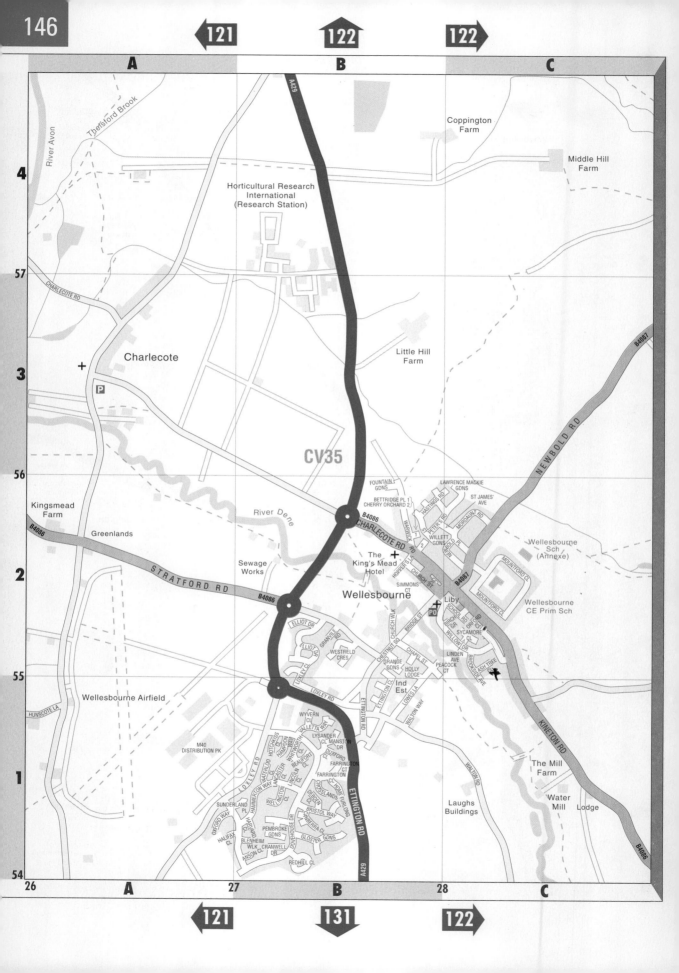

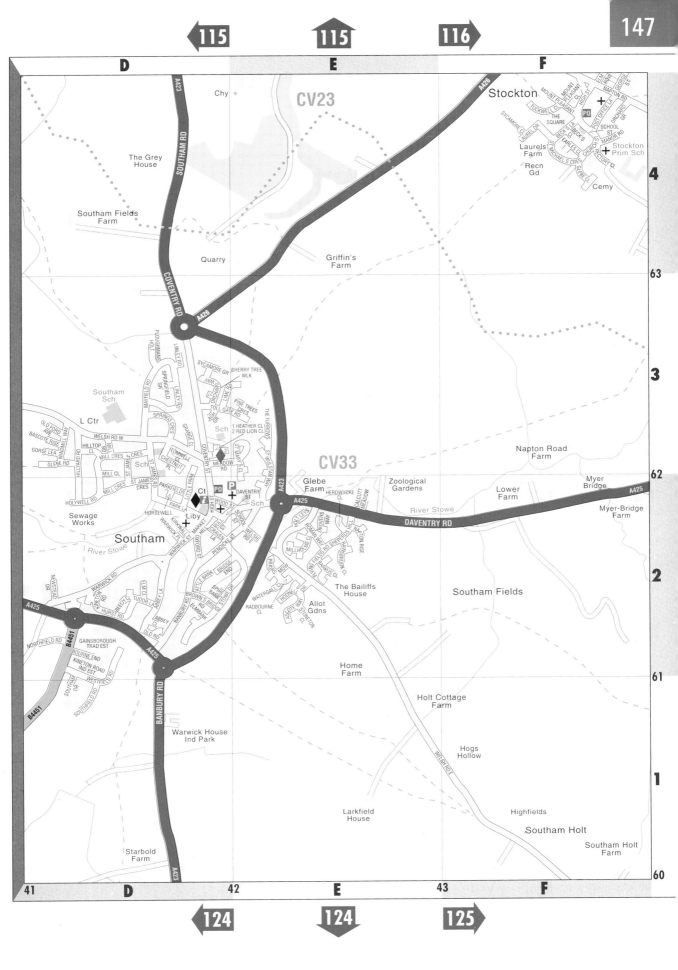

← 115   115   116 →

124 ←   124   125 →

D   E   F

CV23

A23 SOUTHAM RD

Chy

The Grey House

Southam Fields Farm

COVENTRY RD   A426

Quarry

Griffin's Farm

A426

Stockton

MOUNT PLEASANT   NAPTON RD   ELM ROW   GEORGE ST
TUCKWELL DR   HIGH ST   POST OFFICE LA   ORCHARD CL
THE SQUARE   PO   SCHOOL ST   MANOR RD
SYCAMORE CL   LAUREL DR   BECK'S CL   BECK'S CL   CHURCH ST   RECTORY CL
Laurels Farm   ST MICHAEL'S CRES   GLEBE CL   Stockton Prim Sch
Recn Gd   Cemy

PLOUGHMANS HOLT
LINLEY RD
SPRINGFIELD GR
MAYFIELD RD
SYCAMORE GR   CHERRY TREE WLK
AVM CL
LIME RD   PINE TREES CRES
TOLL GATE RD
Southam Sch
L Ctr
SPRINGS CRES   GRANGE CL   1 HEATHER CL
2 RED LION CL
THE FURROWS
OLD FORD AVE
BASCOTE RISE
WELSH RD W
HILLTOP CL
WINDMILL WAY
GORSE LEA
GLEBE RD
HILLYARD RD
MILL CRES
ST JAMES CRES
TOMWELL CL
CHESTNUT PL
Sch
ST MARY'S CL
Sch
ST WULSTAN WY
HOLYWELL RD
MILL CRES
ST JAMES CRES
PARKFIELDS
LITTLE PARK
PARK LA
PO
P
DAVENTRY ST
Sch
HORSEWELL
Ct
Liby
MARKET
HIGH ST
SCHOOL ST
WELSH RD E
Sewage Works
KIRWALL CT
WARWICK ST
OXFORD ST
BELL ST
CRAVEN LA
River Stowe
Southam
WARWICK RD
BRIDGE END
PENDUCKE ST
PRIORS MDW
NEWSTEAD DR
WARWICK RD
KINETON RD
HURST RD
ELM CL
TUDOR LA
ABBEY LA
TATTLE BANK
SPIRE BANK
STONE DR
BROWN'S BRIDGE
BANBURY RD
ELMBANK
OLD RD
WATERGALL CL
RADBOURNE CL
ASCOTE WAY
HODNEL DR
STONETON CL
Allot Gdns
FLAMVILLE RD
FIELDS RD
ROMAN WAY
GROVERS WAY
SHEPFOLDS RD
RAINBROOK CL
BARKUS CL
MILLHOME
NAPTON RISE

CV33

Glebe Farm
HERDWYCKE CL
CALCUTT MEADOW
Zoological Gardens
A423
A425
DAVENTRY RD
River Stowe

Napton Road Farm
Lower Farm
Myer Bridge
A425
Myer-Bridge Farm

The Bailiffs House
Southam Fields

A425
B4451
Gainsborough Trad Est
NORTHFIELD RD
BOURNE END
KINETON ROAD IND EST
SOUTHAM DR
WESTFIELD
SOUTHFIELD RD
B4451
A425

BANBURY RD

Warwick House Ind Park

Home Farm

Holt Cottage Farm

WELSH RD

Hogs Hollow

Larkfield House

Highfields

Southam Holt

Southam Holt Farm

Starbold Farm
A423

41   42   43

4   63   3   62   2   61   1   60

D   E   F

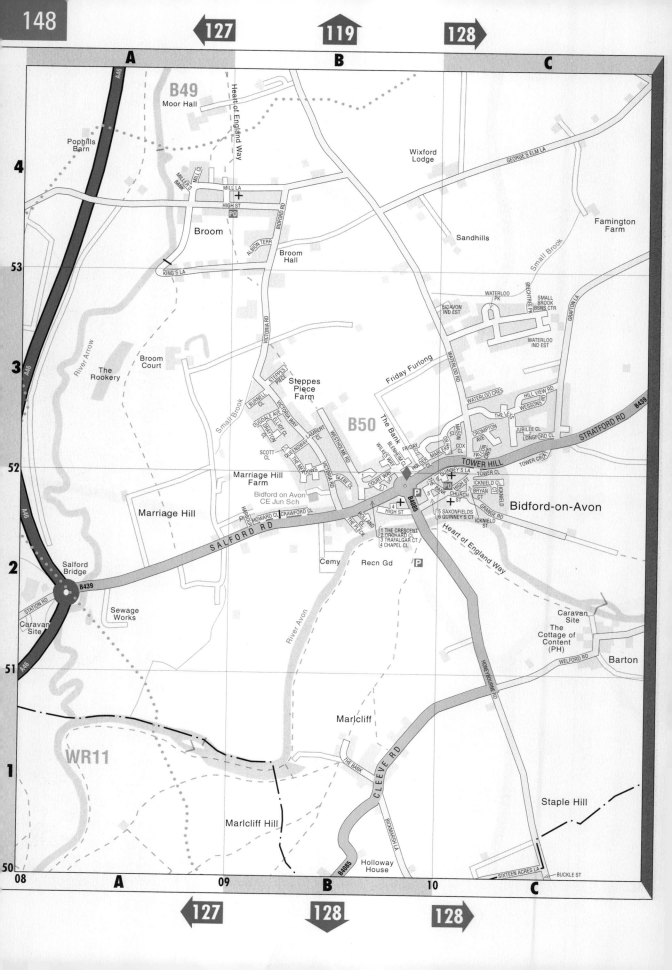

A　　　　B　　　　C

B49

Moor Hall

Pophills Barn

Heart of England Way

MILLER'S BANK

MILL CL

MILL LA

HIGH ST

PO

Broom

BIDFORD RD

ALBION TERR

Wixford Lodge

GEORGE'S ELM LA

Famington Farm

Sandhills

Broom Hall

KING'S LA

4

53

VICTORIA RD

Small Brook

Waterloo Pk

BEECHTREE LA

SMALL BROOK BSNS CTR

GRAFTON LA

BIDAVON IND EST

WATERLOO IND EST

The Rookery

River Arrow

A46

Broom Court

STEPPES PIECE

BURNELL CL

Steppes Piece Farm

VICTORIA WAY

DUGDALE AVE

ELLIOT CL

DRAYTON

QUEENSWAY

LAMBERT CL

SCOTT CL

THE NEND

DOWS

WESTHOLME RD

GLEBE CL

VICTORIA RD

Friday Furlong

WATERLOO RD

WATERLOO CRES

HILL VIEW RD

WESSONS RD

THE LEYS

JUBILEE CL

LONGFORD CL

B50

The Bank

WILKES WAY

COURT WAY

BLENHEIM CL

FRIDAY

NOLDER CL

MARLEES CL

MASON RD

CROMPTON AVE

COX CL

FAL CRES

BRYAN CT

ST

HIGH ST

ICKNIELD CL

ICKNIELD CL

GRANGE RD

3

STRATFORD RD

B439

Marriage Hill Farm

Bidford on Avon CE Jun Sch

Marriage Hill

HARBOUR

HOWARD CL

CRAWFORD CL

SALFORD RD

HOLLAND

THE PLECK

B4085

HIGH ST

CHURCH ST

TOWER HILL

QUINNEY'S LA

PO

TOWER CL

TOWER CROFT

Bidford-on-Avon

5 SAXONFIELDS

6 QUINNEY'S CT

ICKNIELD CL

52

1 THE CRESCENT

2 ORCHARD CL

3 TRAFALGAR CT

4 CHAPEL CL

Cemy

Recn Gd

P

Heart of England Way

Salford Bridge

B439

STATION RD

A46

Caravan Site

Sewage Works

River Avon

Caravan Site

The Cottage of Content (PH)

WELFORD RD

Barton

2

51

WR11

Marlcliff

THE BANK

CLEEVE RD

BICKMARSH LA

HONEYBOURNE RD

Staple Hill

1

Marlcliff Hill

B4085

Holloway House

SIXTEEN ACRES LA

BUCKLE ST

50

08　　　A　　　09　　　B　　　10　　　C

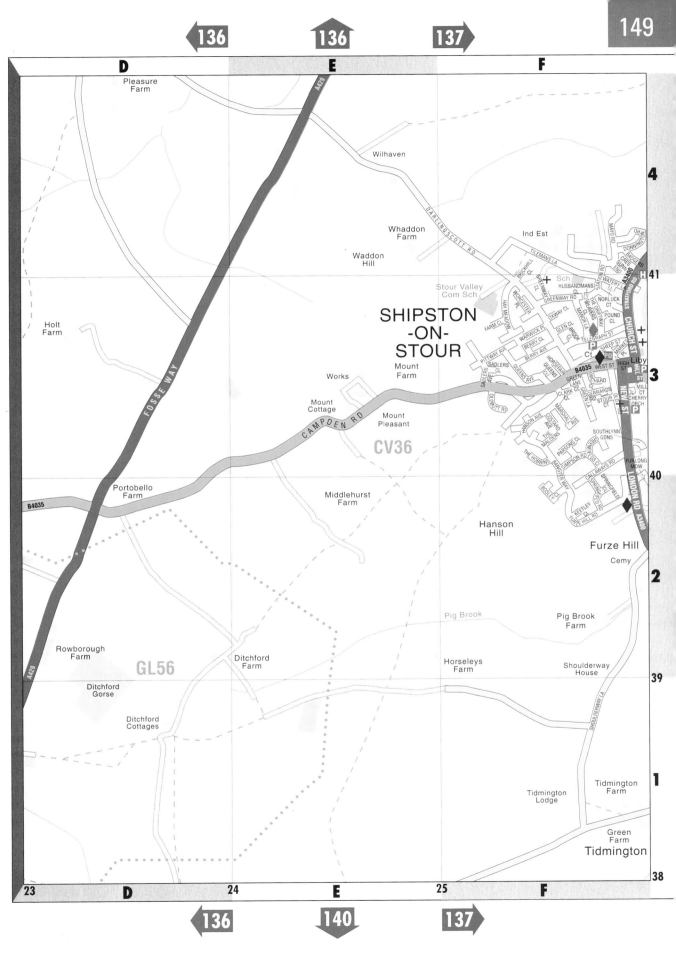

136 136 137

D E F

4

Pleasure Farm

Wilhaven

Whaddon Farm

Waddon Hill

Ind Est

DARLINGSCOTT RD

Stour Valley Com Sch

TILEMANS LA

BRICKHILL CL
GREENWAY RD

MAYO RD

DONNINGTON

STATION RD

BADGERS

LONDON

HUSBANDMANS CL

NORLUCK CT

A3400 STRATFORD RD

H 41

Sch

Holt Farm

SHIPSTON
-ON-
STOUR

THE DRIFTWAY

POUND CL

WATERY LA

WORCESTER CL

OXWAY CL

CHURCH LA

GLEN CL

BROOK

MAUR LA

TELEGRAPH ST

CHURCH ST

P

SHEEP ST

MARKET PL

Ct

RD

High St

Lib

P

WARWICK CL

FARM CL

HAY MEADOW

PITTWAY AVE

SADLERS AVE

BERRY CL

BERRY AVE

QUEENS AVE

HORSEFAIR

SADLERS CL

B4035 WEST ST

ORCHARD

MILL CT

CHERRY ORCH

P

+ +

3

Works

Mount Cottage

Mount Farm

Mount Pleasant

CAMPDEN RD

CV36

GREEN LANE

CLARK CL

GREEN LA

MARSHALL AVE

GERRARDS CT

STOUR TCE

NEW ST

HANSON AVE

COLLARD AVE

PARSONS CL

SOUTHLYNN GDNS

FURLONG MDW

LONDON RD A3400

P

Portobello Farm

B4035

THE MALDENS

SIMPSON RD

SPRINGFIELD

SPRINGS CL

40

Middlehurst Farm

THE HOBBINS

BANSTER WAY

BUSK CL

CALLAWAY'S CL

SPRINGFIELD RD

KETTLEY

FURZE HILL RD

Hanson Hill

Furze Hill

Cemy

2

Pig Brook

Pig Brook Farm

A429

FOSSE WAY

Rowborough Farm

GL56

Ditchford Gorse

Ditchford Farm

Horseleys Farm

Shoulderway House

39

SHOULDERWAY LA

Ditchford Cottages

1

Tidmington Lodge

Tidmington Farm

Green Farm

Tidmington

38

23 D 24 E 25 F

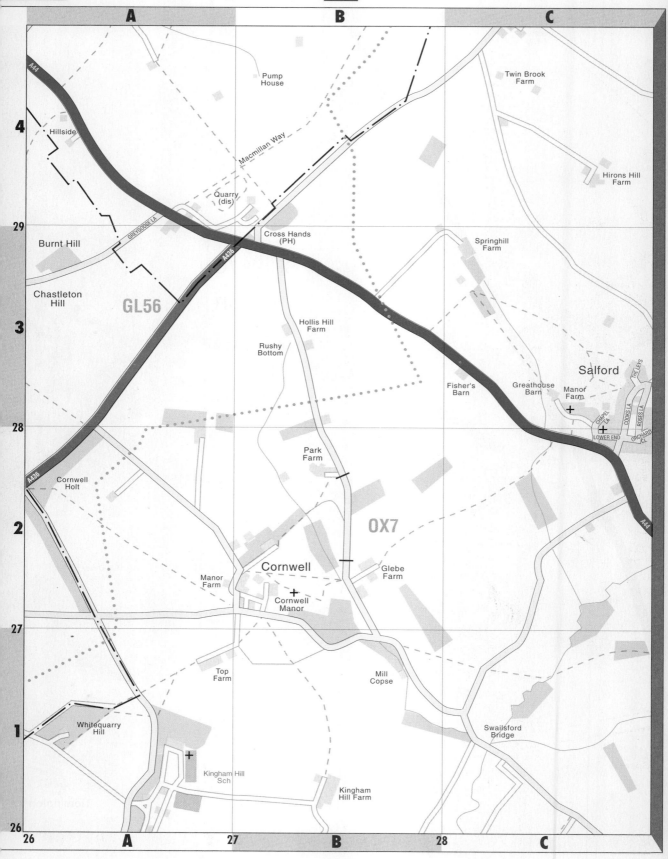

Pump House

Twin Brook Farm

Macmillan Way

Hirons Hill Farm

Quarry (dis)

Cross Hands (PH)

Springhill Farm

Burnt Hill

GREYGOOSE LA

A436

Chastleton Hill

GL56

Hollis Hill Farm

Rushy Bottom

Fisher's Barn

Greathouse Barn

Salford

THE LEYS

Manor Farm

CHAPEL LA

COOKS LA

ROSES LA

LOWER END

ORCHARD CL

A436

Cornwell Holt

Park Farm

OX7

A44

Manor Farm

Cornwell

Glebe Farm

Cornwell Manor

Top Farm

Mill Copse

Swailsford Bridge

Whitequarry Hill

Kingham Hill Sch

Kingham Hill Farm

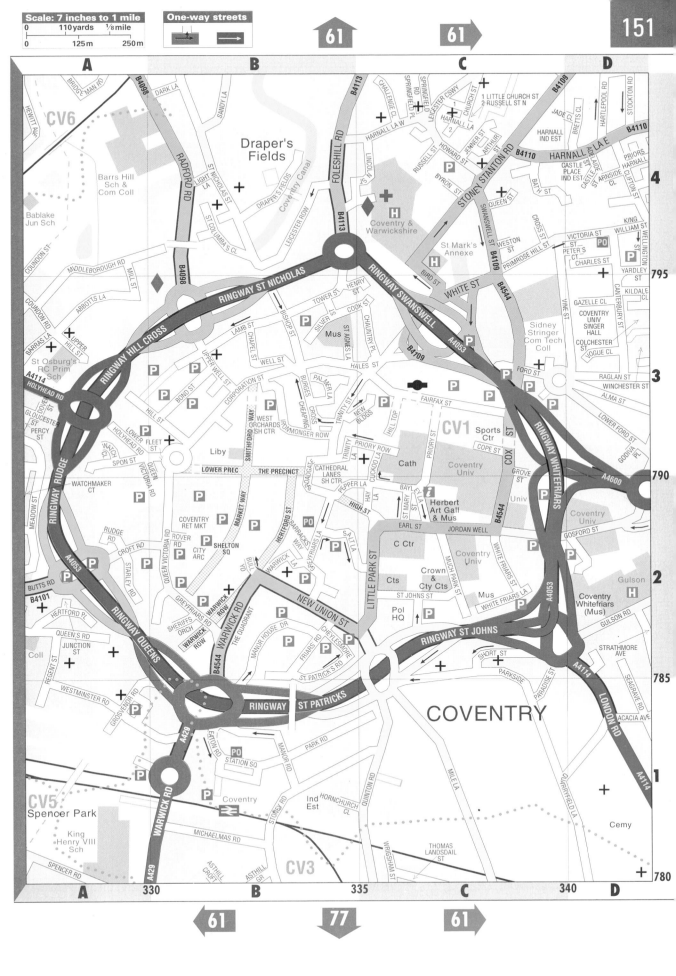

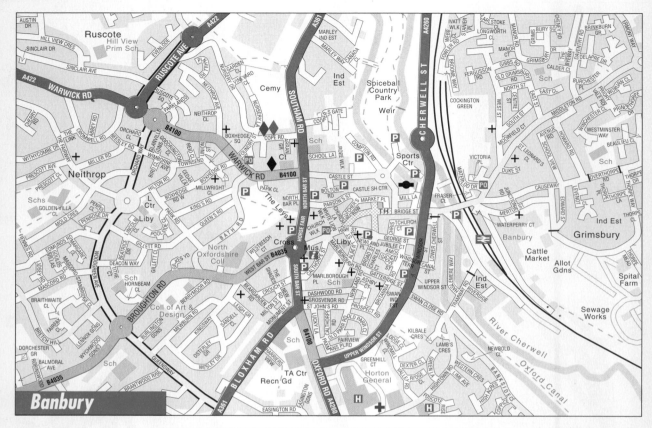

Banbury

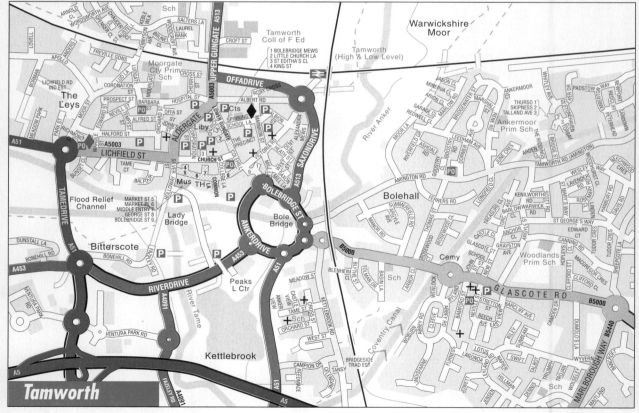

Tamworth

Street names are listed alphabetically and show the locality, the Postcode District, the page number and a reference to the square in which the name falls on the map page

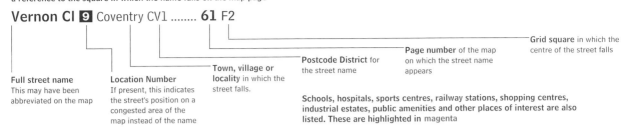

Vernon Cl **9** Coventry CV1 .... **61** F2

Full street name
This may have been abbreviated on the map

Location Number
If present, this indicates the street's position on a congested area of the map instead of the name

Town, village or locality in which the street falls.

Postcode District for the street name

Page number of the map on which the street name appears

Grid square in which the centre of the street falls

Schools, hospitals, sports centres, railway stations, shopping centres, industrial estates, public amenities and other places of interest are also listed. These are highlighted in magenta

Abbreviations used in the index

App **Approach**	Comm **Common**	Est **Estate**	N **North**	Sq **Square**
Arc **Arcade**	Cnr **Corner**	Gdns **Gardens**	Orch **Orchard**	Strs **Stairs**
Ave **Avenue**	Cotts **Cottages**	Gn **Green**	Par **Parade**	Stps **Steps**
Bvd **Boulevard**	Ct **Court**	Gr **Grove**	Pk **Park**	St **Street, Saint**
Bldgs **Buildings**	Ctyd **Courtyard**	Hts **Heights**	Pas **Passage**	Terr **Terrace**
Bsns Pk **Business Park**	Cres **Crescent**	Ho **House**	Pl **Place**	Trad Est **Trading Estate**
Bsns Ctr **Business Centre**	Dr **Drive**	Ind Est **Industrial Estate**	Prec **Precinct**	Wlk **Walk**
Bglws **Bungalows**	Dro **Drove**	Intc **Interchange**	Prom **Promenade**	W **West**
Cswy **Causeway**	E **East**	Junc **Junction**	Ret Pk **Retail Park**	Yd **Yard**
Ctr **Centre**	Emb **Embankment**	La **Lane**	Rd **Road**	
Cir **Circus**	Ent **Enterprise**	Mans **Mansions**	Rdbt **Roundabout**	
Cl **Close**	Espl **Esplanade**	Mdw **Meadows**	S **South**	

Town and village index

Alcester 143 E2	Burton Green 75 E2	Grendon 11 E2	Middleton 8 A1
Alderminster 130 D3	Burton Hastings 41 D4	Halford 137 A8	Mile Oak 8 A4
Allesley 60 A4	Butlers Marston 131 F5	Hampton in Arden 57 D4	Minworth 22 B3
Alvecote 4 B3	Catherine de Barnes 56 A3	Hampton Lucy 121 F4	Mollington 134 A2
Alveston 121 D3	Catthorpe 68 B1	Hampton Magna 114 F4	Monks Kirby 53 F1
Ansley 27 D2	Chadwick End 90 A4	Hanwell 139 F6	Moreton Morrell 122 F2
Ansty 51 E2	Charwelton 126 D2	Harborough Magna 66 A2	Moreton-in-Marsh 140 C3
Appleby Magna 3 F4	Cherington 141 D7	Harbury 123 E7	Napton 125 C8
Arley 26 C1	Chesterton 123 D5	Hartshill 19 D1	Nether Whitacre 25 D3
Ash Green 49 E3	Cheswick Green 70 C2	Harvington 127 C4	Newbold on Stour 130 E1
Astley 37 F4	Chipping Campden 135 B2	Hatton 114 E6	Newton 68 A1
Aston Cantlow 119 F6	Chipping Warden 134 F3	Henley-in-Arden 113 B5	Newton Regis 2 B2
Aston Flamville 32 C3	Church Lawford 81 D3	Higham-on-the-Hill 21 D2	North Newington 139 D2
Aston le Walls 134 F5	Church Lench 127 A6	Hinckley 31 E4	Northend 133 B7
Aston Magna 140 A6	Churchover 67 E3	Hockley Heath 88 B3	Norton 127 C2
Astwood Bank 102 C1	Claverdon 113 F3	Hollywood 69 D4	Norton Lindsey 114 C2
Austrey 3 D1	Claybrooke Magna 43 F3	Honiley 91 E3	Nuneaton 29 D3
Avon Dassett 133 C5	Claybrooke Parva 43 F2	Honington 137 A5	Offchurch 111 E4
Badby 126 F5	Claydon 134 B5	Hook Norton 142 D4	Offenham 127 D1
Baddesley Ensor 11 E1	Cleeve Prior 128 A4	Horley 139 D6	Orton-on-the-Hill 6 C2
Baginton 77 F2	Cliff 9 D1	Hornton 139 B8	Oxhill 137 F8
Balsall Common 74 A4	Clifford Chambers 129 F6	Hurley 16 B2	Pailton 66 A4
Banbury 139 F3	Clifton upon Dunsmore 84 A3	Ilmington 136 B6	Pebworth 128 F1
Barby 101 E1	Coleshill 33 F3	Kenilworth 92 C2	Piccadilly 9 F1
Barford 122 B7	Combrook 131 E6	Keresley 48 C3	Pillerton Hersey 131 E3
Barnacle 51 D3	Cookhill 118 D5	Kilsby 101 F2	Pillerton Priors 131 D2
Barston 57 D1	Corley 48 A4	Kineton 132 C6	Polesworth 5 D1
Barton-on-the-Heath ... 140 F1	Coughton 118 F7	Kingsbury 15 F3	Portway 86 A3
Bascote 115 C2	Coventry 61 D2	Knightcote 124 B1	Preston Bagot 113 D5
Baxterley 17 E3	Coventry 151 C1	Knowle 72 A3	Princethorpe 96 C1
Bearley 120 E7	Cropredy 134 C1	Ladbroke 124 D5	Priors Hardwick 125 D3
Beausale 91 E1	Cubbington 106 B3	Lapworth 88 C2	Priors Marston 125 F4
Bedworth 39 D1	Curdworth 23 D3	Lawford Heath 98 B4	Radford Semele 110 C3
Bentley Heath 71 F3	Darlingscott 136 D5	Lea Marston 24 A4	Ratley 133 A2
Berkswell 58 B2	Daventry 117 F1	Leamington Hastings 116 A6	Redditch 102 C4
Bickenhill 44 B1	Dordon 10 C3	Leek Wootton 104 C4	Rowington 114 A8
Bidford-on-Avon 148 C2	Dorridge 71 F2	Lighthorne 123 B2	Rowington Green 90 A1
Binley Woods 79 E4	Drayton 139 E4	Lighthorne Heath 123 D2	Royal Leamington Spa ... 109 F4
Binton 120 A1	Drayton Bassett 8 B3	Lilbourne 84 C3	Rugby 83 D1
Birchmoor 10 B4	Dunchurch 99 E2	Little Compton 140 F1	Ryton-on-Dunsmore 79 D1
Birdingbury 115 F7	Dunnington 127 E8	Little Packington 45 E3	Salford 150 C3
Birmingham 33 E3	Earlswood 70 A1	Littleton 127 F1	Salford Priors 127 F6
Bishops Itchington 124 B4	Easenhall 65 F2	Long Compton 141 C3	Sambourne 118 D8
Bishops Tachbrook 122 E7	Ebrington 135 E3	Long Itchington 115 D4	Shawell 68 B3
Blackdown 105 F3	Epwell 138 D3	Long Lawford 82 A2	Sheepy Magna 12 C4
Bourton on Dunsmore 97 F1	Ettington 131 B3	Long Marston 129 B3	Shenington 138 F5
Bradnock's Marsh 57 C2	Farnborough 133 E4	Lower Boddington 134 E7	Sherbourne 121 F8
Bramcote 40 C3	Fazeley 8 C4	Lower Brailes 137 F2	Shilton 51 F3
Brandon 79 F3	Fenny Compton 133 D7	Lower Quinton 129 D2	Shipston-on-Stour 149 E3
Braunston 117 E5	Fenny Drayton 20 A3	Lower Shuckburgh 116 F1	Shotteswell 139 E8
Bretford 80 B4	Fillongley 36 C2	Lowsonford 113 E6	Shrewley 114 B6
Brinklow 64 C2	Flecknoe 117 B2	Loxley 130 F8	Shustoke 24 C1
Broadwell 116 B4	Frankton 97 E1	Luddington 129 C7	Shutford 139 A3
Broom 148 A4	Furnace End 25 F2	Lutterworth 55 F3	Shuttington 4 C1
Broughton 139 E1	G Wolford 140 F5	Mappleborough Green .. 112 B6	Sibford Ferris 142 D7
Bubbenhall 95 E3	Gaydon 123 E1	Marton 115 C7	Sibford Gower 142 D8
Bulkington 40 A1	Grandborough 116 C3	Maxstoke 35 D1	Snitterfield 121 B6
Burmington 141 A8	Great Alne 119 D6	Meriden 46 B1	Southam 147 D2
	Great Rollright 142 B1	Mickleton 135 C6	Staverton 126 D7
			Stockton 147 F4
			Stoke Golding 21 E3
			Stoneleigh 94 A3
			Stratford-upon-Avon ... 145 D2
			Stretton on Dunsmore 97 D3
			Stretton on Fosse 136 B3
			Stretton under Fosse 65 E4
			Studley 103 F2
			Sutton Coldfield 13 D2
			Swalcliffe 142 F8
			Swerford 142 F1
			Tamworth 9 E3
			Tanworth-in-Arden 87 D1
			Temple Grafton 119 E2
			Temple Herdewyke 132 C6
			Thorpe Constantine 1 C3
			Thurlaston 98 C2
			Tidbury Green 69 F2
			Tiddington 145 E2
			Todenham 140 E7
			Tredington 136 F6
			Twycross 6 C4
			Tysoe 138 B6
			Ufton 111 F5
			Ullenhall 112 D6
			Upper Boddington 134 D8
			Upper Brailes 137 E2
			Upper Quinton 129 D1
			Wardington 134 F1
			Warmington 133 D2
			Warton 5 F2
			Warwick 108 C4
			Water Orton 23 E2
			Welford on Avon 129 A6
			Wellesbourne 146 B2
			Weston under Wetherley 107 E4
			Whatcote 137 D7
			Whateley 9 F2
			Whichford 141 F5
			White Stitch 46 B2
			Whitnash 110 B2
			Wibtoft 43 D2
			Wigston Parva 42 C4
			Willey 54 C3
			Willoughby 117 B6
			Wilmcote 120 C4
			Wishaw 14 A1
			Witherley 19 D4
			Withybrook 52 C3
			Wolston 80 A2
			Wolvey 41 E2
			Wood End 10 B1
			Wootton Wawen 113 B1
			Wroxall 90 C2
			Wroxton 139 D4
			Wythall 69 D2

154 1st – Ath

1st Ave GL56 140 B4
2nd Ave GL56 140 B4
3rd Ave GL56 140 B3
4th Ave GL56 140 C3
5th Ave GL56 140 C4
6th Ave GL56 140 B4
7th Ave GL56 140 B3
8th Ave GL56 140 B3
Ab Lench Rd WR11 127 A6
Abberley B77 4 B1
Abberton Gr B90 71 D4
Abberton Way CV4 76 C2
Abbey CE Fst Sch CV11 29 D3
Abbey Cl Alcester B49 143 D3
Southam CV33 147 D2
Abbey Croft B78 5 D1
Abbey End CV8 92 C2
Abbey Est CV2 62 C3
Abbey Gate CV11 29 E2
Abbey Gate Sh Ctr CV11 29 E2
Abbey Gn CV11 29 D3
Abbey Hill CV8 92 C3
Abbey La CV33 147 D2
Abbey Rd CV3 78 A3
Abbey St Nuneaton CV11 29 D3
Rugby CV21 83 E2
Abbey View B78 11 D4
Abbey Way CV3 77 F3
Abbeydale Cl CV3 62 C1
Abbeyfields Dr B80 103 F3
Abbots Cl B93 72 A4
Abbots Farm Jun & Inf Schs CV21 83 F1
Abbots Wlk CV8 80 A2
Abbots Wood Cl B98 112 A6
Abbotsbury Cl CV2 63 D2
Abbotsford Rd CV11 29 F1
Abbotsford Sch CV8 92 C3
Abbotts Gn LE10 31 F3
Abbotts La CV1 151 A3
Abbotts St 15 CV31 109 F4
Abbotts Way CV21 83 F1
Abbotts Wlk CV3 79 E4
Abeles Way CV9 12 B1
Abelia B77 4 A2
Abercorn Rd CV5 60 C1
Aberdeen Cl CV5 60 A3
Aberdeen Rd CV11 29 F1
Aberfoyle Rd CV35 132 D4
Abergavenny Wlk CV3 78 C3
Abingdon Way
Birmingham B35 22 A2
Nuneaton CV11 29 F4
Abu Sultan Rd CV35 132 F5
Acacia Ave CV1 61 F1
Acacia Gr CV21 83 D2
Acacia Rd Nuneaton CV10 28 C3
Royal Leamington Spa CV32 105 E1
Achal Cl CV6 49 F1
Achilles Rd CV6 62 A4
Acorn Cl Bedworth CV12 49 E4
Stoneleigh CV8 94 A4
Acorn Dr CV22 82 A1
Acorn St CV3 78 A4
Acre Cl CV31 110 A2
Acre Ditch OX15 142 D8
Adam Rd CV6 61 F4
Adams St CV21 82 C2
Adare Dr CV3 77 E4
Adcock Dr CV8 93 D3
Addenbrooke Rd CV7 49 D3
Adderley St CV1 61 F2
Addingham Cl 2 CV34 104 C1
Addison Cl CV10 28 A3
Addison Pl B46 23 D2
Addison Rd Coventry CV6 61 D4
Rugby CV22 82 B1
Adelaide Rd CV31 109 F4
Adelaide St CV1 151 D4
Adkins Croft CV7 36 C2
Adkinson Ave CV22 99 E2
Admington La CV36 135 E7
Admiral Gdns CV8 93 E3
Admirals Way CV11 40 C3
Agincourt Rd CV3 77 F4
Ainsbury Rd CV5 76 C4
Ainsdale Cl CV6 50 A2
Aintree Cl Bedworth CV12 39 D2
Coventry CV6 61 F3
Aintree Dr CV32 106 B2
Aintree Rd CV37 144 B1
Airport Way B26 44 B2
Akon Ho CV6 48 C1
Alan Bray Cl LE10 30 B4
Alan Higgs Way CV4 75 E4
Alandale Ave CV5 59 F2
Alauna Ave B49 143 E3
Albany Rd Coventry CV5 61 D1
Stratford-u-A CV37 144 C1
Albany Terr CV32 105 F1
Albert Cl B80 103 F2
Albert Cres CV6 49 D2
Albert Rd Allesley CV5 59 D4
Fazeley B78 9 D4
Albert Sq CV21 83 D2
Albert St Coventry CV1 61 F2
Nuneaton CV10 28 C1
Royal Leamington Spa CV32 105 E1
Rugby CV21 83 D2
Warwick CV34 108 B4
Albion Ind Est CV6 61 E4
Albion St CV8 93 D3
Albion Terr B50 148 B4
Albrighton Wlk CV11 30 A1
Albury Rd B80 103 F2
Alcester By-Pass B49 143 D2
Alcester Gram Sch B49 143 D2
Alcester Heath B49 118 E6
Alcester High Sch B49 143 E3
Alcester Highway B98 102 C4
Alcester Hospl B49 143 E2
Alcester Inf Sch B49 143 D2
Alcester Rd Hollywood B47 69 D4
Portway B48 85 F4
Stratford-u-A CV37 144 B2
Studley B80 103 F2
Wootton Wawen B95 113 A1
Wootton Wawen B95 113 B2
Alcester Southern By-Pass B49 143 E1
Alcocks Rd B49 143 E2
Alcott Cl B93 71 F1
Alcott Hall Prim Sch B37 33 D1
Aldbourne Rd CV1 61 E3
Aldbury Rise CV5 60 B2
Alder Cl B47 69 D3
Alder Dr B37 33 D1
Alder La CV7 74 B3
Alder Meadow Cl CV6 49 E2
Alder Rd CV6 50 A1
Alderbrooke Dr CV11 30 A1
Alderhanger La B98 112 B8
Alderman Callow Sch & Com Coll CV4 76 A3
Alderman Harris Prim Sch CV4 75 F4
Alderman Smith Sch CV10 28 B1
Alderman Way CV33 107 E4
Alderman's Green Ind Est CV2 50 B1
Alderman's Green Prim Sch CV2 50 B2
Alderman's Green Rd CV2 50 A2
Alderminster Gr CV35 114 F5
Alderminster Rd
Coventry CV5 60 A2
Solihull B90 71 E4
Aldermoor Farm Prim Sch CV3 78 A4
Aldermoor La CV3 62 A1
Alderney Cl Bramcote CV11 40 C3
Coventry CV6 49 D1
Alders Dr B98 112 A6
Alders Gr CV34 108 B2
Alders La CV10 28 A4
Alders The CV12 38 C1
Aldersgate B78 15 E4
Alderton Mews CV31 110 B3
Aldrich Ave CV4 59 F1
Aldridge Cl B78 10 C4
Aldridge Rd LE10 31 E3
Aldrin Way CV4 76 B3
Aldwick Cl CV32 106 A2
Alesworth Dr LE10 31 F2
Alex Grierson Cl CV3 78 C4
Alexander Rd CV12 39 E2
Alexandra Ct CV9 18 C4
Alexandra Hospl The B98 103 E3
Alexandra Rd Coventry CV1 61 F2
Royal Leamington Spa CV31 110 A3
Rugby CV21 83 D2
Alexandra St CV11 29 D2
Alfall Rd CV2 62 A3
Alfred Green Cl CV22 83 D1
Alfred Rd CV1 61 F2
Alfred St CV21 82 C1
Alfreda Ave B47 69 D4
Alfreton Cl LE10 31 F3
Alfriston Rd CV3 77 E2
Alice Cl CV12 38 C1
Alice Stevens Sch CV3 78 A3
Alison Sq CV6 50 A2
All Saints CE Fst Sch
Bedworth CV12 39 E1
Nuneaton CV10 29 E1
All Saints CE Mid Sch CV34 105 D1
All Saints CE Prim Sch CV1 61 F1
All Saints Cl CV7 52 C3
All Saints La CV1 61 F2
All Saints Rd Bedworth CV12 38 C1
Warwick CV34 109 D4
All Saints Sq CV12 39 D2
All Souls RC Prim Sch CV5 60 C2
Allan Rd CV6 60 C2
Allans Cl CV23 84 A3
Allans La CV23 84 A3
Allard Way CV3 78 B4
Allen Cl B80 103 F2
Allendale Ave B80 103 F2
Allendale Cres B80 103 F2
Allendale Ct B80 103 F2
Allens Cl CV9 17 E4
Allens Orch OX17 134 F3
Allerton Cl CV2 62 C1
Allesley Croft CV5 60 A4
Allesley Cty Prim Sch CV5 60 A4
Allesley Hall Dr CV5 60 B2
Allesley Hall Prim Sch CV5 60 A2
Allesley Old Rd CV5 60 B2
Allesley Rd CV21 82 C3
Alliance Cl CV11 29 F2
Alliance Way CV2 62 A3
Allibone Cl CV31 110 A2
Allied Cl CV6 49 E1
Allitt Gr CV8 93 D3
Allwood Cl B49 143 D2
Alma Ct CV11 40 C3
Alma St CV1 151 D3
Almond Ave Nuneaton CV10 28 B3
Royal Leamington Spa CV32 105 F2
Almond Cl CV23 101 E1
Almond Gr Rugby CV21 82 C4
Warwick CV34 105 D1
Almond Tree Ave CV2 50 B1
Almshouses B78 8 A1
Alne Bank Rd B49 143 E2
Alne Cl B95 113 B4
Alpha Bsns Pk CV2 50 B1
Alpine Ct CV8 93 D3
Alpine Rise CV3 77 D3
Alspath La CV5 59 F2
Alspath Rd CV7 46 B1
Althorpe Dr B93 71 F2
Althorpe Ind Est 7 CV31 110 A4
Althorpe St CV31 110 A4
Alton Cl CV2 50 B1
Alum Cl CV6 61 E4
Alvecote Pools Nature Reserve B79 4 B4
Alverstone Rd CV2 62 A2
Alveston CE Prim Sch CV37 145 F2
Alveston Gr B93 72 A4
Alveston La CV37 121 D3
Alveston Rd B47 69 D4
Alvin Cl CV3 62 C1
Alvis Gate OX16 139 F4
Alvis Ret Pk CV5 61 D2
Alvis Way NN11 117 F2
Alvis Wlk B36 22 C1
Alwyn B77 9 F4
Alwyn Rd CV22 99 E3
Alwynne Freeman Ct CV7 49 D3
Amber Bsns Village B77 4 A2
Amber Cl B77 4 A2
Amberley Ave CV12 40 B1
Ambien Rd CV9 18 B4
Ambler Gr CV2 62 B2
Ambleside Coventry CV2 50 C1
Rugby CV21 83 E4
Ambleside Way CV11 29 F3
Ambrose Cl CV21 83 E3
Amersham Cl CV5 60 A2
Amherst Rd CV8 92 C3
Amhurst Bsns Ctr CV34 108 A4
Amicombe B77 4 B1
Amington Heath Prim Sch B77 4 A2
Amington Ind Est B77 4 A1
Amington Rd B90 70 A4
Amos Ave CV10 29 D1
Amos Jacques Rd CV12 39 D2
Amroth Mews 1 CV31 110 B3
Amy Cl CV6 49 F2
Anchor La WR11 127 E3
Anchorway Rd CV3 77 D2
Anderson Ave CV22 100 A4
Anderson Dr CV31 110 A1
Anderton Rd Bedworth CV12 38 B1
Coventry CV6 50 A2
Andrew Cl CV13 21 E4
Angela Ave CV2 50 C1
Anglesey Ave B36 33 D3
Anglesey Cl CV5 60 A4
Angless Way CV8 92 C2
Angus Cl Coventry CV5 60 A2
Kenilworth CV8 93 E3
Anker Dr CV23 82 A3
Anker St CV11 29 E2
Anker View B78 11 D4
Ankerside B78 5 D2
Ann Rd B47 69 D2
Anne Cres CV3 78 B3
Annie Osborn Prim Sch CV2 62 B4
Ansell Rd CV34 108 B4
Ansley Comm CV10 28 A4
Ansley La CV7 26 C2
Ansley Rd CV10 27 F2
Anson Cl Rugby CV22 82 B1
Wellesbourne CV35 146 B1
Anson Way CV2 62 C4
Ansty Rd CV2 62 C3
Antelope Gdns CV34 108 B4
Anthony Way CV2 62 B1
Anton Dr B76 22 A3
Antrim Cl CV5 60 A4
Antrobus Cl CV35 114 C5
Apollo Way CV34 109 E3
Appian Cl B77 9 E4
Appian Way B90 70 B2
Apple Gr CV22 82 A1
Apple Pie La CV10 19 D1
Applebee Rd LE10 31 E3
Appleby Cl Banbury OX16 139 F4
Great Alne B49 119 D6
Appleby Gr 9 B90 71 D3
Appleby Hill CV9 3 D2
Applecross Cl CV4 75 F3
Appledore Dr CV5 59 F3
Appletree Cl B91 56 A3
Appletree La Cookhill WR7 118 A3
Cropredy NN11 134 F5
Appletree Rd OX17 134 F3
Approach The CV31 109 F3
Apsley Gr B93 71 F1
Aragon Dr CV34 109 E3
Arbor Way B37 33 E1
Arboretum The CV4 76 B2
Arbour Cl Kenilworth CV8 93 D2
Mickleton GL55 135 B6
Rugby CV22 99 E4
Arbour Tree La B93 89 F4
Arbury Ave Bedworth CV12 39 D2
Coventry CV6 49 F1
Arbury Banks OX17 134 F3
Arbury Cl CV32 106 A2
Arbury Ct B95 113 B5
Arbury Hall Rd B90 70 B4
Arbury Rd CV10 28 B1
Arbury Wlk B76 22 B3
Arch Rd CV2 62 C3
Archer Ave NN11 117 E5
Archer Cl B80 103 E2
Archer Rd CV8 92 C2
Archers Spinney CV21 101 D4
Archery Fields CV34 108 C3
Archery Rd Meriden CV7 46 A1
Royal Leamington Spa CV31 109 F4
Arches Bsns Ctr CV21 83 E3
Arches Ind Est CV21 83 E3
Arches Ind Est The CV5 61 D2
Arches La CV21 83 E3
Arden Ave CV9 18 C4
Arden Bsns Ctr B49 143 D3
Arden Cl Balsall Common CV7 74 A4
Henley-in-A B95 113 B4
Meriden CV7 46 B1
Royal Leamington Spa CV31 110 A3
Rugby CV22 99 E3
Warwick CV34 105 D1
Wilmcote CV37 120 C5
Arden Croft B46 23 F1
Arden Ct B49 143 D3
Arden Dr Dorridge B93 72 A1
Sutton Coldfield, Falcon Lodge B75 13 D3
Arden Forest Est CV10 18 A1
Arden Forest Ind Est B49 143 E3
Arden Forest Inf Sch CV12 40 A2
Arden Hill Inf Sch CV9 18 C4
Arden Lawn Sch B95 113 A4
Arden Leys B94 86 B1
Arden Meads B94 88 B3
Arden Rd Alcester B49 143 D3
Bulkington CV12 40 B1
Dorridge B93 71 F1
Henley-in-A B95 113 B4
Hollywood B47 69 D3
Kenilworth CV8 93 D2
Nuneaton CV11 30 A1
Tamworth B77 9 F3
Arden Sch B93 72 A3
Arden St Atherstone CV9 18 C4
Coventry CV5 76 C4
Stratford-u-A CV37 144 C2
Arden Vale Rd B93 72 A4
Ardens Cl B98 112 A5
Arderne Dr B37 33 D1
Argyle St CV21 83 E2
Argyle Way 5 CV33 122 F8
Argyll St CV2 62 A2
Ariel Way CV22 99 E3
Arkle B77 9 E2
Arkle Dr CV2 62 C4
Arleston Way B90 70 C4
Arley Ind Est CV7 36 C4
Arley La CV10 27 E2
Arley Mews CV32 105 F1
Arlidge Cres CV8 93 E3
Arlington Ave CV32 105 F1
Arlington Mews 14 CV32 105 F1
Arlington Way CV11 29 F1
Arlon Ave CV10 28 B4
Armarna Dr CV5 59 D4
Armfield St CV6 62 A4
Armorial Rd CV3 77 D4
Armour Cl LE10 31 E3
Armscote Rd
Ilmington CV36 136 B6
Tredington CV36 136 E6
Armscott Rd CV2 62 B3
Armson Rd CV7 39 D1
Armstrong Ave CV3 62 A1
Armstrong Cl Rugby CV22 82 C1
Whitnash CV31 110 A1
Armstrong Dr B36 22 C1
Arncliffe Cl CV11 30 A1
Arncliffe Way 11 CV34 104 C1
Arne Rd CV2 63 D3
Arnhem Cnr CV3 78 B3
Arnold Ave CV3 77 E3
Arnold Cl CV22 83 D1
Arnold Lodge Prep Sch CV32 105 F1
Arnold Rd CV13 21 E3
Arnold St CV21 83 D2
Arnolds La B46 34 C2
Arnside Cl CV1 151 D4
Arran Cl CV10 29 D2
Arran Way B36 33 D4
Arras Bvd CV35 108 A4
Arrow Cl B93 72 A3
Arrow Cres B49 143 E3
Arrow End WR11 128 A2
Arrow La WR11 127 F2
Arthingworth Cl CV3 62 C1
Arthur Rd CV37 145 D2
Arthur St Coventry CV1 151 C4
Kenilworth CV8 93 D3
Artillery Rd CV11 40 C3
Arun Way B76 13 D1
Arundel B77 9 E4
Arundel Cl 2 CV34 108 C4
Arundel Pl OX16 139 F3
Arundel Rd Bulkington CV12 40 B2
Coventry CV3 77 E3
Asbury Rd CV7 74 A3
Ascot Cl Bedworth CV12 39 D2
Coventry CV3 78 B3
Stratford-u-A CV37 144 B1
Ascot Rd CV35 132 D3
Ascot Ride CV32 106 B2
Ascote Way CV33 147 E2
Ascott Hill CV36 142 A5
Ascott Rd CV36 141 F5
Asfare Bsns Pk LE10 31 F1
Ash Cl CV35 114 C5
Ash Ct CV22 99 F4
Ash Dr Hartshill CV10 28 A4
Kenilworth CV8 93 D2
Ash Gr Arley CV7 26 C1
Ash Green CV7 49 E4
Kingsbury B78 15 E4
Southam CV33 147 D3
Stratford-u-A CV37 144 C3
Tamworth B77 9 F3
Ash Green La CV7 49 E3
Ash Green Sch CV7 49 E3
Ash La CV37 120 E7
Ash Priors Cl CV4 60 A1
Ash Tree Ave CV4 60 A1
Ash Tree Cl CV35 146 C2
Ash Tree Gr CV7 51 F3
Ash Way NN11 117 D5
Ashborough Dr B91 71 E4
Ashbourne Way B90 70 C4
Ashbridge Rd CV5 60 B2
Ashbrook Cres B91 71 E4
Ashbrook Rise CV10 19 D1
Ashburton Cl LE10 32 A3
Ashburton La OX15 142 D3
Ashburton Rd CV2 62 C4
Ashby Cl CV3 78 C4
Ashby Ct CV11 29 E2
Ashby Rd NN11 117 E5
Ashcombe Dr CV4 59 F2
Ashcroft Cl CV2 63 D4
Ashcroft Way CV2 63 D4
Ashdale Cl CV3 79 F4
Ashdene Gdns CV8 93 D2
Ashdown Cl CV3 78 B4
Ashdown Dr CV10 28 C1
Ashe Rd CV10 28 A2
Ashfield Ave CV4 59 E1
Ashfield Rd CV8 93 D2
Ashford Dr CV12 39 D2
Ashford Gdns CV31 109 F2
Ashford La B94 88 A4
Ashford Rd Hinckley LE10 31 D4
Whitnash CV31 109 F1
Ashfurlong Cl CV7 74 A3
Ashington Gr CV3 78 A3
Ashington Rd CV12 38 B1
Ashlawn Rd CV22 100 B4
Ashlawn Sch CV22 100 C4
Ashlea B78 10 C3
Ashleigh Cl CV23 101 E1
Ashleigh Dr Nuneaton CV11 29 F1
Tamworth B77 9 F4
Ashley Cres CV34 109 D3
Ashman Ave CV23 82 A3
Ashmore Rd CV6 61 D2
Ashmores Cl B97 102 B3
Ashorne Cl Coventry CV2 50 B1
Redditch B98 103 E4
Ashorne Hill Coll CV33 122 E5
Ashow Cl CV8 93 D2
Ashridge Cl CV11 39 F4
Ashstead Cl B76 22 A3
Ashwood Ave CV6 60 C3
Ashwood Dr B37 33 E2
Ashwood Rd CV10 28 C3
Aspbury Croft B36 22 B1
Aspen Cl Alcester B49 143 D3
Coventry CV4 59 E1
Aspen Dr B37 44 B4
Aspen Gr B47 69 D3
Aspens The B78 15 E4
Asplen Ct CV8 93 E2
Aspley Ct CV35 114 F6
Aspley Heath B94 86 B1
Aspley Heath La B94 86 B1
Asra Cl CV2 61 F2
Assheton Cl CV22 99 E4
Aster Cl Hinckley LE10 31 F3
Nuneaton CV11 30 A1
Aster Way LE10 31 E3
Asthill Croft CV3 77 E4
Asthill Gr CV3 77 E4
Astley Ave CV6 49 F1
Astley Cl Redditch B98 103 D4
Royal Leamington Spa CV32 105 E1
Astley La Bedworth CV12 38 B2
Fillongley CV7 37 D2
Nuneaton CV10 28 A1
Astley Wlk CV33 133 A7
Astley's Pl CV21 101 D4
Aston Cantlow Rd CV37 120 B5
Aston Flamville Rd LE10 32 B4
Aston Hill CV37 120 B5
Aston Ind Est CV12 39 E1
Aston La LE10 32 A3
Aston Pk Ind Est CV11 29 D3
Aston Rd
Chipping Campden GL55 135 B3
Coventry CV5 60 C1
Nuneaton CV11 29 D3
Astwood Bank Fst Sch B96 102 C1
Astwood La B96 102 B1
Atch Lench Rd WR11 127 A6
Atcheson Cl B80 103 F2
Athena Dr CV34 109 F3
Athena Gdns CV6 50 A1
Atherston Pl CV4 76 B3
Atherstone Coll CV9 18 C4
Atherstone La CV9 16 C3
Atherstone Rd
Appleby Magna DE12 3 F3
Fenny Drayton CV13 20 A3
Furnace End B46 25 F3
Hartshill CV10 19 D1
Hurley CV9 16 B2
Sheepy Magna CV9 12 B2
Twycross DE12 3 F3

Atherstone St B78 .... 9 D4
Atherstone Sta CV9 .... 18 B4
Athol Rd CV2 .... 63 D3
Atholl Cres CV10 .... 28 C1
Atkins Way LE10 .... 31 F4
Atterton La CV9 .... 19 E4
Attleborough Fields Ind Est
  CV11 .... 29 F2
Attleborough Fst Sch CV11 29 F2
Attleborough La B46 .... 23 D1
Attleborough Rd CV11 ...... 29 E2
Attoxhall Rd CV2 .... 62 C2
Attwood Cres CV2 .... 62 B4
Auckland Dr B36 .... 33 D4
Auden Cl CV10 .... 27 F2
Augusta Pl CV32 .... 109 F4
Augustine Ave B80 .... 103 E2
Augustus Cl B46 .... 23 F1
Augustus Dr B49 .... 143 D2
Augustus Rd CV1 .... 61 F2
Austcliff Cl B97 .... 102 B3
Austcliff Dr B91 .... 71 E4
Austen Cl CV10 .... 27 F3
Austen Ct CV32 .... 106 C3
Austin Cl CV9 .... 18 B4
Austin Croft B36 .... 22 C1
Austin Dr Banbury OX16 .. 139 F4
  Coventry CV6 .... 62 A4
Austin Edwards Dr [2]
  CV34 .... 109 D4
Austin Way NN11 .... 117 F2
Austrey CE Prim Sch CV9 .. 3 D1
Austrey Cl B93 .... 72 A3
Austrey La Austrey B79 .... 3 D3
  Newton Regis B79 .... 2 C2
Austrey Rd Appleby Magna CV9 3 E3
  Warton B79 .... 5 F3
Austwick Cl CV34 .... 104 C1
Auxerre Ave B98 .... 103 D4
Avebury Cl CV11 .... 29 F1
Aventine Way CV21 .... 82 C4
Avenue B93 .... 72 A2
Avenue Farm CV37 .... 144 C3
Avenue Field Ind Est CV37 144 C2
Avenue Rd
  Astwood Bank B96 .... 102 C1
  Dorridge B93 .... 72 A2
  Kenilworth CV8 .... 92 B3
  Nuneaton CV11 .... 29 E1
  Royal Leamington Spa CV31 .. 109 F4
  Rugby CV21 .... 82 C2
  Stratford-u-A CV37 .... 145 D2
Avenue The Coventry CV3 78 A3
  Rowington Green CV35 .... 90 A1
  Stratford-u-A CV37 .... 144 B3
Aviemore Cl CV10 .... 29 D1
Avill B77 .... 10 A3
Avocet Cl CV2 .... 50 A2
Avon B77 .... 10 A3
Avon Aquatics CV37 .... 130 A3
Avon Ave CV35 .... 138 B6
Avon Carrow CV33 .... 133 D4
Avon Cl Barford CV35 ...... 122 B8
  Bulkington CV12 .... 40 A3
  Ettington CV37 .... 131 B3
Avon Cres Alcester B49 .. 143 E3
  Stratford-u-A CV37 .... 145 E1
Avon Ct CV8 .... 92 C3
Avon Dassett Rd CV33 .... 133 D6
Avon Ind Est Rugby CV21 .. 83 E3
  Stratford-u-A CV37 .... 144 C2
Avon Rd Kenilworth CV8 .. 92 C2
  Lighthorne Heath CV35 .. 123 D2
  Whitnash CV31 .... 110 A2
Avon St Clifton u D CV21 .. 83 F2
  Coventry CV2 .... 62 A3
  Rugby CV21 .... 83 D2
  Warwick CV34 .... 109 D4
Avon Valley High Sch CV21 82 C3
Avon Way CV35 .... 138 B6
Avonbank B97 .... 102 B3
Avonbank Dr CV37 .... 129 E8
Avonbank Paddocks CV37 145 D1
Avonbrook Cl CV37 .... 144 B2
Avondale Rd Brandon CV8 .. 79 F3
  Coventry CV5 .... 77 D4
  Royal Leamington Spa CV32 .. 106 B2
Avonfields Cl CV37 .... 121 D3
Avonlea Rise CV32 .... 105 E1
Avonmeadow Cl CV37 ...... 144 C1
Avonmere CV21 .... 82 C4
Avonside CV37 .... 145 D1
Awson St CV6 .... 61 F3
Axholme Rd CV2 .... 62 C2
Axminster Cl CV11 .... 29 F3
Aylesbury Cl B94 .... 88 B3
Aylesbury Rd B94 .... 88 B4
Aylesford Dr B37 .... 44 A4
Aylesford Sch CV34 .... 108 B2
Aylesford St Coventry CV1 61 F2
  Royal Leamington Spa CV31 110 A3
Aylstone Cl CV37 .... 129 D2
Aynho Cl CV5 .... 60 A2
Aysgarth Cl CV11 .... 30 A1
Azalea Cl LE10 .... 31 F3
Azalea Dr LE10 .... 31 F3
Azalea Wlk LE10 .... 31 F3

Babbacombe Rd CV3 ...... 77 D3
Bablake Cl CV6 .... 60 C4
Bablake Jun Sch CV1 ...... 151 A4
Bablake Sch CV1 .... 61 D2
Bachelors Bench CV9 ...... 18 B4
Back Ends GL55 .... 135 B2
Back La Birdingbury CV23 .. 115 F7
  Claverdon CV35 .... 114 A6
  Claybrooke Magna LE17 .. 43 F3

Back La continued
  Cleeve Prior WR11 .... 128 A4
  Harborough Magna CV23 .. 66 A2
  Henley-in-A B95 .... 113 B5
  Long Compton CV36 ...... 141 D3
  Long Lawford CV23 .... 82 A2
  Lower Quinton CV37 ...... 129 E3
  Meriden CV7 .... 58 C3
  Mickleton GL55 .... 135 B6
  Pebworth CV37 .... 128 E1
  Pillerton Priors CV35 .... 131 D2
  Shustoke B46 .... 24 C1
  Sibford Ferris OX15 ...... 142 D8
  Warwick CV34 .... 108 C3
Back St Ilmington CV36 .. 136 B6
  Nuneaton CV11 .... 29 E3
Backside La OX15 .... 142 D8
Badbury CE Prim Sch CV23 .. 117 E8
Badbury Cl B80 .... 103 E2
Badby Cty Prim Sch NN11 126 F6
Badby Leys CV22 .... 100 A4
Baddesley Cl [30] CV31 .. 110 B3
Baddesley Clinton B93 .... 89 F2
Baddesley Ensor CE
  Inf Sch CV9 .... 11 E1
Baddesley Ensor Jun Sch
  CV9 .... 11 E1
Badger Cl B90 .... 70 B2
Badger Rd CV3 .... 78 B4
Badgers Cres CV9 .... 149 F4
Badgers Farm La CV35 .. 138 C8
Badgers Field GL55 .... 135 B2
Baffin Cl CV22 .... 82 C1
Baginton Fields Sch CV3 .. 78 A2
Baginton Rd Birmingham B35 22 A2
  Coventry CV3 .... 77 E3
Bagshaw Cl CV8 .... 79 D1
Bailey Ave B77 .... 9 F3
Bailey's La CV23 .... 82 A2
Bakehouse La
  Chadwick End B93 .... 90 A3
  Nether Whitacre B46 ...... 24 C3
  Rugby CV21 .... 82 C2
  Shotteswell OX17 .... 139 E8
Baker Ave
  Royal Leamington Spa CV31 109 F3
  Stratford-u-A CV37 .... 144 B2
Baker St CV6 .... 50 A3
Baker's Hill GL55 .... 135 C5
Bakers Croft CV9 .... 11 E1
Bakers Ct CV9 .... 18 B4
Bakers La Coventry CV5 .. 60 C1
  Knowle B93 .... 72 B1
  Swadcliffe OX15 .... 142 F8
Bakers Wlk B77 .... 9 F3
Bakewell Cl CV3 .... 78 C4
Balcombe Ct CV22 .... 100 C4
Balcombe Rd CV22 .... 100 B4
Baldwin Croft CV6 .... 50 A1
Baldwins La CV35 .... 138 B6
Balfour CF LE10 .... 31 F4
Ballantine Rd CV6 .... 61 D3
Ballard Wlk B37 .... 33 D3
Ballards Cl GL55 .... 135 B6
Ballards La CV36 .... 136 B6
Ballingham Cl CV4 .... 60 A1
Balliol Rd Coventry CV2 .. 62 B2
  Hinckley LE10 .... 31 F3
Balmoral Ave Banbury OX16 139 F3
  Banbury, Crouch Hill OX16 .. 139 F2
Balmoral Cl CV2 .... 62 C3
Balmoral Rd B36 .... 33 D4
Balmoral Way CV32 .... 106 A3
Balsall Common Prim Sch
  CV7 .... 74 A3
Balsall St B93, CV7 .... 73 E4
Balsall St E CV7 .... 74 A3
Bamburgh B77 .... 9 E4
Bamburgh Gr CV32 .... 105 F2
Ban Brook Rd WR11 .... 127 F6
Banbury Rd
  Bishops Tachbrook CV33 122 E7
  Chipping Warden OX17 .. 134 F3
  Ettington CV37 .... 131 B3
  Kineton CV35 .... 132 C5
  Ladbroke CV33 .... 124 D4
  Lower Boddington NN11 .. 134 E7
  North Newington OX15 .. 139 E2
  Shutford OX15 .... 139 A3
  Southam CV33 .... 147 D1
  Southam CV33 .... 147 D2
  Stratford-u-A CV37 .... 130 D7
  Swerford OX7 .... 142 E1
  Warmington OX17 .... 133 D1
  Warwick CV34 .... 109 D2
Banbury St CV35 .... 132 B5
Bancroft Pl CV37 .... 145 D2
Bangley La Drayton Bassett B78 7 F3
  Mile Oak B78 .... 8 A1
Banister Way CV36 .... 149 F3
Bank Cl CV35 .... 131 F5
Bank Croft CV31 .... 110 B3
Bank Rd CV9 .... 18 C4
Bank St CV21 .... 83 D2
Bank The Bidford-on-A B50 148 B2
  Bidford-on-A, Marlcliff B50 .. 148 B1
  Lighthorne CV35 .... 123 B2
Bank View CV35 .... 131 F5
Bankfield Dr CV31 .... 105 E1
Banks Rd CV6 .... 61 D3
Bankside CV3 .... 78 A3
Banky Mdw LE10 .... 32 A4
Banner La CV4 .... 59 E1
Banners La B97 .... 102 C3
Bantam Gr CV6 .... 49 D2
Bantock Rd CV4 .... 59 F1
Barber Wlk CV35 .... 114 F4
Barbers La B91 .... 56 B3
Barbican Rise CV2 .... 62 C1

Barbourne Cl B91 .... 71 D4
Barbridge Cl CV12 .... 40 B1
Barbridge Rd CV12 .... 40 B2
Barby CE Prim Sch CV23 .. 117 E8
Barby La CV22 .... 101 D2
Barby Rd Kilsby CV23 .... 101 F2
  Rugby CV22 .... 100 A4
Barcheston Rd B93 .... 72 A2
Barcombe Cl CV6 .... 139 F5
Bardon View Rd B78 ...... 11 D4
Barford App CV31 .... 110 A1
Barford Cl CV3 .... 78 B4
Barford Rd B36 .... 93 D2
Barham Cl [7] B90 .... 71 D3
Bari Rd CV35 .... 132 E5
Barker's Butts La CV6 .... 61 D2
Barkers' Butts La CV1 .... 61 D3
Barkers La B47 .... 69 D1
Barkus Cl CV33 .... 147 E2
Barle Gr B36 .... 33 D4
Barley Cl Henley-In-A B95 .. 113 B4
  Rugby CV21 .... 101 D4
  Sibford Gower OX15 ...... 142 D8
Barley Lea The CV3 .... 78 B4
Barlichway B49 .... 143 E2
Barlow Rd CV2 .... 50 B1
Barn Cl
  Clifford Chambers CV37 129 F7
  Dordon B78 .... 10 C3
  Whitnash CV31 .... 110 A2
Barn End Rd B79 .... 5 F2
Barn La CV23 .... 96 B1
Barnack Ave CV3 .... 77 D3
Barnack Dr CV34 .... 104 C1
Barnacle La CV12 .... 40 B1
Barnard Cl Birmingham B37 33 E1
  Royal Leamington Spa CV32 106 B2
Barnbrook Rd B93 .... 72 A4
Barncroft CV36 .... 141 C3
Barne Cl CV11 .... 40 A4
Barnfield Ave CV5 .... 60 A3
Barnsley Cl CV9 .... 18 B4
Barnstaple Cl CV5 .... 59 F3
Barnwell Cl CV22 .... 99 E2
Baron's Croft CV3 .... 77 F4
Baron's Field Rd CV3 ...... 77 F4
Barons Croft CV10 .... 28 B2
Barpool Rd CV10 .... 28 C2
Barr La Brinklow CV23 .... 64 C2
  Higham-on-t-H CV13 .... 21 D2
Barra Croft B35 .... 22 A2
Barrack St CV34 .... 108 C4
Barracks Gn CV35 .... 130 F7
Barracks La CV35 .... 91 E1
Barracks Way CV1 .... 151 B2
Barras Gn CV2 .... 62 A2
Barras La CV1 .... 61 D2
Barretts La CV7 .... 74 B3
Barrington Rd CV22 .... 82 B1
Barrow Cl CV2 .... 63 D3
Barrow Rd CV8 .... 92 C2
Barrowfield La CV8 .... 92 C3
Barrs Hill Sch & Com Coll
  CV1 .... 151 A4
Barsby Cl CV9 .... 18 B4
Barston Cl CV6 .... 50 A1
Barston La
  Balsall Common CV7 ...... 73 E4
  Barston B92 .... 57 E1
  Catherine de B B91 .... 56 A1
  Hampton in A B92 .... 56 B2
Bartleet Rd B98 .... 103 F4
Bartlett Cl Coventry CV6 .. 49 F1
  [8] Warwick CV34 .... 108 C4
Barton Cres CV31 .... 110 B3
Barton Dr B93 .... 72 A2
Barton Fields CV37 .... 129 A6
Barton Rd Bedworth CV12 39 D2
  Coventry CV6 .... 49 F1
  Long Compton CV36 ...... 141 B4
  Nuneaton CV10 .... 29 E1
  Rugby CV22 .... 99 E4
Barton's Mdw CV2 .... 62 A3
Barwell Cl Dorridge B93 .. 71 F2
  Royal Leamington Spa CV32 105 F2
Basant Cl CV34 .... 109 D4
Bascote Cl CV33 .... 115 C3
Bascote Rise CV33 .... 147 D3
Basford Brook Dr CV6 .... 49 F4
Basildon Wlk [3] CV2 .... 63 D4
Basin Bridge La CV13 .... 21 E2
Basley Way CV6 .... 49 E2
Bassett Rd CV6 .... 61 D3
Bastyan Ave CV37 .... 129 D2
Bateman Rd B46 .... 23 F1
Bateman's Acre S [1] CV6 .. 61 D2
Bates Cl B76 .... 22 A4
Bates La B94 .... 86 C1
Bates Rd CV5 .... 76 C4
Bath Pl [14] CV1 .... 109 F4
  Nuneaton CV11 .... 29 E3
Bath Rd Atherstone CV9 .. 18 C4
  Nuneaton CV11 .... 29 E3
Bath St Coventry CV1 .... 151 C4
  Royal Leamington Spa CV31 .. 109 F4
  Rugby CV21 .... 83 D2
Bathurst Rd CV6 .... 61 D3
Bathway Rd CV3 .... 77 D2
Batsford Cl B98 .... 103 D3
Batsford Rd CV6 .... 60 C2
Battle Ct CV35 .... 132 B6
Baulk La CV7 .... 58 B1
Bawnmore Ct CV22 .... 99 E3
Bawnmore Cty Fst Sch CV22 99 F4
Bawnmore Pk CV22 .... 99 E3
Bawnmore Rd CV22 .... 99 E4
Baxter Cl CV4 .... 60 A1
Baxter Ct [9] CV31 .... 110 A4
Baxters Gn B90 .... 70 A4

Baxters Rd B90 .... 70 A4
Bay Tree Cl CV2 .... 50 B1
Bayley La CV1 .... 151 C2
Bayton Rd CV7 .... 50 A4
Bayton Road Ind Est CV7 .. 50 A4
Bayton Way CV7 .... 50 B4
Baywell Cl [8] B90 .... 71 D4
Bazzard La CV11 .... 40 C3
Beacon Cl B49 .... 143 E3
Beacon Rd CV6 .... 49 E2
Beaconsfield Ave CV22 .. 83 D1
Beaconsfield Ct CV11 .... 29 E3
Beaconsfield Rd CV2 ...... 62 A1
Beaconsfield St CV31 .... 110 A4
Beaconsfield St W CV31 110 A4
Beake Ave CV6 .... 61 D4
Beamish Cl CV2 .... 63 D3
Beanacre Rd OX15 .... 142 D3
Beanfield Ave CV3 .... 76 C2
Bear Cl B95 .... 113 B5
Bear La B95 .... 113 A5
Bear La B78 .... 5 D1
Bearcroft Gdns GL55 ...... 135 C6
Bearley Croft B90 .... 70 B4
Bearley Cty Jun & Inf Sch
  CV37 .... 120 D7
Bearley Gn CV37 .... 120 E7
Bearley Halt B95 .... 120 D7
Bearley Rd
  Aston Cantlow B95 .... 120 A7
  Snitterfield CV37 .... 121 A7
Beatty Dr CV22 .... 82 B1
Beauchamp Ave CV32 .... 105 F1
Beauchamp Cl
  [1] Birmingham B37 ...... 33 D1
  Sutton Coldfield B76 .... 22 A4
Beauchamp Gdns CV34 .. 109 D3
Beauchamp Hill CV32 .... 105 F1
Beauchamp Ind Pk B77 .. 9 E4
Beauchamp Rd
  Alcester B49 .... 143 E3
  Kenilworth CV8 .... 92 C1
  Royal Leamington Spa CV32 .. 9 F3
  Tamworth B77 .... 9 F3
  Warwick CV34 .... 109 D4
Beaudesert Cl
  Henley-in-A B95 .... 113 B4
  Hollywood B47 .... 69 D3
Beaudesert La B95 .... 113 B5
Beaudesert Rd Coventry CV5 69 D1
  Hollywood B47 .... 69 D3
Beaudesert St Mary's RC
  Prim Sch B95 .... 113 B4
Beaufell Cl CV34 .... 104 C1
Beaufort Ave CV32 .... 106 B3
Beaufort Cl Hinckley LE10 31 D4
  Wellesbourne CV35 ...... 146 B1
Beaufort Dr CV3 .... 78 C4
Beaulieu Pk CV31 .... 110 B1
Beaumaris Cl Banbury OX16 139 F4
  Coventry CV5 .... 59 F3
Beaumont Ave LE10 ...... 31 D4
Beaumont Cl CV33 .... 133 D4
Beaumont Cres CV6 ...... 61 D2
Beaumont Pl CV11 .... 29 D2
Beaumont Rd Keresley CV7 49 D3
  Nuneaton CV11 .... 29 D2
Beausale Croft CV5 .... 60 A2
Beausale Dr B93 .... 72 B4
Beausale La CV35 .... 114 E7
Beck's La CV23 .... 147 F4
Beck's La CV23 .... 147 F4
Beckbury Rd CV2 .... 62 C3
Becket Cl GL56 .... 140 E7
Beckfoot Cl CV21 .... 83 E4
Beckfoot Dr CV2 .... 50 C1
Beckford Croft B93 .... 71 F2
Beconsfield Cl B93 .... 71 F1
Bedale Rd B35 .... 132 D4
Bede Rd Bedworth CV12 .. 39 D2
  Coventry CV6 .... 61 D3
  Nuneaton CV10 .... 28 B2
Bedford Cl OX16 .... 139 F4
Bedford Pl CV32 .... 109 F4
Bedford St Coventry CV1 61 D1
  Royal Leamington Spa CV32 .. 109 F4
Bedlam La CV6 .... 49 F1
Bedworth Cl CV12 .... 40 A1
Bedworth La CV12 .... 38 B2
Bedworth Rd Bedworth CV12 39 F1
  Bulkington CV12 .... 40 A1
  Coventry CV6 .... 50 A3
Bedworth Sta CV12 .... 39 E1
Beech Ave B37 .... 33 D1
Beech Cl Alcester B49 .... 143 E1
  Hartshill CV10 .... 28 A4
  Hurley CV9 .... 16 B3
  Kingsbury B78 .... 15 E4
  Rowington B95 .... 114 A8
  Southam CV33 .... 147 D2
  Stratford-u-A CV37 .... 145 D1
Beech Cliffe CV34 .... 108 C4
Beech Ct
  Royal Leamington Spa CV34 109 F1
  Rugby CV22 .... 100 C4
  Stratford-u-A CV37 .... 145 D1
Beech Dr Kenilworth CV8 .. 93 D4
  Rugby CV22 .... 99 E4
  Thurlaston CV23 .... 98 C2
Beech Gr Arley CV7 .... 26 C1
  Warwick CV34 .... 105 D1
Beech Rd Coventry CV6 .. 61 D3
  Hollywood B47 .... 69 D3
  Oxhill CV35 .... 137 F8
Beech Tree Ave CV4 ...... 60 A1
Beecham Wlk CV37 .... 144 B2
Beechcroft Birmingham B36 .. 22 B1
  Long Itchington CV23 .. 115 D4
Beecher's Keep CV8 ...... 79 F3
Beeches The Bedworth CV12 38 C1
  Harbury CV33 .... 123 E7
  Polesworth B78 .... 11 D4
Beeches Wlk CV37 .... 145 F2
Beechtree Pk B50 .... 148 C3
Beechwood Ave
  Coventry CV5 .... 76 C4
  Hinckley LE10 .... 31 F3
Beechwood Cl B90 .... 70 B2
Beechwood Croft CV8 .... 92 C1
Beechwood Rd
  Bedworth CV12 .... 39 E2
  Nuneaton CV10 .... 28 B3
Beehive Hill CV8 .... 92 C4
Beehive La B76 .... 23 E3
Beeston Cl CV3 .... 78 C4
Begonia Cl LE10 .... 31 F3
Begonia Dr LE10 .... 31 F3
Belcony GL56 .... 136 C1
Belgrave Dr CV21 .... 83 E3
Belgrave Rd Coventry CV2 62 C2
  Tamworth B77 .... 9 F4
Belgrave Sq CV2 .... 62 C2
Bell Brook CV37 .... 121 B6
Bell Cl B36 .... 33 D3
Bell Ct CV37 .... 145 D1
Bell Dr CV7 .... 49 F4
Bell Green Rd CV6 .... 62 A4
Bell Hill OX15 .... 142 D4
Bell La Monks Kirby CV23 .. 53 F1
  Snitterfield CV37 .... 121 B6
  Stratford-u-A CV37 .... 144 B1
  Studley B80 .... 103 F2
Bell Mead B80 .... 103 F2
Bell St Claybrooke Magna LE17 43 F3
  Hornton OX15 .... 139 B7
Bell Tower Mews CV32 .. 105 F2
Bell Wlk CV21 .... 101 D4
Bell's La OX15 .... 142 D4
Bellairs Ave CV12 .... 38 C1
Bellam Rd CV35 .... 114 F4
Bellbrooke Cl CV6 .... 50 A1
Belle Cotts B94 .... 88 C3
Belle Vue CV10 .... 28 C2
Belle Vue Terr B92 .... 57 D3
Bellemere Rd B92 .... 57 D3
Bellfield B94 .... 87 D1
Bellingham B77 .... 4 B1
Bellington Croft [5] B90 71 D3
Bells La OX15 .... 137 E3
Bellview Way CV6 .... 50 A1
Belmont Dr CV32 .... 106 A2
Belmont Rd Coventry CV6 62 A4
  Rugby CV21 .... 83 D1
  Tamworth B77 .... 9 F4
Belton Cl B94 .... 88 B3
Belvedere Rd CV5 .... 77 D4
Belvoir B77 .... 9 E4
Benedictine Rd CV3 ...... 77 E4
Bengrove Cl B98 .... 103 D4
Benn Cl CV12 .... 40 A1
Benn St CV22 .... 83 E1
Bennet Cl CV13 .... 21 E4
Bennett Ct CV8 .... 79 F2
Bennett Dr CV34 .... 109 E4
Bennett Pl CV36 .... 136 B6
Bennett St CV21 .... 82 C2
Bennett's Rd CV7 .... 48 C2
Bennett's Rd N CV7 ...... 48 C4
Bennett's Rd S CV6 ...... 48 C1
Bennfield Rd CV21 .... 83 D2
Benson Rd Coventry CV6 49 D1
  Stratford-u-A CV37 .... 145 D2
Benthall Rd CV6 .... 49 F2
Bentley Cl Banbury OX16 139 F4
  Royal Leamington Spa CV32 106 A2
Bentley Ct CV6 .... 49 E2
Bentley Farm Cl B93 ...... 71 F2
Bentley Heath CE Jun &
  Inf Sch B93 .... 71 F3
Bentley La B46 .... 35 E2
Bentley Rd Bedworth CV7 39 D1
  Nuneaton CV11 .... 29 D2
Bentley Way NN11 .... 117 F2
Benton Green La CV7 .... 58 C1
Bentree The CV3 .... 78 A4
Beoley La B98 .... 86 A1
Berenska Dr CV32 .... 106 A1
Beresford Ave CV6 .... 49 F1
Bericote Rd CV32 .... 105 F4
Berkeley Cl Banbury OX16 139 F4
  Nuneaton CV11 .... 29 E2
  Redditch B98 .... 112 A6
Berkeley Rd CV8 .... 92 C3
Berkeley Rd N CV5 .... 61 D1
Berkeley Rd S CV5 .... 77 D4
Berkett Rd CV6 .... 49 D1
Berkshire Cl CV10 .... 29 D3
Berners Cl CV4 .... 59 F1
Berrills La CV9 .... 141 D7
Berrington Rd
  Chipping Campden GL55 .. 135 C2
  Nuneaton CV10 .... 28 B4
  Royal Leamington Spa CV31 110 A3
Berry Ave CV36 .... 149 F3

Berry Cl CV36 149 F3
Berry Hall La B91 56 A2
Berry Mdw CV33 133 E7
Berry St CV1 61 F2
Berryfields CV7 36 C2
Berryfields La CV37 136 C7
Berrymound View B47 69 E4
Bertie Rd CV8 93 D2
Berwick Cl Coventry CV5 60 A2
Warwick CV34 104 C1
Berwicks La B37 33 D1
Berwyn Ave CV6 49 D1
Berwyn Way CV10 28 B2
Besbury Cl B93 71 F1
Besford Gr B90 71 D3
Best Ave CV8 93 E4
Beswick Gdns CV22 99 E4
Bettina Cl CV10 28 A3
Bettman Cl CV3 77 F3
Bettridge Pl CV35 146 B2
Beverley Ave CV10 28 A2
Beverley Cl
Astwood Bank B96 102 C1
Balsall Common CV7 74 B4
Beverley Rd CV32 105 E1
Beverly Dr CV4 76 B1
Bevington Cres CV6 60 C3
Bexfield Cl CV5 60 A3
Beyer Cl B77 4 A1
Biart Pl CV21 83 E2
Bicester Sq B35 22 A2
Bickenhill La Birmingham B40 44 B2
Catherine de B B91 56 B3
Bickenhill Parkway B37 44 B3
Bickenhill Rd B37 44 A4
Bickmarsh La B50 148 B1
Bidavon Ind Est B50 148 C3
Biddles Hill B94 86 B3
Bideford Rd CV2 62 B4
Bidford on Avon CE Jun Sch B50 148 B2
Bidford Rd B50 148 B4
Bigbury Cl CV3 77 F3
Biggin Cl B35 22 A2
Biggin Hall Cres CV3 62 A1
Biggin Hall La CV23 98 C1
Bignolds Cl OX17 134 B4
Bigwood Dr B75 13 D3
Bilberry Rd CV2 50 B1
Bilbury Cl B97 102 B3
Billesden Cl CV3 78 C4
Billesley La B48 85 F3
Billesley Rd CV37 120 C4
Billing Rd CV5 60 B2
Billingham Cl B91 71 D4
Billington Cl CV2 62 C1
Bills La B90 69 F4
Bilton CE Mid Sch CV22 99 E3
Bilton Cty Fst Sch CV22 99 E4
Bilton Grange Sch CV22 99 F2
Bilton High Sch CV22 82 A1
Bilton Ind Est CV3 61 F1
Bilton La Dunchurch CV22 99 E2
Long Lawford CV23 82 A2
Bilton Rd CV22 82 C1
Binley Ave CV3 78 C4
Binley Cl B90 70 A4
Binley Gr CV3 78 C4
Binley Ind Est CV3 79 D4
Binley Rd CV2, CV3 62 B1
Binley Woods Cty Prim Sch CV3 79 F4
Binns Cl CV4 75 F4
Binswood Ave CV32 105 F1
Binswood Cl CV2 50 B1
Binswood End CV33 123 E7
Binswood Mans 15 CV32 105 F1
Binswood St CV32 105 F1
Binton Rd Coventry CV2 50 B1
Welford on A CV37 129 A7
Bintonhill CV37 120 A1
Birch Abbey B49 143 D2
Birch Cl Bedworth CV12 39 E2
Coventry CV5 59 F3
Kingsbury B78 15 E4
Birch Croft B37 33 E1
Birch Ct CV34 109 F1
Birch Dr CV22 82 A1
Birch Gr Birchmoor B78 10 B4
Wellesbourne CV35 146 C2
Birches La CV8 93 D2
Birches The CV12 40 A2
Birchfield Cl CV9 10 B1
Birchfield Rd Coventry CV6 60 C4
Stratford-u-A CV37 145 D3
Birchgrave Cl CV6 62 A4
Birchley Heath Rd CV10 17 F1
Birchmoor Rd B78 10 C4
Birchtree Rd CV10 28 B3
Birchway Cl 2 CV32 105 E1
Birchwood Ave B78 10 C4
Birchwood Prim Sch B78 10 C4
Birchwood Rd CV3 79 E4
Birchy Cl B90 69 F3
Birchy Leasowes La B90 69 F3
Bird Grove Ct CV1 61 E3
Bird Rd
Lighthorne Heath CV35 123 D2
Royal Leamington Spa CV34 109 E2
Bird St CV1 151 C3
Birdhaven Cl CV35 123 D2
Birdhope B77 4 B1
Birdingbury La CV23 115 E8
Birdingbury Rd
Birdingbury CV23 115 F8
Marton CV23 115 D7
Birds Bush Cty Prim Sch B77 9 F4
Birds Bush Rd B77 9 F4
Birds La OX15 138 D3
Birkdale Cl CV11 30 A1
Birmingham Bsns Pk B37 44 C4
Birmingham Int Airport B40 44 A2
Birmingham Int Sta B40 44 B2
Birmingham Rd
Alcester B49 143 D2
Allesley CV5 59 F4
Ansley CV10 27 D2
Burton Green CV8 75 D1
Coleshill B46 33 F3
Henley-In-A B95 113 B6
Kenilworth CV8 92 B4
Little Packington CV7 45 F2
Nether Whitacre B46 24 B4
Shrewley CV35 114 D6
Stoneleigh CV8 94 A3
Stratford-u-A CV37 144 C3
Studley B80 103 F4
Warwick CV34 108 B4
Water Orton B46 23 D2
Wilmcote CV37 120 D6
Wroxall B93, CV35 90 B2
Birstall Dr CV21 83 E3
Bishop Carpenter CE Prim Sch Ox15 139 D2
Bishop St CV1 151 B3
Bishop Ullathorne RC Sch CV3 76 C2
Bishop Wilson CE Prim Sch B37 33 E2
Bishop Wulstan RC High Sch CV22 83 D1
Bishop's Hill CV35 123 B2
Bishop's Itchington Sch CV33 124 B4
Bishop's Tachbrook CE Prim Sch CV35 122 F8
Bishopgate Bsns Pk CV1 61 E3
Bishopgate Ind Est CV1 61 E3
Bishops Bowl Lakes Water Sports Ctr CV33 124 A5
Bishops Cl
16 Bishops Tachbrook CV33 122 F8
Stratford-u-A CV37 144 B2
Bishops Cleeve CV9 3 D1
Bishops Gate CV33 124 B5
Bishops Wlk CV5 77 D4
Bishopton Cl CV5 60 A2
Bishopton La CV37 144 B3
Bishopton Prim Sch CV37 144 B2
Bisset Cres 21 CV31 110 B3
Bitham Rd CV35 123 D3
Bixhill La B46 25 D2
Black Bank CV7 39 D1
Black Hall La CV7 36 B2
Black Horse Hill DE12 3 F4
Black Horse Rd CV6 50 A3
Black La CV32 106 B1
Black Prince Ave CV3 77 F3
Black-A-Tree Rd CV10 28 C2
Blackberry Ave B94 88 B3
Blackberry Cl CV23 83 E4
Blackberry La Ash Green CV7 49 E3
Coventry CV2 62 B3
Blackbird Croft B36 33 D4
Blackburn Rd CV6 49 F2
Blackcat Cl B37 33 D2
Blackdown B77 4 B1
Blackdown Rd B93 72 A3
Blackfirs La B37, B46 44 B4
Blackford Hill B95 113 B4
Blackford Rd B90 70 B4
Blackford Way CV35 137 F8
Blackgreaves La B76 14 C1
Blacklow Rd CV34 105 D1
Blackman Way CV21 82 C2
Blackshaw Dr CV2 62 C3
Blacksmith's La NN11 134 F5
Blacksmiths Cl WR11 127 F1
Blacksmiths La
Hockley Heath B94 88 B3
Littleton WR11 127 F1
Mollington OX17 134 A2
Blacksmiths Yd CV13 21 E4
Blackthorn Cl CV4 76 B3
Blackthorn Gr CV11 29 F1
Blackthorn Rd CV37 145 D3
Blackthorn Way B49 143 D3
Blackthorne Rd CV8 93 D2
Blackwatch Rd CV6 61 E4
Blackwell Rd Coventry CV6 61 F4
Tredington CV36 136 F6
Blackwood Ave CV22 82 B1
Blackwood Rd B77 9 E4
Blacon Way CV37 144 B2
Bladon Cl CV11 29 F4
Bladon Wlk 14 CV31 110 B3
Blair Dr CV12 38 B1
Blair Gr B37 33 E1
Blake Cl Nuneaton CV10 28 A3
Rugby CV22 82 B1
Blake's Hill WR11, CV37 128 B1
Blakelands Ave CV31 110 A3
Blakenhurst WR11 127 C4
Blandford Ave B36 22 C1
Blandford Dr CV2 62 C3
Blandford Rd 1 CV32 105 E1
Blandford Way CV35 108 A4
Blaze La B96, B97 102 A2
Bleaberry CV21 83 E4
Bleachfield St B49 143 D2
Blenheim Ave CV6 49 E1
Blenheim Cl
Bidford-on-A B50 148 B3
Nuneaton CV11 29 F1
Blenheim Cres 29 CV31 110 B3
Blenheim Wlk CV35 146 B1
Bletchley Dr CV5 60 A2
Blewgates OX15 137 F2
Blewitt Cl B36 22 B1
Blick Rd CV34 109 E2
Blind La Berkswell CV7 58 B2
Chipping Campden GL55 135 A1
Tanworth-In-A B94 86 B1
Blindpit La B76 23 D4
Bliss Cl CV4 59 F2
Blockley Rd CV12 39 E2
Blondvil St CV3 77 E4
Bloxam Gdns CV22 82 C1
Bloxam Mid Sch CV22 82 C1
Bloxam Pl CV21 83 D2
Bloxham Rd OX16 139 F1
Blue Cap Rd CV37 145 D3
Blue Coat CE Sch CV1 61 F1
Blue La CV35 130 E6
Blue Lake Rd B93 72 A1
Bluebell Cl CV23 83 E4
Bluebell Dr B37 33 F1
Bluebellwood Cl B76 13 D2
Blundells Croft CV37 129 A7
Blundells The CV8 93 D3
Blyth Ave CV7 74 B3
Blyth Cl CV12 38 B1
Blythe Cl B97 102 B4
Blythe Rd Coleshill B46 34 A4
Coventry CV1 61 F2
Boar Croft CV4 59 F1
Boat La CV37 129 A7
Bockendon Rd CV4 75 F3
Boddington Cl CV32 106 C3
Boddington Rd OX17 134 B5
Bodmin Rd CV2 62 C3
Bodnant Way CV8 93 E3
Bodymoor Heath La B76 15 D2
Bohun St CV4 59 F1
Boleyn Cl CV34 109 E3
Bolingbroke Rd CV3 62 A1
Bolton Cl CV3 77 F3
Bolyfant Cl CV31 110 A1
Bond Dr B35 22 A2
Bond End CV23 53 F2
Bond Gate CV11 29 E2
Bond St Coventry CV1 151 B3
Nuneaton CV11 29 E3
Rugby CV21 82 C2
Boningale Way B93 71 F2
Bonington Dr CV12 39 D2
Bonneville Cl CV5 59 D4
Bonniksen Cl CV31 109 F3
Bonnington Cl CV21 84 A1
Boot Hill CV9 11 E1
Booths Fields CV6 49 F1
Bordesley Ct CV32 106 A2
Bordon Hill CV37 144 B1
Bordon Pl CV37 144 C1
Borough The LE10 31 E4
Borrowdale CV21 83 E4
Borrowdale Cl CV6 61 D4
Borrowdale Dr CV32 105 E1
Borrowell La CV8 92 C2
Boscobel Rd B90 70 B3
Bosley Cl CV36 149 F2
Bostock Cres CV33 107 E4
Boston Pl CV6 61 E4
Boswell Dr CV2 63 D4
Boswell Gr CV34 104 B1
Boswell Rd CV22 99 F4
Bosworth Dr B37 33 D1
Bosworth Wood Jun & Inf Sch B36 22 C1
Boteler Cl B49 143 D2
Botoner Rd CV1 61 F1
Bott Rd CV5 76 B4
Bott's La DE12 3 F4
Bottrill St CV11 29 D3
Botts Green La B46 25 E3
Boucher Cl CV37 144 B1
Boughton Leigh Cty Inf Sch CV21 83 E4
Boughton Leigh Jun Sch CV21 83 E4
Boughton Rd CV21 83 E3
Boulters La CV9 10 B1
Boultons La B97 102 B3
Boundary Rd CV21 83 E1
Bourne Brook Cl CV7 36 C2
Bourne Cl CV9 12 C1
Bourne End CV33 147 D2
Bourne La OX15 142 D4
Bourne Rd CV3 62 B1
Bourne The OX15 142 D4
Bournebrook View CV7 26 C1
Bourton Dr CV31 110 A3
Bourton La CV23 115 F8
Bourton Rd Frankton CV23 97 E1
Moreton-in-M GL56 140 A3
Bouts La WR7 118 B5
Bovey Croft B76 22 A4
Bovingdon Rd B35 22 A3
Bow Fell CV21 83 E4
Bow La CV7 53 D2
Bowbrook Ave B90 71 D3
Bowden Way CV3 62 C1
Bowen Rd CV22 83 E1
Bowers Croft CV32 106 A3
Bowes Lyon Cl GL56 140 A2
Bowfell Cl CV5 60 A2
Bowley's La DE12 3 F4
Bowling Green Ave B77 9 F4
Bowling Green Ct GL56 140 A3
Bowling Green La CV7, CV12 49 F4
Bowling Green St CV34 108 B3
Bowls Ct CV5 60 C2
Bowman Gn LE10 31 F3
Bowness Cl CV6 61 D4
Bowshot Cl B36 22 B1
Box Cl CV31 110 A2
Box Rd B37 44 B4
Box Trees Rd B93 71 E1
Boxhill The CV3 62 A1
Boyce Way CV23 82 A3
Boyd Cl CV2 63 D4
Boyslade Rd LE10 31 F3
Boyslade Rd E LE10 31 F3
Bracadale Cl CV3 63 D1
Bracebridge Cl CV7 74 A3
Bracebridge Rd
Atherstone CV9 18 B4
Kingsbury B78 15 E3
Bracebridge St CV11 29 D2
Bracken Cl CV22 82 C1
Bracken Croft 1 B37 33 E2
Bracken Dr Rugby CV22 82 C1
Sutton Coldfield B75 13 D3
Wolvey LE10 41 E2
Brackendale Dr Barby CV23 101 E1
Nuneaton CV10 28 C2
Brackenhurst Rd CV6 61 D4
Bracklesham Way B77 4 A3
Brackley Cl CV6 60 C4
Bracknell Wlk 1 CV2 63 D4
Braddock Cl CV3 63 D1
Brade Dr CV2 63 D4
Bradestone Rd CV11 29 E1
Bradewell Rd B36 22 B1
Bradford Rd 6 CV33 122 E8
Brading Rd CV10 29 E3
Bradley Croft CV7 74 A3
Bradney Gn CV4 75 F4
Bradnick Pl CV4 59 F1
Bradnock's Marsh La B92 57 F1
Braemar Cl CV2 62 C3
Braemar Rd CV32 106 A2
Braemar Way CV10 29 D1
Braeside Croft B37 33 E1
Brafield Leys CV22 100 A3
Braggington La CV37 128 F5
Braggs Farm La B90 70 A2
Brailes CE Prim Sch OX15 137 E2
Brain St B77 4 A1
Brakesmead CV31 109 F3
Bramber Cl OX16 139 F4
Bramble Cl 4 Coleshill B46 33 F4
Nuneaton CV11 29 F1
Bramble St CV1 61 F1
Brambles The B76 22 A4
Brambling B77 10 A4
Bramcote Cl CV12 40 B1
Bramcote Hospl CV11 40 C4
Bramdene Ave CV10 29 E4
Bramley Dr B47 69 D3
Bramley Rd CV35 132 E6
Brampton Way CV12 40 A2
Bramshall Dr B93 71 F2
Bramston Cres CV4 59 F1
Bramwell Gdns CV6 49 F3
Brancaster Cl B77 4 A3
Brandfield Rd CV6 60 C4
Brandon La CV3, CV8 79 E3
Brandon Marsh Nature Reserve CV8 79 D2
Brandon Marsh Visitor Ctr CV8 79 D2
Brandon Par CV32 110 A4
Brandon Rd Bretford CV23 80 B3
Coventry CV3 79 D4
Hinckley LE10 31 D4
Branksome Rd CV6 60 C3
Bransdale Ave CV6 49 E2
Bransford Ave CV4 76 B3
Bransford Rise B91 56 A3
Branstree Dr CV6 49 E1
Brascote Rd LE10 30 C4
Bratches The GL55 135 B3
Brathay Cl CV3 77 E3
Braunston Cl B76 13 D1
Braunston Jun & Inf Sch NN11 117 E5
Braunston La NN11 126 E8
Braunston Pl CV22 100 B4
Braunston Rd NN11 117 F2
Bray Bank B46 25 E2
Bray's La CV2 62 A2
Brayford Ave CV3 77 E3
Brays Cl CV23 64 C2
Braytoft Cl CV6 49 E1
Brazil St CV4 59 F1
Breach La CV35 113 F3
Breach Oak La CV7 37 E2
Breaches La B98 103 E4
Bream B77 9 E4
Bream Cl B37 33 E1
Brechin Cl LE10 31 D4
Bredon Ave CV3 78 C4
Bredon View B97 102 B4
Bree Cl CV5 60 A4
Bree's La CV8 74 A1
Breeden Dr B76 23 D3
Brendan Cl B46 34 A3
Brendon B77 4 A1
Brendon Way CV10 28 A2
Brenfield Dr LE10 31 D4
Brent B77 9 F4
Brentwood Ave CV3 77 E2
Brese Ave CV34 104 C1
Bretch Hill OX16 139 F3
Bretford Rd CV2 50 B1
Bretshall Cl B90 70 C3
Bretts Cl CV1 151 D4
Brewer Rd CV12 40 B1
Brewers Cl CV3 63 D1
Brewery La OX15 142 C4
Brewery Row GL56 140 F1
Brewery St CV37 144 C2
Brewster Cl CV2 62 C1
Briansway CV6 49 F2
Briar B77 4 A2
Briar Cl Hinckley LE10 31 F3
Royal Leamington Spa CV32 106 A1
Briar Hill Cty Fst Sch CV31 110 A2
Briardene Ave CV12 39 D1
Briarmead LE10 31 F2
Briars Cl Coventry CV2 62 B1
Long Lawford CV23 82 A2
Nuneaton CV11 29 F3
Briarwood Cl B90 70 B2
Brick Hill OX15 142 D3
Brick Hill La CV5 59 F4
Brick Kiln La Middleton B78 14 B3
Solihull B90 70 C4
Brick Kiln St LE10 31 E4
Brickhill Cl CV36 149 F3
Brickhill Dr B37 33 D1
Brickkiln La CV9 16 A2
Brickyard La B80 103 E2
Bridal Path The CV5 60 A3
Bridge End Southam CV33 147 D2
Warwick CV34 108 C3
Bridge Foot CV37 145 D1
Bridge La Ladbroke CV33 124 D5
Witherley CV9 19 D4
Bridge Meadow Dr B93 71 F3
Bridge Rd LE10 31 E4
Bridge St Barford CV35 122 A7
Coventry CV6 62 A4
Fenny Compton CV33 133 D7
Hampton Lucy CV35 121 F4
Hurley CV9 16 B2
Kenilworth CV8 92 C3
Kineton CV35 132 B5
Nuneaton CV11 29 E2
Nuneaton, Chilvers Coton CV11 29 E1
Polesworth B78 5 D1
Rugby CV21 83 E2
Stratford-u-A CV37 145 D1
Warwick CV34 109 E4
Wellesbourne CV35 146 B2
Bridge Town Prim Sch CV37 145 D1
Bridgeacre Gdns CV3 62 C1
Bridgecote CV3 78 C3
Bridgeman Rd CV6 61 D2
Bridget St CV22 82 C2
Bridgetown Rd CV37 145 D1
Bridgeway CV37 145 D2
Bridle Brook La CV5, CV7 48 A2
Bridle Rd
Lighthorne Heath CV35 123 D2
Rugby CV21 82 C2
Bridport Cl CV2 63 D2
Brierley Rd CV2 62 B4
Briggs Cl OX16 139 F2
Bright St CV6 61 F3
Brightmere Rd CV6 61 D2
Brighton St CV2 61 F2
Brightwalton Rd CV3 77 E4
Brightwell Cres B93 71 F2
Brill Cl CV4 76 B3
Brindle Ave CV3 62 B1
Brindley Rd Bedworth CV7 50 A4
Hinckley LE10 30 C4
Rugby CV21 84 A1
Brinklow CE Fst Sch CV23 64 C2
Brinklow Cl B98 103 E4
Brinklow Rd Coventry CV3 63 D1
Easenhall CV23 65 F2
Brisbane Cl CV3 77 F3
Briscoe Rd CV6 49 E2
Bristol Rd CV5 60 C1
Bristol Way CV35 146 B1
Britannia Rd LE10 32 A3
Britannia St CV2 61 F2
Briton Rd CV2 62 A2
Brittania Sh Ctr 2 LE10 31 E4
Britten Cl CV11 40 A4
Brittons La CV35 114 C2
Brixham Cl CV11 29 F3
Brixham Dr CV2 62 B4
Brixworth Cl CV3 78 C4
Broad Cl CV33 123 F8
Broad Heath Com Prim Sch CV6 61 F4
Broad La Coventry CV5 59 E2
Fillongley CV7 35 F2
Tanworth-in-A B98 86 C2
Broad Marston Rd
Mickleton CV37,GL55 135 B7
Pebworth CV37 128 F1
Broad Oaks B76 13 D1
Broad Park Rd CV2 62 B4
Broad St Brinklow CV23 64 C2
Coventry CV6 61 F4
Long Compton CV36 141 C3
Stratford-u-A CV37 144 C1
Warwick CV34 108 C4
Broad Wlk CV37 144 C1
Broadfern Rd B93 72 A4
Broadgate CV1 151 B3
Broadhaven Cl CV31 110 B4
Broadlands Cl CV5 60 B1
Broadlee B77 4 B1
Broadmeadow La CV37 144 C3
Broadmere Rise CV5 60 A1

Broadmoor La CV36 .... 141 A6
Broadsword Way LE10 .... 31 E2
Broadwater CV5 .... 77 D4
Broadway Coventry CV5 ...... 61 D1
  Cubbington CV32 .... 106 C3
Broadway Rd GL55 .... 135 B6
Broadwell Ct CV4 .... 75 F3
Broadwells Cres CV4 .... 76 A3
Brockhill La B98 .... 85 F1
Brockhurst Ave LE10 .... 31 E2
Brockhurst Dr CV4 .... 59 E1
Brockhurst La
  Monks Kirby CV23 .... 53 F2
  Sutton Coldfield B75 .... 7 D4
Brodick Cl LE10 .... 31 D4
Brodick Rd LE10 .... 30 C4
Brodick Way CV10 .... 28 C2
Bromage Ave B78 .... 15 E3
Brome Hall La B94 .... 89 E1
Bromford Way CV37 .... 144 B2
Bromleigh Dr CV2 .... 62 B1
Bromley Cl CV8 .... 92 C3
Bromsgrove Highway B98 102 C4
Bromsgrove Rd B80 .... 103 E1
Bromwich Cl CV3 .... 78 C4
Bromwich Rd CV21 .... 83 F1
Bromyard Ave B76 .... 22 A4
Bronte Cl Nuneaton CV10 .... 27 F3
  Rugby CV21 .... 83 E2
Bronze Cl CV11 .... 39 F4
Brook Ave B77 .... 10 A4
Brook Cl Coventry CV1 .... 61 F2
  Kingsbury B78 .... 15 E3
  Shipston-on-S CV36 .... 149 F3
Brook Croft B37 .... 44 A4
Brook End B78 .... 9 D4
Brook End Cl B95 .... 113 A4
Brook End Dr B95 .... 113 A4
Brook Farm Wlk B37 .... 33 E1
Brook Green La B92 .... 57 D1
Brook La
  Moreton Morrell CV35 .... 122 F3
  Newbold-on-S CV37 .... 130 C1
  Nuneaton CV10 .... 29 E3
Brook Piece Wlk B35 .... 22 A2
Brook St Bedworth CV12 ..... 39 D3
  Fenny Compton CV33 .... 133 D7
  Warwick CV34 .... 108 C3
  Wolston CV8 .... 80 A2
Brook View CV22 .... 99 E2
Brook Wlk CV9 .... 18 C4
Brookdale Harvington WR11 127 C4
  Hinckley LE10 .... 31 D4
Brookdale Rd CV10 .... 29 F4
Brooke Cl CV34 .... 108 C3
Brooke Rd CV8 .... 93 D2
Brooke Specl Sch CV22 ...... 82 C1
Brookfield Cl B97 .... 102 B2
Brookfield Dr LE10 .... 41 E2
Brookfield Rd
  Cubbington CV32 .... 106 C3
  Hinckley LE10 .... 31 E3
Brookford Ave CV6 .... 49 D2
Brookhurst Ct CV32 .... 105 E1
Brookhurst Cty Comb Sch
  CV32 .... 105 E1
Brookhus Farm Rd B76 ...... 22 A4
Brooklea CV12 .... 38 C1
Brooklime Dr CV23 .... 83 F4
Brooklyn Rd CV1 .... 61 E3
Brooks Cl CV23 .... 117 B6
Brooks Croft B35 .... 22 A1
Brooksby Gr B93 .... 72 A1
Brookshaw Way CV2 .... 62 C4
Brookside
  Cheswick Green B90 .... 70 B2
  Hinckley LE10 .... 31 F4
  Hook Norton OX15 .... 142 D4
  Snitterfield CV37 .... 121 B7
  Stretton on D CV23 .... 96 C3
Brookside Ave Coventry CV5 60 B2
  Kenilworth CV8 .... 92 C2
  Pailton CV23 .... 66 A4
  Wellesbourne CV35 .... 146 C2
Brookside Cl Rugby CV22 .... 83 D1
  Stratford-u-A CV37 .... 144 B2
Brookside Rd CV37 .... 144 B2
Brookside Way B77 .... 10 A3
Brookvale Ave CV3 .... 62 C1
Brookvale Rd CV37 .... 144 C1
Brookweed B77 .... 4 A2
Broom Cl CV22 .... 82 C1
Broome Croft CV6 .... 49 D2
Broomey Croft Farm B76 .. 15 D4
Broomfield Ave B78 .... 9 D4
Broomfield Pl CV5 .... 61 D1
Broomfield Rd CV5 .... 61 D1
Broomfield Rise CV10 .... 28 C1
Broomybank CV8 .... 93 D3
Broughton Rd OX16 .... 139 F2
Browett Rd CV6 .... 60 C4
Brown's Bridge Rd CV33 .. 147 D2
Brown's La Allesley CV5 ...... 48 B1
  Dordon B78 .... 11 D3
Browning Ave CV34 .... 108 B3
Browning Cl CV10 .... 28 A3
Browning Rd Coventry CV2 62 B2
  Rugby CV21 .... 101 D4
Brownley Rd B90 .... 70 C4
Brownlow St 5 CV32 .... 106 A1
Browns La B93 .... 71 F3
Browns Rd NN11 .... 117 F1
Brownshill Ct CV6 .... 60 C4
Brownshill Green Rd CV6 .. 48 C1
Brownsover Cl B36 .... 22 A1
Brownsover Com Inf Sch
  CV3 .... 83 E4
Brownsover La CV21 .... 83 D4

Brownsover Rd CV21 .... 82 C4
Broxell Cl CV34 .... 104 B1
Bruce Rd Bedworth CV7 ...... 49 F4
  Coventry CV6 .... 61 D4
Bruce Williams Way CV22 .. 83 D1
Brunel Cl Coventry CV2 ...... 61 F2
  Daventry NN11 .... 117 F2
  Whitnash CV31 .... 110 A1
Brunel Rd LE10 .... 31 E4
Brunel Wlk B78 .... 5 D2
Brunswick Cl CV21 .... 83 E3
Brunswick Rd CV1 .... 61 D1
Brunswick St CV31 .... 110 A3
Bruntingthorpe Way CV3 .. 78 C4
Brunton Cl CV3 .... 63 D1
Brutus Dr B46 .... 23 F1
Bryan Ct B50 .... 148 C2
Bryanston Cl CV2 .... 63 D2
Bryant Rd CV7 .... 50 A4
Brympton Rd CV3 .... 62 B1
Bryn Jones Cl CV3 .... 78 C4
Bryn Rd CV6 .... 61 F4
Buccleuch Cl CV22 .... 99 E2
Buchan Cl CV10 .... 27 F2
Buchannan Rd CV22 .... 82 C1
Buck La CV35 .... 138 B7
Buckbury Croft B90 .... 71 D3
Buckden B77 .... 4 B1
Buckden Cl 9 CV34 .... 104 C1
Buckfast Cl CV3 .... 77 F3
Buckhold Dr CV5 .... 60 A3
Buckingham Cl CV10 .... 29 D1
Buckingham Rd CV33 .... 132 F5
Buckingham Rise CV5 .... 60 A2
Buckland Rd CV6 .... 49 D1
Buckle St WR11,B50 .... 128 C3
Buckley Rd CV32 .... 106 B1
Buckminster Dr B93 .... 71 F2
Bucks Hill CV10 .... 28 B3
Buckwell La CV23 .... 84 A3
Budbrooke Cl CV2 .... 50 B1
Budbrooke Ind Est CV34 ... 108 A4
Budbrooke Prim Sch CV35 114 F4
Budbrooke Rd CV34 .... 108 A4
Bufferys Cl B91 .... 71 D4
Bulkington Fst Sch CV12 ... 40 B1
Bulkington La CV11 .... 40 A4
Bulkington Rd
  Bedworth CV12 .... 39 E1
  Shilton CV7 .... 51 F3
  Wolvey LE10 .... 41 E2
Bull Ring Harbury CV33 ..... 123 F6
  Nuneaton CV10 .... 29 D1
Bull Ring Farm Rd CV33 .. 123 F7
Bull St Nuneaton CV11 ...... 29 E1
  Southam CV33 .... 147 D2
  Stratford-u-A CV37 .... 144 C1
Bull Yd CV1 .... 151 B2
Bull's Head La CV3 .... 62 A1
Bull's La B76 .... 13 F1
Bullaces La LE17 .... 68 B2
Bullfield Ave CV4 .... 59 F1
Bullfurlong La LE10 .... 31 F2
Bullimore Gr CV8 .... 93 D1
Bullivents Cl B93 .... 71 F3
Bulls Head Yd B49 .... 143 D2
Bulwer Rd CV6 .... 61 D3
Bulwick Cl CV3 .... 63 D1
Bunkers Hill NN11 .... 126 F5
Burbage Ave CV37 .... 144 C3
Burbage Cty Jun Sch LE10 . 31 F3
Burbage Rd
  Aston Cantlow B95 .... 119 F6
  Hinckley LE10 .... 32 A4
Burbages La CV6 .... 49 E2
Burberry Gr CV7 .... 74 A3
Burbury Cl Bedworth CV12 39 E2
  Royal Leamington Spa CV32 . 106 B1
Burford La B49 .... 112 C1
Burford Mews 22 CV31 .... 110 B3
Burford Rd Hollywood B47 .. 69 D3
  Stratford-u-A CV37 .... 145 E1
Burgage Pl CV11 .... 29 E2
Burgage Wlk CV11 .... 29 D3
Burges CV1 .... 151 B3
Burges Gr CV34 .... 104 C1
Burghley Cl CV11 .... 29 F1
Burhill Way B37 .... 33 D3
Burleigh Cl CV7 .... 74 A4
Burlington Rd Coventry CV2 . 61 F2
  Nuneaton CV10 .... 39 D4
Burman Dr B46 .... 34 A3
Burnaby Cl CV10 .... 28 A3
Burnaby Rd CV6 .... 49 D1
Burnaston Cres B90 .... 71 E3
Burnell Cl B50 .... 148 B3
Burnett Rd CV35 .... 123 D2
Burnham Rd CV3 .... 78 A3
Burnham Rise CV11 .... 30 A3
Burns Ave CV34 .... 108 B3
Burns Cl B97 .... 102 B4
Burns Rd Coventry CV2 ...... 62 A2
  Royal Leamington Spa CV32 106 A2
Burns Wlk CV12 .... 39 E1
Burnsall Gr CV5 .... 76 B4
Burnsall Rd CV5 .... 76 B4
Burnside Coventry CV3 .... 63 D1
  Rugby CV22 .... 82 C1
Burnthurst Cres B90 .... 71 D4
Burrow Hill La CV7 .... 48 B4
Burrows Cl CV31 .... 110 A1
Burton Cl CV5 .... 48 B1
Burton Dassett Hills
  Ctry Pk CV33 .... 133 B7
Burton Green CE
  Jun & Inf Sch CV8 .... 75 D2
Burton La CV11 .... 40 C4
Burton Rd CV9 .... 3 F1

Burtons Farm Prim Sch
  B36 .... 33 D4
Bury Rd CV31 .... 109 F4
Burycroft Rd OX15 .... 142 D3
Buryway La CV36 .... 141 C4
Busby Cl CV3 .... 78 C4
Bush Cl CV4 .... 59 F2
Bush Heath La CV33 .... 123 F6
Bush Hill La CV23 .... 117 B2
Bush La B77 .... 9 E2
Bushbery Ave CV4 .... 59 F1
Bushbury Croft B37 .... 33 E2
Bushley Cl B98 .... 103 D4
Bushley Croft B91 .... 71 D4
Bushwood Dr B93 .... 72 A2
Bushwood La B94 .... 113 C8
Butcher's Cl CV23 .... 64 C2
Butcher's La CV5 .... 60 B3
Butchers La OX15 .... 137 F2
Butchers Rd B92 .... 57 D3
Butler Cl CV8 .... 93 E4
Butler St B96 .... 102 C1
Butlers Cl Aston le W NN11 . 134 F5
  Long Compton CV36 .... 141 D3
Butlers Cres CV7 .... 39 D1
Butlers End CV35 .... 91 E1
Butlers La Grendon CV9 ..... 11 E1
  Long Compton CV36 .... 141 C3
Butlers Leap CV21 .... 83 E3
Butlers Leap Ind Est CV21 . 83 E2
Butlers Rd CV36 .... 141 E3
Butlin Rd Coventry CV6 ...... 49 E2
  Rugby CV21 .... 83 E2
Butt Hill CV23 .... 125 C8
Butt La Allesley CV5 .... 60 A4
  Harbury CV33 .... 123 F6
Butter St B49 .... 143 E2
Buttermere Rugby CV21 ..... 83 E4
  Tamworth B77 .... 10 A3
Buttermere Ave CV11 .... 30 A3
Buttermere Cl CV3 .... 78 C4
Buttermilk La CV35 .... 113 F5
Butterworth Dr CV4 .... 76 A3
Butts CV1 .... 61 D1
Butts Cl B99 .... 3 D1
Butts La B94 .... 87 C1
Butts Rd CV1 .... 61 D1
Butts The
  Long Compton CV36 .... 141 C3
  Napton CV23 .... 125 C8
  Warwick CV34 .... 108 C4
Buxton Ave B78 .... 9 D4
By Pass Rd B77 .... 4 A3
Byfield Rd
  Chipping Warden OX17 ..... 134 F4
  Coventry CV6 .... 60 C3
  Priors Marston CV23 .... 125 C4
Byford St CV10 .... 28 C2
Bygones Mus OX17 .... 134 B4
Byron Ave Bedworth CV12 .. 39 E1
  Warwick CV34 .... 108 A3
Byron Rd Redditch B97 ..... 102 B4
  Stratford-u-A CV37 .... 145 E1
Byron St CV1 .... 151 C4
Byron Wlk CV33 .... 132 F7
Bywater Cl CV3 .... 77 D3

Cable & Wireless Coll CV4 . 75 F3
Cadbury Dr B35 .... 22 A1
Cadden Dr CV4 .... 60 A1
Cadman Cl CV12 .... 39 E2
Cadogan Rd CV3 .... 9 E3
Caen Cl CV35 .... 108 A4
Caernarfon Dr CV11 .... 29 E2
Caernarvon Way OX16 ..... 139 F3
Caesar Rd CV8 .... 92 C2
Caesar Way B46 .... 23 F1
Caister B77 .... 4 A3
Caistor Cl B78 .... 8 A4
Caithness Cl CV5 .... 60 A2
Calcutt Mdw CV33 .... 147 E2
Caldecote Cl CV10 .... 29 E4
Caldecote Hall Dr CV10 .... 19 F2
Caldecote Rd CV6 .... 61 E3
Caldecott Pl CV21 .... 83 E1
Caldecott St CV21 .... 83 E1
Caldeford Ave B90 .... 71 D4
Calder B77 .... 4 A1
Calder Cl Bulkington CV12 . 40 A1
  Coventry CV3 .... 77 F4
Calder Dr B76 .... 22 A4
Calder Wlk CV31 .... 110 B3
Caldon Cl LE10 .... 31 D4
Caldwell Rd CV11 .... 29 E1
Calf's La GL55 .... 135 B2
Callaways Rd CV36 .... 149 F2
Calendar Cl CV11 .... 30 A4
Callow Hill La B97 .... 102 A3
Calmere Cl CV2 .... 62 C4
Caludon Castle Sch CV2 .... 62 C2
Caludon Park Ave CV2 .... 62 C3
Caludon Rd CV2 .... 62 A2
Calvert Cl Coventry CV3 ..... 77 E3
  Rugby CV21 .... 83 F4
Camberwell Terr CV31 ..... 110 A4
Camborne Dr CV11 .... 29 F3
Cambourne Rd LE10 .... 32 A3
Cambria Cl B90 .... 69 F4
Cambrian B77 .... 4 A1
Cambridge Dr
  Birmingham B37 .... 33 D1
  Nuneaton CV10 .... 28 C2
Cambridge St Coventry CV1 61 F3
  Rugby CV21 .... 83 E2
Camden Cl GL56 .... 140 F3
Camden St CV2 .... 62 A2
Camellia Rd CV2 .... 50 A1
Camelot Gr CV8 .... 93 E3

Cameron Cl Allesley CV5 .... 60 A4
  Royal Leamington Spa CV32 106 A2
Camhouses B77 .... 4 A1
Camp Hill Cty Jun Sch CV10 28 C3
Camp Hill Dr CV10 .... 28 B4
Camp Hill Rd CV10 .... 28 B4
Camp La Henley-in-A B95 .. 113 B6
  Warmington OX17 .... 133 B2
Campbell St CV21 .... 82 C2
Campden Cl B97 .... 102 B3
Campden Lawns CV37 ...... 130 D3
Campden Pitch CV36 .... 136 A6
Campden Rd
  Ebrington GL55 .... 135 D3
  Lower Quinton CV37 .... 129 D4
  Mickleton GL55 .... 135 B4
  Shipston-on-S CV36 .... 149 E3
Campden St CV36 .... 136 A6
Campion Cl CV3 .... 77 E3
Campion Gn CV32 .... 106 A1
Campion Rd CV32 .... 106 A1
Campion Sch & Com Coll
  CV31 .... 110 B3
Campion Terr CV32 .... 106 A1
Campion Way CV23 .... 83 E4
Camplea Croft B37 .... 33 D1
Campling Cl CV12 .... 40 A1
Campton Cl LE10 .... 31 F4
Camville CV3 .... 63 D1
Canada La CV35 .... 114 C5
Canal La CV35 .... 114 C5
Canal Rd CV6 .... 61 F4
Canberra Cl CV35 .... 146 B1
Canberra Rd CV2 .... 50 B2
Canford Cl CV3 .... 77 E2
Canley Ford CV5 .... 76 C4
Canley Rd CV5 .... 76 B4
Canley Sta CV5 .... 60 B1
Cannocks La CV5 .... 76 B3
Cannon Cl CV4 .... 76 C3
Cannon Hill Rd CV4 .... 76 B3
Cannon Park District Ctr
  CV4 .... 76 B3
Cannon Park Prim Sch CV4 76 B3
Cannon Park Rd CV4 .... 76 C3
Canon Dr CV7 .... 49 E3
Canon Evans CE Fst Sch
  CV12 .... 39 D1
Canon Hudson Cl CV3 .... 78 B3
Canon Maggs CE Mid Sch
  CV12 .... 39 D1
Canon Young Rd CV31 ..... 110 B3
Canterbury Cl Kenilworth CV8 93 E2
  Studley B80 .... 103 E2
Canterbury Dr B37 .... 44 A4
Canterbury St CV1 .... 151 D3
Canterbury Way CV11 .... 30 A4
Cantlow Cl CV5 .... 60 A2
Canton La B76 .... 24 A3
Canwell Dr B75 .... 7 D3
Cape Ind Est CV34 .... 108 C4
Cape Rd CV34 .... 108 B4
Capmartin Rd CV6 .... 61 E4
Captain's Hill B49 .... 143 E3
Capulet Cl Coventry CV3 ..... 78 B3
  Rugby CV22 .... 99 F3
Caradoc B77 .... 4 A1
Caradoc Cl CV2 .... 62 B4
Cardale Croft 1 CV3 .... 78 C4
Cardiff Cl CV3 .... 78 B3
Cardigan Rd CV12 .... 38 B1
Cardinal Newman RC Sch
  CV6 .... 48 C1
Cardinal Wiseman RC Sch
  CV2 .... 50 C1
Carding Cl CV5 .... 59 F2
Carew Cl CV37 .... 144 C3
Carey B77 .... 10 A3
Carey St CV6 .... 62 A4
Cargill Cl CV6 .... 49 F3
Carhampton Rd B75 .... 13 D4
Carisbrook Cl CV11 .... 4 A1
Carisbrook Rd CV10 .... 29 E3
Carisbrooke Ave B37 .... 33 E1
Carlcroft B77 .... 4 A1
Carlton Cl CV12 .... 40 A2
Carlton Rd Coventry CV6 ... 49 F1
  Rugby CV22 .... 82 B1
Carlyle Cl CV10 .... 27 F3
Carlyon Rd CV9 .... 18 C4
Carlyon Road Ind Est CV9 . 12 C1
Carmelite Rd CV1 .... 61 F1
Carnbroe Ave CV3 .... 78 C4
Carnegie Cl CV3 .... 78 A3
Carnoustie B77 .... 4 B3
Carnoustie Cl CV11 .... 40 B4
Caroline Cl CV11 .... 39 F4
Carpenters Cl LE10 .... 31 F3
Carroway Head Hill B78 ..... 7 E2
Carsal Cl CV7 .... 49 E3
Carson Cl GL56 .... 136 C1
Cart's La CV9 .... 11 E1
Carter Dr CV3 .... 122 A4
Carter Rd CV3 .... 78 A4
Carters La CV37 .... 145 F2
Carters Leaze CV36 .... 140 E5
Carthusian Rd CV3 .... 77 E4
Cartmel Cl CV5 .... 60 A2
Carver Cl CV2 .... 62 C1
Cascade Cl CV3 .... 77 F2
Case La CV35 .... 114 B8
Cash's Bsns Ctr CV1 .... 61 E3
Cash's La CV1 .... 61 E3
Cashmore Ave CV31 .... 109 F3
Cashmore Mid Sch CV31 .. 109 F3
Cashmore Rd Bedworth CV12 38 B1
  Kenilworth CV8 .... 93 E2
Casia Gr CV8 .... 93 E3

Caspian Way CV2 .... 63 D4
Cassandra Cl CV4 .... 76 B2
Cassandra Gr CV34 .... 109 E2
Castello Dr B36 .... 22 B1
Castle Bromwich Bsns Pk
  B35 .... 22 A1
Castle Cl Coventry CV3 ...... 77 E4
  Fillongley CV7 .... 36 C1
  Henley-in-A B95 .... 113 B4
  Warwick CV34 .... 108 C3
Castle Cres CV35 .... 132 B5
Castle Ct LE10 .... 31 E3
Castle Dr Astley CV10 .... 37 F4
  Coleshill B46 .... 33 F3
Castle Gdns GL55 .... 135 C2
Castle Gn CV8 .... 92 B3
Castle Hill Kenilworth CV8 .. 92 C3
  Upper Brailes OX15 .... 137 E3
  Warwick CV34 .... 108 C3
Castle Hill La OX15 .... 137 E3
Castle La Maxstoke B46 ...... 34 C4
  Warwick CV34 .... 108 C3
Castle Mound CV23 .... 101 E3
Castle Place Ind Est CV1 .. 151 D4
Castle Rd Alcester B49 ...... 143 D3
  Henley-in-A B95 .... 113 B4
  Kenilworth CV8 .... 92 C3
  Kineton CV35 .... 132 B6
  Nuneaton CV10 .... 29 E4
  Studley B80 .... 103 F2
  Tamworth B77 .... 9 F3
Castle St Astwood Bank B96 102 C1
  Coventry CV1 .... 151 C4
  Hinckley LE10 .... 31 E4
  Rugby CV21 .... 83 D2
  Warwick CV34 .... 108 C3
Castle Vale Sec Sch CV11 .. 22 A2
Castle Vale Sports Ctr B35 . 22 A1
Castle View CV10 .... 19 E1
Castleditch La B98 .... 102 C4
Castlehall B77 .... 4 A1
Caswell Rd CV31 .... 110 A3
Catbrook Cl GL55 .... 135 B1
Catesby La B94 .... 89 D1
Catesby Rd Coventry CV6 .. 61 D4
  Rugby CV22 .... 83 E1
Cathedral Lanes Sh Ctr
  CV1 .... 151 B3
Catherine de Barnes La
  Bickenhill B92 .... 44 B1
  Catherine de B B92 .... 56 B1
Catherine St CV2 .... 61 F2
Catherines Cl B91 .... 56 A2
Cathiron La CV23 .... 65 E1
Cattell Dr B75 .... 13 D3
Cattell Rd CV34 .... 108 C3
Catthorpe Manor LE17 ...... 68 C1
Catthorpe Rd LE17 .... 68 B2
Cavalier Cl CV11 .... 29 F1
Cavans Way CV3 .... 79 D4
Cavendish Rd CV4 .... 59 F1
Caversham Cl CV11 .... 30 A4
Cawdon Gr B93 .... 71 F2
Cawnpore Rd CV6 .... 49 D1
Cawston La CV22 .... 99 D3
Cawston Way CV22 .... 99 E4
Cawthorne Cl 1 CV1 .... 61 F2
Cecil Leonard Knox Cres
  CV11 .... 40 C3
Cecily Rd CV3 .... 77 F4
Cedar Cl Kingsbury B78 ...... 15 E3
  Royal Leamington Spa CV32 106 A2
  Stratford-u-A CV37 .... 145 D2
Cedar Ct LE10 .... 32 A3
Cedar Dr CV37 .... 121 B7
Cedar Gr CV34 .... 105 E2
Cedar Rd Mickleton GL55 .. 135 C6
  Nuneaton CV10 .... 28 B3
Cedar Wlk 5 B37 .... 33 D1
Cedar Wood Dr CV7 .... 74 A3
Cedars Ave CV6 .... 60 C3
Cedars Fst Sch CV7 .... 50 A4
Cedars Rd CV7 .... 39 D1
Cedric Cl CV3 .... 78 B3
Celandine CV23 .... 83 E4
Celandine Rd CV2 .... 50 B1
Centaur Rd CV5 .... 60 C1
Centenary Bsns Ctr CV11 .. 29 F2
Centenary Rd CV4 .... 76 B4
Central Ave Coventry CV2 .. 62 A1
  Nuneaton CV11 .... 29 D3
  Royal Leamington Spa CV31 . 109 F3
Central City Ind Est CV6 .... 61 F3
Central Dr CV33 .... 124 B4
Centrovell Ind Est CV11 ..... 29 E1
Centurion Cl B46 .... 23 F1
Centurion Pk B77 .... 10 A3
Centurion Way B77 .... 10 A3
Ceolmund Cres B37 .... 33 D1
Chace Ave CV3 .... 78 B3
Chace Prim Sch CV3 .... 78 B3
Chaceley Cl CV2 .... 63 D4
Chadbury Croft 1 B91 .... 71 D4
Chadbury Rd WR11 .... 127 A1
Chadshunt Cl B36 .... 22 B1
Chadstone Cl B90 .... 71 D3
Chadwick Cl CV5 .... 60 A2
Chadwick La
  Chadwick End B93 .... 90 A4
  Knowle B93 .... 73 D1
Chadwick Mews B93 .... 90 A3
Chadworth Ave B93 .... 71 F2
Chaffinch Dr B36 .... 33 D4
Chalcot Cl Bedworth CV12 . 39 D2
  Coventry CV5 .... 60 A2

Challenge Bsns Pk CV1 .... 61 E3
Challenge Cl CV1 .... 151 C4
Chamberlain Cl CV32 .... 106 C3
Chamberlain La B49 .... 118 D5
Chamberlain Rd CV21 .... 101 D4
Chamberlain St CV12 .... 39 D2
Chance Fields CV31 .... 110 C3
Chancery La CV10 .... 28 A4
Chanders Rd CV34 .... 104 B1
Chandlers Cl B97 .... 102 B4
Chandlers Dr B77 .... 4 A3
Chandlers Rd CV31 .... 110 A1
Chandos St Coventry CV2 ..... 62 A2
  Nuneaton CV11 .... 29 D2
  Royal Leamington Spa CV32 . 105 F1
Change Brook Cl CV11 .... 29 F4
Chantries The CV1 .... 61 F3
Chantry Cl B47 .... 69 D4
Chantry Cres B49 .... 143 D2
Chantry Heath Cres B93 ...... 72 B4
Chantry The CV34 .... 105 D1
Chapel Cl B50 .... 148 B2
Chapel Ct B96 .... 102 C1
Chapel Dr
  Balsall Common CV7 .... 74 A4
  Wythall B47 .... 69 D2
Chapel End OX7 .... 142 A2
Chapel Gdns GL56 .... 136 C1
Chapel Gn CV23 .... 125 C2
Chapel Hill OX7 .... 142 F2
Chapel La Aston Cantlow B95 119 F7
  Barnacle CV7 .... 51 D3
  Cropredy OX17 .... 134 C1
  Great Rollright OX7 .... 142 A2
  Lapworth B94 .... 89 E4
  Mickleton GL55 .... 135 B6
  Newbold-on-S CV37 .... 130 E1
  Pillerton Priors CV35 .... 131 D2
  Ratley OX15 .... 133 A2
  Ryton-on-D CV8 .... 79 D1
  Salford OX7 .... 150 C3
  Stratford-u-A CV37 .... 145 D1
  Ullenhall B95 .... 112 E6
  Witherley CV9 .... 19 E4
Chapel Rd B96 .... 102 C1
Chapel Row 14 CV34 .... 108 C4
Chapel St
  Astwood Bank B96 .... 102 C1
  Bedworth CV12 .... 39 E2
  Bishops Itchington CV33 .... 124 A4
  Charwelton NN11 .... 126 D2
  Coventry CV1 .... 151 B3
  Harbury CV33 .... 123 F6
  Hook Norton OX15 .... 142 D4
  Long Lawford CV23 .... 82 A2
  Nuneaton CV11 .... 29 E2
  3 Royal Leamington Spa
  CV31 .... 110 A4
  Rugby CV21 .... 83 D2
  Stratford-u-A CV37 .... 145 D1
  Warmington OX17 .... 133 D2
  Warwick CV34 .... 108 C4
  Welford on A CV37 .... 129 B6
  Wellesbourne CV35 .... 146 B2
Chapelhouse Rd B37 .... 33 D1
Chapelon B77 .... 4 A1
Chapman Cl CV31 .... 110 C3
Chapman Way B49 .... 143 E3
Chard Rd CV3 .... 78 B4
Chariot Way CV21 .... 83 D4
Charity Rd CV7 .... 49 D4
Charlbury Mews CV31 .... 110 B3
Charlecote Cl CV37 .... 145 F2
Charlecote Croft B90 .... 70 B4
Charlecote Gdns 27 CV31 .. 110 B3
Charlecote Park 121 F3
Charlecote Rd Coventry CV6 . 49 D1
  Wellesbourne CV35 .... 146 B2
  Wellesbourne, Charlcote
  CV35 .... 146 A3
Charlecote Wlk CV11 .... 39 F4
Charles Eaton Rd CV12 ...... 38 C2
Charles Gardner Rd CV31 . 109 F3
Charles Lakin Cl CV7 .... 51 E3
Charles Rd CV9 .... 18 C4
Charles St Arley CV7 .... 37 D4
  Coventry CV1 .... 151 D4
  Hurley CV9 .... 16 B3
  Nuneaton CV11 .... 29 D3
  Rugby CV21 .... 82 C2
  Warwick CV34 .... 109 D4
Charles Warren Cl CV21 ..... 83 D2
Charlesfield Rd CV22 .... 100 A4
Charlesworth Ave B90 .... 71 D3
Charlewood Rd CV6 .... 49 D1
Charlotte St
  Royal Leamington Spa CV31 . 109 F3
  Rugby CV21 .... 83 D2
Charminster Dr CV34 .... 77 E2
Charnwood Ave CV10 .... 28 C1
Charnwood Dr CV10 .... 19 D1
Charnwood Way CV32 .... 106 B2
Charter App CV34 .... 108 B3
Charter Ave CV4 .... 76 A4
Charter Rd CV22 .... 100 C4
Charterhouse Rd CV1 .... 61 F1
Chartley Cl B93 .... 71 F2
Chartwell Cl CV11 .... 29 F1
Chartwell Dr B90 .... 70 B3
Charwelton Dr CV21 .... 83 F3
Chase Cl CV11 .... 29 F3
Chase La CV8 .... 92 A4
Chater Dr B76 .... 13 D1
Chatham Cl CV3 .... 78 B4

Chatsworth Cl
  Cheswick Green B90 .... 70 C3
  Hinckley LE10 .... 31 F3
Chatsworth Dr CV11 .... 29 F1
Chatsworth Gr
  Kenilworth CV8 .... 93 B3
  Royal Leamington Spa CV31 . 110 B3
Chatsworth Rise CV3 .... 77 F3
Chattaway Dr CV7 .... 74 A3
Chattle Hill B46 .... 23 F1
Chaucer Dr CV10 .... 28 A2
Chaucer Rd CV22 .... 99 F3
Chauntry Pl CV1 .... 151 C3
Chauson Gr B91 .... 71 D4
Chaytor Rd B78 .... 11 D4
Cheadle Cl CV2 .... 50 A2
Cheam Cl CV6 .... 50 A1
Cheedon Cl B93 .... 71 F1
Chelmsley Ave B46 .... 33 F3
Chelmsley Circ B37 .... 33 D2
Chelmsley La B37 .... 44 A4
Chelmsley Rd B37 .... 33 E1
Chelney Wlk CV3 .... 63 D1
Chelsea Cl CV11 .... 29 F4
Chelsey Rd CV2 .... 62 C4
Cheltenham Cl CV12 .... 39 D2
Cheltenham Croft CV2 .... 62 C4
Chelveston Rd CV6 .... 60 C3
Chelwood Gr CV2 .... 50 C1
Chenies Cl CV5 .... 60 A2
Chepstow Cl Coventry CV3 ... 78 B3
  Stratford-u-A CV37 .... 144 C1
Chepstow Gdns OX16 .... 139 F3
Chequer St CV12 .... 40 B1
Cheriton Cl CV5 .... 60 B2
Cherry Blossom Gr CV31 ... 110 A1
Cherry Cl Coventry CV6 ...... 49 E1
  Ettington CV37 .... 131 A3
  Hurley CV9 .... 16 B2
  Offenham WR11 .... 127 D1
Cherry Gr CV22 .... 99 F4
Cherry La Bearley CV37 ..... 120 E7
  Hampton Magna CV35 ..... 114 F4
Cherry Orch
  Henley-in-A B95 .... 113 B5
  Kenilworth CV8 .... 93 D3
  Shipston-on-S CV36 .... 149 F3
  Stratford-u-A CV37 .... 144 C1
  Wellesbourne CV35 .... 146 B2
Cherry Orchard Cl GL55 .... 135 B1
Cherry Pit La B98 .... 86 A1
Cherry Rd OX16 .... 139 F4
Cherry St
  Stratford-u-A CV37 .... 144 C1
  Warwick CV34 .... 108 C4
Cherry Tree Ave CV10 .... 28 C3
Cherry Tree Cres WR11 ..... 127 F6
Cherry Tree Wlk CV33 .... 147 D3
Cherry Way CV8 .... 93 D3
Cherry Wlk B47 .... 69 D3
Cherrybrook Way CV2 .... 50 B1
Cherryfield Cl CV10 .... 19 D1
Cherrywood Cres 8 B91 ..... 71 E4
Cherrywood Gr CV5 .... 59 F3
Cherwell Cl LE10 .... 31 D4
Cherwell The NN11 .... 117 F1
Cherwell Way CV23 .... 82 A2
Chesford Cres Coventry CV6 . 50 A1
  Warwick CV34 .... 105 D1
Chesford Gr CV37 .... 144 B2
Chesham St CV31 .... 110 A4
Cheshire Cl CV22 .... 99 E4
Chesholme Rd CV6 .... 49 D1
Chesils The CV3 .... 77 E3
Chessetts Wood Rd B94 ..... 89 E4
Chester Cl B37 .... 33 D1
Chester Rd Birmingham B36 . 33 D1
  Birmingham, Chelmsley Wood
  B37 .... 44 C4
  Hampton in A B46, B92, CV7 .. 45 D3
Chester St Coventry CV1 ...... 61 D2
  Rugby CV21 .... 83 E2
Chester Way OX16 .... 139 F3
Chesterton Cl B97 .... 102 B2
Chesterton Dr
  Nuneaton CV10 .... 28 A3
  Royal Leamington Spa CV31 . 110 B3
Chesterton Hill CV35 .... 123 C3
Chesterton Rd Coventry CV6 . 61 D4
  Lighthorne CV35 .... 123 B2
Chesterwood B47 .... 69 D3
Chestnut Ave CV8 .... 92 C2
Chestnut Cl Ettington CV37 . 131 B3
  Kingsbury B78 .... 15 E3
Chestnut Cres CV10 .... 28 C3
Chestnut Ct Alcester B49 ... 143 E2
  Royal Leamington Spa CV31 . 109 F1
Chestnut Dr CV11 .... 29 F2
Chestnut Field CV21 .... 83 D2
Chestnut Gr Coleshill B46 ... 34 A4
  Coventry CV4 .... 60 A1
  Moreton Morrell CV35 ...... 122 E3
  Wolston CV8 .... 80 A2
Chestnut Pl CV33 .... 147 D3
Chestnut Rd
  Astwood Bank B96 .... 102 C1
  Bedworth CV12 .... 39 E2
  Mollington OX17 .... 134 A2
Chestnut Sq
  6 Royal Leamington Spa
  CV32 .... 106 A1
  Wellesbourne CV35 .... 146 B2
Chestnut Tree Ave CV4 .... 60 A1
Chestnut Wlk
  2 Birmingham B37 .... 33 D1
  Henley-in-A B95 .... 113 A5
  Stratford-u-A CV37 .... 144 C1
Chestnuts The CV12 .... 38 C1

Cheswick Cl Coventry CV6 ... 62 A4
  Redditch B98 .... 112 A6
Cheswick Green
  Jun & Inf Sch B94 .... 70 C2
Cheswick Way B90 .... 70 B2
Cheswood Dr B76 .... 22 A3
Chetwode Cl CV5 .... 60 A2
Chetwynd Dr CV11 .... 40 A4
Chetwynd Mid Sch CV11 ..... 40 A4
Chetwynd Rd B78 .... 11 D4
Cheval Ave CV6 .... 61 D3
Cheveral Rd CV12 .... 39 D2
Cheverel Pl CV11 .... 29 D1
Cheverel St CV11 .... 29 D2
Cheviot B77 .... 4 B1
Cheviot Cl CV10 .... 28 A2
Cheviot Rise CV32 .... 106 B2
Cheviot Way OX16 .... 139 F5
Cheylesmore CV1 .... 151 B2
Chicory Dr CV23 .... 83 E4
Chideock Hill CV3 .... 77 D3
Chiel Cl CV5 .... 59 F2
Chigwell Cl B35 .... 22 A2
Childs Cl CV37 .... 144 C3
Childs Oak Cl CV7 .... 74 A3
Chilham Dr B37 .... 33 E1
Chillaton Rd CV6 .... 49 D1
Chillingham B77 .... 9 E4
Chilling Rd CV23 .... 83 B7
Chilterns The CV5 .... 60 A2
Chilton Cl
  CV11 .... 29 E1
Chilvers Coton Fst Sch
  CV11 .... 29 E1
Chilworth Cl CV11 .... 39 F4
Chingford Rd CV6 .... 50 A2
Chingley Bank B95 .... 113 B4
Chipping Campden Sch
  GL55 .... 135 B2
Chipping Norton Rd OX15 .. 142 D4
Chipstone Cl 1 B91 .... 71 E4
Chiswick Wlk B37 .... 33 F1
Chivenor Prim Sch B35 ...... 22 A1
Chivington Cl B90 .... 71 D3
Choyce Cl CV9 .... 12 B1
Christ the King RC Inf Sch
  CV6 .... 60 C3
Christ the King RC Jun Sch
  CV6 .... 60 C4
Christchurch Rd CV6 .... 61 D3
Christine Ledger Sq 3
  CV31 .... 110 A3
Chub B77 .... 9 E4
Chudleigh Rd CV2 .... 62 C4
Church Ave B46 .... 23 D2
Church Ct Binton CV37 ..... 129 A8
  Temple Grafton B49 .... 119 E1
Church Cl Arley CV10 .... 26 C1
  Birmingham B37 .... 33 D3
  Bishops Itchington CV33 . 124 A4
  Drayton Bassett B78 .... 8 C3
  Hartshill CV10 .... 28 A4
  Hinckley LE10 .... 32 A3
  Luddington CV37 .... 129 C7
  Stoke Golding CV13 .... 21 E4
  Wardington OX17 .... 134 F1
  Whitnash CV31 .... 110 A2
  Wolvey LE10 .... 41 F2
  Wood End CV9 .... 10 B1
Church Down Cl B97 .... 102 B3
Church Dr B49 .... 118 D5
Church End
  Great Rollright OX7 .... 142 A2
  Radford Semele CV31 ..... 110 C3
Church Farm Ct CV35 .... 138 C7
Church Farm La GL56 ...... 140 A6
Church Fields NN11 .... 126 E8
Church Hill Badby NN11 .... 126 F5
  15 Bishops Tachbrook CV33 . 122 F8
  Coleshill B46 .... 34 A3
  Combrook CV35 .... 131 E6
  Cubbington CV32 .... 106 C3
  Royal Leamington Spa CV32 . 109 F4
  Stretton on D CV23 .... 96 C3
  Ullenhall B95 .... 112 E6
  Warmington OX17 .... 133 D2
  Wolvey LE10 .... 41 F2
Church La Alveston CV37 ... 121 D3
  Ansley CV10 .... 27 E1
  Arley CV7 .... 26 C1
  Ash Green CV7 .... 49 F4
  Aston Cantlow B95 .... 119 F6
  Austrey CV9 .... 3 D1
  Austrey, No Man's Heath CV9 .. 3 D3
  Barford CV35 .... 122 B7
  Bearley CV37 .... 120 E7
  Berkswell CV7 .... 58 B2
  Bickenhill B92 .... 44 C1
  Cookhill B49 .... 118 D5
  Corley CV7 .... 48 A4
  Coventry, Middle Stoke CV2 . 62 A2
  Coventry, Upper Eastern Green
  CV5 .... 59 E3
  Cropredy OX17 .... 134 C1
  Cubbington CV32 .... 106 C3
  Curdworth B76 .... 23 D3
  Ettington CV37 .... 131 A3
  Fenny Drayton CV13 .... 19 F3
  Fillongley CV7 .... 36 C2
  Gaydon CV35 .... 132 E8
  Hanwell OX17 .... 139 F6
  Hornton OX15 .... 139 B7
  Kingsbury B78 .... 15 E3
  Lapworth B94 .... 88 C2

Church La continued
  Lea Marston B76 .... 24 A4
  Lighthorne CV35 .... 123 B2
  Littleton WR11 .... 127 F1
  Meriden CV7 .... 58 C4
  Middleton B78 .... 8 B1
  Mollington OX17 .... 134 A2
  Newbold-on-S CV37 .... 130 E1
  Norton WR11 .... 127 C2
  Nuneaton CV10 .... 29 E4
  Oxhill CV35 .... 137 F8
  Royal Leamington Spa CV32 106 A2
  Shawell LE17 .... 68 B3
  Shuttington B79 .... 4 C4
  Snitterfield CV37 .... 121 B7
  Stoneleigh CV8 .... 94 B3
  Stratford-u-A CV37 .... 144 B2
  Thurlaston CV23 .... 98 C1
  Welford on A CV37 .... 129 A7
  Whatcote CV36 .... 137 D7
  Whitnash CV31 .... 110 A2
  Wigston Parva LE10 .... 42 C4
  Wishaw B76 .... 14 A1
Church Lees 7 CV33 .... 122 F8
Church Lench Fst Sch
  WR11 .... 127 A6
Church Mews CV33 .... 132 B6
Church Park Cl CV6 .... 48 C1
Church Path CV35 .... 114 F3
Church Rd
  Astwood Bank B96 .... 102 C1
  Baginton CV8 .... 77 F1
  Braunston NN11 .... 117 D5
  Bubbenhall CV8 .... 95 E3
  Church Lawford CV23 ...... 81 E3
  Claverdon CV35 .... 113 F3
  Dordon B78 .... 11 D3
  Gaydon CV35 .... 132 E8
  Grandborough CV23 ...... 116 F5
  Hartshill CV10 .... 28 A4
  Ladbroke CV33 .... 124 D5
  Long Itchington CV23 ..... 115 D4
  Newbold-on-S CV37 .... 130 E1
  Norton Lindsey CV35 ...... 114 C2
  Nuneaton CV10 .... 28 B2
  Pebworth CV37 .... 128 F1
  Ryton-on-D CV8 .... 79 D1
  Shilton CV7 .... 51 F3
  Shustoke B46 .... 25 D1
  Snitterfield CV37 .... 121 B6
  Tamworth B77 .... 9 E2
  Ullenhall B95 .... 112 D5
  Upper Boddington NN11 .. 134 E8
  Warton B79 .... 5 E2
  Wilmcote CV37 .... 120 C4
  Witherley CV9 .... 19 D4
Church St Alcester B49 ..... 143 E2
  Appleby Magna DE12 .... 3 F4
  Atherstone CV9 .... 18 B4
  Barford CV35 .... 122 B7
  Bidford-on-A B50 .... 148 C2
  Bulkington CV12 .... 40 B1
  Charwelton NN11 .... 126 D2
  Chipping Campden GL55 .. 135 B2
  Churchover CV23 .... 67 E3
  Clifton u D CV23 .... 84 A3
  Coventry CV1 .... 151 C4
  Fenny Compton CV33 ..... 133 D7
  Hampton Lucy CV35 ...... 121 F4
  Harbury CV33 .... 123 F6
  Harvington WR11 .... 127 D3
  Hinckley LE10 .... 32 A3
  Marton CV23 .... 115 C7
  Moreton-in-M GL56 .... 140 A3
  Nuneaton CV11 .... 29 E2
  Offenham WR11 .... 127 D1
  Royal Leamington Spa CV31 110 A4
  Rugby CV21 .... 83 D2
  Shipston-on-S CV36 .... 149 F3
  Staverton NN11 .... 126 D8
  Stockton CV23 .... 147 F4
  Stratford-u-A CV37 .... 144 C1
  Studley B80 .... 103 F2
  Warwick CV34 .... 108 C3
  Welford on A CV37 .... 129 A7
  Wellesbourne CV35 .... 146 B2
  Wroxton OX15 .... 139 B7
Church Terr Harbury CV33 . 123 F7
  Royal Leamington Spa CV31 110 A4
Church View
  Aston Magna GL56 .... 140 A6
  Tamworth B77 .... 9 F4
  Warton B79 .... 5 F2
Church Way CV12 .... 39 D1
Church Wlk Allesley CV5 ..... 60 B3
  Atherstone CV9 .... 18 C4
  Barby CV23 .... 101 E1
  Hinckley LE10 .... 31 E4
  12 Royal Leamington Spa
  CV31 .... 109 F4
  Rugby CV22 .... 83 D1
  Rugby, Bilton CV22 .... 99 E4
  Thurlaston CV23 .... 98 C2
  Wellesbourne CV35 .... 146 B2
Church Wlks CV31 .... 21 E4
Churchdale Cl CV10 .... 28 B2
Churchfield CV37 .... 129 A7
Churchill Ave Coventry CV6 . 61 F4
  Kenilworth CV8 .... 93 D3
Churchill Cl CV37 .... 131 A4
Churchill Rd Rugby CV22 .... 83 D1
  Sutton Coldfield B75 .... 13 D3
Churchlea OX17 .... 134 A2
Chylds Ct CV5 .... 60 A3
Cicey La CV11 .... 41 D4
Cinder La CV9 .... 6 A4
Cinderhill La GL55 .... 135 B2
Circle The CV10 .... 28 C2

Circuit The CV37 .... 129 C8
Circus Ave B37 .... 33 E1
City Arc CV1 .... 151 B2
City Tech Coll The B37 .... 33 D2
Cladswell Cl B49 .... 118 D5
Cladswell La B49 .... 118 C6
Clapham Sq CV31 .... 110 A4
Clapham St CV31 .... 110 A3
Clapham Terr CV31 .... 110 A4
Clapham Terrace
  Com Prim Sch CV31 .... 110 A4
Clara St CV2 .... 62 A1
Clare Cl CV32 .... 106 B1
Clare Ct CV21 .... 82 C2
Claremont Cl CV12 .... 40 A2
Claremont Rd
  Royal Leamington Spa CV31 . 109 F3
  Rugby CV21 .... 83 E2
Claremont Wlk CV5 .... 60 B3
Clarence Rd Hinckley LE10 . 31 F4
  Rugby CV21 .... 82 C2
  Stratford-u-A CV37 .... 144 B2
Clarence St 4 Coventry CV1 . 61 F2
  Nuneaton CV11 .... 29 D1
  Royal Leamington Spa CV31 110 A4
Clarence Terr 6 CV32 ...... 105 F1
Clarendon Ave CV32 .... 105 F1
Clarendon Cres CV32 .... 105 F1
Clarendon Pl CV32 .... 105 F1
Clarendon Rd Hinckley LE10 . 31 E4
  Kenilworth CV8 .... 93 D2
Clarendon Sq CV32 .... 105 F1
Clarendon St Coventry CV5 . 60 C1
  Royal Leamington Spa CV32 105 F1
Clarewell Ave B91 .... 71 D4
Clark Cl CV36 .... 149 F3
Clark St CV6 .... 50 A1
Clarke Ave GL56 .... 140 C3
Clarke's Ave CV8 .... 93 D2
Clarks La CV36 .... 141 D3
Clarkson Dr CV31 .... 110 A2
Claverdon Cl B97 .... 102 B2
Claverdon Jun & Inf Sch
  CV35 .... 113 F3
Claverdon Rd CV5 .... 60 A2
Claverdon Sta CV35 .... 114 A3
Clay Ave CV11 .... 29 F4
Clay Bank OX15 .... 142 D4
Clay La Allesley CV5 .... 47 F2
  Coventry CV2 .... 62 A2
Claybrook Dr B98 .... 103 F4
Claybrook Prim Sch LE17 ... 43 F2
Claydon Rd OX17 .... 134 C2
Claymore B77 .... 9 E4
Clayton Rd CV6 .... 60 C3
Clayton Wlk B35 .... 22 A1
Cleasby B77 .... 4 B1
Cleaver Gdns CV10 .... 29 E3
Cleeve Prior CE Fst Sch
  WR11 .... 128 A4
Cleeve Rd Bidford-on-A B50 . 148 B1
  Littleton WR11 .... 127 F2
Cleeves Ave CV34 .... 109 E3
Clemens St CV31 .... 110 A4
Clement St CV11 .... 29 D2
Clements St CV2 .... 62 A2
Clennon Rise CV2 .... 62 B4
Clent Ave B97 .... 102 B4
Clent Dr CV10 .... 28 A2
Cleobury La B94 .... 70 A2
Clevedon Gn WR11 .... 128 A1
Cleveland Rd
  Bulkington CV12 .... 40 A2
  Coventry CV2 .... 62 A2
  Hinckley LE10 .... 31 E4
Cleveley Dr CV10 .... 28 B4
Clews Rd B98 .... 102 C4
Clifden Gr CV8 .... 93 E3
Cliff Hall La B78 .... 9 E1
Cliffe Ct CV32 .... 105 E1
Cliffe Rd CV32 .... 105 E1
Cliffe Way CV34 .... 109 D4
Clifford Bridge Prim Sch
  CV3 .... 63 D2
Clifford Bridge Rd CV3 ...... 63 D2
Clifford La CV37 .... 130 A8
Clifford Rd B93 .... 71 F2
Clifton B98 .... 103 F4
Clifton La B79 .... 1 A2
Clifton Rd Nuneaton CV10 ... 28 C2
  Rugby CV21 .... 83 E2
Clifton St CV1 .... 151 D4
Clifton-on-Dunsmore
  CE Prim Sch CV23 .... 83 F3
Clinic Dr CV11 .... 29 E2
Clinton Ave Kenilworth CV8 . 92 B3
  Warwick CV35 .... 108 A4
Clinton Comb Sch CV8 .... 92 C2
Clinton La CV8 .... 92 B3
Clinton Rd Coleshill B46 ..... 33 F3
  Coventry CV6 .... 49 F1
  Solihull B90 .... 70 B4
Clinton St CV31 .... 110 A4
Clipstone Rd CV6 .... 60 C3
Clive Rd CV7 .... 74 B3
Cliveden Wlk CV11 .... 39 F4
Clock La B92 .... 44 B1
Cloister Croft CV2 .... 62 C3
Cloister Crofts CV32 .... 105 F2
Cloister Way CV32 .... 105 F2
Cloisters The Atherstone CV9 18 C4
  Studley B80 .... 103 E2
Clopton Cres B37 .... 33 E2
Clopton Ct CV37 .... 144 C2
Clopton Rd CV37 .... 144 C2
Close The Brandon CV8 ...... 79 F3
  Chipping Warden OX17 ... 134 F3
  Cleeve Prior WR11 .... 128 A4

Close The continued
Epwell OX15 .... 138 D3
Halford CV36 .... 137 A8
Hampton Lucy CV35 .... 121 F4
Hollywood B47 .... 69 D3
Kenilworth CV8 .... 93 D3
Lower Quinton CV37 .... 129 E2
Royal Leamington Spa CV31 110 A3
Closers Bsns Ctr CV11 ...... 29 E1
Closter Gn CV35 .... 132 B6
Cloud Gn CV4 .... 76 B3
Cloudsley Bush La LE10 .... 42 A3
Clovelly Gdns CV2 .... 62 B3
Clovelly Rd CV2 .... 62 A3
Clovelly Way CV11 .... 29 F3
Clover B37 .... 33 E1
Clover Cl Rugby CV23 .... 83 E4
Stratford-u-A CV37 .... 144 C3
Cloweswood La B94 .... 86 C4
Clumber Park Rd CV35 .. 132 D3
Clunes Ave CV11 .... 29 F3
Clyde Rd Bulkington CV12 ... 40 A1
Dorridge B93 .... 72 A1
Co-operative St CV2 .... 50 A2
Coach House Rise B77 .... 9 F4
Coal Pit La Willey CV23 ...... 54 B3
Wolvey LE10 .... 41 E1
Coalpit Fields Rd CV12 ...... 39 E1
Coalpit La CV8 .... 80 C1
Coat Of Arms Bridge Rd
CV3 .... 77 D3
Cobbs Rd CV8 .... 92 B3
Cobden Ave CV31 .... 110 B3
Cobden St CV6 .... 61 F3
Cobia B77 .... 9 E4
Cockerills Mdw CV21 .... 101 D4
Cockermouth Cl CV32 ...... 105 E1
Cocksfoot Cl CV37 .... 144 C3
Cockspur St B78 .... 10 C4
Coffee Pot La CV35 .... 114 C6
Colbourne Grove Dr
CV32 .... 105 E1
Cold Comfort La B49 .... 143 D2
Coldfield Dr B98 .... 102 C4
Coldicotts Cl GL55 .... 135 B2
Cole Ct B37 .... 33 D1
Colebridge Cres B46 .... 33 F4
Colebrook Rd Alcester B49 .. 143 E2
Coventry CV3 .... 62 C1
Coleby Cl CV4 .... 75 E4
Coleford Dr B37 .... 33 D1
Colehurst Croft B90 .... 70 C3
Coleman St CV4 .... 59 F2
Colemeadow Rd B46 .... 33 F4
Coleridge Cl B97 .... 102 B4
Coleridge Rd CV2 .... 62 B2
Coleshill Blythe Specl Sch
B46 .... 34 A2
Coleshill CE Prim Sch
Coleshill B46 .... 33 F3
Coleshill B46 .... 34 A2
Coleshill Cl B97 .... 102 B3
Coleshill Heath Rd
Birmingham B37 .... 44 B4
Birmingham B37, B46 .... 33 F1
Coleshill Heath Sch B37 .... 33 E1
Coleshill Ind Est B46 .... 23 F1
Coleshill Rd Ansley CV10 .... 27 E4
Atherstone CV9 .... 18 B3
Birmingham, Marston Green
B37 .... 44 A4
Curdworth B76 .... 23 E3
Fazeley B78 .... 9 D4
Furnace End B46 .... 25 E2
Maxstoke B46 .... 34 C3
Shustoke B46 .... 24 C1
Water Orton B46 .... 23 D1
Coleshill Sch The B46 .... 34 A2
Coleshill St B78 .... 9 D4
Colesleys The B46 .... 34 A3
Coleville Rd B76 .... 22 A3
Coley Cl LE10 .... 31 E4
Colina Cl CV3 .... 78 B3
Colledge Cl CV23 .... 64 C2
Colledge Rd CV6 .... 49 E1
College Dr CV32 .... 105 F1
College La
Balsall Common CV8 .... 73 F1
Long Compton CV36 .... 141 D2
Stratford-u-A CV37 .... 144 C1
College Mews CV37 .... 144 C1
College Rd CV23 .... 117 C6
College St Nuneaton CV10 .. 29 E1
Stratford-u-A CV37 .... 144 C1
Collets Brook B75 .... 7 D1
Collett B77 .... 4 A1
Collett Wlk CV1 .... 61 D2
Colliers Way CV7 .... 36 C4
Colliery La CV7 .... 39 D1
Colliery La N CV7 .... 39 D1
Colling Wlk B37 .... 33 D3
Collingham La CV5 .... 115 E4
Collingwood Ave CV22 ...... 82 B1
Collingwood Rd CV5 .... 61 D1
Collins Gr CV4 .... 76 B3
Collins Rd CV34 .... 109 E3
Collins Way B49 .... 143 E2
Colmore Dr B75 .... 13 D3
Colony Rd OX15 .... 142 D8
Colts Cl LE10 .... 31 E2
Columbia Gdns CV12 .... 39 F1
Colyere Cl CV7 .... 49 D3
Combe Fields Rd CV3 .... 63 F2
Combroke Gr CV35 .... 114 F5
Commainge Cl CV34 .... 108 B4
Commander Cl CV33 .... 122 F8
Commissary Rd B26 .... 44 A2

Common La Claverdon CV35 113 F4
Corley CV7 .... 47 F4
Mappleborough Green B80 .. 112 A6
Polesworth B78 .... 11 D4
Common The CV9 .... 11 E1
Common Way CV2 .... 62 A3
Compass Ct 8 CV1 .... 61 D2
Compton Cl CV32 .... 106 B1
Compton Croft B37 .... 33 E1
Compton Ct CV36 .... 141 C4
Compton District
Prim Sch The CV36 .... 141 C3
Compton Hill CV35 .... 131 E7
Compton Rd Coventry CV6 .. 49 E1
Lighthorne Heath CV35 ...... 123 D2
Compton Verney House
CV35 .... 131 F7
Comrie Cl CV2 .... 62 C3
Comyn St CV32 .... 106 A1
Conduit Hill GL55 .... 135 A1
Coneybury Wlk B76 .... 22 B3
Congleton Cl CV6 .... 49 F1
Congrave Cl CV12 .... 39 D1
Congreve Cl CV34 .... 104 C1
Conifer Cl CV12 .... 39 E2
Conifer Gr CV31 .... 109 F3
Conifer Paddock CV3 .... 62 C1
Coningsby Cl 5 CV31 ...... 110 B3
Coniston B77 .... 10 A4
Coniston Cl Bulkington CV12 . 40 B2
Rugby CV21 .... 83 E3
Coniston Dr CV5 .... 59 E2
Coniston Rd Coventry CV5 .. 60 C1
Royal Leamington Spa CV32 105 E1
Coniston Way CV11 .... 29 F4
Conrad Cl CV22 .... 99 F3
Conrad Rd CV6 .... 49 F2
Constable Cl CV12 .... 39 D3
Constable Rd CV21 .... 84 A1
Constance Cl CV12 .... 49 F4
Constance Dr CV33 .... 123 F6
Constantine La B46 .... 23 F1
Consul Rd CV21 .... 83 D3
Convent Cl Atherstone CV9 .. 18 C4
Kenilworth CV8 .... 93 D4
Convent La CV9 .... 18 C4
Conway Ave CV4 .... 75 E4
Conway Croft B49 .... 127 E8
Conway Dr OX16 .... 139 F3
Conway Rd
Birmingham, Fordbridge B37 .. 33 D2
Royal Leamington Spa CV32 109 E4
Conwy Cl CV11 .... 29 E2
Rugby CV21 .... 83 E4
Cook Cl Knowle B93 .... 72 B3
Rugby CV21 .... 83 E4
Cook St CV1 .... 151 C3
Cook's Hill OX15 .... 139 A3
Cooke Cl CV34 .... 104 C1
Cooks Cl CV9 .... 18 B4
Cooks La Birmingham B37 .. 33 D2
Frankton CV23 .... 97 E1
Salford OX7 .... 150 C3
Coombe Abbey
Ctry Pk CV3 .... 63 F2
Coombe Ave CV3 .... 78 C4
Coombe Cl CV3 .... 63 D1
Coombe Dr CV3 .... 79 E4
Coombe Park Rd CV3 .... 62 C1
Coombe St CV3 .... 62 A1
Cooper St CV11 .... 29 E2
Cooper's Way CV33 .... 132 F6
Coopers Wlk CV8 .... 95 E3
Cope Arnolds Cl CV6 .... 49 F2
Cope St CV1 .... 151 C3
Copeland CV21 .... 83 E4
Copeland Cl B79 .... 5 F2
Copland Pl CV4 .... 59 F1
Coplow Cl CV7 .... 74 A3
Copper Beech Cl CV6 .... 49 F1
Copperfield Rd CV2 .... 62 A2
Coppice Cl
Cheswick Green B90 .... 70 B2
Stratford-u-A CV37 .... 145 D3
Coppice Dr B78 .... 11 D3
Coppice La Middleton B78 .... 7 E1
Thorpe Constantine B79 ...... 1 C4
Coppice Prim Sch The B47 69 D3
Coppice Rd CV31 .... 110 A1
Coppice The Atherstone CV9 19 D3
Coventry CV3 .... 78 A4
Hinckley LE10 .... 31 F4
Nuneaton CV10 .... 29 E4
Coppice Way 6 B37 .... 33 D1
Coppice Wlk B90 .... 70 B2
Copps Rd CV32 .... 109 E4
Copse Cl CV5 .... 59 D4
Copse The CV7 .... 50 A4
Copsewood Ave CV11 .... 40 A4
Copsewood Terr CV3 .... 62 B1
Copston La LE10 .... 42 A3
Copstone Dr B93 .... 71 F2
Copt Heath Croft B93 .... 72 A4
Copt Heath Dr B93 .... 72 A4
Copt Oak Cl CV4 .... 75 E3
Copthorne Rd CV6 .... 60 C4
Coral Cl Coventry CV5 .... 60 B1
Hinckley LE10 .... 31 F2
Coralin Cl B37 .... 33 E1
Corbett Rd B47 .... 69 D4
Corbett St CV21 .... 83 E2
Corbetts Cl B92 .... 57 D4
Corbin Rd B78 .... 11 D3
Corbison Cl CV34 .... 104 B1
Corbizum Ave B80 .... 103 E2
Cord La CV23 .... 65 D2
Cordelia Gn CV34 .... 109 F2

Cordelia Way CV22 .... 99 F3
Corfe Cl CV2 .... 62 C3
Corinne Croft B37 .... 33 D2
Corley Cl B98 .... 102 C4
Corley Sch CV7 .... 48 A3
Corley View CV7 .... 49 E3
Corncrake Dr B36 .... 33 D4
Cornel B37 .... 44 B4
Cornelius St CV3 .... 77 E4
Cornet's End La CV7 .... 58 A3
Cornets End La CV7 .... 57 F4
Cornfield Croft B37 .... 33 E2
Cornfield The CV3 .... 62 B1
Cornflower Dr CV23 .... 83 E4
Cornhill Gr CV8 .... 93 E3
Cornish Cl CV10 .... 27 E4
Cornish Cres CV10 .... 29 D1
Cornwall Cl 3 CV34 .... 108 C4
Cornwall Pl CV32 .... 105 E1
Cornwall Rd CV1 .... 61 F1
Cornwallis Rd CV22 .... 82 B1
Cornwell Cl B98 .... 103 D3
Coronation Ave B78 .... 5 D1
Coronation Cl GL55 .... 135 A2
Coronation Cres B79 .... 4 C4
Coronation Rd
Church Lawford CV23 .... 81 D3
Coventry CV1 .... 61 F2
Hurley CV9 .... 16 B3
Coronel Ave CV6 .... 49 F2
Corporation St
Coventry CV1 .... 151 B3
Nuneaton CV11 .... 29 D3
Rugby CV21 .... 83 D2
Corpus Christi RC Prim Sch
CV3 .... 78 B4
Correen B77 .... 4 B1
Corsham Rd CV33 .... 132 F6
Corston Mews CV31 .... 110 B3
Cosford Cl CV32 .... 106 A2
Cosford Cres B35 .... 22 A2
Cosford La CV21 .... 82 C4
Costard Ave CV36 .... 149 F3
Coten End CV34 .... 108 C4
Coten End Cty Fst Sch
CV34 .... 109 D4
Coten End Prim Sch CV34 108 C4
Cotes Rd LE10 .... 31 F3
Cotheridge Cl B90 .... 71 E3
Cotman Cl CV12 .... 39 D2
Coton House Coll CV23 ...... 67 F2
Coton Rd Churchover CV23 .. 67 E2
Nether Whitacre B46 .... 15 E1
Nuneaton CV11 .... 29 E2
Rugby CV21 .... 84 A1
Cotsmore Cl GL56 .... 140 B3
Cotswold Bsns Village
GL56 .... 140 B3
Cotswold Cl
Sibford Ferris OX15 .... 142 D8
Tredington CV36 .... 136 F6
Cotswold Cnr OX7 .... 142 A2
Cotswold Cres CV10 .... 28 A2
Cotswold Dr CV3 .... 77 E2
Cotswold Edge GL55 .... 135 B6
Cottage Cl CV31 .... 110 B3
Cottage Farm Ct GL56 ...... 136 C1
Cottage Farm Rd
Coventry CV6 .... 49 D1
Tamworth B77 .... 9 E4
Cottage La Minworth B76 .... 22 B3
Nether Whitacre B46 .... 24 B3
Stratford-u-A CV37 .... 144 B1
Cottage Leap CV21 .... 83 E3
Cottage Wlk B77 .... 9 F3
Cotterell Rd CV21 .... 82 C3
Cotterill's Cl CV31 .... 110 A2
Cotters Croft CV33 .... 133 D7
Cottesbrook Cl CV3 .... 62 C1
Cotton Dr CV8 .... 93 E3
Cotton Mill Spinney CV32 106 C3
Coughton CE Jun &
Inf Schs B49 .... 118 F7
Coughton Court B49 .... 119 A7
Coughton Dr CV31 .... 110 B3
Coughton Fields La B49 .... 143 E4
Coughton La B49 .... 118 F7
Coundon Court Sch &
Com Coll CV6 .... 60 C4
Coundon Gn CV6 .... 60 C4
Coundon Prim Sch CV6 ...... 60 C3
Coundon Rd CV1 .... 61 D2
Coundon St CV1 .... 151 A4
Coundon Wedge Dr CV5 .... 60 B4
Countess Rd CV11 .... 29 D2
Countess's Croft The CV3 .. 77 E4
Countryside NN11 .... 117 D5
Court Cl
7 Bishops Tachbrook CV33 .. 122 E8
Warmington OX17 .... 133 D2
Court La WR11 .... 127 D1
Court Leet CV3 .... 79 E4
Court Leet Rd CV3 .... 77 F4
Court St CV31 .... 110 A4
Court Way B50 .... 148 B2
Courtaulds Way CV6 .... 61 E3
Courthouse Croft CV8 .... 93 E2
Courthouse Green Prim Sch
CV6 .... 50 A1
Courtland Ave CV6 .... 60 C3
Courtney Cl CV11 .... 29 F4
Courtyard The B46 .... 23 F1
Cove Pl CV2 .... 62 B4
Coventry Airport CV8 .... 78 A1
Coventry Cath Church
of St Michael CV1 .... 151 C3
Coventry City FC CV1 .... 61 F2
Coventry Golf Course CV8 .. 77 F1
Coventry Highway B98 .... 112 A7

Coventry Prep Sch CV3 ...... 77 D4
Coventry Rd Baginton CV8 .. 77 F1
Barnacle CV7 .... 51 D4
Bedworth, Hawkesbury
CV2, CV7 .... 50 C3
Bedworth, Springfield CV12 .. 39 D1
Berkswell CV7 .... 58 C2
Brinklow CV23 .... 64 B2
Bulkington CV12 .... 40 A1
Church Lawford CV23 .... 80 C3
Coleshill B46 .... 34 A3
Cubbington CV32 .... 106 C4
Dunchurch CV23 .... 99 D2
Hampton in A B92 .... 45 D2
Hinckley LE10 .... 31 D4
Hinckley, Sketchley LE10 .... 31 F3
Kenilworth CV8 .... 93 D4
Kingsbury B78 .... 15 F2
Long Lawford CV23 .... 81 D3
Lutterworth LE17 .... 55 E3
Marton CV23 .... 115 C8
Nuneaton CV10 .... 39 E4
Pailton CV23 .... 66 A4
Solihull B26, B92 .... 44 B1
Southam CV33 .... 147 D3
Stoneleigh CV8 .... 94 B4
Warwick CV34 .... 108 C4
Wigston Parva LE10 .... 32 C1
Coventry Ret Mkt CV1 ...... 151 B2
Coventry St Coventry CV2 .. 62 A2
Nuneaton CV11 .... 29 E2
Southam CV33 .... 147 D3
Coventry Sta CV1 .... 151 B1
Coventry Tech Coll CV1 ...... 61 D1
Coventry Univ CV1 .... 151 C3
Coventry Univ Singer Hall
CV1 .... 151 D3
Coventry Walsgrave
Triangle Bsns Pk CV2 .... 51 D1
Coventry & Warwickshire
Hospl CV1 .... 151 C4
Coventry Whitefriars
(Mus) CV1 .... 151 D2
Coverley Pl CV22 .... 82 C2
Covers The B80 .... 103 F3
Cow La Lower Brailes OX15 .. 137 F2
Whateley B78 .... 9 F2
Cowan Cl CV22 .... 82 B1
Cowdray Cl CV31 .... 110 B4
Cowley Cl B36 .... 22 C1
Cowley Rd CV2 .... 62 B2
Cowley Way CV23 .... 101 F1
Cowper Cl CV34 .... 104 C1
Cowper Rd LE10 .... 31 E3
Cox Cl B50 .... 148 C3
Cox Cres CV22 .... 99 E2
Cox St CV1 .... 151 C3
Cox's Cl CV10 .... 29 D2
Cox's La CV23 .... 125 C7
Cozens Cl CV12 .... 39 D2
Crabbs Cross La B97 .... 102 C3
Crabmill Cl B93 .... 72 B4
Crabmill La CV6 .... 61 F4
Crabtree Gr 19 CV31 .... 110 B3
Crackley La Coventry CV4 .... 75 F2
Kenilworth CV8 .... 93 D4
Craddock Dr CV10 .... 28 B4
Craig Cl CV21 .... 110 A3
Craig Croft B37 .... 33 E1
Craigends Ave CV3 .... 78 C3
Crakston Cl CV2 .... 62 C1
Crammond Cl LE10 .... 31 D4
Cramper's Field CV6 .... 61 D3
Cranborne Chase CV2 .... 63 D3
Cranbourne Cl CV6 .... 49 F2
Cranbrook Hall B78 .... 7 F3
Craner's Rd CV1 .... 61 F2
Cranford Rd CV5 .... 60 B2
Cranham Cl B97 .... 102 A4
Cranmore Ave B90 .... 70 C4
Cranmore Bvd B90 .... 70 B4
Cranmore Rd
Birmingham B36 .... 22 C1
Solihull B90 .... 70 B4
Crantock Way CV11 .... 29 F2
Cranwell Dr CV35 .... 146 B1
Cranwell Rise B78 .... 8 A4
Cranwell Way B35 .... 22 A2
Crathie Cl CV2 .... 62 C3
Craven B77 .... 4 A1
Craven Arms Rd CV35 ...... 132 D3
Craven Ave CV3 .... 79 E4
Craven La CV33 .... 147 D2
Craven Rd CV21 .... 83 E2
Craven St CV5 .... 60 C1
Crawford Cl
Bidford-on-A B50 .... 148 B2
Royal Leamington Spa CV32 106 A3
Crawshaws Rd B36 .... 22 B1
Creampot Cl OX17 .... 134 C1
Creampot Cres OX17 .... 134 C1
Creampot La OX17 .... 134 C1
Crecy Rd CV3 .... 77 F4
Crediton Cl CV11 .... 29 F3
Crendon Cl B80 .... 103 F3
Crescent Ave CV3 .... 62 B1
Crescent St CV22 .... 99 E4
Crescent The
Baddesley Ensor CV9 .... 11 E2
Bidford-on-A B50 .... 148 B2
Birmingham, Coleshill Heath
B37 .... 44 C4
Brinklow CV23 .... 64 C3
Hampton in A B92 .... 44 C4
Keresley CV7 .... 48 C3
Lawford Heath CV23 .... 98 B3

Crescent The continued
Napton CV23 .... 125 C7
Wootton Wawen B95 .... 120 C7
Cressage Rd CV2 .... 63 D3
Cresswell Cl CV10 .... 29 E4
Crest Hill WR11 .... 127 D3
Crest The CV32 .... 106 B2
Crestwood B77 .... 4 A3
Crew La CV8 .... 93 F3
Creynolds Cl B90 .... 70 B2
Creynolds La B90 .... 70 C2
Crick Rd CV21 .... 101 E4
Cricket Cl CV5 .... 60 C2
Crigdon B77 .... 4 B1
Crimscote Cl B90 .... 70 C3
Cringlebrook B77 .... 9 E4
Critchley Dr CV22 .... 99 E2
Crockwell St CV36 .... 141 C4
Croft Cl
6 Bishops Tachbrook CV33 .. 122 F8
Stretton on D CV23 .... 96 C3
Warwick CV34 .... 109 E4
Wolvey LE10 .... 41 F2
Croft Field CV23 .... 125 C7
Croft Fields CV12 .... 39 D1
Croft Holm GL56 .... 140 B3
Croft Ind Est B37 .... 33 E1
Croft La Shrewley CV35 ...... 114 C6
Staverton NN11 .... 126 D8
Temple Grafton B49 .... 119 E2
Croft Mead CV10 .... 27 E2
Croft Mid Sch CV10 .... 28 C2
Croft Pool CV12 .... 38 C1
Croft Rd Atherstone CV9 ...... 12 B1
Bedworth CV12 .... 38 C1
Coventry CV1 .... 151 A2
Leek Wootton CV35 .... 105 D4
Littleton WR11 .... 127 F2
Nuneaton CV10 .... 28 C2
Croft Sch The CV37 .... 144 C1
Croft The Bulkington CV12 .. 40 A1
Church Lench WR11 .... 127 A6
Coventry CV6 .... 49 F2
Meriden CV7 .... 46 B1
Warton B79 .... 5 F2
Croft's La OX15 .... 142 D3
Crofts La B96 .... 102 A1
Crofts The B76 .... 22 A4
Cromarty Cl CV5 .... 60 A3
Cromdale B77 .... 4 B1
Cromdale Cl CV10 .... 28 A2
Cromer Rd CV32 .... 106 A1
Cromes Wood CV4 .... 59 E1
Crompton Ave B50 .... 148 C3
Crompton St CV34 .... 108 B3
Cromwell La CV4 .... 75 E3
Cromwell Pl CV35 .... 123 D2
Cromwell Rd CV22 .... 83 E1
Cromwell St CV6 .... 61 F3
Crondal Rd CV7 .... 50 A4
Crook House Yd CV23 .... 64 C2
Crooks La Alcester B49 ...... 143 E3
Studley B80 .... 103 E2
Croome Cl CV6 .... 60 C2
Cropredy CE Prim Sch
OX17 .... 134 C1
Cropthorne Cl B98 .... 103 D4
Cropthorne Dr B47 .... 69 D4
Crosbie Rd CV5 .... 60 C2
Cross Cheaping CV1 .... 151 B3
Cross Fields Rd 4 CV34 .. 108 C4
Cross La Braunston NN11 .. 117 E5
Cubbington CV32 .... 106 C2
Cross Leys CV36 .... 136 B6
Cross Rd Alcester B49 ...... 143 D2
Coventry CV6 .... 61 F4
Keresley CV7 .... 48 C3
12 Royal Leamington Spa
CV32 .... 105 E1
Cross Road Ind Est CV1 .. 61 F4
Cross St Coventry CV1 ...... 151 C4
Long Lawford CV23 .... 82 A3
Nuneaton CV10 .... 28 B2
Royal Leamington Spa CV32 106 A1
Rugby CV21 .... 83 E2
12 Warwick CV34 .... 108 C4
Cross Wlk B78 .... 11 D3
Crossfell B77 .... 4 A1
Crossgate Rd B98 .... 103 E4
Crossland Row LE10 .... 32 A3
Crosslands CV35 .... 146 B1
Crossley Ct CV6 .... 61 F4
Crossway Rd CV3 .... 77 D2
Crossways LE10 .... 31 F3
Crow Hill CV9 .... 11 E1
Crow Thorns CV21 .... 83 E3
Crowberry La B78 .... 14 B4
Crowden Rd B77 .... 4 A1
Crowhill Rd CV11 .... 30 A1
Crowleys Cl B95 .... 112 E6
Crowmere Rd CV2 .... 62 C4
Crown St CV33 .... 123 F7
Crown Terr CV31 .... 109 F4
Crown Way CV32 .... 106 A2
Crownhill Rd LE10 .... 31 E2
Croxall Dr B46 .... 25 D1
Croxhall St CV12 .... 39 E2
Croy Dr B35 .... 22 A2
Croydon Cl CV3 .... 77 D3
Crummock Cl CV6 .... 49 E2
Crutchley Way CV31 .... 110 A1
Cryersoak Cl 7 B90 .... 71 D4
Cryfield Grange Rd CV4 .... 76 B1
Cubbington CE Comb Sch
CV32 .... 106 C3

Cubbington Rd
Coventry CV6 ..... 50 A1
Royal Leamington Spa CV32 106 A2
Cuckoo La CV1 ..... 151 C3
Culey Wlk B37 ..... 33 E1
Culpepper Cl CV10 ..... 28 C2
Culverley Cres B93 ..... 71 F3
Culworth Cl
Royal Leamington Spa CV31 . 109 F3
Rugby CV21 ..... 83 F4
Culworth Ct CV6 ..... 61 F4
Culworth Row CV6 ..... 61 F4
Cumberland Cres CV32 ..... 106 B2
Cumberland Dr CV10 ..... 28 C2
Cumberland Wlk B75 ..... 13 D3
Cumbernauld Wlk 7 CV2 ... 63 D4
Cumbria Cl CV1 ..... 61 D2
Cumming St 6 CV31 ..... 110 A4
Cumsey The CV35 ..... 114 A5
Cundall Cl CV31 ..... 110 A3
Cunningham Way N CV22 ... 82 B1
Cunningham Way S CV22 ... 82 B1
Cup & Saucer OX17 ..... 134 C1
Curdworth La B76 ..... 23 D4
Curdworth Prim Sch B76 ..... 23 E3
Curie Cl CV21 ..... 83 E2
Curlew B77 ..... 10 A4
Curlew Cl
Stratford-u-A CV37 ..... 144 B2
Warton B79 ..... 5 F2
Curlieu Cl CV35 ..... 108 A4
Curlieu La CV35 ..... 114 C2
Curran Cl CV31 ..... 110 A2
Curriers Cl CV4 ..... 75 E4
Curtis Rd CV2 ..... 62 B3
Curzon Ave CV6 ..... 61 F4
Curzon Cl LE10 ..... 31 F4
Curzon Gr CV31 ..... 110 B3
Cut Throat La B94 ..... 87 E4
Cuttle Mill La B76 ..... 14 B2
Cuttle Pool La B93 ..... 72 C2
Cutworth Cl B76 ..... 13 D2
Cymbeline Way CV22 ..... 99 E3
Cypress Croft CV3 ..... 78 C4
Cypress La CV31 ..... 110 A1
Cyprus Ave B96 ..... 102 B1

D'Aubeny Rd CV4 ..... 76 B4
Dace B77 ..... 9 E4
Dadglow Rd CV33 ..... 124 B4
Daffern Ave CV7 ..... 37 D4
Daffern Rd CV7 ..... 39 D1
Dagtail La B97 ..... 102 B2
Dahlia Cl LE10 ..... 31 F3
Daimler Ave OX16 ..... 139 F4
Daimler Cl B36 ..... 22 C1
Daimler Rd CV6 ..... 61 E3
Daintree Croft CV3 ..... 77 E4
Dairyground The OX15 ..... 139 A3
Dalby Cl CV3 ..... 78 C4
Dale Ave CV37 ..... 145 E1
Dale Cl
10 Bishops Tachbrook CV33 . 122 F8
Long Itchington CV23 ..... 115 C4
Warwick CV34 ..... 109 D4
Dale End CV10 ..... 28 C3
Dale End Cl LE10 ..... 31 D4
Dale Meadow Cl CV7 ..... 74 A3
Dale St
Royal Leamington Spa CV32 . 109 F4
Rugby CV21 ..... 83 D2
Dale The B95 ..... 113 B2
Dalehouse La CV8 ..... 93 E4
Dales Cty Jun &
Inf Schs The B77 ..... 10 A4
Daleway Rd CV3 ..... 77 D2
Dalkeith Ave CV22 ..... 99 E4
Dallington Rd CV6 ..... 60 C3
Dalmahoy Cl CV11 ..... 40 B4
Dalmeny Rd CV4 ..... 75 E4
Dalton Cl CV23 ..... 81 D3
Dalton Gdns CV2 ..... 62 C2
Dalton Rd Bedworth CV12 ..... 39 D1
Coventry CV5 ..... 61 D1
Dalwood Way CV6 ..... 50 A2
Daly Ave CV35 ..... 114 F3
Dama Rd B78 ..... 8 C4
Dame Agnes Gr CV6 ..... 62 A4
Damson Cl B97 ..... 102 B3
Damson Ct LE10 ..... 31 D4
Damson Rd CV35 ..... 114 F3
Danbury Cl B76 ..... 13 D1
Dane Rd CV2 ..... 62 A2
Danesbury Cres CV31 ..... 110 B3
Daneswood Rd CV3 ..... 79 F4
Daniel Ave CV10 ..... 28 B2
Daniel Rd CV9 ..... 18 C4
Danvers Cl OX15 ..... 139 E1
Danvers Rd OX15 ..... 139 E1
Danzey Cl B98 ..... 103 D3
Danzey Green La B94 ..... 112 E8
Danzey Green Rd B36 ..... 22 A1
Danzey Sta B94 ..... 112 E8
Daphne Cl CV2 ..... 50 B2
Darfield Ct CV8 ..... 95 E3
Dark La Astwood Bank B96 ... 102 B1
Bedworth CV12 ..... 38 B1
Birchmoor B78 ..... 10 C4
Braunston NN11 ..... 117 E5
Coventry CV1 ..... 151 B4
Hollywood B47 ..... 69 D4
Tiddington CV37 ..... 145 F2
Wroxton OX15 ..... 139 D4
Darley Green Rd B93 ..... 72 A1
Darley Rd LE10 ..... 31 F3
Darlingscott Rd CV36 ..... 149 E2
Darnbrook B77 ..... 4 B1
Darnford Cl CV2 ..... 62 C4
Darrach Cl CV2 ..... 50 C1
Dart B77 ..... 10 A3
Dart Cl LE10 ..... 31 D4
Dartmouth Rd CV2 ..... 62 B3
Dartmouth Sch CV2 ..... 62 B3
Darwell Pk B77 ..... 4 A1
Darwin Cl CV2 ..... 63 D3
Dassett CE Prim Sch The
CV33 ..... 133 D7
Dassett Rd B93 ..... 71 F2
Datchet Cl CV5 ..... 60 B2
Davenport Dr B35 ..... 22 B2
Davenport Rd CV5 ..... 77 D4
Davenport Terr LE10 ..... 31 F4
Daventry Rd Barby CV23 ..... 101 E1
Coventry CV3 ..... 77 E4
Rugby CV22, CV23 ..... 99 F1
Southam CV33 ..... 147 E2
Staverton NN11 ..... 126 D8
Staverton NN11 ..... 126 E8
Daventry St CV33 ..... 147 D2
David Rd Bedworth CV7 ..... 49 F4
Coventry CV1 ..... 61 F1
Rugby CV22 ..... 99 E4
Davidson Ave CV31 ..... 110 A4
Davies Rd Bedworth CV7 ..... 49 F4
Moreton-in-M GL56 ..... 140 B3
Davis Cl CV32 ..... 105 E1
Dawes Cl CV2 ..... 62 A2
Dawley Cres B37 ..... 33 D1
Dawley Wlk 9 CV2 ..... 63 D4
Dawlish Cl CV11 ..... 29 F3
Dawlish Dr CV3 ..... 77 E3
Dawson Cl Redditch B97 ..... 102 B3
Whitnash CV31 ..... 110 A1
Dawson Rd CV3 ..... 62 A1
Day's La CV2 ..... 61 F2
Days Cl CV1 ..... 61 F2
Daytona Dr CV5 ..... 59 D4
De Mohun Cres CV36 ..... 141 F5
De Montfort Rd CV8 ..... 92 C3
De Montfort Way CV4 ..... 76 B3
De-Compton Cl CV7 ..... 49 D4
De-La-Bere Cres LE10 ..... 32 A3
Deacon Cl CV22 ..... 83 E1
Deacon St CV11 ..... 29 E2
Dean St CV2 ..... 62 A2
Deanbrook Cl B90 ..... 71 D3
Deane Par CV21 ..... 101 D4
Deane Rd CV21 ..... 101 D4
Deans Way CV7 ..... 49 E3
Deanston Croft CV2 ..... 50 C1
Deansway CV34 ..... 104 C1
Debden Cl Dorridge B93 ..... 71 F1
Wellesbourne CV35 ..... 146 B1
Dee Wlk Birmingham B36 ..... 33 D4
Daventry NN11 ..... 117 F1
Deedmore Rd CV2 ..... 50 B1
Deedmore Sch CV2 ..... 62 B4
Deegan Cl CV2 ..... 62 A3
Deeley B77 ..... 4 A1
Deep La B46 ..... 24 C3
Deepdale B77 ..... 4 B1
Deepmore Rd CV22 ..... 99 E4
Deer Leap The CV8 ..... 93 D3
Deerdale Way CV3 ..... 78 C4
Deerhill B77 ..... 4 B1
Deerhurst Cl GL56 ..... 140 F1
Deerhurst Mews CV22 ..... 99 E2
Deerhurst Rd CV6 ..... 49 D1
Deerings Rd CV21 ..... 101 D4
Deerpark Dr CV34 ..... 108 C4
Delage Cl CV6 ..... 50 A2
Delamere Cl B36 ..... 22 B1
Delamere Rd CV12 ..... 38 C1
Delamere Way CV32 ..... 106 B2
Delancey Keep B75 ..... 13 D3
Delaware Rd CV3 ..... 77 E3
Delhi Ave CV6 ..... 49 E1
Delius St CV4 ..... 59 F2
Dell Cl CV3 ..... 78 B3
Dell Ct B95 ..... 113 B5
Dell Farm Cl B93 ..... 72 A3
Delmore Way B76 ..... 22 A3
Delphl Cl CV34 ..... 109 F2
Deltic B77 ..... 4 A1
Delves Cres CV9 ..... 10 B1
Dempster Rd CV12 ..... 39 D2
Denbigh Cl OX16 ..... 139 F2
Denbigh Cnr B46 ..... 45 D3
Denbigh Rd CV6 ..... 60 C3
Denby Cl CV32 ..... 106 B2
Denby Croft B90 ..... 71 D3
Dencer Dr CV8 ..... 93 E2
Dene Cl CV35 ..... 132 B5
Denegate Cl B76 ..... 22 A3
Denehurst Way CV10 ..... 28 C2
Denewood Way CV8 ..... 93 E3
Denham Ave CV5 ..... 60 B2
Denham Ct CV9 ..... 18 C4
Denis Rd LE10 ..... 31 E3
Denne Cl CV37 ..... 145 D3
Dennett Cl CV34 ..... 104 C1
Dennis Rd CV2 ..... 62 A3
Denshaw Croft CV2 ..... 63 D4
Denton Cl CV8 ..... 92 B3
Denton Croft B93 ..... 71 E2
Denville Rd CV32 ..... 106 A2
Deppers Bridge CV33 ..... 124 B6
Derby Dr B37 ..... 33 D1
Derby La CV9 ..... 18 B4
Dereham Ct CV32 ..... 106 A1
Derek Ave B78 ..... 11 D3
Dering Cl CV2 ..... 62 B4
Deronda Cl CV12 ..... 39 D2
Derry Cl CV8 ..... 80 A2
Dersingham Dr CV6 ..... 50 A1
Derwent Cl Coventry CV5 ..... 59 F2
Royal Leamington Spa CV32 . 105 E1
Rugby CV21 ..... 83 E3
Derwent Rd Bedworth CV12 .. 39 D1
Coventry CV6 ..... 49 D1
Derwent Way CV11 ..... 29 F3
Despard Rd CV5 ..... 59 E2
Devereux Cl CV4 ..... 59 E1
Devitts Cl B90 ..... 70 C4
Devon Cl CV10 ..... 28 C2
Devon Gr CV2 ..... 62 A3
Devon Ox Rd CV23 ..... 101 F1
Devonish Cl B49 ..... 143 E3
Devoran Cl CV7 ..... 50 A4
Dew Cl CV22 ..... 99 E2
Dewar Gr CV21 ..... 83 F1
Dewsbury Ave CV3 ..... 77 D3
Dexter La CV9 ..... 16 B2
Dexter Way B78 ..... 10 C4
Dial House La CV5 ..... 59 F2
Diana Dr CV2 ..... 50 C1
Dickens Cl CV10 ..... 28 A2
Dickens Heath Rd B90 ..... 70 A3
Dickens Rd Coventry CV6 ..... 61 D4
Harbury CV33 ..... 123 E6
Rugby CV22 ..... 99 F3
Dickins Rd CV34 ..... 105 D1
Dickinson Ct CV22 ..... 83 D1
Didcot Cl B97 ..... 102 B3
Didcot Way DE12 ..... 3 F4
Diddington La B92, CV7 ..... 45 E1
Didgley Gr B37 ..... 33 D3
Didsbury Rd CV7 ..... 39 D1
Digbey Cl CV5 ..... 60 A3
Digby Cres B46 ..... 23 D2
Digby Dr B37 ..... 44 A3
Digby Pl CV7 ..... 46 B1
Digby Rd B46 ..... 33 F3
Dighton Cl CV37 ..... 129 F7
Dilcock Way CV4 ..... 75 F4
Dillam Cl CV6 ..... 50 A2
Dillotford Ave CV3 ..... 77 E3
Dingle Cl CV6 ..... 61 D3
Dingle La Appleby Magna CV9 ... 3 E3
Nether Whitacre B46 ..... 24 C3
Dingle The
Cheswick Green B90 ..... 70 B3
Nuneaton CV10 ..... 28 C3
Dingles Way CV37 ..... 145 D3
Dingleside Mid Sch B98 ... 103 D4
Dingley Rd CV12 ..... 40 A1
Discovery Way CV3 ..... 79 D4
Ditchford Cl B97 ..... 102 B2
Ditton Cl CV22 ..... 82 B1
Dixon Cl B35 ..... 22 A1
Dobbie Rd CV37 ..... 129 D1
Dobson La CV31 ..... 110 A2
Dockers Cl CV7 ..... 74 B4
Doctors La B95 ..... 113 B5
Dodd Ave CV34 ..... 109 E4
Dodwells Bridge Ind Est
LE10 ..... 30 C4
Dodwells Rd LE10 ..... 30 C4
Doe Bank La CV1 ..... 61 D2
Dog Kennel La B90 ..... 70 B4
Dog La Fenny Compton CV33 133 D7
Napton CV23 ..... 125 C8
Nether Whitacre B46 ..... 25 D4
Tamworth B77 ..... 4 A3
Dogberry Cl CV3 ..... 78 B3
Doglands The CV31 ..... 110 A2
Doily Cl OX15 ..... 142 D4
Doll Mus CV34 ..... 108 C3
Doncaster Cl CV2 ..... 62 B4
Done Cerce Cl CV22 ..... 99 E2
Donegal Cl CV4 ..... 76 A4
Dongan Rd CV34 ..... 108 C4
Donibristle Croft B35 ..... 22 A2
Donnington Ave CV6 ..... 60 C3
Donnington Rd CV36 ..... 149 F4
Donnithorne Ave CV10, CV11 29 E1
Doone Cl CV2 ..... 62 C3
Dorado B77 ..... 9 E3
Dorcas Cl CV11 ..... 40 B4
Dorchester Ave CV35 ..... 114 F3
Dorchester Gr OX16 ..... 139 F2
Dorchester Rd LE10 ..... 32 A4
Dorchester Way
Coventry CV2 ..... 63 D2
Nuneaton CV11 ..... 30 A4
Dordon Prim Sch B78 ..... 11 D3
Dordon Rd B78 ..... 10 C4
Doris Rd B46 ..... 33 F4
Dorlecote Pl CV10 ..... 39 E4
Dorlecote Rd CV10 ..... 39 E4
Dormer Harris Ave CV4 ..... 59 F1
Dormer Pl CV32 ..... 109 F4
Dormston Cl B91 ..... 71 E4
Dorney Cl CV5 ..... 76 C4
Dorothy Powell Way CV2 ..... 50 C1
Dorridge Croft B93 ..... 71 F1
Dorridge Jun & Inf Schs
B93 ..... 72 A2
Dorridge Rd B93 ..... 72 A1
Dorridge Sta B93 ..... 71 F1
Dorset Cl CV10 ..... 28 C2
Dorset Rd CV1 ..... 61 E3
Dorsington Rd CV37 ..... 128 E2
Dosthill Rd
(Two Gates) B77 ..... 9 E4
Dosthill Sch B77 ..... 9 E3
Douglas Rd Hollywood B47 .... 69 D4
Rugby CV21 ..... 83 E3
Doulton Cl CV2 ..... 50 C1
Dove Cl Bedworth CV12 ..... 38 C2
Hinckley LE10 ..... 31 D4
Dovecote Cl CV6 ..... 60 B3
Dovedale CV21 ..... 83 E4
Dovedale Ave CV6 ..... 49 F1
Dovehouse Dr CV35 ..... 146 B1
Dover Ave OX16 ..... 139 F3
Dover Farm Cl B77 ..... 10 A4
Dover St CV1 ..... 151 A3
Doverdale Cl B98 ..... 103 D4
Doverhouse La CV33 ..... 123 F7
Dovestone B77 ..... 4 B1
Dovey Dr B76 ..... 22 A4
Dowler's Hill Cres B98 ..... 103 D4
Dowley Croft CV3 ..... 63 D1
Down End OX15 ..... 142 D4
Downderry Way CV6 ..... 62 A3
Downing Cl B93 ..... 72 A2
Downing Cres CV12 ..... 39 E2
Downton Cl CV2 ..... 63 D4
Dowty Ave CV12 ..... 38 B1
Doyle Dr CV6 ..... 49 F2
Dr Phillips Sh Ctr The CV2 . 50 B1
Drake St CV6 ..... 61 E4
Drakes Cl B97 ..... 102 B3
Drakes Cross B47 ..... 69 D3
Draper Cl CV8 ..... 93 E2
Draper's Fields CV1 ..... 151 B4
Drawbridge Rd B90 ..... 69 F4
Draycote Water Ctry Pk
CV23 ..... 116 C8
Draycott Rd CV2 ..... 62 B4
Drayton Ave CV37 ..... 144 B2
Drayton Cl Bidford-on-A B50 148 B3
Fenny Drayton CV13 ..... 19 F3
Hartshill CV10 ..... 28 A4
Redditch B98 ..... 103 E4
Stratford-u-A CV37 ..... 144 B2
Drayton Cres CV5 ..... 59 E3
Drayton Ct CV34 ..... 104 C1
Drayton Fields Ind Est
NN11 ..... 117 F2
Drayton La Drayton Bassett
B78 ..... 8 B3
Fenny Drayton CV13 ..... 19 F3
Drayton Leys CV22 ..... 100 A4
Drayton Manor Dr
Fazeley B78 ..... 8 C4
Stratford-u-A CV37 ..... 120 C2
Drayton Manor Pk B78 ..... 8 C4
Drayton Rd Bedworth CV12 ... 39 E1
Solihull B90 ..... 70 C4
Drayton Sch OX16 ..... 139 F4
Drayton Way Daventry NN11 117 F2
Nuneaton CV10 ..... 28 B4
Drem Croft B35 ..... 22 A1
Drew Cres CV8 ..... 93 D2
Dreyer Cl CV22 ..... 82 B1
Driftway The CV36 ..... 149 F3
Drinkwater Cl CV33 ..... 123 F6
Drive The Coleshill B46 ..... 34 A3
Coventry CV2 ..... 62 C2
Dunchurch CV22 ..... 99 F2
Drivers La GL56 ..... 141 A1
Dronfield Rd CV2 ..... 62 A2
Drovers Way CV33 ..... 147 E2
Droylsdon Park Rd CV3 ..... 77 D2
Druid Rd CV2 ..... 62 A2
Drummond Cl CV6 ..... 60 C4
Drummond Way B37 ..... 33 E1
Drury La CV21 ..... 83 D2
Drybrooks Cl CV7 ..... 74 A3
Dryden Cl Kenilworth CV8 ..... 92 C2
Nuneaton CV10 ..... 27 F3
Dryden Pl CV22 ..... 82 C2
Dryden Wlk CV22 ..... 82 C2
Drymen Rd CV35 ..... 132 D3
Duck La CV37 ..... 129 B7
Duck Lake DE12 ..... 3 F4
Dudley Gn CV32 ..... 106 A1
Dudley Rd CV8 ..... 92 C1
Dudley Rise LE10 ..... 31 E3
Dudley St Atherstone CV9 ..... 18 B4
Coventry CV6 ..... 50 A1
Duffy Pl CV21 ..... 101 D4
Dugard Pl CV35 ..... 122 B7
Dugdale Ave
Bidford-on-A B50 ..... 148 B3
Stratford-u-A CV37 ..... 145 D3
Dugdale Rd CV6 ..... 61 D3
Dugdale St CV11 ..... 29 E2
Duggins La CV4, CV7 ..... 75 D4
Duke Barn Field CV2 ..... 62 A3
Duke St Coventry CV5 ..... 60 C1
Nuneaton CV11 ..... 29 D2
Royal Leamington Spa CV32 106 A1
Rugby CV21 ..... 83 D2
Dukes Jetty CV21 ..... 83 D3
Dukes Rd B78 ..... 11 D3
Dulverton Ave CV5 ..... 60 B2
Dulverton Pl GL56 ..... 140 B3
Dumble Pit La B48 ..... 85 F4
Dumphouse La B48 ..... 85 E2
Dunblane Dr CV32 ..... 106 B3
Duncan Dr CV22 ..... 99 E3
Dunchurch Boughton
CE Mid Sch CV22 ..... 99 E2
Dunchurch Cl CV7 ..... 74 A4
Dunchurch Cty Fst Sch
CV22 ..... 99 E2
Dunchurch Hall CV22 ..... 99 E2
Dunchurch Highway CV5 ..... 60 A2
Dunchurch Rd CV22 ..... 99 F3
Dunchurch Trad Est CV23 ..... 98 B2
Duncombe Gn 7 B46 ..... 33 F4
Duncroft Ave CV6 ..... 60 C4
Duncumb Rd B75 ..... 13 D3
Dunedin B77 ..... 4 A1
Dunhill Ave CV4 ..... 59 F2
Dunley Croft B90 ..... 70 C3
Dunlop Rd B97 ..... 102 B3
Dunn's La B78 ..... 11 D3
Dunnerdale CV21 ..... 83 E4
Dunnington CE Prim Sch
B49 ..... 127 E8
Dunnose Cl CV6 ..... 61 F4
Dunrose Cl CV2 ..... 62 C1
Dunsmore Ave Coventry CV3 78 B3
Rugby CV22 ..... 100 C4
Dunsmore Heath CV22 ..... 99 E2
Dunstall Cres 2 CV33 ..... 122 E8
Dunstan Croft B90 ..... 70 B4
Dunster B77 ..... 9 E4
Dunster Pl CV6 ..... 49 E2
Dunster Rd B37 ..... 33 E1
Dunsville Dr CV2 ..... 62 C4
Dunton Hall Rd B90 ..... 70 A4
Dunton La B76 ..... 14 B1
Dunvegan Cl Coventry CV3 .... 63 D1
Kenilworth CV8 ..... 93 E2
Duport Rd LE10 ..... 31 F4
Durbar Ave CV6 ..... 61 E4
Durham Cl CV7 ..... 48 C2
Durham Cres CV5 ..... 60 A4
Durham Croft B37 ..... 33 D1
Durlston Cl B77 ..... 4 A3
Dursley La B98 ..... 112 A6
Dutton Rd CV2 ..... 50 B2
Duttons Cl CV37 ..... 121 B7
Duxford Cl Redditch B97 ..... 102 A4
Wellesbourne CV35 ..... 146 B1
Dwarris Wlk CV34 ..... 104 C1
Dyas Rd B47 ..... 69 D4
Dyce Cl B35 ..... 22 A2
Dyer's La
Chipping Campden GL55 ..... 135 A2
Wolston CV8 ..... 80 A2
Dyers La B94 ..... 87 E4
Dyers Rd CV11 ..... 40 C3
Dymond Rd CV6 ..... 49 E2
Dysart Cl CV1 ..... 61 F2
Dyson Cl CV21 ..... 83 F1
Dyson St CV4 ..... 59 F2

Eacott Cl CV6 ..... 49 D2
Eadie St CV10 ..... 28 B2
Eagle Cl CV11 ..... 40 A4
Eagle Dr B77 ..... 4 B2
Eagle Gr B36 ..... 33 D4
Eagle Ho CV1 ..... 61 E3
Eagle La CV8 ..... 92 C2
Eagle St Coventry CV1 ..... 61 E3
Royal Leamington Spa CV31 110 A3
Eagle St E CV1 ..... 61 E3
Ealingham B77 ..... 4 A1
Earl St Bedworth CV12 ..... 39 E1
Coventry CV1 ..... 151 C2
Royal Leamington Spa CV32 106 A1
Rugby CV21 ..... 83 D2
Earl's Croft The CV3 ..... 77 E4
Earl's Wlk CV3 ..... 79 E4
Earles Cl CV23 ..... 147 F4
Earls Rd CV11 ..... 29 D3
Earlsdon Ave N CV5 ..... 60 C1
Earlsdon Ave S CV5 ..... 77 D4
Earlsdon Bsns Ctr CV5 ..... 76 C4
Earlsdon Prim Sch CV5 ..... 61 D1
Earlsdon St CV5 ..... 76 C4
Earlsmere B94 ..... 70 A1
Earlswood Comm B94 ..... 87 D3
Earlswood Rd B93 ..... 71 E1
Earlswood Sta B94 ..... 69 E1
Earlswood Trad Est B94 ..... 86 B3
Easedale Cl Coventry CV3 ..... 77 D3
Nuneaton CV11 ..... 30 A3
Easenhall Cl B93 ..... 72 A2
Easenhall Rd CV23 ..... 66 A1
Easingwold Rd CV35 ..... 132 D4
East Ave Bedworth CV12 ..... 39 E1
Coventry CV2 ..... 62 A1
East Car Park Rd B40 ..... 44 C2
East Cl LE10 ..... 31 E4
East Dene CV32 ..... 106 A1
East End OX15 ..... 142 D4
East Gr CV31 ..... 110 A3
East Green Dr CV37 ..... 144 B2
East House Dr CV9 ..... 16 B2
East Side WR11 ..... 128 A2
East St Coventry CV1 ..... 61 F2
Long Compton CV36 ..... 141 C3
Moreton-in-M GL56 ..... 140 A3
Rugby CV21 ..... 83 E2
Tamworth B77 ..... 9 E3
East Union St CV22 ..... 83 D1
East Way B92 ..... 45 D2
Eastboro Way CV11 ..... 29 F1
Eastbourne Cl CV6 ..... 60 C3
Eastcote La B92 ..... 56 C2
Eastcotes CV4 ..... 60 A1
Eastern Green Jun Sch
CV5 ..... 59 E3
Eastern Green Rd CV5 ..... 59 F2
Eastern Hill B96 ..... 102 C1
Eastfield Cl CV37 ..... 144 C3
Eastfield Pl CV21 ..... 83 D2
Eastfield Rd Nuneaton CV10 .. 29 E3
Royal Leamington Spa CV32 110 A4
Eastgate OX15 ..... 139 B8
Eastlands Cty Prim Sch
CV21 ..... 83 E1
Eastlands Gr CV5 ..... 60 C2
Eastlands Pl CV21 ..... 83 E2
Eastlands Rd CV21 ..... 83 E2
Eastlang Rd CV7 ..... 36 C2
Eastleigh Ave CV5 ..... 76 C4
Eastleigh Croft B76 ..... 22 A4
Eastley Cres CV34 ..... 108 A4
Eastnor Gr CV31 ..... 110 A4

Easton Gr B47 .... 69 D4
Eastway B40 .... 44 C2
Eastwood Cl **9** CV31 ..... 110 B3
Eastwood Gr CV21 .... 101 E4
Easy La CV21 .... 82 C2
Eathorpe Cl Coventry CV2 .. 50 B1
Redditch B98 .... 103 F4
Eaton Cl CV32 .... 105 E1
Eaton Rd CV1 .... 151 B1
Eaves Green La CV7 .... 46 C1
Eborall Cl CV34 .... 104 C1
Ebourne Cl CV8 .... 93 D2
Ebrington Dr CV35 .... 114 F5
Ebrington & St James
  CE Prim Sch GL55 .... 135 B1
Ebro Cres CV3 .... 62 C1
Eburne Prim Sch CV2 ...... 50 B1
Eburne Rd CV2 .... 50 B2
Eccles Cl CV2 .... 62 B4
Eckington Cl B98 .... 103 D4
Eclipse Rd B49 .... 143 D2
Eclipse Trad Est B49 ...... 143 D2
Ecton Leys CV22 .... 100 A4
Edale P 4 A1
Edale Gn LE10 .... 31 F3
Edale Way CV6 .... 62 A4
Eddenswood Cl B78 .... 8 C3
Eden Cl B80 .... 103 E2
Eden Croft CV8 .... 93 D2
Eden Gr B37 .... 33 E1
Eden Rd Coventry CV2 ..... 63 D4
Rugby CV21 .... 83 F1
Eden St CV6 .... 61 F4
Edge Hill CV9 .... 10 A1
Edge La B95 .... 113 C5
Edgecote CV21 .... 83 F1
Edgefield Rd CV2 .... 63 D4
Edgehill Ctry Pk OX17 .... 133 B3
Edgehill Pl CV4 .... 59 E1
Edgehill Rd CV35 .... 123 C2
Edgewick Com Prim Sch
  CV6 .... 61 F4
Edgioake La B96 .... 118 C7
Edgwick Park Ind Est CV6 .. 61 F4
Edgwick Rd CV6 .... 61 F4
Edinburgh Cl OX16 .... 139 F4
Edinburgh Cres CV31 ...... 109 F3
Edinburgh Rd Hurley CV9 .. 16 B3
Nuneaton CV10 .... 28 B3
Edinburgh Way
  Banbury OX16 .... 139 F3
  Long Lawford CV23 .... 82 A3
Edingale Rd CV2 .... 62 C4
Edison Rd B76 .... 24 A2
Edmondes Cl CV34 .... 104 C1
Edmonds Cl CV37 .... 129 D1
Edmondscote Rd CV32 .... 109 E4
Edmondson Cl CV22 .... 99 E2
Edmund Rd CV1 .... 61 E3
Edmunds Rd
  Banbury OX16 .... 139 F3
  Wroxton OX15 .... 139 D4
Edstone Cl B93 .... 71 F2
Edward Bailey Cl CV3 ..... 78 C4
Edward Rd Bedworth CV12 .. 39 E2
Coventry CV6 .... 49 D2
Water Orton B46 .... 23 E2
Edward St Coventry CV6 .. 61 F3
Nuneaton CV11 .... 29 E2
3 Royal Leamington Spa
  CV32 .... 105 E1
Rugby CV21 .... 82 C2
Warwick CV34 .... 108 B4
Edward Tyler Rd CV7 ...... 39 E3
Edwards Gr CV8 .... 93 E3
Edyth Rd CV2 .... 62 C2
Edyvean Cl CV22 .... 99 F3
Egerton Cl CV21 .... 82 C3
Eileen Gdns B37 .... 33 D2
Elan Cl CV32 .... 106 B2
Elborow St CV21 .... 83 D2
Elbury Croft B93 .... 71 F3
Eld Rd CV6 .... 61 F4
Elder Cl Kingsbury B78 .... 15 E4
Rugby CV22 .... 82 A1
Elderberry Way CV2 .... 62 A3
Eldersfield Gr B91 .... 71 D4
Eldorado Cl B80 .... 103 E2
Elford Gr B37 .... 33 D1
Elgar Cl CV11 .... 40 A4
Elgar Rd CV6 .... 62 A4
Eliot Cl CV34 .... 104 C1
Eliot Ct CV22 .... 82 C2
Elizabeth Ave B78 .... 5 D1
Elizabeth Ct CV34 .... 109 D3
Elizabeth Rd CV31 .... 109 F3
Elizabeth Way
  Kenilworth CV8 .... 92 C3
  Long Lawford CV23 .... 82 A3
Elkington Croft **8** B90 .. 71 D3
Elkington La CV23 .... 101 D1
Elkington St CV6 .... 61 F4
Ell La CV23 .... 64 C2
Ellacombe Rd CV2 .... 62 B4
Ellen Badger Com Hospl
  CV36 .... 137 A4
Ellerbeck B77 .... 4 A1
Ellerdene Cl B98 .... 102 B4
Ellesmere Rd CV12 .... 39 D1
Ellice Dr B36 .... 33 D4
Elliot Cl B50 .... 148 B3
Elliot Dr CV35 .... 146 B2
Elliot's Field Ret Pk CV21 .. 83 D3
Elliotts Orch CV37 .... 122 A7
Elliston Gr CV31 .... 110 B3
Ellys Rd CV1 .... 61 E3
Elm Bank CV32 .... 106 A2

Elm Cl Binley Woods CV3 ... 79 E4
  Ilmington CV36 .... 136 B6
  Pebworth CV37 .... 128 F1
  Southam CV33 .... 147 D2
Elm Dr B49 .... 143 E2
Elm Gr Arley CV7 .... 26 C1
  Balsall Common CV7 ..... 74 B3
  Ebrington GL55 .... 135 F3
  Hurley CV9 .... 16 B2
Elm Rd
  Royal Leamington Spa CV32 .. 106 A2
  Stratford-u-A CV37 ...... 144 C3
Elm Row CV23 .... 115 F3
Elm Tree Ave CV4 .... 60 A1
Elm Tree Cl B78 .... 15 E3
Elm Tree Dr LE10 .... 31 F4
Elm Tree Rd CV12 .... 40 B1
Elm Tree Rise B92 .... 57 D3
Elmbank CV33 .... 147 D2
Elmbank Rd CV8 .... 92 C3
Elmbridge Dr B90 .... 71 D3
Elmdene Cl Hatton CV35 .. 114 C5
  Wolston CV8 .... 80 A2
Elmdene Rd CV8 .... 93 D2
Elmdon Cl B37 .... 44 A4
Elmdon La Birmingham B37 .. 44 A3
  Solihull B26 .... 44 A2
Elmdon Rd B37 .... 44 A4
Elmdon Trad Est B37 ..... 44 B3
Elmfield Rd CV10 .... 29 E4
Elmhurst Cl B97 .... 102 B2
Elmhurst Rd CV6 .... 50 A2
Elmore Cl CV3 .... 78 B4
Elmore Rd CV22 .... 82 C1
Elms Ct CV9 .... 3 D1
Elms Dr Austrey CV9 ...... 3 D1
  Rugby CV22 .... 100 C4
Elms Paddock The CV23 ... 83 F3
Elms The Bedworth CV12 .. 38 C1
  Leek Wootton CV35 ...... 104 C3
  Stratford-u-A CV37 ...... 145 D2
Elmsdale Ave CV6 .... 49 F1
Elmstone Cl B97 .... 102 B3
Elmwood Ave CV6 .... 60 C3
Elmwood Cl CV7 .... 74 A3
Elmwood Gr B47 .... 69 D3
Elphin Cl CV6 .... 49 D2
Elsee Rd CV21 .... 83 D2
Eltham Rd CV3 .... 77 F4
Elton Cl CV32 .... 106 B1
Elton Croft B93 .... 71 F2
Elva Croft B36 .... 22 C1
Elvers Green La B93 ...... 72 C4
Elwy Circ CV7 .... 49 E3
Ely Cl Birmingham B37 .... 33 D1
  Coventry CV2 .... 63 D3
Ely St CV37 .... 145 D1
Embassy Wlk CV2 .... 62 B4
Emerald Way CV31 .... 109 F3
Emerson Rd CV2 .... 62 B2
Emery Cl CV2 .... 62 C4
Emmott Dr CV31 .... 110 A3
Emperor Way CV21 .... 82 C4
Empire Rd CV4 .... 59 F1
Emscote Cty Fst Sch CV34 .. 109 D4
Emscote Lawn Prep Sch
  CV34 .... 109 D4
Emscote Rd Coventry CV3 .. 62 B1
  Warwick CV34 .... 109 D4
Ena Rd CV1 .... 61 E3
End The OX7 .... 142 A2
Endemere Rd CV6 .... 61 E4
Endsleigh Gdns CV31 ..... 110 A3
Enfield Rd Coventry CV2 .. 62 A2
  Redditch B97 .... 102 B3
Engine La B77 .... 4 A1
England Cres CV31 .... 109 F4
Engleton Rd CV6 .... 61 D3
English Martyrs
  RC Prim Sch CV21 ...... 101 D4
Ennerdale CV21 .... 83 E4
Ennerdale Cl CV32 .... 105 E1
Ennerdale Cres CV11 ..... 29 F3
Ennerdale La CV2 .... 62 C2
Ennersdale Bglws B46 .... 23 F1
Ennersdale Cl B46 .... 23 F1
Ennersdale Rd B46 .... 23 F1
Enright Cl CV32 .... 105 F1
Ensign Bsns Ctr CV4 ..... 75 F3
Ensign Cl CV4 .... 59 E1
Ensor Cl CV11 .... 30 A3
Ensor Dr B78 .... 4 C1
Epping Way CV32 .... 106 B2
Epsom Cl Bedworth CV12 .. 39 D2
  Redditch B97 .... 102 B4
Epsom Rd
  Royal Leamington Spa CV32 .. 106 B2
  Rugby CV22 .... 82 B1
Epwell Rd Shutford OX15 .. 138 F3
  Upper Tysoe CV35 .... 138 B6
Erdington Rd CV9 .... 18 B4
Eric Grey Cl CV2 .... 62 A3
Erica Ave CV12 .... 38 C1
Erica Dr CV31 .... 110 A1
Eringden B77 .... 4 A1
Erithway Rd CV3 .... 77 D2
Ernesford Grange Prim Sch
  CV3 .... 62 C1
Ernesford Grange Sch &
  Com Coll CV3 .... 78 B4
Ernest Richards Rd CV12 .. 39 D2
Ernsford Ave CV3 .... 62 A1
Ernsford Cl B93 .... 71 F1
Errington GL56 .... 140 B3
Esher Dr CV3 .... 77 F4
Eskdale CV21 .... 83 E4
Eskdale Rd LE10 .... 31 D4

Eskdale Wlk CV3 .... 78 B4
Essen La CV23 .... 101 F2
Essex Cl Coventry CV5 ... 60 A2
  Kenilworth CV8 .... 92 C1
Essex Gn CV33 .... 132 F7
Essex St CV21 .... 83 D2
Esterton Cl CV6 .... 49 E1
Ethelfield Rd CV2 .... 62 A2
Ethelfleda B77 .... 9 F3
Eton Rd CV37 .... 145 E1
Ettingley Dr B98 .... 103 D3
Ettington CE Prim Sch
  CV37 .... 131 B3
Ettington Cl Dorridge B93 .. 71 E1
  Wellesbourne CV35 ...... 146 B1
Ettington Rd Coventry CV5 .. 60 A2
  Wellesbourne CV35 ...... 146 B1
Eunal Ct B97 .... 102 C3
Europa Way
  Birmingham B26 .... 44 B2
  Royal Leamington Spa CV34 .. 109 E3
Eustace Rd CV12 .... 40 B1
Euston Cres CV3 .... 78 B3
Euston Pl CV32 .... 109 F4
Evans Cl Bedworth CV12 .. 39 E2
  Stratford-u-A CV37 ...... 144 B1
Evans Gr CV31 .... 110 A1
Evans Rd CV22 .... 82 B1
Evelyn Ave CV6 .... 49 F1
Evenlode Cl CV37 .... 145 E1
Evenlode Cres CV6 .... 60 C3
Evenlode Gdns GL56 ..... 140 B3
Evenlode Rd GL56 .... 140 B3
Everard Cl CV23 .... 84 A3
Everard Ct CV11 .... 29 F1
Everdon Cl CV22 .... 100 C4
Everdon Rd CV6 .... 49 D1
Everest Rd CV22 .... 99 F4
Everglade Rd CV9 .... 10 B1
Everitt Dr B93 .... 72 A3
Eversleigh Rd CV6 .... 60 C4
Evesham Pl CV37 .... 144 C1
Evesham Rd
  Bidford-on-A B50 .... 128 E8
  Church Lench WR11 .... 127 A6
  Cookhill B49 .... 118 D5
  Harvington WR11 .... 127 D4
  Littleton WR11 .... 127 F3
  Offenham WR11 .... 127 F3
  Redditch,Dagtail End
    B96, B97 .... 102 C2
  Redditch,Headless Cross
    B97 .... 102 B4
  Salford Priors WR11 .... 127 F5
  Stratford-u-A CV37 ...... 144 B1
Evesham St B49 .... 143 D2
Evesham Wlk CV4 .... 76 B3
Evreux Way CV21 .... 83 D2
Exbury Way CV11 .... 39 F4
Exeter Cl CV3 .... 78 B4
Exhall Cl CV37 .... 145 E1
Exhall Fst Sch CV7 ...... 49 F4
Exhall Gn CV7 .... 49 F4
Exhall Grange Sch CV7 .. 49 E3
Exhall Rd CV7 .... 49 D3
Exham Cl CV34 .... 104 C1
Exhibition Way B40 ...... 44 B2
Exis Ct CV11 .... 29 F1
Exminster Rd CV3 .... 77 F3
Exmoor Dr CV32 .... 106 B2
Exmouth Cl CV2 .... 62 B4
Exton Cl CV7 .... 49 E3
Eydon Cl CV21 .... 83 F3
Eyffler Cl CV34 .... 108 B4

Fabian Cl CV3 .... 78 B4
Fair Cl CV23 .... 97 E1
Fair Isle Dr CV10 .... 28 C1
Fairbanks Cl CV2 .... 63 D4
Fairbourne Way CV6 ..... 60 C4
Faircroft CV8 .... 92 C2
Faircroft Rd B36 .... 22 B1
Fairfax Cl CV35 .... 122 A7
Fairfax St CV1 .... 151 C3
Fairfield Ct CV3 .... 78 A4
Fairfield Rise CV7 .... 46 B1
Fairfields Hill B78 .... 10 C4
Fairfields Wlk CV37 ..... 144 B2
Fairhurst Dr CV32 .... 105 F2
Fairlands Pk CV4 .... 76 C3
Fairlawn Cl CV32 .... 105 E1
Fairlawns B76 .... 22 A4
Fairmile Cl CV3 .... 78 B4
Fairview Mews **6** B46 .. 33 F4
Fairwater Cres B49 ..... 143 E2
Fairway Nuneaton CV11 .. 40 A4
  Tamworth B77 .... 9 F3
Fairway Ct B77 .... 4 A2
Fairway Rise CV8 .... 93 E3
Fairway The Banbury OX16 .. 139 F4
  Hinckley LE10 .... 31 F4
Fairways CV5 .... 60 A3
Fairways The CV32 ...... 105 E1
Falcon B77 .... 10 A3
Falcon Ave CV3 .... 78 C4
Falcon Cl CV11 .... 40 A4
Falcon Cres B50 .... 148 C3
Falcon Lodge Cres B75 .. 13 C3
Falconers Gn LE10 ...... 31 F3
Falcons The B75 .... 13 D3
Falkland Cl CV4 .... 75 E4
Falkland Pl CV33 .... 133 A7
Falkland Way B36 ...... 33 D3
Falkwood Gr B93 .... 71 F2
Fallow Hill CV31 .... 110 B3
Falmouth Cl CV11 .... 30 A4
Falmouth Rd CV2 .... 62 C2
Falstaff B47 .... 69 D3

Falstaff Cl Nuneaton CV11 .. 30 A1
  Sutton Coldfield B76 .... 22 A4
Falstaff Dr CV22 .... 99 E3
Falstaff Rd CV4 .... 59 F1
Fancott Dr CV8 .... 92 C3
Fant Hill OX15 .... 137 E3
Far Gosford St CV1 ...... 61 F1
Far Lash LE10 .... 31 F4
Far Moor La B98 .... 112 A6
Faraday Ave B76 .... 24 A2
Faraday Rd Hinckley LE10 .. 30 C4
  Rugby CV22 .... 83 E1
Farber Rd CV2 .... 63 D3
Farcroft Ave CV5 .... 59 E2
Fareham Ave CV22 ...... 100 C4
Farley Ave CV33 .... 123 E6
Farley St CV31 .... 110 A4
Farlow Cl CV6 .... 62 A3
Farm Cl Coventry CV6 ... 49 D2
  Harbury CV33 .... 123 E6
  Shipston-on-S CV36 .... 149 F3
Farm Gr CV22 .... 83 E1
Farm La Easenhall CV23 .. 65 F2
  Grendon CV9 .... 11 F3
  Littleton WR11 .... 127 F1
Farm Rd Hinckley LE10 .. 31 F3
  Kenilworth CV8 .... 92 C1
  Royal Leamington Spa CV32 .. 106 A2
Farm St CV33 .... 123 E6
Farm Stile NN11 .... 134 E8
Farm Wlk **2** CV33 ... 122 F8
Farman Rd CV5 .... 61 D1
Farmcote Cl B97 .... 102 B2
Farmcote Rd CV2 .... 50 A2
Farmer Ward Rd CV8 ... 93 D2
Farmhouse Way B90 ... 71 D4
Farmside CV3 .... 78 B3
Farmstead The CV3 .... 78 A4
Farnborough CE Jun &
  Inf Sch OX17 .... 133 F4
Farnborough Dr B90 .... 70 C3
Farnborough Hall OX17 .. 133 F4
Farnborough Rd B35 ... 22 A2
Farndale Ave CV6 ...... 49 E2
Farndon Ave B37 ...... 44 A4
Farndon Cl CV12 ...... 40 A2
Farnworth Gr B36 ..... 22 C1
Farr Dr CV4 .... 60 A1
Farren Rd CV2 .... 62 C3
Farriers Ct CV23 .... 65 E4
Farriers Way Hinckley LE10 .. 31 F3
  Nuneaton CV11 .... 29 F1
Farrington Cl CV35 .... 146 B1
Farrington Ct CV35 .... 146 B1
Farther Sand Cl CV35 .. 121 F4
Farthing La B76 .... 23 E3
Farvale Rd B76 .... 22 B3
Faseman Ave CV4 ..... 59 F2
Faulconbridge Ave CV5 .. 59 F2
Faultlands Cl CV11 .... 39 F4
Fawley Cl CV3 .... 78 B3
Fawsley Leys CV22 .... 100 A4
Faygate Cl CV2 .... 62 C2
Featherbed La
  Bascote CV33 .... 115 B1
  Cherington CV36 ...... 141 D7
  Coventry CV4 .... 76 A3
  Redditch B97 .... 102 B3
  Rugby CV21 .... 84 A1
  Wilmcote CV37 .... 120 D5
  Withybrook CV7 ...... 52 C3
Featherston Rd LE10 .. 31 F3
Featherstone Cl CV10 .. 29 E1
Feckenham Rd
  Astwood Bank B96 .... 102 C1
  Redditch, Headless Cross
    B97 .... 102 B4
  Redditch, Hunt End B97 .. 102 B2
Feilding Cl CV2 .... 63 D3
Feilding Way CV10 .... 28 A3
Feldon Mid Sch CV23 .. 115 E3
Felgate Cl B90 .... 71 D3
Fell Gr CV32 .... 106 B2
Fell Mill La CV36 ..... 137 A3
Fell's La CV23 .... 125 C8
Fellmore Gr CV31 .... 110 B4
Fellows Way CV21 .... 100 C4
Felspar Rd B77 .... 4 A2
Felton Cl CV2 .... 50 C1
Fen End Rd CV8 ...... 73 F2
Fencote Ave B37 ..... 33 D2
Fenn Lanes CV13 .... 20 B4
Fennis Cl B93 .... 71 F2
Fenny Compton Rd OX17 .. 134 B5
Fenside Ave CV3 ..... 77 F2
Fentham Cl B92 ...... 57 D3
Fentham Gn B92 ..... 57 D3
Fentham Rd B92 ..... 57 D3
Fenton Rd B47 .... 69 D4
Fenwick Cl B49 ...... 143 E3
Fenwick Dr CV21 .... 101 D4
Fern Cl Coventry CV2 .. 50 B1
  Salford Priors WR11 .. 127 D6
Fern Dale Rd CV7 .... 73 F3
Fern Hill Way LE10 .. 41 E2
Ferncumbe CE Prim
  Sch The CV35 .... 114 D6
Ferndale Cl CV11 .... 40 A4
Ferndale Ct B46 ..... 34 A3
Ferndale Dr CV8 ..... 93 D1
Ferndale Mews B46 .. 34 A3
Ferndale Rd Banbury OX16 .. 139 F4
  Binley Woods CV3 .... 79 E4
Ferndown Cl CV4 .... 60 A2
Ferndown Ct CV22 ... 82 C1
Ferndown Rd CV22 .. 82 C1
Ferndown Terr CV22 .. 82 C1
Fernhill Cl CV8 .... 92 C3

Fernhill Dr CV32 ...... 106 A1
Fernhill La CV7 .... 73 F3
Fernwood B98 .... 103 D3
Ferrers Cl CV4 .... 59 F1
Ferrieres Cl CV22 .... 99 E2
Ferry La CV37 .... 121 D3
Fetherston Cres CV8 .. 79 D1
Fiddlers Gn B92 ..... 57 D4
Field Barn Rd
  Hampton Magna CV35 .. 114 F4
  Warwick CV35 .... 108 A4
Field Cl Kenilworth CV8 .. 93 D3
  Warwick CV34 .... 109 D4
Field Gate La CV33 .. 133 E7
Field Head La CV34 .. 109 D3
Field La B91 .... 56 A3
Field March CV3 .... 78 C3
Field View Braunston NN11 .. 117 E5
  Ryton-on-D CV8 ..... 79 D1
Field View Cl CV7 ... 50 A4
Field Way B94 ...... 88 B3
Fieldfare Croft B36 .. 33 D4
Fieldgate La Kenilworth CV8 .. 92 C3
  Whitnash CV31 ...... 110 A1
Fieldhouse Cl B95 .. 113 B4
Fielding Cl CV9 .... 12 B1
Fields Ct CV34 .... 108 C4
Fields Park Dr B49 .. 143 E2
Fieldside La CV3 ... 62 C2
Fieldways Cl B47 ... 69 D4
Fife Rd CV5 .... 60 C1
Fife St CV11 ...... 29 D2
Fifield Cl CV11 ... 29 E1
Fighting Cl CV35 .. 132 B6
Fillingham Cl B37 .. 33 E1
Fillongley CE Fst Sch CV7 .. 36 C2
Fillongley Rd Maxstoke B46 .. 35 E2
  Meriden CV7 .... 46 C2
Filton Croft B35 ... 22 A2
Finch Cl CV6 ...... 49 E1
Finch La WR11 .... 127 D3
Findon Cl CV12 ... 40 B2
Fineacre La CV8,CV23 .. 96 B3
Finford Croft CV7 .. 74 A3
Fingal Cl CV3 .... 78 B3
Fingest Cl CV5 .. 60 A2
Finham Cres CV8 .. 93 D3
Finham Gr CV3 .. 77 E2
Finham Green Rd CV3 .. 77 D2
Finham Park Comp Sch
  CV3 .... 77 D2
Finham Prim Sch CV3 .. 77 D2
Finham Rd CV8 .. 93 D3
Finmere CV21 ... 83 E3
Finnemore Cl CV3 .. 77 D3
Finwood Rd CV35 .. 113 D3
Fir Gr CV4 .... 60 A1
Fir Tree Ave CV4 .. 60 A1
Fir Tree Gr CV11 .. 39 E4
Fircroft B78 ..... 15 E4
Fire Service Tech Coll
  GL56 .... 140 C3
Fire Station Rd B26 .. 44 B3
Firethorn Cres CV31 .. 110 A1
Firleigh Dr CV12 .. 40 B1
Firs Dr CV22 .... 82 C1
Firs The Bedworth CV12 .. 38 C1
  Coventry CV5 ...... 77 D4
  Kingsbury B78 ..... 15 E4
  Lower Quinton CV37 .. 129 E2
  Wroxton OX15 ..... 139 D4
First Ave
  Birmingham, Tyburn B76 .. 22 A3
  Coventry CV3 ...... 62 B1
First Exhibition Ave B40 .. 44 B2
Firth Ave GL56 .... 140 C3
Firtree Cl OX16 ... 139 F5
Firtree La CV7 .... 37 D4
Fisher Ave CV22 .. 100 C4
Fisher Rd
  Bishops Itchington CV33 .. 124 A4
  Coventry CV6 ...... 61 F4
Fisher's Ct CV34 .. 108 B2
Fishers Cl CV23 .. 101 F1
Fishers Dr B90 ... 69 F3
Fishponds Rd CV8 .. 92 C2
Fishpool La CV7 ... 45 D3
Fitton St CV11 ... 29 D2
Fitzalan Cl CV23 .. 81 D3
Fitzroy Cl CV2 ... 63 D3
Five Ways CV35 .. 90 C1
Five Ways Rd CV35 .. 114 C7
Fivefield Rd CV7 .. 48 C3
Fladbury Cl B98 .. 103 D4
Flamboro' Cl CV3 .. 78 C4
Flamville Rd LE10 .. 32 A3
Flats La CV3 ..... 3 D1
Flaunden Cl CV5 .. 60 A2
Flavel Cres CV31 .. 109 F4
Flavel Ct CV9 .... 3 D1
Flax Cl B47 ...... 69 D3
Flaxley Cl B98 ... 112 A6
Flecknoe Cl B36 .. 22 B1
Flecknose St CV3 .. 78 B3
Fleet Cres CV21 .. 83 F1
Fleet St CV1 ..... 151 B3
Fleming Rd CV35 .. 30 C4
Fletchamstead Highway
  CV5 .... 76 B4
Fletcher Gr B93 .. 72 A2
Fletcher Rd LE10 .. 31 F4
Fletchworth Gate CV5 .. 76 B4
Flint Cl CV9 ..... 12 C1
Florence Cl Atherstone CV9 .. 12 B1
  Bedworth CV12 .... 49 F4

Flower Rd CV37 144 C3
Flowerdale Dr CV2 62 A3
Flude Rd CV7 49 E3
Flying Fields Rd CV33 147 E2
Flynt Ave CV5 60 A3
Foldyard Cl B76 22 A4
Foleshill CE Prim Sch CV6 50 A1
Foleshill Rd CV1, CV6 61 E3
Folkland Gn CV6 61 D4
Folly Ct OX15 142 E8
Folly La Baddesley Ensor CV9 17 E4
Napton CV23 125 B7
Fontmell Cl CV2 63 D2
Ford Cotts CV33 106 C1
Ford La CV37 113 F1
Ford St Coventry CV1 151 C3
Nuneaton CV10 28 C2
Fordbridge Inf Sch B37 33 D3
Fordbridge Rd B37 33 D3
Forde Hall La B94,B95 112 D7
Fordham Ave CV37 145 D2
Fordrift The B37 44 A3
Fordrough The B90 69 E4
Fords Rd B90 69 F4
Fordwell Cl CV5 60 C2
Foredraught B80 103 F2
Foregate St B96 102 C1
Foreland Way CV6 49 D2
Forest Oak Specl Sch B36 22 C1
Forest Rd Dorridge B93 71 F2
Hinckley LE10 31 F4
Forest View B97 102 C3
Forest Way Hollywood B47 69 D3
Nuneaton CV10 28 C1
Forester's Rd CV3 77 F3
Foresters Pl CV21 101 D4
Forfield Pl CV31 110 A4
Forfield Rd CV6 60 C3
Forge Croft B76 22 A3
Forge La B76 22 A3
Forge Rd Kenilworth CV8 93 D3
Shustoke B46 25 D1
Forge Way CV6 49 E2
Forknell Ave CV2 62 B3
Fornside Cl CV21 83 E4
Forrest Rd CV8 92 C2
Forresters Cl LE10 31 F3
Forresters Rd LE10 31 F3
Forryan Rd LE10 31 F4
Forshaw Heath La B94 86 A4
Forshaw Heath Rd B94 69 E1
Forth Dr B37 33 D2
Forties B77 9 F4
Forum Dr CV21 83 E3
Forum Rd B40 44 C2
Forward Rd B26 44 A2
Fosberry Cl CV34 109 D4
Fossdale Rd B77 10 A4
Fosse Cres CV23 96 C2
Fosse Way Chesterton CV33 123 C6
Ettington CV35, CV37 131 C5
Moreton Morrell CV35 123 A3
Shipston-on-S CV36 149 D3
Stretton u F CV23 65 D4
Tredington CV36 136 F6
Ufton CV31,CV33 111 E3
Wolvey CV23 42 C1
Fosseway Ave GL56 140 A2
Fosseway Cl GL56 140 A2
Fosseway Cres CV36 136 F6
Fosseway Dr GL56 140 A2
Fosseway Gdns LE17 43 F3
Fosseway Rd CV3 77 D2
Foster Ave B80 103 F2
Foster Rd CV6 61 D4
Fosterd Rd CV21 82 C3
Founder Cl CV4 76 A4
Fountain Gdns CV35 146 B2
Fountain Way CV37 145 D1
Four Ashes Rd B93 71 F2
Four Oaks Cl B98 102 B4
Four Pounds Ave CV5 60 C2
Fourfields Way CV7 37 D4
Fourways CV9 18 C4
Fowey Cl B76 22 A4
Fowler Rd Coventry CV6 61 D2
Sutton Coldfield B75 13 E3
Fox Ave CV10 29 E4
Fox Cl Harbury CV33 123 F6
Rugby CV21 84 A1
Fox Hill Rd B75 7 D1
Fox Hollies Rd B76 13 D1
Fox's Covert CV13 19 F3
Foxbury Dr B93 72 A2
Foxcote Cl B90 70 B4
Foxcote Dr B90 70 B4
Foxcote Hill CV36 136 B6
Foxcovert La CV13 21 D4
Foxdale Wlk 16 CV31 110 B3
Foxes La CV37 120 C5
Foxes Mdw B76 22 A4
Foxes Way
Balsall Common CV7 74 A3
Warwick CV34 108 B2
Foxfield CV23 66 A4
Foxford Cl B36 22 B1
Foxford Cres CV2 50 A2
Foxford Sch CV6 50 A3
Foxglove B77 4 A2
Foxglove Cl Coventry CV6 49 E1
Rugby CV23 83 F4
Foxhills Cl CV11 30 B1
Foxholes La B97 102 A3
Foxland Cl Birmingham B37 33 E1
Cheswick Green B90 70 B2
Foxon's Barn Rd CV21 83 E3
Foxtail Cl CV37 144 B3
Foxton Rd CV3 62 C1
Foxwood Rd
Birchmoor B78 10 C4
Polesworth B78 4 C1
Framlingham Gr CV8 93 E3
Frampton Cl B37 33 E2
Frampton Wlk CV2 62 C2
Frances Ave CV34 109 D4
Frances Cres CV12 39 D2
Frances Rd Baginton CV8 77 F2
Harbury CV33 123 F6
Francis Cl B78 5 D1
Francis St CV6 61 F4
Franciscan Rd CV3 77 E4
Frank St CV11 29 D2
Frank Whittle Prim Sch
CV2 62 C4
Frankholmes Dr B90 71 D3
Frankland Rd CV6 50 A1
Franklin Gr CV4 59 F1
Franklin Rd Nuneaton CV11 29 E1
Whitnash CV31 110 A2
Frankpledge Rd CV3 77 F4
Frankton Ave CV3 77 E3
Frankton Cl B98 103 F4
Frankton La CV23 97 D3
Frankton Rd CV23 97 F1
Frankwell Dr CV2 50 C1
Fraser Cl CV10 28 A3
Fraser Rd CV6 49 D1
Frasers Way CV37 129 B6
Fred Lee Gr CV3 77 E2
Frederick Bird Prim Sch
CV1 61 F3
Frederick Neal Ave CV5 59 E2
Frederick Press Way 5
CV21 82 C2
Frederick Rd CV7 37 D4
Frederick St CV21 82 C2
Freeboard La CV23 96 C4
Freeburn Cswy CV4 76 B4
Freehold St CV1 61 F2
Freeman Cl CV10 28 B2
Freeman St CV6 61 F3
Freeman's La LE10 32 A3
Freemans Cl CV32 105 F1
Freemantle Rd CV22 82 B1
Freer St CV11 29 F1
Freesland Rise CV10 28 A3
Frensham Cl B37 33 E1
Frensham Dr CV10 28 A3
Freshfield Cl CV5 48 B1
Freshwater Gr 2 CV31 110 B3
Fretton Cl CV6 61 F4
Frevill Rd CV6 62 A4
Friar's Gate CV9 18 B4
Friars Cl CV3 79 F4
Friars La OX15 137 F2
Friars' Rd CV1 151 B2
Friars St CV34 108 B3
Friars Wlk B37 33 E1
Friary Ave B90 71 D3
Friary Cl CV35 114 F3
Friary Rd CV9 12 B1
Friary St CV11 29 D3
Friday Cl B50 148 B3
Friday La B92 56 B2
Friday St
Lower Quinton CV37 129 E2
Pebworth CV37 128 F1
Frilsham Way CV5 60 A2
Frisby Ct CV11 29 F1
Frisby Rd CV4 59 F1
Friswell Dr CV6 61 F4
Friz Hill CV35 131 D8
Frobisher Rd Coventry CV3 77 E3
Rugby CV22 82 B1
Frog La
Balsall Common CV7 74 A3
Ilmington CV36 136 A6
Upper Boddington NN11 134 E8
Welford on A CV37 129 B6
Froglands La WR11 128 A4
Frogmere Cl CV5 60 B3
Frogmore La CV8 73 F1
Frogmore Rd CV37 121 B6
Frolesworth La LE17 43 F4
Front St Ilmington CV36 136 B6
Pebworth CV37 128 E1
Froxmere Cl B91 71 E4
Fryer Ave CV32 105 F2
Frythe Cl CV8 93 E3
Fulbrook La CV35 121 F8
Fulbrook Rd CV2 50 B1
Fulford Dr B76 22 A3
Fulford Hall Rd B94 69 E2
Fullbrook Cl B90 71 D3
Fuller Pl CV35 122 F3
Fullers Cl CV6 60 C4
Fullwood Cl CV2 50 C1
Furlong Mdw CV36 149 F2
Furnace Rd CV12 39 E2
Furndale Rd B46 34 A3
Furness Cl CV21 83 E4
Furrows The CV33 147 E3
Furze Hill Rd CV36 149 F2
Furze La
Chipping Campden GL55 135 C4
Redditch B98 112 A6
Fynford Rd CV6 61 D3

Gables Cl CV22 99 E4
Gables The B78 5 D1
Gadsby St CV11 29 F2
Gadshill CV31 109 F2
Gainford Rise CV3 63 D2
Gainsborough Cres
Knowle B93 72 A3
Rugby CV21 84 A1
Gainsborough Dr
Bedworth CV12 39 D2
Mile Oak B78 8 A4
Royal Leamington Spa CV31 110 B3
Gainsborough Rd CV37 144 B1
Gainsborough Trad Est
CV33 147 D2
Galey's Rd CV3 77 E4
Gallagher Bsns Pk CV6 49 F3
Gallagher Rd CV12 39 D1
Galley Common Fst Sch
CV10 27 F3
Galliards The CV4 76 B2
Gallows Hill CV34 109 D2
Galmington Dr CV3 77 D3
Gannaway Rd CV35 114 B3
Garden Cl Hinckley LE10 31 E3
Knowle B93 71 F3
Mickleton GL55 135 B6
Garden Ct 11 CV34 108 C4
Garden Gr CV12 49 F4
Gardenia Dr CV5 60 A3
Gardens The Kenilworth CV8 93 D2
Radford Semele CV31 110 C3
Rugby CV22 99 E4
Thurlaston CV23 98 C2
Garlick Dr CV8 93 E3
Garnette Cl CV10 28 A3
Garrard Cl WR11 127 F6
Garratt Cl CV23 82 A3
Garrett St CV11 29 F1
Garrick Cl CV5 59 E2
Garrick Way CV37 144 C1
Garrigill B77 4 A1
Garth Cres CV3 78 B4
Garway Cl CV32 105 F2
Garyth Williams Cl CV22 99 F4
Gas House La B49 143 E2
Gas St
Royal Leamington Spa CV31 109 F4
Rugby CV21 83 D2
Gate Farm Dr CV23 53 F2
Gate La Dorridge B93 71 E2
Nether Whitacre B46 24 C3
Gatehouse Cl CV21 101 D4
Gatehouse La CV12 39 D1
Gateley Cl B98 112 A6
Gateside Rd CV6 49 F1
Gatwick Rd B35 22 A2
Gaulby Wlk CV3 63 D1
Gaveston Cl 7 CV34 108 C4
Gaveston Rd Coventry CV6 60 C3
Royal Leamington Spa CV32 105 F1
Gaydon Cl CV6 62 A4
Gaydon Cty Prim Sch
CV35 123 D2
Gaydon Rd CV33 124 A3
Gayer St CV6 50 A1
Gayhurst Cl CV3 78 C4
Gayle B77 4 A1
Gaza Cl CV4 60 A1
Gazelle Cl CV1 151 D3
Geeson Cl B35 22 A2
Gentian Way CV23 83 F4
Gentlemans La B94 112 E7
Geoffery Cl CV2 62 A3
Geoffrey Cl B76 22 A4
George Bach Cl CV23 64 C2
George Eliot Ave CV12 39 E1
George Eliot Hospl CV10 29 D1
George Eliot Rd CV1 61 E3
George Eliot Sch
Nuneaton CV11 29 E1
Nuneaton CV11 39 E4
George Eliot St CV11 29 E1
George Fentham Prim Sch
B92 57 D3
George Fox La CV13 20 A3
George Hodgkinson Cl CV4 59 F2
George La GL55 135 B1
George Marston Rd CV3 62 C1
George Park Cl Ansty CV7 51 E2
Coventry CV2 50 B1
George Rd Warwick CV34 109 D4
Water Orton B46 23 E2
George Robertson Cl CV3 78 C4
George St Arley CV7 37 D4
Coventry CV1 61 F3
Hinckley LE10 31 E4
Nuneaton CV11 29 F1
Royal Leamington Spa CV31 110 A4
Rugby CV21 82 C2
Stockton CV23 115 F3
George Street Ringway
CV12 39 D2
George's Elm La B50 148 C4
Georgian Cl B49 143 D2
Gerard Ave CV4 76 A4
Gerard Rd B49 143 E2
Gerrard St 4 CV34 108 C3
Gerrards Rd CV36 149 F3
Gibbet Hill Rd CV4 76 A2
Gibbet La LE17 68 A3
Gibbons Cl CV4 59 F1
Gibbs Cl CV2 63 D3
Gibbs La WR11 127 D1
Gibson Cres CV12 39 D1
Gibson Dr CV21 84 A1
Gielgud Way CV2 63 D4
Giffard Way CV34 104 C1
Gifford Rd CV35 123 D3
Gifford Wlk CV37 144 B2
Gigg La B76 14 A2
Gilberry Cl B93 72 A2
Gilbert Ave CV22 82 B1
Gilbert Cl 7 Coventry CV1 61 F2
Stratford-u-A CV37 144 C3
Gilberts Rugby Football
Mus CV21 83 D2
Giles Cl CV6 49 E1
Gilfil Rd CV10 29 D1
Gilkes La CV35 137 F8
Gillet Cl CV11 29 D2
Gillett's La OX15 137 E2
Gillians Wlk CV2 63 D4
Gillows Croft B90 71 D4
Gilson Dr B46 33 E4
Gilson Rd B46 33 F4
Gilson Way B37 33 D3
Gingko Wlk CV31 109 F3
Gipsy Cl CV7 74 A3
Gipsy La Balsall Common CV7 74 B3
Nuneaton CV10, CV11 39 E4
Girdlers Cl CV3 77 D3
Girtin Cl CV12 39 D2
Girvan Gr CV32 106 B3
Gisburn Cl CV34 104 C1
Glade The CV5 59 F2
Gladiator Way CV21 82 C4
Gladstone Rd B93 72 A1
Gladstone St CV21 82 C2
Gladstone Terr LE10 31 F4
Glaisdale Ave CV6 49 F2
Glamis Pl OX16 139 F3
Glamorgan Cl CV3 78 B3
Glarmara Cl CV21 83 E4
Glascote Heath Prim Sch
B77 4 A1
Glascote La B77 9 F4
Glascote Rd B77 4 A1
Glasshouse La
Kenilworth CV8 93 E2
Lapworth B94 88 C3
Gleave Rd CV31 110 A2
Glebe Ave CV12 38 C1
Glebe Cl Bidford-on-A B50 148 B2
Coventry CV4 76 A4
Stockton CV23 147 F4
Glebe Cres Kenilworth CV8 93 D2
Rugby CV21 82 C2
Glebe Est CV37 120 B5
Glebe Farm Ind Est CV21 82 C4
Glebe Farm (Mus) CV37 120 C5
Glebe Farm Rd CV21 82 C4
Glebe Fields B76 23 D3
Glebe La Nuneaton CV11 29 F3
Staverton NN11 126 E8
Glebe Pl CV31 110 A4
Glebe Rd Claverdon CV35 113 F3
Hinckley LE10 31 F4
Nuneaton CV11 29 E2
Southam CV33 147 D3
Stratford-u-A CV37 144 B2
Glebe Rise CV9 3 D1
Glebe The Corley CV7 48 B4
Hook Norton OX15 142 D4
Wootton Wawen B95 113 B2
Glebe Way CV7 74 A4
Glebefarm Gr CV3 62 C2
Gleeson Dr CV34 104 C1
Glen Cl CV36 149 F3
Glenbarr Cl LE10 31 D4
Glenbarr Dr LE10 31 D4
Glencoe Rd CV3 62 A1
Glendale Ave CV8 93 D3
Glendale Fst Sch CV10 28 C1
Glendon Gdns CV12 40 B2
Glendon Way B93 71 F2
Glendower Ave CV5 60 B2
Gleneagles B77 4 A3
Gleneagles Cl CV11 30 B1
Gleneagles Rd CV2 62 C3
Glenfield Ave CV10 29 E4
Glenfield Cl Redditch B97 102 B3
2 Solihull B91 71 E4
Glenhurst Rd B95 113 A4
Glenmore Dr CV6 49 F3
Glenmount Ave CV6 49 F3
Glenn St CV6 49 E2
Glenridding Cl CV6 49 F3
Glenrosa Wlk CV4 76 A4
Glenroy Cl CV2 62 C3
Glentworth Ave CV6 49 D1
Glentworth Dr B76 13 D1
Glenville Ave CV9 10 B1
Glenwood Dr B90 70 B2
Glenwood Gdns CV12 39 D3
Gloster Dr CV8 92 C3
Gloster Gdns CV35 146 A4
Gloucester Cl CV11 30 A4
Gloucester La GL55 135 B6
Gloucester St
Coventry CV1 61 D2
1 Royal Leamington Spa
CV31 110 A4
Gloucester Way B37 33 D1
Glover Cl CV34 108 A2
Glover Rd B75 13 D3
Glover St CV3 77 E4
Glover's Cl CV9 18 C4
Glovers Cl CV7 46 B1
Godfrey Cl CV31 110 C3
Godiva Pl CV1 151 D3
Godiva Trad Est CV6 61 F4
Godsons La CV23 125 C8
Gofton B77 10 A4
Gold Cl CV11 39 F4
Goldcrest B77 10 A3
Goldcrest Croft B36 33 D4
Golden Acres La CV3 78 C4
Golden End Dr B93 72 B3
Goldicote Rd CV35 130 F7
Goldsborough B77 4 A1
Goldsmith Ave Rugby CV22 99 F3
Warwick CV34 108 B3
Goldthorn Cl CV5 59 E2
Golf Dr CV11 30 A1
Golf La CV31 110 A1
Good Shepherd Prim Sch
CV6 49 F1
Goodacre Cl CV23 84 A3
Goode Croft CV4 59 F1
Goodere Ave B78 11 D4
Goodere Dr B78 5 D1
Goodeve Wlk B75 13 D3
Goodfellow St CV32 105 E1
Goodman Way CV4 59 E1
Goodyers End Fst &
Mid Schs CV12 49 F4
Goodyers End La CV12 49 E4
Goose La CV37 129 D1
Goosehills Rd LE10 31 F3
Gorcott Hill B98 112 B7
Gordon Cl CV12 39 E2
Gordon St Coventry CV1 61 D1
Royal Leamington Spa CV31 110 A4
Goring Rd CV2 62 A2
Gorse Cl CV22 82 C1
Gorse Farm Rd CV11 40 A4
Gorse La B95 113 A2
Gorse Lea CV33 147 D3
Gorseway CV5 60 B2
Gorsey Cl B96 118 C8
Gorsey La Coleshill B46 23 F1
Wythall B47 69 D2
Gorsey Way B46 23 F1
Gorsy Bank Rd B77 9 F3
Gorsy Way CV10 28 B3
Gosford Ind Est CV1 61 F1
Gosford Park Prim Sch
CV1 61 F1
Gosford St CV1 151 D2
Gospel Oak La CV37 120 F5
Gospel Oak Rd CV6 49 D2
Gosport Rd CV6 61 F4
Gould Cl NN11 117 D5
Gould Rd CV35 108 A4
Grace Rd CV5 59 D4
Grafton Cl B98 103 D4
Grafton La B50 148 C3
Grafton Rd B50 128 C8
Grafton St CV1 61 F1
Graham Cl CV6 50 A1
Graham Rd CV21 83 E2
Graham St CV11 29 E3
Granborough Cl CV3 78 C4
Granbrook La GL55 135 C7
Granby Cl LE10 31 E4
Granby Rd Hinckley LE10 31 E4
Honington CV36 137 A5
Nuneaton CV10 28 C2
Grand Depot Rd CV11 40 C3
Grange Ave
Coventry, Binley CV3 78 C4
Coventry, Finham CV3 77 E2
Kenilworth CV8 92 C4
Grange Cl Nuneaton CV10 28 B4
Ratley OX15 132 F2
Southam CV33 147 D3
Tamworth B77 9 E4
Warwick CV34 109 E4
Grange Dr LE10 31 F3
Grange Farm Prim Sch
CV3 77 D3
Grange Gdns CV35 146 B2
Grange La Harvington WR11 127 D3
Sibford Ferris OX15 142 E8
Grange Pk CV37 145 D2
Grange Rd
Balsall Common CV7 73 F4
Bearley CV37 120 E7
Bidford-on-A B50 148 C2
Coventry CV6 50 A3
Dorridge B93 71 F1
Hartshill CV10 19 E1
Lapworth B94 88 C4
Royal Leamington Spa CV32 106 A2
Rugby CV21 82 C3
Grange The
Cubbington CV32 106 C3
Royal Leamington Spa CV32 106 A1
Grangehurst Prim Sch
CV6 50 A2
Grangemouth Rd CV6 61 D4
Grangers La B98 102 C3
Granhill Cl B98 103 D4
Granoe Cl CV3 78 C4
Grant Rd Bedworth CV7 39 D1
Coventry CV3 62 A1
Grantham St CV2 61 F2
Grantley Dr B37 33 D2
Grants Cl CV33 133 D7
Granvile Rd CV35 146 B2
Granville Gdns LE10 31 E4
Granville Rd Dorridge B93 72 A1
Hinckley LE10 31 E4
Granville St CV32 106 A1
Grapes Cl CV6 61 D3
Grasmere Ave CV3 76 C3
Grasmere Cl CV21 83 E3
Grasmere Cres CV11 29 F4
Grasmere Rd CV12 39 D1
Grasscroft Dr CV3 77 F3
Grassholme B77 10 A4
Grassington Ave CV34 104 C1
Grassington Dr CV11 30 A1
Gratton Ct CV3 76 C3
Gravel Hill CV4 59 F1
Gravel The B76 14 A1
Gray's La GL56 140 A3
Graylands The CV3 77 E2

Grayling B77 .... 9 E3
Grayling Wlk B37 .... 33 E2
Grays Orch CV23 .... 98 C1
Grayswood Ave CV5 .... 60 B2
Great Alne Sch B49 .... 119 D6
Great Balance CV23 .... 64 C2
Great Borne CV21 .... 83 E4
Great Central Way CV21 .... 83 E3
Great Rollright CE
  Prim Sch OX7 .... 142 A2
Great William St CV37 .... 145 D2
Greatheed Rd CV32 .... 105 F1
Greaves Cl CV34 .... 109 E4
Greaves Way The CV34 .... 124 B4
Green Cl Long Lawford CV23 .. 81 F2
  Studley B80 .... 103 F2
  Whitnash CV31 .... 110 A2
  Wythall B47 .... 69 D2
Green End CV23 .... 115 D4
Green Farm Rd CV35 .... 132 B6
Green Field The CV3 .... 78 A4
Green Gables B47 .... 69 D4
Green Gates B95 .... 113 B5
Green La Arley CV10 .... 26 C4
  Balsall Common CV7 .... 74 A4
  Brinklow CV23 .... 64 B2
  Church Lawford CV23 .... 81 E3
  Corley CV7 .... 47 E3
  Coventry CV3 .... 77 D2
  Grendon CV9 .... 11 F2
  Middleton B78 .... 14 A3
  Nuneaton CV10 .... 28 B4
  Oxhill CV35 .... 137 F8
  Redditch B97 .... 102 A4
  Shipston-on-S CV36 .... 149 F3
  Shrewley CV35 .... 114 C6
  Shutford OX15 .... 139 A1
  Studley B80 .... 103 D3
  Swalcliffe OX15 .... 139 A1
  Tamworth B78 .... 10 B4
  Warwick CV34 .... 108 C4
  Wibtoft CV23,LE17 .... 43 D2
  Wolvey LE10 .... 42 B3
Green Lane Cl CV36 .... 149 F3
Green Lanes Prim Sch B36 .. 33 D4
Green Lea B77 .... 10 A4
Green The Austrey CV9 .... 3 D1
  Barby CV23 .... 101 E1
  Chipping Campden GL55 .... 135 B1
  Cleeve Prior WR11 .... 128 A4
  G Wolford CV36 .... 140 E5
  Great Rollright OX7 .... 142 A2
  Hook Norton OX15 .... 142 D4
  Hornton OX15 .... 139 B7
  Kineton CV35 .... 132 F3
  Kingsbury B78 .... 15 E3
  Lighthorne CV35 .... 123 B2
  Long Itchington CV23 .... 115 D4
  Nuneaton CV11 .... 29 F1
  Orton-on-t-H CV9 .... 6 B2
  Priors Marston CV23 .... 125 E4
  Rugby CV22 .... 99 E4
  Shawell LE17 .... 68 B3
  Shrewley CV35 .... 114 D6
  Shustoke B46 .... 24 C1
  Stoke Golding CV13 .... 21 F4
  Stoneleigh CV8 .... 94 B3
  Swalcliffe OX15 .... 142 F8
  Tamworth B77 .... 4 A3
  Wood End B78 .... 10 B2
Greenacre Cl B77 .... 4 A3
Greenacres B76 .... 22 A4
Greenacres Prim Sch B77 .. 4 A3
Greenbank Rd CV7 .... 73 F3
Greendale Cl CV9 .... 18 C4
Greendale Rd Atherstone CV9 18 C4
  Coventry CV5 .... 60 B2
Greenfield Ave CV7 .... 74 A4
Greenfields Cl CV36 .... 149 F3
Greenfinch Cl B36 .... 33 D4
Greenfinch Rd B36 .... 33 D4
Greenhart B77 .... 4 A2
Greenhill Cl B77 .... 9 E3
Greenhill Rd Rugby CV22 .... 82 C1
  Stoke Golding CV13 .... 21 E4
  Whitnash CV31 .... 110 A2
Greenhill St CV37 .... 144 C2
Greenland Ave CV5 .... 59 F3
Greenland Ct CV5 .... 59 F3
Greenlands Dr B98 .... 102 C4
Greenlands Rd B37 .... 33 E1
Greenleaf Cl CV5 .... 60 A2
Greenmoor Rd Hinckley LE10 31 E3
  Nuneaton CV10 .... 29 D2
Greenodd Dr CV6 .... 49 F3
Greens Rd CV6 .... 49 D1
Greenside B90 .... 70 B2
Greenside Cl CV11 .... 30 B1
Greensleeves Cl CV6 .... 49 D1
Greensward Cl CV8 .... 93 D3
Greensward The
  Coventry CV3 .... 63 D1
  Wardington OX17 .... 134 F1
Greenswood CV37 .... 120 E7
Greenway Braunston NN1 .. 117 D5
  Nuneaton CV11 .... 40 A4
  Polesworth B78 .... 5 D2
  Warwick CV34 .... 104 C1
Greenway Cl CV36 .... 149 F3
Greenway Nature Trail The
  CV37 .... 129 C5
Greenway Rd CV36 .... 149 F3
Greenway The B37 .... 44 A3
Greenways The CV32 .... 106 A2
Greenwood Cl CV23 .... 82 A3
Greenwood Ct CV11 .... 29 F2
Greenwood Rd CV13 .... 21 F4
Greenwood Sq 4 B37 .... 33 D1

Greenwood Way B37 .... 33 D1
Gregory Ave CV3 .... 77 D3
Gregory Hood Rd CV3 .... 77 F2
Grenden Hall Rd CV35 .... 132 D3
Grendon Cl CV4 .... 59 E1
Grendon Dr CV21 .... 83 F4
Grendon Rd B78 .... 11 D4
Grenfell Cl 7 CV31 .... 110 B3
Grenville Ave CV2 .... 62 A2
Grenville Cl CV22 .... 82 B1
Gresham Ave CV32 .... 106 A1
Gresham Pl 7 CV32 .... 106 A1
Gresham Rd CV10 .... 39 D4
Gresham St CV2 .... 62 A1
Gresley Rd CV2 .... 62 B4
Greswold Cl CV4 .... 59 F1
Greswoldes The CV31 .... 110 C3
Gretna Rd CV3 .... 76 C2
Grevel La GL55 .... 135 B2
Greville Rd Alcester B49 .... 143 D3
  Kenilworth CV8 .... 92 C2
  Warwick CV34 .... 105 D1
Greville Smith Ave CV31 .... 110 A2
Grewcock Cl LE17 .... 43 F3
Grey Mill Cl B90 .... 70 C3
Grey Tree Cres B93 .... 71 F2
Grey's Rd B80 .... 103 F2
Greycoat Rd CV6 .... 49 D1
Greyfriars La CV1 .... 151 B2
Greyfriars Rd CV1 .... 151 B2
Greygoose La GL56 .... 150 A3
Greyhurst Croft 5 B91 .... 71 D4
Greyrick Ct GL55 .... 135 B6
Greys Cl OX16 .... 139 F3
Griff La CV10 .... 38 C3
Griffin Rd CV34 .... 109 E4
Griggs Cl GL55 .... 135 B2
Grimston Cl CV3 .... 63 D1
Grindle Rd CV6 .... 49 F2
Grindsbrook B77 .... 10 A4
Grizebeck Dr CV5 .... 60 A3
Grizedale CV21 .... 83 E4
Grosvenor Cres LE10 .... 32 A3
Grosvenor Rd Coventry CV1 151 A1
  Royal Leamington Spa CV31 110 A3
  Rugby CV21 .... 83 E2
Grouse Cl CV37 .... 144 B3
Grove Croft CV35 .... 114 F3
Grove Fields CV10 .... 29 E4
Grove La Keresley CV7 .... 48 C4
  Lapworth B94 .... 88 C2
  Wishaw B76 .... 13 F1
Grove Pk
  Hampton Magna CV35 .... 114 F3
  Hinckley LE10 .... 32 A3
Grove Pl Nuneaton CV10 .... 28 B2
 1 Royal Leamington Spa
  CV31 .... 110 A3
Grove Rd Ansty CV7 .... 51 E2
  Atherstone CV9 .... 18 B4
  Dorridge B93 .... 72 A2
  Hinckley LE10 .... 32 A3
  Nuneaton CV10 .... 28 B2
  Stratford-u-A CV37 .... 144 C1
Grove St Coventry CV1 .... 151 C3
  Royal Leamington Spa CV32 . 109 F4
Grove The Bedworth CV12 .... 39 E2
  Coleshill B46 .... 33 F2
  Hampton in A B92 .... 45 D1
  Hinckley LE10 .... 31 E4
  Studley B80 .... 103 E2
Grovelands Ind Est CV7 .... 50 A3
Grump St CV36 .... 136 B6
Guardhouse Rd CV6 .... 61 D4
Guernsey Dr B36 .... 33 D3
Guild Rd Aston Cantlow B95 . 119 F6
  Coventry CV6 .... 61 E4
Guild St CV37 .... 145 D2
Guilsborough Rd CV3 .... 78 C4
Guinness Cl B98 .... 102 B4
Gulistan Rd CV32 .... 105 F1
Gullet The B78 .... 4 C1
Gullicote La OX17 .... 139 F6
Gulliver's Cl OX15 .... 139 D6
Gulson Hospl CV1 .... 151 D2
Gulson Rd CV1 .... 61 F1
Gun Hill CV7 .... 37 D4
Gun Hill Fst Sch CV7 .... 37 D4
Gun La CV2 .... 62 A3
Gundry Cl CV31 .... 110 A4
Gunn Ct B49 .... 119 E6
Gunn End CV36 .... 149 F4
Gunners La B80 .... 103 F2
Gunnery Terr 5 CV32 .... 105 E1
Gunnings Rd B49 .... 143 E2
Gunton Ave CV3 .... 78 B3
Guphill Ave CV5 .... 60 B1
Guphill La CV5 .... 60 B2
Gurnard B77 .... 9 E3
Gurney Cl CV4 .... 59 F2
Gutteridge Ave CV6 .... 49 D1
Guy Pl E 10 CV32 .... 105 F1
Guy Pl W 9 CV32 .... 105 F1
Guy Rd CV8 .... 92 C1
Guy St
  Royal Leamington Spa CV32 . 105 F1
  Warwick CV34 .... 108 C4
Guy's Cl CV34 .... 109 D4
Guy's Cliffe Ave CV32 .... 105 E1
Guy's Cliffe Rd CV32 .... 109 F4
Guy's Cliffe Terr CV34 .... 108 C4
Guy's Cross Park Rd CV34 108 C4
Gypsy La Atherstone CV9 .... 12 B1
  Dordon B78 .... 11 D2
  Kenilworth CV8 .... 92 C1
  Water Orton B46 .... 23 E1

Hack La CV36 .... 141 C5

Hackwell St CV23 .... 125 C8
Haddon End CV3 .... 77 F3
Haddon Rd CV32 .... 106 A1
Haddon St CV6 .... 62 A4
Hadfield Cl CV23 .... 84 A3
Hadleigh Croft B76 .... 22 A3
Hadleigh Rd CV3 .... 77 E2
Hadley Cl B47 .... 69 D3
Hadrian Cl CV32 .... 106 A2
Hadrian Dr B46 .... 23 F1
Hadrians Cl B77 .... 9 E4
Hadrians Way CV21 .... 82 C4
Hadrians Wlk B49 .... 143 D2
Halberd Cl LE10 .... 31 E3
Hales Cl CV37 .... 121 B7
Hales Park Ind Est CV6 .... 49 F2
Hales St CV1 .... 151 C3
Halford La CV6 .... 49 D1
Halford Rd Ettington CV37 .. 131 A3
  Stratford-u-A CV37 .... 144 C1
  Whatcote CV36 .... 137 C7
Halfpenny Field Wlk B35 .... 22 A2
Halfway La CV23 .... 99 D2
Halifax Cl Allesley CV5 .... 60 A4
  Wellesbourne CV35 .... 146 A1
Hall Brook Rd CV6 .... 49 D2
Hall Cl CV8 .... 94 A3
Hall Cl The CV22 .... 99 E1
Hall Dr Baginton CV8 .... 77 F2
  Birmingham B37 .... 44 A4
  Stoke Golding CV13 .... 21 F4
Hall End CV11 .... 29 E1
Hall End Pl CV11 .... 29 E1
Hall Gr CV23 .... 64 C2
Hall Green Rd CV6 .... 50 A1
Hall La Coventry CV2 .... 62 C3
  Harbury CV33 .... 123 F7
  Witherley CV9 .... 19 D4
  Wolvey LE10 .... 41 E2
Hall Rd Hinckley LE10 .... 31 E3
  Royal Leamington Spa CV32 . 105 F1
  Wolvey LE10 .... 41 E2
Hall Wlk B46 .... 33 F2
Hall's Cl CV31 .... 110 A2
Hallam Rd CV6 .... 49 D1
Hallcroft Way B93 .... 72 A3
Hallfields CV31 .... 110 C3
Hallway Dr CV7 .... 51 F3
Halstead Gr B91 .... 71 D4
Halston Green Rd B90 .... 69 F4
Haltonlea B77 .... 10 A4
Hamar Way B37 .... 33 D1
Hambridge Rd CV33 .... 124 C3
Hames La B79 .... 2 B2
Hamilton Cl CV12 .... 38 B1
Hamilton Cl CV10 .... 28 B2
Hamilton Dr B80 .... 103 E2
Hamilton Rd Coventry CV2 ... 62 A2
  Radford Semele CV31 .... 110 C3
  Redditch B97 .... 102 B4
  Tiddington CV37 .... 145 F2
Hamilton Terr CV32 .... 109 F4
Hamlet Cl Nuneaton CV11 .. 30 A1
  Rugby CV22 .... 99 E3
Hamlet The CV35 .... 105 D4
Hammersley St CV12 .... 38 C1
Hammerton Way CV35 .... 146 B1
Hammond Bsns Ctr CV11 ... 29 F2
Hammond Cl CV11 .... 29 F2
Hammond Rd CV2 .... 61 F2
Hampden Cl OX16 .... 139 F3
Hampden Cl CV33 .... 133 A7
Hampden Way CV22 .... 99 E4
Hampdon Way CV35 .... 146 B1
Hampshire Cl CV3 .... 78 C4
Hampstead Norreys Rd
  CV35 .... 132 D4
Hampton Ave CV10 .... 28 A2
Hampton Cl Coventry CV6 ... 61 F3
  Redditch B98 .... 103 D4
Hampton Croft CV35 .... 114 F2
Hampton in Arden Sta B92 . 57 D4
Hampton La Meriden CV7 .... 57 F4
  Solihull B91 .... 56 A3
Hampton Lucy CE Prim Sch
  CV35 .... 121 F4
Hampton Rd Coventry CV6 .. 61 F3
  Knowle B93 .... 72 B4
  Warwick CV34 .... 108 A3
Hampton St CV34 .... 108 B3
Hams La Curdworth B76 .... 23 F3
  Lea Marston B76 .... 24 A4
Hanbury Cl CV35 .... 132 B6
Hanbury Rd Bedworth CV12 .. 39 D2
  Dorridge B93 .... 71 F2
Hancock Gr CV4 .... 75 F4
Hancox Cl CV33 .... 107 E4
Handcross Gr CV3 .... 77 D3
Handley Gr CV34 .... 104 B1
Handley's Cl CV8 .... 79 D1
Hands Paddock CV37 .... 130 E1
Handsworth Cres CV5 .... 59 F2
Hanford Cl CV6 .... 61 F3
Hanger Rd B26 .... 44 A2
Hangmans La B79 .... 2 A1
Hanlith B77 .... 10 A4
Hanover Ct Hinckley LE10 ... 31 F3
  Redditch B98 .... 102 B4
Hans Cl CV2 .... 61 F2
Hansell Dr B93 .... 71 F1
Hanson Ave CV36 .... 149 F3
Hanwell Cl B76 .... 22 A4
Hanwell Ct OX17 .... 139 F6
Hanwood Cl CV5 .... 59 E2
Hanworth Cl CV32 .... 106 B1
Hanworth Rd CV34 .... 108 B4
Harbet Dr B40 .... 44 C2
Harborough Dr B36 .... 22 B1

Harborough Rd
  Coventry CV6 .... 49 D1
  Long Lawford CV21 .... 82 B4
Harbour Cl B50 .... 148 B2
Harbury CE Sch CV33 .... 123 F6
Harbury Cl B76 .... 22 A3
Harbury La
  Bishops Tachbrook CV33 .... 123 B7
  Royal Leamington Spa
    CV33,CV34 .... 109 F1
Harbury Rd CV33 .... 124 C6
Harcourt CV3 .... 78 C3
Harcourt Gdns CV11 .... 29 E2
Hardwick CE CV5 .... 60 A2
Hardwick La B80 .... 112 B3
Hardwick Pk OX16 .... 139 F5
Hardwick Rd CV23 .... 125 E4
Hardwyn Cl CV3 .... 63 D1
Hardy Rd CV6 .... 61 D4
Hare & Hounds La CV10 .... 29 D1
Harebell B77 .... 4 A2
Harebell Way CV23 .... 83 E4
Harebell Wlk 1 B37 .... 33 E1
Harefield La CV12 .... 38 C4
Harefield Rd Coventry CV2 ... 62 A2
  Nuneaton CV11 .... 29 E2
Hareway La CV35 .... 122 C7
Harewood Rd CV5 .... 60 B1
Harger Ct CV8 .... 92 C2
Hargrave Cl Coventry CV3 ... 63 D1
  Water Orton B46 .... 23 D2
Harington Rd CV6 .... 61 D3
Harlech Cl Banbury OX16 .... 139 F3
  Kenilworth CV8 .... 93 E3
Harley St CV2 .... 62 A2
Harlow Wlk 8 CV2 .... 63 D4
Harmar Cl CV34 .... 104 B1
Harmer Cl CV2 .... 63 D4
Harnall Cl B90 .... 70 C4
Harnall Ind Est CV1 .... 151 C4
Harnall La CV1 .... 151 C4
Harnall La E CV1 .... 61 F2
Harnall La W CV1 .... 151 C4
Harnall Row Coventry CV1 ... 61 F1
  Coventry CV1 .... 61 F2
Harold Cox Pl CV22 .... 99 F3
Harold Rd CV2 .... 62 B1
Harold St CV11 .... 29 E2
Harpenden Dr CV5 .... 60 A3
Harper Rd CV1 .... 61 F1
Harpers La CV9 .... 19 D4
Harriott Dr CV34 .... 109 E2
Harris CE High Sch CV22 ... 82 C1
Harris Cl B95 .... 113 B4
Harris Dr CV22 .... 99 F4
Harris Mews B95 .... 113 B4
Harris Rd Coventry CV3 .... 62 A1
  Warwick CV34 .... 108 B4
Harrison Cl CV21 .... 101 D4
Harrison Cres CV12 .... 39 D1
Harrison Rd B97 .... 102 B4
Harrow La CV37 .... 144 C1
Harrow Rd CV31 .... 110 A2
Harrowbrook Ind Est LE10 .. 30 C4
Harrowbrook Rd LE10 .... 30 C4
Harry Rose Rd CV2 .... 62 C2
Harry Taylor Fst Sch B97 . 102 C3
Harry Truslove Cl CV6 .... 61 D4
Harry Weston Rd CV3 .... 63 D1
Hart Cl CV21 .... 83 E1
Hartington Cl B93 .... 71 F2
Hartington Cres CV5 .... 60 C1
Hartington Gn LE10 .... 31 F3
Hartland Ave CV2 .... 62 A3
Hartlebury Cl B93 .... 71 F2
Hartlepool Rd CV1 .... 151 D4
Hartleyburn B77 .... 10 A4
Hartridge Wlk CV5 .... 60 A2
Hartshill Hayes Ctry Pk
  CV10 .... 18 C1
Hartshill Hayes Visitors Ctr
  CV10 .... 18 C1
Hartshill Sch CV10 .... 28 A4
Harvard Cl CV35 .... 146 B1
Harvest Hill 15 CV31 .... 110 B3
Harvest Hill La CV5, CV7 ... 47 E2
Harvesters Cl CV3 .... 63 D1
Harvey Cl CV5 .... 60 A4
Harvington CE Fst Sch
  WR11 .... 127 D4
Harvington Dr B90 .... 71 D3
Harvington Way B76 .... 22 A4
Harwood Gr B90 .... 70 B4
Haselbech Rd CV3 .... 62 C1
Haseley Bsns Ctr CV35 .... 114 D7
Haseley Cl CV31 .... 110 A3
Haseley Rd CV2 .... 50 B1
Haselor Cl B49 .... 143 E2
Haselor Jun & Inf Sch
  B49 .... 119 D4
Hasilwood Sq CV3 .... 62 A1
Haslucks Green Rd B90 .... 69 F4
Hassall Cl 9 CV33 .... 122 F8
Hastings Cl Banbury OX16 .. 139 F3
  Tamworth B77 .... 9 F3
Hastings High Sch LE10 .... 31 F4
Hastings Rd Banbury OX16 .. 139 F4
  Coventry CV2 .... 62 A2
  Wellesbourne CV35 .... 146 B2
Hatchford Wlk B37 .... 33 D1
Hathaway Cl
  Balsall Common CV7 .... 74 A4
  Littleton WR11 .... 127 F1
Hathaway Dr Nuneaton CV11 30 A1
  Warwick CV34 .... 104 C1
Hathaway Green La CV37 . 144 C3
Hathaway Hamlet CV37 .... 144 B1
Hathaway La CV37 .... 144 B1
Hathaway Rd CV4 .... 59 E1
Hatherden Dr B76 .... 13 D1
Hatherell Rd CV31 .... 110 C3
Hatters Dr CV9 .... 12 B1
Hatton Bank La CV37 .... 121 D5
Hatton Cl CV35 .... 114 F5
Hatton Ctry World
  CV35 .... 114 C5
Hatton Sta CV35 .... 114 C5
Hatton Terr CV35 .... 114 F5
Haunch B76 .... 24 A4
Haunchwood Rd CV10 .... 28 B2
Havendale Cl CV6 .... 61 D3
Hawbridge Cl B90 .... 71 D3
Hawfinch B77 .... 10 A3
Hawk Cl CV11 .... 40 A4
Hawke's La OX15 .... 142 E8
Hawkes Dr CV34 .... 109 E4
Hawkes Mill La CV5 .... 48 A1
Hawkesbury Fields Sch
  CV2 .... 50 B2
Hawkesbury La CV2 .... 50 B3
Hawkeshead CV21 .... 83 E4
Hawkeswell La B46 .... 34 A2
Hawkesworth Dr CV8 .... 93 D3
Hawkinge Dr B35 .... 22 A2
Hawkins Cl CV22 .... 82 C1
Hawkins Rd CV5 .... 61 D1
Hawkshead Dr B93 .... 71 F3
Hawkside B77 .... 10 A4
Hawkswood Dr CV7 .... 74 A4
Hawksworth Dr 6 CV1 .... 61 D2
Hawlands CV21 .... 83 E3
Hawley Rd LE10 .... 31 E4
Hawnby Gr B76 .... 13 D1
Hawthorn Ave CV9 .... 16 B3
Hawthorn Cl B49 .... 143 D3
Hawthorn Cres LE10 .... 31 F2
Hawthorn La CV4 .... 59 F1
Hawthorn Rd CV31 .... 109 F3
Hawthorn Way
  Hartshill CV10 .... 28 A4
  Rugby CV22 .... 82 A1
Hawthorne Ave CV7 .... 37 D4
Hawthorne Cl CV8 .... 80 A2
Hawthorne Dr B47 .... 69 D3
Hawthorne Terr CV10 .... 28 C3
Hawthorns The B78 .... 15 E4
Hay La Coventry CV1 .... 151 C2
  Solihull B90 .... 71 D3
Hay Meadow CV36 .... 149 F3
Hay Pool OX17 .... 133 F5
Hay Wood La B93, CV35 .... 90 A2
Haybarn The B76 .... 22 A4
Haydock Cl Coventry CV6 ... 50 A2
  Stratford-u-A CV37 .... 144 C1
Haydon Cl B93 .... 71 F1
Haydon Way B49 .... 118 F3
Haydons Cl GL55 .... 135 B2
Haye La B80 .... 112 A5
Hayes Cl CV21 .... 83 E4
Hayes Green Rd CV12 .... 49 F4
Hayes La CV7 .... 50 A4
Hayes Rd CV10 .... 28 A4
Hayle Ave CV34 .... 104 C1
Hayle Cl CV11 .... 30 A3
Haynes Way CV21 .... 82 C4
Haynestone Rd CV6 .... 60 C3
Hays La LE10 .... 31 D4
Haysum's Cl GL55 .... 135 B1
Hayton Gn CV4 .... 75 F4
Hayton Rise CV2 .... 62 B4
Hayward Cl CV35 .... 114 F3
Hayward's Gn CV6 .... 61 D4
Hayway La CV23 .... 116 B4
Hazel Cl Hartshill CV10 .... 28 A4
  Royal Leamington Spa CV32 . 106 A1
Hazel Croft
  Birmingham, Chelmsley Wood
    B37 .... 33 D1
  Braunston NN11 .... 117 C5
Hazel Dr B47 .... 69 D3
Hazel Gr Bedworth CV12 .... 39 E2
  Hockley Heath B94 .... 88 B3
Hazel Rd Coventry CV6 .... 50 A1
  Nuneaton CV10 .... 28 B3
Hazelcroft B78 .... 15 E4
Hazelgarth B77 .... 10 A4
Hazelhead St Georges
  (Ind Est) CV1 .... 61 F1
Hazell Way CV10 .... 29 D1
Hazeltree Gr B93 .... 71 F2
Hazelwood Cl CV22 .... 99 D2
Hazlemere Cl CV5 .... 60 A2
Headborough Rd CV2 .... 62 A3
Headington Ave CV6 .... 49 D1
Headland Cl CV37 .... 129 A6
Headland Rd CV37 .... 129 A6
Headland Rise CV37 .... 129 A6
Headlands The CV5 .... 60 B2
Healey Cl CV21 .... 83 E4
Health Centre Rd CV8 .... 76 B2
Heanley La CV9 .... 16 B3
Hearsall Com Prim Sch
  CV5 .... 60 C1
Hearsall Comm CV5 .... 60 C1
Hearsall Golf Course CV5 .. 76 C4
Hearsall La CV5 .... 60 C1
Heart of England Sch CV7 . 74 B4
Heart of England Way
  CV11 .... 29 F2
Heath Ave CV12 .... 38 C1

Heath Cres CV2 .... 62 A3
Heath End La CV37 .... 121 D7
Heath End Rd CV10 .... 28 C1
Heath Farm La CV35 .... 123 C3
Heath La CV23 .... 64 C1
Heath Rd Bedworth CV12 .. 38 C1
Coventry CV2 .... 62 A2
Hollywood B47 .... 69 D4
Heath Terr CV32 .... 105 F1
Heath The CV22 .... 99 E2
Heath Way CV22 .... 100 B4
Heathcote Ind Est CV34 .. 109 E3
Heathcote La
Royal Leamington Spa CV34 . 109 E2
Warwick CV34 .... 109 D3
Heathcote Rd CV31 .... 110 A2
Heathcote St CV6 .... 61 D4
Heathcote Way CV34 ...... 109 E2
Heather Cl Birmingham B36 .. 33 D4
Nuneaton CV10 .... 28 C2
Rugby CV22 .... 82 C1
Southam CV33 .... 147 D3
Stratford-u-A CV37 ...... 144 B2
Heather Dr CV12 .... 38 C1
Heather Rd Binley Woods CV3 79 E4
Coventry CV2 .... 50 B1
Heathfield Cl B93 .... 72 A3
Heathfield Rd Coventry CV5 .. 60 B1
Norton WR11 .... 127 B2
Heathfields Cty Inf Sch B77 .. 9 F3
Heathgreen Cl B37 .... 33 E2
Heathley La B78 .... 8 C3
Hebden B77 .... 10 A4
Hebden Ave CV34 .... 104 C1
Hebden Way CV11 .... 30 A1
Heber Dr CV33 .... 123 E6
Heckley Rd CV7 .... 50 A4
Heddle Gr CV6 .... 62 A4
Hedgerow Wlk CV6 .... 49 D2
Hedgerows The CV10 ...... 28 C3
Hedges CV33 .... 124 D6
Hedgetree Croft B37 ...... 33 E1
Hedging La B77 .... 9 F3
Hedging Lane Ind Est B77 .. 9 F3
Hedingham Gr B37 .... 33 E1
Hedley Croft B35 .... 22 A2
Heemstede La CV32 ...... 106 A1
Heera Cl CV6 .... 61 E4
Hele Rd CV3 .... 77 E3
Helen St CV6 .... 61 F3
Helena Cl CV10 .... 28 C2
Hellidon Cl 4 CV32 ...... 106 A1
Hellidon Rd CV23 .... 125 F4
Helmdon Cl CV21 .... 83 E3
Helmsdale Rd CV32 ...... 106 A3
Helmswood Dr B37 .... 44 B4
Helston Cl CV11 .... 30 A3
Helvellyn Way CV21 .... 83 E4
Hemdale CV11 .... 30 A2
Heming Rd B98 .... 103 F4
Hemingford Rd CV2 .... 63 D4
Hemingford Croft B37 ..... 44 B4
Hemlingford Rd
Kingsbury B78 .... 15 E2
Sutton Coldfield B76 .... 22 A3
Hemmings Cl CV31 .... 110 C3
Hemmings Mill CV35 ..... 122 A7
Hemsby Cl CV4 .... 76 A4
Hemsworth Dr CV12 .... 40 A1
Hen La CV6 .... 49 E2
Henbrook La OX15 .... 137 E2
Hendre Cl CV5 .... 60 B1
Henley Cl CV11 .... 29 F4
Henley Coll CV2 .... 62 B4
Henley Mill La CV2 .... 62 B4
Henley Park Ind Est CV2 .. 62 C4
Henley Rd Claverdon CV35 .. 113 E4
Coventry CV2 .... 62 B4
Lowsonford B95 .... 113 D6
Norton Lindsey CV35 .... 114 D3
Royal Leamington Spa CV31 110 A3
Stratford-u-A CV37 ...... 145 D2
Henley-in-Arden High Sch
B95 .... 113 B4
Henley-in-Arden Prim Sch
B95 .... 113 B4
Henley-in-Arden Sta B95 113 A4
Henrietta St CV6 .... 61 F3
Henry Bellairs CE Mid Sch
CV12 .... 39 E2
Henry Boteler Rd CV4 ..... 76 A4
Henry Hinde Fst Sch CV22 .. 82 B1
Henry Hinde Mid Sch CV22 82 B1
Henry St Coventry CV1 ... 151 B3
Kenilworth CV8 .... 93 D3
Nuneaton CV11 .... 29 E1
Rugby CV21 .... 83 D2
Henson Rd CV12 .... 38 C1
Henwood La B91 .... 56 A2
Hepworth Rd CV3 .... 63 D1
Herald Bsns Pk CV3 .... 78 C4
Herald Way Coventry CV3 .. 79 D4
Hinckley LE10 .... 31 E2
Herbert Art Gall & Mus
CV1 .... 151 C2
Herbert Fowler Mid Sch
CV10 .... 26 C1
Herbert St CV10 .... 28 C2
Herbert's La CV8 .... 93 D3
Herdwycke Cl CV33 ...... 147 E2
Hereford Rd CV11 .... 40 C3
Hereward Coll of FE CV4 .. 59 F1
Herford Way LE10 .... 31 F3
Heritage Ct CV4 .... 76 B2

Heritage Motor Ctr CV35 .. 123 D1
Hermes Cl CV34 .... 109 F3
Hermes Cres CV2 .... 62 C3
Hermit's Croft CV3 .... 77 E4
Hermitage Dr B76 .... 13 D2
Hermitage La B78 .... 4 C1
Hermitage Rd CV2 .... 62 B2
Hermitage Way CV8 .... 93 D2
Heron Cl Alcester B49 .... 143 D3
Cheswick Green B90 ...... 70 B2
Heron La CV37 .... 144 B3
Herrick Rd CV2 .... 62 B2
Hertford Cl CV10 .... 28 C2
Hertford Pl CV1 .... 151 A2
Hertford Rd Alcester B49 .. 143 E3
Stratford-u-A CV37 ...... 144 C1
Hertford St CV1 .... 151 B2
Hertford Way B93 .... 72 A2
Hesleden B77 .... 10 A4
Heslop Cl CV3 .... 78 C4
Hetton Cl 8 CV34 .... 104 C1
Hewitt Ave CV6 .... 61 D2
Hexby Cl CV2 .... 63 D3
Hexworthy Ave CV3 .... 77 D3
Heybrook Cl CV2 .... 62 B4
Heycroft CV4 .... 76 B2
Heydons Terr OX17 ...... 133 F4
Heyford Gr B91 .... 71 E4
Heyford Leys CV22 .... 99 F3
Heyford Way B35 .... 22 A3
Heyville Croft CV8 .... 93 E2
Heywood Cl CV6 .... 62 A4
Hibberd Ct CV8 .... 92 C2
Hibbert Cl CV22 .... 83 D1
Hickman Rd CV10 .... 27 F3
Hicks Cl CV34 .... 104 C1
Hidcote Ave B76 .... 22 A4
Hidcote Cl Nuneaton CV11 .. 39 F4
28 Royal Leamington Spa
CV31 .... 110 B3
Hidcote Gr B37 .... 44 A4
Hidcote Manor Garden
GL55 .... 135 D5
Hidcote Rd Ebrington GL55 . 135 D3
Kenilworth CV8 .... 93 E3
High Ash Cl CV7 .... 49 F4
High Beech CV5 .... 60 A3
High Brink Rd B46 .... 33 F4
High Cross La
Claybrooke Magna LE17 .. 43 E3
Lowsonford CV35 .... 113 F6
High La OX15 .... 137 E2
High Mdw OX15 .... 138 D1
High Meadow Fst Sch B46 .. 33 F4
High Park Cl CV5 .... 59 F2
High St Alcester B49 ...... 143 D2
Astwood Bank B96 .... 102 C1
Barford CV35 .... 122 B8
Bedworth CV12 .... 39 D1
Bidford-on-A B50 .... 148 C2
Bidford-on-A,Broom B50 148 A4
Bishops Itchington CV33 124 A4
Braunston NN11 .... 117 D5
Charwelton NN11 .... 126 D2
Chipping Campden GL55 135 B2
Coleshill B46 .... 34 A3
Coventry CV1 .... 151 C2
Coventry, Keresley CV6 .. 48 C1
Cropredy OX17 .... 134 C1
Cubbington CV32 .... 106 C3
Fenny Compton CV33 ... 133 D7
Great Rollright OX7 ...... 142 A2
Hampton in A B92 .... 57 D4
Harbury CV33 .... 123 F6
Henley-in-A B95 .... 113 B5
Hook Norton OX15 .... 142 D4
Hurley CV9 .... 16 B3
Kenilworth CV8 .... 92 C3
Knowle B93 .... 72 B3
Lower Brailes OX15 ...... 137 F2
Marton CV23 .... 115 C7
Mickleton GL55 .... 135 C6
Moreton-in-M GL56 ...... 140 A3
Napton CV23 .... 125 C7
Nuneaton CV11 .... 29 D2
Polesworth B78 .... 5 D1
Ratley OX15 .... 133 A2
Royal Leamington Spa CV31 110 A3
Rugby CV21 .... 83 D2
Rugby,Hillmorton CV21 . 101 D4
Ryton-on-D CV8 .... 79 D1
Shipston-on-S CV36 ..... 149 F3
Shutford OX15 .... 139 A3
Southam CV33 .... 147 D2
Stockton CV23 .... 147 F4
Stoke Golding CV13 ...... 21 E4
Stratford-u-A CV37 ...... 145 D1
Studley B80 .... 103 F2
Tamworth B77 .... 9 E2
Warwick CV34 .... 108 C3
Welford on A CV37 ...... 129 A7
High Trees Cl B98 .... 102 C4
High Trees Rd B93 .... 72 A4
High View Dr CV7 .... 49 E4
High View Rd CV32 .... 106 B3
Higham La Nuneaton CV11 .. 29 F4
Stoke Golding CV13 ...... 21 E3
Stoke Golding,Wykin LE10 21 F2
Higham Lane Sch CV10 .. 29 E3
Higham on the Hill
CE Prim Sch CV13 ...... 21 D2
Higham Way LE10 .... 31 F4
Highbury Gn CV10 .... 28 B4
Highclere Gdns OX16 ... 139 F3
Highcliffe Rd B77 .... 9 E4
Highcroft CV35 .... 113 F3
Highcroft Cres CV32 ..... 105 E1
Highdown Cres 3 B90 ... 71 D3

Highdown Rd CV31 .... 110 A3
Highfield CV7 .... 46 B1
Highfield Ave Redditch B97 . 102 B4
Tamworth B77 .... 4 A3
Highfield Cl Kenilworth CV8 .. 92 C2
Snitterfield CV37 .... 121 B3
Highfield Rd Coventry CV2 .. 61 F2
Nuneaton CV11 .... 29 F1
Redditch B97 .... 102 B4
Stratford-u-A CV37 ...... 144 C3
Studley B80 .... 103 E2
Highfield Terr CV32 ...... 105 E1
Highgrove Coventry CV4 .. 75 F3
Rugby CV22 .... 99 E4
Highland Rd Coventry CV5 .. 60 C1
Kenilworth CV8 .... 93 E4
Royal Leamington Spa CV32 106 A2
Highland Way B98 .... 103 D4
Highlands OX16 .... 139 F5
Highlands Cl CV34 .... 109 D4
Highlands Rd B90 .... 70 C4
Highview CV9 .... 16 B2
Highwaymans Croft CV4 .. 76 B3
Hiker Gr 8 B37 .... 33 E1
Hilary Bevins Cl CV13 .... 20 C2
Hilary Dr B76 .... 13 D3
Hilary Rd Coventry CV4 .. 76 C3
Nuneaton CV10 .... 28 C3
Hill Cl Northend CV33 ... 133 B7
Royal Leamington Spa CV32 106 A2
Hill Cres CV23 .... 96 C3
Hill Crest CV32 .... 106 C3
Hill Crest Hospl B98 ..... 103 E3
Hill Farm Ave CV11 .... 30 A1
Hill Farm Prim Sch CV6 .. 61 D4
Hill Fray Dr CV3 .... 78 A3
Hill La Middleton B75 .... 7 D1
Upper Brailes OX15 ..... 137 E3
Upper Quinton CV37 .... 129 D1
Hill Rd Grandborough CV23 .. 116 E6
Keresley CV7 .... 48 C3
Lower Boddington NN11 134 E7
Hill Rise OX7 .... 142 A2
Hill Row NN11 .... 117 E4
Hill Side Coventry CV2 ... 62 A3
Kingsbury B78 .... 15 E2
Hill St Bedworth CV12 ... 39 D3
Coventry CV1 .... 151 B3
Hinckley LE10 .... 31 F4
Nuneaton CV10 .... 28 B2
Royal Leamington Spa CV32 106 A1
Rugby CV21 .... 83 D2
Warwick CV34 .... 109 D4
Hill Top Baddesley Ensor CV9 . 11 D1
Coventry CV1 .... 151 C3
Hill Top Ave CV9 .... 11 D1
Hill View CV33 .... 124 A4
Hill View Rd B50 .... 148 C3
Hill Wootton Rd CV35 ... 105 E3
Hillary Rd CV22 .... 99 F4
Hillborough La B50 .... 128 E7
Hillcrest Rd Nuneaton CV10 .. 28 C3
Polesworth B78 .... 11 D4
Hillfield Mews 8 B91 .... 71 E4
Hillfield Rd CV22 .... 82 B1
Hillhurst Gr B36 .... 22 B1
Hilliard Cl CV12 .... 39 D2
Hillman Gr B36 .... 22 C1
Hillmorton La
Clifton u D CV23 .... 84 A1
Lilbourne CV23 .... 84 C4
Hillmorton Prim Sch CV21 101 D4
Hillmorton Rd Coventry CV2 . 50 B1
Knowle B93 .... 72 A3
Rugby CV22 .... 83 E1
Hillrise LE10 .... 31 F4
Hillside Appleby Magna DE12 .. 3 F4
Hartshill CV10 .... 28 A4
Napton CV23 .... 125 C8
Hillside Dr CV10 .... 28 B4
Hillside N CV2 .... 62 A3
Hillside Rd Hinckley LE10 .. 31 E3
Stratford-u-A CV37 ...... 144 B2
Hilltop Cl Honiley CV8 .... 90 C4
Southam CV33 .... 147 D3
Hillwood Ave B90 .... 71 D3
Hillyard Rd CV33 .... 147 D3
Hilton Ave CV10 .... 28 A3
Himbleton Croft 1 B90 .. 71 D3
Himley Rd CV12 .... 38 B1
Hinckley Bsns Pk LE10 .. 30 C4
Hinckley CE Jun & Inf Sch
LE10 .... 31 E4
Hinckley & District Hospl
LE10 .... 31 E4
Hinckley La CV13 .... 21 E2
Hinckley Rd Ansty CV2,CV7 .. 51 E1
Aston Flamville LE10 ..... 32 B4
Burton Hastings LE10 .... 31 F1
Burton Hastings LE10 .... 41 E4
Coventry CV2 .... 63 D4
Hinckley LE10 .... 32 A3
Nuneaton CV11 .... 29 F3
Stoke Golding CV13 ...... 21 F4
Hinckley Sta LE10 .... 31 E4
Hind Cl CV34 .... 104 C1
Hinde Cl CV21 .... 83 E4
Hindlip Cl B98 .... 112 A6
Hintons Coppice B93 ..... 71 F3
Hipsley Cl B36 .... 22 B1
Hipsley La CV9 .... 16 C3
Hipswell Highway CV2 ... 62 B2
Hipton Hill WR11 .... 127 B3
Hiron Croft CV3 .... 77 E4
Hiron The CV3 .... 77 E4
Hiron Way CV34 .... 108 A4
Hirst Cl CV23 .... 82 A3

Hitchman Mews CV31 ... 110 A3
Hitchman Rd CV31 .... 110 A3
Hithersand Cl CV31 ...... 121 F4
Hoarestone Ave CV11 .... 40 A4
Hob La Balsall Common CV7 .. 74 C2
Burton Green CV8 .... 75 D2
Knowle B92 .... 73 D4
Hob Lane CE Fst Sch CV12 . 39 E2
Hobbins The CV36 .... 149 F3
Hobley Cl CV22 .... 99 E4
Hockett St CV3 .... 77 E4
Hocking Rd CV2 .... 62 C2
Hockley Cl CV23 .... 116 F5
Hockley Heath Prim Sch
B94 .... 88 B3
Hockley La Coventry CV5 .. 59 E3
Ettington CV37 .... 131 B3
Hockley Rd Shrewley CV35 . 114 C6
Tamworth B77 .... 9 F3
Hoden La WR11 .... 128 B3
Hodge La B77 .... 4 A3
Hodgett's La Berkswell CV7 .. 74 C3
Coventry CV7 .... 75 D3
Hodgson Rd CV37 .... 144 C3
Hodnell Cl B36 .... 22 B1
Hodnell Dr CV33 .... 147 E2
Hodnet Cl CV8 .... 93 D3
Hogarth Cl CV12 .... 39 D2
Hogarth Rd CV37 .... 144 B1
Hogg End OX17 .... 134 F3
Hoggrills End La B46 ..... 25 D2
Holbeche Cres CV7 .... 36 C2
Holbeche Rd Knowle B93 .. 72 A4
Sutton Coldfield B75 ..... 13 D3
Holbein Cl CV12 .... 39 D2
Holborn Ave CV6 .... 49 E1
Holbrook Ave CV21 .... 83 D2
Holbrook La CV6 .... 49 E1
Holbrook Park Est CV6 .. 61 E4
Holbrook Prim Sch CV6 .. 49 F1
Holbrook Rd
Long Lawford CV23 .... 82 A3
Stratford-u-A CV37 ...... 144 B2
Holbrook Way CV37 .... 49 E1
Holcot Leys CV22 .... 100 A4
Holder Cl B50 .... 148 B3
Hole House La B94 .... 88 C1
Holioak Dr CV34 .... 109 D3
Holland Ave B93 .... 72 A4
Holland Cl B50 .... 148 B2
Holland Rd CV6 .... 61 D3
Hollberry Cl B98 .... 112 A6
Hollick Cres CV7 .... 37 D4
Hollicombe Terr CV2 ..... 62 B4
Hollies Inf Sch The CV10 .. 28 C3
Hollies Rd B78 .... 11 D4
Hollies The CV23 .... 67 F1
Hollin Brow Cl B93 .... 72 A2
Hollings Gr B91 .... 71 D4
Hollington Way B90 .... 71 E4
Hollinwell Cl CV11 .... 40 B4
Hollis La CV8 .... 92 C4
Hollis Rd CV3 .... 62 A1
Hollow Cres CV6 .... 61 D3
Hollow Way CV23 .... 125 C8
Holloway Field CV6 .... 61 D3
Holloway Hill OX15 ...... 138 A1
Holloway La OX15 .... 138 A1
Holloway The
Mollington OX17 .... 134 A2
Priors Marston CV23 .... 125 E4
Warwick CV34 .... 108 B3
Hollowell Way CV21 ...... 83 E4
Holly Bank Est CV9 .... 3 D1
Holly Cl LE10 .... 31 F3
Holly Dr Hollywood B47 .. 69 D4
Hurley CV9 .... 16 B2
Holly Farm Bsns Pk CV8 . 91 D4
Holly Gr
Church Lawford CV23 .... 81 D3
Coventry CV4 .... 60 A1
Holly La Atherstone CV9 .. 12 B1
Balsall Common CV7 .... 74 A2
Portway B48 .... 85 F3
Wishaw B76 .... 13 E2
Holly Lane Ind Est CV9 .. 12 B1
Holly Lodge CV35 .... 146 B2
Holly St CV32 .... 106 A1
Holly Stitches Rd CV10 .. 28 C3
Holly Tree Wlk LE17 ...... 43 F3
Holly Wlk Baginton CV8 .. 77 F1
Nuneaton CV11 .... 29 F1
Royal Leamington Spa CV32 106 A1
Stratford-u-A CV37 ...... 144 B2
Hollyberry Ave B91 .... 71 D4
Hollybush La Coventry CV6 . 50 A2
Priors Marston CV23 .... 125 E4
Hollybush Rd OX15 ...... 142 D4
Hollyfast La CV7 .... 48 B2
Hollyfast Prim Sch CV6 .. 60 C4
Hollyfast Rd CV6 .... 60 C3
Hollyhurst B46 .... 23 E1
Hollyland B46 .... 24 C1
Hollywood Rd B93 .... 72 A3
Hollywood La B47 .... 69 D4
Holman Way CV11 .... 29 E2
Holmcroft CV2 .... 62 C4
Holme Cl CV21 .... 83 E3
Holme Way CV23 .... 101 E1
Holmes Dr CV5 .... 59 E3
Holmes Rd CV31 .... 110 A3
Holmewood Cl CV8 .... 93 D3
Holmfield Rd CV2 .... 62 A2
Holmsdale Rd CV6 .... 61 F4
Holsworthy Cl CV11 ...... 29 F3
Holt Ave CV33 .... 122 E8
Holt Gdns B80 .... 103 F1
Holt Leys CV33 .... 147 E2

Holt Rd Hinckley LE10 .... 31 F3
Studley B80 .... 103 F1
Holt The Mollington OX17 . 133 F2
Royal Leamington Spa CV32 106 A2
Holte Rd CV9 .... 18 B4
Holtom St CV37 .... 144 C1
Holwick B77 .... 10 A4
Holy Cross RC Jun &
Inf Sch B76 .... 13 D2
Holy Family RC Prim Sch
CV6 .... 49 D2
Holyhead Rd CV5 .... 60 C3
Holyoak Cl Bedworth CV12 . 38 C1
Rugby CV22 .... 99 E4
Holywell Cl CV4 .... 59 E1
Holywell Rd CV33 .... 147 D2
Home Cl Bubbenhall CV8 .. 95 E3
Staverton NN11 .... 126 E8
Home Farm CV35 .... 104 C3
Home Farm Cl CV9 .... 19 D4
Home Farm Cres CV31 .. 110 A2
Home Furlong CV35 ..... 146 B1
Home Mdw CV35 .... 113 F3
Home Park Rd CV11 ...... 29 E2
Homefield La CV22 .... 99 F2
Homefield Sch CV22 ...... 99 F2
Homeward Way CV3 ...... 63 D1
Honeybourne Cl CV5 ..... 60 A2
Honeybourne Rd B50 ... 148 C2
Honeyfield Rd CV1 .... 61 E3
Honeysuckle Cl CV23 .... 83 E4
Honeysuckle Dr CV2 ...... 50 A1
Honiley Rd Honiley CV8 .. 91 D3
Meer End CV8 .... 74 A1
Honiley Way CV2 .... 50 B1
Honington Hall CV36 ... 137 A5
Honiton Rd CV2 .... 62 B3
Honiwell Cl CV33 .... 123 E6
Hoo La GL55 .... 135 A2
Hood St CV1 .... 61 F2
Hood's Way CV22 .... 82 B1
Hook Norton CE Sch
OX15 .... 142 D4
Hook Norton Rd OX15 .. 142 D8
Hoopers La B96 .... 102 C1
Hope Cl CV7 .... 49 D4
Hope St CV1 .... 61 D1
Hopedale Cl CV2 .... 62 C2
Hopkins Field CV37 ..... 129 B3
Hopkins Prec The B49 .. 143 E2
Hopkins Rd CV6 .... 61 D2
Hopper's La CV35 .... 146 B2
Hopton Cl CV5 .... 60 A2
Hopton Crofts CV32 ..... 105 E1
Horley Path Rd OX15 ... 139 D5
Hornbeam B77 .... 4 A2
Hornbeam Dr CV4 .... 59 E1
Hornbeam Gr CV31 ...... 110 B3
Hornchurch Cl CV1 ...... 151 B1
Horndean Cl CV6 .... 61 F4
Horne Cl CV21 .... 101 D4
Horninghold Cl CV3 ...... 78 C4
Hornsey Cl CV2 .... 62 C4
Horse Shoe Rd CV6 .... 50 A2
Horsefair CV36 .... 149 F3
Horsefair The 4 LE10 .. 31 E4
Horsepool LE10 .... 32 A3
Horsewell CV33 .... 147 D2
Horsfall Rd B75 .... 13 D3
Horsford Rd CV3 .... 77 F3
Horsham Cl OX16 .... 139 F5
Horton Cl B49 .... 143 E3
Horton Cres CV22 .... 83 D1
Horton Gr B90 .... 71 D3
Hosiery St CV12 .... 39 E1
Hoskyn Cl CV21 .... 100 C4
Hospital La CV12 .... 38 A1
Hospital of St Cross CV22 .. 83 D1
Hospl Rd (West St) GL56 . 140 B3
Hotchkiss Cl CV35 ...... 146 B1
Hotchkiss Way CV3 .... 79 D4
Hothorpe Cl CV3 .... 62 C1
Houldsworth Cres CV6 .. 49 E2
Houndsfield Cl B47 .... 69 D3
Houndsfield Gr B47 .... 69 D3
Houndsfield La B47 .... 69 D3
Houston Rd CV21 .... 83 E3
Houting B77 .... 9 E3
Hove Ave CV5 .... 59 F2
Hovelands Cl CV2 .... 62 B4
Howard Cl Bidford-on-A B50 148 B2
Coventry CV5 .... 59 F2
Dunchurch CV22 .... 99 C2
Howard Rd Nuneaton CV10 . 29 D2
Redditch B98 .... 103 D4
Howard St CV1 .... 151 C4
Howard Wlk CV31 .... 109 E4
Howat Rd CV7 .... 48 C4
Howcombe La CV23 ..... 125 C7
Howcotte Gn CV4 .... 75 F4
Howe Green La CV7 .... 37 E2
Howells Cl CV12 .... 38 B1
Howes Croft B35 .... 22 A1
Howes La CV3 .... 77 E2
Howes Prim Sch CV3 ..... 77 F3
Howkins Rd CV21 .... 83 E3
Howlette Rd CV4 .... 59 F1
Hoylake B77 .... 4 A2
Hoylake Cl CV11 .... 30 A1
Huckson Rd CV33 .... 124 B4
Huddisdon Cl 12 CV34 .. 104 C1
Hudson Ave B46 .... 33 F3
Hudson Rd CV22 .... 82 C1
Hugh Rd CV3 .... 62 A1
Hughes Cl Harvington WR11 127 D4
Warwick CV34 .... 104 B1
Whitnash CV31 .... 110 A1
Hughes Hill CV35 .... 114 B6

Hughes La WR11 .... 127 D4
Hulme Cl CV3 .... 63 D1
Humber Ave Coventry CV1 .... 61 F1
  Sutton Coldfield B76 .... 22 A4
Humber Cl NN11 .... 117 F2
Humber Gr B36 .... 22 C1
Humber Rd CV3 .... 78 A4
Humber Wlk OX16 .... 139 F4
Humberstone Rd 3 CV6 ..... 61 D3
Humphrey Burton's Rd CV3 77 E4
Humphrey-Davy Rd CV12 .... 49 E4
Humphris St CV34 .... 109 D3
Hungerfield Rd B36 .... 22 B1
Hunningham Gr 6 B91 ..... 71 D4
Hunscote La CV35 .... 121 F1
Hunt Cl CV35 .... 114 F3
Hunt End La B97 .... 102 B3
Hunt Hall La CV37 .... 129 A6
Hunt La CV9 .... 19 D4
Hunt Paddocks CV8 .... 92 C1
Hunt Terr CV4 .... 76 A4
Hunter St CV21 .... 83 E2
Hunter Terr CV5 .... 76 B4
Hunters Cl CV3 .... 63 D1
Hunters La
  Fenny Drayton CV13 .... 20 A3
  Rugby CV21 .... 83 D3
Hunters Lane Ind Est CV21 . 83 D3
Hunters Pk CV5 .... 11 E1
Hunters Wlk CV9 .... 19 D4
Huntingdon Rd CV5 .... 77 D4
Huntingdon Way CV10 ...... 28 C2
Hunts Rd CV37 .... 145 E1
Hurdlers La CV37 .... 121 B6
Hurlbutt Rd CV34 .... 109 E2
Hurley Cl CV32 .... 106 A1
Hurley Comm CV9 .... 16 B3
Hurley La B46 .... 25 F3
Hurley Prim Sch CV9 ..... 16 B2
Hurn Way CV6 .... 50 A2
Hurst Green Rd
  Bentley Heath B93 .... 71 F2
  Minworth B76 .... 22 B3
Hurst Rd Bedworth CV12 .... 39 D2
  Coventry CV6 .... 50 A2
  Hinckley LE10 .... 31 E4
  Southam CV33 .... 147 D2
Hurst The B47 .... 69 D3
Husbandmans Cl CV36 ...... 149 F3
Hyacinth Way LE10 .... 31 E3
Hyde Pl CV32 .... 109 F4
Hyde Rd Coventry CV2 .... 62 C2
  Kenilworth CV8 .... 93 D3
Hydes La LE10 .... 30 C2

Ibex Cl CV3 .... 62 C1
Ibstock Rd CV6 .... 50 A3
Icknield Cl B50 .... 148 C2
Icknield Ct B50 .... 148 C2
Icknield Row B49 .... 143 D2
Icknield St
  Bidford-on-A B50 .... 148 C2
  Portway B48 .... 85 D3
Icknield Street Dr B98 ...... 103 E4
Iden Rd CV1 .... 61 F2
Idlicote Rd CV36 .... 137 B8
Ilam Pk CV8 .... 93 E3
Ilex Ct CV34 .... 109 D4
Ilford Cl CV12 .... 39 D2
Ilford Dr CV3 .... 77 D3
Ilfracombe Gr CV3 .... 77 D3
Illshaw Cl B98 .... 112 A6
Illshaw Heath Rd B94 ...... 70 B1
Ilmer Cl CV21 .... 83 F4
Ilmington Cl CV3 .... 77 D3
Ilmington Prim Sch CV36 . 136 A6
Ilmington Rd
  Ilmington CV36 .... 136 D7
  Tredington CV36 .... 136 E6
Ilminster Cl LE10 .... 32 A4
Imperial Rise B46 .... 23 F1
Inca Cl CV3 .... 78 C4
Inchbrook Rd CV8 .... 93 E4
Inchford Ave CV34 .... 104 C1
Inchford Cl CV11 .... 29 F1
Ingleton Cl CV11 .... 30 A1
Inglewood Cl CV32 .... 106 A2
Ingon La CV37 .... 121 B5
Ingram Pit La B77 .... 4 A3
Ingram Rd CV5 .... 76 B4
Innace Park Small Ind Units
  CV9 .... 12 B1
Innage Cl CV10 .... 110 A4
Innage Terr CV9 .... 18 B4
Innage The B47 .... 69 D3
Innis Rd CV5 .... 76 C4
Innisfree House Sch B47 ... 69 E2
Innsworth Dr B35 .... 22 A2
Instone Rd CV6 .... 49 D1
International Dr B26 ...... 44 B2
Inveraray Cl CV8 .... 93 E2
Inverlea Ct GL55 .... 135 B6
Inverness Cl CV5 .... 60 A2
Invicta Rd CV3 .... 78 C4
Ipsley Fst Sch B98 .... 102 C4
Ipswich Wlk B37 .... 33 D1
Irelands La B95 .... 113 D7
Ireton Cl CV4 .... 59 E1
Iris Cl LE10 .... 31 F3
Ironmonger Row CV1 ...... 151 B3
Ironstone Hollow OX15 .... 142 E4
Irving Rd CV1 .... 61 F1
Isis B36 .... 33 D4
Islington Cres CV9 .... 10 B1
Ivanhoe Ave CV11 .... 29 F1
Ivor Rd Atherstone CV9 ..... 18 C4
  Coventry CV6 .... 49 F1

Ivy Cl CV13 .... 21 E4
Ivy Farm La CV4 .... 76 B3
Ivy La Ettington CV37 ...... 131 A3
  Harbury CV33 .... 123 F6
  Mollington OX17 .... 134 A2
Ivy Lodge Cl B37 .... 44 A4
Ivybridge Rd CV3 .... 77 E3
Ivycroft Rd B79 .... 5 F2
Ivyhouse Wlk B77 .... 9 F3
Izod's Cl GL55 .... 135 A1

Jack O'Watton Bsns Pk
  B46 .... 23 E2
Jack Thomson Croft WR11 127 F6
Jackdaw Dr B36 .... 33 D4
Jacker's Rd CV2 .... 50 A2
Jacklin Dr CV3 .... 77 E2
Jacknell Rd LE10 .... 30 B4
Jackson Cl
  Hampton Magna CV35 ..... 114 F3
  Keresley CV7 .... 49 D4
Jackson Rd Coventry CV6 ... 49 E1
  Rugby CV21 .... 84 A1
Jackson Wlk B35 .... 22 A1
Jacobean La B93 .... 56 A1
Jacox Cres CV8 .... 93 E3
Jade Cl CV1 .... 151 D4
James Dawson Dr CV5 ..... 59 D4
James Galloway Cl CV3 .... 78 C4
James Green Rd CV4 ...... 59 F1
James Rd B46 .... 33 F4
James St Arley CV7 .... 37 D4
  Nuneaton CV11 .... 29 D3
  Rugby CV21 .... 83 D2
James Watt Cl NN11 ...... 117 F2
Jamescroft CV3 .... 78 C3
Jaques Cl B46 .... 23 D1
Jardine Cres CV4 .... 59 F1
Jasmine Gr Coventry CV3 ... 78 B4
  Royal Leamington Spa CV32 106 A1
Jasmine Rd B77 .... 4 A2
Jays Cl B98 .... 112 A6
Jean St CV9 .... 11 E1
Jedburgh Gr CV3 .... 77 D2
Jeff's Cl OX15 .... 137 F2
Jeffrey Cl CV12 .... 49 E4
Jeliff St CV4 .... 59 F1
Jenkins Ave CV5 .... 59 F2
Jenkins Rd CV21 .... 84 A1
Jenner St CV1 .... 151 C4
Jenton Rd CV31 .... 110 A3
Jephcott Cl B49 .... 143 D2
Jersey Croft B36 .... 33 D3
Jervis Rd B77 .... 9 F3
Jesmond Rd CV1 .... 61 F2
Jesson Rd B75 .... 13 D3
Jill La B96 .... 103 D1
Jim Forrest Cl 4 CV3 ...... 78 C4
Joan Ward St CV3 .... 77 E4
Joan's Cl 20 CV31 .... 110 B3
Joanna Dr CV3 .... 77 E2
Job's La CV4 .... 60 A1
Jodrell St CV11 .... 29 D3
Joe Williams Cl 7 CV3 ..... 78 C4
John Grace St CV3 .... 77 E4
John Gulson Prim Sch CV1 61 E3
John Knight Rd CV12 ...... 39 D3
John McGuire Cres CV3 .... 78 C4
John Nash Sq CV8 .... 92 C2
John Nichols St LE10 ...... 31 D4
John O'Gaunt Rd CV8 ...... 92 C2
John Rous Ave CV4 .... 76 A4
John Shelton Prim Sch
  CV6 .... 49 E2
John Simpson Cl CV8 ...... 80 A2
John St Bedworth CV12 .... 39 D1
  Nuneaton, Coton CV11 .... 29 E1
  Nuneaton, Stockingford CV10 . 28 C1
  Royal Leamington Spa CV32 109 F4
  Stratford-u-A CV37 ...... 145 D2
John Taylor Way CV35 ..... 122 E3
John Thwaites Cl CV22 .... 83 D1
John's Cl LE10 .... 31 E3
Johndory B77 .... 9 E3
Johns Cl B80 .... 103 E2
Johnson Ave CV22 .... 82 C1
Johnson Pl B95 .... 113 B5
Johnson Rd Bedworth CV12 . 39 E2
  Coventry CV6 .... 62 A4
Johnson St CV9 .... 10 B1
Jolyffe Park Rd CV37 ...... 145 D2
Jon Baker Ct LE10 .... 31 F4
Jonathan Rd CV2 .... 62 C4
Jones Rd CV7 .... 39 D1
Jones Wood Cl B76 .... 22 A4
Jonkel Ave B77 .... 10 A3
Jordan Cl CV8 .... 93 D1
Jordan Well CV1 .... 151 C2
Jordans Cl B97 .... 102 B3
Jordans The CV5 .... 60 B2
Joseph Cash Prim Sch
  CV6 .... 61 D4
Joseph Creighton Cl CV3 .. 78 C3
Joseph Luckman Rd CV12 . 39 D2
Joseph Way CV37 .... 144 C3
Joyce Pool 15 CV34 ...... 108 C4
Jubilee Ave
  Lower Shuckburgh NN11 ... 116 A1
  Redditch B97 .... 102 B4
Jubilee Cl B50 .... 148 C3
Jubilee Cres CV6 .... 61 D4
Jubilee Ct B78 .... 15 E3
Jubilee St CV21 .... 82 C2
Jubilee Terr CV12 .... 39 D2
Judd Cl CV12 .... 38 C2
Judds La CV6 .... 49 F2
Judge Cl CV23 .... 82 A3
Juggins La B94 .... 86 A4

Julian Cl CV2 .... 62 C4
Juliet Cl CV11 .... 30 A1
Juliet Dr CV34 .... 99 E3
Julius Dr B46 .... 23 F1
Junction St CV1 .... 151 A2
Junewood Cl CV21 .... 83 E4
Juniper B77 .... 4 A2
Juniper Dr Coventry CV5 ... 59 F3
  Sutton Coldfield B76 ...... 22 A4
Jury St CV34 .... 108 C3
Justins Ave CV37 .... 144 C3

Kanzan Rd CV2 .... 50 A2
Kareen Gr CV3 .... 79 E4
Karen Cl CV10 .... 28 C4
Karlingford Cl CV5 .... 76 B4
Kathleen Ave CV12 .... 38 C1
Kay Cl CV21 .... 83 E4
Kaysbrook Dr CV23 .... 97 D3
Keats Cl CV10 .... 28 A2
Keats Rd Coventry CV2 ...... 62 B1
  Stratford-u-A CV37 ...... 145 D1
Keble Rd GL56 .... 140 A2
Kebull Gn CV4 .... 75 F4
Keeling Rd CV8 .... 93 D3
Keenan Dr CV12 .... 38 B1
Keepers Cl B46 .... 34 A2
Keepers Wlk CV12 .... 38 B1
Keetley Cl CV36 .... 149 F2
Kegworth Cl CV6 .... 50 A2
Keir Cl CV32 .... 106 A1
Keith Rd CV32 .... 106 A2
Kele Rd CV4 .... 76 A4
Kelmscote Rd CV6 .... 60 C4
Kelsey Cl CV11 .... 29 F2
Kelsey La CV7 .... 74 B3
Kelsey's Cl CV8 .... 79 F2
Kelsull Croft B37 .... 33 D1
Kelvin Ave CV2 .... 62 B3
Kelvin Rd CV32 .... 106 B3
Kelway CV3 .... 63 D1
Kem St CV11 .... 29 F1
Kemble Dr B35 .... 22 A2
Kemerton Way B90 .... 70 C3
Kempley Ave CV2 .... 62 B1
Kemps Green Rd
  Balsall Common CV7 ...... 74 A3
  Tanworth-in-A B94 ...... 88 A1
Kempsey Cl B98 .... 103 D4
Kempsford Cl B98 .... 102 C3
Kempton Cres CV32 ...... 106 B2
Kendal Ave Coleshill B46 .... 33 F4
  Royal Leamington Spa CV32 105 E1
Kendal Cl Nuneaton CV11 ... 30 A3
  Redditch B98 .... 112 A6
Kendal Rise CV5 .... 60 B2
Kendall Ave CV37 .... 145 D2
Kendon Ave CV6 .... 60 C3
Kendrick Cl CV6 .... 50 A2
Kenhill Rd OX15 .... 138 F5
Kenilworth Castle CV8 ..... 92 B3
Kenilworth Cl B97 .... 102 B3
Kenilworth Ct CV3 .... 77 E4
Kenilworth Dr CV11 .... 29 D2
Kenilworth Rd
  Balsall Common CV7, CV8 .. 74 B2
  Coventry CV3 .... 76 C2
  Cubbington CV32 .... 106 B3
  Hampton in A B92 .... 57 F3
  Kenilworth CV8 .... 93 E4
  Knowle B93 .... 72 C3
  Lighthorne Heath CV35 .... 123 D2
  Meriden CV7 .... 45 E1
  Royal Leamington Spa CV32 105 F3
Kenilworth Sch Castle
  Sixth Form Ctr CV8 ...... 92 C1
Kenilworth St 12 CV32 ...... 105 F1
Kenilworth Way OX16 ...... 139 F3
Kennan Ave CV34 .... 109 F3
Kennedy Dr CV22 .... 82 B1
Kennedy Sq 11 CV32 ...... 106 A1
Kennel La CV9 .... 19 D4
Kennet Cl CV2 .... 62 B4
Kenning Cl CV23 .... 115 C4
Kenpas Highway CV3 ...... 77 D3
Kensington Rd CV5 .... 61 D1
Kent Cl CV3 .... 77 F3
Kent Rd CV33 .... 132 F5
Kent The CV11 .... 84 A1
Kenthurst Cl CV5 .... 59 E2
Kentmere Cl CV2 .... 50 C1
Kents La CV37 .... 131 A4
Kenway B47 .... 69 D4
Kenwyn Gdns CV7 .... 50 A4
Keppel Cl CV22 .... 82 B1
Keppel St CV1 .... 61 F3
Keresley Brook Rd CV6 .... 49 D1
Keresley Cl CV6 .... 49 D1
Keresley Grange Prim Sch
  CV6 .... 48 C1
Keresley Green Rd CV6 .... 48 C1
Keresley Newland
  Comb Sch CV7 .... 48 C4
Keresley Rd CV6 .... 61 D4
Kerns Terr CV37 .... 145 D2
Kerr Way GL56 .... 140 C3
Kerria Ctr B77 .... 4 A2
Kerria Rd B77 .... 4 A2
Kerrls Way CV3 .... 63 D1
Kerswell Dr B90 .... 71 D3
Kestrel B77 .... 10 A3
Kestrel Cl Hinckley LE10 ... 31 F3
  Stratford-u-A CV37 ...... 145 D3
Kestrel Croft 2 CV3 ...... 78 C4
Kestrel Rd CV10 .... 30 A1
Keswick Cl CV11 .... 30 A3
Keswick Dr CV21 .... 83 E4

Keswick Gn CV32 .... 105 E1
Keswick Wlk CV2 .... 62 C2
Kettlebrook Rd B90 ...... 71 E3
Kettlewell Cl CV34 ...... 104 C1
Keviliok St CV3 .... 77 E3
Kew Cl CV8 .... 93 E3
Kew Rd CV21 .... 83 D2
Keys Dr CV22 .... 82 B1
Keys Hill CV9 .... 11 E1
Keys La CV23 .... 125 F4
Keyte Rd CV36 .... 136 B6
Keyte's La CV35 .... 122 B7
Keytes Acre GL55 .... 135 E3
Kiblers La CV35 .... 131 D2
Kielder Dr CV10 .... 28 C1
Kiftsgate Court Gardens
  GL55 .... 135 C6
Kilburn Dr CV5 .... 60 C2
Kilby Gn LE10 .... 31 F3
Kilby Gr CV31 .... 110 B3
Kilbye Cl B77 .... 9 F3
Kildale Cl CV1 .... 151 D3
Kildwick Way 5 CV34 ...... 104 C1
Killworth Rd CV21 .... 101 D4
Kiln Cl
  Royal Leamington Spa CV32 106 A1
  Studley B80 .... 103 E2
Kiln Way Polesworth B78 .... 4 C1
  Shilton CV12 .... 51 F4
Kilnsey Gr CV34 .... 104 C1
Kilsby Gr B91 .... 71 E4
Kilsby La CV21 .... 101 E4
Kilsby Rd CV23 .... 101 E1
Kimbell Cl CV33 .... 124 B1
Kimberley B77 .... 9 F4
Kimberley Cl CV5 .... 59 F2
Kimberley Rd Baginton CV8 .. 77 F1
  Bedworth CV12 .... 39 E2
  Rugby CV21 .... 83 D2
Kimberley Wlk B76 ...... 22 B3
Kimble Cl CV5 .... 60 A2
Kinchford Cl B91 .... 71 D4
Kineton CE Jun & Inf Sch
  CV35 .... 132 B6
Kineton High Sch CV35 .... 132 C6
Kineton La B94 .... 71 D1
Kineton Rd Coventry CV2 ... 62 B3
  Kenilworth CV8 .... 93 E2
  Southam CV33 .... 147 D2
  Wellesbourne CV35 ...... 146 C1
Kineton Road Ind Est
  CV33 .... 147 D2
King Edward Rd
  Coventry CV1 .... 61 F2
  Nuneaton CV11 .... 29 E2
  Rugby CV21 .... 83 D2
King Edward VI Coll CV11 .. 29 E2
King Edward VI Gram Sch
  CV37 .... 145 D1
King George's Ave
  Bedworth CV12 .... 39 D3
  Coventry CV6 .... 49 F1
King George's Ct CV23 .... 82 A3
King George's Way LE10 .. 31 D4
King Henry VIII Sch CV1 .. 151 A1
King John's La CV35 ...... 132 E2
King John's Rd CV35 ...... 132 B6
King Richard St CV2 ...... 61 F2
King St Bedworth CV12 .... 39 E1
  Royal Leamington Spa CV32 106 A1
  Rugby CV21 .... 83 D2
King William St CV1 ...... 61 F3
King's Hill La CV8 .... 77 D1
King's La Broom B50 ...... 148 A3
  Newton Regis B79 .... 2 B2
  Norton WR11 .... 127 B2
  Snitterfield CV37 .... 121 B6
  Stratford-u-A CV37 ...... 144 C4
Kingcomb La GL55 ...... 135 A2
Kingfield Rd CV1, CV6 .... 61 E4
Kingfisher B77 .... 10 A3
Kingfisher Ave CV10 ...... 28 B3
Kingfisher Dr B36 .... 33 D4
Kingfisher Way B49 ...... 143 D3
Kingham Cl B98 .... 112 A6
Kingham Hill Sch OX7 ..... 150 A1
Kingland Dr CV32 .... 105 E1
Kingley Ave B49 .... 143 E3
Kings Ave CV9 .... 18 C4
Kings Coughton La B49 .. 143 D3
Kings Gdns CV12 .... 39 E1
Kings Gr CV2 .... 62 A2
Kings High Sch for Girls
  CV34 .... 108 C4
Kings Newnham La CV23 .. 80 C3
Kings Newnham Rd CV23 .. 81 D3
Kingsbridge Rd CV10 ...... 29 E3
Kingsbrook Dr B91 ...... 71 D4
Kingsbury Bsns Pk B76 .... 22 C3
Kingsbury Cl B76 .... 22 B3
Kingsbury Fst Sch B78 .... 15 E3
Kingsbury Mid Sch B78 .... 15 E3
Kingsbury Rd Coventry CV6 . 60 C3
  Curdworth B76 .... 23 D4
  Minworth B76 .... 22 B3
  Sutton Coldfield B35, B76 .. 22 A4
Kingsbury Sch B78 .... 15 D3
Kingsbury Water Park B76 . 15 D2
Kingscote Gr CV3 .... 77 D2
Kingscote Rd B93 .... 71 F1
Kingsfield Ind Est CV1 .... 61 E3
Kingsford Cl B36 .... 22 B1
Kingshurst CV31 .... 110 C3
Kingshurst Inf Sch B37 .... 33 D2
Kingshurst Jun Sch B37 ... 33 D2
Kingsland Ave CV5 .... 60 C1
Kingsland Dr B93 .... 71 F2
Kingsley Ave CV21 .... 83 F1

Kingsley Cres CV12 ...... 40 A2
Kingsley Orch CV21 ...... 83 F1
Kingsley Prep Sch B93 .... 72 A2
Kingsley Rd 12 CV21 ...... 122 F8
Kingsley Sch The CV32 .... 105 F1
Kingsley Terr CV2 .... 62 C4
Kingsley Wlk CV2 .... 62 C4
Kingston Rd CV35 .... 113 E3
Kingston Mews CV31 ...... 110 B3
Kingston Rd CV5 .... 60 C1
Kingsway Coventry CV2 ... 62 A2
  Kingsbury B78 .... 15 E3
  Lighthorne Heath CV35 .... 123 D2
  Nuneaton CV11 .... 29 D2
  Royal Leamington Spa CV31 . 109 F3
  Rugby CV22 .... 83 D1
Kingswood Ave CV7 ...... 48 A4
Kingswood Cl Coventry CV6 . 49 E1
  Lapworth B94 .... 89 F3
Kingswood Rd CV10 ...... 28 A2
Kington Rise CV35 .... 113 E2
Kinman Way CV21 .... 83 E3
Kinross Cl CV10 .... 28 C1
Kinross Rd CV32 .... 106 A2
Kinsall Gn B77 .... 10 B3
Kinsham Dr B91 .... 71 D4
Kintyre The CV2 .... 63 D4
Kinver Cl CV2 .... 50 C1
Kinver Croft B76 .... 22 A4
Kinwalsey La CV7 .... 46 C3
Kinwarton Dovecote B49 .. 143 F3
Kinwarton Farm Rd B49 .. 143 E3
Kinwarton Rd B49 .... 143 E2
Kinwarton Workshops
  B49 .... 143 F3
Kipling Ave CV34 .... 108 B2
Kipling Cl CV10 .... 28 A3
Kipling Rd Coventry CV6 ... 61 D4
  Stratford-u-A CV37 ...... 130 A8
Kirby Ave CV34 .... 104 C1
Kirby Cl Brandon CV8 ...... 79 F3
  Coventry CV1 .... 61 E3
Kirby Cnr CV4 .... 76 A3
Kirby Corner Rd CV4 ...... 76 A3
Kirby Rd Coventry CV5 .... 60 C1
  Rugby CV21 .... 83 F1
Kirigushi Rd CV35 .... 132 E5
Kirkby Cl CV21 .... 83 F3
Kirkdale Ave CV6 .... 49 E2
Kirkland Way B78 .... 8 A4
Kirkstone CV21 .... 83 E4
Kirkstone Rd CV12 ...... 39 D1
Kirkstone Wlk CV11 ...... 30 A3
Kirkwall CV33 .... 147 D2
Kirtland Cl CV37 .... 3 D1
  Whitnash CV31 .... 110 A2
Kissing Tree La CV37 ...... 121 D3
Kitchener Rd CV6 .... 61 F4
Kitebrook Cl 9 B90 ...... 71 D4
Kites Cl CV34 .... 104 C1
Kites Nest La CV35 .... 114 C8
Kittermaster Rd CV7 ...... 46 B1
Kitwood Ave B78 .... 10 C3
Kixley La B93 .... 72 B3
Klevedon Cl CV11 .... 30 A1
Knebley Cres CV10 ...... 29 E1
Knibbs Sh Ctr The 13
  CV34 .... 108 C4
Knight Ave CV1 .... 61 F1
Knightcote Dr
  Royal Leamington Spa CV32 . 109 F4
  Solihull B91 .... 71 D4
Knightley Cl CV32 .... 106 C3
Knightlow Ave CV3 ...... 78 B3
Knightlow CE Mid Sch
  CV23 .... 96 C4
Knightlow Cl CV8 .... 93 E2
Knightlow Way CV33 ...... 123 F6
Knights Cl LE10 .... 31 E2
Knights Ct LE10 .... 30 C4
Knights La CV37 .... 145 F2
Knightsbridge Ave CV12 .. 39 E2
Knob Hill CV23 .... 96 C3
Knoll Croft
  Cheswick Green B90 ...... 70 B2
  Coventry CV3 .... 77 E3
Knoll Dr Coventry CV3 .... 77 E3
  Warwick CV34 .... 104 C1
Knottesford Cl B80 ...... 103 E2
Knowlands Rd B90 ...... 71 D4
Knowle CE Jun & Inf Sch
  B93 .... 72 B3
Knowle Hill Hurley CV9 .... 16 B2
  Kenilworth CV8 .... 93 E3
Knowle Rd B92 .... 56 C1
Knowle Wood Rd B93 .... 72 A2
Knowles Ave CV10 .... 28 B2
Knox Cres CV11 .... 29 F4
Kranji Rd CV33 .... 132 F5
Kurtus B77 .... 9 E3
Kyetts Cnr OX17 .... 134 C1
Kynner Way CV3 .... 79 D4
Kyter La B35 .... 22 A1

Laburnum Ave
  Coventry CV6 .... 60 C3
  Kenilworth CV8 .... 93 D2
Laburnum Cl
  Bedworth CV12 .... 38 C1
  Hollywood B47 .... 69 D2
  Kingsbury B78 .... 15 E3
Laburnum Dr
  Sutton Coldfield B76 ...... 13 D2
  Whitnash CV31 .... 110 A2

Laburnum Gr
Nuneaton CV10 ... 28 B3
Rugby CV22 ... 99 F4
Warwick CV34 ... 105 D1
Lacell Cl CV34 ... 104 C1
Ladbroke By – Pass CV33 . 124 D5
Ladbroke Pk CV34 ... 104 C1
Ladbroke Rd CV33 ... 124 B4
Ladbrook Cl B98 ... 102 C4
Ladbrook Rd CV5 ... 60 A2
Lady Byron La Knowle B93 ... 71 F4
Knowle,Copt Heath B93 ... 56 A1
Lady Katherine Leveson CE Prim Sch B93 ... 73 D3
Lady La Coventry CV6 ... 49 F2
Earlswood B90, B94 ... 70 A2
Lady Warwick Ave CV12 ... 39 E1
Ladycroft CV32 ... 106 C3
Ladyfields Way CV6 ... 49 D2
Ladygrove Cl B98 ... 103 D4
Ladymead Dr CV6 ... 49 D1
Lair The B78 ... 10 C4
Lake View Rd CV5 ... 60 C2
Lakeland Dr B77 ... 10 A4
Lakes Sta The B94 ... 86 C4
Lakeside CV12 ... 39 D1
Lakeside Dr B90 ... 70 C4
Lakin Ct CV34 ... 108 C4
Lakin Dr CV33 ... 124 A4
Lamb St CV1 ... 151 B3
Lambert Cl B50 ... 148 B3
Lambert Specl Sch CV37 .. 145 D3
Lambeth Cl Birmingham B37 . 33 D2
Coventry CV2 ... 62 C4
Lambourn Cres CV31 ... 110 B3
Lambourne Cl CV5 ... 60 A2
Lamerton Cl CV2 ... 62 B3
Lamintone Dr CV32 ... 105 E1
Lammas Croft CV31 ... 110 A2
Lammas Ct CV8 ... 80 A2
Lammas Rd CV6 ... 60 C2
Lammas Wlk CV34 ... 108 B4
Lamorna Cl CV11 ... 29 F2
Lamp La CV7 ... 36 C3
Lampitts Gn OX15 ... 139 D4
Lamprey B77 ... 9 E3
Lancaster Cl Atherstone CV9 . 12 C1
Wellesbourne CV35 ... 146 B1
Lancaster Pl CV8 ... 92 C1
Lancaster Rd Hinckley LE10 .. 31 E4
Rugby CV21 ... 83 D2
Lance Cl LE10 ... 31 E3
Lanchester Dr OX16 ... 139 F4
Lanchester Rd CV6 ... 61 D3
Lanchester Way
Birmingham B36 ... 22 C1
Daventry NN11 ... 117 F2
Lancia Cl CV6 ... 50 A2
Lancing Rd CV12 ... 40 B1
Land La B37 ... 44 A4
Landor Rd Knowle B93 ... 72 A3
Redditch B98 ... 103 D4
Warwick CV34 ... 108 B4
Whitnash CV31 ... 110 A2
Landrail Wlk B36 ... 33 D4
Landsdowne Pl CV21 ... 83 E1
Landseer Cl CV21 ... 84 A1
Lane Cl OX15 ... 139 D6
Lane Croft B76 ... 22 A4
Lane The Burmington CV36 . 137 A1
Little Compton CV36 ... 141 A6
Laneside CV3 ... 78 C3
Langbank Ave CV3 ... 78 B4
Langcliffe Ave CV34 ... 104 C1
Langcomb Rd B90 ... 70 A4
Langdale Ave CV6 ... 49 E2
Langdale Cl
Royal Leamington Spa CV32 . 106 B2
Rugby CV21 ... 83 E4
Langdale Dr CV11 ... 30 A3
Langdale Rd LE10 ... 31 D4
Langfield Rd B93 ... 72 A4
Langlands The CV35 ... 121 F4
Langley Croft CV4 ... 60 A1
Langley Dr B35 ... 22 A1
Langley Hall Dr B75 ... 13 D3
Langley Hall Rd B75 ... 13 D3
Langley Heath Dr B76 ... 13 D2
Langley Rd Claverdon CV35 . 113 E3
Whitnash CV31 ... 110 A2
Langley Sch B75 ... 13 D3
Langley Wlk B37 ... 33 E1
Langlodge Rd CV6 ... 49 D1
Langnor Rd CV2 ... 62 B3
Langton Cl CV3 ... 78 C4
Langton Rd CV21 ... 83 F1
Langwood Cl CV4 ... 76 A4
Lankett The CV33 ... 133 D7
Lansbury Cl CV2 ... 62 C4
Lansdowne Cir CV32 ... 106 A1
Lansdowne Cl CV12 ... 39 D2
Lansdowne Cres
13 Royal Leamington Spa CV32 ... 106 A1
Studley B80 ... 103 E2
Tamworth B77 ... 9 E4
Lansdowne Rd 10
Royal Leamington Spa CV32 106 A1
Studley B80 ... 103 E2
Lansdowne St Coventry CV2 ... 61 F2
Royal Leamington Spa CV32 106 A1
Lant Cl CV7 ... 75 D4
Lapwing B77 ... 10 A3
Lapwing Dr B92 ... 57 D4
Lapworth CE Jun & Inf Sch B94 ... 89 E2
Lapworth Cl B98 ... 102 C4
Lapworth Oaks B94 ... 89 E2
Lapworth Rd CV2 ... 50 B1
Lapworth St B94 ... 89 D1
Lapworth Sta B94 ... 89 E2
Larch Cl Alcester B49 ... 143 D3
Rugby CV22 ... 82 A1
Stratford-u-A CV37 ... 145 D2
Larch Croft B37 ... 33 D1
Larch Gr CV34 ... 105 D1
Larch Tree Ave CV4 ... 60 A1
Larches The Bedworth CV7 ... 50 A4
Kingsbury B78 ... 15 E4
Larchfields CV8 ... 80 A2
Larchwood Rd CV7 ... 39 D1
Larkfield Way CV5 ... 60 A3
Larkin Cl CV12 ... 40 A2
Larkspur Rugby CV23 ... 83 E4
Tamworth B77 ... 9 E2
Latham Rd CV5 ... 61 D1
Latimer Cl CV8 ... 92 C1
Latymer Cl B76 ... 22 A4
Lauderdale Ave CV6 ... 49 E2
Lauderdale Cl CV23 ... 82 A2
Launceston Dr CV11 ... 29 F2
Laurel Ave B78 ... 11 D4
Laurel Cl CV2 ... 50 C1
Laurel Dr Hartshill CV10 ... 28 A4
Rugby CV22 ... 82 A1
Stockton CV23 ... 147 F4
Laurel Gdns CV22 ... 99 F4
Laurels Cres CV7 ... 74 B3
Laurels The Bedworth CV12 .. 38 C1
Kingsbury B78 ... 15 E4
Lavender Ave CV6 ... 60 C3
Lavender Cl CV23 ... 83 F4
Lavender Hall La CV7 ... 58 B1
Lavenham Cl CV11 ... 40 B4
Lawford Cl CV3 ... 62 C1
Lawford Heath Ind Est CV23 ... 98 B4
Lawford Heath La CV23 ... 98 B3
Lawford La CV22 ... 82 A1
Lawford Rd
Royal Leamington Spa CV31 110 A3
Rugby CV21 ... 82 B2
Lawley Cl CV4 ... 60 A1
Lawns The Bedworth CV12 ... 38 B1
Hinckley LE10 ... 31 F4
Lawnsdale Cl B46 ... 33 F4
Lawnswood Hinckley LE10 ... 31 D4
Sutton Coldfield B76 ... 22 A4
Lawrence Dr B76 ... 22 B3
Lawrence Gdns CV8 ... 93 D3
Lawrence Mackie Gdns CV35 ... 146 C2
Lawrence Rd Bedworth CV7 .. 50 A4
Rugby CV21 ... 83 E2
Lawrence Saunders Rd CV6 ... 61 D3
Lawrence Sheriff Sch CV21 ... 83 D2
Lawrence Sherriff St CV22 . 83 D1
Lawson Ave CV37 ... 145 F2
Lawton Cl LE10 ... 30 C4
Lay Gdns CV31 ... 110 C3
Le Hanche Cl CV7 ... 49 D4
Lea Cl Alcester B49 ... 143 E3
Stratford-u-A CV37 ... 144 A2
Lea Cres CV21 ... 82 B3
Lea Croft Rd B97 ... 102 B3
Lea Green La B47 ... 69 E3
Leacrest Rd CV6 ... 49 D1
Leaf La Coventry CV3 ... 77 E5
Coventry CV3 ... 77 F3
Leafield Cl CV2 ... 62 C4
Leagh Cl CV8 ... 93 D4
Leam Cl CV11 ... 29 F1
Leam Gn CV4 ... 76 B3
Leam Rd
Lighthorne Heath CV35 ... 123 D2
Royal Leamington Spa CV31 . 109 E4
Leam St CV31 ... 110 A4
Leam Terr CV31 ... 110 A4
Leam The NN11 ... 117 F1
Leamington Hastings CE Inf Sch CV23 ... 116 B6
Leamington Rd Coventry CV3 ... 77 E3
Kenilworth CV8 ... 93 D1
Long Itchington CV23 ... 115 C4
Princethorpe CV23 ... 96 B1
Ryton-on-D CV23 ... 96 A4
Southam CV33 ... 124 C8
Leamington Spa Sta CV31 . 109 F4
Lear Gr CV34 ... 109 F2
Leas Cl CV12 ... 39 D2
Leasowe's Ave CV3 ... 76 C2
Leasowes Children's Farm The B94 ... 87 E1
Leather St CV23 ... 115 D4
Leathermill La CV10 ... 19 E2
Leaward Cl CV10 ... 28 C1
Ledbrook Rd CV32 ... 106 C3
Ledbury Rd CV31 ... 110 B3
Ledbury Way B76 ... 22 A4
Lee Cl CV34 ... 104 C1
Lee Rd Hollywood B47 ... 69 D4
Royal Leamington Spa CV31 . 109 F3
Lee The CV5 ... 60 B2
Leeder Cl CV6 ... 49 E1
Leek Wootton CE Fst Sch CV35 ... 105 D3
Leeming Cl CV4 ... 76 B3
Leicester Cswy CV1 ... 61 E3
Leicester Ct CV12 ... 40 B1
Leicester La Cubbington CV32 ... 94 C1
Royal Leamington Spa CV32 . 106 B3
Leicester Rd Atherstone CV9 ... 12 C1
Bedworth CV12 ... 39 D2
Nuneaton CV11 ... 29 E3
Rugby CV21 ... 83 D4
Shilton CV7 ... 51 F3
Leicester Row CV1 ... 151 B4
Leicester St Bedworth CV12 .. 39 D2
Bulkington CV12 ... 40 B1
Royal Leamington Spa CV32 106 A1
Leigh Ave CV3 ... 77 E2
Leigh CE Prim Sch CV4 ... 75 E4
Leigh Cres CV23 ... 115 D3
Leigh Rd Rugby CV21 ... 82 C4
Sutton Coldfield B75 ... 13 D3
Leigh St 3 CV1 ... 61 F2
Leighton Cl Coventry CV4 ... 76 B1
Royal Leamington Spa CV32 . 106 B2
Leisure Wlk B77 ... 9 F3
Lennon Cl CV21 ... 101 E4
Lennox Cl CV3 ... 78 C3
Lenton's La CV2 ... 50 C2
Leofric St CV6 ... 61 D3
Leopold Rd CV1 ... 61 F2
Lesingham Dr CV4 ... 59 F1
Lestock Cl CV22 ... 82 B1
Letchlade Cl CV2 ... 62 B4
Level The OX15 ... 138 F5
Leven Cl LE10 ... 31 D4
Leven Croft B76 ... 22 A4
Leven Way CV2 ... 63 D4
Lever Rd CV21 ... 84 A1
Leveson Cres CV7 ... 74 A3
Levett Rd B77 ... 4 A3
Levy Cl CV21 ... 82 C2
Lewis Ct CV9 ... 18 C3
Lewis Rd Coventry CV1 ... 61 E3
Radford Semele CV31 ... 110 C3
Leyburn Cl Coventry CV6 ... 49 F1
Nuneaton CV11 ... 30 A1
10 Warwick CV34 ... 104 C1
Leycester Pl CV34 ... 108 C3
Leycester Rd CV8 ... 93 D1
Leyes La CV8 ... 93 E3
Leyes The CV23 ... 68 A1
Leyfields Cres CV34 ... 108 B2
Leyland Rd Bulkington CV12 .. 40 A1
Coventry CV5 ... 60 B2
Nuneaton CV11 ... 29 F1
Leyland Specl Sch CV11 ... 29 F1
Leymere Cl CV7 ... 46 B1
Leys Cl Northend CV33 ... 133 B7
Wroxton OX15 ... 139 D4
Leys High Sch The B98 ... 103 E3
Leys La CV7 ... 46 B1
Leys Rd Harvington WR11 ... 127 B5
Rugby CV21 ... 101 E4
Leys The Bidford-on-A B50 ... 148 C3
Halford CV36 ... 137 A8
Salford OX7 ... 150 C3
Upper Boddington NN11 ... 134 E8
Leysbourne GL55 ... 135 B2
Leysfield WR11 ... 127 C4
Leyside CV3 ... 78 C3
Libbards Gate 4 B91 ... 71 E4
Libbards Way B91 ... 71 D4
Liberty Rd B77 ... 9 F3
Liberty Way CV11 ... 29 F2
Library Cl LE10 ... 32 A3
Lichen Gn CV4 ... 76 B3
Lichfield Cl Arley CV7 ... 37 D4
Nuneaton CV11 ... 30 A4
Lichfield Rd Coventry CV3 ... 77 E4
Water Orton B46, B76 ... 23 E2
Wishaw B76 ... 14 A2
Lichfield St B78 ... 9 D4
Liecester Rd LE10 ... 41 F3
Lifford Way CV3 ... 79 D4
Light Hall Sch B90 ... 70 A4
Light La CV1 ... 151 B4
Lighthorne Rd CV35 ... 132 B6
Lightoak Cl B97 ... 102 B3
Lightwood Cl B93 ... 72 A4
Lilac Ave CV6 ... 60 C3
Lilac Cl LE10 ... 31 F3
Lilac Dr CV22 ... 82 A1
Lilac Gr CV34 ... 105 D1
Lilac Rd CV12 ... 39 E3
Lilbourne Rd CV23 ... 84 B3
Lilley Cl CV6 ... 49 E1
Lilley Green Rd B48 ... 85 E3
Lillington Ave CV32 ... 105 F1
Lillington CE Fst Sch CV32 ... 106 A2
Lillington Cl
Royal Leamington Spa CV32 106 A2
Sutton Coldfield B75 ... 13 D2
Lillington Prim Sch CV32 . 106 A2
Lillington Rd Coventry CV2 ... 50 B1
Royal Leamington Spa CV32 106 A2
Solihull B90 ... 70 A4
Limbrick Ave CV4 ... 60 A1
Limbrick Wood Prim Sch CV4 ... 59 F2
Lime Ave CV32 ... 106 A2
Lime Cl B47 ... 69 D3
Lime Gr
Birmingham, Chemsley Wood B37 ... 33 D1
Coventry CV4 ... 60 A1
Hurley CV9 ... 16 B2
Kenilworth CV8 ... 93 D2
Nuneaton CV10 ... 28 C3
Lime Kiln B78 ... 11 D4
Lime Rd CV33 ... 147 D3
Lime Tree Ave Coventry CV4 . 60 A1
Rugby CV22 ... 99 D4
Limekiln La B94 ... 70 B1
Limes Ave CV37 ... 144 B1
Limes Coppice CV10 ... 27 F4
Limes The CV12 ... 38 C1
Limestone Hall La CV23 ... 81 D2
Linaker Rd CV3 ... 78 B3
Lincoln Ave CV10 ... 28 A4
Lincoln Cl Warwick CV34 ... 104 C1
Wellesbourne CV35 ... 146 B1
Lincoln Gr B37 ... 33 D1
Lincoln St CV1 ... 151 C4
Lincroft Cres CV5 ... 60 C2
Lindale CV21 ... 83 E4
Linden Ave CV35 ... 146 C2
Linden Cl CV34 ... 104 C1
Linden Lea CV12 ... 39 D2
Lindera B77 ... 4 A2
Lindfield The CV3 ... 78 B4
Lindhurst Dr B94 ... 88 B3
Lindisfarne Dr CV8 ... 93 E2
Lindley Rd Bedworth CV12 ... 38 B1
Coventry CV3 ... 62 A1
Lindridge Cl B98 ... 112 A6
Lindridge Dr B76 ... 22 B3
Lindridge Jun Sch B75 ... 13 D3
Lindridge Rd B75 ... 13 D3
Lindsay Wlk CV33 ... 132 F7
Lindsey Cres CV8 ... 93 D1
Lineholt Cl B98 ... 103 D3
Linen St CV34 ... 108 B3
Linford Wlk CV2 ... 50 C1
Lingard Rd B75 ... 13 D3
Lingwood Dr CV10 ... 28 C2
Links Rd CV6 ... 61 D4
Linkway CV31 ... 109 F3
Linley Rd CV33 ... 147 D3
Linnell Rd CV21 ... 83 F1
Linnet Cl CV3 ... 78 B3
Linstock Way CV6 ... 50 A2
Linthouse Wlk B77 ... 9 F3
Lintly B77 ... 4 A1
Linwood Dr CV2 ... 50 C1
Lion Fields Ave CV5 ... 60 A3
Liskeard Cl CV11 ... 30 A3
Liskeard Rd CV35 ... 132 D3
Lisle Gdns 4 CV35 ... 122 F8
Lister Cres CV9 ... 12 C1
Lister St CV11 ... 29 E2
Little Acre B97 ... 102 B3
Little Brom CV9 ... 11 E1
Little Church St
Coventry CV1 ... 151 C4
Rugby CV21 ... 83 D2
Little Duke St CV11 ... 29 D2
Little Elborow St CV21 ... 83 D2
Little Farm CV3 ... 78 B3
Little Field CV2 ... 62 A3
Little Forge Rd B98 ... 103 E4
Little Gr CV22 ... 83 E1
Little Heath Ind Est CV6 ... 50 A1
Little Lawford La CV21 ... 82 A4
Little London La CV23 ... 68 A1
Little Park St CV1 ... 151 C2
Little Pennington St 3 CV21 ... 82 C2
Little Pittern CV35 ... 132 B6
Little Pk CV33 ... 147 D2
Little South St CV1 ... 61 F2
Little Woods B97 ... 102 C3
Littlemead Rd B90 ... 69 F4
Littleshaw Croft B47 ... 69 E2
Littleshaw La B47 ... 69 E2
Littlethorpe CV3 ... 78 B3
Littleton CE Fst Sch WR11 127 F1
Littleton Cl Kenilworth CV8 ... 93 D4
Sutton Coldfield B76 ... 13 D1
Littleton Croft 6 B91 ... 71 E4
Littlewood Cl 2 B91 ... 71 D4
Littlewood Gn B80 ... 103 E2
Littleworth
Chipping Campden GL55 ... 135 A2
Henley-in-A B95 ... 113 B4
Litton B77 ... 4 B1
Liveridge Cl B93 ... 71 F3
Liveridge Hill B95 ... 113 B7
Livery St CV32 ... 109 F4
Livingstone Ave CV23 ... 81 F2
Livingstone Rd CV6 ... 61 F4
Liza Ct CV21 ... 83 E4
Llewellyn Rd CV31 ... 110 A3
Lloyd Cl
Hampton Magna CV35 ... 114 F3
Norton WR11 ... 127 C2
Nuneaton CV11 ... 29 E1
Lloyd Cres CV2 ... 62 C2
Lloyd Rd CV21 ... 83 E3
Loach Dr CV2 ... 50 A2
Lobelia Cl LE10 ... 31 F3
Lochmore Cl LE10 ... 31 D4
Lochmore Dr LE10 ... 31 D4
Lochmore Way LE10 ... 31 D4
Lock Cl CV37 ... 145 D2
Lock La CV34 ... 108 B4
Locke Cl CV6 ... 49 D1
Lockhart Cl CV8 ... 93 D2
Lockheed Cl CV31 ... 109 F3
Lockhurst La CV6 ... 61 E4
Locking Croft B35 ... 22 A2
Locks The CV21 ... 84 A1
Loder Cl CV4 ... 59 F2
Lodge Cl Atherstone CV9 ... 19 D3
Hinckley LE10 ... 32 A3
Lodge Cres CV34 ... 108 B2
Lodge Croft B93 ... 72 A3
Lodge Green La CV7 ... 46 C1
Lodge Green La N CV7 ... 46 C2
Lodge Rd Coventry CV3 ... 62 A1
Knowle B93 ... 72 A3
Rugby CV21 ... 83 D2
Stratford-u-A CV37 ... 144 C2
Logan Rd CV2 ... 62 C4
Lollard Croft CV3 ... 77 E4
Lomita Cres B77 ... 9 E4
Lomond Cl LE10 ... 31 D4
London End NN11 ... 134 E8
London Rd
Coventry, Cheylesmore CV3 ... 77 F4
Coventry, Willenhall CV3 ... 78 A3
Hinckley LE10 ... 31 F4
Middleton B75, B78 ... 13 E4
Moreton-in-M GL56 ... 140 B3
Ryton-on-D CV8 ... 79 D1
Shipston-on-S CV36 ... 149 F2
Stretton on D CV23 ... 96 C4
Sutton Coldfield B75 ... 7 D2
Willoughby CV23 ... 117 C6
Long Brook La CV7 ... 73 F3
Long Close Ave CV5 ... 60 A3
Long Close Wlk B35 ... 22 A2
Long Furlong CV22 ... 100 A4
Long Hyde Rd WR11 ... 127 F1
Long Itchington CE Prim Sch CV23 ... 115 D4
Long La CV5, CV7 ... 48 B1
Long Lawson Comb Sch CV23 ... 82 A3
Long Marston Rd
Mickleton CV37 ... 135 B8
Pebworth CV37 ... 128 F2
Welford on A CV37 ... 129 B5
Long Shoot The CV11 ... 30 B3
Long St Atherstone CV9 ... 18 B4
Bulkington CV12 ... 40 B1
Dordon B78 ... 11 D3
Longborough Cl B97 ... 102 A3
Longcroft Cl B35 ... 22 A1
Longdon Cl B98 ... 103 D4
Longdon Rd B93 ... 72 A3
Longdown La CV23 ... 117 D7
Longfellow Ave CV34 ... 108 B2
Longfellow Cl B97 ... 102 B4
Longfellow Rd CV2 ... 62 B2
Longfield Rd CV31 ... 110 A3
Longford Cl
Bidford-on-A B50 ... 148 C3
Dorridge B93 ... 72 A2
Longford Park Prim Sch CV6 ... 50 A2
Longford Rd Bedworth CV7 ... 50 A3
Coventry CV6 ... 50 A2
Longford Sq CV6 ... 50 A2
Longhope Cl B98 ... 112 A6
Longleat Dr B90 ... 70 C3
Longleat Gr 25 CV31 ... 110 B3
Longley Ave B76 ... 22 B3
Longrood Rd CV22 ... 99 E3
Longstone Cl B90 ... 71 D3
Longwood Cl CV4 ... 75 F3
Lonscale Dr CV3 ... 77 D3
Lonsdale Rd CV32 ... 106 A2
Lord Lytton Ave CV2 ... 62 B1
Lord St CV5 ... 60 C1
Lords La B80 ... 103 F1
Lorenzo Cl CV3 ... 78 B3
Lothersdale B77 ... 10 B4
Loudon Ave CV6 ... 61 D3
Loughshaw B77 ... 4 B1
Louisa Ward Cl CV23 ... 115 C7
Love La LE10 ... 32 A3
Love Lyne B97 ... 102 A3
Loveday Cl Atherstone CV9 ... 12 B1
Royal Leamington Spa CV32 . 105 F1
Lovelace Ave B91 ... 71 E4
Lovell Cl CV7 ... 50 A4
Lovell Rd CV12 ... 39 D2
Loverock Cres CV21 ... 83 F1
Lovetts Cl LE10 ... 30 C4
Low Rd WR11 ... 127 A6
Lowbrook La B90 ... 69 E2
Lowdham B77 ... 4 B1
Lowe Rd CV6 ... 49 D1
Lower Ave CV31 ... 109 F4
Lower Cape CV34 ... 108 B4
Lower Cladswell La B49 ... 118 C5
Lower Eastern Green La CV5 ... 59 F2
Lower End Bubbenhall CV8 ... 95 E3
Salford OX7 ... 150 C2
Shutford OX15 ... 139 A3
Lower Farm La OX17 ... 133 F2
Lower Ford St CV1 ... 151 D3
Lower Grinsty La B97 ... 102 A4
Lower High St GL55 ... 135 A2
Lower Hillmorton Rd CV21 ... 83 E1
Lower Holyhead Rd CV1 ... 151 A3
Lower House La CV9 ... 11 D2
Lower Ladyes Hills CV8 ... 93 D3
Lower Leam St CV31 ... 110 A4
Lower Prec CV1 ... 151 B3
Lower Rd CV7 ... 51 E3
Lower St Rugby CV21 ... 101 D4
Willoughby CV23 ... 117 B6
Lower Villiers St 9 CV32 . 106 A1
Lowes Ave CV34 ... 104 C1
Lowes La CV35 ... 146 B1
Loweswater Cl CV11 ... 30 A3
Loweswater Rd CV3 ... 62 C1
Lowforce B77 ... 10 B4
Lowry Cl CV12 ... 39 D2
Lowther St CV2 ... 61 F2
Loxley CE Prim Sch CV35 ... 130 F7
Loxley Cl Coventry CV2 ... 50 B1
Wellesbourne CV35 ... 146 B2

Loxley Rd Alveston CV37 ..... 121 D1
Stratford-u-A CV37 ..... 145 E1
Wellesbourne CV35 ..... 146 B1
Loxley Way CV32 ..... 106 A1
Lucas Rd CV10 ..... 31 E3
Luce Cl B35 ..... 22 A2
Lucian Cl CV2 ..... 63 D4
Luddington Rd CV37 ..... 129 E8
Ludford Cl Ansley CV10 ..... 27 D2
Stratford-u-A CV37 ..... 144 B2
Ludford Rd CV10 ..... 28 B3
Ludgate Ct B77 ..... 4 A3
Ludlow Cl B37 ..... 33 E1
Ludlow Rd CV5 ..... 61 D1
Ludlow's La CV35 ..... 114 C7
Luff Cl CV3 ..... 78 A4
Lugtrout La B91 ..... 56 A3
Lulworth Pk CV8 ..... 93 E3
Lumley Gr B37 ..... 33 E1
Lumsden Cl CV2 ..... 62 C4
Lunar Cl CV4 ..... 76 B3
Lundy View B36 ..... 33 D3
Lunn Ave CV8 ..... 92 C2
Lupin Cl LE10 ..... 31 E3
Lupton Ave CV3 ..... 77 E4
Luscombe Rd CV2 ..... 62 C4
Luther Way CV5 ..... 59 F2
Lutterworth Rd
Brinklow CV23 ..... 64 C2
Churchover CV23 ..... 67 E3
Coventry CV2 ..... 62 B3
Hinckley LE10 ..... 32 B2
Nuneaton CV11 ..... 40 B4
Pailton CV23 ..... 54 B1
Shawell LE17 ..... 68 B3
Wolvey LE10 ..... 41 F3
Lutterworth Road
Commercial Est LE10 ..... 32 A3
Luxor La CV5 ..... 59 D4
Lychgate Cl LE10 ..... 32 A3
Lychgate La LE10 ..... 32 B3
Lydd Croft B35 ..... 22 A2
Lydford Cl CV2 ..... 62 B4
Lydgate Rd CV6 ..... 61 D3
Lydstep Gr CV31 ..... 110 B4
Lye Green Rd CV35 ..... 113 F4
Lyecroft Ave B37 ..... 33 E1
Lymesy St CV3 ..... 77 E4
Lymington Cl CV6 ..... 61 E4
Lymore Croft CV2 ..... 63 D4
Lynbrook Cl B47 ..... 69 D4
Lynbrook Rd CV5 ..... 76 B4
Lynch The Nuneaton CV11 ..... 29 E1
Polesworth B78 ..... 4 C1
Lynchgate Rd CV4 ..... 76 B3
Lyndale B77 ..... 9 F3
Lyndale Rd CV5 ..... 60 B2
Lyndhurst Cl LE10 ..... 32 A4
Lyndhurst Croft CV5 ..... 59 E2
Lyndhurst Rd CV21 ..... 83 F1
Lyndon Croft B37 ..... 44 A4
Lyneham Gdns B76 ..... 22 A3
Lyng Cl CV5 ..... 60 A2
Lyng Hall Sch CV2 ..... 62 B3
Lynmouth Cl CV11 ..... 29 F3
Lynmouth Rd CV2 ..... 62 C4
Lynton Cl CV34 ..... 104 C1
Lynton Rd CV6 ..... 49 F1
Lynwood Wlk 18 CV31 ..... 110 B3
Lysander Cl CV35 ..... 146 B1
Lysander Ct CV37 ..... 145 D1
Lysander St CV3 ..... 78 B3
Lyster Cl CV34 ..... 108 A4
Lythall Cl CV31 ..... 110 C3
Lythalls La CV6 ..... 49 F1
Lythalls Lane Ind Est CV6 ..... 49 F1
Lytham B77 ..... 4 B3
Lytham Cl B76 ..... 22 A3
Lytham Rd CV22 ..... 82 C1
Lyttelton Rd CV34 ..... 108 C4
Lyttleton Cl CV3 ..... 63 D1

M40 Distribution Pk CV35 ..... 146 A1
Macaulay Rd Coventry CV2 ..... 62 B2
Rugby CV22 ..... 99 F4
Macbeth App CV34 ..... 109 E2
Macbeth Cl CV22 ..... 99 F3
Macdonald Rd CV2 ..... 62 B2
Macefield Cl CV2 ..... 50 B1
Mackenzie Cl CV5 ..... 60 A4
Mackley Way CV33 ..... 123 E6
Madam's Hill Rd B90 ..... 70 B4
Madden Pl CV22 ..... 82 B1
Madeira Croft CV5 ..... 60 C1
Madrona B77 ..... 4 A2
Magdalen Cl CV37 ..... 129 D2
Magdalen Rd CV23 ..... 117 C6
Magna Park LE17 ..... 55 E3
Magnet La CV22 ..... 99 E4
Magnolia B77 ..... 4 A2
Magnolia Cl CV3 ..... 77 D3
Magnus B77 ..... 9 F3
Magpie La CV7 ..... 73 F3
Maguire Ind Est CV4 ..... 75 F4
Magyar Cres CV11 ..... 40 A4
Maidavale Cres CV3 ..... 77 E2
Maidenhair Dr CV23 ..... 83 E4
Maidenhead Cl CV37 ..... 145 D2
Maidenhead Rd CV37 ..... 145 D2
Maidwell Dr B90 ..... 70 C4
Main Ave B26 ..... 44 B2
Main Cl Ansty CV7 ..... 51 E2
Austrey CV9 ..... 3 D1
Baxterley CV9 ..... 17 D4
Binton CV37 ..... 120 A1
Broughton OX15 ..... 139 E1
Claybrooke Magna LE17 ..... 43 F3
Kilsby CV23 ..... 101 F2

Main Rd continued
Lower Quinton CV37 ..... 129 E2
Meriden CV7 ..... 58 B4
Newton Regis B79 ..... 2 B2
Main St Aston le W NN11 ..... 134 F5
Badby NN11 ..... 126 F5
Birdingbury CV23 ..... 115 F7
Burmington CV36 ..... 141 A8
Church Lench WR11 ..... 127 A6
Cleeve Prior WR11 ..... 128 A4
Clifton u D CV23 ..... 83 F3
Easenhall CV23 ..... 65 F2
Frankton CV23 ..... 97 E1
Grandborough CV23 ..... 116 F6
Hanwell OX17 ..... 139 F6
Harborough Magna CV23 ..... 66 A2
Higham-on-t-H CV13 ..... 21 D2
Littleton WR11 ..... 127 F1
Long Lawford CV21 ..... 82 A3
Long Lawford,Newbold on A
CV21 ..... 82 B4
Mollington OX17 ..... 134 A2
Monks Kirby CV23 ..... 53 F2
Newton LE17 ..... 68 A1
North Newington OX15 ..... 139 D2
Offenham WR11 ..... 127 D1
Orton-on-t-H CV9 ..... 6 B2
Rugby CV23 ..... 99 E4
Shawell LE17 ..... 68 B3
Sibford Gower OX15 ..... 142 D8
Stoke Golding CV13 ..... 21 E4
Stretton u F CV23 ..... 65 D4
Thurlaston CV23 ..... 98 C2
Tiddington CV37 ..... 145 F2
Tysoe CV35 ..... 138 B7
Willey CV23 ..... 54 C3
Willoughby CV23 ..... 117 C6
Withybrook CV7 ..... 52 C3
Wolston CV8 ..... 80 A2
Wroxton OX15 ..... 139 D4
Makepeace Ave CV34 ..... 104 C1
Malam Cl CV4 ..... 60 A1
Maldale B77 ..... 4 B1
Maldens The CV36 ..... 149 F3
Malham Cl CV11 ..... 30 A1
Malham Rd Tamworth B77 ..... 10 B4
Warwick CV34 ..... 104 C1
Malins The CV34 ..... 109 D3
Mallaby Cl B90 ..... 70 A4
Mallard Ave CV10 ..... 28 B3
Mallard Cl CV37 ..... 144 B3
Mallard Rd B80 ..... 103 F2
Mallender Dr B93 ..... 71 F3
Mallerin Croft CV11 ..... 28 A3
Mallory Dr CV34 ..... 108 B4
Mallory Rd
Bishops Tachbrook CV33 ..... 122 F8
Lighthorne Heath CV35 ..... 123 D2
Mallory Way CV6 ..... 49 F2
Mallow Way CV23 ..... 83 E4
Malmesbury Rd CV6 ..... 49 D2
Malt House Cl CV33 ..... 133 B7
Malt House La WR11 ..... 127 A6
Malthouse Cl Ansley CV10 ..... 27 D2
Harvington WR11 ..... 127 D3
Malthouse La Earlswood B94 ..... 86 C4
Kenilworth CV8 ..... 92 C3
Long Compton CV36 ..... 141 C3
Shutford OX15 ..... 139 A3
Malthouse Row B37 ..... 44 A4
Maltings The Nuneaton CV11 ..... 29 E1
Royal Leamington Spa CV32 ..... 105 F1
Studley B80 ..... 103 E2
Maltmill La B49 ..... 143 E2
Malvern Ave Nuneaton CV10 ..... 28 A2
Rugby CV22 ..... 83 E1
Malvern Dr B76 ..... 22 A4
Malvern Rd
Balsall Common CV7 ..... 74 B3
Coventry CV5 ..... 60 C2
Redditch B97 ..... 102 B4
Manby Rd B35 ..... 22 A2
Mancetter Rd Atherstone
CV9 ..... 19 D3
Nuneaton CV10 ..... 28 B4
Mander Gr CV34 ..... 108 B2
Manderley Cl CV5 ..... 59 E3
Manfield Ave CV2 ..... 63 D4
Mann's Cl CV8 ..... 96 A4
Manning Wlk CV21 ..... 83 D2
Mannings Cl OX15 ..... 142 D8
Manor Barns B36 ..... 136 B6
Manor Cl Charwelton NN11 ..... 126 D2
Hinckley LE10 ..... 31 E3
Manor Court Ave CV11 ..... 29 D3
Manor Court Rd CV11 ..... 29 D3
Manor Ct Cleeve Prior WR11 ..... 128 A4
Ettington CV37 ..... 131 A3
Fenny Compton CV33 ..... 133 D7
Manor Cty Prim Sch B78 ..... 8 C3
Manor Dr Stretton on D CV23 ..... 96 C3
Ullenhall B80 ..... 112 D4
Wilmcote CV37 ..... 120 C4
Manor Est CV8 ..... 79 F2
Manor Farm Cl CV23 ..... 101 E1
Manor Farm Rd CV36 ..... 136 F6
Manor Gn CV37 ..... 145 E1
Manor Ho B96 ..... 102 C2
Manor House Cl
Aston Flamville LE10 ..... 32 C3
Rugby CV21 ..... 82 B4
Manor House Dr CV1 ..... 151 B2
Manor House La B46 ..... 23 D2
Manor La Claverdon CV35 ..... 114 A4
Clifton u D CV23 ..... 84 A3
Ettington CV37 ..... 131 A3
Honiley CV8 ..... 91 D3
Kineton CV35 ..... 132 B5

Manor La continued
Shipston-on-S CV36 ..... 149 F3
Wroxall CV35 ..... 90 C2
Manor Mews B80 ..... 103 F2
Manor Orch Harbury CV33 ..... 123 E6
Horley OX15 ..... 139 D6
Manor Park CV11 ..... 134 B4
Manor Park Jun & Inf Sch
CV3 ..... 77 E4
Manor Park Rd CV11 ..... 29 D3
Manor Pk Sch CV11 ..... 29 D3
Manor Pk WR11 ..... 127 D3
Manor Rd Atherstone CV9 ..... 18 C3
Bishops Itchington CV33 ..... 124 A4
Claybrooke Magna LE17 ..... 43 E3
Coventry CV1 ..... 151 B1
Dorridge B93 ..... 71 F2
Harbury CV33 ..... 123 F6
Kenilworth CV8 ..... 92 C3
Littleton WR11 ..... 127 F1
Loxley CV35 ..... 130 F7
Royal Leamington Spa CV32 ..... 106 A2
Rugby CV21 ..... 83 D2
Staverton NN11 ..... 126 D8
Stockton CV23 ..... 147 F4
Stratford-u-A CV37 ..... 145 E1
Studley B80 ..... 103 F2
Wythall B47 ..... 69 D2
Manor Rd Ind Est CV9 ..... 18 C4
Manor Way LE10 ..... 31 E3
Mansard Ct B46 ..... 34 A4
Manse Cl CV7 ..... 39 D1
Mansel St CV6 ..... 61 F4
Mansell Rd B97 ..... 102 B4
Mansell St CV37 ..... 144 C2
Mansion St 1 LE10 ..... 31 E4
Mansions Cl CV33 ..... 124 A4
Mansley Bsns Ctr The
CV37 ..... 144 B2
Manson's Bridge Rd B35 ..... 22 A2
Manston Dr CV35 ..... 146 B1
Manta Rd CV3 ..... 9 E3
Mantilla Dr CV3 ..... 77 D3
Manton Croft B93 ..... 71 F2
Maple Ave CV7 ..... 39 D1
Maple Cl LE10 ..... 31 F3
Maple Dr B78 ..... 15 E4
Maple Gr Rugby CV21 ..... 83 D2
Stratford-u-A CV37 ..... 144 C3
Warwick CV34 ..... 105 D1
Maple Leaf Dr B37 ..... 44 B4
Maple Rd Nuneaton CV10 ..... 28 C3
Royal Leamington Spa CV31 ..... 109 F3
Maple Rise B77 ..... 4 A2
Maple Wlk 3 B37 ..... 33 D1
Maplebeck Cl CV5 ..... 61 D2
Mapleton Rd CV6 ..... 60 C4
Maplewood B76 ..... 22 A4
Mapperley Cl CV2 ..... 63 D4
Mappleborough Green
Jun & Inf Sch B98 ..... 112 A5
Marble Alley B80 ..... 103 F2
March Rd OX17 ..... 133 E2
March Way CV3 ..... 78 B4
Marchant Rd LE10 ..... 31 E4
Marchfont Cl CV11 ..... 30 A1
Marcos Dr B36 ..... 22 C1
Marcroft Pl CV31 ..... 110 B3
Mardol Cl CV2 ..... 62 B4
Marfield Cl B76 ..... 22 A3
Margaret Ave CV12 ..... 39 D2
Margaret Cl CV33 ..... 123 F6
Margaret Rd CV9 ..... 18 C4
Margeson Cl CV2 ..... 62 C1
Margetts Cl CV8 ..... 92 C2
Marie Brock Cl CV4 ..... 60 A1
Marie Cl CV9 ..... 19 D4
Marie Corelli Sch CV37 ..... 144 B2
Marigold Dr LE10 ..... 31 F3
Marina Cl CV4 ..... 75 F4
Marion Rd CV6 ..... 61 E4
Mark Antony Dr CV34 ..... 109 E2
Market End Cl CV12 ..... 38 B1
Market Hill CV33 ..... 147 D2
Market Mall CV21 ..... 83 D2
Market Pl Alcester B49 ..... 143 D2
Hinckley LE10 ..... 31 E4
Nuneaton CV11 ..... 29 E2
Rugby CV21 ..... 83 D2
Shipston-on-S CV36 ..... 149 F3
2 Warwick CV34 ..... 108 C3
Market Sq CV35 ..... 132 B6
Market St Atherstone CV9 ..... 18 B4
Polesworth B78 ..... 5 D1
Rugby CV21 ..... 83 D2
Warwick CV34 ..... 108 B3
Market Way CV1 ..... 151 B2
Markham Dr CV31 ..... 110 A2
Marlborough Cl LE10 ..... 32 A4
Marlborough Dr CV31 ..... 110 B3
Marlborough Rd
Coventry CV2 ..... 62 A2
Nuneaton CV11 ..... 29 D2
Rugby CV22 ..... 99 F4
Marlborough Way B77 ..... 9 F4
Marlcroft CV3 ..... 78 C3
Marleigh Rd B50 ..... 148 B3
Marlene Croft B37 ..... 33 E1
Marler Rd CV4 ..... 75 F4
Marlin B77 ..... 9 E3
Marlissa Dr CV6 ..... 49 F1
Marloes Wlk CV31 ..... 110 B3
Marlow Cl CV5 ..... 60 A2
Marlow Rd CV9 ..... 16 B3
Marlowe Cl Banbury OX16 ..... 139 F3
Nuneaton CV10 ..... 27 F3
Marlston Wlk CV5 ..... 60 A1

Marlwood Cl CV6 ..... 49 F2
Marner Cres CV6 ..... 61 D3
Marner Rd Bedworth CV12 ..... 39 D2
Nuneaton CV10 ..... 29 D1
Marnhull Cl CV2 ..... 62 C2
Marrick B77 ..... 4 B1
Marriners La CV5 ..... 60 A3
Marriott Rd Bedworth CV12 ..... 38 B1
Coventry CV6 ..... 61 D2
Marsdale Dr CV10 ..... 28 C2
Marsett B77 ..... 10 B4
Marsh La
Bradnock's Marsh B92 ..... 57 E3
Curdworth B76 ..... 23 E3
Hampton in A B92 ..... 57 D3
Water Orton B46 ..... 23 E2
Marsh Rd CV37 ..... 120 B5
Marshall Ave CV36 ..... 149 F3
Marshall Lake Rd B90 ..... 70 B4
Marshall Rd CV7 ..... 49 F4
Marshalls Cl OX15 ..... 138 F5
Marsham Cl CV34 ..... 109 D4
Marshbrook Cl CV2 ..... 50 C2
Marshdale Ave CV6 ..... 49 F2
Marshfield Dr CV4 ..... 76 B1
Marston Ave CV35 ..... 123 D2
Marston Cl 8 CV32 ..... 106 A1
Marston Dr B37 ..... 33 D3
Marston Green Jun &
Inf Sch B37 ..... 44 A4
Marston La Bedworth CV12 ..... 39 E3
Nuneaton CV11 ..... 39 F4
Wishaw B76 ..... 14 C1
Marten Cl CV35 ..... 108 A4
Martin Cl Coventry CV5 ..... 59 F2
Stratford-u-A CV37 ..... 145 D1
Martin La CV22 ..... 99 E4
Martindale Rd CV7 ..... 50 B4
Martins Dr CV9 ..... 12 C1
Martins Rd CV12 ..... 38 C1
Martlesham Sq B35 ..... 22 A2
Martley Cl B98 ..... 103 D4
Martley Croft B91 ..... 71 D4
Marton Rd Birdingbury CV23 ..... 115 E7
Long Itchington CV23 ..... 115 D5
Martyrs' Cl The CV3 ..... 77 E4
Mary Arden's House
CV37 ..... 120 D5
Mary Herbert St CV3 ..... 77 E4
Mary Slessor St CV3 ..... 78 B4
Marystow Cl CV5 ..... 60 A4
Masefield Ave CV34 ..... 108 A2
Masefield Rd CV37 ..... 145 D1
Maseley Ct CV37 ..... 129 D2
Mason Ave CV32 ..... 106 B2
Mason Cl Bidford-on-A B50 ..... 148 C3
Redditch B97 ..... 102 B4
Mason Croft The Shakespeare
Inst (Univ of Birmingham)
CV37 ..... 144 C1
Mason Ct LE10 ..... 31 D4
Mason Rd Coventry CV6 ..... 49 F1
Redditch B97 ..... 102 B4
Masons Rd CV37 ..... 144 B2
Masons Way CV37 ..... 144 B2
Masser Rd CV6 ..... 49 E2
Massey Shan Ave GL56 ..... 140 C3
Master's Yd CV23 ..... 115 F7
Masters Rd CV31 ..... 110 B3
Mathe Croft CV31 ..... 110 B3
Matlock Cl CV21 ..... 83 E4
Matlock Rd CV1 ..... 61 E3
Matterson Rd CV6 ..... 61 D3
Matthews Cl CV37 ..... 145 D2
Maud Rd B46 ..... 23 E2
Maudslay Rd CV5 ..... 60 C1
Maureen Cl CV4 ..... 59 E1
Mavor Dr CV12 ..... 38 B1
Mawby's La DE12 ..... 3 F4
Mawnan Cl CV7 ..... 50 A4
Max Rd CV6 ..... 60 C3
Maxstoke Cl Meriden CV7 ..... 46 A1
Tamworth B77 ..... 9 E2
Maxstoke Croft B90 ..... 70 B4
Maxstoke La Coleshill B46 ..... 34 A3
Meriden CV7 ..... 46 A1
May Farm Cl B47 ..... 69 D2
May La Ebrington GL55 ..... 135 E2
Hollywood B47 ..... 69 D4
Rugby CV22 ..... 82 B1
May St CV6 ..... 61 F4
May's Hill B95 ..... 113 A4
Mayama Rd B78 ..... 8 C4
Maybird Ctr CV37 ..... 144 C2
Maybridge Dr B91 ..... 71 D4
Maybrook Ind Est CV37 ..... 144 C2
Maybrook Rd
Stratford-u-A CV37 ..... 144 C2
Sutton Coldfield B76 ..... 22 A3
Maycock Rd CV6 ..... 61 E4
Mayfair Dr CV10 ..... 27 F2
Mayfield B77 ..... 10 B4
Mayfield Ave CV37 ..... 145 D2
Mayfield Cl Bedworth CV7 ..... 39 D2
17 Royal Leamington Spa
CV31 ..... 110 B3
Mayfield Ct CV37 ..... 145 D2
Mayfield Dr Henley-in-A B95 ..... 113 A5
Kenilworth CV8 ..... 93 E2
Mayfield Rd Coventry CV5 ..... 61 D1
Nuneaton CV11 ..... 29 F1
Southam CV33 ..... 147 D3
Mayflower Dr CV2 ..... 62 C1
Mayhurst Cl B47 ..... 69 E3
Mayhurst Rd B47 ..... 69 D3
Maynard Ave Bedworth CV12 ..... 49 E4
Warwick CV34 ..... 109 D4

Mayne Cl CV4 ..... 114 F3
Mayo Rd CV36 ..... 149 F3
Mayor's Croft CV4 ..... 76 A4
Maypole La CV9 ..... 11 E1
Maypole Rd B79 ..... 5 F2
Mayswood Rd B95 ..... 113 A3
Maythorn Ave B76 ..... 22 A3
Maythorn Gr 4 B91 ..... 71 D4
Maytree Cl B37 ..... 33 D1
Mc Kinnell Cres CV21 ..... 83 F2
McDonnell Dr CV6 ..... 49 F3
McMahon Rd CV12 ..... 49 F4
Mead The OX17 ..... 133 F2
Meadfoot Rd CV3 ..... 78 C3
Meadow Cl Ansty CV7 ..... 51 E2
Hockley Heath B94 ..... 88 B3
Kingsbury B78 ..... 15 E3
Royal Leamington Spa CV32 ..... 106 B2
Stratford-u-A CV37 ..... 144 B2
Stretton on D CV23 ..... 97 D3
Wolvey LE10 ..... 41 E2
Meadow Croft Arley CV7 ..... 26 C1
Wythall B47 ..... 69 D2
Meadow Crofts CV33 ..... 124 B5
Meadow Ct CV11 ..... 29 D2
Meadow Dr Hampton in A
B92 ..... 57 D4
Hinckley LE10 ..... 32 A4
Meadow Gdns CV9 ..... 17 E4
Meadow Green Prim Sch
B47 ..... 69 D2
Meadow La B94 ..... 89 E2
Meadow Rd Alcester B49 ..... 143 D3
Coventry CV6 ..... 49 D2
Hartshill CV10 ..... 28 A4
Henley-in-A B95 ..... 113 B4
Hurley CV9 ..... 16 B3
Rugby CV21 ..... 82 C3
Southam CV33 ..... 147 D3
Warwick CV34 ..... 109 D4
Wolston CV8 ..... 80 A2
Wythall B47 ..... 69 D2
Meadow Rise B95 ..... 112 E6
Meadow St Atherstone CV9 ..... 18 B4
Coventry CV1 ..... 151 A2
Nuneaton CV11 ..... 29 D3
Meadow Sweet Rd CV37 ..... 144 C2
Meadow Way
Fenny Compton CV33 ..... 133 E7
Harborough Magna CV23 ..... 66 A2
Meadows Sch CV4 ..... 59 F2
Meadows The
Bidford-on-A B50 ..... 148 B3
Hinckley LE10 ..... 32 A4
Leek Wootton CV35 ..... 105 D4
Meadowside CV11 ..... 40 A4
Meadowsweet CV23 ..... 83 E4
Meadway CV2 ..... 62 A3
Meadway N CV2 ..... 62 A3
Meadway The Hinckley LE10 ..... 31 F4
Redditch B97 ..... 102 B4
Mearse La WR7 ..... 118 B5
Medhurst Cl CV22 ..... 99 E2
Medina Rd CV6 ..... 49 F1
Medland Ave CV3 ..... 76 C3
Meer End Rd CV8 ..... 74 B1
Meer St CV37 ..... 145 D2
Meerhill Ave B90 ..... 71 D3
Meeting House La CV7 ..... 74 B2
Meeting La B49 ..... 143 E2
Meir Rd B98 ..... 103 E4
Melbourne Cl CV11 ..... 39 F4
Melbourne Rd CV5 ..... 61 D1
Meldrum Ct CV33 ..... 132 F7
Meldrum Rd CV10 ..... 28 B2
Melfort Cl CV3 ..... 62 C1
Melksham Sq B35 ..... 22 A2
Mellish Ct CV22 ..... 82 C1
Mellish Rd CV22 ..... 82 C1
Mellor Rd CV21 ..... 101 D4
Mellowdew Rd CV2 ..... 62 B2
Mellowship Rd CV5 ..... 59 E3
Mellwaters B77 ..... 10 B4
Melmerby B77 ..... 10 B4
Melrose Ave CV12 ..... 49 E4
Melrose Cl LE10 ..... 31 D4
Melton Rd CV32 ..... 106 A2
Melville Cl Bedworth CV7 ..... 50 A4
Rugby CV22 ..... 82 C1
Melville Rd CV1 ..... 61 D2
Memorial Rd CV33 ..... 133 D7
Menai Wlk B37 ..... 33 D2
Mendip Dr CV10 ..... 28 A2
Mendip Way B77 ..... 4 B1
Meon Cl CV37 ..... 129 D1
Meon Rd GL55 ..... 135 C7
Mercer Ave Coventry CV2 ..... 62 A3
Water Orton B46 ..... 23 D2
Mercia Ave CV8 ..... 92 C2
Mercia Bsns Village CV4 ..... 75 F3
Mercia Way CV34 ..... 109 D4
Mercian Pk B77 ..... 4 A2
Mercian Way B77 ..... 4 A2
Mercot Cl B98 ..... 103 D3
Mercury Ct B77 ..... 4 A2
Mere Ave B35 ..... 22 A2
Mere La LE10 ..... 42 B2
Meredith Rd CV2 ..... 62 B1
Merevale Ave Hinckley LE10 ..... 31 E4
Nuneaton CV11 ..... 29 D2
Merevale Cl Hinckley LE10 ..... 31 E4
Redditch B98 ..... 103 E4
Merevale La CV9 ..... 17 F4
Merevale Rd CV9 ..... 12 B3
Merevale View CV9 ..... 18 B4

Merganser B77 10 A3
Meriden CE Prim Sch CV7 .. 46 B1
Meriden Cl B98 112 A6
Meriden Dr B37 33 D3
Meriden Hill CV7 58 C4
Meriden Rd Berkswell CV7 ... 58 B2
Fillongley CV7 36 B1
Hampton in A B92 57 D4
Meriden St CV1 61 D2
Merlin Ave CV10 28 A3
Merlin Cl B77 10 A3
Merrifield Gdns LE10 31 F3
Merrington Cl 5 B91 71 E4
Merrivale Rd CV5 60 C2
Merryfields Way CV2 50 C1
Mersey Rd CV12 40 A2
Merstone Sch B37 33 D1
Merttens Dr CV22 82 C1
Meryton Ave CV4 76 C3
Meschines St CV3 77 E3
Metalloys Ind Est B76 22 A3
Metcalfe Cl OX15 139 E4
Metchley Croft B90 70 C3
Mews Rd CV32 109 E4
Mews The Atherstone CV9 18 B4
Bedworth CV12 39 D1
Kenilworth CV8 92 C2
Rugby CV21 84 A1
Mica Cl B77 4 A1
Michael Blanning Gdns
B93 71 F2
Michael Drayton Mid Sch
CV10 28 A4
Michaelmas Rd CV3 151 B1
Michell Cl CV3 78 A4
Mickle Mdw B46 23 D2
Micklehill Dr B90 70 A4
Mickleton Cl B98 102 C4
Mickleton Cty Prim Sch
GL55 135 B6
Mickleton Dr CV35 114 F5
Mickleton Rd Coventry CV5 .. 77 D4
Ilmington CV36 136 A7
Middelburg Cl CV11 30 A1
Middle Bickenhill La B92 ... 45 D2
Middle Hill OX15 142 D4
Middle La
Nether Whitacre B46 24 C3
Shotteswell OX17 139 E8
Wroxton OX15 139 B4
Middle Lock La CV35 114 E5
Middle Rd CV33 123 D7
Middle Ride CV3 78 C3
Middle St Ilmington CV36 136 B6
Tredington CV37 136 E7
Middleborough Rd CV1 151 A4
Middlecotes CV4 60 A1
Middlefield Ave B93 72 A2
Middlefield Dr CV3 63 D1
Middlefield La CV37 130 E1
Middlefleld Dr CV3 63 D1
Middlemarch Bsns Pk
CV3 78 B1
Middlemarch Mid Sch
CV10 29 D1
Middlemarch Rd
Coventry CV6 61 E4
Nuneaton CV10 29 E1
Middlemore Cl B80 103 E2
Middlesmoor B77 10 B4
Middleton Cl CV35 138 B6
Middleton Hall B78 8 C1
Middleton La B78 13 F3
Middletown
Moreton Morrell CV35 122 F3
Studley B80 103 E1
Middletown La B96 103 E1
Midland Air Mus CV3 78 A2
Midland Oak Trad Est CV6 .. 49 F1
Midland Rd Coventry CV6 61 F3
Nuneaton CV11 29 D3
Midland Trad Est CV21 83 D3
Midpoint Park Ind Est
B76 22 B3
Milburn B77 10 B4
Milburn Hill Rd CV4 76 A3
Milby Dr CV11 30 A4
Milby Fst & Mid Sch CV11 ... 29 F4
Milcote Cl B98 103 D4
Milcote Rd CV37 129 C6
Mildmay Cl CV37 144 C1
Mile La CV1 151 C1
Mile Tree La CV2 50 C4
Milebush Ave B36 22 B1
Miles Mdw CV6 50 A1
Milestone Dr CV22 99 F4
Milestone Rd CV37 130 B8
Milford Cl Allesley CV5 60 A3
Redditch B97 102 B3
Milford Gr B90 71 E4
Milford St CV10 29 D1
Mill Bank B46 25 E2
Mill Bank Mews CV8 93 D3
Mill Cl Braunston NN11 117 D5
Broom B50 148 A4
Coventry CV2 50 A2
Hollywood B47 69 D4
Norton Lindsey CV35 114 C2
Nuneaton CV11 29 F1
Southam CV33 147 D3
Mill Cres Kineton CV35 132 B6
Kingsbury B78 15 E2
Southam CV33 147 D3
Mill Ct CV36 149 F3
Mill End CV8 93 D3
Mill Farm Cl CV22 99 E2
Mill Hill CV8 77 E2
Mill House Cl CV32 109 E4
Mill House Dr CV32 109 E4
Mill House Terr CV32 109 E4
Mill La Alcester B49 143 D1
Aston Cantlow B95 119 F6
Barford CV35 122 A7
Bentley Heath B93 71 F2
Bramcote CV11 40 C4
Broom B50 148 A4
Bulkington CV12 40 A2
Chipping Warden OX17 134 F3
Cleeve Prior WR11 128 A4
Clifton u D CV23 83 F3
Coventry CV3 62 C1
Cubbington CV32 106 C3
Drayton OX15 139 E4
Earlswood B94 86 A4
Fazeley B78 9 D4
Fenny Compton CV33 133 D7
Fillongley CV7 36 B3
Halford CV36 136 F8
Harbury CV33 123 F7
Kineton CV35 132 B6
Lapworth B94 89 E2
Lowsonford,Finwood CV35 ... 113 E7
Lowsonford,Turner's Green
CV35 113 F8
Mickleton GL55 135 B6
Newbold-on-S CV37 130 F1
Shrewley CV35 114 C6
Stratford-u-A CV37 145 D1
Tredington CV36 136 F6
Welford on A CV37 129 A7
Witherley CV9 19 D3
Wolvey LE10 41 F3
Wythall B47 69 D1
Mill Pleck B80 103 F2
Mill Pool La B93 89 D4
Mill Race La CV6 50 A2
Mill Race View CV9 12 B1
Mill Rd
Royal Leamington Spa CV31 110 A4
Rugby CV21 83 E3
Southam CV33 147 D3
Mill Row LE10 41 F3
Mill St Bedworth CV12 39 D2
Coventry CV1 151 A3
Harbury CV33 123 E7
Kineton CV35 132 B6
Nuneaton CV11 29 E2
Royal Leamington Spa CV31 110 A4
Shipston-on-S CV36 149 F3
Warwick CV34 108 C3
Mill Terr CV12 39 D3
Mill Wlk CV11 29 E2
Millais Cl CV12 39 D2
Millbank CV34 105 D1
Millbeck CV21 83 E4
Miller's Bank B50 148 A4
Millers Cl Dunchurch CV22 ... 99 D2
Lower Boddington NN11 134 E6
Welford on A CV37 129 B6
Millers Dale Cl CV21 83 E4
Millers Gn LE10 31 F3
Millers La Hornton OX15 139 B8
Monks Kirby CV23 53 E2
Millers Rd CV34 108 C4
Millfield Prim Sch B78 9 D4
Millfields Ave CV21 100 C4
Millholme Cl CV33 147 E2
Millhouse Ct CV6 61 F4
Milliners Ct CV9 18 B4
Millison Gr B90 71 D4
Mills La OX15 139 D4
Millway Dr 1 CV33 122 F8
Milner Cl CV12 40 B1
Milner Cres CV2 50 C1
Milner Dr B79 4 C4
Milrose Way CV4 75 F4
Milton Ave CV34 108 B3
Milton Cl Bedworth CV12 39 E1
Bentley Heath B93 71 F2
Redditch B97 102 B4
Milton Rd B93 71 F2
Milton St CV2 62 A2
Milverton Comb Sch
CV32 105 F1
Milverton Cres 1 CV32 105 F1
Milverton Cres W 2
CV32 105 F1
Milverton Hill CV32 109 F4
Milverton House Prep Sch
CV11 29 E2
Milverton Rd Coventry CV2 ... 50 B1
Knowle B93 72 B3
Milverton Terr CV32 109 F4
Miners Wlk B78 4 C1
Minions Cl CV9 18 B4
Miniva Dr B76 13 D1
Minster Cl
Hampton Magna CV35 114 F3
Knowle B93 72 A4
Minster Rd CV1 61 D2
Minton Rd CV2 50 C1
Minworth Ind Pk B76 22 A3
Minworth Jun & Inf Sch
B76 22 B3
Minworth Rd B46 23 D2
Mira Dr CV10 20 B2
Miranda Cl CV3 78 B4
Mistral Cl LE10 31 F4
Mitcheldean Cl B98 102 C4
Mitchell Ave CV4 76 A4
Mitchell Rd CV12 39 E1
Mitchison Cl CV23 117 E8
Moat Ave CV3 76 C3
Moat Cl Bubbenhall CV8 95 E3
Thurlaston CV23 98 C1
Moat Croft Birmingham B37 ... 33 D1
Sutton Coldfield B76 22 A4
Moat Dr B78 8 C3
Moat Farm Dr
Bedworth CV12 49 E4
Rugby CV21 101 D4
Moat Farm La B95 112 E6
Moat Gn CV35 108 A1
Moat House Ct B80 103 F4
Moat House La Coventry
CV4 76 B4
Shustoke B46 25 D1
Moat La LE10 41 F3
Mobbs La OX15 142 D4
Mockley Wood Rd B93 72 A4
Modbury Cl CV3 77 E3
Model Village The CV23 ... 115 D3
Molesworth Ave CV3 62 A1
Mollington La OX17 133 D2
Mollington Prim Sch
OX17 133 F2
Mollington Rd CV31 110 A2
Momus Bvd CV2 62 B1
Moncrieff Dr CV31 110 B3
Monk's Croft The CV3 77 E4
Monks Dr B80 103 E2
Monks Kirby La CV23 53 F3
Monks Rd Binley Woods CV3 .. 79 E4
Coventry CV1 61 F1
Monks Way CV34 108 B3
Monkspath B90 71 D3
Monkspath Bsns Pk B90 70 C4
Monkspath Cl B90 70 B4
Monkspath Hall Rd B90 71 D4
Monkspath Jun & Inf Sch
B90 71 D3
Monkswood Cres CV2 62 B4
Monmouth Cl Coventry CV5 .. 60 A2
Kenilworth CV8 92 C3
Monmouth Gdns CV10 28 C2
Montague Rd Rugby CV22 99 E3
Warwick CV34 109 D4
Montague's Cnr CV37 129 A6
Montalt Rd CV3 77 F4
Montana Wlk CV10 28 C2
Montfort Rd B46 33 F3
Montgomery Ave CV35 114 F3
Montgomery Cl Coventry
CV3 78 B2
Stratford-u-A CV37 144 C1
Montgomery Dr CV22 82 B1
Montilo La CV23 66 B3
Montjoy Cl CV3 78 B4
Montley B77 10 B4
Montpellier Cl CV3 77 E3
Montrose Ave CV32 106 A3
Montrose Dr Birmingham
B35 22 A2
Nuneaton CV10 28 C2
Montrose Rd CV22 83 D1
Montsford Cl B93 71 F3
Monument Way CV37 145 D3
Monwode Lea La B46 26 A2
Moor Burgess Activity Ctr
B77 4 A1
Moor Farm Cl CV23 96 C3
Moor Fields B49 143 E2
Moor La
Tamworth, Amington B77 4 A3
Willoughby CV23 117 B6
Moor Rd CV10 28 A4
Moor St CV5 60 C1
Moor The B76 22 A4
Moor Wood Farm CV10 18 C1
Moorcroft Cl Nuneaton
CV11 30 A1
Redditch B97 102 A3
Moore Cl Appleby Magna
DE12 3 F4
Warwick CV34 104 C1
Moore Wlk CV34 109 E4
Moorend Ave B37 33 D1
Moorfield Ave B93 71 F3
Moorfield Rd B49 143 D2
Moorfield The CV3 78 A4
Moorhill Rd CV31 110 A2
Moorhills Croft B90 70 A4
Moorlands Ave CV8 92 C2
Moorpark Cl CV11 40 B4
Moorwood Cres CV10 28 A4
Moorwood La Hartshill CV10 28 A4
Nuneaton CV10 27 F4
Morar Cl B35 22 B2
Moray Cl LE10 31 D4
Mordaunt Rd CV35 146 C2
Moreall Mdws CV4 76 B2
Moreland Croft B76 22 A3
Moreton Cl CV37 145 E1
Moreton Hall Ag Coll
CV35 122 E2
Moreton Morrell La CV35 .. 123 B2
Moreton-in-Marsh
District Hospl GL56 140 A3
Moreton-in-Marsh Sta
GL56 140 A3
Morgan Cl Arley CV7 36 C4
Banbury OX16 139 F4
Norton Lindsey CV35 114 C2
Studley B80 103 F1
Morgan Gr B36 22 C1
Morgans Rd CV5 59 E2
Morgrove Ave B93 71 F3
Morland Cl CV12 40 B1
Morland Rd CV6 49 E1
Morningside CV5 77 D4
Mornington Ct B46 34 A4
Morpeth B77 9 E4
Morrell St CV32 105 F1
Morris Ave CV2 62 B2
Morris Cl CV21 82 C3
Morris Croft B36 22 C1
Morris Dr Banbury OX16 139 F4
Nuneaton CV11 29 E1
Whitnash CV31 110 A1
Morris Hill B78 11 D4
Morris Rd NN11 117 F2
Morse Rd CV31 110 A2
Morson Cres CV21 83 F1
Morston B77 9 E2
Mortimer Rd CV8 92 C1
Morton Cl CV6 49 D1
Morton Gdns CV21 83 E1
Morton La B97 102 A4
Morton Morrell CE
Prim Sch CV35 122 F2
Morton St CV32 105 F1
Morville Cl B93 71 E2
Mosedale
Moreton-in-M GL56 140 B3
Rugby CV21 83 E4
Moseley Ave CV6 61 D2
Moseley Prim Sch CV6 61 D2
Moseley Rd CV8 93 D2
Moss Cl CV22 82 C1
Moss La Beoley B98 112 A8
Newbold-on-S CV37 130 E1
Moss St 8 CV31 110 A4
Mossdale B77 10 B4
Mossdale Cl CV6 61 D3
Mossdale Cres CV10 28 C1
Mosspaul Cl CV32 105 E1
Mottistone Cl CV3 77 E3
Moultrie Rd CV22 83 D1
Mount Cres CV37 144 B2
Mount Dr CV12 39 D2
Mount Nod Prim Sch CV5 ... 60 A2
Mount Nod Way CV5 60 A2
Mount Pleasant
Bishops Itchington CV33 124 A4
Stockton CV23 147 F4
Stratford-u-A CV37 144 B2
Tamworth B77 9 E4
Mount Pleasant Cl CV23 147 F4
Mount Pleasant La B95 112 E6
Mount Pleasant Rd CV12 39 D2
Mount Pleasant Terr CV10 .. 28 C3
Mount Rd Henley-In-A B95 ... 113 B4
Hinckley LE10 31 E4
Mount St Coventry CV5 60 C1
Nuneaton CV11 29 D2
Mount Street Pas CV11 29 D2
Mount The Coventry CV3 77 F4
Curdworth B76 23 E3
Mountbatten Ave CV8 93 E2
Mountbatten Cl CV37 144 B1
Mountford Cl CV35 146 C2
Mountford Rise CV35 123 B2
Mowbray St CV2 61 F2
Mowe Croft B37 44 A4
Mows Hill Rd B94 113 A8
Moxhull Rd B37 33 D3
Moyeady Ave CV22 100 C4
Moyle Cres CV5 59 E2
Much Park St CV1 151 C2
Muirfield B77 4 A3
Muirfield Cl CV11 40 B4
Mulberry Cl CV32 106 A1
Mulberry Ctr The CV37 145 D2
Mulberry Dr 5 CV34 108 C4
Mulberry Rd Coventry CV6 ... 62 A4
Rugby CV22 82 A1
Mulberry St CV37 145 D2
Mull Croft B36 33 D4
Mullard Dr CV31 110 A2
Mullensgrove Rd B37 33 D3
Mulliner St CV6 61 F3
Mulliners Cl 2 B37 33 E1
Muntz Cres B94 88 B3
Murcott Rd CV31 110 A2
Murcott Rd E CV31 110 A2
Murray Rd Coventry CV6 61 D4
Rugby CV21 83 D2
Murrayian Cl CV21 83 D2
Murton B77 10 B4
Musborough Cl B36 22 B1
Myatt Rd WR11 127 D1
Myatt's Field WR11 127 D4
Myers Rd CV21 101 E4
Mylgrove CV3 77 E2
Mynors Cres B47 69 D3
Myrtle Gr CV5 60 C1
Mythe La CV9 19 D4
Mythe View CV9 12 C1
Myton Cres CV34 109 E3
Myton Crofts CV31 109 E4
Myton Gdns CV34 109 D3
Myton La CV34 109 E3
Myton Rd CV31, CV34 109 D3
Myton Sch CV34 109 D3
Mytton Rd B46 22 C2
Nailcote Ave CV4 75 E4
Nailcote La CV7 75 D4
Nailsworth Rd B93 71 E1
Nairn Cl CV10 29 D1
Napier St CV1 61 F2
Naples Rd CV35 132 F5
Napton Dr CV32 106 A1
Napton Gn CV5 60 A2
Napton Rd CV23 147 F4
Napton Rise CV33 147 E2
Narberth Way CV2 62 C4
Nares Cl CV22 82 C1
Narrow La B95 113 F6
Narrows The LE10 31 F4
Naseby Cl CV3 78 C4
Naseby Rd CV22 83 E1
Nash's La GL55 135 E3
Nashes The CV37 129 F7
Nathaniel Newton Fst Sch
CV10 28 A4
National Ag Ctr CV8 94 A2
National Ex Ctr B40 44 C2
National Motorcycle
Mus The B92 45 D1
Navigation Way CV6 62 A4
Neal Ct CV2 63 D4
Neale Ave CV5 60 A3
Neale Cl CV12 40 B1
Neale's Cl CV33 123 F7
Nebsworth La CV36 135 F5
Needhill Cl B93 71 F3
Needle Cl B80 103 F2
Needlers End La CV7 74 A4
Neilston St CV31 110 A4
Nellands Cl CV36 136 B6
Nelson Ave CV34 109 D4
Nelson Cl CV37 131 A4
Nelson La CV34 109 D4
Nelson St 5 CV1 61 F2
Nelson Way CV22 82 B1
Nemesia B77 4 A2
Nene Cl CV3 78 B4
Nene Side Cl NN11 126 F6
Nene Wlk NN11 117 F1
Nesfield Gr B92 57 D4
Nesscliffe Rd CV33 132 F5
Netherfield B98 103 D4
Nethermill Rd 1 CV6 61 D3
Nethersole Sch The B78 5 D1
Nethersole St B78 5 D1
Netherwood La B93 90 A4
Netting St OX15 142 D4
Nevada Way B37 33 E1
Nevill Cl CV31 109 F3
Neville Gr CV34 104 C1
Neville Rd
Birmingham, Castle Bromwich
B36 22 C1
Hollywood B90 69 F4
Neville Wlk B35 22 A1
New Ash Dr CV5 59 F3
New Bldgs CV1 151 C3
New Broad St CV37 144 C1
New Brook St 2 CV32 109 F4
New Century Pk CV3 62 B1
New Century Way CV11 29 D2
New Cl CV35 114 F3
New End Rd B46 35 D2
New Inn La WR11 127 D5
New Leasow B76 22 A4
New Mill La B78 9 D4
New Park Cotts OX15 137 F2
New Rd Alderminster CV37 .. 130 D3
Appleby Magna DE12 3 F4
Ash Green CV7 49 D3
Astwood Bank B96 118 C8
Bedworth CV12 38 A2
Coventry CV6 48 C1
Ebrington GL55 135 E3
Henley-in-A B95 113 A4
Hinckley LE10 32 A3
Hollywood B47 69 D4
Kineton CV33 132 F6
Lowsonford CV35 113 E6
Norton Lindsey CV35 114 C2
Pebworth CV37 128 F1
Ratley OX15 133 A2
Shotteswell OX17 139 E8
Shuttington B79 1 B1
Studley B80 103 F2
Tamworth B77 9 F4
Temple Grafton B49 119 E1
Temple Herdewyke CV33 133 A6
Water Orton B46 23 D2
New Row B78 8 C3
New St Baddesley Ensor CV9 .. 11 E1
Bedworth CV12 39 E1
Birchmoor B78 10 C4
Bulkington CV12 40 B1
Cubbington CV32 106 C3
Dordon CV9 11 D3
Fazeley B78 9 D4
Kenilworth CV8 92 C3
Napton CV23 125 C7
Royal Leamington Spa CV31 110 A4
Rugby CV22 82 C2
Shipston-on-S CV36 149 F3
Stratford-u-A CV37 144 C1
Tiddington CV37 145 F2
Warwick CV34 108 C3
New Union St CV1 151 B2
Newall Cl CV23 83 F3
Newbold Avon Mid Sch
CV21 82 C3
Newbold Cl
Bentley Heath B93 71 F3
Coventry CV3 62 C1
Newbold Comyn Pk CV32 .. 110 B4
Newbold Pl
Royal Leamington Spa CV32 110 A4
Wellesbourne CV35 146 C2
Newbold Rd Rugby CV21 82 C3
Wellesbourne CV35 146 C3
Newbold St CV32 110 A4
Newbold Terr CV32 110 A4
Newbold Terr E CV32 110 A4
Newbold & Tredington
CE Prim Sch Newbold-on-S
CV37 130 E1
Tredington CV36 136 F6
Newborough Cl CV9 3 D1

Newburgh Cres CV34 .... 108 C4
Newburgh Prim Sch CV34 ... 108 B2
Newbury [12] CV31 .... 110 B3
Newby Cl CV3 .... 77 F3
Newby Gr B37 .... 33 D2
Newcastle Croft B35 .... 22 B2
Newcombe Cl CV22 .... 99 E2
Newcombe Rd CV5 .... 61 D1
Newcomen Cl CV12 .... 49 E4
Newcomen Rd CV12 .... 38 B1
Newdegate Pl CV11 .... 29 E2
Newdegate Rd CV12 .... 39 D2
Newdegate St CV11 .... 29 E2
Newdigate CV31 .... 110 B3
Newdigate Cty Fst &
   Mid Sch CV12 .... 38 B1
Newdigate Rd Coventry CV6 . 61 F3
   Sutton Coldfield B75 .... 13 D3
Newent Cl B98 .... 112 A6
Newey Ave CV12 .... 49 E4
Newey Rd CV2 .... 62 B2
Newfield Ave CV8 .... 93 D2
Newfield Rd CV1 .... 61 E3
Newgale Wlk CV31 .... 110 B4
Newhall Rd CV2 .... 62 B4
Newhaven Cl CV6 .... 60 C3
Newhouse Croft CV7 .... 74 A3
Newington Cl CV6 .... 60 B3
Newington Rd B37 .... 44 A4
Newland Cl B98 .... 103 D4
Newland La CV7 .... 49 D4
Newland Rd Coventry CV1 .... 61 E3
   Royal Leamington Spa CV32 . 106 B2
Newland St CV22 .... 82 C2
Newlands La B37 .... 44 A3
Newlands Rd
   Baddesley Ensor CV9 .... 11 E1
   Bentley Heath B93 .... 71 F2
Newlands The B80 .... 103 E2
Newlyn Cl CV11 .... 29 F2
Newman Cl CV12 .... 39 D2
Newmarket Cl CV6 .... 50 A2
Newmarsh Rd B76 .... 22 A3
Newnham La B95 .... 120 C7
Newnham Rd Coventry CV1 ... 61 F3
   Royal Leamington Spa CV32 . 106 A2
Newport Cl B97 .... 102 A3
Newport Dr B49 .... 143 D2
Newport Rd CV6 .... 49 E1
Newquay Cl CV11 .... 29 F3
Newscut La OX17 .... 134 C1
Newsholme Cl [1] CV34 ..... 104 C1
Newstead Ave LE10 .... 31 E2
Newstead Cl CV11 .... 29 F1
Newstead Dr CV33 .... 147 D2
Newstead Way CV3 .... 63 D1
Newton Cl Coventry CV2 ...... 62 C4
   Hartshill CV10 .... 19 D1
   Redditch B98 .... 103 D3
Newton La Newton CV23 ..... 68 A2
   Newton Regis B79 .... 2 A2
   Newton Regis B79 .... 2 C1
Newton Manor La CV21 ...... 83 F4
Newton Rd Hinckley LE10 .... 30 C4
   Knowle B93 .... 72 A4
   Newton CV23 .... 84 A4
Newton Regis CE Prim Sch
   B79 .... 2 B2
Newtown Rd Bedworth CV12 . 39 D1
   Nuneaton CV11 .... 29 E3
Nibbits La NN11 .... 117 E5
Nicholas Chamberlaine
   Comp Sch CV12 .... 39 E2
Nicholls St CV2 .... 61 F2
Nicholson Cl CV34 .... 104 C1
Nickson Rd CV4 .... 59 F1
Nightingale B77 .... 10 A3
Nightingale Ave B36 .... 33 D4
Nightingale Cl
   Atherstone CV9 .... 12 C1
   Great Alne B49 .... 119 D6
Nightingale La
   Cleeve Prior WR11 .... 128 A4
   Coventry CV5 .... 76 C4
Nimbus B77 .... 9 E2
Nine Days La B98 .... 103 D3
Nineacres Dr B37 .... 33 D2
Ninefoot La B77 .... 9 F4
Ninian Pk B77 .... 9 E3
Ninian Way B77 .... 9 F3
Niton Rd CV10 .... 29 E3
Niven Cl CV5 .... 60 A3
No Man's Heath La CV9 ...... 3 D2
Noble Cl CV34 .... 108 B3
Nod Rise CV5 .... 60 A2
Node Hill Cl B80 .... 103 E2
Nolans Cl CV6 .... 49 E2
Nook The CV11 .... 29 F1
Norcombe Gr B90 .... 71 D3
Nordic Drift CV2 .... 63 D3
Norfolk Cl LE10 .... 31 E2
Norfolk Cres CV10 .... 28 C2
Norfolk St Coventry CV1 ..... 61 D2
   Royal Leamington Spa CV32 . 106 A1
Norfolk Terr CV4 .... 76 A4
Norluck Ct CV36 .... 149 F3
Norman Ashman Coppice
   CV3 .... 79 E4
Norman Ave Coventry CV2 .... 50 C1
   Nuneaton CV11 .... 29 D2
Norman Place Rd CV6 .... 60 C4
Norman Rd CV21 .... 82 C3
Normandy Mdws CV31 ...... 110 A1
Normandy Cl CV35 .... 108 A4
North Ave Bedworth CV12 .... 39 E1
   Birmingham B40 .... 44 C3
   Coventry CV2 .... 62 A2

North Brook Rd CV5 .... 60 B4
North Cl Braunston NN11 .... 117 E5
   Cubbington CV32 .... 106 C3
   Hinckley LE10 .... 31 F3
North Leamington Sch
   CV32 .... 105 F2
North Leamington Sch
(Binswood Hall) CV32 ...... 105 F1
North Rd CV21 .... 83 F3
North St Atherstone CV9 ..... 18 C4
   Coventry CV2 .... 62 A3
   Kilsby CV23 .... 101 F2
   Marton CV23 .... 115 C7
   Nuneaton CV10 .... 28 C2
   Rugby CV21 .... 83 D2
North View CV7 .... 51 D1
North Villiers St CV32 ...... 106 A1
North Warwickshire &
   Hinkley Coll Hinckley LE10 . 31 F4
   Nuneaton CV11 .... 29 F3
Northampton La CV22 .... 99 E2
Northcote Rd CV21 .... 82 C1
Northcote St [12] CV31 ..... 110 A4
Northcote Wlk CV9 .... 12 B1
Northend Rd CV33 .... 133 C7
Northey Rd CV6 .... 61 E4
Northfield Rd Coventry CV1 .. 61 F1
   Hinckley LE10 .... 31 E4
   Southam CV33 .... 147 D2
Northgate St CV34 .... 108 C4
Northlands Cty Prim Sch
   CV21 .... 83 D2
Northolt Dr B35 .... 22 A2
Northside Cl B98 .... 102 C4
Northumberland Ave CV10 . 28 C2
Northumberland Rd
   Coventry CV1 .... 61 D2
   Royal Leamington Spa CV32 105 F1
Northvale Cl CV8 .... 93 D3
Northway Birmingham B40 ... 44 C3
   Royal Leamington Spa CV31 110 A3
   Rugby CV21 .... 83 D2
Norton Curlieu La CV35 .... 114 C3
Norton Dr CV34 .... 104 C1
Norton Green La B93 .... 72 B1
Norton Hill 3 E1
Norton Hill Dr CV2 .... 62 C3
Norton La B47, B94 .... 69 F2
Norton Lea CV35 .... 114 C2
Norton Leys CV22 .... 99 F3
Norton Rd B46 .... 33 F4
Norton View GL55 .... 135 B6
Nortons Cl CV33 .... 133 B7
Norwich Cl CV11 .... 30 A4
Norwich Dr CV3 .... 77 D3
Norwood Gr CV2 .... 50 C1
Nova Croft CV5 .... 59 E2
Novotel Way B26 .... 44 B2
Nuffield Rd Coventry CV6 .... 62 A4
   Hinckley LE10 .... 30 C4
Nugent Gr B90 .... 70 B2
Nuneaton La CV13 .... 20 C1
Nuneaton Rd Bedworth CV12 39 D2
   Bulkington CV12 .... 40 A2
   Fillongley CV7 .... 36 C2
   Furnace End B46,CV10 ...... 26 B3
   Hartshill CV10 .... 19 D1
Nuneaton Trent Valley Sta
   CV11 .... 29 E3
Nunts La CV6 .... 49 D2
Nunts Park Ave CV6 .... 49 D2
Nunwood La CV23 .... 96 A1
Nursery Cl Mickleton GL55 . 135 C7
   Moreton-in-M GL56 .... 140 A4
Nursery Hill Fst Sch CV10 . 27 F4
Nursery La CV31 .... 110 A3
Nursery Rd Ansley CV10 ..... 27 F4
   Atherstone CV9 .... 18 C4
Nutbrook Ave CV4 .... 59 F1
Nuthurst B75 .... 13 D2
Nuthurst Cres CV10 .... 27 E2
Nuthurst Gr B93 .... 72 A2
Nuthurst Grange Rd B94 .... 88 B2
Nuthurst La CV10 .... 27 E1
Nuthurst Rd B94 .... 113 B8
Nutt's La LE10 .... 31 D4
Nymet B77 .... 9 F4

Oak Avenue Woodside
   CV7 .... 26 C1
Oak Cl Baginton CV8 .... 77 F1
   Bedworth CV12 .... 39 E2
   Hinckley LE10 .... 31 F3
Oak Ct CV34 .... 109 F1
Oak Farm Cl B76 .... 22 A4
Oak La Allesley CV5 .... 47 F1
   Barston B92 .... 57 D1
Oak Leigh CV35 .... 123 D2
Oak Rd CV37 .... 145 F2
Oak Rise B46 .... 33 F3
Oak St CV22 .... 83 D1
Oak Tree Ave CV3 .... 77 D3
Oak Tree Cl
   Bentley Heath B93 .... 71 F2
   Royal Leamington Spa CV31 106 A1
Oak Tree La Cookhill B49 ... 118 D5
   Hollywood B47 .... 69 D3
   Sambourne B96 .... 103 D1
Oak Tree Rd Coventry CV3 ... 79 D4
   Harvington WR11 .... 127 C4
Oak Way CV4 .... 59 E1
Oakdale Rd CV3 .... 79 E4
Oakdene Cl CV35 .... 113 F3
Oakdene Cres Hatton CV35 114 C5
   Nuneaton CV10 .... 29 E4
Oakenhayes Cres B76 .... 22 B3
Oakey Cl CV6 .... 49 F2
Oakfield Gdns CV9 .... 18 C4

Oakfield Jun Sch CV9 .... 18 C4
Oakfield Rd Coventry CV6 ... 60 C3
   Rugby CV22 .... 82 C1
Oakfields Way B91 .... 56 A3
Oakford Dr CV5 .... 59 F3
Oakhall Dr B93 .... 71 F2
Oakham Cl B98 .... 103 D3
Oakham Cres CV12 .... 40 B1
Oakham La 126 D8
Oakham Rd GL56 .... 141 A1
Oaklands 23 D3
Oaklands Croft B76 .... 22 A4
Oaklands The
   Birmingham B37 .... 44 A4
   Coventry CV4 .... 60 A1
Oakleigh Rd CV37 .... 144 C3
Oakley CV8 .... 73 F1
Oakley Wood Rd CV33 ..... 122 F7
Oakmoor Rd CV6 .... 50 A2
Oakridge Rd CV32 .... 106 B2
Oakroyd Cres CV10 .... 28 B4
Oaks Pl CV6 .... 50 A2
Oaks Rd CV8 .... 92 C1
Oaks The CV12 .... 38 C1
Oakthorpe Dr B37 .... 33 D3
Oaktree Cl Bearley CV37 ... 120 D7
   Kingsbury B78 .... 15 E3
   Moreton Morrell CV35 .... 122 E3
Oaktree Farm
   Mobile Homes Pk B94 ..... 86 A4
Oakwood Cl CV9 .... 11 E1
Oakwood Gr CV34 .... 105 D1
Oakwood Rd B47 .... 69 D3
Oakworth Cl CV2 .... 62 C4
Oaston Rd CV11 .... 29 E2
Oban Dr CV10 .... 29 D1
Oban Rd Coventry CV6 ...... 49 F3
   Hinckley LE10 .... 31 D4
Oberon Cl Nuneaton CV11 ... 30 A1
   Royal Leamington Spa CV34 . 109 F2
   Rugby CV22 .... 99 E3
Occupation Rd CV2 .... 62 B2
Oddicombe Croft CV3 ...... 77 E3
Odingsel Dr CV23 .... 115 C4
Odstone Dr LE10 .... 30 C4
Offa Dr CV8 .... 93 D2
Offa Rd CV31 .... 110 A3
Offchurch La CV31 .... 110 C3
Offchurch Rd CV32 .... 106 C2
Offenham CE Fst Sch
   WR11 .... 127 D1
Ogley Dr B75 .... 13 D3
Okehampton Rd CV3 .... 77 F3
Okement Gr CV23 .... 82 A3
Oken Rd CV34 .... 108 B4
Olaf Pl CV2 .... 63 D4
Old Brewery Cl CV36 ..... 137 A4
Old Budbrooke Rd
   Hampton Magna CV35 .... 114 F4
   Warwick CV35 .... 108 A4
Old Church Rd Coventry
   CV6 .... 50 A1
   Water Orton B46 .... 23 D2
Old Crown Mews CV2 .... 50 B3
Old Damson La B92 .... 44 A1
Old Farm La B46 .... 25 D3
Old Farm Rd CV9 .... 18 C3
Old Ford Ave CV33 .... 147 D4
Old Forge Dr B98 .... 103 E4
Old Forge Rd
   Fenny Drayton CV13 .... 20 A3
   Great Rollright OX7 ...... 142 A2
Old Green La CV8 .... 73 E1
Old Hedging La B77 .... 9 E3
Old Hinckley Rd CV10 ...... 29 E3
Old House La CV7 .... 48 A4
Old Kingsbury Rd B76 ...... 22 B3
Old La B48 .... 85 E2
Old Leicester Rd CV21 ..... 83 D4
Old Manor Cl B78 .... 8 C3
Old Meeting Yd CV12 .... 39 D2
Old Mill Ave CV4 .... 76 B3
Old Mill Rd B46 .... 33 F4
Old Milverton La CV32 ..... 105 E3
Old Milverton Rd CV32 .... 105 E1
Old Orchard The GL55 .... 135 E3
Old Rd
   Bishops Itchington CV33 .. 124 B4
   Braunston NN11 .... 117 E4
   Meriden CV7 .... 46 C1
   Ratley OX15 .... 132 F2
   Shipston-on-S CV36 ...... 149 F3
   Southam CV33 .... 147 D2
Old Rectory Cl CV23 .... 67 E3
Old Rectory Gdn B49 ...... 143 D2
Old Red Lion Ct CV37 ..... 145 D1
Old School Cl WR11 .... 127 C1
Old School End OX15 ..... 142 D4
Old School La
   Hampton Magna CV35 .... 114 F3
   Lighthorne CV35 .... 123 C2
   Wilmcote CV37 .... 120 C4
Old School Mews CV32 .... 106 A2
Old Snitterfield Rd CV37 .. 120 E7
   Warton B79 .... 5 F2
Old Sq [1] CV34 .... 108 C3
Old Station Rd B92 .... 57 D4
Old Town CV37 .... 145 D1
Old Town Mews CV37 ..... 144 C1
Old Tramway Wlk CV37 .... 145 D1
Old Tree La CV35 .... 138 B6
Old Warwick Rd
   Lapworth B94, CV35 .... 89 E2
   Rowington CV35 .... 114 A7
   Royal Leamington Spa CV31 109 F4
Old Winnings Rd CV7 .... 48 C3
Oldany Way CV10 .... 28 C1
Oldberrow Cl [4] B90 ...... 71 D4
Oldbury Rd CV10 .... 18 C1

Oldbury View CV10 .... 19 D1
Oldbutt Rd CV36 .... 149 F3
Oldfield Rd CV5 .... 60 C2
Oldham Ave CV2 .... 62 C2
Oldham Way CV23 .... 82 A2
Oldington Gr B91 .... 71 D4
Oldwich La E Honiley CV8 ... 90 C4
   Knowle CV8 .... 73 E1
Oldwich La W B93 .... 90 B4
Olive Ave CV2 .... 62 B3
Oliver St Coventry CV6 ...... 61 F3
   Rugby CV21 .... 82 C2
Olivier Way CV2 .... 63 D4
Olney Rd CV35 .... 132 D3
Olton Ave CV5 .... 59 F2
Olton Cl CV11 .... 41 D4
Olton Pl CV11 .... 28 C2
Olympus Ave CV34 .... 109 E3
Olympus Cl CV5 .... 59 D4
Omar Rd CV2 .... 62 B1
Ombersley Cl B98 .... 103 C4
Omega Pl CV21 .... 83 D2
Onley La CV22 .... 100 B3
Onley Terr CV4 .... 76 B4
Onslow Croft CV32 .... 105 F1
Openfield Croft B46 .... 23 E1
Oratory Dr CV3 .... 78 B3
Orchard Cl Austrey CV9 ..... 3 D1
   Badby NN11 .... 126 F6
   Bidford-on-A B50 .... 148 B2
   Bishops Itchington CV33 .. 124 B4
   Bubbenhall CV8 .... 95 E3
   Coleshill B46 .... 33 F4
   Curdworth B76 .... 23 D4
   Hartshill CV10 .... 28 A4
   Hinckley LE10 .... 32 A3
   Hurley CV9 .... 16 B2
   Lower Brailes OX15 ...... 137 F2
   Mickleton GL55 .... 135 C7
   Polesworth B78 .... 5 D2
   Salford OX7 .... 150 C2
   Shipston-on-S CV36 ...... 149 F3
   Tamworth B77 .... 9 E3
   Welford on A CV37 .... 129 B6
   Witherley CV9 .... 19 D4
   Wolvey LE10 .... 41 E2
Orchard Cres CV3 .... 77 E4
Orchard Ct Atherstone CV9 . 18 B4
   Coventry CV3 .... 63 D1
Orchard Dr Alcester B49 ... 143 D2
   Coventry CV5 .... 59 E2
Orchard Gr
   Astwood Bank B96 .... 118 C8
   Stockton CV23 .... 147 F4
Orchard Meadow Wlk B35 . 22 A2
Orchard Piece OX17 ...... 134 A2
Orchard Pl
   Harvington WR11 .... 127 D4
   Redditch B80 .... 103 D4
Orchard Rd
   Hockley Heath B94 .... 88 B3
   Hook Norton OX15 ...... 142 D4
Orchard Rise CV9 .... 11 E1
Orchard St Bedworth CV12 . 39 D2
   Hinckley LE10 .... 31 F4
   Nuneaton CV11 .... 29 E2
Orchard The Baxterley CV9 . 17 E4
   Lower Quinton CV37 ..... 129 D2
   Marton CV23 .... 115 C2
   Staverton NN11 .... 126 D8
   Whatcote CV36 .... 137 E2
Orchard View OX17 .... 134 A2
Orchard Way Hollywood B47 . 69 D4
   Long Itchington CV23 .... 115 C4
   Nuneaton CV10 .... 28 B3
   Rugby CV22 .... 99 E4
   Southam CV33 .... 147 D3
   Stratford-u-A CV37 ...... 144 C1
   Stretton on D CV23 ...... 96 C3
   Studley B80 .... 103 F1
Orchards The
   Cheswick Green B90 ...... 70 B2
   Hollywood B47 .... 69 D4
   Newton CV23 .... 68 A1
Orchid Way CV23 .... 83 E4
Ordnance Rd CV6 .... 61 F3
Orford Cl CV37 .... 146 C2
Orford Rise CV10 .... 27 F2
Oriel Gr GL56 .... 140 A2
Orion Cres CV2 .... 50 C1
Orkney Cl CV10 .... 29 D1
Orkney Croft B36 .... 33 D4
Orlando Cl CV22 .... 99 E3
Orlescote Rd CV4 .... 76 C3
Orpington Dr CV6 .... 49 E2
Orrian Cl CV37 .... 144 C3
Orson Leys CV22 .... 99 F4
Orton Ave B76 .... 23 D2
Orton Hill CV9 .... 6 C4
Orton La Austrey CV9 .... 6 B3
   Orton-on-t-H CV9 .... 6 C1
   Twycross CV9 .... 3 F1
Orton Rd Coventry CV6 ..... 60 C4
   Nuneaton CV10 .... 28 B3
Orton Way B35 .... 22 A1
Orwell Cl Clifton u D CV23 .. 84 A3
   Nuneaton CV10 .... 28 B3
Orwell Rd CV1 .... 61 F1
Osbaston Cl CV9 .... 59 F2
Osborne Ct CV31 .... 110 A2
Osborne Rd CV5 .... 77 D4
Osbourne Croft B90 .... 70 B3
Oslo Gdns CV2 .... 63 D4
Osney Cl OX15 .... 142 D4
Osprey B77 .... 10 A3
Osprey Cl Coventry CV2 ..... 63 D4
   Nuneaton CV11 .... 40 A4

Ossetts Hole La CV35 ...... 113 E4
Oswald Rd CV32 .... 109 E4
Oswald Way CV22 .... 82 B2
Oswestry Cl B97 .... 102 B4
Oswin Gr CV2 .... 62 B2
Othello Cl CV22 .... 99 E3
Ottery B77 .... 10 A3
Our Lady of the Angels
   RC Fst Sch CV11 .... 29 E2
Our Lady of the Assumption
   RC Prim Sch CV4 .... 59 F1
Our Lady Of the Wayside
   RC Prim Sch B90 .... 70 B4
Our Lady & St Teresa's
   RC Comb Sch CV32 ...... 106 B3
Our Lady's RC Prim Sch
   Alcester B49 .... 143 D3
   Princethorpe CV23 .... 96 B1
Ousterne La CV7 .... 36 B2
Outermarch Rd CV6 .... 61 E4
Outwood Cl B98 .... 102 C4
Outwoods Cl CV9 .... 18 B4
Oval Rd CV22 .... 100 B4
Over St CV6 .... 62 A4
Overbare Cl B94 .... 87 D1
Overberry Cl CV2 .... 50 B1
Overberry Orch [5] CV33 .. 122 F8
Overdale B96 .... 102 C1
Overdale Rd CV5 .... 60 B2
Overell Gr CV32 .... 105 E1
Overslade Cres CV6 .... 60 C4
Overslade Manor Dr CV22 .. 99 F4
Oversley Rd B76 .... 22 A3
Overstone Rd CV7 .... 52 C3
Overton Dr B46 .... 23 E2
Overtons Cl CV31 .... 110 C3
Overwoods Rd B77 .... 10 A2
Owen Sq CV9 .... 18 B4
Owen St CV9 .... 18 B4
Owenford Rd CV6 .... 61 E4
Owl End La NN11 .... 134 E7
Owl End Way NN11 .... 134 E7
Ox Cl CV2 .... 62 A3
Ox Leys Rd B75, B76 .... 13 E2
Oxendon Way CV3 .... 78 C4
Oxford Cl CV11 .... 29 F4
Oxford Rd Marton CV23 ... 115 C8
   Marton CV23 .... 115 D7
   Princethorpe CV8,CV23 .... 96 B2
Oxford Row [11] CV32 .... 105 F1
Oxford St Coventry CV1 ..... 61 F2
   Moreton-in-M GL56 ...... 140 A3
   Royal Leamington Spa CV32 . 105 F1
   Rugby CV21 .... 83 D2
   Southam CV33 .... 147 D2
Oxford Way CV35 .... 146 A1
Oxhayes Cl CV7 .... 74 B3
Oxhey Hill OX17 .... 134 B2
Oxhill Bridle Rd CV35 .... 131 E3
Oxhill Rd CV35 .... 138 B6
Oxley Dr CV3 .... 77 E2
Oxstall Cl B76 .... 22 B3
Oxway Cl CV36 .... 149 F3

Packington Ave CV5 .... 60 A3
Packington La Coleshill B46 . 34 A1
   Little Packington CV7 ..... 45 E3
   Maxstoke B46 .... 35 D1
   White Stitch CV7 .... 46 A2
Packington Pl [4] CV31 .... 110 A4
Packmore St CV34 .... 108 C4
Packsaddle Hill CV37 ..... 145 F4
Packwood Ave CV21 ...... 101 E4
Packwood Cl
   Bentley Heath B93 .... 71 F2
   [26] Royal Leamington Spa
   CV31 .... 110 B3
Packwood Cotts B93 .... 71 F1
Packwood Gn CV5 .... 60 A2
Packwood House B94 ...... 89 D3
Packwood La B94 .... 89 D4
Packwood Rd B94 .... 89 D4
Paddiford Pl CV10 .... 28 B2
Paddock Cl CV23 .... 125 C8
Paddock Dr B93 .... 72 A1
Paddock La Redditch B98 .. 102 C4
   Stratford-u-A CV37 ...... 144 C1
Paddock The
   Lower Boddington NN11 .. 134 E7
   Newton CV23 .... 68 A1
Paddocks Cl Polesworth B78 . 4 C1
   Wolston CV8 .... 80 A2
Paddocks The
   Bulkington CV12 .... 40 A2
   Mollington OX17 .... 133 F2
   Norton WR11 .... 127 C4
   Stretton on D CV23 ...... 96 C3
   Warwick CV34 .... 108 A4
Paddox Cl CV22 .... 100 C4
Paddox Mid Sch CV22 .... 100 B4
Paddox Prim Sch CV22 ... 100 C4
Padgate Cl B35 .... 22 A2
Padmore Ct CV31 .... 110 A3
Padstow Cl CV11 .... 29 F3
Padstow Rd CV4 .... 75 F4
Page Rd CV4 .... 75 F4
Pages La OX15 .... 139 D7
Paget Ct CV2 .... 50 A2
Paget's La CV8 .... 95 E3
Pailton Cl CV2 .... 50 B1
Pailton Rd B90 .... 70 B4
Painswick Cl B98 .... 102 C3
Pake's Croft [2] CV6 .... 61 D3
Palefield Rd B90 .... 70 C3
Palermo Ave CV3 .... 77 F3

Pallett Dr CV11 .... 29 F4
Palm Tree Ave CV2 .... 50 B1
Palmer La CV1 .... 151 B3
Palmer Rd CV31 .... 110 A2
Palmer's Cl CV21 .... 101 D4
Palmerston Rd CV5 .... 76 C4
Pampas Cl CV37 .... 144 C3
Pancras Cl CV2 .... 50 C1
Pandora Rd CV2 .... 62 C4
Pangbourne Cl CV11 .... 29 F4
Pangbourne Rd CV2 .... 62 B4
Pangfield Pk CV5 .... 60 B2
Pantolf Pl CV21 .... 82 C4
Papenham Gn CV4 .... 76 A4
Parade CV32 .... 109 F4
Parade The Birmingham B37 .. 33 D3
  Nuneaton CV11 .... 29 E2
Paradise St Coventry CV1 ..... 151 C1
  Rugby CV21 .... 83 E2
  Warwick CV34 .... 108 C4
Paradise Way CV7 .... 51 D1
Paragon Way CV7 .... 50 A4
Parbrook Cl CV4 .... 75 F4
Parbury B77 .... 9 E3
Park Ave Coleshill B46 .... 33 F3
  Coventry CV6 .... 49 E2
  Nuneaton CV11 .... 29 E2
  Polesworth B78 .... 11 D4
  Studley B80 .... 103 F1
Park Cl Avon Dassett CV33 .. 133 C4
  Claverdon CV35 .... 113 F3
  Hanwell OX17 .... 139 F6
  Hook Norton OX15 .... 142 D3
  Kenilworth CV8 .... 93 D3
Park Croft B47 .... 69 D3
Park Ct CV37 .... 144 C2
Park Dr Claverdon CV35 ...... 113 F3
  Royal Leamington Spa CV31 . 109 F4
Park Farm Ind Est B98 .... 103 E4
Park Gr B46 .... 23 E1
Park Hall WR11 .... 127 E6
Park Hall Cres B36 .... 22 B1
Park Hall Mews WR11 .... 127 E6
Park Hall Sch B36 .... 22 C1
Park Hill Hook Norton OX15 . 142 D4
  Kenilworth CV8 .... 93 D3
  Lower Shuckburgh NN11 ... 116 F1
Park Hill Cty Mid Sch CV8 .. 93 F3
Park Hill N Allesley CV5 .... 60 A3
  Coventry CV5 .... 60 A3
Park Hill Prim Sch CV5 .... 60 A2
Park La Astley CV10 .... 37 E3
  Berkswell CV7 .... 58 A1
  Birmingham B26 .... 44 B2
  Birmingham, Castle Vale B35 . 22 B2
  Great Alne B49 .... 119 D6
  Harbury CV33 .... 123 F6
  Ilmington CV36 .... 135 F7
  Lower Shuckburgh NN11 ... 116 F1
  North Newington OX15 ...... 139 E2
  Nuneaton CV7 .... 27 F2
  Snitterfield CV37 .... 121 C6
  Southam CV33 .... 147 D2
  Swalcliffe OX15 .... 142 F8
Park Paling The CV3 .... 77 F4
Park Piece CV35 .... 132 B6
Park Rd Baddesley Ensor B78 . 11 D1
  Bedworth CV12 .... 39 D1
  Chipping Campden GL55 ... 135 A1
  Coleshill B46 .... 33 F3
  Coventry CV1 .... 151 B1
  Hinckley LE10 .... 31 F4
  Hook Norton OX15 .... 142 D4
  Kenilworth CV8 .... 93 D3
  Polesworth B78 .... 11 D4
  Royal Leamington Spa CV32 . 106 A2
  Rugby CV21 .... 83 D2
  Stratford-u-A CV37 .... 144 C2
  Tamworth B77 .... 9 E3
Park Sq B37 .... 44 B4
Park St Coventry CV6 .... 61 F4
  Nuneaton CV11 .... 29 E2
  Royal Leamington Spa CV32 . 105 F1
Park Street Ind Est CV6 .... 61 E4
Park The OX15 .... 137 F3
Park View Cookhill B96 .... 118 F3
  Hockley Heath B94 .... 88 B3
Park View CV7 .... 50 A4
Park Wood La CV4 .... 75 E4
Parkend CV21 .... 83 E4
Parkers La CV35 .... 140 A3
Parkes St CV34 .... 108 B4
Parkfield Cl B77 .... 9 E4
Parkfield Cres B77 .... 9 E4
Parkfield Dr Birmingham B36 . 22 B1
  Kenilworth CV8 .... 93 D3
Parkfield Prim Sch B77 .... 9 E4
Parkfield Rd Coleshill B46 ..... 33 F3
  Keresley CV7 .... 49 D3
  Rugby CV21 .... 82 C3
Parkfields CV33 .... 147 D2
Parkgate Prim Sch CV6 .... 49 E2
Parkgate Rd CV6 .... 49 E2
Parkhill Dr CV5 .... 60 A3
Parkinson Dr CV9 .... 12 C1
Parkland Cl CV6 .... 49 E2
Parklands Ave CV32 .... 106 B2
Parkside CV1 .... 151 C1
Parkstone Rd CV6 .... 49 F1
Parkville Cl CV6 .... 49 E2
Parkville Highway CV6 .... 49 D2
Parkway CV2 .... 63 D4
Parmington Cl B97 .... 102 A3
Parnell Cl CV21 .... 82 C3
Parr Cl CV34 .... 109 E3

Parrotts Gr CV2 .... 50 B3
Parry Rd CV2 .... 62 B4
Parson St B77 .... 9 F4
Parson's La LE10 .... 31 F4
Parson's Nook CV2 .... 62 A3
Parsonage Cl 13 CV33 .... 122 F8
Parsons Cl CV36 .... 149 F3
Partridge Cl B37 .... 33 E2
Partridge Croft CV6 .... 50 A1
Partridge La B97 .... 102 A4
Partridge Rd CV37 .... 144 B2
Patch La B98 .... 102 C3
Patrcia Cl CV4 .... 59 E1
Pattens Rd CV34 .... 105 D1
Patterdale CV21 .... 83 E4
Patterton Dr B76 .... 22 A4
Pattison Coll CV3 .... 62 A1
Pauline Ave CV5 .... 50 A1
Pavilion Way CV5 .... 60 C2
Paxmead CV10 .... 49 D1
Paxton Rd CV6 .... 61 D2
Paybody Hospl CV5 .... 60 B3
Payne Cl CV32 .... 106 A1
Payne's La CV1 .... 61 F2
Paynell Cl CV6 .... 49 D1
Paynes La CV7 .... 82 B2
Payton St CV37 .... 145 D2
Peace Wlk B37 .... 33 D1
Peacock Ave CV2 .... 50 C1
Peacock Ct CV35 .... 146 B2
Peacock La CV35 .... 138 C7
Peacocks The CV34 .... 108 A1
Peake CV11 .... 29 F4
Pear Tree Ave Kingsbury
  B78 .... 15 E3
  Nuneaton CV10 .... 28 C3
Pear Tree Cl
  Chipping Campden GL55 ... 135 B1
  Shuttington B79 .... 4 C4
Pear Tree Way CV22 .... 82 A1
Pearl Hyde Prim Sch CV2 ..... 63 D3
Pearmans Croft B47 .... 69 D3
Pears Cl CV8 .... 92 C3
Pearson Ave CV6 .... 50 A1
Peat Cl CV22 .... 82 C1
Pebble Cl B77 .... 4 A2
Pebworth Ave B90 .... 71 D3
Pebworth Cl CV5 .... 60 A2
Pebworth Cty Fst Sch
  CV37 .... 128 F1
Peddimore La B76 .... 22 B4
Pedmore Cl B98 .... 103 D4
Peel Cl Coventry CV6 .... 61 F3
  Drayton Bassett B78 .... 8 C3
  Hampton in A B92 .... 57 D3
Peel La CV6 .... 61 F3
Peel Rd CV34 .... 108 C4
Peel St CV6 .... 61 F3
Pegasus Jun & Inf Sch
  B35 .... 22 A2
Pegmill Cl CV3 .... 77 F4
Pelham La B49 .... 119 D5
Pembridge Rd B93 .... 71 F2
Pembroke Cl Bedworth
  CV12 .... 38 B1
  1 Warwick CV34 .... 108 C4
Pembroke Gdns CV35 .... 146 B1
Pembroke Way CV11 .... 29 E2
Pembrook Rd CV6 .... 49 E1
Pembury Ave CV6 .... 50 A1
Penarth Gr CV3 .... 78 C4
Pencraig Cl CV8 .... 93 E3
Pendenis Cl CV6 .... 62 A4
Pendicke St CV33 .... 147 D2
Pendigo Way B40 .... 44 C2
Pendred Rd CV22 .... 82 C2
Pendrell Cl B37 .... 33 D2
Penelope Cl CV3 .... 123 F6
Penfold Cl 3 CV33 .... 122 F8
Penmire Cl CV9 .... 11 E2
Penn La Tanworth-in-A B94 ... 86 B2
  Wibtoft LE17 .... 43 E1
Pennant Rd LE10 .... 31 E3
Pennine Way Nuneaton
  CV10 .... 28 A2
  Tamworth B77 .... 10 A4
Pennington Mews 4 CV21 . 82 C2
Pennington St 1 CV21 .... 82 C2
Pennington Way CV6 .... 61 F4
Penns Cl CV32 .... 106 C3
Penns La B46 .... 33 F4
Penny Park La CV6 .... 49 D2
Pennyford La B95 .... 113 B1
Pennymoor Rd B77 .... 10 A4
Pennystone Cl CV31 .... 110 B3
Penrhyn Cl OX16 .... 139 F4
Penrith Cl Coventry CV6 .... 49 E1
  Royal Leamington Spa CV32 . 105 E1
Penrith Gr B37 .... 33 E1
Penrose Cl CV4 .... 76 A4
Penrhyn Cl CV8 .... 93 E3
Penryn Cl CV11 .... 30 A2
Pensham Croft B90 .... 71 D3
Penshurst Way CV11 .... 39 F4
Pensilva Way 2 CV1 .... 61 F2
Pentire Cl CV11 .... 29 F3
Penzance Way CV11 .... 30 A3
Pepper La CV1 .... 151 B2
Pepys Cr CV4 .... 59 F2
Perch Ave B37 .... 33 D2
Percival Dr CV33 .... 123 F6
Percival Rd CV22 .... 100 B4
Percy Cres CV8 .... 92 C1
Percy Rd Kenilworth CV8 ...... 92 C1
  Warwick CV34 .... 108 C4
Percy St Coventry CV1 .... 151 A3
  Stratford-u-A CV37 .... 145 D2
Percy Terr 7 CV32 .... 105 E1

Peregrine Dr CV5 .... 60 A3
Perimeter Rd
  Birmingham B40 .... 44 B2
  Birmingham B40 .... 44 C2
Perkins Cl Hornton OX15 ... 139 B8
  Salford Priors WR11 .... 127 E6
Perkins Gr CV21 .... 83 F1
Permian Cl CV21 .... 83 E3
Perry Mill La B95 .... 112 E6
Perryfields Cl B98 .... 102 C3
Perryford Dr B91 .... 71 E4
Perryman Dr B78 .... 15 F4
Perrymill La B96 .... 103 D1
Pershore Pl CV4 .... 76 C3
Perth Rise CV5 .... 60 A2
Peter Hall La
  Brinklow CV7,CV23 .... 64 A3
  Coventry CV7 .... 63 F3
Peterbrook Cl B98 .... 102 C4
Peterbrook Rd B90 .... 69 F4
Peterlee Wlk 6 CV2 .... 63 D4
Petitor Cres CV2 .... 50 B1
Pettiford La B95 .... 113 C3
Pettiver Cres CV21 .... 83 F1
Pettyfields Cl B93 .... 72 A3
Peveril Dr CV3 .... 77 D3
Peyto Cl CV6 .... 49 E1
Pheasant Cl Bedworth CV12 .. 38 B1
  Stratford-u-A CV37 .... 144 B2
Pheasant Croft B36 .... 33 D4
Pheasant La B98 .... 102 C4
Phillippes Rd 13 CV34 .... 104 C1
Phipps Av CV21 .... 83 F1
Phoenix Bsns Pk LE10 .... 30 C4
Phoenix Way CV6 .... 49 F2
Piccadilly B78 .... 9 F1
Piccadilly Cl B37 .... 33 E1
Piccadilly Cres B78 .... 9 F1
Pickard Cl CV21 .... 83 F4
Pickard St CV34 .... 109 D4
Pickford Cl CV11 .... 30 A1
Pickford Grange La CV5 .... 59 E4
Pickford Green La CV5 .... 59 E4
Pickford Way CV5 .... 60 A3
Picton Croft 4 B37 .... 33 E1
Piers Cl CV34 .... 108 C4
Pike Cl LE10 .... 31 E3
Pike Dr B37 .... 33 E2
Pikehorne Croft B36 .... 22 B1
Pikers La CV7 .... 48 A2
Pilgrims Gate LE10 .... 32 A3
Pilgrims La CV23 .... 67 F1
Pilkington Rd CV5 .... 76 B4
Pill La GL56 .... 140 F1
Pilling Cl CV2 .... 62 C4
Pimlico La CV37 .... 121 D2
Pinbury Croft B37 .... 33 D1
Pinchester Cl GL56 .... 141 A1
Pinders La CV21 .... 83 D2
Pine Cl Stoke Golding CV13 ... 21 F4
  Stratford-u-A CV37 .... 144 B1
Pine Ct CV32 .... 106 A2
Pine Gr CV21 .... 84 A1
Pine Sq B37 .... 33 D1
Pine Tree Ave CV4 .... 60 A1
Pine Tree Rd CV12 .... 39 E2
Pine Trees Cres CV33 .... 147 E3
Pineham Ave CV33 .... 123 F6
Pinehurst CV32 .... 106 C3
Pines The Bedworth CV12 ...... 38 C1
  Cheswick Green B90 .... 70 B3
  Coventry CV4 .... 75 E4
Pinewood Ave CV9 .... 10 B1
Pinewood Dr CV3 .... 79 E4
Pinewood Gr CV5 .... 77 D4
Pinfold Gn NN11 .... 126 F6
Pinfold St CV21 .... 82 C2
Pingle Ct CV11 .... 29 E1
Pink Green La B98 .... 112 A8
Pinley Fields CV3 .... 78 A4
Pinner's Croft CV2 .... 62 A3
Pinnock Pl CV4 .... 59 F1
Pinwall La CV9 .... 12 C2
Pioneer Units CV11 .... 29 F2
Pipe La CV9 .... 6 B2
Piper's End LE10 .... 41 E2
Piper's La CV8 .... 93 D3
Pipers La CV10 .... 27 E4
Pipers Rd B98 .... 103 E4
Pipewell Cl CV22 .... 82 B1
Pirie Cl CV33 .... 123 F6
Pit Hill CV8 .... 95 E3
Pitt La B92 .... 44 B1
Pittons La CV23 .... 101 E1
Pittway Ave CV36 .... 149 F3
Pixhall Wlk B35 .... 22 A2
Plain Rd The OX15 .... 139 A3
Plane Gr B37 .... 33 D1
Plank La B46 .... 23 D1
Plantagenet Dr CV22 .... 99 F3
Plantation The OX17 .... 134 C1
Plants Brook Rd B76 .... 22 A4
Plants Hill Cres CV4 .... 59 F1
Pleasant Way CV32 .... 106 A1
Pleck The B50 .... 148 B2
Plexfield Rd CV22 .... 82 B1
Pleydell Cl CV3 .... 78 B3
Plomer Cl CV22 .... 99 E4
Plot Rd OX15 .... 139 A3
Plott La CV23 .... 96 C3
Plough Hill Rd CV10 .... 28 A3
Plough La CV33 .... 124 A4
Ploughmans Holt CV33 ...... 147 D3
Plover Cl Alcester B49 .... 143 D3
  Stratford-u-A CV37 .... 144 B3
Plowden Cl NN11 .... 134 F5
Plowman St CV21 .... 82 C2
Plymouth Cl CV2 .... 62 B4

Plymouth Pl CV31 .... 110 A4
Poitiers Rd CV3 .... 77 E3
Polesworth High Sch B78 ... 10 C4
Polesworth Sta B78 .... 5 D2
Polperro Dr CV5 .... 60 A3
Pomeroy Cl CV4 .... 75 E4
Pondthorpe CV3 .... 78 C3
Pontrilas Rd CV35 .... 132 D4
Pontypool Ave CV3 .... 78 C3
Pool Bank St CV11 .... 29 D2
Pool Cl Little Compton GL56 . 140 F1
  Rugby CV22 .... 99 E4
  Welford on A CV37 .... 129 B6
Pool Close Cotts GL56 .... 140 F1
Pool End Cl B93 .... 71 F3
Pool Mdw B78 .... 22 A4
Pool Mdw Cl B80 .... 103 F2
Poole Rd CV6 .... 61 D3
Pooley La B78 .... 4 C1
Pooley Veiw B78 .... 5 D1
Poolgate CV35 .... 138 B6
Poolhead La Earlswood B94 .. 86 B4
  Tanworth-in-A B94 .... 86 C3
Poolside Gdns CV3 .... 77 D3
Pope St CV22 .... 82 C2
Popes La B96 .... 102 C1
Poplar Ave Bedworth CV12 ... 39 E1
  Birmingham, Coleshill Heath
  B37 .... 44 B4
Poplar Cl Alcester B49 .... 143 E2
  Knightcote CV33 .... 124 B1
Poplar Gr CV21 .... 83 D2
Poplar Rd
  Bishops Itchington CV33 .. 124 B4
  Coventry CV5 .... 60 C1
  Dorridge B93 .... 71 F2
  Napton CV23 .... 125 C8
Poplars Cl GL55 .... 135 A1
Poplars La B96 .... 102 A1
Poplars The CV10 .... 28 B2
Poplars Trad Est B80 .... 103 E3
Poppy Dr CV23 .... 83 F4
Poppyfield Ct CV4 .... 76 B2
Porchester Cl CV3 .... 63 D1
Porlock Cl CV3 .... 77 F3
Porter Cl CV4 .... 75 F4
Portia Cl CV11 .... 30 A1
Portland Dr CV10 .... 28 B2
Portland Pl
  6 Royal Leamington Spa
  CV32 .... 109 F4
  Rugby CV21 .... 83 E1
Portland Pl E 5 CV32 .... 109 F4
Portland Pl W 4 CV32 .... 109 F4
Portland St CV32 .... 109 F4
Portleys La B78 .... 8 B2
Portree Ave CV3 .... 62 C1
Portsea Cl CV3 .... 77 E3
Portway Cl Coventry CV4 ...... 75 F4
  Royal Leamington Spa CV31 . 110 B3
Portwrinkle Ave CV3 .... 62 A3
Post House Gdns CV23 .... 66 A4
Post Office La
  Lighthorne CV35 .... 123 B2
  Stockton CV23 .... 147 F4
  Witherley CV9 .... 19 D4
Post Office Rd CV9 .... 11 E1
Post Office Wlk B96 .... 102 C1
Post Office Yd CV23 .... 64 C2
Postbridge Rd CV3 .... 77 E3
Postle Cl CV23 .... 101 F1
Potters Cl CV23 .... 64 C2
Potters Green Prim Sch
  CV2 .... 50 C1
Potters Green Rd CV2 .... 50 C1
Potters La Darlingscott
  CV36 .... 136 D5
  Polesworth B78 .... 11 D4
Potters Rd CV12 .... 38 C1
Potton Cl CV3 .... 78 C3
Potts Cl CV8 .... 93 E2
Poultney Rd CV6 .... 61 D3
Pound Cl Berkswell CV7 .... 58 B2
  Lapworth B94 .... 89 D2
  Shipston-on-S CV36 .... 149 F3
Pound House La
  Tanworth-in-A B94 .... 87 F2
  Tanworth-in-A B94 .... 88 A2
Pound La Badby NN11 .... 126 F6
  Coleshill B46 .... 34 A2
  Furnace End B46 .... 25 E2
  Mickleton GL55 .... 135 B6
  Royal Leamington Spa CV32 . 106 A2
  Sibford Gower OX15 .... 138 D1
Pound The OX15 .... 139 D2
Powell Rd CV2 .... 62 A2
Powell Way CV11 .... 29 E2
Powis Gr CV8 .... 93 E3
Powys Gr OX16 .... 139 F4
Poyser Rd CV10 .... 39 E4
Pratts La B80 .... 112 A4
Prebend The CV33 .... 133 B7
Precinct The CV1 .... 151 B3
Precision Way B49 .... 143 E3
Prescelly Cl CV10 .... 28 A2
Prescott Ave OX16 .... 139 F3
President Kennedy Sch &
  Com Coll CV6 .... 49 D2
Prestbury Cl B98 .... 112 A6
Preston Cl CV4 .... 75 F4
Preston Fields La B95 .... 113 D6
Preston La OX17 .... 134 A4
Prestwick Rd B35 .... 22 A2
Pretorian Way CV21 .... 83 D4
Price Rd CV32 .... 106 C3
Pridmore Rd CV6 .... 61 E4

Priest Meadow Cl B96 .... 102 B1
Priestfield Rd B97 .... 102 C3
Priesthills Rd LE10 .... 31 E4
Primley Ave B77 .... 9 F3
Primrose Ct GL56 .... 140 A3
Primrose Dr Br LE10 .... 31 F3
Primrose Hill CV34 .... 104 C1
Primrose Hill St CV1 .... 151 C4
Primrose La B49 .... 143 E1
Primsland Cl B90 .... 71 E4
Prince Harry Rd B95 .... 113 B4
Prince Of Wales Rd CV5 ..... 60 C2
Prince William Cl CV6 .... 60 C3
Prince's Ave CV11 .... 29 D2
Prince's Dr CV31 .... 109 E4
Prince's Rd B78 .... 5 D1
Prince's St Nuneaton CV11 ... 29 E2
  Royal Leamington Spa CV32 . 106 A1
Princes Cl CV3 .... 78 A4
Princes Dr CV8 .... 93 D4
Princes Rd CV9 .... 16 B3
Princes St CV21 .... 83 D2
Princess Rd Atherstone CV9 . 18 C4
  Hinckley LE10 .... 31 F4
Princess St CV6 .... 61 F4
Princethorpe Coll CV23 ...... 96 B2
Princethorpe Way CV3 .... 78 C4
Prior Deram Wlk CV4 .... 76 B4
Priors Cl CV7 .... 74 A3
Priors Field Comb Sch
  CV8 .... 92 B4
Priors Harnall CV1 .... 151 D4
Priors Mdw CV33 .... 147 E2
Priors The CV12 .... 39 E1
Priorsfield Rd
  4 Coventry CV6 .... 61 D2
  Kenilworth CV8 .... 92 B3
Priorsfield Rd N 3 CV6 .... 61 D2
Priorsfield Rd S CV6 .... 61 D2
Priory Cl Coleshill B46 .... 34 A3
  Lapworth B94 .... 89 E3
Priory Croft CV8 .... 93 D2
Priory Ct B80 .... 103 F3
Priory La CV35 .... 131 D2
Priory Mews CV34 .... 108 C4
Priory Rd Alcester B49 .... 143 D2
  Kenilworth CV8 .... 93 D2
  Warwick CV34 .... 108 C4
  Wolston CV8 .... 80 A2
Priory Row CV1 .... 151 C3
Priory St Coventry CV1 ...... 151 C3
  Nuneaton CV10 .... 28 B2
  Royal Leamington Spa CV31 . 109 F3
Priory Terr CV31 .... 110 A4
Priory Wlk CV9 .... 18 C3
Privet Rd CV2 .... 50 A1
Proffitt Ave CV6 .... 50 A1
Progress Cl CV3 .... 79 D4
Progress Way CV3 .... 79 D4
Prospect Rd CV31 .... 110 A4
Prospect Way
  Daventry NN11 .... 117 F2
  Rugby CV21 .... 83 E3
Prossers Wlk B46 .... 33 F4
Providence St CV5 .... 76 C4
Provost Williams CE
  Prim Sch CV8 .... 79 D4
Provost Williams CE
  Prim Sch (annexe) CV8 ...... 95 E3
Ptarmigan Pl CV11 .... 29 F2
Puckering's La 3 CV34 ..... 108 C3
Pudding Bag La CV23 .... 98 C1
Pudlicott La GL55 .... 135 E1
Pughe's Cl LE10 .... 32 A3
Pullman Cl B77 .... 4 A1
Pump La CV7 .... 36 B2
Purbrook B77 .... 9 F4
Purcell Ave CV11 .... 40 A4
Purcell Cl CV32 .... 110 A4
Purcell Rd CV6 .... 62 A4
Purefoy Rd CV3 .... 77 E4
Purley Chace La CV9 .... 18 B2
Purley Way CV9 .... 18 C3
Purlieu La CV8 .... 92 B3
Purnells Way B93 .... 72 A3
Purser Dr CV34 .... 108 A2
Purton Cl B49 .... 143 E3
Purton Mews CV31 .... 110 B3
Putney Wlk B37 .... 33 D2
Pyeharps Rd LE10 .... 31 F3
Pyt Pk CV5 .... 60 B2
Pytchley Rd CV22 .... 83 E1
Pytman Dr B76 .... 22 A4

Quadrant The Coventry CV1 151 B2
  Nuneaton CV11 .... 29 F2
Quail La CV37 .... 144 B2
Quaker Cl CV13 .... 20 A3
Quantock Dr CV10 .... 28 A2
Quarry Cl
  Leek Wootton CV35 .... 104 C4
  Rugby CV21 .... 82 C3
Quarry Fields CV35 .... 104 C4
Quarry La Atherstone CV9 .... 19 D3
  Chadwick End CV35 .... 90 B1
  Cleeve Prior WR11 .... 128 A4
  Nuneaton CV11 .... 29 F1
Quarry Rd CV8 .... 92 C3
Quarry St CV32 .... 109 E4
Quarry Yd CV10 .... 28 B2
Quarry Cl CV1 .... 151 C1
Quarrywood Gr CV2 .... 62 A2
Queen Eleanors Dr B93 .... 72 A4
Queen Elizabeth Rd CV10 ... 28 B3
Queen Isabel's Ave CV3 ...... 77 E4
Queen Margaret's Rd CV4 .. 76 B4

Queen Mary's Rd
Bedworth CV12 .... 39 E3
Coventry CV6 .... 61 F4
Queen Philippa St CV3 .... 77 E3
Queen St Astwood Bank B96 ... 102 C1
Bedworth CV12 .... 39 E1
Coventry CV1 .... 151 C4
Cubbington CV32 .... 106 C3
Hook Norton OX15 .... 142 D4
Royal Leamington Spa CV32 ... 106 A1
Rugby CV21 .... 83 D2
Queen Victoria Rd CV1 .... 151 B2
Queen Victoria St CV21 .... 83 E2
Queen's Cl CV8 .... 92 C2
Queen's Cres OX15 .... 139 E4
Queen's Dr CV35 .... 114 A8
Queen's Rd Atherstone CV9 ... 18 C4
Coventry CV1 .... 151 A2
Hinckley LE10 .... 31 F4
Kenilworth CV8 .... 92 C2
Nuneaton CV11 .... 29 D2
Queen's Sq CV34 .... 108 B3
Queens Arc CV11 .... 29 E2
Queens Ave CV36 .... 149 F3
Queens CE Mid Sch CV11 ... 29 D2
Queens Cl Harbury CV33 ...... 123 F6
Shipston-on-S CV36 .... 149 F3
Queens Rd Bretford CV23 ...... 80 C4
Tredington CV36 .... 136 F6
Queens St CV36 .... 136 F8
Queens Way Dordon B78 .... 10 C3
Hurley CV9 .... 16 B2
Queensferry Cl CV22 .... 99 E4
Queensland Ave CV5 .... 60 C1
Queenspark CV31 .... 109 F3
Queensway
Bidford-on-A B50 .... 148 B3
Nuneaton CV10 .... 29 E3
Royal Leamington Spa CV31 . 109 F3
Queensway Trad Est CV31 ... 109 F3
Quilletts Cl CV6 .... 50 A1
Quince B77 .... 4 A2
Quince Tree Specl Sch
B77 .... 4 A2
Quiney's Leys CV37 .... 129 A7
Quiney's Rd CV37 .... 144 B1
Quinn Cl CV3 .... 78 A4
Quinney's Ct B50 .... 148 B2
Quinney's La B50 .... 148 C3
Quinneys La B98 .... 103 D3
Quinton Par CV3 .... 77 E4
Quinton Pk CV3 .... 77 E4
Quinton Prim Sch CV37 ..... 129 D2
Quinton Rd CV1 .... 151 C1
Quorn Way CV3 .... 78 C4

Race Leys Fst Sch CV12 .... 39 D2
Race Leys Mid Sch CV12 ..... 39 D2
Racemeadow Prim Sch
CV9 .... 12 C1
Racemeadow Rd CV9 .... 12 C1
Radbourn La CV33 .... 124 E5
Radbourne Cl CV33 .... 147 E2
Radbrook Way CV31 .... 110 B3
Radcliffe Rd CV5 .... 76 C4
Radford Cl CV9 .... 12 C1
Radford Prim Sch CV6 .... 61 D3
Radford Rd Coventry CV1 ..... 61 D2
Royal Leamington Spa CV31 . 110 B4
Radford Semele
CE Prim Sch CV31 .... 110 C3
Radley Dr CV10 .... 29 D1
Radnor Dr CV10 .... 28 C1
Radnor Wlk CV2 .... 62 C4
Radway Rd B90 .... 70 C4
Raglan Cl CV11 .... 29 E2
Raglan Gr CV8 .... 93 D3
Raglan St CV1 .... 151 D3
Raglan Way B37 .... 33 E1
Ragley Cl B93 .... 72 A4
Ragley Hall B96 .... 118 F2
Ragley Mill La B49 .... 143 D2
Ragley Rd WR11 .... 127 D4
Ragley Way CV11 .... 29 F1
Railway St CV23 .... 82 A2
Railway Terr Atherstone CV9 . 18 B4
Rugby CV21 .... 83 D2
Rainsbrook Ave CV22 .... 100 C4
Rainsbrook Cl CV33 .... 147 E2
Rainsbrook Dr
Nuneaton CV11 .... 30 A1
Solihull B90 .... 70 C3
Rainsbrook Valley Rly
CV22 .... 100 B3
Rainscar B77 .... 10 A4
Rainsford Cl CV37 .... 129 F7
Raison Ave CV11 .... 29 F4
Raleigh Rd CV2 .... 62 A1
Ralph Cres B78 .... 15 E3
Ralph Rd CV6 .... 60 C3
Ramp Rd B26 .... 44 B3
Ramsay Cres CV5 .... 60 A4
Ramsden Ave CV10 .... 28 B3
Ramsden Rd CV9 .... 19 D4
Ramsey Rd CV31 .... 110 A4
Ramshill La B94 .... 112 E7
Ran-tan The B97 .... 102 C3
Ranby Rd CV2 .... 61 F2
Rance Way B78 .... 15 E3
Randall Rd CV8 .... 92 C2
Randle Rd CV10 .... 28 B2
Randle St CV6 .... 61 D3
Randolph Cl CV31 .... 110 B3
Ranelagh St CV31 .... 110 A3
Ranelagh Terr CV31 .... 109 F3
Range Meadow Cl CV32 ..... 105 E2
Rangemoor CV3 .... 78 B3

Rangeworthy Cl B97 .... 102 B4
Rankine Cl CV21 .... 82 B4
Rannoch Cl LE10 .... 31 D4
Rannock Cl CV3 .... 62 C1
Ransom Rd CV6 .... 61 F4
Ransome Rd CV7 .... 37 D4
Ranulf Croft CV3 .... 77 E4
Ranulf St CV3 .... 77 E4
Raphael Cl CV5 .... 60 B2
Ratcliffe La CV9 .... 12 C2
Ratcliffe Rd Atherstone CV9 . 12 C1
Hinckley LE10 .... 31 F3
Ratcliffe St CV9 .... 18 B4
Rathbone Cl Keresley CV7 ... 49 D3
Rugby CV21 .... 101 D4
Rathlin Croft B36 .... 33 D3
Ratliffe Rd CV22 .... 99 F4
Rattlecombe Rd OX15 .... 138 E5
Raveloe Dr CV11 .... 29 E1
Raven Cragg Rd CV5 .... 76 C4
Raven Way CV11 .... 29 F1
Ravenglass CV21 .... 83 E4
Ravensdale Ave CV32 .... 105 E1
Ravensdale Prim Sch ... 62 B2
Ravensdale Rd CV2 .... 62 B2
Ravenshaw La B91 .... 56 A2
Ravenshaw Way B91 .... 56 A2
Ravensthorpe Cl CV3 .... 78 C4
Ravenstone B77 .... 10 A4
Ravenswood Hill B46 .... 33 F4
Rawlins Croft B35 .... 22 B2
Rawlinson Rd CV32 .... 106 A1
Rawn View CV9 .... 18 C3
Rawnsley Dr CV8 .... 93 E3
Raygill B77 .... 10 A4
Raymond Cl CV6 .... 49 F3
Raynor Cres CV12 .... 38 B1
Raynsford Wlk CV34 .... 104 B1
Raywoods The CV10 .... 28 C2
Read St CV1 .... 61 F2
Reading Ave CV11 .... 29 F4
Reading Cl CV2 .... 50 A2
Readings The CV33 .... 133 E7
Reardon Ct CV34 .... 104 C1
Recreation Rd CV6 .... 50 A2
Rectory Cl Allesley CV5 .... 60 B3
Barby CV23 .... 101 E1
Bedworth CV7 .... 39 D1
Drayton Bassett B78 .... 8 C3
Harvington WR11 .... 127 D4
Stockton CV23 .... 147 F4
Warmington OX17 .... 133 D2
Whitnash CV31 .... 110 A2
Rectory Dr CV7 .... 39 D1
Rectory Gdns OX15 .... 139 E4
Rectory La Allesley CV5 .... 60 B3
Barby CV23 .... 101 E1
Lower Brailes OX15 .... 137 F2
Rectory Rd Arley CV7 .... 26 C1
Hook Norton OX15 .... 142 D4
Sutton Coldfield B75 .... 13 D3
Red Deeps CV11 .... 39 E4
Red Deeps Specl Sch CV10 . 39 D4
Red Hill CV35 .... 131 B8
Red Hill Cl B80 .... 103 F3
Red La Astley CV10 .... 37 F4
Burton Green CV8 .... 75 E1
Coventry CV6 .... 61 F3
Kenilworth CV8 .... 92 B4
Red Lion Cl CV33 .... 147 D3
Red Lion St OX17 .... 134 C1
Red Lodge Dr CV22 .... 99 F4
Red Rd CV35 .... 132 B5
Red Wing Wlk B36 .... 33 D4
Redcap Croft CV6 .... 49 E2
Redcar Cl CV32 .... 106 B2
Redcar Rd CV1 .... 61 F3
Reddicap Heath Rd B75 ...... 13 D2
Reddings La B46 .... 25 D3
Reddings The B47 .... 69 D3
Redditch Rd B80 .... 103 E3
Redditch Wlk CV2 .... 63 D4
Redesdale Ave CV6 .... 60 C3
Redesdale Pl GL56 .... 140 A2
Redfern Ave CV8 .... 93 D3
Redhill Bank CV37 .... 130 B3
Redhill Cl CV35 .... 146 B1
Redhouse Cl B93 .... 71 F4
Redlake B77 .... 9 F4
Redland Ct CV2 .... 50 C1
Redland Rd CV31 .... 110 A3
Redlands Cres CV37 .... 144 B2
Redmoor Way B76 .... 22 B3
Redruth Cl Coventry CV6 ...... 62 A4
Nuneaton CV11 .... 30 A2
Redwing B77 .... 10 A3
Redwing Cl CV37 .... 144 B3
Redwood Croft CV10 .... 29 D1
Redwood Dr B78 .... 15 E4
Reed Sq B35 .... 22 A2
Reeds Pk CV33 .... 111 F1
Rees Dr CV3 .... 77 E2
Reeve Dr CV8 .... 93 D2
Reeves Rd LE10 .... 31 F3
Regal Cl CV9 .... 18 C4
Regal Rd CV37 .... 144 C2
Regal Road Trad Est
CV37 .... 144 C2
Regency Cl Henley-in-A
B95 .... 113 B4
Nuneaton CV10 .... 29 E3
Regency Ct CV5 .... 76 C3
Regency Dr Alcester B49 .... 143 D3
Coventry CV3 .... 76 C3
Kenilworth CV8 .... 92 C2
Regency Ho CV32 .... 110 A4
Regent Gr CV32 .... 109 F4

Regent Pl
[2] Royal Leamington Spa
CV31 .... 110 A4
Rugby CV21 .... 83 D2
Regent St Bedworth CV12 ..... 39 E2
Coventry CV1 .... 151 A2
Hinckley LE10 .... 31 E4
Nuneaton CV11 .... 29 E3
Royal Leamington Spa
CV32 .... 109 F4
Rugby CV21 .... 83 D2
Regina Cres CV2 .... 63 D4
Regis Wlk CV2 .... 62 C4
Reindeer Rd B78 .... 8 C4
Relay Dr B77 .... 10 B4
Relton Mews CV6 .... 61 F3
Rembrandt Cl CV5 .... 60 B2
Remburn Gdns CV34 .... 108 C4
Remembrance Rd CV3 .... 78 B3
Renfrew Sq B35 .... 22 A2
Renfrew Wlk CV4 .... 76 A4
Renison Rd CV12 .... 38 C1
Repington Ave CV9 .... 12 B1
Repington Rd N B77 .... 4 A3
Repington Rd S B77 .... 4 A3
Repington Way B75 .... 13 D3
Repton Dr CV6 .... 50 A1
Reservoir Dr B46 .... 24 C1
Reservoir Rd CV21 .... 83 E3
Retreat St B96 .... 102 C1
Revel CE Prim Sch The
CV23 .... 53 F1
Rex Cl CV4 .... 75 E4
Reynolds Cl CV21 .... 84 A1
Reynolds Rd CV12 .... 39 D2
Rhoose Croft B35 .... 22 A2
Rhyl Rd CV11 .... 40 C3
Ribble Cl CV12 .... 40 A1
Ribble Rd CV3 .... 61 F1
Ribblesdale B77 .... 10 A4
Ribbonfields CV11 .... 29 E2
Rich Cl CV34 .... 109 D4
Richard Joy Cl CV6 .... 49 E1
Richard Lee Prim Sch CV2 . 62 C2
Richards Cl CV8 .... 92 C3
Richardson Cl CV34 .... 104 C1
Richman Gdns OX16 .... 139 F4
Richmond Rd Atherstone
CV9 .... 18 B4
Hollywood B47 .... 69 E4
Nuneaton CV11 .... 29 D2
Rugby CV21 .... 83 E1
Richmond St CV2 .... 62 A2
Richmond Way **[2]** B37 .... 33 E2
Rickard Cl B93 .... 71 F3
Riddell Cl CV34 .... 143 E2
Riddings Gdns B78 .... 11 D4
Riddings La CV9 .... 11 E2
Riddings The Coventry CV5 ... 76 C4
Grendon CV9 .... 11 E1
Sutton Coldfield B76 .... 22 A4
Riddon Dr LE10 .... 31 D4
Ridge Ct CV5 .... 60 A3
Ridge La CV10 .... 18 A1
Ridgeley Cl CV34 .... 104 C1
Ridgethorpe CV3 .... 78 C3
Ridgeway Ave CV3 .... 77 E3
Ridgeway Cl B80 .... 103 F1
Ridgeway Mid Sch B96 ...... 118 C8
Ridgeway Specl Sch CV34 . 105 D1
Ridgeway The
Astwood Bank B96 .... 118 D6
Barby CV23 .... 117 F8
Hinckley LE10 .... 31 E3
Warwick CV34 .... 105 D1
Ridgewood Cl CV32 .... 105 E1
Ridgewood Rise B77 .... 4 A3
Ridgley Rd CV4 .... 75 F4
Ridgway The CV37 .... 120 C3
Ridley La B46 .... 25 D3
Ridsdale Cl WR11 .... 127 F6
Rigby Cl CV34 .... 109 E2
Rigdale Cl CV2 .... 62 C1
Riley Cl Daventry NN11 .... 117 F2
Kenilworth CV8 .... 93 E2
Riley Dr Banbury OX16 .... 139 F4
Birmingham B36 .... 23 D1
Riley Sq CV2 .... 50 A1
Rimell Cl CV37 .... 130 E1
Ringway Hill Cross CV1 ..... 151 A3
Ringway Queens CV1 .... 151 A2
Ringway Rudge CV1 .... 151 A2
Ringway St Johns CV1 .... 151 C2
Ringway St Nicholas CV1 .. 151 B3
Ringway St Patricks CV1 .. 151 B1
Ringway Swanswell CV1 .... 151 C3
Ringway Whitefriars CV1 .. 151 C1
Ringwood Highway CV2 ...... 50 C1
Rinhill Gr **[8]** CV31 .... 110 B3
Riplingham **[13]** CV32 ...... 105 F1
Ripon Cl CV5 .... 60 A4
Risborough Cl CV5 .... 60 B2
Risdale Cl CV32 .... 105 E1
Rise The B37 .... 44 A4
Rising La Chadwick End B93 ... 90 A3
Lapworth B94 .... 89 F3
Rising Rd B94 .... 89 E3
River Cl Bedworth CV12 .... 38 C1
Royal Leamington Spa CV32 . 109 E4
River House Specl Sch
B95 .... 113 B4
River Way CV36 .... 137 A3
River Wlk CV2 .... 50 B1
Riverford Croft CV4 .... 76 B2
Rivermead CV11 .... 29 D2
Rivermead Dr CV37 .... 145 F2
Riversdale Rd CV9 .... 19 D4

Riverside Alcester B49 .... 143 E2
Studley B80 .... 103 F2
Witherley CV9 .... 19 D4
Riverside Cl CV3 .... 78 A4
Riverside Ct **[1]** B46 .... 33 F4
Riverside Gdns B95 .... 113 B4
Riverside Ind Est B78 .... 9 D4
Riversleigh Rd CV32 .... 105 E1
Riversley Rd CV11 .... 29 E2
Ro-Oak Rd CV6 .... 60 C3
Roach B77 .... 9 E3
Roach Cl B37 .... 33 E2
Roanne Ringway CV11 .... 29 D2
Robert Cl CV3 .... 78 B2
Robert Cramb Ave CV4 .... 75 F4
Robert Hill Cl CV21 .... 84 A1
Robert Rd CV7 .... 49 F4
Roberts Cl CV23 .... 96 C3
Roberts La WR11 .... 127 F1
Robertson Cl CV23 .... 84 A3
Robey's La B78 .... 4 B2
Robin Cl B36 .... 33 D4
Robin Hood Rd CV3 .... 78 B3
Robinia Cl CV32 .... 106 A1
Robins Cl OX7 .... 142 A2
Robins Gr CV34 .... 108 B2
Robins Way CV10 .... 28 A2
Robinson Rd CV12 .... 49 E4
Robinson Way LE10 .... 31 F2
Robinson's End Mid Sch
CV10 .... 28 A2
Robinson's Way B76 .... 22 B3
Robotham Cl CV21 .... 82 C3
Rocheberie Way CV22 .... 99 F4
Rochester Cl CV11 .... 29 D2
Rochester Rd CV5 .... 76 C4
Rochford Cl B76 .... 22 A4
Rochford Ct B90 .... 71 D3
Rock Cl Coventry CV6 .... 50 A1
Nuneaton CV10 .... 27 F2
Rock La CV7 .... 48 B4
Rock Mill La CV32 .... 109 E4
Rocken End CV6 .... 61 E4
Rockford Cl B98 .... 102 C3
Rockingham Cl B93 .... 71 E1
Rocky La CV8 .... 93 E1
Rodborough Rd B93 .... 71 F2
Rodhouse Cl CV4 .... 59 E1
Rodney Cl CV22 .... 82 B1
Rodway Dr CV5 .... 59 E2
Roe Cl CV34 .... 108 C4
Roebuck Pk B49 .... 143 D3
Rogers La CV37 .... 131 A3
Rogers Way CV34 .... 108 A2
Rokeby County Inf Sch
CV22 .... 100 A4
Rokeby Ct CV22 .... 99 F4
Rokeby Jun Sch CV22 .... 100 A4
Rokeby St CV21 .... 83 E2
Rolan Dr B90 .... 69 F4
Roland Ave CV6 .... 49 E2
Roland Mount CV6 .... 49 E2
Rollason Cl CV6 .... 61 E4
Rollason Rd CV6 .... 61 D4
Rolling Stones GL55 .... 135 B2
Rollright Stones OX7 .... 141 D1
Roman Ct CV17 .... 43 F3
Roman Ct B77 .... 9 F4
Roman Rd CV2 .... 62 A2
Roman Row CV36 .... 141 F5
Roman Way Alcester B49 ..... 143 D2
Coleshill B46 .... 23 F1
Coventry CV3 .... 77 E2
Dordon B78 .... 11 D3
Halford CV36 .... 136 F8
Rugby CV21 .... 83 D4
Southam CV33 .... 147 E2
Romford Rd CV6 .... 49 D1
Romilly Cl B76 .... 13 D2
Romney B77 .... 9 F4
Romney Rd OX16 .... 139 F5
Romsey Ave CV10 .... 29 E4
Ronald Gr B36 .... 22 B1
Rookery Cl CV13 .... 20 A4
Rookery La Coventry CV6 ...... 49 D2
Ettington CV37 .... 131 A3
Newbold-on-S CV37 .... 130 E1
Preston Bagot B95 .... 113 E5
Rookery The
Birchley Heath CV10 .... 17 F1
Nuneaton CV10 .... 27 F3
Rooks Nest CV22 .... 64 C2
Roosevelt Dr CV4 .... 59 F1
Rope Way OX15 .... 142 D3
Roper Cl CV21 .... 101 D4
Ropewalk B49 .... 143 D2
Rosaville Cres CV5 .... 60 A3
Rose Ave Coventry CV6 .... 60 C3
Henley-in-A B95 .... 113 B5
Rose Croft CV8 .... 92 C3
Rose Hill CV9 .... 18 C4
Rose La Napton CV23 .... 125 C7
Nuneaton CV11 .... 29 E2
Rose Rd B46 .... 33 F4
Roseberry Ave CV2 .... 50 B1
Rosebery Rd B77 .... 9 E2
Rosefield Pl **[10]** CV32 ..... 109 F4
Rosefield St CV32 .... 110 A4
Rosefield Wlk **[9]** CV32 ... 109 F4
Rosegreen Cl CV3 .... 77 F3
Rosehall Cl B98 .... 102 C3
Roseship Dr CV2 .... 62 A3
Roseland Rd CV8 .... 92 C2
Roselands Ave CV2 .... 62 B4
Rosemary Cl CV4 .... 59 F2
Rosemary Hill CV8 .... 92 C3
Rosemary Way LE10 .... 31 D4
Rosemount Cl CV2 .... 62 C4

Rosemullion Cl CV7 .... 50 A4
Roses La OX7 .... 150 C3
Roseway CV13 .... 21 E4
Rosewood CV11 .... 29 F1
Rosewood Ave CV22 .... 100 A4
Rosewood Cl LE10 .... 31 F3
Rosewood Cres CV32 .... 106 A1
Ross Cl CV5 .... 60 A3
Ross Way CV11 .... 40 A4
Rossendale Way CV10 .... 28 C1
Rosslyn Ave CV6 .... 60 C3
Roston Dr LE10 .... 31 D4
Rothay B77 .... 9 F4
Rother Rd OX16 .... 139 F5
Rother St CV37 .... 144 C1
Rotherby Gr B37 .... 44 A4
Rotherfield Cl CV31 .... 110 A4
Rotherham Rd CV6 .... 49 E1
Rotherhams Oak La B94 .... 87 F4
Rothermans Hill CV9 .... 17 E4
Rothesay Ave CV4 .... 60 A1
Rothesay Cl CV10 .... 29 D1
Rothley Dr CV21 .... 83 F4
Rothwell Rd CV34 .... 104 B1
Rough Coppice Wlk B35 ...... 22 A1
Rough Hill Dr B98 .... 102 C3
Rough The B97 .... 102 B4
Roughknowles Rd CV4 .... 75 E3
Council La CV8 .... 104 B4
Round Ave CV23 .... 82 A3
Round Close Rd OX15 .... 142 D4
Round House Rd CV3 .... 78 A4
Round Moor Wlk B35 .... 22 A2
Round Oak Specl Sch
CV32 .... 106 A2
Round St **[2]** CV21 .... 82 C2
Roundhill Rd OX17 .... 134 A2
Rounds Gdns CV21 .... 82 C2
Rounds Hill CV8 .... 92 C1
Rouse La CV35 .... 137 F8
Rover Dr B36 .... 22 C1
Rover Rd CV1 .... 151 B2
Row The CV7 .... 51 E2
Rowan Cl Binley Woods CV3 ... 79 E4
Hollywood B47 .... 69 D3
Kingsbury B78 .... 15 E3
Stratford-u-A CV37 .... 144 C3
Rowan Gr Rugby CV22 .... 82 A1
[6] Warwick CV34 .... 108 C4
Rowan Gr CV2 .... 50 C1
Rowan Rd CV10 .... 28 B3
Rowan Way B37 .... 33 E1
Rowans The Bedworth CV12 ... 38 C1
Harvington WR11 .... 127 D4
Rowborough Cl CV35 .... 114 F5
Rowbrook Cl B90 .... 69 F4
Rowcroft Rd CV2 .... 63 D3
Rowington Cl CV6 .... 60 B3
Rowington Gn CV35 .... 89 F1
Rowland Ave Polesworth B78 .. 5 D2
Studley B80 .... 103 F2
Rowland Ct CV7 .... 26 C1
Rowland St CV21 .... 82 C2
Rowland Way CV9 .... 12 B1
Rowley Cres CV37 .... 145 D2
Rowley Dr CV3 .... 78 A2
Rowley La CV3 .... 78 A2
Rowley Rd Coventry CV3, CV8 78 A2
Whitnash CV31 .... 110 A1
Rowley's Green La CV6 .... 49 F2
Rowleys Green Lane
Ind Est CV6 .... 49 F2
Rowse Cl CV21 .... 83 E4
Rowthorn Dr B90 .... 71 D3
Roxburgh Croft CV32 .... 106 B3
Roxburgh Rd CV11 .... 29 F1
Royal Cres CV3 .... 78 B3
Royal Ct LE10 .... 31 E4
Royal Leamington Spa
Rehabilitation Hospl
CV34 .... 109 F2
Royal Oak Ind Est NN11 ...... 117 F2
Royal Oak La CV12 .... 49 E4
Royal Oak Way N NN11 .... 117 F2
Royal Oak Way S NN11 ...... 117 F2
Royal Oak Yd CV12 .... 39 D2
Royal Shakespeare
Theatre CV37 .... 145 D1
Royston Cl CV3 .... 63 D2
Rubens Cl CV5 .... 60 B2
Rudge Rd CV1 .... 151 A2
Rufford Cl Alcester B49 .... 143 E3
Hinckley LE10 .... 31 E2
Rugby Coll CV21 .... 83 E1
Rugby High Sch CV22 .... 99 E3
Rugby La CV23 .... 97 D3
Rugby Midland Sta CV21 ...... 83 E2
Rugby Rd Barby CV23 .... 101 E1
Binley Woods CV3 .... 79 E4
Brandon CV8 .... 80 A3
Brinklow CV23 .... 64 C2
Bulkington CV12 .... 40 B1
Church Lawford CV23 .... 81 E3
Clifton u D CV23 .... 83 F3
Dunchurch CV22 .... 99 E2
Easenhall CV23 .... 65 F2
Harborough Magna CV23 .... 66 A1
Hinckley LE10 .... 31 E3
Kilsby CV21,CV23 .... 101 F3
Lilbourne CV23 .... 84 C3
Long Lawford CV23 .... 82 A2
Pailton CV23 .... 66 A4
Princethorpe CV23 .... 96 C1
Royal Leamington Spa CV32 . 105 E1
Shawell LE17 .... 68 A4

Rugby Sch CV22 .... 83 D1
Ruislip Cl B35 .... 22 A2
Rumbush La B94 .... 69 F2
Rumer Cl CV37 .... 129 B4
Runcorn Cl Birmingham B37 .. 33 E2
Redditch B98 .... 102 C4
Runcorn Wlk **10** CV2 .... 63 D4
Runneymede Gdns CV10 ... 28 C2
Runnymede Dr CV7 .... 74 B3
Rupert Brooke Rd CV22 ..... 99 F4
Rupert Kettle Dr CV33 .... 124 B4
Rupert Rd CV6 .... 61 D4
Rush La B77 .... 9 D4
Rushbrook La B94 .... 86 B2
Rushbrook Rd CV37 .... 145 E1
Rushford Cl B90 .... 71 D4
Rushleigh Rd B90 .... 69 F4
Rushmoor Dr CV5 .... 60 C2
Rushmore St CV31 .... 110 A4
Rushmore Terr **13** CV31 .... 110 A4
Rushock Cl B98 .... 103 E4
Rushton Cl CV7 .... 74 B4
Rushwick Gr B90 .... 71 D3
Ruskin Cl Coventry CV6 ..... 60 B3
Nuneaton CV10 .... 28 A3
Rugby CV22 .... 99 F3
Russell Ave CV22 .... 99 E2
Russell Cl CV23 .... 115 D4
Russell St Coventry CV1 ... 151 C4
Royal Leamington Spa CV32 . 105 F1
Russell St N CV1 .... 151 C4
Russell Terr CV31 .... 110 A4
Russelsheim Way CV22 ... 83 D1
Rutherford Glen CV11 ...... 29 F1
Rutherglen Ave CV5 .... 78 A3
Rutland Ave Hinckley LE10 .. 31 E4
Nuneaton CV10 .... 28 C2
Rutland Croft **8** CV3 .... 78 C4
Rydal B77 .... 10 A4
Rydal Ave CV11 .... 30 A3
Rydal Cl Allesley CV5 .... 60 A4
Hinckley LE10 .... 30 C4
Rugby CV21 .... 83 E3
Ryde Ave CV10 .... 29 E4
Ryder Cl CV35 .... 114 F3
Ryder Row CV7 .... 37 D4
Ryders Hill Cres CV10 ...... 28 B4
Rye Cl Banbury OX16 .... 139 F5
Stratford-u-A CV37 .... 144 C3
Rye Croft B47 .... 69 D3
Rye Fields **1** CV33 .... 122 E8
Rye Grass Wlk B35 .... 22 A2
Rye Hill CV5 .... 60 A3
Rye Piece Ringway CV12 .. 39 E2
Ryeclose Croft B37 .... 33 E2
Ryefield La B76 .... 14 A1
Ryegrass La B97 .... 102 B3
Ryelands The CV23 .... 98 B4
Ryhope Cl CV12 .... 38 B1
Ryknild St B49 .... 143 D3
Ryland Cl CV31 .... 110 B3
Ryland Rd CV35 .... 122 B8
Ryland St CV37 .... 144 C1
Rylston Ave CV6 .... 49 D1
Rylstone Way **4** CV34 .... 104 C1
Ryon Hill CV37 .... 145 F4
Ryton Cl CV4 .... 9 F4
Ryton Cl CV4 .... 76 A4
Ryton Gardens CV8 .... 79 F1

Sabin Cl CV23 .... 115 C4
Sabin Dr CV33 .... 107 E4
Sackville Cl Hanwell OX17 . 139 F6
Stratford-u-A CV37 .... 144 B2
Sacred Heart RC Prim Sch
CV2 .... 62 A2
Saddington Rd CV3 .... 78 C4
Saddlebow La CV35 .... 114 B2
Saddlers Cl LE10 .... 31 F3
Saddleton St CV35 .... 138 C7
Sadler Cl CV37 .... 144 C3
Sadler Rd CV6 .... 61 D4
Sadlers Ave CV36 .... 149 F3
Sadlers Cl CV36 .... 149 F3
Sadlerswell La B94 .... 88 A3
Saffron B77 .... 4 A2
Saffron Cl CV23 .... 83 F4
Saffron Mdw CV37 .... 144 C1
Saffron Wlk CV37 .... 144 C1
Saintbury Cl CV37 .... 145 E1
Saintbury Dr B91 .... 71 E4
Saints Way CV10 .... 29 E3
SS Peter & Paul
RC Prim Sch CV2 .... 62 C4
St Agatha's Rd CV2 .... 62 A2
St Agnes Cl B80 .... 103 E2
St Agnes La CV1 .... 151 B3
St Agnes Way CV11 .... 29 F2
St Albans Cl CV32 .... 105 E1
St Andrew's CE Inf Sch
CV5 .... 59 E3
St Andrew's Cres CV34 ... 144 C1
St Andrew's Rd Coventry
CV5 .... 76 C4
Royal Leamington Spa
CV32 .... 106 A3
St Andrews B77 .... 4 A2
St Andrews Benn
CE Fst Sch CV21 .... 83 E2
St Andrews Benn
CE Fst Sch CV21 .... 83 E2
St Andrews Cres CV22 ..... 100 A4
St Andrews Dr CV11 .... 30 A1
St Ann's Cl CV31 .... 110 B4
St Ann's Rd CV2 .... 62 A2

St Anne's RC Prim Sch
Birmingham B37 .... 33 D1
Coventry CV3 .... 78 B3
Nuneaton CV10 .... 28 B4
St Anne's Rd CV22 .... 82 C1
St Annes Gr B93 .... 72 A3
St Anthony's
RC Comb Sch CV31 ..... 110 B4
St Antony's RC Prim Sch
B37 .... 33 D3
St Asaphs Rd B80 .... 103 E2
St Athan Croft B35 .... 22 A2
St Augustine's
RC Comb Sch CV8 .... 92 C4
St Augustine's
RC Prim Sch CV6 .... 61 D4
St Augustine's RC Sch
B97 .... 102 B3
St Augustine's Wlk CV6 ... 61 D4
St Austell Cl CV11 .... 30 A3
St Austell Rd CV2 .... 62 C2
St Bartholemews Cl CV3 .. 63 D1
St Bartholomew's
CE Prim Sch CV3 .... 78 C4
St Benedict's
RC High Sch B49 .... 143 E2
St Benedict's RC Prim Sch
Atherstone CV9 .... 18 C4
Coventry CV1 .... 61 F2
St Benedicts Cl CV9 .... 18 B4
St Bernards Wlk CV3 .... 78 B3
St Blaise Ave B46 .... 23 E1
St Bride's Cl **3** CV31 ...... 110 B3
St Catherine's LE10 .... 31 F4
St Catherine's Cl CV3 ...... 78 A4
St Catherine's Cres CV37 . 109 F2
St Catherine's RC Prim Sch
GL55 .... 135 A2
St Chads Rd
3 Bishops Tachbrook CV33 . 122 E8
Studley B80 .... 103 E2
St Christian's Croft CV3 ... 77 F4
St Christian's Rd CV3 ...... 77 F4
St Christopher Prim Sch
CV5 .... 60 B2
St Christopher's Cl CV34 . 108 B4
St Columba's Cl CV1 ..... 151 B4
St David's Cl CV31 .... 110 B4
St David's Prim Sch GL54 . 140 A3
St Davids Orch CV3 .... 78 C4
St Davids Way CV10 .... 39 D3
St Edith's Cl CV23 .... 53 F2
St Edith's Gn **1** CV34 ... 109 D4
St Editha's Ct CV9 .... 5 D1
St Edithas Rd B78 .... 11 D4
St Edmonds Rd CV9 .... 5 B6
St Edward's RC Prim Sch
B46 .... 34 A3
St Edwin's Cl WR11 .... 127 B2
St Elizabeth's RC Prim Sch
CV6 .... 61 F4
St Elizabeth's Cl CV6 .... 61 F4
St Faith's CE Jun Sch B49 . 143 E2
St Faith's Rd B49 .... 143 E3
St Francis RC Comb Sch
CV12 .... 39 E2
St George & St Teresa
RC Sch B93 .... 72 A4
St George's Cl
Moreton-in-M GL56 ...... 140 A3
Stratford-u-A CV37 .... 144 B2
St George's Rd
Atherstone CV9 .... 12 C1
Coventry CV1 .... 61 F1
Royal Leamington Spa CV31 . 109 F3
Solihull B90 .... 70 B4
St Georges Ave CV22 .... 99 F4
St Georges Way CV10 ...... 39 D4
St Gerard's (Warwickshire)
Orthopaedic Hospl B46 .. 34 A3
St Gerards RC Jun &
Inf Sch B35 .... 22 A2
St Giles Cty Mid Sch CV7 .. 49 E4
St Giles Rd Coventry CV7 .. 49 E3
Gaydon CV35 .... 132 E8
St Govan's Cl **4** CV31 .... 110 B3
St Gregory's RC Prim Sch
Coventry CV2 .... 62 C2
Stratford-u-A CV37 .... 145 E3
St Gregory's Rd CV37 .... 145 D2
St Helen's Rd CV31 .... 110 A3
St Helen's Way CV5 .... 60 A4
St Helena Rd B78 .... 11 D4
St Ives Rd CV2 .... 62 C2
St Ives Way CV11 .... 29 F3
St James' Ave CV35 .... 146 C2
St James CE Fst Sch
CV33 .... 147 D3
St James CE Mid Sch
CV12 .... 40 B1
St James Cl WR11 .... 127 D3
St James Cres CV33 ...... 147 D3
St James Ct GL56 .... 140 A2
St James Gdns CV12 .... 40 B1
St James La CV3 .... 78 B3
St James Meadow Rd
CV32 .... 105 E1
St James Rd CV33 .... 147 D3
St James's Cl LE10 .... 31 E1
St John Fisher RC Prim Sch
CV2 .... 62 B3
St John St CV21 .... 83 D2
St John the Baptist
CE Fst Sch CV37 .... 109 F4
St John the Baptist
RC Prim Sch B36 .... 33 D4
St John the Divine
CE Prim Sch CV3 .... 78 B3

St John Vianney
RC Prim Sch CV5 .... 60 A2
St John's Ave CV8 .... 93 D2
St John's CE Prim Sch CV5 . 60 B2
St John's Cl
Cherington CV36 .... 141 D7
Henley-in-A B95 .... 113 A4
St John's Ct **9** CV34 ...... 108 C4
St John's La CV23 .... 82 A3
St John's Rd
Cherington CV36 .... 141 D7
Royal Leamington Spa CV31 . 110 A3
St John's St Coventry CV1 . 151 C2
Kenilworth CV8 .... 93 D2
St Johns CV34 .... 108 C4
St Johns Ave CV2 .... 100 C4
St Johns Cl Knowle B93 ... 72 A3
Stratford-u-A CV37 .... 144 C1
St Johns Mid Sch CV8 ..... 92 C1
St Johns Rd CV10 .... 27 F4
St Joseph's RC Comb Sch
CV31 .... 110 A2
St Joseph's RC Mid Sch
CV11 .... 29 E2
St Joseph's RC Prim Sch
OX16 .... 139 F3
St Joseph's RC Sch CV23 . 53 F2
St Joseph's Sch CV8 .... 93 D4
St Jude's Cles CV3 .... 78 B4
St Judes Ave B80 .... 103 E2
St Laurence Ave CV34 .... 108 B3
St Laurence Cl CV35 ...... 114 A8
St Lawrence CE Prim Sch
CV23 .... 125 C7
St Lawrence Cl Knowle B93 . 72 A3
Napton CV23 .... 125 C8
St Lawrence Rd CV10 ...... 27 D2
St Lawrence's Rd CV11 .... 49 F1
St Leonard's Wlk CV8 ...... 79 D1
St Leonards Cl
Birmingham B37 .... 44 A4
Dordon B78 .... 11 D3
St Leonards View B78 ...... 10 C4
St Luke's Rd CV6 .... 49 E2
St Margaret Rd Coventry CV1 . 61 F1
Stoke Golding CV13 .... 21 F4
St Margaret's CE Mid Sch
CV31 .... 110 A3
St Margaret's CE Prim Sch
CV8 .... 80 A2
St Margaret's Rd CV31 .... 110 A3
St Margaret's Specl Sch
CV12 .... 39 D2
St Margarets CE Prim Sch
CV13 .... 21 E4
St Marie's RC Inf Sch CV22 . 83 D1
St Marie's RC Mid Sch
CV22 .... 82 C1
St Mark's Annexe (Coventry
& Warwickshire Hospl)
CV1 .... 151 A4
St Mark's Ave CV22 .... 99 E4
St Mark's Cl Gaydon CV35 . 132 E8
Ullenhall B95 .... 112 E6
St Mark's Mews CV32 .... 105 F1
St Mark's Rd CV32 .... 105 E1
St Martin's LE10 .... 31 F3
St Martin's Catholic
High Sch CV31 .... 21 F4
St Martin's Cl CV37 .... 144 C1
St Martin's Rd CV8 .... 77 E1
St Martins Ave B80 .... 103 E2
St Mary St CV1 .... 151 C2
St Mary's CE Jun Sch B80 . 103 F2
St Mary's Cl
Priors Hardwick CV23 .... 125 D3
Southam CV33 .... 147 D3
Ullenhall B95 .... 112 E6
Warwick CV34 .... 108 B4
St Mary's Cres CV31 ..... 110 A4
St Mary's La OX7 .... 142 F2
St Mary's RC Comb Sch
CV33 .... 147 E2
St Mary's RC Jun & Inf Sch
B80 .... 103 F2
St Mary's RC Prim Sch
Aston le W NN11 .... 134 F5
Coventry CV1 .... 61 F2
St Mary's Rd Alcester B49 . 143 E2
Atherstone CV9 .... 18 C4
Fillongley CV7 .... 36 C2
Hinckley LE10 .... 31 E4
Nuneaton CV11 .... 29 D3
Royal Leamington Spa CV31 . 110 A4
Stratford-u-A CV37 .... 145 D2
St Peter's Terr CV31 .... 110 A4
St Marys Acre CV37 ...... 120 E7
St Marys Gr B79 .... 2 B2
St Matthews Cl WR11 .... 127 E6
St Matthews St CV21 ...... 83 D2
St Mawgen Cl B35 .... 22 B2
St Michael's Cl Arley CV7 .. 37 D4
Bishops Itchington CV33 . 124 A4
Claverdon CV35 .... 113 F3
Weston u W V33 .... 107 E4
Wood End CV9 .... 10 B1
St Michael's Cres CV23 .. 147 F4
St Michael's Dr DE12 .... 3 F4
St Michael's Hospl CV34 . 108 C4
St Michael's Rd
Claverdon CV35 .... 113 F3
Coventry CV2 .... 62 A2
Warwick CV34 .... 108 B4
St Michael's Way CV10 .... 28 B2
St Michaels Cl CV9 .... 12 C1
St Michales Cl CV33 ...... 111 F1
St Milburgh Cl WR11 ..... 127 D1
St Nicholas Ave CV8 .... 92 C2

St Nicholas CE Comb Sch
CV8 .... 92 C3
St Nicholas Church St
CV34 .... 108 C4
St Nicholas Cl Alcester B49 . 143 E2
Austrey CV9 .... 3 D1
Coventry CV1 .... 61 E3
St Nicholas Est CV9 .... 11 E1
St Nicholas Rd
Henley-in-A B95 .... 113 B4
Radford Semele CV31 ... 110 C3
St Nicholas St CV1 .... 151 B4
St Nicholas Wlk B76 .... 23 D3
St Nicolas CE Fst Sch
CV11 .... 29 F3
St Nicolas Park Dr CV11 .. 29 F4
St Nicolas Rd CV11 .... 29 E3
St Osburg's RC Prim Sch
CV1 .... 151 A3
St Osburg's Rd CV2 .... 62 A2
St Oswalds CE First Sch
CV31 .... 82 B2
St Patrick's CE Prim Sch
B94 .... 70 B1
St Patrick's RC Prim Sch
Birmingham B37 .... 33 E1
Coventry CV2 .... 50 B1
St Patrick's Rd CV1 .... 151 B1
St Patricks RC Comb Sch
CV31 .... 109 F3
St Paul's CE Comb Sch
CV32 .... 106 A1
St Paul's CE Comb Sch
(Annexe) CV32 .... 106 A1
St Paul's CE Fst Sch CV10 . 28 B2
St Paul's Cl CV34 .... 108 B3
St Paul's Cres **3** B46 ..... 33 F4
St Paul's Ct B77 .... 9 E2
St Paul's Rd Coventry CV6 . 61 F3
Nuneaton CV10 .... 28 B2
St Paul's Sq **12** CV32 .... 106 A1
St Paul's Terr CV34 .... 108 B3
St Peter's Ave CV9 .... 19 D4
St Peter's CE Prim Sch
CV35 .... 122 F8
St Peter's Cl Redditch B97 . 102 C3
Water Orton B46 .... 23 D1
Witherley CV9 .... 19 D4
St Peter's Ct CV1 .... 151 D4
St Peter's Dr CV10 .... 27 F2
St Peter's Rd
7 Royal Leamington Spa
CV32 .... 109 F4
Rugby CV21 .... 83 E2
Wellesbourne CV35 ...... 146 B2
St Peters La CV8 .... 44 B1
St Peters Rd Atherstone CV9 . 19 D4
Kineton CV35 .... 132 B6
St Swithin's Dr CV37 ..... 129 D2
St Thomas More
RC Fst Sch B98 .... 103 D4
St Thomas More
RC Prim Sch CV3 .... 77 E3
St Thomas More Sch
CV10 .... 29 D2
St Thomas' Rd CV6 .... 50 A2
St Thomas's Ct CV1 .... 61 D1
St Wulstan Way CV33 .... 147 E3
Salcombe Cl Coventry CV3 . 78 B3
Nuneaton CV11 .... 29 E3
Salem Rd LE10 .... 31 F3
Salford Cl Coventry CV2 ... 62 A3
Redditch B98 .... 103 E4
Salford Priors CE Prim Sch
WR11 .... 127 F6
Salford Rd B50 .... 148 B2
Salisbury Ave CV3 .... 77 E3
Salisbury Dr Nuneaton CV10 . 28 A4
Water Orton B46 .... 23 E2
Salisbury Rd LE10 .... 32 A4
Salt La CV1 .... 151 B2
Salt Way B96 .... 118 B7
Salt Way La OX15 .... 137 F2
Salter St B94 .... 70 B1
Salters La B95 .... 120 C7
Saltisford CV34 .... 108 B4
Saltisford Gdns CV34 .... 108 B4
Salts La B78 .... 8 C2
Sam Gault Cl CV3 .... 78 C4
Sambourne La
Astwood Bank B96 .... 102 C1
Coughton B49 .... 118 E7
Sambourne B96 .... 103 D1
Sambourne Park La B96 . 118 D8
Sammons Way CV4 .... 59 E1
Sampson Cl CV2 .... 62 B4
Sanby Cl CV12 .... 39 D2
Sanctus Dr CV37 .... 144 C1
Sanctus Rd CV37 .... 144 C1
Sanctus St CV37 .... 144 C1
Sand Barn La CV37 .... 121 D6
Sanda Croft B36 .... 33 D3
Sandbarn Cl B90 .... 70 C3
Sandel Cl CV37 .... 144 C2
Sanders Cl Atherstone CV9 . 12 C1
Braunston NN11 .... 117 D5
Sanders Rd Bedworth CV6 . 50 A3
Salford Priors WR11 ...... 127 F6
Sandfield Cl B90 .... 70 A4
Sandfield Rd CV37 .... 144 C1
Sandfine Rd OX15 .... 139 D1
Sandford Cl CV2 .... 50 C2
Sandford Gn OX16 .... 139 F4
Sandford Way CV22 .... 99 E2
Sandgate Cres CV2 .... 62 C1
Sandhills Cres B91 .... 71 D4
Sandhurst Gr CV6 .... 61 D3
Sandilands CV2 .... 62 C2

Sandon Rd CV11 .... 29 D3
Sandown Ave CV6 .... 49 F1
Sandown Cl CV32 .... 106 B2
Sandown Rd CV21 .... 83 E2
Sandpiper B77 .... 10 A3
Sandpiper Cl CV37 .... 144 B3
Sandpiper Rd CV2 .... 50 A2
Sandpits Cl Curdworth B76 . 23 D3
Tysoe CV35 .... 138 B6
Sandpits La CV6 .... 48 C1
Sandpits Rd CV35 .... 138 B7
Sandpits The CV12 .... 40 B1
Sandwick Cl CV3 .... 78 C4
Sandy La Blackdown CV32 . 105 F3
Coventry CV1 .... 61 E3
Furnace End B46 .... 25 F2
Marton CV23 .... 115 D7
Monks Kirby CV23 .... 53 F2
Newton Regis B79 .... 2 B3
Royal Leamington Spa CV32 . 105 E2
Rugby CV21 .... 82 C2
Sandy Lane Bsns Pk CV1 ... 61 E3
Sandy Way Barford CV35 . 122 B7
Tamworth B77 .... 4 A2
Sandy Way La B78 .... 11 E4
Sandythorpe CV3 .... 78 C3
Sankey Gr GL56 .... 140 A2
Santos Cl CV3 .... 78 C4
Sapcote Rd LE10 .... 32 A4
Saplings The B76 .... 22 A4
Sapphire Dr CV31 .... 109 F3
Sapphire Gate CV2 .... 62 B1
Saracen Dr CV7 .... 73 F3
Sargeaunt St CV31 .... 109 F4
Sark Dr B36 .... 33 D3
Satchwell Wlk **8** CV32 .. 109 F4
Saumur Way CV35 .... 109 E3
Saunders Ave CV12 .... 39 D1
Saunton Ave CV5 .... 60 A4
Saunton Rd CV22 .... 82 C1
Savages Cl CV33 .... 122 F8
Savernake Rd CV35 .... 132 C4
Saville Gr CV8 .... 93 E3
Sawbridge Rd CV23 ...... 116 F5
Saxon Cl Binley Woods CV3 . 79 E4
Polesworth B78 .... 4 C1
Stratford-u-A CV37 .... 145 E1
Studley B80 .... 103 F3
Tamworth B77 .... 9 F3
Saxon Mdws CV32 .... 105 E1
Saxon Rd CV2 .... 62 A2
Saxon Wood Rd B90 .... 70 B3
Saxonfields B50 .... 148 B2
Scafell CV21 .... 83 E4
Scafell Cl CV5 .... 60 A2
Scammerton B77 .... 10 A4
Scar Bank CV34 .... 104 C1
Scarborough Way CV4 ..... 75 F4
Schofield Rd B37 .... 33 D3
Scholars La CV37 .... 144 C1
Scholfield Rd CV7 .... 49 D3
School Ave WR11 .... 127 F6
School Cl Birmingham B37 . 33 D3
Braunston NN11 .... 117 E5
Coventry CV3 .... 61 F1
Great Alne B49 .... 119 D6
Hinckley LE10 .... 32 A3
Long Compton CV36 ...... 141 C3
School Dr B47 .... 69 D2
School Gdns CV21 .... 84 A1
School Hill Hartshill CV10 . 28 A4
Mollington OX17 .... 133 F2
Napton CV23 .... 125 C8
Offchurch CV33 .... 111 D4
School House La CV2 ...... 63 D3
School La Badby NN11 .... 126 F6
Bearley CV37 .... 120 E7
Bedworth CV7 .... 49 F4
Kenilworth CV8 .... 92 C3
Ladbroke CV33 .... 124 D5
Lea Marston B76 .... 24 A4
Littleton WR11 .... 127 F1
Lower Brailes OX15 .... 137 F2
North Newington OX15 .. 139 E2
Nuneaton CV10 .... 27 F3
Priors Marston CV23 .... 125 E4
Radford Semele CV31 ... 110 C3
Shuttington B79 .... 4 C1
Stretton on D CV23 .... 96 C3
Tamworth B77 .... 9 E3
Tiddington CV37 .... 145 F2
Warmington OX17 .... 133 D2
Wolvey LE10 .... 41 F2
Wroxall CV35 .... 90 C2
School Rd Alcester B49 ... 143 D2
Bulkington CV12 .... 40 B1
Great Alne B49 .... 119 D6
Henley-in-A B95 .... 113 B4
Hockley Heath B94 .... 88 A4
Pebworth CV37 .... 128 F1
Salford Priors WR11 ...... 127 F6
Snitterfield CV37 .... 121 B6
Wellesbourne CV35 ...... 146 C2
School St
Church Lawford CV23 ..... 81 D3
Churchover CV23 .... 67 E3
Dunchurch CV22 .... 99 E2
Long Lawford CV23 .... 82 A2
Rugby CV21 .... 84 A1
Southam CV33 .... 147 D3
Stockton CV33 .... 147 F4
Wolston CV8 .... 80 A2
School Wlk CV11 .... 29 F1
Scotchill The CV6 .... 49 D1
Scotland End OX15 .... 142 D4
Scots Cl CV22 .... 99 E4
Scots La CV6 .... 60 C3
Scott Ave CV10 .... 29 E4

Scott Cl B50 148 B3
Scott Rd Kenilworth CV8 92 C1
Redditch B97 102 B4
Royal Leamington Spa CV31 110 A3
Seabroke Ave CV22 82 C2
Seafield La B48 85 F2
Seaford Cl CV6 50 A2
Seagrave Rd CV1 151 D1
Sealand Dr CV12 39 D2
Sear Hills Cl CV7 74 A3
Seathwaite CV21 83 E4
Seaton B77 9 F4
Seaton Cl Hinckley LE10 32 A4
Nuneaton CV11 29 F3
Sebastian Cl CV3 78 A3
Seckington La B79 2 B2
Second Ave CV3 62 B1
Second Exhibition Ave B40 44 B2
Sedgemere Gr CV7 74 B3
Sedgemoor Rd CV3 78 A3
Sedlescombe Pk CV22 99 F4
Seed Field Croft CV3 77 F4
Seekings The CV31 110 A2
Seeney La B76 15 D1
Seeswood Cl CV10 28 B1
Sefton Rd Coventry CV4 76 C3
Tamworth B77 9 E2
Seggs La B49 143 D2
Segrave Cl CV35 132 B6
Selborne Rd CV22 99 E4
Selby Way CV10 28 A3
Selsdon Cl B47 69 E3
Selsey Cl CV3 78 B2
Selside CV21 83 E4
Selworthy Rd CV6 49 F2
Semele Cl CV31 110 C3
Seneschal Rd CV3 77 F4
Sennen Cl CV11 30 A3
Seven Acre Cl 4 CV33 122 E8
Seven Meadows Rd CV37 144 C1
Severn Ave LE10 31 D4
Severn Cl CV32 106 B2
Severn Rd Bulkington CV12 40 A2
Coventry CV1 61 F1
Severn Stars Ind Est CV3 78 A4
Sevincott Cl CV37 144 B2
Sevington Cl B91 71 E4
Sewall Highway CV2 62 A3
Seymour Cl Coventry CV3 78 B3
Hampton Magna CV35 114 F3
Seymour Gate GL55 135 B2
Seymour Gr CV34 109 E3
Seymour Rd Alcester B49 143 E3
Nuneaton CV11 29 E2
Rugby CV21 83 E3
Stratford-u-A CV37 144 B1
Shackleton Way LE17 55 E3
Shadow Brook La B92 56 C4
Shadowbrook Rd CV6 61 D3
Shaft La CV7 47 D2
Shaftesbury Ave CV7 49 D4
Shaftesbury Rd CV5 76 C4
Shakers La CV23 115 C5
Shakesfield Cl CV36 136 F6
Shakespeare Ave
Bedworth CV12 39 E1
Warwick CV34 108 B2
Shakespeare Ctr Mus The
CV37 145 D2
Shakespeare Dr CV11 30 A1
Shakespeare Gdns CV22 99 F4
Shakespeare La WR11 127 D3
Shakespeare Rd B90 70 B4
Shakespeare St
Coventry CV2 62 A2
Stratford-u-A CV37 145 D2
Shakespeares Birthplace
Mus CV37 145 D2
Shakleton Rd CV5 61 D1
Shanes Castle Rd CV35 132 D3
Shanklin Dr CV10 29 E3
Shanklin Rd CV3 78 A2
Shannon B77 9 F4
Shap Fell CV21 83 E4
Sharnford Rd LE10 32 C3
Sharp Cl CV6 49 E1
Sharpe Cl CV34 108 C4
Sharpe St B77 4 A3
Sharpless Rd LE10 31 F4
Sharpley Ct CV2 63 D4
Sharratt Rd CV12 39 D1
Shaw's La CV35 114 C8
Shawberry Ave B35 22 A2
Shawbury La B46 35 E4
Shawbury Village B46 35 F3
Shawe Ave CV10 29 E4
Shawell Rd LE17 68 B4
Shawfield B47 69 D3
Shawhurst Croft B47 69 D4
Shawhurst La B47 69 D3
Shearings The OX15 142 D4
Sheep Dip La CV23 96 C1
Sheep St
Chipping Campden GL55 135 A1
Rugby CV21 83 D2
Shipston-on-S CV36 149 F3
Stratford-u-A CV37 145 D1
Sheepclose Dr B37 33 D2
Sheepcote Cl CV32 106 A1
Sheepy La CV9 6 C2
Sheepy Rd Atherstone CV9 12 B1
Sheepy Magna CV9 12 C3
Shefford Rd CV35 132 D3
Shelbourne Rd CV37 144 A2
Sheldon Gr 6 CV34 104 C1
Sheldon Rd B98 103 D4
Shelfield Cl CV5 60 A2
Shelley Ave CV34 108 B2
Shelley Cl Bedworth CV12 39 E1
Redditch B97 102 B4
Shelley Rd Coventry CV2 62 B2
Stratford-u-A CV37 145 D1
Shellon Cl CV3 78 C4
Shelly Cres B90 71 D3
Shelly La B90 71 D3
Shelton Sq CV1 151 B2
Shelton St B77 9 F4
Shelwick Gr B93 71 F2
Shenington CE Prim Sch
OX15 138 F5
Shenstone Ave CV22 83 F1
Shenstone Dr CV7 74 A3
Shenton Cl CV13 21 F4
Sheperds Hill CV33 147 E2
Shepherd Cl CV4 59 F2
Shepherd Pl CV35 132 B5
Shepherd St CV23 115 C7
Shepherds Cl CV23 115 D3
Shepperton Bsns Pk CV11 29 E1
Shepperton St CV11 29 E1
Sheppey Dr B36 33 D3
Sherard Croft B36 33 D3
Sherborne Cl B46 34 A2
Sherborne Rd LE10 32 A4
Sherbourne Ave CV10 28 A2
Sherbourne Cres CV5 60 C2
Sherbourne Fields Sch CV6 60 B3
Sherbourne St CV1 61 D1
Sherbrooke Ave B77 9 F3
Sherdmore Croft B90 70 C3
Sheridan Cl CV22 99 F4
Sheridan Dr CV10 27 F3
Sheridan Wlk B35 22 A2
Sheriff Ave CV4 76 A4
Sheriff Rd CV21 83 E2
Sheriffs Orch CV1 151 B2
Sheringham Cl CV11 29 F1
Sherington Ave CV5 60 B2
Sherlock Rd CV5 60 B2
Sherwell Dr B49 143 D2
Sherwood Cl CV9 10 B1
Sherwood Jones Cl CV6 61 D3
Sherwood Rd CV13 21 F4
Sherwood Wlk CV32 106 B2
Shetland Cl CV5 60 A2
Shetland Dr CV10 29 D1
Shetland Wlk B36 33 D3
Shevlock Way CV6 62 A3
Shillingstone Cl CV2 63 D2
Shilton & Ansty Fst Sch
CV7 51 F3
Shilton Cl B90 70 C3
Shilton Ind Est CV7 51 F4
Shilton La Barnacle CV2, CV7 51 D2
Bulkington CV12 40 B1
Coventry CV2 50 C2
Shilton CV7, CV12 51 E4
Shinehill La WR11 128 A1
Shipston Rd
Alderminster CV37 130 B5
Coventry CV2 62 B3
Long Compton CV36 141 C4
Upper Tysoe CV35 138 B6
Shipton-on-Stour
Prim Sch CV36 149 F3
Shire Cl CV6 50 A1
Shirebrook Cl CV2 50 B1
Shires Gate Ret Pk CV31 109 F3
Shires Ret Pk CV34 109 E3
Shires The CV23 81 D3
Shirlett Cl CV2 50 A2
Shirley La CV7 59 D3
Shirley Rd CV2 63 D4
Shirrall Dr B78 7 F2
Shopping Ctr The CV31 110 A3
Shopping Prec The CV34 105 D1
Shorncliffe Rd CV6 60 C3
Short Acres CV35 132 C6
Short La CV23 115 C4
Short St Coventry CV1 151 C2
Nuneaton CV10 28 B2
Shortland Cl B93 72 A4
Shortlands CV7 49 E3
Shortley Rd CV3 77 F4
Shortwoods The B78 11 D3
Shottery CV37 144 B1
Shottery CE Prim Sch
CV37 144 B1
Shottery Cl CV5 60 A2
Shottery Rd CV37 144 C1
Shotteswell Rd B90 70 A4
Shoulderway La CV36 149 F1
Showell La CV7 47 D1
Shrewley Comm CV35 114 B6
Shrubberies The CV4 76 C2
Shrubland St CV31 110 A3
Shrubland Street
Com Prim Sch CV31 110 A3
Shuckburgh Cres
Bourton on D CV23 97 F1
Rugby CV22 100 B4
Shuckburgh Gr 3 CV32 106 A1
Shuckburgh Rd
Napton CV23 125 C8
Priors Marston CV23 125 E4
Shulman's Wlk CV2 62 B4
Shultern La CV4 76 B3
Shuna Croft CV2 63 D4
Shustoke CE Prim Sch
B46 25 D1
Shutford Rd
North Newington OX15 139 D2
Shutford OX15 139 B1
Shutt La B94 70 A1
Shuttington Rd B79 4 A3
Shuttle St CV6 62 A4
Shuttleworth Rd CV23 83 F3
Sibford Gower Rrim Sch
OX15 142 D8
Sibford Rd
Hook Norton OX15 142 D4
Shutford OX15 138 F2
Sibford Sch OX15 142 D8
Sibree Rd CV3 78 A2
Sibton Cl CV2 50 B1
Sidbury Gr B93 71 F2
Siddeley Ave Coventry CV3 62 A1
Kenilworth CV8 92 C2
Siddeley Way NN11 117 F2
Sidelands Rd CV37 144 B2
Sidenhill Cl B90 70 A4
Sidmouth Cl Coventry CV2 62 B4
Nuneaton CV11 29 F3
Sidney Rd CV22 100 B4
Sidney Stringer
Com Tech Coll CV1 151 C3
Signal Hayes Rd B76 13 D1
Signal Wlk B77 4 A1
Silica Rd B77 4 A1
Silksby St CV3 77 E4
Silver Birch Ave CV12 38 C1
Silver Birch Dr B47 69 D3
Silver Birch Gr CV31 109 F3
Silver Link Rd B77 4 A1
Silver St Coventry CV1 151 B3
Newton CV23 68 A1
Wroxton OX15 139 D4
Silver Trees Dr CV12 40 A2
Silver Wlk CV10 28 C2
Silverbirch Cl CV10 28 A4
Silverdale Cl CV2 50 A2
Silverstone Dr CV6 49 F3
Silverton Rd CV6 61 F4
Simmonds Way CV9 12 B1
Simmons Cl B78 8 A1
Simmons Ct CV35 146 B2
Simms La B47 69 D3
Simon Cl CV11 29 E1
Simon Rd B47 69 D4
Simon Stone St CV6 61 F4
Simpkins Cl CV33 107 E4
Simpson Rd CV36 149 F3
Sinclair Ave OX16 139 F4
Singer Cl CV6 62 A4
Singer Croft B36 22 C1
Sir Henry Parkes Prim Sch
CV4 76 B4
Sir Henry Parkes Rd CV5 76 B4
Sir John Moore CE Sch
DE12 3 F4
Sir Thomas White's Rd
CV5 60 C1
Sir William Lyons Rd CV4 76 B3
Sir Winston Churchill Pl
CV3 79 E4
Siskin Dr CV3 78 B2
Siskin Parkway E CV3 78 B1
Siskin Parkway W CV3 78 B1
Sitwell Ave CV23 115 D3
Sixteen Acres La B50 148 C1
Skelwith Rise CV11 30 A3
Sketchley Hall Gdns LE10 31 E3
Sketchley Hill Cty Prim Sch
LE10 31 F3
Sketchley La LE10 31 E3
Sketchley La Ind Est LE10 31 D3
Sketchley Manor La LE10 31 E3
Sketchley Mdws LE10 31 E3
Sketchley Meadows
Bsns Pk LE10 31 E2
Sketchley Old Village LE10 31 E3
Sketchley Rd LE10 31 F3
Skiddaw CV21 83 E4
Skidmore Ave B77 9 E3
Skilts Sch B98 112 B6
Skipton Gdns CV2 62 A3
Skipwith Cl CV23 64 B2
Skipworth Rd CV3 63 D1
Sky Blue Way CV1 61 F2
Skye Cl Birmingham B36 33 D3
Nuneaton CV10 28 C1
Slack's Ave CV9 18 B4
Slade Cl CV11 40 B4
Slade Gr B93 71 F3
Slade Hill CV35 114 F4
Slade La Sutton Coldfield
B75 7 D2
Tamworth B77 9 E2
Slade Mdw CV31 110 C3
Slade Rd CV21 83 E1
Slade The CV33 133 E6
Slateley Cres B90 70 C3
Slater Rd B93 71 F2
Sleath's Yd CV12 39 D2
Sledmere Cl CV2 50 A2
Sleets Yd CV12 39 D1
Slimbridge Cl Redditch
B97 102 C3
2 Solihull B90 71 D3
Slingates Rd CV37 145 D2
Slingsby B77 9 E4
Slingsby Cl CV11 29 F1
Slough The B97 103 D2
Slowley Hill CV7 26 A1
Small Brook Bsns Ctr
B50 148 C3
Small Ho OX15 142 D8
Small La B94 86 C3
Smalley Pl CV8 92 C2
Smarts La CV35 138 B6
Smarts Rd CV12 38 C1
Smeaton La CV23 64 C3
Smercote Cl CV12 38 B1
Smite Cl CV23 53 F2
Smith St Bedworth CV12 38 C1
Coventry CV6 61 F3
13 Royal Leamington Spa
CV31 109 F4
Warwick CV34 108 C4
Wood End CV9 10 B1
Smith's La CV37 121 B6
Smith's Way B49 143 E3
Smithford Way CV1 151 B3
Smiths La B93 71 F4
Smiths Way B46 23 D2
Smiths Wood Sch B36 33 D3
Smithy La Aston Flamville LE9 32 B4
Church Lawford CV23 81 E3
Tamworth B77 9 F4
Smithy Rd CV9 17 E3
Smockington La LE10 42 A4
Smorrall La CV12 38 B1
Smythe Gr CV34 104 C1
Snape Rd CV2 62 C3
Snarestone Rd DE12 3 F4
Snitterfield La CV37 121 C7
Snitterfield La CV37 114 C1
Snitterfield Prim Sch
CV37 121 B6
Snitterfield Rd CV37 120 E7
Snitterfield St CV35 121 F4
Snowdon Cl CV10 28 A2
Snowford Hill CV33 115 A5
Snows Drive Hill B90 70 B3
Snowshill Cl CV11 39 F4
Snuff La OX17 139 E8
Soar Way LE10 31 D4
Soden Cl CV3 78 B3
Soden's Ave CV8 79 D1
Solent Dr CV2 50 C1
Solihull Coll
Chelmsley Campus B37 33 E2
Solihull Parkway B37 44 C4
Solihull Rd B92 56 C3
Solway Cl CV31 110 B3
Somerby Dr B91 71 D4
Somerly Cl CV3 78 C4
Somers Pl 3 CV32 109 F4
Somers Rd Keresley CV7 49 D3
Meriden CV7 45 F1
Rugby CV22 82 B2
Somerset Dr CV10 28 C2
Somerset Rd CV1 61 E3
Somerton Dr B37 44 A4
Sommerville Rd CV2 62 B2
Soot La OX17 133 D2
Sopwith Croft B35 22 A1
Sorbus B77 4 A2
Sorrel B77 4 A3
Sorrel Cl CV4 75 F4
Sorrel Dr Kingsbury B78 15 E4
Rugby CV23 83 E4
Sorrell Rd CV10 39 E4
South Ave CV2 62 A1
South Car Park Rd B40 44 C2
South Cl NN11 117 E5
South Dr B46 33 F3
South End OX7 142 A2
South Green Dr CV37 144 B2
South Par CV33 123 F6
South Rd CV23 84 A3
South Ridge CV5 60 A2
South St Atherstone CV9 18 B4
Coventry CV1 61 F2
Rugby CV21 83 E2
South Terr CV31 110 A2
South View B78 15 E2
South View Rd
Long Lawford CV23 81 F2
Royal Leamington Spa CV32 106 B3
South Way B40 44 C2
Southam Cl CV4 75 F4
Southam Cres CV35 123 D2
Southam Dr CV33 147 D1
Southam Prim Sch CV33 147 D3
Southam Rd Cropredy OX17 134 A2
Dunchurch CV22 99 D1
Kineton CV35 132 B6
Ladbroke CV33 124 D6
Long Itchington CV23 115 D3
Mollington OX17 134 A2
Priors Marston CV23 125 E4
Southam CV33 124 B8
Ufton CV33 111 E2
Ufton CV33 115 A1
Southam Sch CV33 147 D3
Southam St CV35 132 B6
Southbank Rd Coventry CV6 60 C3
Kenilworth CV8 92 C2
Southbrook Rd CV22 83 D1
Southcott Way CV2 50 C1
Southern La CV37 145 D1
Southey Cl B91 71 D4
Southey Rd CV22 99 F4
Southfield Cl CV10 29 E3
Southfield Dr CV8 93 D3
Southfield Rd Hinckley LE10 31 F4
Rugby CV22 83 E1
Southam CV33 147 D1
Southfields Cl B46 34 A2
Southlands Atherstone CV9 18 C4
11 Royal Leamington Spa
CV31 110 A4
Southlea Ave CV31 109 F3
Southlea Cl CV31 109 F3
Southleigh Ave CV5 76 C4
Southlynn Gdns CV36 149 F3
Southmead Gdns B80 103 F2
Southport Cl CV3 78 A3
Southrop Rd OX15 142 D3
Southway CV31 110 A3
Sovereign Cl CV8 92 C1
Sovereign Rd CV5 61 D1
Sovereign Row CV1 61 D1
Sowe Valley Prim Sch CV3 78 B4
Spa View CV31 110 A2
Sparkbrook St CV1 61 F2
Sparrow Cock La B93 73 E1
Sparrowdale Specl Sch
CV9 11 E2
Sparta Cl CV21 83 D3
Spartan Cl CV34 109 F2
Speedway La CV8 79 F4
Speedwell Dr CV7 74 A3
Speedwell La CV9 11 D1
Speedwll Cl CV23 83 F4
Spencer Ave CV5 61 D1
Spencer Rd CV5 151 A1
Spencer St CV31 109 F4
Spencer Yd CV31 109 F4
Spencer's La CV7 58 C1
Spernal Ash B49 103 F1
Spernal La Great Alne B80 119 C7
Studley B80 112 A1
Spetchley Cl B97 102 B3
Sphinx Dr CV3 62 A1
Spicer Pl CV22 82 B1
Spiers Cl B93 72 A3
Spilsbury Cl CV32 105 F1
Spilsbury Croft B91 71 D4
Spindle St CV1 61 E3
Spindles The LE10 31 F3
Spinney Cl Arley CV7 36 C4
Binley Woods CV3 79 F4
Birchmoor B78 10 C4
Spinney Dr B90 70 B2
Spinney Hill
Braunston NN11 117 E5
Warwick CV34 105 D1
Spinney La CV10 28 B2
Spinney Rd LE10 31 E3
Spinney The Atherstone CV9 19 D4
Bishops Itchington CV33 124 B4
Coventry CV4 76 B2
Long Lawford CV23 82 A3
Royal Leamington Spa CV32 105 E1
Wythall B47 69 D2
Spire Bank CV33 147 D2
Spires The CV10 28 B2
Spon End CV1, CV5 61 D2
Spon Gate Prim Sch CV1 61 D2
Spon La CV9 11 F3
Spon St CV1 151 A3
Spring Cl 10 Coventry CV1 61 F2
Ettington CV37 131 A3
Spring Coppice Dr B93 72 A2
Spring Ct CV8 95 E3
Spring Hill Arley CV7 36 C4
Bubbenhall CV8 95 E3
Combrook CV35 131 F7
Spring Hill Rd CV10 28 B3
Spring La Combrook CV35 131 E6
Lapworth B94 88 B2
Radford Semele CV31 110 C3
Tanworth-in-A B94 88 A3
Spring Pool CV34 108 C4
Spring Rd Barnacle CV7 51 D3
Coventry CV6 49 F1
Spring St CV21 83 D2
Springbrook Cl B36 22 B1
Springbrook La B94 87 D4
Springfield OX17 139 F6
Springfield Cl CV36 149 F3
Springfield Cres
Bedworth CV12 39 D1
Sutton Coldfield B76 13 D2
Springfield Gr CV33 147 D3
Springfield House
Specl Sch B93 73 D3
Springfield Pl CV1 151 C4
Springfield Rd
Coventry CV1 151 C4
Hinckley LE10 31 E4
Nuneaton CV11 29 F1
Shipston-on-S CV36 149 F2
Sutton Coldfield B76 13 D2
Tamworth B77 9 E4
Springfields B46 33 F3
Springfields Rd B49 143 D3
Springhill CV10 28 A4
Springs Cres CV33 147 D3
Springside B98 103 E4
Springwell Rd 6 CV31 110 B3
Spruce B77 4 A2
Spruce Gr CV31 109 F3
Squadron Cl B35 22 B2
Square La CV7 37 D1
Square The Dunchurch CV22 99 E2
Ettington CV37 131 A3
Fazeley B78 9 D4
Kenilworth CV8 92 C2
Nuneaton CV11 29 F1
Stockton CV33 147 F4
Swalcliffe OX15 142 F8
Tysoe CV35 138 B7
Wolvey LE10 41 E2
Wootton Wawen B95 113 A3
Squire Pl CV33 133 D7
Squires Croft Coventry CV2 50 C1
Sutton Coldfield B76 13 D1
Squires Gate Wlk B35 22 A2
Squires Gn LE10 31 F3
Squires Rd CV23 96 C3
Squires Way CV4 76 B3
Squirrel Hollow B76 13 D1
Spring La CV8 93 D3
Stable Wlk CV11 29 F1

Stableford Cl B97 .... 102 B4
Stacey Ct CV22 .... 99 E3
Stadium Cl CV6 .... 49 E1
Stafford Cl CV12 .... 40 B1
Stafford St CV9 .... 18 C4
Staines Cl CV11 .... 29 F4
Stainforth Cl CV11 .... 30 A1
Stainsby Croft B90 .... 71 D3
Staircase La CV5 .... 60 B4
Stamford Ave CV3 .... 77 E3
Stamford Gdns CV32 .... 105 E1
Stanbrook Rd B90 .... 71 D3
Stand St CV34 .... 108 B3
Standard Ave CV4 .... 60 A1
Standedge B77 .... 10 A4
Standish Cl CV2 .... 62 C1
Standlake Mews **23** CV31 . 110 B3
Stanford Cl B97 .... 102 A3
Stanier Ave CV1 .... 61 D2
Stanley Ct CV31 .... 110 B4
Stanley Rd Atherstone CV9 .. 18 B4
  Coventry CV5 .... 76 C4
  Nuneaton CV11 .... 29 D3
  Rugby CV21 .... 83 F1
Stannells Cl CV37 .... 129 E8
Stansfield Gr CV8 .... 93 E2
Stanton Bridge Prim Sch
  CV6 .... 61 F3
Stanton Rd **13** CV31 .... 110 B3
Stanton Wlk CV34 .... 104 B1
Stanway Rd CV5 .... 77 D4
Stapenhall Rd B90 .... 71 D3
Stapledon Gn CV33 .... 132 F7
Staples Cl CV12 .... 40 B2
Stapleton Cl Studley B80 ... 103 E2
  Sutton Coldfield B76 .... 22 A3
Stapleton Dr B37 .... 33 D2
Stapleton La CV13 .... 21 F4
Stapleton Rd B80 .... 103 E2
Star Cnr CV23 .... 101 E1
Star Ind Pk CV2 .... 62 C3
Star La CV35 .... 114 A4
Starbold Cres B93 .... 72 A3
Starbold Rd CV33 .... 124 A4
Starcross Cl CV2 .... 62 B4
Stare Gn CV4 .... 76 B3
Stareton Cl CV4 .... 76 C3
Starkey Croft B37 .... 33 E1
Starley Pk CV7 .... 50 A4
Starley Rd CV1 .... 151 A2
Starley Way B37 .... 44 B3
Starmer Pl CV35 .... 114 D6
Startin Cl CV7 .... 49 F4
Station App Dorridge B93 .. 71 F1
  Royal Leamington Spa CV31 .109 F4
Station Ave Coventry CV4 ... 75 E4
  Warwick CV34 .... 108 C4
Station Dr B94 .... 69 E1
Station La B94 .... 89 E2
Station Rd Alcester B49 .... 143 D2
  Arley CV7 .... 36 B4
  Balsall Common CV7 .... 74 A4
  Birmingham B37 .... 44 A4
  Bishops Itchington CV33 .... 124 A4
  Chipping Campden GL55 .... 135 C2
  Claverdon CV35 .... 114 A3
  Clifton u D CV23 .... 83 F3
  Coleshill B46 .... 23 F1
  Cropredy OX17 .... 134 C1
  Fenny Compton CV33 .... 133 E7
  Hampton in A B92 .... 57 D4
  Harvington WR11 .... 127 D3
  Hatton CV35 .... 114 C5
  Henley-in-A B95 .... 113 A5
  Higham-on-t-H CV13 .... 20 C2
  Hinckley LE10 .... 31 E4
  Hook Norton OX15 .... 142 E4
  Kenilworth CV8 .... 92 C2
  Knowle B93 .... 72 A2
  Lapworth B94 .... 89 E2
  Long Marston CV37 .... 129 C2
  Moreton-in-M GL56 .... 140 A3
  Polesworth B78 .... 5 D1
  Salford Priors WR11 .... 127 F6
  Shipston-on-S CV36 .... 149 F3
  Shustoke B46 .... 24 B2
  Stockton CV23 .... 116 A3
  Stoke Golding CV13 .... 21 E4
  Stratford-u-A CV37 .... 144 C2
  Studley B80 .... 103 E2
  Warwick CV34 .... 108 C4
  Wilmcote CV37 .... 120 C5
  Wythall B47 .... 69 D2
Station Sq CV1 .... 151 B1
Station St CV9 .... 18 B4
Station St E CV6 .... 61 F4
Station St W CV6 .... 61 F4
Station Way B26 .... 44 B2
Staunton Rd CV31 .... 110 A3
Staveley Rd CV31 .... 83 E3
Staverton CE Prim Sch
  NN11 .... 126 E8
Staverton Cl CV5 .... 60 A2
Staverton Leys CV22 .... 100 A4
Staverton Rd NN11 .... 126 F8
Staverton Sports Ctr NN11 117 F1
Steele St CV22 .... 82 C2
Steels La CV36 .... 141 D7
Steeping Rd CV32 .... 82 A3
Steeplefield Rd CV6 .... 61 D3
Steeples The CV23 .... 116 F5
Stefen Way NN11 .... 126 F8
Stella Croft B37 .... 33 E1
Stennels Cl CV6 .... 60 C4
Stephen St CV21 .... 82 C2

Stephens Rd B76 .... 13 D2
Stephenson Cl
  Daventry NN11 .... 117 F2
  Royal Leamington Spa CV32 . 105 E1
  Tamworth B77 .... 4 A1
Stephenson Dr B37 .... 33 D1
Stephenson Rd
  Bedworth CV7 .... 50 B4
  Hinckley LE10 .... 30 C4
Stepney Rd CV2 .... 62 A2
Steppes Piece B50 .... 148 B3
Stepping Stones Rd CV5 .... 60 C2
Sterling Way CV11 .... 39 F4
Stevenage Wlk **2** CV2 .... 63 A4
Stevenson Rd CV6 .... 61 D4
Stewart Cl CV4 .... 60 B1
Stewart St CV11 .... 29 E2
Stidfall Gr CV31 .... 110 B3
Stileman Cl CV37 .... 129 D2
Stiper's Hill B78 .... 5 D1
Stirling Ave CV32 .... 106 A3
Stirling Cl CV3 .... 78 C4
Stirling St OX16 .... 139 F3
Stirling Rd B90 .... 70 C4
Stivichall Croft CV3 .... 77 D3
Stivichall Prim Sch CV3 .. 77 D3
Stocking La OX15 .... 138 E5
Stocking Mdw CV23 .... 53 F2
Stockingford Fst &
  Mid Sch CV10 .... 28 B2
Stocks La CV23 .... 98 C2
Stockton Cl Birmingham B36 . 22 B3
  Knowle B93 .... 72 A2
Stockton Gr **1** CV32 .... 106 A1
Stockton Prim Sch CV23 . 147 F4
Stockton Rd Coventry CV1 . 151 D4
  Long Itchington CV23 .... 115 E3
Stockwells GL56 .... 140 A3
Stoke Gn CV3 .... 62 A1
Stoke Heath Prim Sch
  CV2 .... 62 A3
Stoke La CV11 .... 21 F4
Stoke Park Sch &
  Com Coll CV2 .... 62 A2
Stoke Prim Sch CV2 .... 62 A2
Stoke Rd Fenny Drayton
  CV13 .... 20 C4
  Stoke Golding CV13 .... 21 F3
Stoke Row CV2 .... 62 A2
Stokesay Cl CV11 .... 29 D2
Stone Ave B75 .... 13 D3
Stone Bridge GL56 .... 140 D7
Stone Cross B46 .... 23 D2
Stone Ct OX7 .... 142 A2
Stone Pits Mdw CV37 .... 120 C5
Stonebow Ave CV37 .... 71 D4
Stonebridge Highway CV3 . 77 F2
Stonebridge Rd Coleshill
  B46 .... 33 F3
  Lighthorne Heath CV35 ..... 123 C3
  Little Packington B46 .... 45 D4
  Long Itchington CV23 .... 115 B4
Stonebridge Trad Est CV3 . 78 A2
Stonebrook Way CV6 .... 49 F2
Stonebury Ave CV5 .... 59 F2
Stonefield Cl CV2 .... 63 D4
Stonehaven Dr CV3 .... 77 E2
Stonehill Croft B90 .... 70 C3
Stonehill Wlk B77 .... 9 F3
Stonehills CV21 .... 83 E4
Stonehouse Cl CV32 .... 106 B3
Stonehouse La CV3 .... 78 B2
Stoneleigh Ave CV8 .... 93 D3
Stoneleigh Rd Hartshill CV10 . 19 D1
  Redditch B98 .... 102 C3
  Stoneleigh CV8 .... 94 B3
Stoneleigh Rd
  Blackdown CV32 .... 106 A4
  Coventry CV4 .... 76 C1
  Kenilworth CV8 .... 93 D3
  Stoneleigh CV8 .... 94 A2
Stonely Rd CV13 .... 21 E3
Stonepits La B97 .... 102 B2
Stoneton Cl CV33 .... 147 E2
Stoneton Cres CV7 .... 74 A3
Stoneway NN11 .... 126 F5
Stoneway Gr **11** CV31 .... 110 B3
Stonewell Cres CV11 .... 40 A4
Stoney Ct CV3 .... 79 D4
Stoney La CV35 .... 114 C6
Stoney Rd Coventry CV1 ... 151 B1
  Nuneaton CV10, CV11 .... 29 D3
Stoney Stanton Rd
  CV1, CV6 .... 61 F3
Stoneydelph Inf Sch B77 ... 4 A1
Stoneydelph Jun Sch B77 .... 4 A1
Stoneymoor Dr B36 .... 22 B1
Stoneywood Rd CV2 .... 62 C4
Stonleigh Ave CV5 .... 76 C4
Stonydelph La B77 .... 10 A4
Stornoway Rd B35 .... 22 A2
Storrage La B48 .... 85 D2
Stour B77 .... 10 A3
Stour Ct CV36 .... 149 F3
Stour Valley Com Sch
  CV36 .... 149 F3
Stour View CV36 .... 137 A8
Stourton Cl B93 .... 72 A4
Stow Rd GL56 .... 140 A3
Stowe Dr CV31 .... 147 D2
Stowe Pl CV4 .... 59 E1
Strachey Ave CV32 .... 105 F1
Straight Mile CV23 .... 98 A3
Stratford Ave CV9 .... 18 B4
Stratford Cty Prim Sch
  CV37 .... 144 C1
Stratford Rd Alcester B49 . 143 D2
  Bidford-on-A B50 .... 128 D7

Stratford Rd continued
  Dorridge B94 .... 71 D2
  Drayton OX15 .... 139 F4
  Hampton Lucy CV35 .... 121 E4
  Hampton Lucy CV35 .... 121 F2
  Henley-in-A B95 .... 113 A3
  Hockley Heath B94 .... 88 B3
  Ilmington CV36 .... 136 B7
  Lighthorne Heath CV35 ..... 123 D2
  Loxley CV35 .... 130 F8
  Mickleton GL55 .... 135 B7
  Newbold-on-S CV37 .... 130 E1
  Shenington OX15 .... 138 F7
  Shipston-on-S CV36 .... 149 F3
  Solihull B90 .... 70 B4
  Temple Grafton B49 .... 119 E3
  Warwick CV34 .... 108 B2
  Wellesbourne CV35 .... 146 A2
  Wroxton OX15 .... 139 C4
Stratford Coventry CV2 ..... 62 A4
  Nuneaton CV11 .... 29 E2
Stratford-upon-Avon Coll
  CV37 .... 144 C2
Stratford-upon-Avon
  Gram Sch For Girls CV37 144 B1
Stratford-upon-Avon
  High Sch CV37 .... 144 C2
Stratford-upon-Avon
  Hospl CV37 .... 144 C2
Stratford-upon-Avon
  Racecourse CV37 .... 129 E8
Stratford-upon-Avon Sta
  CV37 .... 144 C2
Strathearn Rd CV32 .... 105 F1
Strathmore Ave CV1 .... 61 F1
Strathmore Rd LE10 .... 31 D4
Strawberry Fields CV7 .... 46 A1
Strawberry Wlk CV2 .... 50 B1
Streamside Cl CV5 .... 60 A4
Stretton Ave CV3 .... 78 B3
Stretton Cl LE10 .... 31 E3
Stretton Cres CV31 .... 110 A3
Stretton Ct Hinckley LE10 ... 31 E2
  Rugby CV21 .... 83 E4
Stretton Rd Nuneaton CV10 . 29 D2
  Solihull B90 .... 70 A4
  Wolston CV8 .... 80 A1
Stroma Way CV10 .... 28 C1
Strutt Rd LE10 .... 32 A3
Stuart Cl CV34 .... 108 B3
Stuart Ct CV6 .... 62 A4
Stuart Gdns CV33 .... 132 F7
Stubbs Cl CV12 .... 39 D2
Stubbs Gr CV2 .... 62 A3
Studland Ave CV21 .... 83 F1
Studland Gn CV2 .... 63 D2
Studley Cty Inf Sch B80 .. 103 F2
Studley High Sch B80 ..... 103 F2
Studley Rd B98 .... 103 D4
Sturley Cl CV8 .... 93 D3
Sturminster Cl CV2 .... 63 D2
Styles Cl CV31 .... 110 A4
Stychbrook Ave CV5 .... 77 D4
Sudbury Cl CV32 .... 106 B2
Sudeley B77 .... 9 E4
Sudeley Cl B36 .... 22 A1
Sudeley Rd CV10 .... 39 E4
Suffolk Cl Bedworth CV12 .. 39 D2
  Coventry CV5 .... 60 A2
  Nuneaton CV10 .... 28 C2
Suffolk St CV32 .... 106 A1
Sugarswell La OX15 .... 138 D7
Sulgrave Cl CV2 .... 62 C4
Sullivan Rd CV6 .... 62 A4
Sumburgh Croft B35 .... 22 A2
Summer La B76 .... 22 B3
Summerhouse Cl B97 .... 102 A3
Summerton Rd CV31 .... 110 A2
Sumner Cl CV35 .... 114 F3
Sumner Rd B46 .... 34 A3
Sun Rising Hill OX15 .... 132 D1
Sun St CV21 .... 83 E2
Sunbeam Cl B36 .... 22 C1
Sunbury Rd CV3 .... 78 B3
Suncliffe Dr CV8 .... 93 D1
Sunderland Pl CV35 .... 146 B1
Sundew Cl CV2 .... 50 B1
Sundorne Cl CV5 .... 60 A2
Sunningdale B77 .... 4 B3
Sunningdale Ave
  Coventry CV6 .... 49 E1
  Kenilworth CV8 .... 93 D2
Sunningdale Cl CV11 .... 30 A1
Sunnybank Ave CV3 .... 78 A3
Sunnydale Cres LE10 .... 31 D4
Sunnydale Rd LE10 .... 30 C4
Sunnyhill LE10 .... 31 F4
Sunnyhill S LE10 .... 31 F3
Sunnyside B95 .... 119 F7
Sunnyside Cl
  Balsall Common CV7 .... 74 B4
  Coventry CV5 .... 60 C2
Sunnyside La CV7 .... 74 B4
Sunset Cl B78 .... 11 D4
Sunshine Cl CV8 .... 93 D1
Sunway Gr CV3 .... 77 D3
Surrey Cl Hinckley LE10 ..... 31 F2
  Nuneaton CV10 .... 28 C2
Sussex Cl CV10 .... 28 C2
Sussex Rd CV5 .... 60 C2
Sutcliffe Ave CV37 .... 130 D3
Sutcliffe Dr CV33 .... 123 E6
Sutherland Ave CV5 .... 60 A4
Sutherland Cl CV34 .... 104 C1
Sutherland Dr CV12 .... 39 D2
Sutton Ave CV5 .... 59 E2
Sutton Cl NN11 .... 134 F6
Sutton La OX15 .... 137 E1

Sutton Rd B78 .... 8 A4
Sutton Sq B76 .... 22 C3
Sutton Stop CV6 .... 50 A3
Swadling St CV31 .... 109 F3
Swain Crofts CV31 .... 110 A3
Swains Gn LE10 .... 31 F3
Swalcliffe St OX15 .... 142 F8
Swale Rd B76 .... 13 D1
Swallow Ave B36 .... 33 D4
Swallow Cl CV37 .... 145 D3
Swallow Rd CV6 .... 49 E1
Swallowdean Rd CV6 .... 60 C4
Swallows' Mdw B90 .... 70 B4
Swan Cl GL56 .... 140 A3
Swan Cr CV37 .... 145 D1
Swan La CV2 .... 61 F2
Swan St Alcester B49 .... 143 D2
  Royal Leamington Spa CV32 106 A1
  Warwick CV34 .... 108 C3
Swan's Nest CV37 .... 145 D1
Swanage Gn CV2 .... 63 D2
Swancroft Rd CV2 .... 62 A3
Swanfold CV37 .... 120 C5
Swans Cl CV37 .... 120 C5
Swanswell St CV1 .... 151 C4
Swanswood Gr **3** B37 ...... 33 E2
Swerford Rd OX15 .... 142 D3
Swift Cl B36 .... 33 D4
Swift Rd CV37 .... 145 D3
Swift Valley Ind Est CV21 ... 82 C4
Swift's Cnr CV3 .... 77 F4
Swillington Rd CV6 .... 61 D3
Swinburne Ave CV2 .... 62 B1
Swinburne Cl CV10 .... 28 A3
Swinburne Rd B97 .... 102 B4
Swindale B77 .... 10 A4
Swindale Croft CV3 .... 78 C4
Swinford Gr B93 .... 71 F2
Swinford Rd
  Lutterworth LE17 .... 68 C4
  Shawell LE17 .... 68 B3
Swinnerton Mid Sch CV1 .. 29 E1
Swiss Lodge Dr B78 .... 8 C4
Sycamore B77 .... 9 F4
Sycamore Ave B78 .... 11 D4
Sycamore Cl Hinckley LE10 ... 31 F3
  Sibford Gower OX15 .... 142 D8
  Stockton CV23 .... 147 F4
  Stratford-u-A CV37 .... 144 C3
  Wellesbourne CV35 .... 146 C2
Sycamore Cres Arley CV7 .. 37 D4
  Birmingham B37 .... 44 A4
Sycamore Dr B47 .... 69 D3
Sycamore Gr Rugby CV21 .. 83 D2
  Southam CV33 .... 147 D3
  Warwick CV34 .... 105 D1
Sycamore Rd Coventry CV2 . 50 A1
  Kingsbury B78 .... 15 E3
  Nuneaton CV10 .... 28 B3
Sycamores The CV12 .... 38 C1
Sydenham Dr CV31 .... 110 A3
Sydenham Ind Est CV31 ... 110 A3
Sydenham Prim Sch
  CV31 .... 110 B3
Sydnall Fields CV6 .... 49 F2
Sydnall Rd CV6 .... 49 F2
Sykesmoor B77 .... 10 A4
Sylvan Dr CV3 .... 76 C3
Synkere Cl CV7 .... 49 D3
Sywell Leys CV22 .... 99 F3
Table Oak La CV8 .... 74 A1
Tachbrook Cl CV2 .... 50 B1
Tachbrook Park Dr CV34 ... 109 F3
Tachbrook Rd CV31 .... 109 F3
Tachbrook St CV31 .... 110 A3
Tackford Cl B36 .... 22 B1
Tackford Rd CV6 .... 62 A4
Tackley Cl B90 .... 70 A4
Tailor's La CV37 .... 129 D1
Tainters Hill CV8 .... 93 D3
Talbot Cl OX16 .... 139 F4
Talbot Rd CV37 .... 145 D2
Talisman Cl CV8 .... 92 C2
Talisman Sq CV8 .... 92 C2
Talland Ave CV6 .... 62 A3
Tallants Cl CV6 .... 62 A4
Tallants Rd CV6 .... 62 A4
Talton Cl B90 .... 71 D3
Tamar Cl CV23 .... 82 A3
Tamar Dr B76 .... 22 A4
Tamar Rd Bulkington CV12 . 40 A1
  Tamworth B77 .... 10 A3
Tame Bank B78 .... 15 E3
Tame Valley Bsns Ctr B77 .... 9 F3
Tame Valley Ind Est B77 ...... 9 F4
Tame Way LE10 .... 31 D4
Tameside Dr B35 .... 22 A1
Tamworth Bsns Ctr B77 .... 4 A2
Tamworth Bsns Pk B77 .... 4 A2
Tamworth Rd Cliff B78 .... 9 E1
  Corley CV7 .... 37 D1
  Fillongley CV7 .... 36 B3
  Keresley CV6, CV7 .... 48 B3
  Kingsbury B78 .... 15 E4
  Polesworth B78 .... 4 C1
  Sutton Coldfield B75 .... 7 D1
  Tamworth B77 .... 9 E4
Tamworth Rd (Dosthill)
  B77 .... 9 E3
Tangmere Dr B35 .... 22 A2
Tanhill B77 .... 10 A4
Tankards Hill GL56 .... 136 B1
Tanners Green La B47 .... 69 D1
Tanners' La CV4, CV7 .... 59 D1
Tannery Cl CV9 .... 18 C4
Tansley Cl B93 .... 71 F2

Tanwood Cl Redditch B97 ... 102 A3
  Solihull B90 .... 71 D4
Tanworth La
  Henley-in-A B95 .... 113 A7
  Redditch B98 .... 112 B8
  Solihull B90 .... 70 B3
Tanworth-in-Arden
  CE Sch B94 .... 87 D1
Tanyard Cl CV4 .... 59 E1
Tapcon Way CV2 .... 62 C3
Tappinger Gr CV8 .... 93 E3
Tapster La B94 .... 88 C1
Tarlington Rd CV6 .... 60 C3
Tarn Cl CV12 .... 39 D1
Tarquin Cl CV3 .... 78 B4
Tarragon Cl CV2 .... 50 B1
Tarrant B77 .... 9 F4
Tarrant Wlk CV2 .... 63 D3
Tatnall Gr CV34 .... 108 C4
Tattle Bank CV33 .... 147 D2
Taunton Way CV6 .... 49 D1
Tavern La CV37 .... 144 B1
Taverners La CV9 .... 18 B4
Tavistock St CV32 .... 105 F1
Tavistock Way CV11 .... 29 F3
Tavistock Wlk CV2 .... 62 B4
Tay Croft B37 .... 33 E2
Tay Rd CV6 .... 61 D3
Taylor Ave CV32 .... 106 A1
Taylor Cl CV8 .... 93 D3
Tea Gdn The CV12 .... 49 F4
Teachers Cl CV6 .... 61 D3
Teal Bsns Ctr LE10 .... 30 B4
Teal Cl CV37 .... 144 B3
Teal Rd B80 .... 103 F2
Teasel Cl CV23 .... 83 E4
Ted Pitts La CV5 .... 48 A1
Teign B77 .... 10 A3
Telegraph St CV36 .... 149 F3
Telephone Rd CV3 .... 62 B1
Telfer Rd CV6 .... 61 D4
Telford Ave CV32 .... 106 A3
Telford Cty Fst & Mid Sch
  CV32 .... 106 B3
Telford Rd CV7 .... 50 B4
Templar Ave CV4 .... 60 A1
Templars' Fields CV4 .... 76 A4
Templars Prim Sch CV4 ... 60 A1
Templars The CV34 .... 108 C3
Temple Ave CV7 .... 73 F3
Temple End CV33 .... 123 E6
Temple Gr CV34 .... 108 B3
Temple Grafton
  CE Prim Sch B49 .... 119 E1
Temple Hill LE10 .... 41 F3
Temple La B93 .... 73 D2
Temple Rd B93 .... 72 A2
Temple St CV21 .... 83 E1
Temple Way B46 .... 23 F1
Templeton Cl B93 .... 72 A2
Ten Acres B49 .... 143 E2
Tenby Cl CV12 .... 38 B1
Teneriffe Rd CV6 .... 49 F1
Tenlons Rd CV10 .... 28 C1
Tennant St CV11 .... 29 F2
Tennyson Ave Rugby CV22 . 99 F4
  Warwick CV34 .... 108 B2
Tennyson Cl CV8 .... 93 E2
Tennyson Rd Coventry CV2 . 62 B2
  Redditch B97 .... 102 B4
  Stratford-u-A CV37 .... 130 A8
Terrace Rd CV9 .... 18 B4
Terrett Cl CV37 .... 145 D1
Terry Ave CV32 .... 105 E1
Terry Rd CV1 .... 61 F1
Tewkesbury Dr CV12 .... 39 E2
Thackeray Cl
  Lower Quinton CV37 .... 129 D2
  Nuneaton CV10 .... 28 A2
  Rugby CV22 .... 99 F4
Thackhall St CV2 .... 61 F2
Thames Cl CV12 .... 40 A2
Thames Rd NN11 .... 117 F1
Thamley Rd CV6 .... 61 D2
Thatchers Cl OX15 .... 138 D3
Theatre St CV34 .... 108 C4
Thebes Cl CV5 .... 59 D4
Theddingworth Cl CV3 .... 78 C4
Thickthorn Cl CV8 .... 93 D1
Thickthorn Orchs CV8 .... 93 D1
Thimble End Rd B76 .... 13 D1
Thimbler Rd CV4 .... 76 B4
Third Exhibition Ave B40 ... 44 B2
Thirlestane Cl CV8 .... 93 E3
Thirlmere CV21 .... 83 E4
Thirlmere Ave CV11 .... 29 F3
Thirlmere Cl CV4 .... 59 F2
Thirlmere Rd Bedworth
  CV12 .... 39 D1
  Hinckley LE10 .... 31 D4
Thirsk Rd CV3 .... 77 F3
Thistle Way CV23 .... 83 E4
Thistledown Gr B93 .... 90 A3
Thistley Field E CV6 .... 61 D4
Thistley Field N CV6 .... 61 D4
Thistley Field S CV6 .... 60 C4
Thistley Field W CV6 .... 60 C4
Thomas Jolyffe
  Cty Prim Sch CV37 .... 145 D3
Thomas Landsdail St CV3 .. 77 D4
Thomas Lane St CV6 .... 50 A1
Thomas Naul Croft CV4 ...... 59 F2
Thomas Sharp St CV4 .... 76 A4
Thomas St Bedworth CV12 . 39 D2
  Royal Leamington Spa CV32 106 A1
Thomas Way CV23 .... 82 A3
Thomas Wlk B35 .... 22 A2
Thompson's Rd CV7 .... 48 C3

Thomson Cl CV21 .... 83 D3
Thorn Cl CV21 .... 83 E3
Thorn Stile Cl CV32 .... 106 C3
Thorn Way CV23 .... 115 D4
Thornby Ave Kenilworth
  CV8 .... 93 D2
  Tamworth B77 .... 9 F4
Thorncliffe Cl B97 .... 102 A3
Thorncliffe Way CV10 ...... 27 F4
Thorney Rd CV2 .... 62 A3
Thornfield Ave CV13 .... 21 F4
Thornfield Way LE10 ...... 31 F4
Thorngrove Ave 7 B91 .... 71 E4
Thornhill Dr CV11 .... 40 B4
Thornhill Rd CV1 .... 61 E3
Thornley Cl CV31 .... 110 C3
Thornley Gr B76 .... 22 B3
Thorns Cty Fst Sch CV8 .. 93 D2
Thornton Cl Coventry CV5 . 59 E2
  Warwick CV34 .... 104 C1
Thornton Rd B90 .... 70 C3
Thorntons La CV23 .... 125 C7
Thorntons Way CV10 ...... 28 A2
Thornycroft Rd LE10 ...... 31 F4
Thorpe Rd OX17 .... 134 F1
Threadneedle St CV1 ...... 61 E3
Three Cocks La WR11 .... 127 D1
Three Corner Cl B90 ...... 69 F4
Three Cornered Cl CV32 . 106 C3
Three Oaks Rd B47 .... 69 D2
Three Pots Rd LE10 .... 31 F2
Three Shires Jct CV6 ..... 49 F1
Three Spires Ave CV6 ..... 61 D3
Three Spires Ind Est CV6 . 50 A3
Three Spires Sch CV5 ..... 60 B3
Throckmorton Rd
  Alcester B49 .... 143 E2
  Redditch B98 .... 103 D4
Thurlestone Rd CV6 .... 60 C4
Thurlow Cl CV9 .... 12 B1
Thurne B77 .... 9 F4
Thurnmill Rd CV23 .... 82 B2
Thursfield Rd CV32 ...... 106 A2
Tibberton Cl B91 .... 71 D4
Tibbetts Cl B49 .... 143 E2
Tiber Cl CV5 .... 59 F2
Tiber Way CV21 .... 82 C4
Tiberius Cl B46 .... 23 F1
Tidbury Cl B97 .... 102 B3
Tidbury Green Jun &
  Inf Sch B90 .... 69 F2
Tiddington Cl B36 .... 22 A1
Tiddington Rd CV37 ..... 145 E2
Tideswell Cl CV3 .... 63 D1
Tidmarsh Cl CV7 .... 74 A3
Tidmarsh Rd CV35 .... 105 D4
Tidmington Cl CV35 ..... 114 F5
Tile Gr B37 .... 33 D3
Tile Hill Coll of FE CV4 .. 59 F1
Tile Hill La
  Coventry, Allesley CV4, CV5 . 60 B1
  Coventry, Tile Hill CV4 .... 60 A1
Tile Hill Sta CV4 .... 75 E4
Tile Hill Wood Sch CV4 .. 59 E1
Tile Hurst Dr CV4 .... 59 E1
Tilehouse Green La B93 .. 71 F3
Tilehouse La B90 .... 69 F3
Tilemans La CV36 .... 149 F4
Tilesford Cl B90 .... 71 D3
Tilewood Ave CV5 .... 59 F2
Tilia Rd B77 .... 4 A3
Tilton Rd LE10 .... 31 F3
Timberlake Cl 10 B90 .... 71 D3
Timothy Gr CV4 .... 60 A1
Timothy's Bridge Rd CV37 144 B2
Timsa Rd CV35 .... 132 E5
Tink-A-Tank CV34 .... 108 C4
Tinkers Green Rd B77 ...... 9 F3
Tinkers La Earlswood B94 .. 87 F4
  Lapworth B94 .... 88 C1
  Mollington OX17 .... 133 F2
Tintagel Cl CV3 .... 78 B3
Tintagel Gr CV8 .... 93 D2
Tintagel Way CV11 .... 30 A3
Tintern Way CV12 .... 39 E2
Tipper's Hill La CV7 ...... 36 C3
Tippett Cl CV11 .... 40 A4
Tipping's Hill B97 .... 102 B3
Tisdale Rise CV8 .... 93 D3
Tite La OX15 .... 142 D4
Tithe Barn Cl CV35 ...... 114 F4
Tithe Barn La B94 .... 87 E3
Tithe Cl CV13 .... 21 E3
Tithe Ct WR11 .... 127 F2
Titheway WR11 .... 127 F2
Tithings The OX15 ...... 142 F8
Tiverton Dr CV11 .... 29 F3
Tiverton Gr CV2 .... 62 B3
Tiverton Rd CV2 .... 62 B3
Tiverton Sch CV6 .... 60 B3
Tiveycourt Rd CV6 .... 50 A2
Tocil Croft CV4 .... 76 B2
Toft Hill CV23 .... 99 D1
Tokchong Rd CV35 ...... 132 E5
Toler Rd CV11 .... 29 D3
Toll Gate Cl CV37 .... 144 A2
Toll Gate Rd CV33 ...... 147 D3
Tollard Cl CV2 .... 62 C3
Tolson Ave B78 .... 9 D4
Tolson Cl B77 .... 9 E3
Tom Brown St CV21 ...... 83 E2
Tom Henderson Cl CV3 .. 78 C4
Tom Hill B94 .... 87 D2
Tom Ward Cl CV3 .... 78 C4
Tomkinson Rd CV10 ...... 28 C2
Tomlinson Rd B36 .... 22 B1
Tommy's Turn La OX15 . 137 E1
Tompson Cl NN11 .... 117 E5

Toms Town La B80 ...... 103 F2
Tomson Ave CV6 .... 61 D2
Tomwell Cl CV33 .... 147 D3
Tonbridge Rd CV3 .... 78 A3
Top Rd CV7 .... 51 D4
Top St DE12 .... 3 F1
Topcliffe Jun & Inf Sch
  B35 .... 22 A2
Topp's Dr CV12 .... 38 C1
Topp's Heath CV12 .... 38 C1
Torbay Rd CV5 .... 60 B2
Torcastle Cl CV6 .... 61 F4
Torcross Ave CV2 .... 62 B3
Torpoint Cl CV2 .... 62 B4
Torrance Rd CV21 .... 82 C2
Torridge B77 .... 10 A3
Torrington Ave CV4 .... 75 F4
Torside B77 .... 10 A4
Torwood Cl CV4 .... 75 F3
Totnes Cl CV2 .... 62 B4
Tove Ct CV23 .... 82 A3
Towbury Cl B98 .... 102 C3
Tower Croft
  Bidford-on-A B50 .... 148 C3
  Birmingham B37 .... 33 D2
Tower Hill B50 .... 148 C3
Tower Rd Bedworth CV12 . 39 D1
  Rugby CV22 .... 83 E1
Tower St Coventry CV1 .. 151 B3
  5 Royal Leamington Spa
  CV31 .... 110 A4
Tower View Cres CV10 ... 28 A2
Towers Cl CV8 .... 92 C1
Town Feilds Cl CV5 .... 60 A4
Town Ground CV35 ..... 131 F5
Town Yd CV23 .... 64 C2
Townesend Cl CV34 .... 104 C1
Townhill OX15 .... 133 A2
Townsend Cl B79 .... 2 B2
Townsend Croft CV3 ..... 77 E4
Townsend Dr CV11 .... 29 F2
Townsend La
  Long Lawford CV23 .... 82 A2
  Upper Boddington NN11 .. 134 E8
Townsend Rd Coventry CV3 . 77 E4
  Rugby CV21 .... 83 E2
  Tiddington CV37 .... 145 F2
Townsends Cl CV11 ...... 31 D1
Trafalgar Ct B50 .... 148 B2
Trafford Cl CV9 .... 12 B1
Trafford Dr CV10 .... 28 B3
Traitor's Ford La OX15 . 142 B6
Trajan Hill B46 .... 23 F1
Travellers Way B37 .... 33 E2
Tredington Cl B98 .... 103 D4
Tredington Rd CV5 .... 59 F2
Treedale Cl CV4 .... 75 E4
Trefoil B77 .... 4 A3
Treforest Rd CV3 .... 78 B4
Tregorrick Rd CV7 .... 50 A4
Tregullan Rd CV7 .... 50 A4
Trehern Cl B93 .... 72 A3
Treherne Rd CV6 .... 61 D4
Trelawney Rd CV7 .... 50 A4
Tremelling Way CV7 ...... 36 C4
Trenance Rd CV7 .... 50 A4
Trench La B49 .... 143 F2
Treneere Rd CV7 .... 50 A4
Trensale Ave CV6 .... 60 C2
Trent Rd Bulkington CV12 . 40 A1
  Hinckley LE10 .... 31 D4
  Nuneaton CV11 .... 29 E3
Trent Wlk NN11 .... 117 F1
Trentham Cl CV11 .... 39 F4
Trentham Gdns CV8 ...... 93 E3
Trentham Rd Coventry CV1 . 61 F2
  Hartshill CV10 .... 19 D1
Tresillian Rd CV7 .... 50 A4
Trevelyan Cl Claverdon
  CV35 .... 113 F3
  Stratford-u-A CV37 .... 144 B2
Trevelyan Cres CV37 ... 144 B2
Treviscoe Cl CV7 .... 50 A4
Trevor Cl CV4 .... 75 E4
Trevor White Dr CV22 ... 83 D1
Trevose Ave CV7 .... 50 A4
Trewint Cl CV7 .... 50 A4
Triangle The CV5 .... 60 A2
Tribune Trad Est CV21 .. 83 D3
Trident Bsns Pk CV11 ... 29 E2
Trimpley Cl B93 .... 71 F2
Trinity Cl Banbury OX16 . 139 F4
  Stratford-u-A CV37 .... 145 D1
  Warton B79 .... 5 F2
Trinity La CV1 .... 151 B3
Trinity RC Sch The
  Royal Leamington Spa CV32 . 105 E1
  Warwick CV34 .... 109 E1
Trinity St Kingsbury B78 .. 15 F4
  Wood End B78 .... 10 A2
Trinity St Coventry CV1 . 151 B3
  Royal Leamington Spa CV32 . 105 F1
  Stratford-u-A CV37 .... 145 D1
Trinity Vicarage Rd LE10 . 31 E4
Trinity Wlk CV11 .... 29 F2
Triton Pk CV21 .... 82 C4
Triumph Cl CV2 .... 62 C2
Triumph Wlk B36 .... 23 D1
Trojan Bsns Ctr CV34 .. 109 F2
Troon CV21 .... 4 B2
Trossachs Rd CV5 .... 59 F2
Troubridge Wlk CV22 .... 82 B1
Troughton Cres CV6 ...... 61 D3
Troutbeck Ave CV32 .... 105 E1
Troutbeck Rd CV5 .... 59 F2
Troy Ind Est B96 .... 103 D2

Troyes Cl CV3 .... 77 F4
Trueman Cl CV34 .... 108 C4
Truemans Heath La B47 . 69 E4
Truggist La CV7 .... 74 C4
Truro Cl CV11 .... 29 F3
Truro Wlk B37 .... 33 D1
Trust Cotts B49 .... 118 D8
Tryan Rd CV10 .... 28 C2
Tuckwell Cl CV23 .... 147 F4
Tudman Cl B76 .... 22 A4
Tudor Ave CV5 .... 59 F2
Tudor Cl CV7 .... 74 A3
Tudor Cres CV9 .... 12 B1
Tudor Ct Coventry CV7 .. 49 F4
  Warwick CV34 .... 108 B3
Tudor La CV33 .... 147 D2
Tudor Rd CV10 .... 28 B3
Tuer The WR11 .... 127 A6
Tulip Tree Ave CV8 .... 93 D3
Tulip Wlk B37 .... 44 B4
Tulliver Cl CV12 .... 39 D2
Tulliver Rd CV10 .... 29 E1
Tulliver St CV6 .... 61 D3
Tunnel Rd CV11 .... 27 E2
Turchill Dr B76 .... 22 A4
Turlands Cl CV2 .... 63 D4
Turnberry B77 .... 4 B3
Turnberry Dr CV11 .... 40 B4
Turnberry Dr CV11 .... 40 B4
Turner Cl Bedworth CV12 . 39 D2
  Rugby CV21 .... 101 D4
  Warwick CV34 .... 108 A2
Turnhouse Rd B35 .... 22 A2
Turnpike Dr B46 .... 23 E1
Turpin Ct CV31 .... 109 F3
Turton Way CV8 .... 93 E2
Tutbury B77 .... 9 E4
Tutbury Ave CV4 .... 76 C3
Tutehill B77 .... 10 A4
Tuttle Hill CV10 .... 28 C3
Tuttle Hill Ind Est CV10 . 28 C4
Twenty One Oaks CV9 .. 17 F3
Twycross La CV9 .... 6 C3
Twycross Rd LE10 .... 31 F3
Twycross Zoo CV9 .... 3 F1
Twyford Ctry Ctr WR11 . 127 C1
Tybalt Cl Coventry CV3 .. 78 B3
  Royal Leamington Spa CV34 . 109 E2
Tyler St CV37 .... 145 D2
Tylers Gr B90 .... 70 C3
Tylney Cl CV3 .... 63 D1
Tyne Cl B37 .... 33 E2
Tyne Rd NN11 .... 126 F8
Tynemouth Cl CV2 .... 50 B3
Tyntesfield Specl Sch
  CV22 .... 99 F4
Tynward Cl CV3 .... 77 D3
Tysoe CE Prim Sch CV35 . 138 C2
Tysoe Cl B94 .... 88 B3
Tysoe Croft CV3 .... 78 C4
Tysoe Rd CV35 .... 132 B4
Tythebarn La B90 .... 69 F3
Tything Rd B49 .... 143 E3

Ufton Croft CV5 .... 60 A2
Ufton Fields CV33 ...... 123 F8
Ufton Hill CV33 .... 111 F1
Ullapool Cl B97 .... 102 B3
Ullenhall La B95 .... 112 D6
Ullenhall Rd Knowle B93 . 72 A3
  Ullenhall B95 .... 112 E6
Ullenhall St B95 .... 112 E6
Ullswater B77 .... 10 A4
Ullswater Ave Nuneaton
  CV11 .... 29 F3
  Royal Leamington Spa CV32 . 105 E1
Ullswater Rd Bedworth
  CV12 .... 39 D1
  Coventry CV3 .... 62 C1
Ulverscroft Rd CV3 .... 77 E4
Ulverston CV21 .... 83 E4
Umberslade Rd
  Earlswood B94 .... 87 E4
  Tamworth-in-A B94 .... 87 F2
Underhill Cl Coventry CV3 . 77 E2
  Redditch B98 .... 102 C3
Underpass The B40 .... 44 C2
Underwood Cl B97 ...... 102 A4
Unicorn Ave CV5 .... 59 F2
Unicorn La CV5 .... 59 F2
Union Pl CV6 .... 49 F2
Union Rd CV32 .... 105 F1
Union St Rugby CV22 .... 83 D1
  Stratford-u-A CV37 .... 145 D1
Univ of Warwick CV5 .... 76 B2
Univ of Warwick
  Science Pk CV4 .... 76 A3
Univ of Warwick
  (Westwood) CV4 .... 76 A3
Upavon Cl B35 .... 22 A2
Uplands CV2 .... 62 A3
Upleadon Cl B97 .... 102 A3
Upper Abbey St CV11 ... 29 D3
Upper Crossgate Rd B98 . 103 E4
Upper Eastern Green La
  CV5 .... 59 F3
Upper Grove St 3 CV32 . 105 F1
Upper Hill St CV1 .... 151 A3
Upper Holly Wlk CV32 . 106 A1
Upper Pk CV3 .... 78 B3
Upper Ride CV3 .... 78 B3
Upper Rosemary Hill CV8 . 92 C3
Upper Spon St CV1 .... 61 D2
Upper Well St CV1 ...... 151 B3
Upper York St CV1 .... 61 D1
Upperfield Way CV3 ...... 63 D1

Upton House OX15 ..... 138 E8
Upton La CV13 .... 21 D4
Upton Rd CV22 .... 82 B2
Utrillo Cl CV5 .... 60 B2
Uxbridge Ave CV3 .... 62 B1

Valanders La CV36 ..... 136 B6
Vale Cl CV21 .... 101 D4
Vale The CV3 .... 78 B4
Vale View CV10 .... 28 C2
Valencia Croft B35 .... 22 A2
Valentine Cl CV37 ...... 129 F8
Vallet Ave B49 .... 143 D3
Valletta Way CV35 ..... 146 B1
Valley Cl B97 .... 102 A3
Valley La Lapworth B94 . 89 F4
  Tamworth B77 .... 9 F4
Valley Rd Coventry CV2 . 62 A3
  Earlswood B94 .... 70 A1
  Nuneaton CV10 .... 27 F2
  Radford Semele CV31 .. 110 C2
  Royal Leamington Spa CV32 . 106 B2
Valley The CV31 .... 110 C2
Van Dyke Cl CV5 .... 60 B2
Vanguard B77 .... 9 E3
Vardon Dr CV3 .... 77 E2
Vauxhall 8 CV1 .... 61 F2
Vauxhall Cres B36 .... 22 C1
Vauxhall St CV1 .... 61 F2
Vaynor Dr B97 .... 102 B4
Vaynor Fst Sch The B97 . 102 B4
  Hurley CV9 .... 16 B2
Veasey Cl CV11 .... 29 F2
Vecqueray St CV1 .... 61 F1
Ventnor Cl CV2 .... 62 C2
Ventnor St CV10 .... 29 E3
Venture Ct LE10 .... 30 C4
Verden Ave CV34 .... 108 A2
Verdon Cl CV35 .... 122 B8
Verdun Cl CV31 .... 110 A1
Vere Rd CV21 .... 83 F1
Vermont Gr CV31 .... 110 B3
Verney Cl
  Butlers Marston CV35 . 131 F4
  Lighthorne CV35 .... 123 B2
Verney Dr CV37 .... 144 C3
Verney Gdns CV37 ..... 144 C3
Verney Rd CV35 .... 123 C3
Vernon Ave CV22 .... 100 C4
Vernon Cl 9 Coventry CV1 . 61 F2
  Royal Leamington Spa
  CV32 .... 105 F2
Vernons La CV10, CV11 . 28 C2
Verona Cl CV11 .... 30 A1
Vesey Cl B46 .... 23 F1
Vicarage Cl Atherstone CV9 . 18 C4
  Dordon B78 .... 10 C3
Vicarage Field CV34 ... 109 D4
Vicarage Gdns CV37 ... 134 C1
Vicarage Hill Badby NN11 . 126 F5
  Clifton u D CV23 .... 83 F3
  Middleton B78 .... 14 A4
  Tanworth-in-A B94 .... 86 C2
Vicarage La Coventry CV7 . 49 E4
  Dunchurch CV22 .... 99 E2
  Harbury CV33 .... 123 F6
  Long Compton CV36 ... 141 C3
  Priors Marston CV23 ... 125 F4
  Warwick CV35 .... 108 A1
  Water Orton B46 .... 23 D1
Vicarage Rd
  Cheswick Green B94 ..... 70 B2
  Dorridge B94 .... 88 C4
  Flecknoe CV23 .... 117 B2
  Napton CV23 .... 125 C8
  Royal Leamington Spa
  CV32 .... 106 A2
  Rugby CV22 .... 82 C2
  Stoneleigh CV8 .... 94 A3
Vicarage Rise 8 CV33 .. 122 F8
Vicarage St CV11 .... 29 E2
Victoria Ave CV21 .... 82 C2
Victoria Bsns Ctr 10 CV31 . 110 A4
Victoria Dr B78 .... 9 D4
Victoria Mews CV34 ... 108 B4
Victoria Rd Atherstone CV9 . 18 C3
  Bidford-on-A B50 .... 148 B3
  Hartshill CV10 .... 28 A4
  Hinckley LE10 .... 31 F3
  Royal Leamington Spa
  CV31 .... 109 F4
Victoria St Coventry CV1 . 151 D4
  Nuneaton CV11 .... 29 E2
  Royal Leamington Spa
  CV31 .... 109 F4
  Rugby CV21 .... 82 C2
  Warwick CV34 .... 108 B4
Victoria Terr 11 CV31 .. 109 F4
Victoria Way B50 .... 148 B3
Victory Rd CV6 .... 49 F1
Vilia Cl LE10 .... 31 F2
Villa Cl CV12 .... 40 B1
Villa Cres CV12 .... 40 B1
Villa Rd CV6 .... 61 D3
Village Hall Yd CV23 ... 115 D4
Village Mews CV22 ...... 99 E4
Village St WR11 .... 127 D4
Villiers Rd CV8 .... 93 D3
Villiers St Coventry CV2 . 62 A2
  Nuneaton CV11 .... 29 D2
  Royal Leamington Spa CV32 . 106 A1
Vincent Ave CV37 .... 145 D2
Vincent St Coventry CV1 . 61 D1
  Royal Leamington Spa
  CV32 .... 106 A1
Vine La CV34 .... 108 C4
Vine St CV1 .... 151 C4
Vinecote Rd CV6 .... 49 F2
Vineyard The LE17 .... 43 F3

Upton House OX15 ..... 138 E8

Violet Cl Coventry CV2 ... 50 B2
  Rugby CV23 .... 83 F4
Virginia Pl CV10 .... 28 C2
Virginia Rd CV1 .... 61 F2
Viscount Cl Birmingham
  B35 .... 22 A1
  Royal Leamington Spa CV31 . 109 F3
Vittle Dr CV34 .... 108 B4
Vogue Cl CV1 .... 151 D3
Vulcan Way LE17 .... 55 E4

Wackrill Dr CV32 .... 106 B2
Wade Ave CV3 .... 77 D3
Wade Gr CV34 .... 104 C1
Wade La CV35 .... 123 D2
Wadebridge Dr CV11 .... 29 F3
Waggoner's La B78 .... 7 F4
Waggoners Cl CV8 .... 95 E3
Wagstaffe Cl CV33 ..... 123 E6
Wain Cl B49 .... 143 E3
Wainbody Ave N CV3 .... 77 D3
Wainbody Ave S CV3 .... 76 C3
Wainbody Wood Sch CV5 . 76 B1
Wainrigg B77 .... 10 A4
Wake Gr CV34 .... 108 A3
Wakefield Cl Coventry CV3 . 78 B4
  Hurley CV9 .... 16 B2
Wakefield Gr B46 .... 23 D2
Wakeford Rd CV10 .... 18 A2
Wakehurst Cl CV11 .... 39 F4
Wakelin Rd B90 .... 70 A4
Walcot Gn B93 .... 72 A1
Walcote Cl LE10 .... 30 C4
Walford Gr CV34 .... 104 C1
Walford Pl CV22 .... 100 C4
Walkers Orch CV8 .... 94 A3
Walkers Rd CV37 .... 145 D3
Walkers Way Bedworth
  CV12 .... 38 C2
  Coleshill B46 .... 34 A3
Walkwood CE Mid Sch
  B97 .... 102 B4
Walkwood Cres B97 .... 102 B3
Walkwood Rd B97 ...... 102 B3
Wall Ave B46 .... 33 F3
Wall Hill Rd CV5, CV7 .. 48 A2
Wallace Rd CV6 .... 61 D4
Waller Cl CV35 .... 104 C4
Waller St CV32 .... 106 A1
Wallingford Ave CV11 ... 29 F4
Wallsgrove Cl CV32 ..... 106 A2
Walmer Way B37 .... 33 E2
Walmley Ash La B76 ..... 22 B3
Walmley Ash Rd B76 .... 22 A4
Walmley Jun & Inf Schs
  B76 .... 22 A4
Walnut Cl Birmingham B37 . 33 D1
  Braunston NN11 .... 117 E5
  Hartshill CV10 .... 28 A4
  Harvington WR11 .... 127 D3
  Nuneaton CV10 .... 28 C3
Walnut Croft CV9 .... 17 E4
Walnut Dr CV32 .... 106 A2
Walnut Paddocks CV35 . 138 B6
Walnut St CV2 .... 50 A1
Walnut Tree Cl CV8 ...... 93 D2
Walnut Way CV22 .... 82 A1
Walsal End La B92 .... 56 C2
Walsall St CV4 .... 76 A4
Walsgrave CE Prim Sch
  CV3 .... 63 D3
Walsgrave Gdns 5 CV2 . 63 D4
Walsgrave Rd CV2 .... 62 A2
Walsh La CV7 .... 46 C1
Walsingham Dr CV10 ... 39 E1
Walter Scott Rd CV12 ... 39 E1
Waltham Cres CV10 ...... 28 A3
Walton Cl Coventry CV3 . 78 C4
  Nuneaton CV11 .... 40 A4
Walton Rd
  Hampton Lucy CV35 ... 121 F4
  Wellesbourne CV35 .... 146 C1
Walton W ay CV35 ...... 146 B1
Wandsbeck B77 .... 9 F4
Wanley Rd CV3 .... 77 E3
Wansfell Cl CV4 .... 76 A4
Wantage Rd B46 .... 23 F1
Wappenbury Cl CV2 ..... 50 B1
Wappenbury Rd CV2 ..... 50 B1
Wapping La B98 .... 112 A7
Ward Gr CV34 .... 109 E4
Warden Rd CV6 .... 61 D3
Wardens Ave The CV5 ... 60 A3
Wardens The CV8 .... 93 E3
Wardour Dr B37 .... 33 E1
Ware Orch CV23 .... 101 E1
Ware Rd CV23 .... 101 E1
Wareham Gn CV2 .... 63 D3
Waring Way CV22 .... 99 E2
Warings Green Rd B94 .. 70 B1
Warkworth Cl OX16 .... 139 F4
Warmington Cl CV3 ...... 78 C4
Warmington Gr CV34 .. 108 A4
Warmington Rd B47 ..... 69 D3
Warmwell Cl CV2 .... 62 C2
Warneford Pl GL56 ..... 140 A3
Warner Cl CV34 .... 104 B1
Warner Row CV6 .... 61 F4
Warren Cl CV32 .... 106 A2
Warren Dr B93 .... 72 A2
Warren Field CV23 .... 79 D1
Warren Gn CV4 .... 75 F4
Warren Rd CV22 .... 83 E1
Warren Cl CV8 .... 93 E2
Warton Cl CV8 .... 93 E2

Warton La Austrey CV9 .... **3** D1
Orton-on-t-H CV9 .... **6** B2
Warton B79 .... **5** F4
Warton Nethersole
CE Fst Sch B79 .... **5** F2
Warwick Ave CV5 .... **77** D4
Warwick By-Pass
Warwick, Hampton Magna
CV35 .... **108** A3
Warwick, Heathcote CV34 ..... **109** D1
Warwick Castle CV34 .... **108** C3
Warwick Cl B80 .... **103** E2
Warwick Cres CV37 .... **145** D2
Warwick Ct CV37 .... **145** D2
Warwick Dr CV9 .... **12** B1
Warwick Gdns CV10 .... **28** C2
Warwick Gn CV12 .... **40** B1
Warwick Highway
Redditch B98 .... **102** C4
Redditch B80 .... **112** A5
Warwick Hospl CV34 .... **108** C4
Warwick La CV1 .... **151** B2
Warwick Mus CV34 .... **108** C4
Warwick New Rd CV32 ...... **109** E4
Warwick Pl
Royal Leamington Spa CV32 . **105** F1
Shipston-on-S CV36 .... **149** F3
Southam CV33 .... **147** D2
Warwick Rd
Chadwick End B93 .... **90** A4
Coventry CV3 .... **151** B1
Ettington CV37 .... **131** A4
Hanwell OX17 .... **139** F5
Henley-in-A B95 .... **113** C4
Kenilworth CV8 .... **93** D1
Kineton CV35 .... **132** B6
Knowle B93 .... **72** B2
Leek Wootton CV35 .... **104** C4
Norton Lindsey CV35 .... **114** C2
Sherbourne CV35 .... **121** E7
Snitterfield CV37 .... **121** C5
Southam CV33 .... **147** D2
Stratford-u-A CV37 .... **145** E3
Upper Boddington NN11 ...... **134** E8
Wellesbourne CV35 .... **146** B2
Wolston CV8 .... **80** A2
Warwick Row CV1 .... **151** B2
Warwick Sch CV34 .... **109** D3
Warwick St Coventry CV5 .. **60** C1
Royal Leamington Spa CV32 . **105** F1
Southam CV33 .... **147** D2
Warwick St Mary's
RC Prim Sch CV34 .... **108** C4
Warwick Sta CV34 .... **108** C4
Warwick Tech Pk CV34 ..... **109** D3
Warwick Terr CV32 .... **105** F1
Warwicks The CV35 .... **114** F3
Warwickshire Coll CV32 ... **109** E4
Warwickshire Coll of Ag
CV11 .... **29** F3
Warwickshire Mus CV34 ... **108** C3
Warwickshire Nuffield
Hospl The CV32 .... **105** F3
Wasdale Cl CV32 .... **105** E1
Washbourne Rd CV31 .... **110** A1
Washbrook La CV5 .... **48** A1
Washbrook Pl CV36 .... **136** B6
Washford Dr B98 .... **103** E4
Washford Ind Est B98 .... **103** F4
Washford La B98 .... **103** E4
Wasperton Cl CV3 .... **78** C4
Wasperton La CV35 .... **122** C7
Waste La Baddesley Ensor
CV9 .... **11** F1
Balsall Common CV7 .... **74** C3
Coventry CV7 .... **48** C1
Watch Cl CV1 .... **151** A3
Watchbury Cl B36 .... **22** B1
Watchmaker Ct CV1 .... **151** A2
Watcombe Rd CV2 .... **62** C4
Water La CV35 .... **131** E3
Water Orton La B76 .... **22** C2
Water Orton Prim Sch B46 . **23** D1
Water Orton Rd B36 .... **22** C1
Water Orton Sta B46 .... **23** D2
Water Tower La CV8 .... **92** C3
Watercall Ave CV3 .... **77** E3
Waterdale B90 .... **70** B3
Waterfall Cl CV7 .... **46** B1
Waterfield Gdns CV31 .... **110** B4
Waterfield Way LE10 .... **31** E3
Watergall Cl CV33 .... **147** E2
Waterloo Ave B37 .... **33** D2
Waterloo Cl
Stratford-u-A CV37 .... **130** B8
Wellesbourne CV35 .... **146** B1
Waterloo Cres B50 .... **148** C3
Waterloo Ct CV37 .... **109** D4
Waterloo Dr CV37 .... **145** E1
Waterloo Ind Est
Bidford-on-A B50 .... **148** C3
Birmingham B37 .... **33** D3
Waterloo Pk B50 .... **148** C3
Waterloo Pl [5] CV32 .... **105** F1
Waterloo Rd
Bidford-on-A B50 .... **148** C3
Hinckley LE10 .... **31** E4
Waterloo St [6] Coventry
CV1 .... **61** F2
Royal Leamington Spa CV31 . **110** A4
Waterman Rd CV6 .... **61** F3
Watersbridge Gdns CV10 .... **29** E1
Waterside Polesworth B78 .... **5** D1
Stratford-u-A CV37 .... **145** D1
Waterside Cl B24 .... **22** A3

Waterside Ct CV31 .... **110** A3
Watersmeet Gr CV2 .... **62** A3
Watersmeet Rd CV2 .... **62** A3
Waterson Croft B37 .... **33** E2
Watery La
Cheswick Green B90 .... **70** B2
Corley CV7 .... **47** E3
Coventry CV6 .... **49** D2
Hook Norton OX15 .... **142** D4
Keresley CV7 .... **48** C2
Knowle B93 .... **72** C2
Portway B48 .... **85** E4
Shipston-on-S CV36 .... **149** F3
Shustoke B46 .... **24** B1
Ullenhall B95 .... **112** E6
Warwick CV35 .... **108** A1
Wathen Rd
Royal Leamington Spa CV32 . **106** A1
Warwick CV34 .... **108** C4
Watling Cl LE10 .... **31** E2
Watling Cres CV23 .... **68** B1
Watling Ct CV11 .... **29** F2
Watling Dr LE10 .... **31** E2
Watling Rd CV8 .... **93** D3
Watling St Atherstone CV9 ... **19** D4
Dordon B78 .... **10** B3
Hinckley CV11, LE10 .... **30** B4
Tamworth B77 .... **9** E4
Watson Cl [3] CV34 .... **104** C1
Watson Rd CV5 .... **60** B1
Wattisham Sq B35 .... **22** A2
Watton Gn B35 .... **22** A2
Watton La B46 .... **23** E1
Watts La CV21 .... **101** D4
Watts Rd B80 .... **103** F1
Waugh Cl B37 .... **33** D1
Wavebeck Ct CV23 .... **82** A3
Waveley Rd CV1 .... **61** D2
Wavendon Cl CV2 .... **50** C1
Waveney B77 .... **9** F4
Waveney Cl LE10 .... **31** D4
Waverley Ave CV11 .... **29** F1
Waverley Rd Kenilworth
CV8 .... **93** D2
Royal Leamington Spa
CV31 .... **110** A3
Rugby CV21 .... **84** A1
Waverley Sq CV11 .... **29** F1
Waverton Ave B79 .... **5** F2
Waverton Mews [24] CV31 .. **110** B3
Wavytree Cl CV34 .... **108** B4
Wawensmere Rd B95 .... **113** A4
Wayside B37 .... **44** A4
Weale Gr [7] CV34 .... **104** C1
Weatheroak Rd B49 .... **143** E2
Weaver Ave B76 .... **13** D1
Weaver Dr CV21 .... **82** B2
Weavers Cl CV36 .... **149** F3
Weavers Hill B97 .... **102** B2
Weavers Row OX15 .... **139** A3
Weavers Wlk CV6 .... **62** A4
Webb Dr CV21 .... **83** E4
Webb Ellis Rd CV22 .... **82** C1
Webb St CV10 .... **28** B2
Webster Ave CV5 .... **93** D3
Webster Steet CV6 .... **61** F4
Webster Way B76 .... **22** A2
Weddington Fst Sch CV10 .... **29** E4
Weddington La CV10 .... **20** A2
Weddington Rd CV10 .... **29** E4
Weddington Terr CV10 .... **29** E3
Wedgnock Gn CV34 .... **108** B4
Wedgnock Ind Est CV34 .... **104** B1
Wedgnock La CV34 .... **104** B1
Wedon Cl CV4 .... **75** F4
Weford Aviation Mus
GL56 .... **140** A3
Weigh Bridge Ct GL55 .... **135** B2
Welbeck Ave LE10 .... **31** E2
Welchman Pl CV35 .... **138** B6
Welcombe Hills Ctry Pk
CV37 .... **145** D4
Welcombe Rd CV37 .... **145** D2
Welcome St CV9 .... **18** C4
Welford Cl B98 .... **102** C3
Welford Pl CV6 .... **61** E4
Welford Rd
Bidford-on-A B50 .... **128** D6
Long Marston CV37 .... **129** B4
Rugby CV21 .... **83** E2
Tamworth B77 .... **9** E3
Welford-on-Avon
Cty Prim Sch CV37 .... **129** A6
Welgarth Ave CV6 .... **60** C3
Welham Croft B90 .... **71** D3
Well Bank OX15 .... **142** D4
Well Cl B97 .... **102** C3
Well La Shenington OX15 .... **138** F5
Staverton NN11 .... **126** D8
Tanworth-in-A B94 .... **87** D1
Well Spring Cl CV9 .... **18** C4
Well St CV1 .... **151** B3
Welland Cl
Long Lawford CV23 .... **82** B3
Water Orton B46 .... **23** D1
Welland Rd CV1 .... **61** F1
Welland Way B76 .... **22** A4
Wellesbourne CE Prim Sch
CV35 .... **146** C2
Wellesbourne Gr CV37 .... **144** C1
Wellesbourne Rd
Alveston CV37 .... **121** D3
Barford CV35 .... **122** B7
Coventry CV5 .... **60** A2
Lighthorne CV35 .... **123** B3
Loxley CV35 .... **130** F8
Wellington Cl CV35 .... **146** B1
Wellington Parkway LE17 .... **55** E3

Wellington Rd
Moreton-in-M GL56 .... **140** B3
Royal Leamington Spa CV32 . **106** B1
Wellington St CV1 .... **151** D4
Wells Cl CV10 .... **27** F2
Wells St CV21 .... **83** D2
Wells Wlk B37 .... **33** D1
Welsh Cl CV34 .... **104** C1
Welsh Rd Aston le W NN11 .. **134** F6
Bascote CV33 .... **115** B2
Coventry CV2 .... **62** A2
Lower Boddington NN11 ...... **134** E7
Napton CV33 .... **125** C5
Offchurch CV33 .... **107** D1
Offchurch CV33 .... **111** F4
Welsh Rd E CV33 .... **147** E1
Welsh Rd W CV33 .... **147** D3
Welton Cl B76 .... **13** D1
Welton Pl CV22 .... **100** B4
Welton Rd Braunston NN11 . **117** E5
Warwick CV34 .... **104** B1
Wembrook Cl CV11 .... **29** E1
Wendiburgh St CV4 .... **76** A4
Wendover Rise CV5 .... **60** B2
Wenlock Way CV10 .... **28** A2
Wensum Cl LE10 .... **31** D4
Wentworth Dr CV11 .... **30** A1
Wentworth Rd
[10] Royal Leamington Spa
CV31 .... **110** B3
Rugby CV22 .... **82** C1
Wesley Rd CV21 .... **101** D4
Wessenden B77 .... **10** A4
Wessex Cl CV12 .... **39** D2
Wessons Rd B50 .... **148** C3
West Ave Bedworth CV12 ...... **39** E1
Coventry CV2 .... **62** A1
West Cl LE10 .... **31** E4
West End Cleeve Prior
WR11 .... **128** A4
Hornton OX15 .... **139** B7
West Green Dr CV37 .... **144** A2
West Leyes CV21 .... **83** D2
West of St Laurence
CV35 .... **114** A8
West Orchards Sh Ctr
CV1 .... **151** B3
West Ridge CV5 .... **60** A3
West Rock CV34 .... **108** B4
West Side WR11 .... **128** A2
West Side Bsns Ctr CV4 ...... **75** F4
West St Coventry CV1 .... **61** F2
Long Lawford CV23 .... **82** A2
Royal Leamington Spa
CV31 .... **110** A4
Shipston-on-S CV36 .... **149** F3
Shutford OX15 .... **139** A3
Stratford-u-A CV37 .... **144** C1
Warwick CV34 .... **108** B3
West View Rd
Royal Leamington Spa CV32 . **106** B3
Rugby CV22 .... **82** C1
Westbourne Gr CV22 .... **82** C1
Westbury Rd Coventry CV5 ... **60** B3
Nuneaton CV10 .... **28** B2
Westcliff Dr CV34 .... **104** C1
Westcliffe Dr CV3 .... **77** D3
Westcotes CV4 .... **60** A1
Westerham CV33 .... **147** E2
Western Dr LE17 .... **43** F3
Western Hill Cl B96 .... **102** C1
Western Rd CV37 .... **144** C2
Western Road Ind Est
CV37 .... **144** C2
Westfield Cl Dorridge B93 .... **71** F1
Nuneaton CV10 .... **29** E3
Stratford-u-A CV37 .... **144** C3
Westfield Cres CV35 .... **146** B2
Westfield Cty Fst Sch
CV22 .... **82** C1
Westfield City
Jun & Inf Schs LE10 .... **31** D4
Westfield Rd Hinckley LE10 .. **31** D4
Rugby CV22 .... **82** C1
Southam CV33 .... **147** D2
Westgate Cl CV34 .... **108** B3
Westgate Cty Prim Sch
CV34 .... **108** B3
Westgate Rd CV21 .... **83** F1
Westgrove Ave [6] B90 .... **71** D3
Westham La CV35 .... **122** A7
Westhill Rd Blackdown
CV32 .... **106** A3
Coventry CV6 .... **60** C3
Westholme Rd B50 .... **148** B3
Westlea Rd CV31 .... **109** F3
Westleigh Ave CV5 .... **76** C4
Westmead Ave B80 .... **103** F2
Westminster Dr
Hinckley LE10 .... **31** F2
Nuneaton CV10 .... **28** A4
Westminster Rd CV1 .... **151** A1
Westmorland Ave CV10 .... **28** C2
Westmorland Rd CV2 .... **62** C2
Weston Cl Dorridge B93 .... **72** A1
Dunchurch CV22 .... **99** E2
Royal Leamington Spa
CV31 .... **110** B3
Warwick CV34 .... **108** C4
Weston Ct CV36 .... **141** D3
Weston La Bubbenhall CV8 ... **95** D2
Bulkington CV12 .... **40** A2
Weston St CV1 .... **151** C4
Westonbirt Cl CV8 .... **93** E3
Westway CV21 .... **83** D2
Westwood Bsns Pk CV4 .... **75** F3
Westwood Heath Rd CV4 ..... **75** F3

Westwood Rd
Atherstone CV9 .... **18** B4
Coventry CV5 .... **60** D1
Rugby CV22 .... **100** C4
Westwood Way CV4 .... **76** A3
Wetherell Way CV23 .... **83** E4
Wexford Rd CV2 .... **50** B1
Weymouth Cl CV3 .... **78** B3
Whaley's Croft CV6 .... **61** D4
Wharf Ind Est The CV23 ...... **65** D4
Wharf La B94 .... **88** B2
Wharf Rd Coventry CV6 .... **61** F3
Stratford-u-A CV37 .... **144** C2
Wharf St CV34 .... **109** D4
Wharf The CV37 .... **120** C5
Wharrage Rd B49 .... **143** E2
Wharrington Cl B98 .... **103** D4
Wharrington Hill B98 .... **103** D4
Whatcote Rd CV35 .... **137** F8
Whateley Hall Cl B93 .... **72** B4
Whateley Hall Rd B93 .... **72** A4
Whateley La B78 .... **9** F2
Whateley's Dr CV8 .... **93** D3
Wheat St CV11 .... **29** E2
Wheatcroft Dr B37 .... **33** E1
Wheate Croft CV4 .... **59** F1
Wheaten Cl B37 .... **33** E2
Wheatfield Cl B36 .... **33** D4
Wheatfield Ct GL55 .... **135** B6
Wheatfield Rd CV22 .... **82** B1
Wheathill Cl CV32 .... **105** F1
Wheatley Grange B46 .... **33** F3
Wheatsheaf La B94 .... **113** C8
Wheelbarrow La CV35 .... **114** A3
Wheeler Cl B93 .... **90** A4
Wheeley Moor Rd B37 .... **33** D3
Wheelwright La CV6 .... **49** E2
Wheelwright Lane
Comb Sch CV7 .... **49** E3
Wheler Rd CV3 .... **78** A4
Whernside CV21 .... **83** E4
Whetstone Dr CV21 .... **83** F4
Whichcote Ave CV7 .... **46** B1
Whiley Cl CV23 .... **83** F3
Whitacre Rd Knowle B93 ...... **72** A4
Nuneaton CV11 .... **29** F2
Whitacre Rd Ind Est CV11 .... **29** F2
Whitaker Rd CV5 .... **60** B2
Whitburn Rd CV12 .... **38** B1
Whitchurch Cl B98 .... **102** C3
Whitchurch Way CV4 .... **75** F4
White Beam Rd B37 .... **44** B4
White Friars La CV1 .... **151** C2
White Friars St CV1 .... **151** C2
White Hart La CV33 .... **111** F1
White Horse Hill CV37 .... **121** B6
White House Hill B95 .... **120** B7
White St CV1 .... **151** C3
Whitebeam Cl CV4 .... **59** E1
Whitefield Cl CV5 .... **75** E3
Whitehall Cl CV10 .... **19** D1
Whitehall Rd CV22 .... **83** D1
Whitehead Dr Kenilworth
CV8 .... **93** E4
Minworth B76 .... **22** B3
Whitehorn Dr CV32 .... **106** A1
Whitehorse Cl CV6 .... **50** A3
Whitehouse Cres CV10 .... **28** B2
Whitehouse Rd B78 .... **11** D3
Whitelaw Cres CV5 .... **60** B3
Whitemoor Dr B90 .... **71** D4
Whitemoor Hill Rd B96 .... **118** D8
Whitemoor Rd B90 .... **93** D3
Whitemoors Cl CV13 .... **21** F4
Whitemoors Rd CV13 .... **21** F4
Whitepits La B48 .... **85** F2
Whitepump La B95 .... **112** E7
Whites Row CV8 .... **93** D2
Whiteside Cl CV3 .... **78** C4
Whiteslade Cl B93 .... **72** A4
Whitestitch La CV7 .... **46** B2
Whitestone Fst Sch CV11 .... **40** A4
Whitestone Rd CV11 .... **40** A4
Whiteway OX17 .... **133** F2
Whitfield Cl CV37 .... **145** F2
Whitford Dr B90 .... **71** E4
Whiting B77 .... **9** E4
Whitley Abbey Comp Sch
CV3 .... **77** F3
Whitley Abbey Prim Sch
CV3 .... **78** A3
Whitley Ct CV3 .... **77** F4
Whitley Rd B95 .... **113** B4
Whitley Village CV3 .... **77** F4
Whitlock's End Halt B90 ...... **69** F4
Whitmore Park Prim Sch
CV6 .... **49** D1
Whitmore Park Rd CV6 .... **49** E2
Whitmore Rd CV31 .... **110** A2
Whitnash Cl CV7 .... **74** A3
Whitnash Cty Comb Sch
CV31 .... **110** A2
Whitnash Gr CV2 .... **62** B3
Whitnash Rd CV31 .... **110** A2
Whittington La CV34 .... **109** D4
Whittington La CV9 .... **12** A1
Whittle Cl Coventry CV3 .... **78** C4
Daventry NN11 .... **117** F3
Rugby CV22 .... **99** F4
Whittle Rd LE10 .... **30** C4
Whittleford Gr B36 .... **22** B1
Whittleford Rd CV10 .... **28** B2
Whittons Cl OX15 .... **142** D4
Whitwell Dr B90 .... **71** D3
Whitworth Ave CV3 .... **62** A1
Whitworth Cl CV35 .... **146** B1

Whoberley Ave CV5 .... **60** B1
Whoberley Hall Prim Sch
CV5 .... **60** B2
Wickham Cl CV6 .... **48** C1
Wicklow Rd B80 .... **103** F2
Wiclif Way CV10 .... **28** A2
Widdecombe Cl CV2 .... **62** B4
Widdrington Rd CV1 .... **61** E3
Widney Cl B93 .... **71** F3
Widney La B91 .... **71** D4
Widney Manor Rd B91 .... **71** E4
Widney Manor Sta B91 .... **71** E4
Widney Rd B93 .... **71** F3
Wigford Rd B77 .... **9** E3
Wiggins Hill Rd B76 .... **22** C4
Wight Croft B36 .... **33** D3
Wigston Hill CV9 .... **17** E3
Wigston Rd Coventry CV2 ..... **50** C1
Rugby CV21 .... **84** A1
Wike La B96 .... **118** E8
Wilcox Cl CV33 .... **124** A4
Wild Goose La B98 .... **103** E4
Wildcroft Rd CV5 .... **60** B2
Wildey Rd CV12 .... **38** B1
Wildmoor Cl CV2 .... **50** A2
Wilford Gr B76 .... **22** A3
Wilkes Way B50 .... **148** B3
Wilkins Cl CV35 .... **122** A7
Wilkinson Way B46 .... **25** D1
Willaby Dr CV9 .... **12** B1
Willenhall La CV3 .... **78** C4
Willenhall Wood Prim Sch
CV3 .... **78** B3
Willes Rd CV31, CV32 .... **110** A4
Willes Terr CV31 .... **110** A4
Willett Gdns CV35 .... **146** B2
William Arnold Cl CV2 .... **62** A2
William Beesley Cres
CV11 .... **40** C3
William Bree Rd CV5 .... **59** E3
William Bristow Rd CV3 .... **77** F4
William Cl OX16 .... **139** F4
William Groubb Cl CV3 .... **78** B4
William Iliffe St LE10 .... **31** D4
William McKee Cl CV3 .... **78** C4
William Morris
Cty Prim Sch OX16 .... **139** F4
William St Bedworth CV12 .... **39** E1
Nuneaton CV11 .... **29** F2
Royal Leamington Spa CV32 . **110** A4
Rugby CV21 .... **83** D2
William Tarver Cl CV34 ...... **109** D4
Williams Rd CV31 .... **110** C2
Willington St CV11 .... **29** D3
Willis Gr CV12 .... **39** E2
Willoughby Ave CV8 .... **92** C2
Willoughby Cl Alcester B49 **143** D3
Coventry CV3 .... **78** C4
Willoughby Pl CV22 .... **100** B4
Willow Bank CV37 .... **129** A7
Willow Bank Rd B93 .... **71** F3
Willow Brook Rd CV8 .... **80** A2
Willow Cl Alcester B49 .... **143** D1
Bedworth CV12 .... **39** D3
Hinckley LE10 .... **31** F3
Kingsbury B78 .... **15** E4
Nuneaton CV10 .... **28** A4
Willow Cytd CV2 .... **62** B4
Willow Dr
Cheswick Green B90 .... **70** B2
Wellesbourne CV35 .... **146** C2
Willow End GL56 .... **141** A1
Willow Gr CV4 .... **60** A1
Willow Meer Cl CV8 .... **93** D3
Willow Park Ind Est CV13 .... **21** E4
Willow Rd CV10 .... **28** C3
Willow Sheets Mdw CV32 .. **106** C3
Willow Tree Gdns CV21 ...... **101** D4
Willow Way B37 .... **33** D1
Willowbank Rd LE10 .... **31** E4
Willowdale LE10 .... **31** D4
Willowfields Rd CV11 .... **30** A1
Willowherb Cl [5] CV3 .... **78** C4
Willows CE Prim Sch The
CV37 .... **144** C1
Willows Dr N CV37 .... **144** C2
Willows The Atherstone
CV9 .... **12** C1
Bedworth CV12 .... **38** C1
Hollywood B47 .... **69** D3
Stratford-u-A CV37 .... **144** C1
Wilmcote CE Prim Sch
CV37 .... **120** C4
Wilmcote Gn CV5 .... **60** A2
Wilmcote La B95 .... **120** A5
Wilmot Ave B46 .... **33** F3
Wilnecote Gr CV31 .... **110** A3
Wilnecote High Sch B77 .... **9** F3
Wilnecote Jun Sch B77 .... **9** F4
Wilnecote Sta B77 .... **9** F4
Wilson Cl CV22 .... **82** B1
Wilson Dr B75 .... **13** D3
Wilson Gn CV3 .... **62** C1
Wilson Gr CV8 .... **93** E2
Wilson's La CV6 .... **49** F3
Wilsons La CV7 .... **50** A3
Wilson Rd B93 .... **72** B3
Wilton Rd CV7 .... **74** A3
Wiltshire Cl Bedworth CV12 . **39** D2
Coventry CV5 .... **60** A2
Wimborne Dr CV2 .... **63** D2
Wimbourne Cl CV10 .... **28** A3
Wimbourne Rd B76 .... **13** D2
Wimpstone La CV37 .... **130** B4
Winceby Pl CV4 .... **59** E1
Winchat CV1 .... **62** C1
Winchcombe Rd B49 .... **143** E2
Winchelsea Cl OX16 .... **139** F5

Winchester Ave CV10 .... 29 E4
Winchester Dr
  Birmingham B37 .... 33 D1
  Hinckley LE10 .... 32 A4
Winchester St CV1 .... 61 F2
Wincott Cl CV37 .... 145 E1
Windermere B77 .... 10 A4
Windermere Ave
  Coventry, Binley CV3 .... 62 C1
  Coventry, Upper Eastern Green
  CV5 .... 59 F2
  Nuneaton CV11 .... 29 F3
Windermere Cl CV21 .... 83 E4
Windermere Dr CV32 .... 105 E1
Windmill Ave 2 B46 .... 33 F4
Windmill Cl Kenilworth CV8 ... 93 D3
  Warton B79 .... 5 F2
Windmill Dr B97 .... 102 B3
Windmill Gdns NN11 .... 126 E8
Windmill Hill
  Bidford-on-A B50 .... 128 E8
  Royal Leamington Spa
  CV32 .... 106 B3
Windmill Hill The CV5 .... 60 A4
Windmill Ind Est CV5 .... 59 F4
Windmill La Astley CV10 .... 37 F3
  Austrey CV9 .... 3 D1
  Balsall Common CV7 .... 74 B2
  Baxterley CV9 .... 17 E3
  Corley CV7 .... 47 E3
  Dorridge B94 .... 89 D4
  Dunchurch CV22 .... 99 D2
  Ladbroke CV33 .... 124 E5
  Staverton NN11 .... 126 E8
Windmill Rd Atherstone
  CV9 .... 12 B1
  Bedworth CV7 .... 50 A4
  Coventry CV6 .... 50 A2
  Nuneaton CV10 .... 28 B4
  Royal Leamington Spa
  CV31 .... 109 F3
Windmill Way
  Southam CV33 .... 147 D3
  Tysoe CV35 .... 138 B6
Windridge Cl CV3 .... 78 B3
Windrush Cl B97 .... 102 B3
Windrush Dr LE10 .... 31 D4
Windrush Rd B47 .... 69 D4
Windrush Way CV23 .... 82 A3
Windsor Ct LE10 .... 32 A3
Windsor Pl 7 CV32 .... 105 F1
Windsor Rd B78 .... 5 D2
Windsor St Coventry CV1 .. 61 D1
  Hinckley LE10 .... 32 A3
  Nuneaton CV11 .... 29 D2
  Royal Leamington Spa
  CV32 .... 109 F4
  Rugby CV21 .... 83 E2
  Stratford-u-A CV37 .... 144 C2
Windward Way B36 .... 33 D3
Windy Arbor Prim Sch
  B37 .... 33 E1
Windy Arbour CV8 .... 93 D2
Windyridge Rd B76 .... 22 A3
Winfield Rd CV11 .... 29 D3
Winfield St CV21 .... 83 E2
Wingfield Rd B46 .... 33 F3
Wingfield Way CV6 .... 49 D1
Wingrave Cl CV5 .... 60 A3
Winifred Ave CV5 .... 61 D1
Winnallthorpe CV3 .... 78 C3
Winsford Ave CV5 .... 60 A2
Winsford Cl CV7 .... 74 A3
Winsham Wlk CV3 .... 77 E2
Winslow Cl Coventry CV5 .... 60 A2
  4 Royal Leamington Spa
  CV32 .... 105 E1
Winspear Cl CV7 .... 46 A1
Winster Ave B93 .... 71 F2
Winster Cl CV7 .... 49 D4
Winston Ave CV2 .... 62 B4

Winston Cl Coventry CV2 .... 62 B4
  Stratford-u-A CV37 .... 144 B1
Winterton Rd CV12 .... 40 B1
Winthorpe Dr B91 .... 71 E4
Winton Gr B76 .... 22 A3
Winwick Pl CV22 .... 99 E4
Winyates Rd CV35 .... 123 D2
Wise Gr Rugby CV21 .... 83 F1
  Warwick CV34 .... 104 C1
Wise St CV31 .... 109 F4
Wise Terr CV31 .... 109 F4
Wishaw Cl B98 .... 103 D4
Wishaw La Curdworth B76 .... 23 D4
  Middleton B78 .... 14 B3
  Minworth B76 .... 22 C4
Wisley Dr CV8 .... 93 E3
Wistaria Cl CV2 .... 50 A1
Witham The NN11 .... 117 F1
Witherley CE Prim Sch
  CV9 .... 19 D4
Witherley Rd Atherstone
  CV9 .... 18 C4
  Witherley CV9 .... 19 D3
Withington Gr B93 .... 71 F2
Withum Cl B76 .... 13 D1
Withy Hill Rd B75 .... 13 D4
Withybrook La CV7 .... 51 F3
Withybrook Rd
  Bulkington CV12 .... 40 B1
  Solihull B90 .... 70 A4
Withycombe Dr OX16 ...... 139 F3
Woburn Cl CV31 .... 110 B3
Woburn Dr CV10 .... 29 D1
Wolds End Cl GL55 .... 135 B2
Wolds La LE10 .... 41 F2
Wolfe Rd CV4 .... 75 F4
Wolford Rd GL56 .... 140 D6
Wolfstan Dr CV23 .... 115 D4
Wolseley Cl B36 .... 23 D1
Wolsey Rd CV22 .... 99 E3
Wolsey St CV3 .... 78 B3
Wolston Bsns Pk CV8 .... 80 A2
Wolston La CV8 .... 79 F1
Wolverton Prim Sch
  CV35 .... 114 B2
Wolverton Rd
  Birmingham, Marston Green
  B37 .... 44 A4
  Coventry CV5 .... 60 A2
  Norton Lindsey CV35 ..... 114 C2
  Snitterfield CV37 .... 121 B7
Wolvey CE Prim Sch LE10 .. 41 E2
Wolvey Rd Bulkington CV12 .. 40 C1
  Hinckley LE10 .... 31 F2
Wood Cl B46 .... 33 F4
Wood Croft B47 .... 69 D3
Wood End Fst Sch CV9 ...... 10 B1
Wood End Jun Sch CV9 ...... 10 B1
Wood End La Fillongley CV7 .. 37 D2
  Tanworth-in-A B94 .... 86 C3
Wood End Sta B94 .... 86 C2
Wood Hill Rise CV6 .... 49 E1
Wood La Arley CV7 .... 26 B1
  Aston Cantlow B95 .... 119 F5
  Astwood Bank B96 .... 118 C6
  Birmingham, Marston Green
  B37 .... 44 A4
  Cherington CV36 .... 141 D7
  Earlswood B94 .... 69 F1
  Hampton in A B92 .... 56 C1
  Hartshill CV10 .... 28 A4
  Higham-on-t-H CV13 .... 20 C2
  Shilton CV7 .... 51 E3
Wood St Bedworth CV12 .... 39 D3
  Nuneaton CV10 .... 28 C2
  Royal Leamington Spa CV32 ... 110 A4
  Rugby CV21 .... 83 D2
  Southam CV33 .... 147 D2
  Stratford-u-A CV37 .... 145 D1
  Wood End CV9 .... 10 B1
Wood Terr B96 .... 118 D8

Woodbank LE10 .... 32 A4
Woodberrow La B97 .... 102 B3
Woodberry Dr B76 .... 13 D1
Woodbine St 1 CV32 ...... 109 F4
Woodbine Wlk B37 .... 33 E1
Woodburn Cl CV5 .... 60 A2
Woodby La LE17 .... 55 F4
Woodchester Rd B93 .... 71 F1
Woodclose Ave CV6 .... 60 C3
Woodclose Rd B37 .... 33 D2
Woodcock Cl B94 .... 86 C2
Woodcot Park Dr CV37 ... 120 B5
Woodcote Ave
  Kenilworth CV8 .... 92 B3
  Nuneaton CV11 .... 29 F4
Woodcote Dr Dorridge B93 .. 72 A1
  Leek Wootton CV35 .... 104 C4
Woodcote La CV35 .... 104 C4
Woodcote Rd
  Royal Leamington Spa CV32 . 105 F3
  Warwick CV34 .... 108 C4
Woodcraft Cl CV4 .... 60 A1
Woodend Croft CV4 .... 75 F4
Woodfield Rd Coventry CV5 .. 76 C4
  Hinckley LE10 .... 31 E3
Woodford Cl Ash Green
  CV7 .... 49 E3
  Nuneaton CV10 .... 28 B2
Woodford La CV10 .... 19 E2
Woodgate Rd LE10 .... 32 A4
Woodgreen Cl B97 .... 102 A4
Woodhall Cl CV11 .... 30 A1
Woodhams Rd CV3 .... 78 B2
Woodhouse Cl CV3 .... 78 C4
Woodhouse High Sch B77 .. 4 A2
Woodhouse La B77 .... 4 A3
Woodhouse St B77 .... 108 B3
Woodington Fst Sch B75 .. 13 D3
Woodington Rd B75 .... 13 D3
Woodland Ave
  Claybrooke Magna LE17 .. 43 F3
  Coventry CV5 .... 76 C4
  Hinckley LE10 .... 32 A4
Woodland Rd Kenilworth
  CV8 .... 93 D4
  Tamworth B77 .... 4 A2
Woodland Way B78 .... 10 C4
Woodlands Ave B46 .... 23 D1
Woodlands Cl B78 .... 11 D3
Woodlands Inf Sch B90 .... 70 A4
Woodlands Jun & Inf Sch
  B36 .... 33 D3
Woodlands La
  Bedworth CV12 .... 38 C2
  Solihull B90 .... 70 A4
Woodlands Rd
  Bedworth CV12 .... 38 C2
  Binley Woods CV3 .... 79 E4
  Stratford-u-A CV37 .... 144 C3
Woodlands Sch The CV4 ... 59 E3
Woodlands The
  Hartshill CV10 .... 28 A4
  Staverton NN11 .... 126 D8
  Wood End CV9 .... 10 B1
Woodlands Way B37 .... 33 E2
Woodloes Ave N CV34 ..... 104 C1
Woodloes Ave S CV34 ..... 104 C1
Woodloes Fst Sch CV34 .. 104 C1
Woodloes La CV34 .... 104 C1
Woodloes Mid Sch CV34 . 104 C1
Woodloes Rd B90 .... 70 A4
Woodman Ct CV37 .... 144 C2
Woodpecker Gr B36 .... 33 D4
Woodridge Ave CV5 .... 60 A3
Woodrow Cres B93 .... 72 A3
Woodrow Ctr B98 .... 103 D3
Woodrow Dr B98 .... 103 D3
Woodrow Fst Sch B98 .... 103 D4
Woodrow N B98 .... 103 D4
Woodrow S B98 .... 103 D4
Woodrow Wlk B98 .... 103 D4
Woodrush Dr B47 .... 69 D3
Woodrush High Sch The
  B47 .... 69 D3
Woodshires Rd CV6 .... 49 F3
Woodsia Cl CV23 .... 83 E4
Woodside Arley CV7 .... 26 B1
  Grendon CV9 .... 11 E1
Woodside Ave N CV3 .... 76 C3
Woodside Ave S CV3 .... 76 C3
Woodside Bsns Pk CV21 .. 83 D2
Woodside Cl CV9 .... 10 B1
Woodside Cres B93 .... 72 A2
Woodside Pk CV21 .... 83 D3
Woodstock Cl LE10 .... 32 A3
Woodstock Cres B93 .... 71 F2
Woodstock Rd Coventry
  CV3 .... 77 E4
  Nuneaton CV11 .... 29 F1
Woodston Gr B91 .... 71 E4
Woodville Rd CV34 .... 108 C4
Woodward Cl CV31 .... 110 A1
Woodward Ct CV37 .... 121 B6
Wooday CV35 .... 114 F3
Woodway Ave CV35 .... 114 F3
Woodway Cl CV2 .... 62 C4
Woodway La
  Claybrooke Parva LE17 .... 43 E2
  Coventry CV2 .... 50 C1
Woodway Park Sch &
Com Coll CV2 .... 50 C1
Woodway Rd OX15 .... 142 D8
Woodway Wlk CV2 .... 62 C4
Woolaston Rd B98 .... 103 E4
Woolgrove St CV6 .... 50 A2
Wooll St CV21 .... 83 D2
Woolpack Way CV9 .... 18 B4
Woolwich Rd CV11 .... 40 C3
Wootton Cl CV37 .... 145 E1
Wootton Ct CV2 .... 62 B4
Wootton Green La CV7 ...... 74 A4
Wootton La B92 .... 57 F1
Wootton St CV12 .... 39 E2
Wootton Wawen Jun &
Inf Sch B95 .... 113 A2
Wootton Wawen Sta B95 . 113 A2
Worcester Cl CV5 .... 60 A4
Worcester Pl CV36 .... 149 F3
Worcester Rd CV8 .... 93 D2
Worcester St CV21 .... 83 D2
Worcester Wlk B37 .... 33 D1
Wordsworth Ave
  Redditch B97 .... 102 B4
  Warwick CV34 .... 108 B3
Wordsworth Dr CV8 .... 93 E2
Wordsworth Rd
  Bedworth CV12 .... 39 E1
  Coventry CV2 .... 62 B2
  Rugby CV22 .... 99 F3
Workhouse La LE10 .... 32 A2
Works Rd B26 .... 44 A2
Worsdell Cl CV1 .... 61 D2
Worsfold Cl CV5 .... 60 A4
Worthy Down Wlk B35 ...... 22 A2
Wren Cl DE12 .... 3 F4
Wren St CV2 .... 61 F2
Wrenbury Dr CV6 .... 50 A2
Wright Cl B78 .... 15 E3
Wright St CV1 .... 61 F2
Wrigsham St CV3 .... 77 E4
Wroxall Abbey (Sch) CV35 . 90 C1
Wroxall CE Jun & Inf Sch
  CV35 .... 90 C2
Wroxall Dr CV3 .... 78 B3
Wroxton CE Prim Sch
  OX15 .... 139 D4
Wroxton Coll OX15 .... 139 D4
Wroxton Ct OX15 .... 139 D4
Wyatt Rd B75 .... 13 D3
Wyatts Ct CV12 .... 39 D2
Wych Elm Dr CV31 .... 109 F3

Wych-Elm Cl CV22 .... 82 A1
Wychbold Cl B97 .... 102 A3
Wychbury B76 .... 13 D1
Wychwood Ave Coventry
  CV3 .... 77 E2
  Knowle B93 .... 72 A4
Wychwood Cl 14 CV33 ... 122 F8
Wychwood Dr B97 .... 102 B3
Wycliffe Gr CV2 .... 62 A3
Wycliffe Rd W CV2 .... 62 B3
Wye Cl Bulkington CV12 .... 40 A1
  Hinckley LE10 .... 31 D4
  Royal Leamington Spa
  CV32 .... 106 B2
  Sutton Coldfield B76 .... 22 A4
Wyke Rd CV2 .... 62 B2
Wykeley Rd CV2 .... 62 B2
Wyken Ave CV2 .... 62 B3
Wyken Cl B93 .... 71 F1
Wyken Croft CV2 .... 62 B3
Wyken Croft Prim Sch
  CV2 .... 62 C3
Wyken Grange Rd CV2 ...... 62 B3
Wyken Way CV2 .... 62 A3
Wykham La OX15 .... 139 F1
Wyld Ct CV5 .... 60 A3
Wyley Rd CV6 .... 61 D3
Wynbrook Gr B90 .... 71 D3
Wyncote Cl CV8 .... 93 D2
Wyndshiels B46 .... 34 A3
Wynter Rd CV22 .... 82 B2
Wyre La CV37 .... 129 B3
Wythall Sta B47 .... 69 E2
Wythburn Way CV21 .... 83 E4
Wythwood Gr B47 .... 69 E3
Wythwood Rd B47 .... 69 E3
Wyver Cres CV2 .... 62 B2
Wyvern Cl CV35 .... 146 B1

Yardley Chase Rd CV35 ... 132 D4
Yardley Cl CV34 .... 104 C1
Yardley St CV1 .... 61 E2
Yarmouth Gn CV4 .... 75 F4
Yarn Cl B47 .... 69 D3
Yarningale Cl B98 .... 102 C3
Yarningale La CV35 .... 113 C5
Yarningale Rd CV3 .... 78 B3
Yarranton Cl CV37 .... 144 C3
Yarrow Cl CV23 .... 83 E4
Yates Ave CV21 .... 82 C3
Yatesbury Ave B35 .... 22 A2
Yelverton Rd CV6 .... 61 E4
Yeomanry Cl 10 CV34 .... 108 C4
Yew Cl CV3 .... 62 B1
Yew Tree Cl B94 .... 89 E2
Yew Tree Ct CV9 .... 3 D1
Yew Tree Gdns B95 .... 113 A4
Yew Tree Hill CV23 .... 64 C2
Yew Tree La B94 .... 113 D8
Yew Trees The B95 .... 113 B4
Yew Wlk B37 .... 33 D1
Yewdale Cres CV2 .... 50 C1
Yews The CV12 .... 38 C1
York Ave Atherstone CV9 .. 12 C1
  Bedworth CV12 .... 39 E1
York Cl Coventry CV3 .... 78 B3
  Studley B80 .... 103 E2
York Rd CV31 .... 109 F4
York St Coventry CV1 .... 61 D1
  Nuneaton CV11 .... 29 D2
  Rugby CV21 .... 82 C2
Yorkminster Dr B37 .... 33 E2
Yorksand Rd B78 .... 8 C4
Young Cl CV34 .... 108 A3
Yule Rd CV2 .... 62 B3
Yvonne Rd B97 .... 102 B4

Zorrina Cl CV10 .... 28 A3

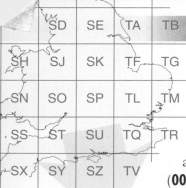

Any feature in this atlas can be given a unique reference to help you find the same feature on other Ordnance Survey maps of the area, or to help someone else locate you if they do not have a Street Atlas. The grid squares in this atlas match the Ordnance Survey National Grid and are at 500 metre intervals. The small figures at the bottom and sides of every other grid line are the National Grid kilometre values (**00** to **99** km) and are repeated across the country every 100 km (see left).

To give a unique National Grid reference you need to locate where in the country you are. The country is divided into 100 km squares with each square given a unique two-letter reference. The atlas in this example falls across the junction of four such squares. Start by working out on which two-letter square the page falls. The Key map and Administrative map are useful for this.

The bold letters and numbers between each grid line (**A** to **F**, **1** to **8**) are for use within a specific Street Atlas only, and when used with the page number, are a convenient way of referencing these grid squares.

Example   The railway bridge over DARLEY GREEN RD in grid square B1 on page 128

Step 1: Identify the two-letter reference, in this case page 128 is in **SP**

Step 2: Identify the 1 km square in which the railway bridge falls. Use the figures in the southwest corner of this square: Eastings **17**, Northings **74**. This gives a unique reference: **SP 17 74**, accurate to 1 km.

Step 3: To give a more precise reference accurate to 100 m you need to estimate how many tenths along and how many tenths up this 1 km square the feature is (to help with this the 1 km square is divided into four 500 m squares). This makes the bridge about **8** tenths along and about **1** tenth up from the southwest corner.

This gives a unique reference: **SP 178 741**, accurate to 100 m.

Eastings (read from left to right along the bottom) come before Northings (read from bottom to top). If you have trouble remembering say to yourself "Along the hall, THEN up the stairs"!

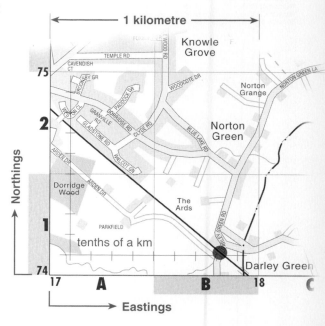

Name and Address	Telephone	Page	Grid Reference

Addresses

Name and Address	Telephone	Page	Grid Reference

STREET ATLASES ORDER FORM

The Street Atlases are available from all good bookshops or by mail order direct from the publisher. Orders can be made in the following ways. **By phone** Ring our special Credit Card Hotline on **01933 443863** during office hours (9am to 5pm) or leave a message on the answering machine, quoting your full credit card number plus expiry date and your full name and address. **By post or fax** Fill out the order form below (you may photocopy it) and post it to: **Philip's Direct, 27 Sanders Road, Wellingborough, Northants NN8 4NL** or fax it to: **01933 443849**. Before placing an order by post, by fax or on the answering machine, please telephone to check availability and prices.

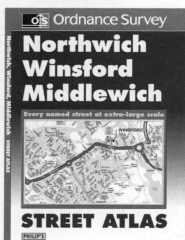

COLOUR LOCAL ATLASES

	PAPERBACK Quantity @ £3.50 each	£ Total
CANNOCK, LICHFIELD, RUGELEY	☐ 0 540 07625 2	➤ ☐
DERBY AND BELPER	☐ 0 540 07608 2	➤ ☐
NORTHWICH, WINSFORD, MIDDLEWICH	☐ 0 540 07589 2	➤ ☐
PEAK DISTRICT TOWNS	☐ 0 540 07609 0	➤ ☐
STAFFORD, STONE, UTTOXETER	☐ 0 540 07626 0	➤ ☐
WARRINGTON, WIDNES, RUNCORN	☐ 0 540 07588 4	➤ ☐

COLOUR REGIONAL ATLASES

	HARDBACK	SPIRAL	POCKET	£ Total
	Quantity @ £10.99 each	Quantity @ £8.99 each	Quantity @ £5.99 each	
BERKSHIRE	☐ 0 540 06170 0	☐ 0 540 06172 7	☐ 0 540 06173 5	➤ ☐
	Quantity @ £10.99 each	Quantity @ £8.99 each	Quantity @ £4.99 each	
MERSEYSIDE	☐ 0 540 06480 7	☐ 0 540 06481 5	☐ 0 540 06482 3	➤ ☐
	Quantity @ £12.99 each	Quantity @ £9.99 each	Quantity @ £4.99 each	
DURHAM	☐ 0 540 06365 7	☐ 0 540 06366 5	☐ 0 540 06367 3	➤ ☐
HERTFORDSHIRE	☐ 0 540 06174 3	☐ 0 540 06175 1	☐ 0 540 06176 X	➤ ☐
EAST KENT	☐ 0 540 07483 7	☐ 0 540 07276 1	☐ 0 540 07287 7	➤ ☐
WEST KENT	☐ 0 540 07366 0	☐ 0 540 07367 9	☐ 0 540 07369 5	➤ ☐
EAST SUSSEX	☐ 0 540 07306 7	☐ 0 540 07307 5	☐ 0 540 07312 1	➤ ☐
WEST SUSSEX	☐ 0 540 07319 9	☐ 0 540 07323 7	☐ 0 540 07327 X	➤ ☐
SOUTH YORKSHIRE	☐ 0 540 06330 4	☐ 0 540 06331 2	☐ 0 540 06332 0	➤ ☐
SURREY	☐ 0 540 06435 1	☐ 0 540 06436 X	☐ 0 540 06438 6	➤ ☐
	Quantity @ £12.99 each	Quantity @ £9.99 each	Quantity @ £5.50 each	
GREATER MANCHESTER	☐ 0 540 06485 8	☐ 0 540 06486 6	☐ 0 540 06487 4	➤ ☐
TYNE AND WEAR	☐ 0 540 06370 3	☐ 0 540 06371 1	☐ 0 540 06372 X	➤ ☐
	Quantity @ £12.99 each	Quantity @ £9.99 each	Quantity @ £5.99 each	
BIRMINGHAM & WEST MIDLANDS	☐ 0 540 07603 1	☐ 0 540 07604 X	☐ 0 540 07605 8	➤ ☐
BUCKINGHAMSHIRE	☐ 0 540 07466 7	☐ 0 540 07467 5	☐ 0 540 07468 3	➤ ☐

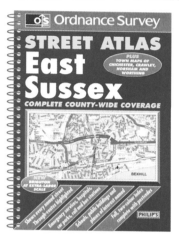

STREET ATLASES ORDER FORM

COLOUR REGIONAL ATLASES

	HARDBACK Quantity @ £12.99 each	SPIRAL Quantity @ £9.99 each	POCKET Quantity @ £5.99 each	£ Total
CHESHIRE	☐ 0 540 07507 8	☐ 0 540 07508 6	☐ 0 540 07509 4	➤ ☐
DERBYSHIRE	☐ 0 540 07531 0	☐ 0 540 07532 9	☐ 0 540 07533 7	➤ ☐
SOUTH HAMPSHIRE	☐ 0 540 07476 4	☐ 0 540 07477 2	☐ 0 540 07478 0	➤ ☐
NORTH HAMPSHIRE	☐ 0 540 07471 3	☐ 0 540 07472 1	☐ 0 540 07473 X	➤ ☐
OXFORDSHIRE	☐ 0 540 07512 4	☐ 0 540 07513 2	☐ 0 540 07514 0	➤ ☐
WARWICKSHIRE	☐ 0 540 07560 4	☐ 0 540 07561 2	☐ 0 540 07562 0	➤ ☐
WEST YORKSHIRE	☐ 0 540 06329 0	☐ 0 540 06327 4	☐ 0 540 06328 2	➤ ☐
	Quantity @ £14.99 each	Quantity @ £9.99 each	Quantity @ £5.99 each	£ Total
LANCASHIRE	☐ 0 540 06440 8	☐ 0 540 06441 6	☐ 0 540 06443 2	➤ ☐
STAFFORDSHIRE	☐ 0 540 07549 3	☐ 0 540 07550 7	☐ 0 540 07551 5	➤ ☐

BLACK AND WHITE REGIONAL ATLASES

	HARDBACK Quantity @ £11.99 each	SOFTBACK Quantity @ £8.99 each	POCKET Quantity @ £3.99 each	£ Total
BRISTOL AND AVON	☐ 0 540 06140 9	☐ 0 540 06141 7	☐ 0 540 06142 5	➤ ☐
	Quantity @ £12.99 each	Quantity @ £9.99 each	Quantity @ £4.99 each	£ Total
CARDIFF, SWANSEA & GLAMORGAN	☐ 0 540 06186 7	☐ 0 540 06187 5	☐ 0 540 06207 3	➤ ☐
EDINBURGH & East Central Scotland	—	☐ 0 540 06181 6	☐ 0 540 06182 4	➤
EAST ESSEX	☐ 0 540 05848 3	☐ 0 540 05866 1	☐ 0 540 05850 5	➤ ☐
WEST ESSEX	☐ 0 540 05849 1	☐ 0 540 05867 X	☐ 0 540 05851 3	➤ ☐
NOTTINGHAMSHIRE	—	☐ 0 540 05859 9	☐ 0 540 05860 2	➤
	Quantity @ £12.99 each	Quantity @ £9.99 each	Quantity @ £5.99 each	£ Total
GLASGOW & West Central Scotland	☐ 0 540 06183 2	☐ 0 540 06184 0	☐ 0 540 06185 9	➤ ☐

Post to: Philip's Direct,
27 Sanders Road, Wellingborough,
Northants NN8 4NL

◆ Free postage and packing

◆ All available titles will normally be dispatched within 5 working days of receipt of order but please allow up to 28 days for delivery

☐ Please tick this box if you do not wish your name to be used by other carefully selected organisations that may wish to send you information about other products and services

Registered Office: Michelin House, 81 Fulham Road, London SW3 6RB

Registered in England number: 3597451

I enclose a cheque / postal order, for a **total** of ☐
made payable to *Octopus Publishing Group Ltd,* or please debit my

☐ Access ☐ American Express ☐ Visa ☐ Diners

Account no   account by ☐

☐☐☐☐☐ ☐☐☐☐ ☐☐☐☐ ☐☐☐☐

Expiry date ☐☐ ☐☐

Signature...

Name...

Address..

....

....

....POSTCODE

PHILIP'S

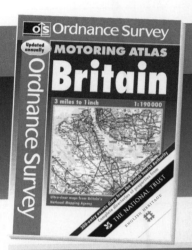